CUSTOM EDITION FOR
Columbus State Community College

DEVIANT BEHAVIOR

By Alex Thio

SOCIOLOGY 210

Taken From:

Deviant Behavior
Eighth Edition
By Alex Thio

PEARSON CUSTOM PUBLISHING
75 Arlington Street, Suite 300, Boston, MA 02116
A Pearson Education Company

CONTENTS

Contents

PART ONE

Perspectives and Theories

1 What Is Deviant Behavior?

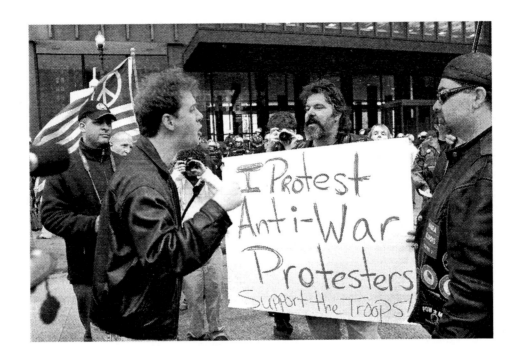

Throughout her life, Aleta Walker, an overweight 36-year-old woman, has been ridiculed and abused for her weight, especially during her childhood and adolescence. Every day, when she walked down the halls at school, boys would step back and yell, "Wide load!" It was worse at lunchtime. As she said, "Every day there was this production of watching me eat lunch." One day, schoolmates threw food at her. Spaghetti splashed on her head and face, and the long greasy strands dripped onto her clothes. "Everyone was laughing and pointing. They were making pig noises. I just sat there," she said (Kolata, 1992).

Is Walker deviant for being overweight? Some people would say yes, but others would say no. In fact, some would say that it is her tormentors—the so-called normal people—who are deviant because they are grossly insensitive, nasty, or cruel. There is, in fact, a great deal of disagreement among people as to what they consider deviant. In a classic study, J. L. Simmons (1965) asked a sample of the general public who they thought was deviant. They mentioned 252 different kinds of people as deviants, including prostitutes, alcoholics, drug users, murderers, the mentally ill, the physically challenged, communists, atheists, liars, Democrats, Republicans, reckless drivers, self-pitiers, the retired, divorcees, Christians, suburbanites, movie stars, perpetual bridge players, pacifists, psychiatrists, priests, liberals, conservatives, junior executives, smart-aleck students, and know-it-all professors. If you are surprised that some of these people are considered deviant, your surprise simply adds to the fact that there is a good deal of disagreement among the public as to the conception of deviant behavior.

A similar lack of consensus exists among sociologists. We could say that the study of deviant behavior is probably the most "deviant" of all the subjects in sociology. Sociologists disagree more over the definition of deviant behavior than they do on any other subject.

Conflicting Definitions

Some sociologists simply say that deviance is a violation of any social rule, while others argue that deviance involves more than rule violation—that it also has the quality of provoking disapproval, anger, or indignation. Some advocate a broader definition, arguing that a person can be a deviant *without* violating any rule or doing something that rubs others the wrong way, such as individuals with physical or mental disabilities. These people are considered deviant in this view because they are disvalued by society. By contrast, some sociologists contend that deviance does not have to be conceived as only negative but instead can also be positive, such as being a genius, saint, creative artist, or glamorous celebrity. Other sociologists disagree, considering "positive deviance" to be an oxymoron, a contradiction in terms (Heckert and Heckert, 2002; Goode, 1991; Dodge, 1985; Harman, 1985).

All these sociologists apparently assume that, whether it is positive or negative, disturbing behavior or disvalued condition, deviance is real in and of itself, that is, endowed with a certain quality that distinguishes it from nondeviance. The logic behind this assumption is that if it is not real in the first place, it cannot be considered positive, negative, disturbing, or devalued. But other sociologists disagree, arguing that deviance does not have to be real in order for behaviors and conditions to be labeled deviant. People can be falsely accused of being criminal, erroneously diagnosed as mentally ill, unfairly stereotyped as dangerous because of their skin color, and so on. Conversely, committing a deviant act does not necessarily make the person a deviant, especially when the act is kept secret, unlabeled by others as deviant. It is, therefore, the label "deviant"—not the act itself—that makes the individual deviant.

Some sociologists go beyond the notion of labeling to define deviance by stressing the importance of power. They observe that relatively powerful people are capable of avoiding the fate suffered by the powerless—being falsely, erroneously, or unjustly labeled deviant. The key reason is that the powerful, either by themselves or through influencing public opinion or both, hold more power for labeling others' behavior as deviant. Understandably, sociologists who hold this view define deviance as any act considered by the powerful at a given time and place to be a violation of some social rule (Ermann and Lundman, 2002; Simon, 2002).

From this welter of conflicting definitions we can discern the influence of two opposing perspectives: positivism and social constructionism. The positivist perspective is associated with the sciences, such as physics, chemistry, or biology. The constructionist perspective is fundamental in the humanities, such as art, language, or philosophy. Each perspective influences how scientists and scholars see, study, and make sense of their subject. The two perspectives have long been transported into sociology, so that some sociologists are more influenced by the positivist perspective while others are more influenced by the constructionist one.

In the sociology of deviance the positivist generally defines deviance as positively real, while the constructionist more often defines deviance as a social construction—an idea imputed by society to some behavior. Each perspective suggests other ideas about deviance, so that it has been referred to in various terms. Thus the positivist perspective has also been called objectivist, absolutist, normative, determinist, and essentialist (Goode, 2001; Wittig, 1990). The constructionist perspective has also been referred to by such terms as humanist, subjectivist, relativist, reactivist, definitionist, and postmodernist (Heckert and Heckert, 2002; Lyman, 1995). Each perspective suggests how to *define* deviance, but reveals through the definitions what *subject* to study, what *method* to use for the study, and what kind of *theory* to use to make sense of the subject.

The Positivist Perspective

The positivist perspective consists of three assumptions about what deviance is. These assumptions are known to positivists as absolutism, objectivism, and determinism.

Absolutism: Deviance as Absolutely Real

The positivist perspective holds deviance to be absolutely or intrinsically real, in that *it possesses some qualities that distinguish it from conventionality.* Similarly, deviant persons are assumed to have certain characteristics that make them different from conventional others. Thus, sociologists who are influenced by such a perspective tend to view deviant behavior as an attribute that inheres in the individual.

This view was first strongly held by the early criminologists who were the progenitors of today's sociology of deviance. Around the turn of this century, criminologists believed that criminals possessed certain biological traits that were absent in law-abiding people. The biological traits were believed to include defective genes, bumps on the head, a long lower jaw, a scanty beard, and a tough body build. Since all these traits are inherited, criminals were believed to be born as such. Thus, if they were born criminals, they would always be criminals. As the saying goes, "If you've had it, you've had it." So, no matter where they might go—they could go anywhere in the world—they would still be criminals.

Then criminologists shifted their attention from biological to psychological traits. Criminals were thought to have certain mental characteristics that noncriminals did not. More specifically, criminals were thought to be feebleminded, psychotic, neurotic, psychopathic, or otherwise mentally disturbed. Like biological traits, these mental characteristics were believed to reside within individual criminals. And like biological traits, mental characteristics were believed to stay with the criminals, no matter what society or culture they might go to. Again, wherever they went, criminals would always remain criminals.

Today's positivist sociologists, however, have largely abandoned the use of biological and psychological traits to differentiate criminals from noncriminals. They recognize the important role of social factors in determining a person's status as a criminal. Such status does not remain the same across time and space; instead, it changes in different periods and with different societies. A polygamist may be a criminal in our society but a law-abiding citizen in Islamic countries. A person who sees things invisible to others may be a psychotic in our society but may become a spiritual leader among some South Pacific peoples. Nevertheless, positivist sociologists still regard deviance as absolutely or intrinsically real. Countering the relativist notion of deviance as basically a *label* imposed on an act, positivist Travis Hirschi (1973), for example, argues: "The person may not have committed a 'deviant' act, but he did (in many cases) do *something*. And it is just possible that what he did was a result of things that had happened to him in the past; it is also possible that the past in some inscrutable way remains with him and that if he were left alone he would *do it again*." Moreover, countering the relativist notion of mental illness as a label imputed to some people's behavior, Gwynn Nettler (1974) explicitly voices his absolutist stance: "Some people *are* more crazy than others; we can tell the difference; and calling lunacy a name does not *cause* it." These positivist sociologists seem to say that just as a rose by any other name would smell as sweet, so deviance by any other label is just as real.

Because they consider deviance real, positivist sociologists tend to focus their study on deviant behavior and deviant persons, rather than on nondeviants who label others deviants, such as lawmakers and law-enforcers, which constructionist sociologists are more likely to study, as will be explained later.

Objectivism: Deviance as an Observable Object

To positivist sociologists deviant behavior is an observable object in that a deviant person is like an object, a real something that can be studied objectively. Positivist sociologists, therefore, assume that they can be as objective in studying deviance as natural scientists can be in studying physical phenomena. The trick is to treat deviants as if they were objects, like those studied by natural scientists.

Nonetheless, positivist sociologists cannot help being aware of the basic difference between their subject, human beings, and that of natural scientists, inanimate objects. As human beings themselves, positivist sociologists must have certain feelings about their subject. However, they try to control their personal biases by forcing themselves not to pass moral judgment on deviant behavior or share the deviant person's feelings. Instead, they try to concentrate on the subject matter as it outwardly appears. Further, these sociologists have tried to follow the scientific rule that all their ideas about deviant behavior should be subject to public test. This means that other sociologists should be able to analyze these ideas to see whether they are supported by facts.

Such a drive to achieve scientific objectivity has made today's positivist sociologists more objective than their predecessors. They have, therefore, produced works that can tell us much more about the nature of deviant behavior. No longer in vogue today are such value-loaded and subjective notions as evil, immorality, moral failing, debauchery, and demoralization, which were routinely used in the past to describe the essence of deviance. Replacing those outmoded notions are such value-free and objective concepts as norm violation, retreatism, ritualism, rebellion, and conflict.

To demonstrate the objective reality of these concepts, positivist sociologists have used official reports and statistics, clinical reports, surveys of self-reported behavior, and surveys of victimization. Positivists recognize the unfortunate fact that the deviants who are selected by these methods do not accurately represent the entire population of deviants. The criminals and delinquents reported in the official statistics, for example, are a special group of deviants, because most crimes and delinquent acts are not discovered and, therefore, not included in the official statistics. Nevertheless, positivists believe that the quality of information obtained by these methods can be improved and refined. In the meantime, they consider the information, though inadequate, useful for revealing at least some aspect of the totality of deviant behavior. A major reason for using the information is to seek out the causes of deviant behavior. This brings us to the next, third assumption of the positivist perspective.

Determinism: Deviance as Determined Behavior

According to the positivist perspective, deviance is determined or caused by forces beyond the individual's control. Natural scientists hold the same deterministic view about physical phenomena. When positivist sociologists follow natural scientists, they adopt the deterministic view and apply it to human behavior.

Overly enthusiastic about the prospect of turning their discipline into a science, early sociologists argued that, like animals, plants, and material objects that natural scientists study, humans do not have any free will. The reason is that acknowledgment of free will would contradict the scientific principle of determinism. If a murderer is thought to will or determine a murderous act, then it does not make sense to say that the murderous act is caused by forces (such as mental condition or family background) beyond the person's control. Therefore, in defending their scientific principle of determinism, early sociologists maintained their denial of free will.

However, today's positivist sociologists assume that humans do possess free will. Still, this assumption, they argue, does not undermine the scientific principle of determinism. No matter how much a person exercises free will by making choices and decisions, the choices and decisions do not just happen but are determined by some causes. If a woman chooses to kill her husband rather than continue to live with him, she certainly has free will or freedom of choice as long as no one forces her to do what she does. Yet some factor may *determine* or *cause* the woman's choice of one alternative over another, that is, determine the way she exercises her free will. One such causal factor may be a long history of abuse at the hands of her husband. Thus, according to today's positivist sociologists, there is no inconsistency between freedom and causality.

Although they allow for human freedom or choice, positivist sociologists do not use it to explain why people behave in a certain way. They will not, for example, explain why the woman kills by saying "because she chooses to kill." This is no explanation at all, since the idea of choice can also be used to explain why another woman does not kill her husband—by saying "because she chooses not to." According to positivists, killing and not killing, or more generally, deviant and conventional behavior, being contrary phenomena, cannot be explained by the same factor, such as choice. Further, the idea of choice simply cannot explain the difference between deviance and conventionality; it cannot explain why one person chooses to kill while the other chooses not to. Therefore, although positivists do believe in human choice, they will not attribute deviance to human choice. Instead, they explain deviance by using such concepts as wife abuse, broken homes, unhappy homes, lower-class background, economic deprivation, social disorganization, rapid social change, differential association, differential reinforcement, and lack of social control. Any one of these causes of deviance can be used to illustrate what positivists consider to be a real explanation of deviance because, for example, wife abuse is more likely to cause a woman to kill her husband than not. Positivist theories essentially point to factors like these as the causes of deviance.

In sum, the positivist perspective on deviant behavior consists of three assumptions. First, deviance is *absolutely real* in that it has certain qualities that distinguish it from conventionality. Second, deviance is an *observable object* in that a deviant person is like an object and thus can be studied objectively. Third, deviance is *determined* by forces beyond the individual's control.

The Constructionist Perspective

Since the 1960s the constructionist perspective has emerged to challenge the positivist perspective, which had earlier been predominant in the sociology of deviance. Let's examine the assumptions of the constructionist perspective that run counter to those of the positivist perspective.

Relativism: Deviance as a Label

The constructionist perspective holds the relativist view that deviant behavior by itself does not have any intrinsic characteristics unless it is thought to have these characteristics. The so-called intrinsically deviant characteristics do not come from the behavior itself; they come instead from some people's minds. To put it simply, an act appears deviant only because some people think it so. As Howard Becker (1963) says, "Deviant behavior is behavior that people so label." So, no deviant label, no deviant behavior. The existence of deviance depends on the label. Deviance, then, is a mental construct (an idea, thought, or image) expressed in the form of a label. Deviance, in other words, is socially constructed, defined as such by society.

Since, effectively, they consider deviance unreal, constructionists understandably stay away from studying it. They are more interested in the questions of whether and why a given act is defined by society as deviant. This leads to the study of people who label others as deviants—such as the police and other law-enforcing agents. If constructionists study so-called deviants, they do so by focusing on the nature of labeling and its consequences.

In studying law-enforcing agents, constructionists have found a huge lack of consensus on whether a certain person should be treated as a criminal. The police often disagree among themselves as to whether a suspect should be arrested, and judges often disagree among themselves as to whether those arrested should be convicted or acquitted. In addition, since laws vary from one state to another, the same type of behavior may be defined as criminal in one state but not so in another. Young adult males who father babies born to unwed teenage females, for example, can be prosecuted for statutory rape in California but not in most other states (Gleick, 1996). There is, then, a *relativity* principle in deviant behavior: Behavior gets defined as deviant relative to a given norm or standard of behavior, which is to say, to the way people react to it. If it is not related to the reaction of other people, a given behavior is in itself meaningless—it is impossible to say whether it is deviant or conforming. Constructionists strongly emphasize this relativistic view, according to which, deviance, like beauty, is in the eye of the beholder.

Subjectivism: Deviance as a Subjective Experience

To constructionists, the supposedly deviant behavior is a subjective, personal experience and the supposedly deviant person is a conscious, feeling, thinking, and reflective subject. Constructionists insist that there is a world of difference between humans (as active subjects) and nonhuman beings and things (as passive objects). Humans feel and reflect, and are thus distinguishable from animals, plants, things, and forces in nature, which cannot. Humans also have sacred worth and dignity, but things and forces do not. It is proper and useful for natural scientists to assume nature as an object and then study it, because this study can produce objective knowledge for controlling the natural world. It can also be useful for social scientists to assume and then study humans as objects because it may produce objective knowledge for controlling humans, but this violates the constructionist's humanist values and sensibilities.

As humanists, constructionists are opposed to the control of humans; instead, they advocate the protection and expansion of human worth, dignity, and freedom. One result of this humanist ideology is the observation that so-called objective knowledge about human behavior is inevitably superficial whenever it is used for controlling people. To control its black citizens, for example, the former white racist regime in South Africa needed only the superficial knowledge that they were identifiable and separable from whites. To achieve the humanist goal of protecting and expanding a certain people's human worth, dignity, and freedom, a deeper understanding is needed. This understanding requires appreciating and empathizing with each individual or group, experiencing what they experience, and seeing their lives and the world around them from their perspective. We must look at their experience from the inside as a participant rather than from the outside as a spectator. In other words, we must adopt the internal, subjective view rather than the external, objective one.

The same principle, according to constructionists, should hold for understanding deviants and their deviant behavior. Constructionists contrast this subjective approach with positivists' objective one. To constructionists, positivists treat deviance as if it were an immoral, unpleasant, or repulsive phenomenon that should be controlled, corrected, or eliminated. In consequence, positivists have used the objective approach by staying aloof from deviants, by studying the external aspects of their deviant behavior, and by relying upon a set of preconceived ideas for guiding their study. The result is a collection of *surface facts* about deviants, such as their poverty, lack of schooling, poor self-image, and low aspirations. All this may be used for controlling and eliminating deviance, but it does not tell us what deviant people think about themselves, society, and their daily activities.

In order to understand the life of a deviant, constructionists believe, we need to use the relatively subjective approach, which requires our appreciation for and empathy with the deviant. The aim of this subjective approach is to understand the deviants' personal views, seeing the world as it appears to them. Thus, constructionists tend to study deviants with such methods as ethnography, participant observation, or open-ended, in-depth interviews.

As a result of their subjective and empathetic approach, constructionists often present an image of deviants as basically the same as conventional people. The deaf, for example, are the same as the nondeaf in being able to communicate and live a normal life. They should therefore be respected rather than pitied. This implies that so-called deviant behavior, because it is like so-called conventional behavior, should not be controlled, cured, or eradicated by society.

Voluntarism: Deviance as a Voluntary Act

The constructionist perspective holds that supposedly deviant behavior is a voluntary act, an expression of human volition, will, or choice. Constructionists take this stand because they are disturbed by what they claim to be the dehumanizing implication of the positivist view of deviant behavior. The positivist view is said to imply that the human being is like a robot, a senseless and purposeless machine reacting to everything in its environment. But constructionists emphasize that human beings, because they possess free will and choice-making ability, determine their own behavior.

To support this voluntarist assumption, constructionists tend to analyze how social control agencies define some people as deviant and carry out the sanctions against them. Such analyses often reveal the arbitrariness of official action, the bias in the administration of law, and the effort of controlling deviants. All these convey the strong impression that control agents, being in positions of power, exercise their free will by actively, intentionally, and purposefully controlling the "deviants."

Constructionists also analyze people who have been labeled deviant. The "deviants" are not presented as if they were robots, passively and senselessly developing a poor self-image as conventional society expects of them. Rather, they are described as actively seeking positive meanings in their deviant activities. In constructionist Jack Katz's (1988) analysis, for example, murderers see themselves as morally superior to their victims. The killing is said to give the murderers the self-righteous feeling of defending their dignity and respectability because their victims have unjustly humiliated them by taunting or insulting them. Katz also portrays robbers as feeling themselves morally superior to their victims—regarding their victims as fools or "suckers" who deserve to be robbed. Such insight into the subjective, experiential world of deviance constitutes a noncausal, descriptive, or analytical theory.

In brief, the constructionist perspective consists of three assumptions. First, deviant behavior is not real in and of itself; it is, basically, a *label*. Second, supposedly deviant behavior is a *subjective* experience and therefore should be studied with subjectivity and empathy. And, third, putatively deviant behavior is a *voluntary, self-willed* act rather than one caused by forces in the internal and external environments.

An Integrated View

To know what deviant behavior is, then, we need both positivist and constructionist perspectives. (See Table 1.1 for a quick review of these two perspectives.) The combination of the two can give us a better picture than either one can by itself. The two perspectives may appear to be in sharp contradiction, but their differences are largely in emphasis. By giving consideration to one side, we do not necessarily deny the reality of the other. Both positivist and constructionist sociologists, in emphasizing their own views, assume in a way their opponents to be correct. Each group merely thinks of the other's argument as less important than its own. Thus, while they accept constructionists' view of deviance as a label, positivists simply take it for granted, considering it less important than their own assumption of deviance as real behavior. On the other hand, while constructionists

TABLE 1.1   A Summary of Two Perspectives

Positivist Perspective	Constructionist Perspective
Absolutism: Deviance is absolutely, intrinsically real; hence, deviance or deviants can be subject of study.	*Relativism:* Deviance is a label, defined as such at a given time and place; hence, labelers, labeling, and impact of labeling can be subject of study.
Objectivism: Deviance is an observable object; hence, objective research methods can be used.	*Subjectivism:* Deviance is a subjective experience; hence, subjective research methods can be used.
Determinism: Deviance is determined behavior, a product of causation; hence, causal, explanatory theory can be developed.	*Voluntarism:* Deviance is a voluntary act, an expression of free will; hence, noncausal, descriptive theory can be developed.

accept positivists' view of deviance as an act that has really occurred, they consider it more worthwhile to focus on society's definition of the act as deviant.

Now that we know the two opposing perspectives, we can bring them together. As Chinese people are fond of saying, "Things that oppose each other also complement each other" (Mao, 1967). Thus we may see deviant behavior as being both a real act and a label. One cannot exist without the other. If there is no real act, there is no deviant *behavior;* if there is no label, there is no *deviant* behavior. In order for us to use the label "deviant," the *behavior* must occur. Similarly, for us to understand that behavior, the *label* "deviant" must be used. Deviance, then, is both behavior and label.

But in complementing each other, the two conflicting perspectives are not necessarily equally applicable to all types of deviant behavior. On the contrary, one perspective seems more relevant than the other in studying the types of deviance that more easily fit its assumptions and the temperaments of the sociologists embracing that perspective.

Specifically, the positivist perspective is more relevant to the study of what society considers relatively *serious* types of deviant behavior, such as murder, rape, armed robbery, and the like. The study of these types of deviance responds well to the positivist perspective for three reasons. First, these forms of deviant behavior, which characteristically enter into the official statistics analyzed by positivists, can be defined as really deviant. Such deviant acts are intrinsically more harmful than conforming behavior, are likely to elicit wide consensus from the public as to their deviant characteristics, and, therefore, are easily distinguishable from conforming behavior. Second, people who commit serious crimes, such as murder and robbery, generally come from the lower classes, quite unlike the positivists who study them. These are crimes that positivists themselves—as researchers, scholars, or professors—generally would not commit or could not conceive themselves capable of committing. It is easy, therefore, for positivists to stay aloof from these criminals, analyzing their behavior objectively, without empathizing with them or romanticizing their behavior. Third, since positivists can easily separate themselves from the people who commit serious deviant acts, it is natural for them to study these deviants as if they were passive objects "out there" rather than active subjects "in here" (like positivists themselves). It is thus natural for positivists to investigate these "passive" individuals with an eye to seeking out the causes of their deviance rather than understanding the operation of their free will.

In the same way, the constructionist perspective is more pertinent to the *less serious* kinds of deviance, particularly those that do not gravely harm other people. Thus this perspective finds itself at home in the world of adulterers, prostitutes, drug users, strippers, sex tourists, tax evaders, and the like. Again, three reasons explain the convenient fit between perspective and subject matter. First, there is a relative lack of consensus in society as to whether the less serious forms of deviant behavior are indeed deviant. Some members of society may label them deviant, while others may not. It is, therefore, logical for constructionists to emphasize that deviant behavior is basically a matter of labeling. Second, those so-called deviants are considered by society as less dangerous than the criminals typically studied by positivists. They also engage in the so-called deviant activities that constructionists themselves could enjoy, participate in, or at least feel themselves capable of engaging in—quite unlike the more dangerous acts committed by "common" criminals. Therefore, constructionists can more easily empathize with these supposed deviants and consider the latter's subjective experience useful for understanding deviance. Third, since they can empathize with these relatively harmless deviants, it is natural for constructionists to consider them active subjects like themselves rather than passive objects. This may be why they emphasize the voluntary, self-willed nature of the putative deviants' experience.

At bottom, the types of deviant behavior—seen through the positivist and constructionist perspectives—differ in the *amount of public consensus* regarding their deviant nature. On the one side, a given deviant act is, from the positivist standpoint, "intrinsically real," largely because there is a relatively great public consensus that it is really deviant. On the other side, a given deviant act is, from the constructionist perspective, "not real in itself but basically a label," largely because there is a relative lack of public consensus supporting it as really deviant. We may integrate the two views by defining deviant behavior with public consensus in mind.

Deviant behavior, we may say, is *any behavior considered deviant by public consensus, which may range from the maximum to the minimum.* Defined this way, deviant behavior should not be regarded as a discrete entity that is clearly and absolutely distinguishable from conforming behavior. Instead, deviance should be viewed as an act located somewhere on a continuum from total conformity at one extreme to total deviance at the other. Given the pluralistic nature of U.S. society, with many different groups having conflicting views of whether a given act is deviant, most of the so-called deviant behaviors can be assumed to fall in the large gray areas between the two poles of the continuum. Hence, deviant behavior actually means being more or less, rather than completely, deviant. It is a matter of degree rather than kind. Keeping this in the back of our minds, we may classify deviant behavior into two types, one more deviant than the other: higher-and lower-consensus deviance. *Higher-consensus deviance* is the type that has often been studied by positivist sociologists. *Lower-consensus deviance* is the type that has more frequently been studied by constructionist sociologists. Today, however, both positivists and constructionists are more interested than before in investigating both types of deviance, as we will see in many of the following chapters. This is probably because positivists are nowadays more likely to regard traditionally lower-consensus deviances (e.g., corporate fraud and governmental abuses) as harmful and dangerous as higher-consensus deviances such as homicide and robbery (Liddick, 2004; Rosoff et al., 2002). And, to be politically correct, constructionists tend more to "define deviancy down," showing greater sensitivity and empathy toward murderers, robbers, and other higher-consensus deviants (Hochstetler, 2004; Skrapec, 2001).

We have seen in this chapter how positivists and constructionists define what deviant behavior is. In Chapter 2 we will see how positivists explain what causes deviance. Then in Chapter 3 we will see how constructionists show what deviance means to certain people and how this meaning affects them or others.

A Word about Deviance and Crime

Students tend to think that deviance is basically the same as crime. Thus, the sociology of deviance is sometimes confused with criminology. But the two fields do differ. Although the sociology of deviance includes crime, it deals much more with deviance that is not crime. Criminology, on the other hand, covers only crime, although it has been profoundly influenced by the sociology of deviance.

How, then, does deviance differ from crime? First, crime *always* involves violating a law, but deviance does not. Deviance may involve breaking the law, so that some deviances such as murder, robbery, and rape are also crimes. So in that sense the sociology of deviance overlaps with criminology. But these two fields are mostly different, because most deviances are not crimes—they merely depart from some societal norm, rule, or standard, such as nude dancing, binge drinking, joining a cult, and being emotionally disturbed. Such subjects clearly distinguish the sociology of deviance from criminology.

Second, crime is a violation of a *formal* norm, which the law is, but deviance is more a violation of an *informal* norm that derives from a popular belief. Thus, crime as a violation of a formal norm is subject to imprisonment, fines, and other punishments by formal control agents such as the police, judges, prison guards, and other law enforcement agents. On the other hand, deviance as a violation of an informal norm is subject to criticism, ridicule, condemnation, rejection, and other negative reactions by informal control agents such as relatives, friends, neighbors, peer groups, and even strangers.

Third, the number and variety of deviances are infinitely greater than those of crimes. Crimes can *only* be *behavioral* in nature, because there are only laws against some unacceptable behaviors, not some strange beliefs and attitudes. But deviances include more than behaviors and even more than beliefs and attitudes. Many deviances involve having certain physical or psychological conditions, characteristics, or traits, such as obesity, mental illness, and being grossly unattractive, for which the individual can in no way be prosecuted.

Fourth, as has been suggested, not all deviances are crimes, but are all crimes deviances? Most crimes, such as murder, rape, and robbery, are deviant because they violate informal norms in addition to breaking the law as a formal norm. But a few crimes are *not* deviant because they are relatively acceptable throughout society. They are, in other words, normative behavior, such as gambling and cohabitation. Such practices hardly raise an eyebrow because they are very common. They are nonetheless criminal because in some places the *old* laws against them are still on the books. Other popular practices such as drinking among older teenagers and twenty-year-olds, smoking inside public buildings, and driving without buckling up have become criminal in many states because of the passing of *new* laws to prohibit them.

The subject of crime was the preoccupation of the positivists in the sociology of deviance before the 1960s. Then the emergence of the constructionist perspective in the 1960s transformed the sociology of deviance into a lively field. The sociology of deviance continues to be vibrant today. Its positivist approach to deviance has revitalized criminology (see, for example, Messner and Rosenfeld, 2001; Tittle, 1995; Hirschi and Gottfredson, 1994), while its constructionist approach has renewed the sociology of deviance. On the one hand, for example, an increasing number of studies delve into the subjective world of deviance, revealing how deviants see themselves and others. On the other hand, the constructionist approach has caused the sociology of deviance to focus less on crime and more on deviance, bringing in many new subjects on deviance for study, such as binge drinking, prescription drug abuse, transgenderism, exotic dancing, physical disabilities, obesity, tattooing, and cyberdeviance, as presented in this text.

Summary

1. How do sociologists define deviant behavior? In sociology there are many different definitions of deviant behavior. They can be divided into two major types, one influenced by the positivist perspective and the other by the constructionist perspective. The positivist perspective holds the absolutist view that deviant behavior is absolutely real, the objectivist view that deviance is an observable object, and the determinist view that deviance is determined behavior, a product of causation. The constructionist perspective consists of the relativist view that the so-called deviance is largely a label applied to an act at a given time and place, the subjectivist view that deviance is itself a subjective experience, and the voluntarist view that deviance is a voluntary, self-willed act.

2. Can we integrate those two perspectives? Yes. We can integrate them into a larger perspective that sees deviant behavior as an act located at some point on a continuum from maximal to minimal public consensus regarding the deviant nature of the act. With this integrated view, we can divide deviant behavior into two major types. One, *higher-consensus deviance,* is generally serious enough to earn a great amount of public consensus that it is really deviant. This type has often been the subject of research by positivist sociologists. The other, *lower-consensus deviance,* is generally less serious and thus receives a lesser degree of public consensus on its deviant reality. This type has more often attracted the interest of constructionist sociologists. The sociology of deviance has been a lively field since the 1960s and continues to be today.

FURTHER READING

Bendle, Mervyn F. 1999. "The death of the sociology of deviance?" *Journal of Sociology,* 35, 42–59. A critical analysis of the problems besetting the sociology of deviance and the emergence of a new paradigm for the field.

Best, Joel. 2004. *Deviance: Career of a Concept.* Belmont, Calif.: Wadsworth. An attempt to argue that deviance is no longer a thriving field of study in sociology.

Conrad, Peter, and Joseph W. Schneider. 1992. *Deviance and Medicalization: From Badness to Sickness.* Philadelphia: Temple University Press. An analysis of the changing definitions of deviance, from religious to criminal to medical definitions.

Cullen, Francis T. 1984. *Rethinking Crime and Deviance Theory: The Emergence of a Structuring Tradition.* Totowa, N.J.: Rowman & Allanheld. Arguing the importance of the "structuring perspective" for understanding deviance, which shows how certain social and social-psychological conditions can determine the transformation of a general deviant tendency into a specific form of deviant behavior.

Dodge, David L. 1985. "The over-negativized conceptualization of deviance: A programmatic exploration." *Deviant Behavior,* 6, 17–37. Argues that sociologists would do well to start studying positive deviance.

Goode, Erich, and Nachman Ben-Yehuda. 1994. *Moral Panics: The Social Construction of Deviance.* Cambridge, Mass.: Blackwell. A constructionist analysis of how societies periodically over-react with excessive fear or outrage to such social events as witchcraft, drug abuse, and satanism.

Henslin, James M. 1988. "Structuralism and individualism in deviance theory." *Deviant Behavior,* 9, 211–223. Illustrating an example of the difference between the positivist and constructionist perspectives in the sociology of deviance.

Lauderdale, Pat (ed.). 2003. *A Political Analysis of Deviance.* Toronto, Canada: de Sitter Publications. A collection of articles dealing with the political nature of deviance and the various aspects of political deviance.

Lyman, Stanford M. 1995. "Without morals or mores: Deviance in postmodernist social theory." *International Journal of Politics, Culture and Society,* 9, 197–235. A critical analysis of the constructionist view that the concept of deviance reflects an unjustifiable attempt to distinguish one group from another.

Pfohl, Stephen J. 1994. *Images of Deviance and Social Control: A Sociological History,* 2d ed. New York: McGraw-Hill. Presents nine perspectives of deviance, ranging from the earliest view of deviance as a demonic act to the latest conception of deviance as a way of "asserting lost power."

Thio, Alex, and Thomas C. Calhoun (eds.). 2006. *Readings in Deviant Behavior,* 4th ed. Boston: Allyn and Bacon. An anthology that includes articles on definitions, images, or notions of deviance.

CRITICAL THINKING QUESTIONS

1. Are liberals more likely than conservatives to hold the positivist or constructionist view of deviance? Why? Which view makes more sense to you and why?

2. Conduct a survey by asking a sample of your fellow students "What is deviant behavior?" and then "Why do you think it is deviant?" How do their responses fit either of the two perspectives of deviance?

CHAPTER
2 Positivist Theories

In October 2002, two men terrorized the residents of the national capital's suburbs for nearly three weeks. They drove around in their car and shot at people whom they picked out randomly. Ten of the victims died instantly and three were critically wounded. During the siege by the serial killers, residents were afraid to go out, causing restaurants, retail stores, and other businesses to suffer a sharp decline in patronage. School children had to run for cover as soon as they got off the bus, and they had to be "locked down," kept inside the building, not allowed to romp in the playground. High-school homecoming games had to be played at some undisclosed places away from the Washington area. Owners of gas stations had to put up large sheets of tarp to shield customers from the snipers. In fact, thanks to the daily reports on national TV about the sniping, Americans all over the country couldn't help feeling less safe than before (Thomas, 2002).

Soon after the snipers were caught, it was reported that before their spree killing in the Washington suburbs they had murdered two other people in Louisiana and Alabama. The killers were identified as John Muhammad, 41, and Lee Malvo, 17. Muhammad was said to treat the teenager as his son, and Malvo was said to be deferential and obedient to the older man. Muhammad was also reported to be "singularly unsuccessful at life," "a two-time loser at money and love." He was twice divorced and lost custody of his children to his ex-wives, who accused him of being abusive. He opened a martial-arts school, which went under, and then a car-repair business, which also failed. He was also arrogant and bad-tempered. When he was in the National Guard, he was court-martialed twice, for disobeying an order and for striking an officer (Duffy and Cannon, 2002). All these experiences were presented in the media as if they caused Muhammad to go on the killing spree. The focus on the causes of behavior like Muhammad's rampage characterizes positivist theories of deviance.

There are many positivist causal theories of deviance. Here we will discuss only the most important ones, namely, anomie-strain theory, social learning theory, and control theory.

Anomie-Strain Theory

In 1938 Robert Merton developed what later became known as anomie theory, attributing deviance to *anomie*, the breakdown of social norms that results from society's urging people to be ambitious while failing to provide them with the opportunities to succeed. In 1955 Albert Cohen (1955) extended Merton's theory to explain the emergence of delinquent boys. Then, two other sociologists, Richard Cloward and Lloyd Ohlin (1960), tried to improve on Merton's theory by adding the concept of differential illegitimate opportunity. Finally, since the early 1990s, other attempts have been made to extend the theory by emphasizing how the *strain* generated in people by anomie or other social conditions causes them to commit deviant acts (Messner and Rosenfeld, 2001; Agnew, 1992). The theory may thus be called anomie-strain theory.

Merton: The Goal–Means Gap

Merton found something wrong with Freud's psychoanalytic theory of deviant behavior. The psychoanalytic theory says that criminal, pathological, or socially dangerous behavior represents the free expression of the libido, biological impulses, or animal desires the individual is born with. The defect of this theory, according to Merton, lies in its assumption that "the structure of society primarily restrains the free expression of man's fixed native impulses." That is, society *discourages* the individual from engaging in deviant activities. Merton called this assumption a "fallacious premise," because he believed just the opposite: Society *encourages* the individual to engage in deviant activities. With such a premise, Merton developed his anomie theory.

Many sociologists have long believed that Merton's theory was inspired by Émile Durkheim, who was the first to use the term *anomie* as a sociological concept. Thus they have called it *anomie theory*. But the implication of Durkheim's concept of anomie is contrary to the premise of Merton's theory. By *anomie* Durkheim referred to the absence of social norms, which he equated with the failure of a society to rein in its members' limitless pursuit of material success. Durkheim assumed that the lack of this normative control causes deviance. This is similar to Freud's assumption that deviance will break out if society fails to discourage it by restraining individuals' impulses. But Merton's theory assumes just the opposite: Deviance will occur if society encourages it by pressuring individuals to commit it. Precisely how does society do this?

In Merton's view U.S. society heavily emphasizes the cultural value of success. From kindergarten to college your teachers motivate you to achieve a high scholastic record and to have great ambition for your future. The books, magazines, and newspapers you read often carry success stories that encourage you to become successful yourself. The games, sports, and athletic events that you watch in the stadium or on television impress you with the supreme importance of winning. If you participate in an athletic event, the coach will prod you to win. If you simply want to enjoy the pleasure of playing the game and sarcastically argue that "winning is not everything," the coach may argue back even more sarcastically: "Right, winning is not everything—winning is the *only* thing!" This cultural value of success is so pervasive in this society that people of *all* classes are expected to be ambitious, to entertain high aspirations; everyone is expected to have the desire to be a winner, to be somebody. Even poor people are told that their children have the chance of becoming president of the United States if they have as much ambition as the young, poverty-stricken Abraham Lincoln did. In this sense, the cultural *goal* of success is freely available to all people, regardless of their social-class backgrounds.

In contrast, the institutionalized, legitimate *means* of achieving the high success goal, such as getting a good job, are not freely available to all classes of people. The society is structured in such a way that people of the lower social classes, when compared with those of the higher, have less opportunity to realize their success aspirations. Lower-class people thus find themselves trapped in a very difficult situation. They have been encouraged by the society to hold high success aspirations, but they are not given the opportunity to realize those aspirations. To get themselves out of that predicament, many lower-class people resort to *illegitimate* means of achieving their success aspirations, such as stealing, robbing, and other similar forms of deviant activities. So, lower-class people are more likely to engage in deviant activities.

We have just seen that the *cause* of those lower-class deviant activities is the societal condition marked by the inconsistency between society's *over*emphasis on the success goal and its *under*emphasis on the use of legitimate means for achieving that goal. Merton (1938) describes this goal–means disjunction in this way: "Contemporary American culture continues to be characterized by a heavy emphasis on wealth as a basic symbol of success, without a corresponding emphasis upon the legitimate avenues on which to march toward this goal." With this

TABLE 2.1   A Typology of Responses to Goal–Means Gap

In U.S. society, according to Merton, there is too much emphasis on success but too little emphasis on the legitimate means for achieving success. Such inconsistency may cause deviant behavior, yet various people respond to it differently.

Response	Success Goal	Legitimate Means
1. Conformity	+	+
2. Innovation	+	−
3. Ritualism	−	+
4. Retreatism	−	−
5. Rebellion	− +	− +

Note: + indicates accepting; − signifies rejecting; and − + means rejecting the old and introducing the new.
Source: Adapted from Robert K. Merton, *Social Theory and Social Structure*. New York: Free Press, 1957.

encouragement of high aspirations and denial of success opportunities, U.S. society produces a great deal of strain that pressures us to commit deviance.

However, given this societal pressure toward deviance, not all of us would respond to it in the same way. Many lower-class people, as the previous discussion has implied, may respond to it by accepting the success goal while rejecting the use of legitimate means for realizing that goal. Merton refers to this deviant behavior as *innovation*. It is also the case that many other individuals of various social classes may respond differently to that same social condition. Therefore, along with innovation, Merton presents other types of response (see Table 2.1).

1. *Conformity* is the most popular form of response. It involves accepting both the cultural goal of success and the use of legitimate means of working toward that goal. Presumably most of us choose this response.

2. *Innovation* is largely found among lower-class people, who reject the use of legal means in favor of illegal ones in their attempts to achieve the high success goal that they have learned to accept. This form of deviant response is the central subject of strain theory, and Merton discusses it much more than any other.

3. *Ritualism* is common among lower-middle-class people who lower their aspirations or abandon high success goals so that they can more easily realize their aspirations. But in their attempts to realize these modest aspirations, they almost compulsively—hence, ritualistically—abide by the institutional norm of toiling as conscientious, loyal workers. They tend to be proud of their hard, honest work while shrugging off their modest incomes.

4. *Retreatism* is a withdrawal from society into the shell of one's self. The retreatist does not care about success, nor does he or she care to work. Examples of such people are psychotics, outcasts, vagrants, vagabonds, tramps, alcoholics, and drug addicts.

5. *Rebellion* involves rejecting the prevailing social expectation that we work hard in the so-called rat race to reach the goal of great success. The rebel also attempts to overthrow the existing system and put in its place a new one with new goals and new means of reaching those goals. Thus, the rebel may abandon both the pursuit of fame and riches and the cutthroat competition needed to achieve this worldly goal. At the same time, the rebel may encourage people to seek goodwill toward others and to cooperate in attaining this heavenly goal.

Cohen: Status Frustration

The version of anomie-strain theory proposed by Cohen (1955) is fundamentally the same as Merton's. Like Merton, Cohen suggests that U.S. society encourages all classes of people to achieve status while at the same time making it difficult for lower-class people to really achieve it. As a consequence, lower-class people are compelled to achieve status in their own way—that is, to engage in deviant acts. Although the theme is the same as in Merton's theory, Cohen tells the story differently, replacing Merton's word *success* with *status*.

According to Cohen, lower-class boys, like their middle-class peers, want to have status. An important place to achieve status is the school, which they are forced to attend. But the school turns out to be a most unlikely place for lower-class boys, because it ensures their failure. How so? The school is run by middle-class teachers, promotes middle-class values and behavior, and judges the student's achievement by middle-class standards of behavior and performance. The school, then, is a middle-class status system. To achieve the status of a successful, competent, or good student in the middle-class setting, youngsters must possess middle-class values, virtues, and traits, such as verbal fluency, academic intelligence, the ability to delay gratification, courtesy, opposition to fistfights, and respect for property. In this status system, middle-class boys obviously have a good chance of becoming successful. Yet lower-class boys, who have not been socialized in the same way as middle-class boys, are thrown into a status system where they are expected to compete with middle-class boys. The result is not surprising: lower-class boys fail disastrously. In Cohen's words, "they are caught up in a game in which others are typically the winners and they are the losers and the also-rans."

Being a loser or also-ran is obviously very frustrating. Driven by this frustration, which Cohen calls *status frustration*, lower-class boys go back to their own lower-class neighborhood and set up their own competitive system, which Cohen refers to as a *delinquent subculture*. In that subculture they can compete more fairly among themselves for high status in accordance with their own criteria of achievement. Their criteria of achievement are in direct opposition to the "respectable" middle-class, conventional criteria. They judge as wrong whatever values and behaviors are considered right by conventional standards, and they judge as right whatever values and behaviors are considered wrong by conventional standards.

Given this, it is obvious that the lower-class boys' very attempt to achieve status among their peers is—according to conventional standards—delinquent. The so-called delinquent activities include stealing "for the hell of it," fighting, terrorizing "good" children, destroying property, and defying various conventional taboos.

In short, Cohen extends Merton's theory by adding the concept of status frustration. As you may remember, Merton suggests that the goal–means gap (discrepancy between success aspiration and opportunity) *by itself* creates a lot of strain that pressures lower-class people into deviance: Goal–means gap → deviance. But Cohen's theory suggests that the goal–means gap can lead lower-class boys toward deviant activities only if the boys encounter *status frustration*. In other words, status frustration serves as the third, intervening variable that enables the goal–means gap to produce delinquent subculture: Goal–means gap → *status frustration* → deviance.

Nevertheless, Cohen's theory is basically the same as Merton's. Both assume that lower-class people are more likely than others to engage in deviant activities because society fails to help them fulfill the aspirations (for success or status) that it has induced in these people.

Cloward and Ohlin: Differential Illegitimate Opportunity

You may recall the way Merton formulates his theory: The lower classes tend to engage in deviance because they, like the middle and upper classes, have been encouraged to hold high success goals but, unlike the higher classes, are denied the *legitimate* means or opportunity of achieving the success goals. Cloward and Ohlin (1960) accept this general idea. At the same time, however, they want to extend it by introducing the concept of differential *illegitimate* opportunity.

First, Cloward and Ohlin point out that Merton correctly directs our attention to the problem of differential legitimate opportunity—that the lower classes have less opportunity than other classes for achieving success in a legitimate, conforming manner. But Merton wrongly assumes that the lower classes, when confronted with the lack of opportunity, would automatically and successfully engage in deviant activities. In other words, Merton fails to recognize the fact that the lower classes, after being confronted with the problem of differential *legitimate* opportunity, are further confronted with the additional problem of differential *illegitimate* opportunity. The fact is that some members of the lower classes have less opportunity than others of the same classes for achieving success in an *illegitimate, deviant* manner. What Cloward and Ohlin want to emphasize is that while all lower-class people suffer from the same lack of opportunity for engaging in legitimate and conforming activities, they do not have the same opportunity for participating in illegitimate and deviant activities. Thus, when some lower-class persons are pressured toward committing a deviant act such as theft or robbery, there is no guarantee that they will actually do it. Whether or not they will actually do it depends on whether they have access to illegitimate opportunity in the lower-class neighborhood.

There are three types of illegitimate opportunity, each provided by a deviant subculture. The *criminal* subculture offers illegitimate opportunities for achieving success goals. If lower-class youngsters are integrated into this subculture, they are able to achieve success by stealing, robbing, and fencing. This is the kind of deviant activity to which Merton assumes all lower-class youngsters will turn when they are denied conventional opportunities in the larger society. But, according to Cloward and Ohlin, many of these lower-class youths are not part of the criminal subculture and therefore do not enjoy criminal opportunities.

Yet some of those youths may find themselves in another neighborhood where the *conflict* subculture flourishes. In this subculture, a youngster has the opportunity to achieve "rep" or status within a violent delinquent gang. But that opportunity is available only to those youngsters who can meet such requirements as possessing great fighting skill and demonstrating enthusiasm for risking injury or death in gang warfare. Some lower-class adolescents fail to meet these requirements and are there-fore denied the opportunity for achieving status within the conflict subculture.

There is, finally, a third, *retreatist* subculture, in which the only requirement for membership is the willingness to enjoy the use of drugs. Persons who are recruited into the retreatist subculture are likely to be those who have failed to achieve success in the criminal subculture or to attain status in the conflict subculture. Because of their failure to achieve success or status in *both* the delinquent underworld and the conventional upperworld, the retreatists have been called "double failures."

In brief, Cloward and Ohlin extend Merton's anomie-strain theory by intro-ducing differential illegitimate opportunity as the third, intervening variable through which the goal–means gap leads to three different kinds of deviant activi-ties: goal–means gap → *differential illegitimate opportunity* → different deviant activi-ties. (Table 2.2 shows how this version of anomie-strain theory compares with the other two.) Nevertheless, Cloward and Ohlin basically agree with Merton that lower-class people are more inclined than others toward deviance because they are more likely to experience the discrepancy between success aspirations and the opportunity for realizing those aspirations.

Recent Developments

Over the last decade a number of sociologists have moved anomie-strain theory in new directions. Steven Messner and Richard Rosenfeld (2001), for example, argue that Merton focused too much on the "inequality in access to the legitimate means for success" as the source of the strain that leads to deviance. It is not so much the

---

TABLE 2.2   Three Versions of Anomie-Strain Theory

Merton: Goal–means gap → deviance

Cohen: Goal–means gap → status frustration → deviance

Cloward and Ohlin: Goal–means gap → differential illegitimate opportunity → different deviant activities

---

Note: The sign "→" indicates "antecedes or causes," as in "*A* antecedes or causes *B*."

relative lack of opportunity that causes people to resort to the illegal means of achieving success, Messner and Rosenfeld contend, rather it is the overwhelming culture of the American Dream that causes deviance by encouraging people to adopt an "anything goes" mentality in the pursuit of success.

Robert Agnew (1992) has also found Merton inadequate for focusing only on failure to achieve economic success goals as the strain that directly causes deviance. There are two other kinds of strain that are non-economic in nature, Agnew theorizes. One is what he calls the "removal of positively valued stimuli," such as "the loss of a boyfriend/girlfriend, the death or serious illness of a friend, moving to a new school district, the divorce/separation of one's parents, and suspension from school." The other form of strain involves the "presentation of negative stimuli," which includes such unpleasant experiences as child abuse and neglect, criminal victimization, physical punishment, and problems with parents or peers. These strains are said to cause frustration and anger, which in turn lead to deviant actions such as theft, aggression, and drug use.

Evaluating Anomie-Strain Theory

This theory has at least two problems. First, there is no reliable evidence to support its claim that people of the lower classes are more likely than those of other classes to engage in deviant activities. It is true that the official statistics on crime and delinquency, which anomie-strain theorists rely on, do support the theory. But the official statistics are largely unreliable and invalid. They are unreliable because law enforcers are much more likely to catch lower-class criminals and delinquents than higher-class ones. They are invalid because they do not reflect the total picture of deviance—they measure instead a very small portion of the totality of deviance, namely, the relatively serious types. If we modify the theory and say that lower-class people are more likely to commit what society considers *serious* types of deviance, then the theory does have adequate empirical support from both the official and unofficial reports on criminality and delinquency.

Second, there is no evidence to support the assumption of anomie-strain theory that lower-class people tend to hold the same level of success aspirations as do upper- and middle-class people. On the contrary, both theoretical analysis and empirical data show that lower-class people hold a significantly lower level of success aspirations. It is true, as anomie-strain theorists claim, that U.S. society *encourages* lower-class people to embrace high-success goals. But it is *not* necessarily true, as anomie-strain theorists assume, that lower-class people will end up embracing high-success goals. Merton and other anomie-strain theorists appear to have ignored the fact that while the manifest, intended function of U.S. success ideology is to get all social classes to entertain high aspirations, its latent, unintended, and real consequence turns out to be the higher social classes holding far higher aspirations than the lower classes.

Whatever its shortcomings, anomie-strain theory does have important redeeming value, aside from its being considered by many sociologists as highly interesting. Foremost to consider is that the theory has contributed greatly to the sociological idea that the society, not the individual, causes deviant behavior. Before the theory was first published in 1938, many sociologists tended to seek the causes of deviance within the individual rather than without. The fact that today many sociologists take for granted the notion of deviance as caused by society is a testament to the contribution of anomie-strain theory.

Further, the theory seems to have a valid premise: The discrepancy between aspirations and the opportunity to realize these aspirations produces pressures toward deviation. This premise suggests that anybody, regardless of their social class backgrounds, tends to engage in deviance if they experience a significant gap between aspiration and opportunity. Indeed, much research has shown that wherever the aspiration–opportunity gap strikes, it tends to generate deviation (Parnaby and Sacco, 2004; Passas and Agnew, 1997; Menard, 1995).

Social Learning Theory

According to social learning theory, the brainchild of Edwin Sutherland (1939), deviant behavior is learned through one's interaction with others. More specifically, Sutherland developed the theory of differential association to explain how the learning of deviance comes about. Later, other sociologists presented different versions of the same theory.

Sutherland: Differential Association

More than 60 years ago—at about the same time that Merton proposed strain theory—Sutherland (1939) introduced the theory of differential association. The heart of the theory is this: If an individual associates with people who hold deviant (or criminal) ideas more than with people who embrace conventional ideas, the individual is likely to become deviant.

We should note two things about the meaning of this statement. First, although deviants typically hold deviant ideas, the people who hold deviant ideas do not have to be deviants—they can be anybody, even those who have not committed any deviance. What counts is the *idea* of committing deviance. If a father tells his children that it's all right to steal when you are poor, he is giving them an idea of committing a deviant act. On the other hand, if the father tells his children that it's wrong to steal, he is giving them an antideviant idea. The emphasis here is on whether the father gives his children deviant or antideviant ideas, not whether the father himself is a deviant or nondeviant. Therefore, if people are given more ideas of committing deviant acts than ideas of performing conventional acts, they are likely to engage in deviance.

Second, the theory does *not* refer to only one type of association, that is, deviant association or exposure to deviant ideas. The theory does not suggest that, if individuals have a lot of contacts with deviant ideas, they will become deviant. Lawyers, for example, may have a lot of contacts with their criminal clients, but they will not necessarily become criminals themselves. The theory instead refers to both deviant and conventional contacts or, more precisely, to the *excess* of deviant over conventional contacts. This means that it is all right to have both kinds of contacts; only if we have a *greater* number of deviant contacts than conventional ones are we likely to become deviant. This is suggested by the term *differential asso- ciation,* which refers to the fact that deviants' *association* with deviant individuals and ideas *differs* from (or, more precisely, occurs more often than) their association with conventional ones. Defined in this way, differential association is theorized to be the cause of deviance: Differential association → deviant behavior.

Glaser: Differential Identification

According to Daniel Glaser (1956), Sutherland's theory actually conveys a "mecha- nistic image" of deviance. Such an image shows the individual as being mechani- cally pushed into deviant involvement by an association with deviants. It ignores the individual's role-taking and choice-making ability. Glaser, then, tries to correct this mechanistic image by suggesting that the experience of associating with deviants is harmless unless the individual *identifies* with them.

Glaser's theory may be taken to suggest that it is all right for us to associate with deviants in real life or get to know them in books and movies, as long as we do not take them so seriously that we identify with them, treating them as our heroes. But if we do identify with them, we are likely to become deviants ourselves. In effect, Glaser suggests that deviance is likely to occur if differential identification inter- venes between it and differential association: Differential association → *differential identification* → deviant behavior.

Burgess and Akers: Differential Reinforcement

According to Robert Burgess and Ronald Akers (1966), Sutherland merely sug- gested, in very broad terms, that people with differential association must go through a learning process before they become deviant. Sutherland failed, they contend, to specify what that learning process entails. In trying to correct this failure, Burgess and Akers offer the idea of *differential reinforcement* as the sub- stance of that learning process.

Burgess and Akers derive their idea from a well-known theory in psychology, which has been variously referred to as *social learning theory, behaviorist theory, operant behavior theory, operant conditioning theory,* and *reinforcement theory.* Gener- ally, the theory says that we are motivated to continue behaving in a certain way if we have been rewarded for doing so, or to discontinue the behavior if we have been punished for it. You are, for example, likely to continue studying hard if you have been rewarded by good grades for studying hard in the past. When applied to deviant behavior, reinforcement theory says that people will continue to engage in deviant activities if they have been rewarded for doing so. Robbers, for example, will continue to rob if they have made much money from their robberies or if they have not been caught for their crimes.

TABLE 2.3   **Three Versions of Social Learning Theory**

Sutherland: Differential association → criminal behavior

Glaser: Differential association → differential identification → criminal behavior

Burgess and Akers: Differential association → differential reinforcement → criminal behavior

Note: The sign "→" indicates "antecedes or causes," as in "*A* antecedes or causes *B*."

One aspect of reinforcement theory that is most relevant to the Burgess–Akers reformulation of Sutherland's differential association theory is the Law of Differential Reinforcement. This law can be expressed in simple terms as follows: If you are given several options, such as studying hard, going to the movies, drinking in a tavern, and attending a wild party the night before an exam, you will most likely choose the option that has been most satisfying to you in the past. When applied to deviant behavior, the law of differential reinforcement would explain that individuals will choose deviance over conventionality if they find deviance more satisfying than conventionality. However, this is likely to occur if they have been exposed to deviant ideas more than to conventional ideas. In short, Burgess and Akers's theory can be expressed as follows: Differential association → *differential reinforcement* → deviant behavior. Table 2.3 summarizes how this version of differential theory differs from the other two discussed earlier.

Evaluating Social Learning Theory

First, it is difficult to determine precisely what "differential association" in Sutherland's theory is in real-life situations. As Sutherland and Cressey (1978) admit, people often cannot identify the persons from whom they have learned deviant and antideviant ideas. Although it is difficult to determine the exact, empirical meaning of differential association, many sociologists have claimed that their research data appear to support Sutherland's theory. But this need not be surprising. Actually, those sociologists have not found any empirical support for Sutherland's theory, but only for their *own* interpretations of the theory. As James Short (1960), who has done considerable research to test the theory, observed: "Much support has been found for the principle of differential association *if* the liberties taken in the process of its operationalization [translation into empirical or testable terms] are granted." One study, for example, treats the concept of "differential association" as if it had to do with "association" only—and nothing to do with "differential." The concept is thus operationalized as a perception of friends' *deviant* attitudes and behaviors alone, not the friends' *excess of deviant over conventional* attitudes and behaviors (Hochstetler, Copes, and DeLisi, 2002).

Second, Glaser's differential identification theory appears to have received some support from empirical data. It has been found, for example, that high school boys who identified with delinquent friends were likely to become delinquent

themselves. But there is no conclusive evidence that identification with delinquent friends is the cause of delinquency or occurs before a person becomes delinquent. It is quite possible that youngsters may identify with delinquent friends only after—not before—having become delinquent themselves.

Third, the Burgess-Akers differential reinforcement theory cannot explain why a person *initially* commits a deviant act. The theory is useful, however, for explaining *repeated* deviance, namely, why some people *continue* to get involved in deviance after committing a deviant act for the first time. The reason, according to differential reinforcement theory, is that they have in the past been rewarded more than punished for their deviance, whereas others do not repeat a deviant act because they have been punished more than rewarded for the act. This formulation has indeed been borne out by many studies (see, for example, Chappell and Piquero, 2004; Akers and Lee, 1999).

Control Theory

Control theory differs in at least two ways from the other major theories discussed above. First, both anomie-strain and learning theorists approach the problem of explaining deviant behavior head-on and ask: What causes deviance? Control theorists approach the problem in a roundabout way: What, they ask, causes conformity? They assume, in other words, that if they find out what causes conformity, they will know what causes deviance, for what causes deviance is simply the *absence* of what causes conformity. Second, both anomie-strain and learning theorists reject the Freudian idea that deviance can naturally, or by itself, burst forth from our inborn animal impulses. Instead, anomie-strain and learning theories maintain that deviance originates from certain social conditions, namely, the discrepancy between goals and means in society and the experience of learning from others. In contrast, control theorists seem to accept the Freudian idea because they assume that people are naturally inclined to commit deviant acts and will do so *unless* they are properly controlled.

In the eyes of control theorists, then, what causes conformity is social control over the individual, and therefore *the absence of social control causes deviance*. There are, however, many different theories about the specific nature of social control. We will focus on only three of the more important ones.

Hirschi: Social Bond and Self-Control

Travis Hirschi (1969) assumes that all of us are endowed like animals with the ability to commit deviant acts. But most of us do not take advantage of this ability, Hirschi suggests, because of our *strong bond* to society. In other words, our strong bond to society ensures our conformity. Conversely, if our social bond is weak, we will commit deviant acts.

According to Hirschi, there are four ways for individuals to bond themselves to society. The first is by *attachment* to conventional people and institutions. In the

case of juveniles, they may show this attachment by loving and respecting their parents, making friends with conventional peers, liking school, and working hard to develop intellectual skills. A *commitment* to conformity is the second way. Individuals invest their time and energy in conventional types of action, such as getting an education, holding a job, developing an occupational skill, improving a professional status, building up a business, or acquiring a reputation for virtue. At the same time, people show a commitment to achievement through these activities. The third way is *involvement* in conventional activities. People simply keep themselves so busy doing conventional things that they do not have time for partaking in deviant activities or even thinking about deviant acts. A *belief* in the moral validity of social rules is the fourth way in which people bond themselves to society. Individuals have a strong moral belief that they should obey the rules of conventional society. A young person may show such moral belief through a respect for the police or through a positive attitude toward the law.

If these four elements of the individual's bond to conventional society are strong, the individual is likely to get stuck in conformity. If these elements are weak, the individual is likely to slide into deviance. In more recent publications, Hirschi, along with Michael Gottfredson, argues that *weak self-control* is more useful for explaining deviance. People with weak self-control are said to be highly impulsive, reckless, and insensitive. They are a product of inadequate socialization. Their parents have often failed, for example, to discipline them in childhood for wrongful behavior. Such people then are likely to commit deviant acts even if their social bond is strong (Hirschi and Gottfredson, 1994; Gottfredson and Hirschi, 1990).

Braithwaite: Reintegrative Shaming

While Hirschi sees how society controls us through bonding, John Braithwaite (2000, 1989) looks at how society controls us through shaming. Shaming involves an expression of social disapproval designed to invoke remorse in the wrongdoer. There are two types of shaming: disintegrative and reintegrative. In *disintegrative shaming*, the wrongdoer is punished in such a way as to be stigmatized, rejected, or ostracized—in effect, banished from conventional society. It is the same as stigmatization. *Reintegrative shaming* is more positive; it involves making wrongdoers feel guilty while showing them understanding, forgiveness, or even respect. It is the kind of shaming that affectionate parents administer to their misbehaving child, or "hating the sin but loving the sinner." Thus, reintegrative shaming serves to reintegrate—or welcome back—the wrongdoer into conventional society.

According to Braithwaite, reintegrative shaming is more common in communitarian societies (marked by strong social relationships but weak individualism), such as Japan, whereas disintegrative shaming is more prevalent in less communitarian societies (characterized by weaker social relationships but stronger individualism), such as the United States. At the same time, reintegrative shaming usually discourages further deviance, while disintegrative shaming or stigmatization encourages it. This is taken to explain why crime rates are higher in the United States than in Japan.

Braithwaite concludes by arguing that the United States can significantly reduce its crime rates if it emphasizes reintegrative shaming rather than stigmatization in dealing with criminals, as Japanese society does. Since the early 1990s reintegrative shaming has appeared in the United States as "shaming penalties," which include drunk drivers being ordered by judges to display "DUI" bumper stickers, people convicted of public urination being ordered to sweep city streets, or men who solicit prostitutes being identified on newspapers, billboards, and radio shows. Dan Kahan (1997), a law professor at the University of Chicago, argues that the shaming is an effective deterrent to deviance.

The Deterrence Doctrine

While Braithwaite's theory deals largely with shaming as an *informal* social control (carried out by relatives, friends, neighbors, and the like), the deterrence doctrine focuses on *formal* social control (executed by judges and other law-enforcement agents). This version of control theory assumes that humans are basically rational, given to calculating the benefit and cost of committing a crime. If they find the cost greater than the benefit, they will refrain from committing the crime. The cost of crime, according to deterrence doctrine, is legal punishment, such as arrest, prosecution, imprisonment, or execution. Thus, the doctrine assumes that punishment (a form of social control) deters crime—and lack of punishment encourages it.

There are three ways in which punishment can be carried out, each being assumed to affect the likelihood of committing crime. First, punishment can be made more or less *severe*. According to deterrence doctrine, the more severe the punishment, the less likely the crime. Murder rates, for example, are expected to be lower in societies where convicted murderers are executed than in societies where the murderers are given a 20-year sentence. Second, punishment can be made more or less *certain*. Deterrence doctrine assumes that the more certain the commission of a crime will result in punishment, the less likely people will be to commit the crime. Shoplifting, for example, is expected to become less common if the chances of getting arrested for it go up from 50–50 to 100. Third, punishment can be made more or less *swift*. The more swiftly punishment is carried out, the less likely the crime is to occur. If it takes only several days for robbers to be arrested in a given city, the robbery rate in this city is likely to be lower than in another city where it takes longer to arrest robbers.

Whatever the mode of punishment, whether it be severe, certain, or swift, it is assumed to achieve two kinds of deterrence: general and specific. In *general deterrence* the punishment of a criminal deters the general public from committing crimes; in *specific deterrence* the punishment of a criminal deters the criminal alone from committing more crimes.

In sum, the three control theories suggest that some form of control prevents people from committing deviant acts, and the lack of controls prompts the commission of such acts. The theories differ largely in regard to what type of control can prevent deviance. Thus, they present various types of control, which include bond to society, weak self-control, reintegrative shaming, and legal punishment.

Evaluating Control Theory

First, many studies have supported Hirschi's social bond and self-control theory. Deviants such as juvenile delinquents, drug users, and drunk drivers have been found to have a weaker social bond or self-control than nondeviants (see, for example, Pratt and Cullen, 2000). But most of these studies, being cross-sectional rather than longitudinal, could not have controlled for (canceled out) the reciprocal effect of deviance on social bond or self-control. Often, it is the deviant experience that causes people to have a weaker social bond and self-control rather than the other way around. Also, many studies that supposedly support the theory turn out to be tautological, using deviant acts (such as smoking, using drugs, speeding, and drunk driving) as the empirical indicators of weak self-control. These studies effectively suggest that deviance causes deviance (Stylianou, 2002; Burton et al., 1998; Kempf, 1993).

Second, Braithwaite is only partly convincing in his argument that the United States can reduce crime with reintegrative shaming—by treating criminals in the same lenient, compassionate way as Japan does. This treatment may work if applied to first-time offenders who have committed relatively minor crimes and still retain a sense of shame for their crimes. But it can hardly have the same positive impact on hardened criminals who have lost their sense of shame for their crimes. Moreover, since reintegrative shaming is part and parcel of a communitarian society, it seems to be the pervasiveness of such society's strong social relationships rather than reintegrative shaming that largely keeps the crime rate low.

Third, the deterrence doctrine has received only conflicting support from research. Various studies show, for example, that arresting wife-beaters deters further violence more than less severe forms of punishment such as ordering the offender to leave the victim for eight hours. However, studies on released prisoners suggest just the opposite: The more severe their punishment (for example, the longer the sentence), the more likely it is that former inmates will commit crimes again (Wright et al., 2004; Heckert and Gondolf, 2000; Berk and Newton, 1985).

Finally, various control theorists share a simplistic view of social control, regarding it as only a *preventer* of deviance. They fail to see control as a possible *cause* of deviance. The great ambition—along with excellent social and intellectual skills—that develops from social bond may prevent juvenile delinquency, as Hirschi's theory suggests, but the same ambition may cause corporate and political crimes. Similarly, contrary to Braithwaite's theory, reintegrative shaming may cause deviance, such as by encouraging judges to presume the accused as guilty, thereby violating the person's right to be presumed innocent. Also, contrary to the deterrence doctrine, the very process of law enforcement to deter crime may trigger lawbreaking acts. In taking action against a suspect, for example, a police officer may cause the suspect to commit such criminal acts as resisting arrest or assaulting an officer (Marx, 1981).

Table 2.4 presents the major points of all the theories discussed in this chapter.

TABLE 2.4   Positivist Theories of Deviance

Anomie-Strain Theory: Social strain causes deviance.

> **Merton's goal–means gap:** Deviance is prevalent in society because the society encourages people to achieve success without providing equal opportunity for achieving it.

> **Cohen's status frustration:** Deviance is prevalent among lower-class youths because they fail to achieve status in a middle-class school environment.

> **Cloward and Ohlin's differential illegitimate opportunity:** Lower-class youths are likely to engage in delinquent activities if they have access to illegitimate opportunity.

> **Latest versions of the theory:** The American Dream contributes to deviance by directly encouraging the use of illegal means to achieve success, while various social strains cause deviance by producing such emotions as frustration and anger.

Social Learning Theory: Deviance is learned through social interaction.

> **Sutherland's differential association:** People are likely to become deviant if they associate with people holding deviant ideas rather than with people holding antide-viant ideas.

> **Glaser's differential identification:** People are likely to become deviant if they identify themselves more with deviants than with nondeviants.

> **Burgess and Akers's differential reinforcement:** Deviants are likely to continue engaging in deviant activities if they have been rewarded rather than punished for their past deviance.

Control Theory: Lack of social control causes deviance.

> **Hirschi's social bond and self-control:** People are likely to become deviant if their bond to society and their self-control are weak.

> **Braithwaite's reintegrative shaming:** People are likely to become deviant if they are not made to feel ashamed for their wrongdoing or to feel they are an integral part of society.

> **The deterrence doctrine:** People are likely to become deviant if they know their deviant acts are not punished with severity, certainty, or swiftness.

Summary

1. How does anomie-strain theory explain the causation of deviant behavior? According to Merton's anomie-strain theory, lower-class people are more likely to get involved in deviant activities because the society has encouraged them to pursue a high-success goal without providing them with the means of achieving it. Cohen extends this theory by proposing that when their aspirations for status are frustrated in the middle-class milieu, lower-class youths are driven to achieve status among themselves by engaging in delinquency. Cloward and Ohlin extend Merton's theory by suggesting that whether potentially delinquent lower-class youth will actually become delinquent depends on whether they have access to illegitimate opportunity. Other sociologists extend Merton's theory by attributing deviance to the American Dream and forms of strain ignored by Merton. **How good is anomie-strain theory?** There is no reliable evidence for its assumption that, compared with middle and upper classes, the lower classes are more prone to deviance while holding the same level of success aspirations. Nevertheless, the theory has been valuable for replacing the psychological with the sociological explanation of deviance and for offering the valid premise that the aspiration–opportunity gap causes deviance.

2. According to various versions of social learning theory, why do some people become deviant? Sutherland's differential association theory states that people will likely become deviant if they associate more with individuals who hold deviant ideas than with those who embrace antideviant ideas. Glaser extends this theory by suggesting that the determining factor for turning the differential association into criminal action is differential identification, while Burgess and Akers designate differential reinforcement the determining factor. **Are**

Sutherland's theory and its extended versions any good? Sutherland's theory has been criticized for lacking a precise, empirical meaning of "differential association," but many researchers claim to have found data supporting the theory. As for Glaser's theory, it has received some, though not conclusive, empirical support. The Burgess–Akers theory cannot explain initial acts of deviance but is useful for explaining repeated deviance.

3. How does control theory explain deviance? According to the theory, what causes conformity is control, and, therefore, the lack of control causes deviance. Hirschi refers to this causal factor of conformity as our *bond to society*, or *self-control*. Braithwaite calls it *reintegrative shaming*, and proponents of deterrence doctrine refer to it as *legal punishment*. **What are the strengths and weaknesses of various control theories?** Hirschi's theory has received a lot of support from research data, but weak social bond or self-control may be the effect rather than the cause of deviance. Braithwaite's theory about reintegrative shaming being able to reduce crime in the United States may work for first-time offenders but not hardened criminals. The deterrence doctrine has received support from some studies but has been refuted by others.

FURTHER READING

Adler, Freda, and William S. Laufer (eds.). 1995. *The Legacy of Anomie Theory.* New Brunswick, N.J.: Transaction. A series of essays that discuss the contribution of Merton's theory to the sociological research and understanding of deviance.

Agnew, Robert. 1992. "Foundation for a general strain theory of crime and delinquency." *Criminology,* 30, 47–87. A revision of Merton's anomie-strain theory that takes into account many forms of strain that lead to deviance.

Akers, Ronald L. 1998. *Social Learning and Social Structure: A General Theory of Crime and Deviance.* Boston: Northeastern University Press. A clear presentation of his social learning theory as well as research data supporting the theory.

Braithwaite, John. 1989. *Crime, Shame and Reintegration.* New York: Cambridge University Press.

A theory about how society deters crime through the imposition of a social control called "reintegrative shaming."

Cullen, Francis T. 1988. "Were Cloward and Ohlin strain theorists? Delinquency and opportunity revisited." *Journal of Research in Crime and Delinquency, 25,* 214–241. Shows why Cloward and Ohlin are more opportunity theorists than strain theorists.

Hirschi, Travis, and Michael R. Gottfredson (eds.). 1994. *The Generality of Deviance.* New Brunswick, N.J.: Transaction. A collection of articles about the editors' theory of self-control, which essentially shows how a lack of self-control can result from ineffective child rearing and then cause deviance.

Liska, Allen E., and Mark D. Reed. 1985. "Ties to conventional institutions and delinquency: Estimating reciprocal effects." *American Sociological Review, 50,* 547–560. Data in this study question the validity of many past studies that claimed to support control theory.

Marx, Gary T. 1981. "Ironies of social control: Authorities as contributors to deviance through escalation, nonenforcement, and covert facilitation." *Social Problems, 28,* 221–246. Discusses how authorities often help bring about deviance that they have set out to control.

Matsueda, Ross L. 1988. "The current state of differential association theory." *Crime & Delinquency, 34,* 277–306. Discusses the development of the theory as well as its strengths and weaknesses.

Messner, Steven F., and Richard Rosenfeld. 2001. *Crime and the American Dream.* Belmont, Calif.: Wadsworth.

Passas, Nikos, and Robert Agnew (eds.). 1997. *The Future of Anomie Theory.* Boston: Northeastern University Press. A collection of articles analyzing, modifying, and expanding Merton's strain theory.

Stylianou, Stelios. 2002. "The relationship between elements and manifestations of low self-control in a general theory of crime: Two comments and a test." *Deviant Behavior, 23,* 531–557. Discusses the tautological problem with low self-control theory and shows the proper way of testing the theory.

Tittle, Charles R. 1995. *Control Balance: Toward a General Theory of Deviance.* Boulder, Colo.: Westview. Presents a complicated theory of how the interaction among deviant motivation, opportunity, and constraint determines the probability of deviance.

CRITICAL THINKING QUESTIONS

1. Which of the positivist theories makes the most sense to you and why?

2. What would you have the government do to fight crime, based on one or more of the positivist theories discussed in this chapter?

CHAPTER

3 Constructionist Theories

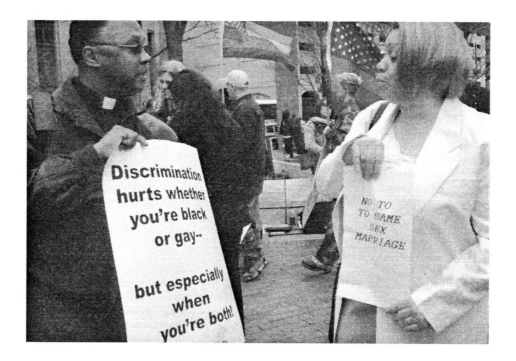

In January, 2000, Richard Pitcher, 35, and Kimberly Henry, 31, began a romance that led to talk of marriage three weeks later. But the sting of his second divorce was still fresh, and her first marriage had also been a disaster. So, they decided to move in together instead of rushing into marriage. After enjoying their lives as a couple for about a month, they found a summons in the mail charging them with violating Article 30-10-2 of the New Mexico criminal code, which covers unlawful cohabitation. They were told that first offenders got a warning but repeat offenders could be sent to jail for six months. "I couldn't believe it," Pitcher said. "I was shocked." Pitcher later found that the complaint to the police had been filed by his second ex-wife. She had just married for the fourth time, but as a newly born-again

Christian, she did not want her five-year-old daughter to see her dad living in sin. The local district attorney, however, said he would dismiss the case, calling the unlawful cohabitation law "weird" (Yardley, 2000).

Is living together really deviant? Positivist sociologists assume that it is because it involves breaking the legal norm that prohibits cohabitation. Because they regard that deviant behavior as real, positivists are inclined to seek out the causes of cohabitation. But constructionist sociologists are not interested in studying cohabitation because they do not really consider it deviant behavior. They are more interested in finding out who thinks of cohabitation as deviant and why. To constructionists, cohabitation is not deviant as an act; it appears deviant only as a mental construction, a figment of human imagination. Thus constructionists have developed theories about how people impute the notion of "deviance" to behaviors like cohabitation and what consequences this has for themselves and for others. This chapter discusses the more important of these theories.

Labeling Theory

In the early 1960s, a group of sociologists developed what soon became widely known as labeling theory. It is actually a version of symbolic interactionism, a well-known sociological theory about social behavior in general (Becker, 1974, 1963; Erikson, 1962; Kitsuse, 1962).

A Version of Symbolic Interactionism

In defining what deviance is, labeling theorists call on two central ideas in symbolic interactionism. These two ideas are suggested by the very two words that make up the name of the theory. First, as suggested by the word *interaction,* deviance—like any other kind of human activity—is a collective action, involving more than one person's act. According to labeling theory, we should not focus on the deviant person alone as positivist sociologists do but rather on the *interaction* between the supposed deviant and other, conventional people. As Becker (1974) says:

> The positivist style of studying deviance has focused on the deviant himself and has asked its questions mainly about him. Who is he? Is he likely to keep being that way? The new [labeling] approach sees it as always and everywhere a process of interaction between at least two kinds of people: those who commit (or are said to have committed) a deviant act and the rest of society, perhaps divided into several groups itself. The two groups are seen in complementary relationship. One cannot exist without the other.

Second, as suggested by the word *symbolic,* the interaction between the supposed deviant and the conformists is governed by the *meanings* that they impute to each other's actions and reactions. The meaning (variously referred to by symbolic interactionists as a symbol, significant gesture, interpretation, definition, or label) that people attach to an act is much more important than the act itself. The meaning, according to labeling theorists, comes through in how people respond to an act: A negative response means deviance; a positive response means nondeviance. As Kitsuse (1962) explains, "Forms of the behavior per se do not differentiate deviants from nondeviants; it is the responses of the conventional and conforming members of the society who identify and interpret behavior as deviant which sociologically transform persons into deviants."

In short, labeling theorists interpret deviance not as a static entity whose causes are to be sought out, but rather as *a dynamic process of symbolic interaction between both deviants and nondeviants.* Consequently, labeling theorists do not ask as positivists do: What causes deviant behavior? Instead, they ask at least two questions: (1) Who applies the *deviant* label to whom? and (2) What consequences does the application of this label have for the person labeled and for the people who apply the label? (These questions can be expressed in terms of symbolic interactionism: Who interprets whose behavior as deviant? And how does this interpretation affect the behavior of both parties involved in the interaction?)

Who Labels Whom?

According to labeling theorists, people who represent the forces of law and order as well as conventional morality typically apply the deviant label to those who have allegedly violated that law and morality. Examples of the *labelers* include the police, judges, prison guards, psychiatrists, mental hospital attendants, and other social control agents. On the other hand, examples of the *labeled* include criminals, juvenile delinquents, drug addicts, mental patients, and prostitutes.

Generally, the rich, white, or powerful and their representatives such as law-enforcing agents are more able to label others as deviant. As Becker (1974) says, "A major element in every aspect of the drama of deviance is the imposition of definitions—of situations, acts, and people—by *those powerful enough or legitimated to be able to do so.*" On the other side of the same coin, the poor, black, or powerless are more likely to be labeled deviant. Thus a poor or black person is more likely than a rich or white person to be arrested, prosecuted, or convicted as a criminal, even if both have committed similar crimes; to be declared insane or committed to a mental institution, even if both suffer from similar psychiatric conditions; and so on. This idea of the powerful labeling the weak as deviant runs through other constructionist theories, especially the various versions of conflict theory, which will be discussed later.

Consequences of Labeling

Labeling a person deviant may have some consequences for the person so labeled and also for the labeler.

Consequences for the Labeled.   According to labeling theorists, being labeled deviant produces *negative* consequences for the individual so labeled. One major consequence is that once people are labeled deviant, they tend to see themselves as deviant, which in turn leads them to continue the so-called deviant behavior. The issue here is not whether they have actually committed deviant acts; rather—whatever the nature of their acts—whenever they are defined as deviant by others, they also tend to define themselves as deviant, then continue to engage in the acts, and, finally, become confirmed deviants. This process of becoming deviant was long ago discussed by Frank Tannenbaum (1938). In his view, a child may engage in many forms of activities—such as breaking windows, annoying people, climbing over the roof, stealing apples, and playing hooky—and innocently consider all these enjoyable. But the parents, teachers, and police may, and often do, define these activities as a type of nuisance, delinquency, or evil. So they may "dramatize the evil" of these activities by admonishing, scolding, spanking, hauling into court, or jailing the child. Thus, dramatically labeled a delinquent, the child will likely become one, and, later, a criminal.

In discussing the process of becoming a criminal, Tannenbaum implied that there are two types of deviant acts. One is the *first* act, which the child considers innocent but which adults define as delinquent, and the second is the *final* behavior, which both the child and adults define as delinquent. Later, Edwin Lemert (1951) made explicit the distinction between these two forms of behavior. He called the first *primary deviation*, and the second, *secondary deviation*.

Like Tannenbaum, Lemert sees the difference between primary and secondary deviance as more than temporal—more than the fact that one occurs earlier than the other, more than that primary deviance is committed only once while secondary deviance is continued or repeated deviance. Lemert sees primary deviance as a matter of value conflict, as a behavior that the society defines as deviant but that the performer of that behavior does not so define. This behavior becomes secondary deviance only when the person comes to agree with the society's definition of the behavior as deviant, seeing himself or herself as a deviant.

Labeling theorists are mostly interested in analyzing the process of becoming a secondary deviant—that is, in how a person goes from primary to secondary deviation. They refer to this analysis as a sequential, career, or identity-stabilizing model of deviance. This model suggests that when people are forced by society to see themselves as deviants, they become secondary deviants by repeatedly engaging in deviation as a way of life. Consider a man who has just been released from prison after serving a sentence for robbery. He is likely to be stigmatized as an "ex-con." As a stigmatized ex-con, he will find it difficult to get a good job. For that reason, he will see himself as an ex-con, feel compelled to commit another robbery, and thus launch his career as a robber.

In short, once labeled a deviant, the individual tends to suffer a negative consequence by continuing to engage in deviant activities as a secondary, confirmed, or career deviant. The individual also suffers other negative consequences, such as being ridiculed, humiliated, degraded, harassed, beaten, imprisoned, or otherwise dehumanized—treated as an object, animal, or nonperson. All this suggests that the deviant is "more sinned against than sinning" (Becker, 1963).

Consequences for the Labeler.   According to labeling theorists, labeling a person deviant tends to create *positive* consequences for the community that applies the label. One consequence is enhanced social order. As Erikson (1962) explains:

> As a trespasser against the group norms, he [the deviant] represents those factors which lie outside the group's boundaries: he informs us, as it were, what evil looks like, what shapes the devil can assume. And in doing so, he shows us the difference between the inside of the group and the outside. It may well be that without this ongoing drama at the outer edges of group space, the community would have no inner sense of identity and cohesion. . . . Thus deviance . . . may itself be, in controlled quantities, an important condition for preserving stability.

If some individuals are periodically singled out to be convicted and punished as criminals, conventional members of the community will know better the distinction between good and evil so that they will ally themselves with good and against evil. The deviant, in effect, does us a great service by teaching us what evil is like, presenting himself or herself as an object lesson for what we shall suffer if we do evil, and thus encouraging us to avoid punishment and do good. Therefore, when some individuals or groups are labeled deviant, there will follow some positive consequences for the community as the labeler, the most important consequence being the preservation and strengthening of social cohesion and social order.

Evaluating Labeling Theory

Labeling theory has enjoyed tremendous popularity among sociologists. They can easily see the significance of labeling in human interaction, and can find considerable research evidence to support the theory (see, for example, Adams, 2003; Davies and Tanner, 2003; Lauderdale et al., 1984). Nevertheless, the theory has also drawn a lot of criticisms, of which only the most important are addressed here.

First, many sociologists have criticized labeling theory for not being able to answer the question of what causes deviance in the first place. This criticism misses the mark, though, because the theory is not meant to explain what causes primary deviance. The theory is intended to be nonetiological; it is not concerned with causal questions about primary deviance, except as they might relate to how labeling causes secondary deviance.

Second, research has failed to produce consistent support to labeling theorists' assumption that the deviant label leads the individual into further deviant involvement. Some studies show that labeling encourages further deviance, but many others do not. According to one researcher, for example, teenagers who are publicly labeled as juvenile delinquents for having been convicted in court for an offense, more than their nonlabeled peers, tend to get involved in delinquent activities again. Another researcher, however, finds that although they are often ridiculed in school as "sluts," "druggies," or "white trash," poor teenage girls with a relatively strong bond to their mothers or grandmothers do *not* engage in promiscuous, unprotected sex or use alcohol and other drugs (Victor, 2004; Farrington, 1977).

Finally, labeling theory cannot logically deal with hidden deviance and powerful deviants (Thio, 1973). By insisting that no behavior can be deviant unless labeled as such, labeling theory inevitably implies that hidden deviance, particularly the kind committed often in secrecy by powerful people, cannot be deviant because it is by definition unknown to others and, therefore, cannot be labeled by others as deviant. In addition, by stating that it is the more powerful people who typically impose the deviant label on the less powerful, labeling theorists in effect suggest that the powerful cannot be deviants because they can only be labelers.

Phenomenological Theory

Many sociologists have been influenced by labeling theory since the early 1960s. But toward the end of that decade, some sociologists took a step beyond labeling theory and developed another, new version of symbolic interactionism called *phenomenological theory*. (It has also been referred to as ethnomethodology, existential sociology, creative sociology, or sociology of everyday life.) As we have noted, labeling theory deals with societal reaction to deviance and the consequences of this reaction for the deviants and their labelers. But the theory does not get into the minds of these people. This is what phenomenological theory does. It delves into people's subjectivity (called a *phenomenon*), including their consciousness, perception, attitudes, feelings, and opinions about deviance. It assumes that all kinds of people, whether deviants or their labelers, are highly subjective in "constructing," defining, or interpreting deviance, although they may claim to be very objective (Rouback, 2004; Handel, 1982; Morris, 1977).

Critique of Positivism

Phenomenologists first launch a philosophical attack on sociologists who adopt the positivist view of deviance. As we saw in Chapter 1, positivists take an objective and deterministic approach to deviance. They view a deviant person as an object whose behavior is determined or caused by various forces in the environment. Consequently, positivists ignore how deviants think and feel about their own deviant experience. By contrast, phenomenologists consider the deviant's subjective experience the heart of deviant reality. At the same time, they regard positivists' supposedly objective notion of deviant behavior as unreal, because it reflects their own preconception of the deviant as an object rather than the reality of the deviant as a thinking and feeling human.

In other words, positivists do not study a phenomenon as it really is but rather study *their own conception* of the phenomenon. They are, in effect, highly subjective—or certainly not as objective as they claim to be. Positivists have long assumed that the real phenomenon and the positivist conception of it are identical. But to phenomenologists, the real phenomenon is different from the positivist conception of it. The real phenomenon, in phenomenologists' view, is the immediate experience and consciousness of the person under study. Consider, for example, how the positivist view of a psychiatrist might differ from the subjective view of quiet, withdrawn Hopi Indians. To the psychiatrist, the Hopi may be abnormal because their withdrawn behavior is defined by the psychiatric profession as a symptom of abnormality. The Hopi, to the contrary, see themselves as perfectly normal because their quiet demeanor is a virtue in Hopi culture.

Subjectivism as the Key to Deviant Reality

To phenomenologists, what deviance means is *fundamentally problematic:* People disagree over the meanings of deviance. Such disagreement frequently occurs among positivists when they try to observe and explain an individual's deviant behavior "objectively." In analyzing suicide, for example, constructionist sociologists find that doctors, coroners, and official statisticians—on whom positivist sociologists rely heavily for their definition of suicide—often disagree among themselves as to whether a given death is "suicide" (Pescosolido and Mendelsohn, 1986; Douglas, 1967). According to general agreement, a self-caused death should be interpreted as suicide if there is "intention to die." But since the *intention* to die is difficult to determine after the person is dead, disagreement is bound to exist over whether the deceased actually had this intention. Thus, those who believe there was intention to die would define the self-caused death as "suicide"; those who do not would interpret it as "accidental death." All this implies that since the meanings of deviance are fundamentally problematic for positivists, their conception of deviance cannot possibly get at the essence of a deviant phenomenon.

The meanings that positivists ascribe to deviance are *abstract* in nature, that is, *independent* of concrete situations in which the deviant person is involved. By contrast, the meanings that the deviant person imputes to his or her own behavior are *situated* in nature, that is, tied to the concrete situations in which the subject is involved. *Abstract meanings* are the positivist's so-called *objective*, scientific interpretation of the deviant subject's behavior, while *situated meanings* are the subject's *subjective* interpretation of the subject's own behavior. Alfred Schutz (1962), a founder of phenomenology, refers to the abstract, objective meanings as "constructs of the *second* degree," and the situated, subjective meanings as "constructs of the *first* degree." Phenomenologists insist that the positivists' supposedly objective idea about deviance is actually their *own* idea, far removed from, and at best a pale representation of, the deviant experience they study. Only the deviant person's subjective interpretation of the person's own experience is real. Thus, phenomenologists emphasize that to understand deviance, we should rely heavily on people's subjective interpretations of their own deviant experiences.

Ethnography: An Application of Phenomenology

Seeking to grasp the reality of deviance, phenomenologists analyze how their subjects feel and think about their deviance, themselves, and others. The method they use is called *ethnography*. Many sociologists who use ethnography to study deviance, however, call themselves ethnographers rather than phenomenologists. And they define ethnography as a style of research that seeks to understand the *meanings* the people under investigation ascribe to their experiences (Maso, 2001; Brewer, 2000; Ferrell and Hamm, 1998). But this is essentially the same thing sought by sociologists who call themselves phenomenologists (see, for example, Skrapec, 2001).

In his classic in-depth interview with 19-year-old Agnes, who had both male genitals and female secondary sex characteristics, Harold Garfinkel (1967) found that Agnes saw himself or herself not as a freak, as most people would, but as a normal person. Agnes was born as a male and raised as a boy until high school. During adolescence Agnes secretly took his mother's hormone medication and eventually developed large breasts, a slim waist, wide hips, and soft skin. At 17 she had an attractive female figure. By then she dropped out of school, left home, moved to another city, and tried to begin a new life as a woman. A year later, she went to the UCLA Medical Center to request a sex-change operation. Before such surgery was approved, Agnes had to be thoroughly investigated to ensure that she really felt like a woman. As a participant in this investigation, Garfinkel interviewed her extensively. He found that she saw herself as a normal woman, and did her best to convince others that she was. She told Garfinkel that she was merely a normal woman who happened to have a physical defect comparable to any other deformity, such as a harelip, clubfoot, or twisted spinal cord. Like any other normal person with a deformity, she felt that it was only natural for her to want to have hers—the penis—removed. Her self-concept as a normal woman further led her to claim that, as a sexual organ, her penis was "dead," that she had no sexual pleasure from it nor sexual attraction to women. She wanted to have it replaced by a surgically constructed vagina. Her self-concept as a normal woman also caused her to make sure that others would not suspect her of having a penis. Thus, on a beach she always wore a bathing suit with a skirt. In the apartment that she shared with a woman, she never undressed in her roommate's presence. On a date she always dodged necking and, in particular, petting below the waist.

Just as Agnes saw and presented herself as a normal person, Jack Katz (1988) found that criminals such as murderers and robbers also see themselves and their deviance in some positive way. More specifically, murderers perceive themselves as morally superior to their victims. This is because, in most cases of homicide, the *victims* have humiliated their killers by teasing, daring, defying, taunting, or insulting them. The resulting rage leads to killing but at the same moment gives the killers the self-righteous feeling of defending their identity, dignity, or respectability.

Katz also found that virtually all robbers feel themselves "morally superior" to their victims, regarding their victims as fools or suckers who deserve to be robbed. If robbers want to rob somebody on the street, they first ask the potential victim for the time, for directions, for a cigarette light, or for change. Each of these requests is intended to determine whether the person is a fool. The request for the time, for example, gives the robber the opportunity to know whether the prospective victim has an expensive watch. Complying with the request, then, is taken to establish the person as a fool and hence the right victim.

Most recently, many ethnographic studies that have delved into the subjective world of various kinds of deviants have come out with basically the same findings as those of Garfinkel and Katz. In his study of a family in which virtually all members were officially certified as "mentally retarded," Steven Taylor (2004) found that these people did not see themselves as mentally challenged. They carried on their daily lives as if they were like everybody else. In his analysis of tattoo collectors, Angus Vail (2004) found that they viewed their tattoos as normal as the car they drove and the hairstyle they wore on any given day. In his examination of the personal accounts of an 18-year-old girl who committed suicide, Thomas Cottle (2004) found that she had gone through many unpleasant experiences in her daily life, but she and other family members seemed not to notice their special significance—they were normal everyday events. Before killing herself, she had even made plans to attend a prestigious university that had admitted her. In her in-depth interviews with serial killers, Candice Skrapec (2001) was impressed by "their apparent ordinariness. They eat breakfast like the rest of us," which implies that they saw themselves as normal and acted accordingly.

Evaluating Phenomenological Theory

Phenomenologists have offered a convincing argument about the inadequacy of positivism: Positivists cannot get at the essence of deviant reality. But phenomenologists' assumption that they themselves can is less convincing. Phenomenologists only create a version of human reality. The phenomenologist version may be unique, but it is not necessarily superior to the positivist or other versions. Since sociologists, whether they are phenomenologists, positivists, or others, differ in their value systems, ideological inclinations, observational methods, and sensitivity to human experience, they are bound to create different, competing, or conflicting versions of human reality. In this regard, however, we may point out the contribution of phenomenological theory. Its view of deviant behavior as comprehensible through the individual's subjective experience does differ, compete, or conflict with the positivist emphasis on the objective side of deviant reality, thereby enabling us to look at the subject with a broader perspective and understanding.

Conflict Theory

More than 60 years ago, a number of sociologists began to point out the pluralistic, heterogeneous, and conflictive nature of modern society (Sellin, 1938; Waller, 1936). In a traditional or simple society, people share the same cultural values and, therefore, can have harmonious relationships with one another. Such value consensus and social harmony are absent in modern industrial societies, particularly in the United States. Instead, there is a great deal of social and cultural conflict. *Social conflict* has to do with the incompatible interests, needs, and desires of such diverse groups as business companies versus labor unions, conservative versus liberal political groups, whites versus blacks, and so on. *Cultural conflict* has to do with the discrepant norms and values that derive from definitions of right and wrong—that is, what is considered right in one culture is considered wrong in another. For example, in the 1930s a Sicilian father in New Jersey, after killing his daughter's 16-year-old seducer, felt proud of having defended his family honor in a traditional way, but was very surprised when the police came to arrest him (Sellin, 1938). Either social or cultural conflict has been said to bring about criminal behavior, not only among immigrants but also among African Americans and other poor or oppressed groups. Therefore, conflict as well as its resulting criminality is an inherent, normal, and integral part of modern society. Those sociologists who held this view 60 years ago may be regarded as *conflict theorists*.

But those conflict theorists failed to develop systematically the notion of conflict as the source of criminal *definition* rather than behavior. They were still very much tied to the traditional positivist concern with the causal explanation of criminal behavior. Only in the mid-1960s did a group of conflict theorists emerge to explore criminality systematically as a matter of definition. Since the mid-1970s, moreover, some of these new conflict theorists have begun to deal with the causation of deviance but in a different way from the early conflict theorists. Let's see how these new conflict theorists view deviance.

Legal Reality Theory

According to William Chambliss (1969), there are two kinds of law. One is the *law on the books*, the ideal of law, and the other is the *law in action*, the reality of law. According to the law on the books, legal authorities *ought* to be fair and just by treating all citizens equally. However, the law in action shows that legal authorities are *actually* unfair and unjust, favoring the rich and powerful over the poor and weak (Chambliss and Seidman, 1971).

Many people may blame the discrepancy between the two types of law on the evil character of lawmaking and law-enforcing individuals, but Chambliss rejects such an individualistic interpretation. He shows how those individuals are heavily influenced by the historical and organizational background of the law, as follows.

Modern Anglo-American law stems from the legal system of early England. The English legal system was established in the eleventh century. Its central feature is that personal wrongs are considered transgressions against the state and that only the state has the right to punish the transgressors. This legal principle replaced the earlier nonlegal norm that personal wrongs, being a highly personal matter, should be settled through reconciliation by the private parties concerned. To carry out the new legal principle, the government used force and coercion as the means for handling wrongs and disputes; created two separate bodies, the lawmakers (legislature) and the law enforcers (judiciary); appointed judges to settle disputes between the state and individual citizens or between individual citizens themselves; and relied on peers (juries) to ultimately decide disputes.

Such was the general structure of the legal system in early England, and it still prevails in contemporary U.S. society. But the specific content of the laws as well as the specific manner of enforcing them has often changed to reflect the interests of the ruling classes. The vagrancy laws in fourteenth-century feudal England, for example, reflected the powerful landowners' need for cheap labor because the law required poor able-bodied men to work at low wages, made it unlawful for them to move from one place to another to avoid the low-paying jobs or to seek higher wages, and prohibited giving alms to able-bodied beggars. Then, in the sixteenth century, the vagrancy laws were changed to protect the interests of prosperous merchants who had to transport their goods from one town to another, as the new vagrancy laws were applied to the rogues, vagabonds, and highwaymen who often preyed on the traveling merchants. Today, in both England and the United States, the vagrancy laws are meant to control down-and-outers, the undesirable, the criminal, and nuisances, thereby reflecting the desire of the influential middle and upper classes to make their streets safe and peaceful. Historically, criminal law has, in effect if not in intent, served the interests of the rich and powerful rather than the interests of the poor and powerless. Under this historical influence, the legislators of today understandably tend to make laws that favor the rich and powerful.

Law enforcers such as police, prosecutors, and judges also tend to become the tools of power and privilege. This tendency is mostly the consequence of *organizational imperative.* It is in the nature of any organization to compel its members to perform tasks that will maximize reward and minimize trouble for the organization. The reward to be sought by the law-enforcing agency is public support; the trouble to be avoided is the withdrawal of such support, or worse. Thus, it is rewarding for the law-enforcing officials to arrest, prosecute, and convict powerless people such as skid-row drunks, vagrants, gamblers, prostitutes, rapists, thieves, and robbers. But it will likely cause trouble for the agency if the law enforcers make the same effort to process respectable middle- and upper-class citizens for their white-collar offenses. In view of such an organizational imperative, the law-enforcing officials are very likely to make the law serve the interests of the rich and powerful (Chambliss, 1969).

Social Reality Theory

While Chambliss attributes the unjust practice of law to historical changes and organizational imperative, Richard Quinney (1974) blames the unjust law itself directly on the capitalist system. "Criminal law," he says, "is used by the state and the ruling class to secure the survival of the capitalist system, and, as capitalist society is further threatened by its own contradictions, criminal law will be increasingly used in the attempt to maintain domestic order."

Such a critical view of capitalism is based on Quinney's (1975) conflict theory of criminality, which he calls "the social reality of crime." According to this theory, four factors jointly produce the capitalist society's high crime rates but also help to consolidate its established legal order as well as its dominant class. First, the dominant class *defines* as criminal those behaviors that threaten its interests. This means that criminal laws are largely made by powerful members of society. Second, the dominant class *applies* those laws to ensure the protection of its interests. This involves having the police, judges, and other members of the criminal justice system enforce the laws. Third, members of the subordinate class are compelled by their unfavorable life conditions to engage in those *actions* that have been defined as criminal. The poor, for example, are likely to commit a crime because their poverty pressures them to do so. And, fourth, the dominant class uses these criminal acts as the basis for constructing and diffusing the *ideology* of crime. This is the belief that the subordinate class contains most of the society's dangerous criminal elements and therefore should most often be arrested, prosecuted, or imprisoned. These four factors are interrelated, supporting each other so as to produce and maintain a certain high level of crime in society. For example, such criminal acts as murder and robbery committed by the poor are likely to cause the dominant class to make and enforce the laws against the poor, which in turn would make life more difficult for the poor, thereby encouraging them to commit more crimes. Figure 3.1 summarizes Quinney's theory.

Quinney (1974) has also tried to turn his theory into a call for political action. As his theory implies, there is something terribly wrong with existing society. What is wrong is that members of the powerful class inevitably criminalize the actions of the powerless so as to exploit, oppress, and subjugate them, thereby preserving, consolidating, and perpetuating the status quo of social inequality. Thus, Quinney calls for the development of a revolutionary consciousness that should eventually lead to the creation of a democratic-socialist society that will end the oppression of the powerless by the powerful. More recently, a "new sociology of social control" has emerged that goes far beyond Quinney's notion about the capitalist state controlling, by itself, the powerless, deviant population. According to this new control theory, many institutions, organizations, professions, and agencies are increasingly involved in controlling troublesome, deviant people on behalf of the state (Garland, 1993; Davis and Stasz, 1990; Scull, 1988).

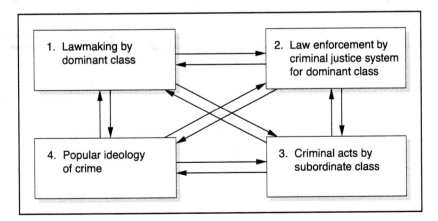

FIGURE 3.1 Quinney's Social Reality Theory. The interaction among these four factors helps produce and maintain a certain high level of crime in society.

Marxist Theory

In describing how the powerful define and control the powerless as deviants, most conflict theorists such as those discussed above have virtually ignored the causes of deviance. More recently, however, a number of conflict theorists have turned their attention to the question of causality. They draw their ideas mostly from Marxism; hence, they are often referred to as *Marxist theorists* (Greenberg, 1981).

According to these theorists, the cause of deviance can be traced to the exploitative nature of capitalism. To increase profit, capitalists must find ways to enhance productivity at low labor costs, including introducing automation and other labor-saving devices, forcing workers to work faster and work overtime, relocating industries to cheap labor locations, such as some nonunionized places in the southern United States or in labor-rich developing countries, and importing workers from poor nations. No matter what method is used, it inevitably throws some of the existing labor force out of work. These unemployed laborers become what Marxists call the *marginal surplus population,* relatively superfluous or useless to the economy. Their inability to maintain decent living conditions pressures them to commit crime.

Capitalism produces not only property crimes (such as robbery and theft) among the unemployed lower-class people; it also causes personal crimes (assault, rape, murder) and various other forms of deviance (alcoholism, suicide, and mental illness). As Sheila Balkan, Ronald Berger, and Janet Schmidt (1980) explained, economic "marginality leads to a lack of self-esteem and a sense of powerlessness and alienation, which create intense pressures on individuals. Many people turn to violence to vent their frustrations and strike out against symbols of authority, and others turn this frustration inward and experience severe emotional difficulties." This means that capitalism pressures people to commit crimes and become deviants by making them poor in the first place. Poverty, however, is not the only means by which capitalism generates deviance. According to Mark Colvin and John Pauly (1983), capitalist society can also produce crimes by exercising "coercive control" over the lower classes. Coercive control involves threatening to fire or actually firing poor workers in order to coerce them to work hard for their capitalist employers. It tends to create resentment. These workers are likely to feel alienated from society, showing an "alienative involvement" in it—a lack of attachment to it. Consequently, they are likely to engage in criminal activities.

However, the capitalistic pressure to commit crime and other forms of deviance is not confined to the lower classes, but reaches upward to affect the higher classes as well. By making possible the constant accumulation of profit, capitalism inevitably creates powerful empires of monopoly and oligopoly in the economy. These economic characteristics are an important cause of corporate crime. The reason is that "when only a few firms dominate a sector of the economy they can more easily collude to fix prices, divide up the market, and eliminate competitors" (Greenberg, 1981).

Feminist Theory

Virtually all theories about deviance are meant to apply to both sexes. The theories assume that what holds true for men also holds true for women. Feminist theorists, however, disagree. They argue that extant theories of deviance are actually about men only. Consequently, the theories may be valid for male behavior but not necessarily for female behavior. Consider, for example, Merton's anomie theory. First, this theory assumes that people are inclined to strive for material success. This may be true for men but not necessarily true for women. In fact, under the influence of patriarchal society, women have been socialized differently than men. Thus, women are traditionally less interested in achieving material success, which often requires one-upmanship, and more interested in attaining emotional fulfillment through close, personal relations with others. Second, the theory assumes that if some women have a strong desire for economic success but no access to opportunities for achieving that goal, they would be as likely as men in the same situation to commit a crime. Today, given the greater availability of high positions for women in the economic world, the number of ambitious women in the "men's" world is on the rise. However, when these women are faced with the lack of opportunities for greater economic success, they are not as likely as men to engage in deviant activities. Finally, Merton's theory explicitly states that people in the United States are likely to commit a crime because their society over-emphasizes the importance of entertaining high success goals while failing to provide the necessary opportunities for all its citizens to realize those goals. This may be relevant to men but less so to women. In fact, despite their greater lack of success opportunities, women still have lower crime rates than men (Heidensohn, 2002, 1995; Morris, 1987; Leonard, 1982).

The lack of relevancy to women in anomie and other conventional theories stems from a male-biased failure to take women into account. In redressing this problem, feminist theory understandably focuses on women. First, the theory deals with women as victims, mostly of rape and sexual harassment. These crimes against women are said to reflect the patriarchal society's attempt to put women in their place so as to perpetuate men's dominance (Heidensohn, 2002, 1995; Messerschmidt, 1986).

Feminist theory also zeroes in on women as offenders. It argues that although the rate of female crime has increased in recent years, the increase is not great enough to be significant. This is said to reflect the fact that gender equality is still far from being a social reality. Like employment opportunities, criminal opportunities are still much less available to women than men, hence women are still much less likely to engage in criminal activities. When women do commit crimes, they tend to commit the types of crime that reflect their continuing sub-ordinate position in society. They are minor property crimes, such as shoplifting, passing bad checks, welfare fraud, and petty credit-card fraud. In fact, most of the recent increases in female crime involve these minor crimes. Largely, this reflects the increasing feminization of poverty—more women are falling below the poverty line today. Not surprisingly, most women criminals are unemployed, without a high school diploma, and single mothers with small children. They hardly fit the popular image of liberated women who benefit from whatever increase there has been in gender equality. There is no increase in female involvement in more profitable crimes, such as burglary, robbery, embezzlement, and business fraud, which are still primarily committed by men (Heidensohn, 2002; Chesney-Lind, 1997; Steffensmeier, 1996; Weisheit, 1992).

Power Theory

It seems obvious that power inequality affects the quality of people's lives: The rich and powerful live better than the poor and powerless. Similarly, power inequality affects the quality of *deviant* activities likely to be engaged in by people. Thus the powerful are more likely to engage in profitable deviant acts, such as corporate crime, while the powerless are more likely to commit less profitable deviant deeds, such as armed robbery. In other words, power—or the lack of it— determines to a large extent the *type* of deviance people are likely to carry out.

Power can also be an important *cause* of deviance. More precisely, the likelihood of powerful people perpetrating profitable deviance is greater than the likelihood of powerless persons committing less profitable deviance. It is, for example, more likely for bank executives to rob customers quietly than for jobless persons to rob banks violently. Analysis of the deviance literature suggests three reasons why the powerful are more likely to commit profitable deviance than the powerless to commit less profitable deviance.

First, the powerful have a *stronger deviant motivation.* Much of this motivation stems from *relative deprivation*—from feeling unable to achieve relatively high aspirations. Compared with the powerless, whose aspirations are typically low, the powerful are more likely to raise their aspirations so high that they cannot be realized. The more people experience relative deprivation, the more likely they are to commit deviant acts (Cookson and Persell, 1985; Harry and Sengstock, 1978; Merton, 1957).

Second, the powerful enjoy *greater deviant opportunity.* Obviously, a rich banker enjoys more legitimate opportunities than a poor worker to make money. But suppose they both want to acquire *illegitimately* a large sum of money. The banker will have access to more and better opportunities that make it easy to defraud customers. The banker, further, has a good chance of getting away with it because the kind of skill needed to pull off the crime is similar to the skills required for holding the bank position in the first place. In contrast, the poor worker would find his or her illegitimate opportunity limited to crudely robbing the bank, an illegitimate opportunity being further limited by a high risk of arrest (Ermann and Lundman, 2002; Vaughan, 1983).

Third, the powerful are subjected to *weaker social control.* Generally, the powerful have more influence in the making and enforcement of laws. The laws against mostly higher-status criminals are, therefore, relatively lenient and seldom enforced, but the laws against largely lower-status criminals are harsher and more often enforced. For example, many lower-class murderers have been executed for killing one person, but not a single corporate criminal, for example, has ever faced the same fate for marketing some untested drug that "cleanly" kills many people. Given the lesser control imposed on them, the powerful are likely to feel freer to use some deviant means to amass their fortune and power.

In sum, due to social inequality, the powerful are likely to have a stronger deviant motivation, enjoy greater deviant opportunity, and encounter weaker social control, as compared with the powerless. As a consequence, the powerful are more likely to get involved in profitable deviancy than the powerless in less profitable deviancy.

Postmodernist Theory

Postmodernist theory is probably the newest attempt in sociology to shed light on the nature of deviance. It first emerged in the early twentieth century as a philosophical movement in France that *questioned* the basic values of *modernism* such as innovation, rationality, objectivity, and other similar values represented by modern science and technology. These modernist values were criticized for encouraging, among other things, objectification, depersonalization, alienation, and other social problems that make it difficult for people to form genuine or close relationships. The French philosophers, then, called for greater attention to postmodernist values including subjectivity, feeling, and intuition, so that a richer, more meaningful life can be attained.

This philosophical thought started to influence the arts and social sciences in the United States in the 1960s, and since the late 1980s it has become a well-known, though poorly understood, theoretical perspective in American sociology.

Postmodernist theory contains both old and new ideas in the sociology of deviance. First is the theory's attack on modern science's emphasis on the search for objective truth. To postmodernists, the so-called objectivity in modern science is actually subjective because it involves the scientists imposing their own "privileged" professional view on the subject under their investigation. The subjective view of the subject, whether the subject is a deviant, victim, or anybody who reacts in some way to the deviant act, is therefore suppressed, discounted, disregarded, or ignored. But, to postmodernists, the subject's own views are important for understanding deviance. By thus attacking positivism (the scientist's so-called objectivity) and advocating subjectivity, postmodernist theory is similar to phenomenological theory.

Another old idea in postmodernist theory is what its developers call "deconstructionism." This term is defined as "tearing a text [which means any phenomenon or event, such as deviance] apart, revealing its contradictions and assumptions" (Rosenau, 1992). In other words, deconstruction is said to involve "the breaking up of something that has been built, as in 'demolition,' and exposing the way in which it is built" (Einstadter and Henry, 1995). This meaning of deconstruction is basically the same as the meaning of what is popularly called "analysis," which involves studying something by separating the whole into its component parts. "Deconstruction" is different, though, in that it serves to destroy, challenge, or question the conventional way of looking at things such as deviance. But, because of its emphasis on the importance of subjectivity, the postmodernist's concept of deconstructionism is similar to the phenomenologist's idea of "phenomenological bracketing," which requires eliminating preconceptions in order to maximize sensitivity to the subject's experiences.

Postmodernist theory does have some new ideas. At the heart of the theory is "linguistic domination," which assumes that a linguistic conflict exists in any social interaction, with the language of the strong dominating that of the weak (Arrigo and Bernard, 1997). To understand the significance of linguistic domination for deviants, consider, for example, the linguistic conflict between the government and rebellious citizens. The government often calls political dissidents "traitors," revolutionaries "criminals," and freedom fighters "terrorists." But the so-called deviants—dissidents, revolutionaries, and freedom fighters—refer to themselves as concerned citizens battling a corrupt government. The first set of words (traitors, criminals, and terrorists) is "privileged," respected, or taken seriously, while the second set (dissidents, revolutionaries, and freedom fighters) is "marginalized," ignored, or suppressed. Thus the government can receive considerable support from the masses and make life extremely difficult for the political deviants.

Evaluating Conflict Theory

In blaming the capitalist or inegalitarian society for the prevalence of deviant labeling and deviant activities, conflict theory seems to hold the *unconvincing* assumption that in the utopian, classless society, deviant labeling will stop and such nasty human acts as killing, robbing, raping, and otherwise hurting one another will disappear. It may be more realistic to assume as Durkheim did that deviance is inevitable, even in a society of saints, but that the type of deviance committed by saints can be expected to be mostly unserious or even trivial. More precisely, if full social equality were achieved, the serious forms of human nastiness would greatly decrease rather than completely disappear. This is because, with the abolition of poverty in a fully egalitarian society, there would not be any poor people left to produce, as they do now, a large volume of serious deviance and thus this volume would greatly shrink. But the formerly poor people would join the formerly rich to engage in less serious—or saintly—forms of deviant activities.

All the same, conflict theory greatly contributes to our understanding of how social inequality—such as in the form of capitalism and patriarchy—influences the making and enforcing of norms, rules, or laws or the definition, production, and treatment of deviance in society (Heidensohn, 2002; Akers, 1985; Williams and Drake, 1980). Moreover, conflict theory is useful for explaining the motivations behind the formulation of laws, even, for example, why the powerful bother to pass laws against such nonpolitical acts as illicit sex, gambling, drinking, and loitering—the kind of deviance that does not seem to threaten their dominant position in society. The reason, according to conflict theory, is that those seemingly

TABLE 3.1 Constructionist Theories of Deviance

Labeling Theory: Relatively powerful persons are more likely to label the less powerful as deviant than vice versa, and being labeled deviant by society leads people to see themselves as deviant and live up to this self-image by engaging in more deviancy.

Phenomenological Theory: Looking into people's subjective interpretation of their own experiences is key to understanding their deviant behavior.

Conflict Theory:

Legal Reality: Law enforcement favors the rich and powerful over the poor and weak.

Social Reality: The dominant class produces crime by making laws, enforcing laws, oppressing subordinate classes, and spreading crime ideology.

Marxist: Deviance and crime stem from the exploitative nature of capitalism.

Feminist: Conventional theories of deviance are largely inapplicable to women, and the status of women as victims and offenders reflects the continuing subordination of women in patriarchal society.

Power: Because of strong deviant motivation, greater deviant opportunity, and weaker social control, the powerful are more likely to engage in profitable deviancy than are the powerless to engage in unprofitable deviancy.

Postmodernist: "Privileged" language of the powerful dominates the "marginalized" language and thus the lives of the weak as deviants.

trivial deviances do threaten powerful people's vested interests by challenging the underlying values of capitalism, such as sobriety, individual responsibility, deferred gratification, industriousness, and the belief that the true pleasures in life can only be found in honest, productive labor. Laws against those "trivial" deviant acts serve to preserve these capitalist values, the capitalist system, and hence the dominant position of the powerful (Hepburn, 1977).

Table 3.1 shows the main points of all the theories discussed in this chapter. These constructionist theories as well as the positivist theories in the preceding chapter are relatively high-level theories. They are, in effect, general analyses of deviance, dealing with deviance in general rather than a specific form of deviant behavior. They assume that all forms of deviant behavior are in some respect similar to one another, and they, as a general theory, are supposed to capture that similarity. This assumption inevitably ignores or misses many unique aspects of each specific form of deviant behavior. Thus, in the following chapters, we will discuss the concrete characteristics of various deviances. Logically, the high-level, general theories can be applied to specific deviances, but to get a closer, sharper view and deeper understanding of the specific deviant behaviors in the following chapters, we will mostly turn to lower-level, more concrete versions of positivist and constructionist theories.

Summary

1. What does labeling theory have to say about deviance? According to labeling theory, superordinate parties apply the deviant label to subordinate parties; being labeled deviant produces unfavorable consequences for the individual so labeled; and labeling some individuals as deviant generates favorable consequences for the community. The theory is generally convincing, and there are considerable data to support it. But it has been criticized for being unable to explain what causes deviance in the first place. It has also failed to receive consistent support from studies on the presumed negative consequences of labeling.

2. What is phenomenological theory all about? It claims that positivist sociologists cannot capture the essence of deviance, while phenomenological sociologists can cut into the heart of deviant experience with the scalpel of subjective interpretation, which they try to demonstrate with analyses of specific deviances. Phenomenologists are convincing in arguing that positivists cannot get into the essence of deviant reality. But their claim that they themselves can is excessive and unjustifiable. What they themselves can capture is only their own version of deviant reality, not necessarily the essence of that reality itself.

3. How do various versions of conflict theory deal with deviance? According to legal reality theory, the enforcement of law is unjust, favoring the rich over the poor, the result of historical changes and organizational imperatives. Social reality theory attributes the capitalist society's high crime rates to the convergence of four forces: lawmaking by the elite, law enforcement for the elite, law violation by the masses, and popular beliefs about the poor as the criminal class. Marxist theory traces the source of lower-class deviance to the exploitative nature of capitalism, and the origin of corporate crime to capitalism-generated monopoly. Feminist theorists criticize all other theories for being mostly relevant to men and, therefore, ignoring women and ascribe the experience of women as offenders and victims to the patriarchal system of gender inequality. Power theory explains that the powerful are more likely to engage in profitable deviance than the powerless in less profitable deviance because the powerful experience stronger deviant motivation, greater deviant opportunity, and weaker social control. Postmodernist theory shows how "privileged" language (like that of the powerful government) influences the lives of deviants (such as political dissidents).

4. What are the weaknesses and strengths of conflict theory? Conflict theory can be faulted for assuming that only capitalism or inequality can produce deviance but the utopian, classless society cannot. Nonetheless, conflict theory contributes greatly to our understanding of the making and enforcement of norms and laws, of the power-influenced definition and production of deviance, and of the motivation behind the formulation of laws against seemingly trivial deviance.

FURTHER READING

Becker, Howard S. 1973. *Outsiders: Studies in the Sociology of Deviance*, enlarged edition. New York: Free Press. A classic collection of articles on the use of labeling theory in studying deviance.

Brewer, John D. 2000. *Ethnography*. Buckingham, Eng.: Open University Press. Explaining what ethnography is and how it is used for theory building and applied research.

Davies, Scott, and Julian Tanner. 2003. "The long arm of the law: Effects of labeling on employment." *Sociological Quarterly*, 44, 385–404. Shows how teenagers who were suspended from school or served time in prison grew up to suffer as adults such negative consequences as low occupational success, small income, and checkered employment.

Hagan, John. 1992. "The poverty of a classless criminology—The American Society of Criminology 1991 presidential address." *Criminology*, 30, 1–19. An effort to convince criminologists that it is important to use the class-related concept of power to understand the nature of crime.

Jensen, Gary F., and Kevin Thompson. 1990. "What's class got to do with it? A further examination of power-control theory." *American Journal of Sociology*, 95, 1009–1023. Reflects the continuing refusal of many sociologists to see the connection between class or power and deviance.

Katz, Jack. 1988. *Seductions of Crime: Moral and Sensual Attractions in Doing Evil*. New York: Basic Books. A phenomenological analysis of how various deviants, such as murderers and robbers, feel about their deviant acts.

Maso, Ilja. 2001. "Phenomenology and Ethnography." In Paul Atkinson et al. (eds), *Handbook of Ethnography*. London: Sage Publications. An analysis of how phenomenology and ethnography are so closely related that they appear nearly identical.

Patterson, E. Britt. 1991. "Poverty, income inequality, and community crime rates." *Criminology, 29,* 755–776. Offers data showing that absolute poverty is significantly associated with higher rates of violent crime.

Regoli, Robert M., Eric D. Poole, and Finn Esbensen. 1985. "Labeling deviance: Another look." *Sociological Focus, 18,* 19–28. Calling for a revision of labeling theory that focuses on the process of labeling before the occurrence of a reaction to certain behavior.

Simpson, Sally S., and Christopher S. Koper. 1992. "Deterring corporate crime." *Criminology, 30,* 347–375. Analyzing the evidence concerning the deterrent impact of legal sanction on criminal corporate behavior.

Sorokin, Pitirim, and Walter Lunden. 1959. *Power and Morality: Who Shall Guard the Guardians?* Boston: Porter Sargent. A classic sociological statement on how power corrupts so that the ruling groups tend to become more criminal than the ruled.

Ward, David A., and Charles R. Tittle. 1993. "Deterrence or labeling: The effects of informal sanctions." *Deviant Behavior 14,* 43–64. Offers data showing how primary deviance leads to secondary deviance as suggested by labeling theory.

Winter, Michael F. 1996. "Social reaction, labeling, and social control: The contribution of Edwin M. Lemert." *History of the Human Sciences,* May, 53–77. Presents the main ideas of a major contributor to labeling theory.

CRITICAL THINKING QUESTIONS

1. In various versions of conflict theory it is always the poor and powerless that suffer as deviants. Is there a way for them to turn their fate around? If so, how? If not, why not?

2. Ask a sample of your fellow students to give a list of behaviors that they believe most people would consider to be deviant but they themselves do not. Then ask them to explain the difference. How would their answers tell you about labeling and phenomenological theories?

PART TWO

Interpersonal Violence

CHAPTER

4 Physical Violence

In March 2002, a Palestinian suicide bomber blew himself up at a café in Jerusalem, taking 11 Israelis with him to the hereafter. Shalita, 25, a member of Israel's Disaster Victims Identification team, arrived at the restaurant a few minutes after the explosion. He saw that "the walls were covered with blood. There were broken tables, plates, salads all over the floor, total chaos. People were lying in a pile, one on top of the other, in a pool of blood" (Derfner, 2002). The Israeli government retaliated by having its soldiers destroy the home of the Palestinian assailant. In August 2002, one day after his 17-year-old son blew himself up in a Jerusalem suicide attack, the Palestinian schoolteacher Ata Sarasra saw his seven-bedroom home reduced to rubble by Israeli soldiers. He mourned for his house, which he had built with savings from wages he had earned working for two decades in the United Arab Emirates. He also mourned for his son but was proud of him for having "died a martyr, thank God." The cycle of violence between the Israelis and the Palestinians has cost the lives of 607 Israelis and 1,702 Palestinians in the last two years (Rees, 2002).

This kind of violence may well spread to the United States and other countries in today's post-9/11 world, as al Qaeda and other Islamic extremists are dead set on inflicting terror on their enemies. We will analyze this horrendous form of deviance under the rubric of terrorism in this chapter. We will also examine other types of violence including assault, homicide, mass and serial murder, school violence, hate-motivated killing, and genocide, along with stalking as a threat of violence.

Assault and Aggravated Assault

Considerably less serious than homicide, assault is understandably far more prevalent. Assault involves the unlawful use of physical force against another person. It can be legally divided into two types: aggravated and simple. Aggravated assault involves an atrocious attack with the intent to kill or the use of a deadly weapon. It is considered a felony carrying a relatively severe penalty. All other forms of assault are simple, hence considered a misdemeanor, for which the punishment is less severe. As an act, aggravated assault is basically similar to homicide. Aggravated assault differs mostly in consequence: The victim survives rather than dies.

Since assault is behaviorally similar in some ways to homicide, most of the research findings about homicide that we will discuss also hold true for assault. Thus, like murderers, assaulters are more likely to be poor than nonpoor, to be black than white, to victimize people of the same race than of a different race, to live in the South than other regions, to reside in large cities than small towns, to be men than women, to have a violent past than not, to commit the crime during the weekend than during the weekday, and so on. At the same time, research has suggested at least two ways in which assault differs from homicide.

First, for obvious reasons, assaulters are less likely than murderers to use firearms in committing the crime. Second, in the summer, the number of homicides increases only slightly, but assault rises significantly. In the hot season, people tend to go out more, especially the poor whose homes are not comfortably air-conditioned. Going out increases social interaction, especially among strangers, who are likely to get involved in assault. Heat stress and increased consumption of alcoholic beverages further heighten aggression. A combination of all these factors enhances the likelihood of assault (Parker with Rebhun, 1995; Harries, 1990).

Who Is More Likely to Kill?

The most striking thing about killers is that they are mostly poor. Not surprisingly, blacks, being generally poorer than whites, are more likely than whites to commit homicide. Poor countries have higher rates of homicide than rich nations. Similarly, societies and individuals with violent pasts have relatively high rates of homicides. The South has more homicides than any other region in the United States. Here and abroad large cities have more killings than smaller cities. Men are far more likely than women to kill, and teenagers are more likely than adults to commit murder. Let us take a closer look at each of these facts.

Class and Race

Various studies have clearly indicated that homicides are concentrated heavily in the lower class. Over 90 percent of the murderers in the United States are semiskilled workers, unskilled laborers, and welfare recipients. Poverty is definitely a factor in homicide. As such, poverty crosses racial lines: Poor whites have higher murder rates than better-off whites, and poor blacks have higher rates than richer blacks. There are several reasons for the strong link between poverty and murder. Compared with people of the higher classes, the poor are more likely to have financial, marital, and other stressful problems, which in turn tend to cause interpersonal conflict. The poor also tend more to resort to physical violence as a way of dealing with interpersonal conflict (Parker with Rebhun, 1995; Parker, 1989; Bailey, 1984a).

Blacks generally have a much higher rate of homicide than whites. This fact makes it appear as if race plays an important role in homicide. Actually, though, being black has nothing to do with such violence. Instead, African Americans' higher rate of homicide simply reflects their higher rate of poverty, which, along with racial discrimination, generates greater frustration and alienation. In expressing their frustration, however, blacks tend more to kill their fellow blacks than to kill whites. In fact, most killings are *intra*racial, for whites also do away with whites more than blacks. *Inter*racial murders—in which blacks kill whites and vice versa— are rare because racial discrimination discourages interaction between blacks and whites (Shihadeh and Flynn, 1996; Greenberg and Schneider, 1994; Messner and Golden, 1992; Rose and McClain, 1990).

Regions, Large Cities, and Rural Areas

Generally, the southern region has the highest murder rate, the western region has the next highest rate, and the northeastern and midwestern states have the lowest rate (FBI, 2004). There is nothing new about these regional differences; they have been around for a long time. What accounts for the southern leadership in homicide rates? Some sociologists have attributed it to the "subculture of violence" in the South, where violent behavior seems more acceptable than in other regions. For example, gun ownership and execution of murderers, which are assumed to reflect a violent subculture, are the most common in the South. Another reason could be the greater prevalence of rurality in the South. A study by Kenneth Wilkinson (1984) shows that the average murder rate in rural areas exceeds the rate in most cities. According to Wilkinson, the dispersion of people in rural areas (as contrasted with the congestion of people in most cities) reduces community integration, thereby forcing family members, friends, and acquaintances to spend too much time with each other. This enhances the opportunity for violent disruption in primary relationships (among relatives and acquaintances), and it is in such relationships that most homicides take place, a strange fact that we will discuss in another section.

The rurality-homicide connection, however, seems to run counter to the popular belief that there are more killings in *large* cities. Actually, it does not, because rurality is related to homicide only if we compare the homicide rates of rural areas with those of *most* cities, which are relatively *small*, having populations of fewer than 50,000 people. Rural areas do have higher homicide rates than these small cities. However, larger cities, with populations exceeding 50,000, have significantly higher murder rates than those for small cities and the rural areas (see Table 4.1).

Paradoxically, like rurality, large city size encourages homicides by reducing community integration. But unlike rurality, which reduces community integration through *population dispersion*, large city size diminishes community integration via *population heterogeneity*. However it comes about, the lack of community integration drives individuals—anonymous urbanites as much as isolated ruralites—into the same matrix of interactions among relatives and acquaintances that is likely to lead to homicides.

Gender and Age

Those homicidal interactions are far more likely to cause men than women to kill because men are far more concerned about defending their manhood. Most of the killings involve a man doing away with another man. If a man and a woman are caught up in a homicidal interaction, he is more likely to be the offender and she the victim. Men who kill their wives or girlfriends do so mostly because they have persistently tried to *keep their victims in an abusive relationship*. Such killing, then, is

TABLE 4.1 **How Urban and Rural Murder Rates Differ**

Where People Live	**Murder Rate in 2003 (per 100,000 population)**
Large cities with population of	
250,000 or more	13.2
100,000 to 249,999	7.9
50,000 to 99,999	4.6
Rural areas	3.4
Small cities with population of	
25,000 to 49,999	3.3
10,000 to 24,999	2.7
Fewer than 10,000	2.8

Source: FBI, *Uniform Crime Reports*, 2003.

the culmination of a long series of physically violent acts perpetrated by the men against their female victims. Moreover, men tend to kill in response to their wives' infidelity. Men would also kill their wives as part of a murder-suicide or a family massacre (Wilson and Daly, 1992).

In the fewer cases where women kill, they differ from their male counterparts in the choice of victims. Unlike male offenders, who are more likely to kill others of the *same sex*, female offenders are more likely to kill members of the *opposite sex*. In these opposite-sex killings, the female and male murderers usually commit the crime for different reasons. The women rarely kill in response to their husbands' infidelity even if their husbands are extremely adulterous. They usually send their husbands to the hereafter as a desperate attempt to *get out of an abusive relationship*. The women basically kill for self-preservation or in self-defense. Violence by women, then, is primarily defensive, in contrast to violence by men, which is distinctly offensive. Such defensive killing serves as "self-help social control" against abusive husbands. Not surprisingly, it often takes place in states where there are no laws requiring mandatory arrests for domestic violence (Gauthier and Bankston, 2004; Peterson, 1999; Mann, 1996; Wilson and Daly, 1992; Goetting, 1989).

Males also kill at a younger age than females. When killing, people are more likely to target others of the same age group than older or younger victims. This is largely because people of about the same age spend more time interacting with one another than with others of a different age. In the few cases where older persons quarrel with younger ones, the older persons are more likely to end up dead, because the younger persons are more impulsive and hence quicker to shoot. While most homicides involve relatives and acquaintances, the younger killers are more likely than their older peers to target strangers and commit murder and robbery together (U.S. Census Bureau, 2004; Eigen, 1981; Mulvihill and Tumin with Curtis, 1969).

The homicide rate in the United States is lower today than ten years ago. But, from the mid-1980s to the early 1990s, there was a stunning upsurge in murders committed by *teenagers*. Most of these killings took place in large cities' poor neighborhoods, where gang violence, drive-by shootings, and crack cocaine were relatively common. More important, many teenagers in poor inner cities carried guns, a new phenomenon in those years. Contrary to popular belief, the primary reason for carrying guns was not seeking status among one's peers or trying to make an impression on others. Teenagers carried guns to protect themselves in their dangerous, high-crime neighborhoods (Fox, 1996; Blumstein, 1995; Wright, Sheley, and Smith, 1992). All the same, the increased possession of guns contributed to the surge in teen murders. Other contributing factors included the larger number of dysfunctional families, the greater prevalence of drugs among the urban poor, the lower quality of public schools, and the increased glorification of violence on television, in the movies, and in video games. Since 1994, however, the teen murder rate has declined, largely as a result of the falloff in the crack market and increased confiscation of handguns from juveniles by police departments (Steinberg, 1999; Kleck and Hogan, 1999; Grossman, 1995).

Patterns of Killing

Various studies have found certain patterns in the majority of murder cases. However, these patterns mainly involve murders committed by lower-class people, not by middle- and upper-class persons. Traditionally, researchers have concentrated on lower-class homicides simply because they make up the overwhelming majority of murders. Thus, in this section, we will focus on the patterns of lower-class homicides, but will also note the characteristics of higher-class murders in cases where they differ.

Time of Killing

Most murders are committed in the heat of passion, and there does seem to be some, though relatively weak, connection between season of the year and murder. The number of homicides increases slightly during the hot late spring and summer, peaking in July and August, during which potential killers and victims, who are relatives, friends, and acquaintances rather than strangers, tend most to get together and drink cold beer in public places such as restaurants and taverns. Homicide decreases during the cool autumn and early spring, and drops even more during the winter months of January and February (U.S. Census Bureau, 2004; Wolfgang, 1958). But the number of homicides peaks again during the cold month of December, primarily due to its being a holiday season, which, like July and August, brings together the kinds of people who are more likely to get involved in homicide (Anderson, 1989).

Far stronger than the association between homicide and season is the link between homicide and days of the week as well as hours of the day. Homicide occurs most frequently during the weekend evenings, particularly on Saturday night. This may explain why the handgun most often used in homicide is popularly called a Saturday night special. These weekend killings are more likely to involve family members than the homicides occurring during the weekdays—the weekday homicides tend more to involve strangers. The reason is that people usually spend more time at home on weekends (Messner and Tardiff, 1985).

All this does not, however, hold true for the minority of cases involving middle-class and upper-class offenders. With these killers, researchers have failed to find any significant variation by the month of the year or day of the week. Why this class difference? Because murders in the middle and upper classes are more likely to be *calculative* or *premeditated*, while lower-class killings are more often carried out in a burst of rage, usually after some heavy drinking (Parker with Rebhun, 1995; Green and Wakefield, 1979).

What about the evening when the moon is full? Does the popularly believed lunar effect on homicide exist? Is it true, as "every policeman, bartender, and emergency-room attendant knows, that people tend to act crazy and become more violent when the moon is full"? One psychiatrist claimed to have found a higher incidence of homicides in Cleveland and Miami at the times of new and full moons. However, in analyzing the same data and other relevant studies, an astronomer found no correlation between lunar phases and homicide rates (*Sky and Telescope*, 1985).

Place of Killing

Men are about equally likely to commit murder in and outside the home, but women are far more likely to kill at home than outside it. In the past women most often did the killing in the kitchen, apparently because it is the place where women traditionally were accustomed to handling a knife—which can turn into a dangerous weapon when a quarrel flares up (Wolfgang, 1958). But nowadays, less likely to be confined to the kitchen as a result of greater gender equality, women tend more to kill in the living room (Mann, 1996). However, the bedroom is a more dangerous place for women than for men, as women are more frequently killed there by their husbands, boyfriends, or exes (Totman, 1978). Perhaps men have been socially conditioned to use the bedroom as a place for demonstrating their "manliness" by sexually conquering women and end up using it as a place for physically subjugating them to death.

While women are more likely to kill at home, they are also more likely to be killed at home. A major reason is simply that they spend more time at home. Other types of people who spend more time at home are also more likely to have the same fate. These include the very young, the very old, minority groups, the married, and the unemployed (Messner and Tardiff, 1985).

Method of Killing

Killing a human may appear extraordinary when compared with, say, killing a rabbit. This consequently fires the imagination of many mystery writers, who help spread the popular notion that murderers often use mysterious, exotic, ingenious, or superclever methods to get rid of their victims. Yet research often shows that there is nothing special about the methods of killing. Most objects can be readily turned into murder weapons, as long as they are conveniently accessible when the murderous anger erupts. In our society firearms are easily available, and so they are most often used as murder weapons (Kristof, 1996b). Perhaps, seeing a gun while embroiled in a heated argument may incite a violent person to murderous action. As Shakespeare has it, "How oft the sight of means to do ill deeds, makes ill deeds done."

Of course, firearms in themselves cannot cause homicide, nor can their absence reduce the motivation to kill. It is true that "guns don't kill people, people do." Still, were guns less available, many heated arguments would have resulted in aggravated assaults rather than murders, thereby reducing the number of fatalities. An analysis of over 20,000 homicides and aggravated assaults in Chicago suggests that attacks with knives are five times *less* likely to result in death than attacks with guns (Wright, Rossi, and Daly, 1983). An enormous number of guns are in private hands: Half of all U.S. households own firearms of some kind, and a quarter of all families have handguns. It is, therefore, not surprising that many deaths in the United States result from gun homicides. Every year, our country has over 10,000 handgun homicides compared with less than 100 in other industrialized nations such as Canada, England, and Japan, where guns are much harder to get (Cook and Moore, 1999; Wright, 1995).

The easy availability of guns in the United States appears to be a great equalizer for the poor. It gives power to the powerless. This may explain why lower-class people are more likely to use firearms than any other weapon when they kill. Shooting is also the most popular mode of murder among people of the higher classes. However, higher-class killers are much more likely than their lower-class peers to use more refined techniques of killing, such as poisoning, staging a hit-and-run car death, and hiring somebody else to do the killing (Green and Wakefield, 1979).

Characteristics of Homicide

Most killings are carried out against family members, friends, or acquaintances rather than strangers. Some killings happen as if the victim asks to be put to death. Some involve an attempt to win a seemingly trivial argument. Some serve as an adjunct to suicide. Let us take a closer look at each characteristic of killing.

Warm-Blooded Murder

Many people are apparently afraid of getting attacked and killed by strangers, particularly in big cities. Such fear came through clearly in the mid-1980s when Bernhard Goetz, the so-called Subway Vigilante, shot four young African Americans on a subway car in New York, though they allegedly had merely approached and asked him for money. It was also the same fear that drove many people to hail him as a hero. The fear that strangers will kill us unless we kill them first does not reflect reality. Compared with other major crimes, such as robbery, rape, and assault, homicide is the least likely to involve strangers. Of all the murders that occur every year, only a small percentage are committed by strangers. In fact, the majority of the murders involve relatives, friends, or acquaintances, as Figure 4.1 indicates. This situation is not unique to our society. It exists in many other countries as well.

It seems incredible that the people we know or even love are more likely to kill us than are total strangers. But, as three sociologists have explained, "This should really not be very surprising. Everyone is within easy striking distance of intimates for a large part of time. Although friends, lovers, spouses, and the like are a main source of pleasure in one's life, they are equally a main source of frustration and hurt. Few others can anger one so much" (Mulvihill and Tumin with Curtis, 1969). Ordinarily, killing requires a great deal of emotion. Therefore, it may be more difficult to kill a stranger about whom we don't have much feeling—unless we are professional killers, who typically dispatch their victims in a cold-blooded, unemotional manner. In sum, we are far less likely to become victims of cold-blooded murders carried out by strangers but more likely to die from warm-blooded, emotional murders at the hands of our relatives, friends, or acquaintances.

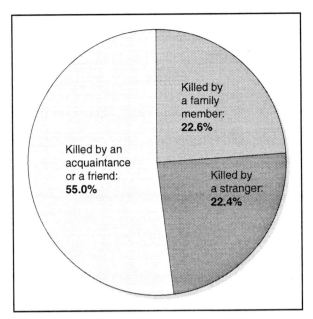

FIGURE 4.1 Most Victims Know Their Killers
Source: FBI, Uniform Crime Reports, 2003.

Doing the Victim a Favor

The general public often sympathizes with the murder victim but not with the offender at all. The public assumes that the murder victim is weak and meek, helplessly slain by the strong and aggressive offender. This assumption is not always correct. In at least one out of four homicides, the victim has first attacked the subsequent slayer, and such murder has been called *victim-precipitated homicide* (Wilbanks, 1984; Felson and Steadman, 1983). The following are typical cases of victim precipitation (Klinger, 2001):

- A drunken husband, beating his wife in the kitchen, gave her a butcher knife and dared her to use it on him. She warned him that she would use it if he should strike her again. At the very instant he heard this warning, he slapped her in the face—and he was fatally stabbed.

- A drunken man, with knife in hand, approached a person during a quarrel. When this person showed a gun, the drunk dared him to shoot. He did.

- A man who had just robbed a jewelry store was fleeing. Outside, he saw three police officers, but he ran toward them. At gunpoint, they ordered him to stop. Instead, he pulled out a gun, whereupon he was shot dead. Later, his gun was found to be unloaded.

Because they provoke another person to kill them, Marvin Wolfgang (1967) assumes that these self-precipitated murder victims may have secretly wanted to kill *themselves.* This assumption may well be correct. But if they have suicide wishes, why do they not take it on themselves to end their own lives? Perhaps they have been influenced by what may be considered a culture of *showy masculinity,* characteristic of sexist society. This culture encourages males to show off their toughness and hide their tenderness, to act like a "man" and avoid acting like a "woman," or to engage in "manly" braggadocio and shun "feminine" quietism. Under the pressure of this culture, suicidally inclined men may *avoid* revealing their "sissy cowardice" or their plea for condescending sympathy from others in quietly ending their own lives. Instead, they are inclined to display masculine bravado and earn from others some "respect" as the worst person imaginable, by making an ostentatious assault on another person that is secretly designed for their own annihilation—the result being a victim-precipitated murder.

Winning a Trivial Argument

Murder is an extremely serious human act, yet the motive for committing it often appears downright trivial. Ordinary quarrels, which often seem to be over nothing, are the most common reason for poor people to kill. As a retired homicide detective in New York reports, "When you get a guy to 'fess up as to why he did it, you get very shoddy answers: 'He took my coat.' 'He stepped on my girlfriend's foot'" (Wilentz, 1985). Similar examples follow (Mulvihill et al., 1969):

- A man was fatally shot in front of a tavern because he had refused to lend his assailant $1.

- Two men were arguing over a $5 bet and became involved in a scuffle. Then one took out a gun and pulled the trigger on the other.

- Two fellow workers were drinking beer; they argued over a $1 pool bet. One wound up in a morgue.

- A man was drunk when he came home. He told his uncle to move over in bed. Seeing that his uncle would not, he stabbed him to death.

- "Hey, you're lookin' at me."
  "No, I ain't."
  "Yes, you are. Why you lookin' at me?"
  Minutes later one of them lay still in a puddle of blood.

Murder, then, is apparently a quick and effective way for the poor to win an argument—over trifles. Middle-class people usually use a much less drastic means, such as verbal or intellectual ability, to settle an argument. But the poor tend more to suffer from lack of such ability, and thus they are more often compelled to use their physical strength to end an argument with—and sometimes the life of—another person.

We may also note that arguments such as those illustrated above may appear trivial to us. Yet the same arguments are apparently taken by poor males as reasons for defending their dignity or honor as men. A dirty look, a little insult, a jostle would not usually get middle-class people into an argument, let alone impel them to spill another person's blood. The same triviality may be perceived differently by the poor. Why would the poor make such a mountain out of a molehill, and with such deadly consequences for themselves?

The explanation can be found in the economic and social oppression of the poor. The poor man's dignity as a man—or, for that matter, as simply a human being—has been substantially diminished by the frustrating and humiliating forces in his life. Some of these forces are impersonal, such as the general condition of poverty, so that the poor man cannot fight back against them. Other humiliating forces can be found in people, such as the police, bureaucrats in a welfare or unemployment office, and employers—who usually treat him with far less respect than they do the more successful, higher-status persons. But since these people are more powerful, the poor man cannot fight back at them either.

As a consequence, he has extremely little dignity left in him, and so, in order to live with at least more worth than an animal, he dearly hangs on to it. Although he cannot maintain this fragile dignity in the larger society or in the presence of those more powerful than himself, he certainly can at his own home and in his neighborhood, among his equally dignity-deprived family members, friends, and acquaintances. Because his dignity as a man is already extremely fragile, the pressure of daily frustration and tension can easily crush it. Thus even a small insult from his relatives, friends, or acquaintances (who are, after all, his last strand of hope for keeping his dignity) can mean, to him, the threat that all his dignity will be taken away. With such a perception, he will very likely fight like mad to defend his dignity, even to the extent of killing the person who has "dissed" him. In fact, as many researchers have found, most homicides result from what they call *character contests,* in which the offender and victim try to defend their honor after it has been threatened by the other (Athens, 1985; Felson and Steadman, 1983).

An Adjunct to Suicide

We have speculated that the so-called victims of victim-precipitated homicide may have wanted to die and contributed greatly to their own deaths. There is yet a different group of offenders with the same suicidal tendency. They are homicide-suicide offenders, who first kill another person and then finish themselves off. The difference between these two types of offenders is obvious. While the "victim" of victim-precipitated homicide conceals the suicide wishes, the homicide-suicide offender reveals them.

Homicide-suicide is relatively rare, no more than 3 or 4 percent of all murders in the United States and approximately 10 percent in Canada. Virtually all homicide-suicides are male. They are usually severely depressed, violent, and jealous people, who impulsively kill their wives and often children as well (Gillespie, Hearn, and Silverman, 1998; Lecomte and Fornes, 1998).

Two conflicting views can be found on the nature of homicide-suicide: one sociological, seeing homicide-suicide as a form of *normality*; the other psychiatric, viewing it as a symptom of *abnormality*. According to the sociological view, the murderer-suicide is a normal person because, after killing the loved one, he is able to feel remorse, just as we would expect normal people to feel after they had done such a horrible thing. By contrast, the psychiatrist sees the murderer-suicide as a psychotic, believing that, instead of feeling remorse, the offender anticipates a reunion with the victim in another world, and, therefore, kills himself in order to achieve that goal.

These two conflicting views can be reconciled. It is true that some murderer-suicides are "normal." It is also true that other murderer-suicides are "psychotic." But these two types of murderer-suicides may have one thing in common—both are unaffected by the culture of showy masculinity discussed before. Instead of acting like "tough guys," as required by that culture, both behave like "weaklings." In effect, the normal one begs the mortally wronged victim (who is usually his wife or girlfriend) for pardon, and the psychotic one dreams for some happy reconciliation in another world. Both behave like—when seen from the standpoint of the "tough guy" culture—mushy characters in a tear-jerking love story.

Sociologist David Phillips (1981, 1980a) has discovered homicide-suicides of a third kind. They resemble the so-called victims of victim-precipitated murder in that they conceal their suicidal wishes, but they carry out these wishes with more ingenuity. They "disguise their homicide-suicides as accidents to protect their survivors from insurance problems and from social stigma." One example of these disguised homicide-suicides is a pilot who deliberately crashes his airplane with passengers onboard, but who makes the crash appear convincingly like an accident. Phillips argues that many plane crashes actually involve the pilots committing murder-suicides. This argument is based on his finding that after a murder-suicide is publicized in the mass media there is an increase in both noncommercial and commercial plane crashes, a trend that persists for approximately nine days. Phillips assumed that the mass media, with their spate of murder-suicide stories, encourage those suicidal pilots to commit murder-suicides. He later reinforced this assumption by showing in another study the impact of mass media on homicides in general. That study indicated that between 1973 and 1978 homicides increased by more than 12 percent on the third day following highly publicized heavyweight championship prizefights (Phillips, 1983; see also Baron and Reiss, 1985; Phillips and Bollen, 1985).

Mass and Serial Murder

In 1997 Andrew Cunanan killed the famous fashion designer Gianni Versace in Miami Beach after having murdered four other men in other cities. In 1992 Jeffrey Dahmer of Milwaukee, Wisconsin, pleaded guilty to killing 15 young men, one after another. He reportedly had sex with some of the corpses, dismembered some of the bodies, and kept in his refrigerator a severed head as well as a heart that he planned to eat later. Earlier, in 1985, another serial killer struck terror in the Los Angeles area. Called the Night Stalker, he sneaked into the homes of 19 people at night and killed them as they slept. Just a year before, a mass murderer walked into a McDonald's restaurant in San Diego carrying a rifle, a shotgun, and a pistol with hundreds of rounds of ammunition. He opened fire on everybody, killing 21 people—mostly children—and wounding 19 others. These types of killing—mass and serial murders—attract considerable attention from the media and public. Just the same, they are extremely rare.

Mass murder involves killing a number of people at about the same time and place. It usually ends with the murderer dying at the scene of the carnage. The murderer's death results from either committing suicide or forcing the police to take lethal action. Despite the shocking nature of their crime, most mass murderers are not mentally ill. As sociologists Jack Levin and James Fox (1985) conclude after studying mass murderers, "The mass killer appears to be *extraordinarily ordinary.* He is indistinguishable from everyone else. Indeed, he may be the neighbor next door, a coworker at the next desk, or a member of the family."

Some mass murderers are *disgruntled employees* who want to get even with their boss who has wronged them in some way, by firing them, for example. But in the process of killing their boss, they end up murdering their coworkers as well. Other mass murderers are *heads of family* who kill their wives and children after having long felt alone, alienated, helpless, and depressed, aggravated by heavy drinking. Some mass murderers are *pseudocommandos,* who turn their home into an arsenal and then lash out at what they consider to be an unjust or evil world. Finally, some mass murderers *work as a team under the direction of a charismatic leader*, such as the September 11 suicide bombers who attacked the United States under the direction of their leader Osama bin Laden (Meloy et al., 2004; Holmes and Holmes, 1992).

Slightly more common than mass murder is serial murder, which involves killing a number of people one at a time. But the media has wildly exaggerated the incidence of serial murder by calling it an "epidemic." This exaggeration originated from the claim by a Justice Department official that serial murder accounts for about 20 percent of all homicides. Actually, the most credible figure, based on careful analysis by sociologists, is only 2 or 3 percent. Another myth about serial murder is that its perpetrators roam from one city to another to carry out their killing. The fact is that most (70 to 75 percent) serial murderers commit their crime in one city alone (Kappeler, Blumberg, and Potter, 1993).

While mass murderers are nearly always caught, serial killers are far more elusive because they are practiced and accomplished at what they do. First, they stalk their victims from a distance, studying the victims' routine activities and habits. Then they win the victims' confidence by befriending them, or gain entry into the victims' house that they have staked out for days. Next, they lure the victims into a trap or simply hold them captive by closing off all possibility of escape. Finally, they kill the victims. In the process of killing, they "often torture their victims, taking delight in the victims' agonies, expressions of terror, cries of despair, and reactions to pain" (Norris, 1989). This should not be surprising, because most serial killers have in their childhood tortured dogs and cats for the thrill of watching them suffer. They have also been subjected to a lot of physical and emotional abuse by their parents. Such experiences have apparently taught the serial killer to become a sociopath, incapable of feeling remorse or guilt for hurting others. Nonetheless, the vast majority of serial killers are not mentally ill. They appear as normal people who go to school or work, come home, and blend into their immediate neighborhood (Fox, Levin, and Quinet, 2005). For more on serial killers, see the Social Profile below.

Social Profile: Serial Killers

According to one popular myth, serial killers are monsters. You would think so too if you had seen many movies like *Friday the 13th,* which portray serial killers as glassy-eyed lunatics bent on getting their kicks from inflicting human destruction. Another myth is just the opposite, regarding serial killers as unusually handsome and charming. This myth may stem from a few well-known cases, such as those involving the debonair "lady killer," Theodore Bundy, who murdered dozens of women, and the "Los Angeles Night Stalker," Richard Rameriz, who attracted many women even after he was in prison and married there. A third myth presents serial killers as extremely brilliant, like Hannibal Lector, the character in the novel and movie, *The Silence of the Lambs.* Contrary to these myths, most serial killers are unusually ordinary.

In one study of 107 serial killers, only 16 percent attended college and only 4 percent graduated with a bachelor's degree; the majority had blue-collar jobs. Despite their relatively low level of education and employment, most serial killers do possess a certain amount of cunning and are especially skillful in presenting themselves as friendly and trustworthy.

Most serial killers are white men in their late twenties or early thirties. In one study of nearly 400 serial killers, 84 percent were found to be male and 80 percent white, with an average age of 28 when their first murder was committed. All this distinguishes serial killings from single-victim homicides, which are more likely to be carried out by non-whites. Also, while murderers with a single victim tend to target people that they know, serial killers are more likely to kill strangers—especially vulnerable ones such as children, prostitutes, and the elderly.

The motive behind most serial murders is an intense desire for power and sadism. Serial murderers typically kill for the fun of it, not for love, money, or revenge. It makes them feel good to kill while also being able to torture the victim in the process.

Source: Fox, Levin, and Quinet, 2005.

Global Perspective: Homicide

The influence of poverty on homicide shows up in comparison between rich and poor countries. In general, developing countries such as those in Latin America, Asia, and Africa have higher homicide rates than do developed countries such as those in North America and Western Europe.

Among the developed countries, however, the United States has by far the highest rate. This is largely due to the greater amount of poverty—and economic inequality—in our society compared to the other developed areas, namely, Western Europe and Japan. If Russia is considered a developed country, it has an even higher homicide rate than the United States, because it has much more poverty. The prevalence of guns can also explain why the homicide rate in the United States is much higher than in Western Europe and Japan. Within Western Europe, countries such as Finland, where many private citizens own guns, have higher homicide rates than those such as England, where guns are scarcer.

But among the poor, developing countries, those in Latin America have unusually high homicide rates, apparently the highest in the world. Some sociologists have attributed these high rates to a "culture of violence," which encourages the use of violence to deal with unbearable interpersonal conflict. This culture seems to have a powerful element of machismo, the belief that men should be concerned about their manhood. In such a culture, men are encouraged to respond aggressively to an insult about their manhood. If they do not respond aggressively, they are made to feel like cowards. In any country, however, killers seem to have developed a similarly tough, macho attitude from a violent past. A killer's violence usually begins with minor assaults against others, gradually escalates to more and more serious assaults, and finally culminates in homicide. Also in every country in the world, men are much more likely than women to kill, which apparently reflects the influence of machismo, though to a lesser degree than in Latin America.

Sources: Pridemore, 2002; Chervyakov et al., 2002; Santtila et al., 2001; LaFree, 1999.

School Violence

Over the last several years, boys as young as 11 have gunned down classmates or teachers in the public schools of such little-known places as Littleton, Colorado; Edinboro, Pennsylvania; Jonesboro, Arkansas; Pearl, Mississippi; West Paducah, Kentucky; and Stamps, Arkansas. It appears that school violence, long known as a phenomenon of large and noisy cities, has now spread to small and tranquil towns, suburbs, and rural areas.

The recent surge of juvenile killing in schools can be attributed to roughly the same factors as those that sociologists have often cited to explain youthful homicides in the larger society. One of these factors is the increased availability of *guns.* Another factor is the glamorization of violence in such *media* as movies, television, and video games. Media violence may not cause actual violence among the overwhelming majority of young men, but it is likely to turn a few susceptible, violence-prone youngsters to violence. A third contributing factor is the *culture* of violence, which favors the possession of guns and accepts the use of force for settling interpersonal conflict. This may explain why every Southern state, with their strong historic culture of violence, has more firearm deaths among children under age 18 than do many Northern states such as New York and New Jersey (Blank, Vest, and Parker, 1998). Under the influence of at least these three factors, youngsters are more likely to commit violence if they have been abused by parents or rejected, taunted, or ostracized by peers (Begley, 1999; Baker, 1998).

In other words, those three factors may produce an environment conducive to school violence, but they do not have the same impact on all students. They seriously affect only a few, particularly those who have been abused by parents or rejected by peers. Consider, for example, the Columbine High School killers, Eric Harris and Dylan Klebold. At the school, they were denigrated as nerds or geeks, excluded from the mainstream student body. They banded together with some fellow outcasts to form what they called the "Trench Coat Mafia" so that they could feel important, powerful, and dominant over the rest of the students. They ultimately decided to show how powerful they were by taking over the school with guns and explosives. As Harris said when he and Klebold were ready to go on the killing spree, "This is just a two-man war against everybody else" (Fox, Levin, and Quinet, 2005).

Despite its horror, schoolboy homicide remains extremely rare. According to the Centers for Disease Control and Prevention, fewer than 1 percent of all youthful homicides take place in or around the school. Besides, school shooting has, along with weapon carrying and physical fighting, gone down in recent years (Fox, Levin, and Quinet, 2005; Brener et al., 2004; Stolberg, 1999).

Stalking and Cyberstalking

Stalking is pursuing someone in a way that creates the fear of being assaulted or killed. The offenders may follow or spy on the victims; send them unsolicited letters; make unsolicited phone calls; stand outside their homes, schools, or workplaces; show up at places where they are present; give them unwanted items; vandalize their property; or kill their pets. Stalkers, if not stopped, may end up assaulting and killing the victim; even if they do not, the stalking may be nearly as bad as being attacked and killed. The ordeal of assault or murder usually lasts only a few minutes, but victims of stalking endure their tormentors' cruelty for nearly two years, the average duration of stalking. Stalking is also more prevalent than nearly all other forms of physical violence discussed in this chapter. According to a survey by the National Institute of Justice, 8 percent of women and 2 percent of men in the United States encounter stalking at some time in their lives (Mullen et al., 2000; Moffatt, 2000).

The majority of stalkers know their victims as ex-intimates, fellow employees, and acquaintances. The following are typical cases (Albrecht, 2001):

- A woman with two young children left her abusive husband to start a new life, but he stalked her and later killed her, saying, "If I can't have her; nobody will."

- A high school girl broke up with her boyfriend. Then he stalked her and eventually set fire to a room in her house, killing an infant her mother babysat.

- A wife had a one-night stand with a man she met in a bar. Later, he stalked, kidnapped, and raped her for getting back together with her husband.

- A man repeatedly asked a female coworker to go out with him but without success. Then he stalked her for many months. After he was dismissed from his job, he killed seven former coworkers and injured four others, including the victim of his stalking.

A few stalkers victimize strangers, especially celebrities. The most well known is probably John Hinckley. Infatuated with movie actress Jodie Foster, he repeatedly sent her letters with poems and messages to get her interested in him. Finally, in 1981, in order to attract her attention, he tried to assassinate President Reagan, wounding the president and two other people. In 1989, Robert Bardo was obsessed with TV actress Rebecca Schaeffer, videotaping every episode of her show *My Sister Sam.* He repeatedly wrote to her, and after seeing her in bed with another actor in one episode, he flew into a rage. He went to her apartment and shot her to death. He later told a court-appointed psychiatrist, "She was a whore, and God appointed me to punish her" (Moffatt, 2000).

Most of the stalkers are male, and most of the victims are female. There is no racial difference in stalking—stalkers are as likely to be white as black. Stalkers are generally older than their victims. The majority of stalkers are loners, mentally unhealthy, and socially incompetent (Moffatt, 2000; Mullen et al., 2000).

Some of these offenders stalk their victims in cyberspace, which is known as cyberstalking. Their numbers are still smaller than the traditional, offline stalkers. But they have been growing fast, since computer technology has become cheaper, more accessible, and easier to use than ever before—helping the cyberstalker avoid arrest by concealing his identity. Cyberstalking involves the use of the Internet or e-mail to repeatedly harass or threaten another person. Lack of physical contact may make online stalking seem more benign than offline stalking, but cyberstalking is often more disturbing and dangerous than traditional stalking. Cyberstalkers have greater access to the victim's personal data—hence more capable of disrupting personal and professional lives—than a prowler lurking in the dark. Cyberstalkers can easily harass the victim anywhere in the world because of the swift global access provided by the Web. While all this can cause the victim serious emotional and mental harm, it may also result in physical or sexual assault, kidnapping, and even murder (Bocij, 2004; Newton, 2004).

Like traditional stalkers, most cyberstalkers are males while their victims are females, and most cyberstalkers are older persons victimizing younger persons. Most cyberstalkers also know their victims. A typical example is a 50-year-old ex-security guard in Los Angeles seeking revenge on a 28-year-old woman who rejected his romantic interest. Posing as his victim, the man posted numerous online messages about "her" fantasies of being raped, along with her real phone number and home address. As a result, six men who saw the messages came on separate occasions to the woman's home at night, knocking on her door and announcing their desire to rape her. The offender was finally arrested, pleaded guilty to stalking and soliciting sexual assaults, and received a six-year sentence (Newton, 2004).

Like traditional stalkers, a few cyberstalkers are strangers to their victims. An example of such an online stalker is a man who had just graduated with honors from a university in San Diego. Convinced that five female students had made fun of him as well as caused others to do the same, he spent 12 months bombarding them with up to four or five threatening e-mails every day, a common cyberstalking tactic called "e-mail bombing." After he was arrested, the police found that he was unbalanced and none of the women had ever met him (Newton, 2004).

Hate Killing

According to the FBI, every year more than 9,000 Americans fall victim to hate or bias crimes, offenses committed because of the victim's race, religion, national origin, or sexual orientation. Slightly more than half of these victims were only intimidated. Nearly half are assaulted and less than 1 percent murdered. Hate-motivated homicides are comparatively rare, but they have received great attention from the media, which presumably reflects the profound concern of many Americans on this issue (Fox, Levin, and Quinet, 2005).

African Americans and gay Americans are more likely than any other group to be victims of hate homicide. Such killing is targeted not only at the particular person but also at all the other members of that person's group. In June 1998, when three white men in Jasper, Texas, dragged James Byrd, an African American, behind their pickup truck to his death, they were in effect telling every black person in town to get out or suffer the same fate as Byrd. Similarly, in October 1998, when two young men in Laramie, Wyoming, beat gay college student Matthew Shepard into a coma and left him to die tied to a fence in the desert, they were effectively warning all gay people that they too could suffer the same fate.

Hate-motivated killers are also more likely than perpetrators of other, less serious hate crimes to have joined an organized hate group. James Byrd's three killers, for example, had met each other in prison and joined the Aryan Brotherhood, a white supremacist group. For someone filled with hate, membership in such a group assures them that they are not alone in their bigotry. They are also likely to feel bolder and more willing to take risks when encouraged by the group to attack the victim of their hate.

In their research on hate killers, James Fox, Jack Levin, and Kenna Quinet (2005) found that the killers can be divided into three types. First are the *thrill* hate killers, who, being young, bored, and idle, are seized with the idea of going out together to look for someone to attack. As marginalized and alienated youngsters, these offenders often feel important and powerful from the thrill attacks. Then, there are the *defensive* hate killers, who feel the need to defend what they consider to be their birthright. A black family moving into a white neighborhood or a gay man attending a predominantly heterosexual party, for example, is seen as encroaching on the hatemonger's birthright of being white or straight. Finally, there are the *mission* hate killers. These are the rarest but the most dangerous of the three types. While the thrill and defensive killers usually target a single victim, the mission killers seek to destroy all members of a hated group. Thus, they may kill members of a group indiscriminately, target many people simultaneously, and carry on a killing spree in various places. Their mission is to eliminate or weaken an entire group of people so that they themselves can attain the most powerful position in society.

Genocide

If the mission hate killers turn out to be the political leaders of a state, they are able to carry out their mission by committing *genocide,* the wholesale killing of members of a racial or ethnic group. There have been numerous cases of genocide around the world. During the nineteenth century, Dutch settlers in South Africa exterminated the native Hottentots, and British settlers on the island of Tasmania, near Australia, wiped out the entire native population, hunting them like wild animals. During the pioneer days of the United States, white settlers from Europe slaughtered many Native American tribes. In the early part of the twentieth century, the Turks massacred more than one million Armenians. Between 1933 and 1945, the Nazi Germans systematically murdered six million Jews. More recently, in the early 1990s, the Serbs in Bosnia killed and tortured numerous Muslims and Croats as part of an "ethnic cleansing" campaign. From 1993 to 1996, thousands of Tutsis were eliminated by Hutus in Rwanda, Africa. In 2004 the Arab government in Sudan killed at least 30,000 of its non-Arab citizens in the Darfur region of western Sudan. In the twentieth century as a whole, the victims of genocide were four times more numerous than the victims of all the wars and revolutions. Since 1968, the number of genocide victims throughout the world has *tripled* (Leaning, 2004; Alvarez, 2001).

One way to grasp the nature of genocide is to take a look at the people who are involved in it as victims, perpetrators, and bystanders. The victims are killed, "not for what they have done, but for who they are." They are, however, seen not as individuals, but as members of a stigmatized category of people. Thus, even if friends and neighbors happen to belong to a despised group, they are perceived as deserving to be killed. This is why, for example, many Muslims in Bosnia were killed by their Serbian friends (Weitz, 2003; Alvarez, 2001).

As for the perpetrators of genocide, common sense would suggest that they are monsters, sadists, and psychopaths, who derive great pleasure from making others suffer. But in reality they are mostly normal, like you and me, except that they have the job of killing others under the order of their superiors. The people who participated in the Holocaust, for example, came from a cross section of German society, representing a variety of careers, religious backgrounds, and socioeconomic classes. They lived normal, law-abiding, family-centered lives before and after the Holocaust. During the Holocaust, many suffered from stress, insomnia, nervous breakdown, or even committed suicide, because they were not psychopathic killers but ordinary people unaccustomed to killing human beings.

Finally, average citizens play the role of bystanders by doing nothing. In virtually all cases of genocide, the majority of citizens stay quiet and let their genocidal government carry out its campaign of exterminating the victims. A typical example is a high official of a university in Rwanda: He closed his eyes to the killing of tens of thousands and turned a deaf ear to the screams of dying people around him (Alvarez, 2001).

Scholars from various disciplines have offered a number of theories to explain genocide. One theory says that the cause of genocide is the *physical and psychological separation* between perpetrators and victims, which makes it easy for the former to kill the latter. A second theory attributes genocide to the *dehumanization* of the victims, who are treated as objects rather than persons. A third theory argues that the syndrome of *"obedience to authority,"* which is widespread in society, causes people to participate in genocide when ordered or asked to do so by the government. A fourth theory traces genocide to the perpetrators' *psychological ability to dissociate* their normal selves from the insanity of mass killing as if the killing is done by somebody else. And a fifth theory blames genocide on *power,* in that the more power the government has, the more able and willing it is to kill on a massive scale, which may explain why genocide occurs far more frequently in authoritarian and totalitarian states than in democratic nations (Valentino, 2004; Alvarez, 2001).

Terrorism

Terrorism is violence aimed at a government, though the victims are usually innocent citizens. Terrorists are basically powerless individuals futilely fighting a powerful government. Some fight their own governments. An example here is Timothy McVeigh, who was convicted of and executed for bombing the Alfred P. Murrah federal office building in Oklahoma City in 1995. Others are international terrorists, who leave their country to attack a foreign government. The Islamic radicals from the Middle East who used hijacked planes to destroy the World Trade Center and damage the Pentagon on September 11, 2001 are a recent example. Here we will discuss international terrorists.

The September 11 Attacks

On September 11, 2001, Muslim terrorists from the Middle East hijacked passenger planes and crashed them into the World Trade Center in New York City and the Pentagon in Washington, D.C., killing about 3,000 innocent people. It was far and away the worst terrorist attack on U.S. soil, the most devastating terrorism in human history. Why did the terrorists commit this heinous crime with the certain knowledge that they would die, too? Were they insane?

The reason for the suicide attacks is that the terrorists believed they were waging a holy war against the infidels, calling the United States "the Great Satan." But they were far from mentally ill. Like the Palestinian suicide bombers who blow themselves up along with innocent Israeli citizens, the September 11 attackers were members of a terrorist organization. But unlike the Palestinians, who belong to local groups, the September 11 terrorists belonged to an international organization called al Qaeda ("the base"), with members spread out all over the world. The September 11 attacks were part of al Qaeda's mission to destroy the United States and its interests abroad. Those terrorists were following the orders of their organization's leader, Osama bin Laden.

According to bin Laden, the U.S. culture of secularism, materialism, and free immorality threatens the traditional Islamic way of life. Moreover, U.S. foreign policy—including support for Israel, the stationing of American troops in Saudi Arabia, and the war and blockade against Iraq—purportedly destroys Muslim lives and wounds Muslim dignity as proud inheritors of a great religion. To redress these wrongs, bin Laden told his followers to engage in a holy war against the United States. He further mesmerized them with the seductive message that should they die as martyrs, they would go to heaven, where they each would be rewarded with 72 virgins (MacFarquhar, 2001). All this apparently resonated well with the young and unattached suicide terrorists who were already intensely religious and patriotic. It should not be surprising, then, that they carried out the horrendous crime on September 11, 2001.

Terrorism in Cyberspace

To plan and carry out their terrorist activities, al Qaeda's members now use mostly the Internet to communicate with one another. Some messages are posted in code on various Web sites. Other messages are transmitted electronically. After they are sent and read by the recipient, however, the whole communication and related files are deleted to maintain secrecy. Moreover, e-mail addresses are generally used only once or twice (Jehl and Rohde, 2004).

The terrorists are further able to launch a direct digital attack on the United States by hacking into its computer networks. The cyberattack could bring the country to its knees by disrupting or disabling a whole slew of its vital facilities and services. These include the power and water supply, gas and oil production and storage facilities, telecommunications and banking networks, air traffic control systems, and transportation and emergency services (Mazzetti, 2004; Hosenball, 2002). For example, a cyberterrorist can break into an air traffic control system, tamper with it, and cause jets to collide, so that hundreds of people die. Such cyberattacks have not taken place yet, but they definitely can happen as suggested by the success of nonpolitical, recreational hackers in briefly disabling Yahoo!, Amazon.com, and other online giants.

By using computers as a weapon of mass disruption, cyberterrorists can reach the United States easier than intercontinental ballistic missiles, disregarding the physical barriers of two broad oceans (the Atlantic and the Pacific) and two large peaceful neighbors (Canada and Mexico) that have long enhanced America's sense of safety. In today's computer-driven world, the terrorists no longer have to physically invade the territory or the airspace of the United States in order to damage its resources and disrupt the lives of its people. Indeed, "cyberterrorism presents a real and growing threat to American security," said Congressperson Jane Harman of California. "What I fear is the combination of a cyberattack coordinated with more traditional terrorism, undermining our ability to respond to an attack when lives are in danger" (Newton, 2004; Will, 2001).

The War on Terrorism

How can the United States stop further attacks from suicide terrorists? Suggestions have been made that the terrorists need to be stopped on three fronts: military, political, and cultural (Zakaria, 2001).

On the military front, the goal should be the total destruction of al Qaeda and other terrorist organizations. The U.S. military must track down and bring to justice any person who plans or helps in a terrorist operation. Even the government of a country that harbors terrorists must be brought down militarily with international support, so that it will be easier to find and capture the terrorists and their leaders.

On the political front, the United States should seek cooperation from around the world to fight terrorism. This will involve getting other governments to make arrests, destroy hideouts, close bank accounts, and share intelligence. To avoid arousing envy, anger, or opposition because of the United States' position as the world's superpower, it should refrain from taking over a country after a military victory but instead work with other nations to help the local people form their own governments. The United States should further provide whatever aid is needed to turn a war-devastated country around, so that goodwill towards Americans can blossom in the Arab world. As for the conflict between the Israelis and Palestinians, the United States should take a more balanced approach to encourage both sides to work for peace.

On the cultural front, the United States should reduce the rage that has fueled terrorist attacks by correcting Arab misperception of U.S. society. To refute the popular Arab belief that the U.S. foreign policy places little value on Muslim lives and priorities, for example, it should be pointed out how the United States has sent soldiers to protect the Muslims in Kuwait, Bosnia, and Kosovo. Messages such as this could be broadcast over the radio and other U.S. media. More American officials should appear on Arab media to counter the anti-American bias in its news and views. The cultural exchange programs that link U.S. students, government officials, and entrepreneurs with their counterparts in the Arab world should be increased. Finally, the American embassies in Arab countries should work with the local education ministries to ensure that teachers and textbooks present a fair view of the United States (Kinzer, 2001).

Since the terrorist attacks in late 2001, the U.S. government has tried to fight the war against the terrorists on those three fronts. The Taliban rulers of Afghanistan, who used to provide sanctuary to the Islamic fundamentalist terrorists, have been eliminated. And with cooperation from other governments, the United States has "hacked" into foreign banks' computer systems to find people who finance terrorist activities. The Americans also have obtained assistance from friendly Muslim intelligence services in tracking down terrorists. While some of the captured terrorists are imprisoned at the U.S. naval base in Guantanamo, Cuba, others have been sent to secret prisons overseas, including those in friendly Muslim countries that do not shy away from using torture as an interrogative aid. Over half of al Qaeda's key operational leaders have been killed or captured, along with some 3,000 of their associates. But al Qaeda has changed from an organization to a movement, made up of a loosely affiliated network joined together by local terrorists in many different countries, the Internet, and a shared hatred of Western governments. Also on the cultural front, not enough has been done to counter the Arab extremist groups' distortion of American actions and intentions (Kaplan and Whitelaw, 2004; Al-Arian, 2004; Kaplan, 2003; Gilgoff and Tolson, 2003).

Why Do People Kill?

Some sociologists have used positivist theories of deviance such as anomie-strain, control, and social learning to explain why people commit homicide (see, for example, Fox, Levin, and Quinet, 2005). The assumption is that whatever causes deviance in general also cause homicide in particular. But here we will discuss two positivist theories that are specifically designed to explain the causes of homicide, theories that are derived from studies on homicide as opposed to other forms of deviance.

External Restraint Theory

Developed by Andrew Henry and James Short (1954), the external restraint theory is intended to explain why some people who are extremely frustrated commit suicide and others who are just as frustrated turn to homicide instead. Henry and Short consider suicide and homicide to be basically the same—both are acts of aggression resulting from frustration. Yet, these sociologists point out, the two acts differ in that suicide is aggression directed inward against oneself, while homicide is aggression directed outward against another person. This theory attempts to explain why intensely frustrated people are likely to choose one type of aggression rather than the other. The explanation is that intensely frustrated people would choose *self*-directed aggression (suicide) if they experience *weak* external restraint, but would choose *other*-directed aggression (homicide) if they suffer *strong* external restraint.

Henry and Short define the *strength of external restraint* as "the degree to which behavior is required to conform to the demands and expectations of other persons." In other words, the strength of external restraint is the amount of social control imposed on people so as to limit their freedom and range of behaviors. According to the theory, people who suffer a great amount of that kind of social control are more inclined toward homicide than suicide because they can legitimately blame others for their frustration.

Martin Gold (1958) has extended the theory of external restraint to include a factor that mediates between strong external restraint and murder. The mediating factor is the *socialization in aggression by physical punishment*. Gold believes that there are two types of socialization—that is, techniques of bringing up a child. One involves the parents using *physical* punishment (spanking, slapping, hitting, or punching) to deter their misbehaving child from further misbehavior. The other involves the parents employing *psychological* punishment (e.g., threatening withdrawal of love, or lecturing to induce guilt) to correct their child's misconduct. Gold theorizes that physical punishment leads to outward aggression against another person, while children psychologically punished turn their aggression against themselves. When they become frustrated adults ready for aggressive action, those who have been physically punished will likely choose murder over suicide, while those who have undergone psychological punishment would choose suicide.

There is some evidence to suggest that strong external restraint is associated with homicide. As we have observed, the lower classes and blacks have significantly higher homicide rates than do the middle classes and whites. Such a finding can be said to support the theory because the lower classes and blacks suffer stronger external restraint. There is also evidence to support Gold's theory that physical punishment received in childhood increases the likelihood of homicide in adulthood (Straus, 1991). Still, all this does not mean, as the theories imply, that external restraint or physical punishment has a direct, causal impact on homicide. Instead, as more recent studies suggest, external restraint can lead to homicide only through a third variable called "external attribution of blame"—blaming others rather than oneself for one's own frustration (Unnithan, Huff-Corzine, Corzine, and Whitt, 1994). In other words, excessive external restraint or physical punishment encourages people to blame others rather than themselves for their own problems in life, which in turn causes them to engage in physical violence against others.

Subculture of Violence Theory

After analyzing his abundant data on homicide, Marvin Wolfgang (1958) concludes:

> There may be a subculture of violence which does not define personal assaults as wrong or antisocial; in which quick resort to physical aggression is a socially approved and expected concomitant of certain stimuli; and in which violence has become a familiar but often deadly partner in life's struggles.

Wolfgang then theorizes that the subculture of violence is the basic cause of high homicide rates in poor neighborhoods.

According to Wolfgang, the violent subculture has such a grip on the poor that they engage in a wider range of violent behavior than the nonpoor. This is because they associate and identify with the model of violence as provided by their parents, peers, and others in the poor neighborhood. At the same time they are discouraged from following the countermodel of nonviolence from the larger society. Consequently, violence becomes a part of their lifestyles and their way of solving interpersonal problems. Not surprisingly, they consider the use of violence not only normal but necessary for survival. They do not feel guilty about their aggression at all (Wolfgang and Ferracuti, 1967).

Critics, however, have questioned the implication that a violent act necessarily reflects the actor's placing a high value on violence. In fact, studies have shown that people who engage in violence do not value violence any more than those who refrain from violence, and that prisoners convicted of murder and other violent crimes do not value violence any more than other inmates convicted of burglary and other nonviolent crimes (Erlanger, 1974; Ball-Rokeach, 1973). Other studies have suggested that the cause of high homicide rates among the poor and African Americans is not the subculture of violence but rather poverty, relative deprivation, or social inequality (Williams, 1984; Messner, 1982). Nevertheless, as it propagates the belief in using violence to solve interpersonal problems, the subculture of violence does encourage—though not cause—homicide, especially among those frustrated by the structural problems of poverty and inequality (Corzine, Huff-Corzine, and Whitt, 1999; Messner, 1983).

Does the Death Penalty Deter Murder?

Nowadays, most people believe that the death penalty is an effective deterrent to murder. Not surprisingly, to win an election, most politicians vow that convicted killers shall be put to death. Many sociologists, however, have observed that the death penalty does not have its hoped-for effect. The evidence supporting this observation has come in several forms.

The first indication is the homicide rates in *states that have retained* the death penalty law are generally much higher than in *states that have abolished* it. (See examples in Figure 4.2.) This clearly suggests that the death penalty does not deter homicide. It might even suggest to some observers that the death penalty causes more homicides. It could be the other way around: That is, the higher homicide rates cause the states to bring back the death penalty. Moreover, the South, where all the states practice the death penalty, has a very large black population and a culture of violence, as reflected by its traditionally high rate of criminal violence and high level of gun ownership. Thus the distinctive population and cultural characteristics of the South, rather than its death penalty, may be responsible for its higher homicide rate.

In view of this, some sociologists have excluded the southern states from analysis of the relationship between capital punishment and murder. Instead, they focused on northern and western states that have about the same population composition and cultural tradition. The result has consistently shown that the death penalty states still have higher homicide rates than their neighboring states without the death penalty. Although this finding does not prove that capital punishment encourages murder, it does show that the death penalty does not deter murder.

A second type of evidence comes from comparing the homicide rates that occurred *before and after abolition* of the death penalty within the same states. Such comparisons have shown no significant difference in homicide rates before and after the states abolished capital punishment. Furthermore, the *restoration* of the

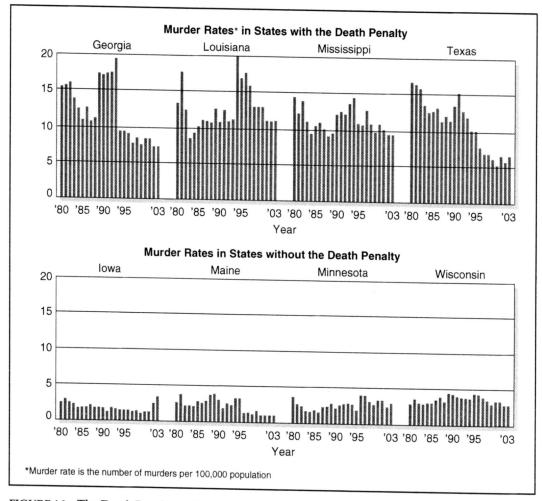

FIGURE 4.2   The Death Penalty and Murder. Murder rates and generally much higher in the 38 states that still retain the death penalty than in the 12 states that have abolished it, as exemplified above.
Sources: FBI, Uniform Crime Reports, 1981–2003.

death penalty in states that had earlier abolished it had *not* led to any significant decrease in homicides. This further suggests that the death penalty does not deter people from committing murder.

A final piece of evidence comes from comparing the numbers of homicides *shortly before and shortly after executions* of convicted murderers that have been widely publicized. If the death penalty has a deterrent effect, the execution should so scare potential killers that they would refrain from killing, and the number of homicides in the area should decrease. Apparently, this is not the case. In Philadelphia during the 1930s, for example, the number of homicides remained about the same in the period from 60 days before to 60 days after a widely publicized execution of five murderers. This finding, among others, suggests that the death penalty, even when the state shows people that it means business with it, apparently does not frighten potential killers from killing.

In fact, publicized executions may have the opposite, *brutalizing effect* on potential murderers, indirectly encouraging them to kill, possibly by diminishing respect for human life or by stimulating imitative violence. In California between 1946 and 1955, the state always chose Friday mornings to carry out executions, and there were more murders during the weekends following executions than during the weekends without the Friday-morning executions. Also, in New York between 1907 and 1963, there was an average increase of two homicides in the month after each execution. The brutalizing effect took place in the 1990s in Oklahoma (Bailey, 1998; Bowers and Pierce, 1980). In a few other cases, the brutalizing effect did not exist, but there was no indication of the deterrent effect either, because the number of homicides remained about the same whether there was a publicized execution or not (King, 1978).

What we have discussed can be summed up by the conclusion from a 14-nation analysis of the death penalty: "If capital punishment is a more effective deterrent than the alternative punishment of long imprisonment, its abolition ought to be followed by homicide rate increases. The evidence examined here fails to support and, indeed, repeatedly contradicts this proposition. In this cross-national sample, abolition was followed more often than not by absolute *decreases* in homicide rates, not by the increases predicted by deterrence theory" (Archer and Gartner, 1984).

Nevertheless, a few studies appear every now and then to challenge that conclusion. The most well-known is economist Isaac Ehrlich's (1975) conclusion from his statistical analysis that one execution can prevent about eight murders. This particular analysis has been criticized for its methodological problems, such as the use of unreliable data on homicides. More devastating to Ehrlich's conclusion is another economist's analysis that uses the same statistical method as Ehrlich's but produces essentially contrary results (Avio, 1979). Like Ehrlich, sociologist David Phillips (1980b) also claims to have found the deterrent effect of capital punishment. In analyzing 22 cases of execution that occurred in London between 1858 and 1921, he found that homicides dropped by 35.7 percent within two weeks following an execution that was widely publicized in the city's leading newspaper. But Phillips has been criticized for analyzing only 22 executions, which can hardly represent the many hundreds of executions that took place between 1858 and 1921 (Zeisel, 1982). Phillips has argued that he analyzed only these few executions because they were heavily publicized in the *Times* of London, but it must be said that the poor and uneducated, who were more likely than others to commit murder, were hardly the readers of that newspaper.

We may conclude that the death penalty does not deter murder, or, more precisely, is no more effective than life imprisonment in deterring murder. But why not? One reason is that murder is a crime of passion, most often carried out under the overwhelming pressure of a volcanic emotion, while capital punishment would more likely be effective if murder were a calmly calculated act. Another reason is that the causal forces of murder, such as exposure to brutality and abuse and economic deprivation, are simply too powerful to be neutralized by the threat of capital punishment.

However, despite its lack of deterrence to murder, capital punishment can be effective for other purposes. It is obviously effective in preventing the murderer from doing harm to others again. It is also effective in satisfying the emotion of outrage against murder. Many people seem to advocate capital punishment for these reasons. As public opinion polls have shown, more than half of the U.S. population would still favor the death penalty even if they know that it does not deter murder. This is particularly true today, as suggested by the growing number of executions in recent years (see Figure 4.3). Nonetheless, our society likes to appear civilized in doing away with convicted murderers. Barbaric methods of execution, such as hangings and firing squads, are for all intents and purposes no longer used; they are replaced by the "more humane" electric chair, gas chamber, and, most recently, lethal injection. Such humane appearances notwithstanding, we remain the only industrialized nation that still executes murderers, and we also have the highest murder rate in the industrialized world.

FIGURE 4.3   The Rising Number of Executions by Year

Source: Bureau of Justice Statistics, 2004–2005.

Summary

1. How do assaults differ from homicide? In assaults the victim survives, and compared to killers, the assaulters are less likely to use firearms and more likely to commit the offense in the summer.

2. What kinds of people are more likely than others to commit homicide? They include the poor, African Americans, men, and young adults. They are also more likely to live in the southern region of the United States, and in large cities and in rural areas rather than in small towns.

3. Are there any patterns to the occurrence of homicide? Yes. Homicides are somewhat more likely to occur during the hot summer months than the cold month of February. They are most likely to occur on Saturday night. They are about as likely to take place in the home as outside if the killers are male, but tend to be at home if the offenders are female. Firearms are more often used than any other weapon.

4. What are the characteristics of homicide? First, homicide is generally warm-blooded killing, involving a relative, a friend, or an acquaintance. Second, it may involve the victim helping to bring about the killing. Third, it often involves killing for trivial reasons. And fourth, it sometimes involves the killer first doing away with the victim and then finishing himself off.

5. What is the nature of mass and serial murder? In mass murder a number of people are killed at the same time, while in serial murder the victims are killed at different times and places. Mass murderers are mostly ordinary people who are disgruntled employees, heads of family, pseudo-commandos, and followers of a charismatic leader. Serial murderers are cleverer in eluding the police and more likely to torture

their victims before killing them. **What is the social profile of serial killers?** Most serial killers have not attended college but are cunning and able to present themselves as friendly and trustworthy. They are mostly white men, generally kill strangers, and are motivated to kill by sadism and a desire for power. **What does homicide look like from the global perspective?** Homicide appears associated with poverty, as shown by its greater prevalence in developing countries than in developed countries. It also has to do with a culture of violence, which characterizes Latin America more than other poor regions in the world.

6. What causes school violence? Contributing factors include the easy availability of guns, the media glamorization of violence, and the culture of violence, which favor the use of force to settle interpersonal problems. Given this environment, youngsters who have been abused by parents or rejected by peers may engage in school violence.

7. What are stalkers like? Most stalkers target ex-intimates, fellow employees, and acquaintances, although a few go after celebrities. Stalkers are more likely to be male than female, and their victims are mostly female. A majority of stalkers are loners, mentally unhealthy, and socially incompetent.

8. How do hate-motivated killers act? They are more likely to target gays and African Americans than any other group. They use their killing to intimidate the entire group of which the victim is a member, and they usually belong to a hate group. They may kill for thrill, for defense of their birthright, or for the mission of eliminating the groups they hate.

9. What kinds of people are involved in genocide? The victims of genocide are members of a stigmatized group, the perpetrators are normal people following orders to kill, and the bystanders are average citizens who do nothing to stop the killing. **What causes genocide?** According to various theories, the causes include the physical and psychological separation between offenders and victims, dehumanization of the victims, widespread obedience to authority, psychological dissociation between the normal self and the insane act of genocidal killing, and the immense power of the state.

10. What is the nature of terrorism? Terrorism is violence aimed at a government and usually involves victimizing innocent citizens. It can serve an instrumental or expressive function, and terrorists can go after foreign or domestic targets. **What caused the September 11 terrorist attacks?** The attacks were directed by Osama bin Laden, the leader of the terrorist organization al Qaeda, who

exhorted or ordered the extremely religious and patriotic young members to attack the United States as "the Great Satan." **What is the nature of cyberterrorism?** It involves using the Internet for communication or hacking into the computer networks in the United States so as to disrupt its vital facilities and services. **How can the suicide terrorists be stopped?** A successful plan must include a combination of military, political, and cultural actions.

11. Why do some people kill? One sociological theory points to strong external restraint as the cause of homicide, while another indicates the subculture of violence as a breeding ground of homicides. **Is the death penalty an effective deterrent to murder?** No, at least no more effective than the life sentence. Nevertheless, it enjoys more popular support in those states that have higher homicide rates.

FURTHER READING

Alvarez, Alex. 2001. *Government, Citizens, and Genocide: A Comparative and Interdisciplinary Approach.* Bloomington: Indiana University Press. Discusses the history of genocide, the political nature of genocide, the institutional and organizational supports of genocide, and the contribution of ordinary men and women to genocide.

Baker, Jean A. 1998. "Are we missing the forest for the trees? Considering the social context of school violence." *Journal of School Psychology,* 36 (Spring), 29–44. Showing how school violence derives from a breakdown of community in schools where students do not feel a sense of belonging.

Beeghley, Leonard. 2003. *Homicide: A Sociological Explanation.* Lanham, MD: Rowman and Littlefield. Discusses the connection of homicide to gun availability, illegal drugs, violence history, racial discrimination, and economic inequality.

Combs, Cindy C. 2000. *Terrorism in the Twentieth-First Century.* Upper Saddle River, N.J.: Prentice

Hall. A systematic discussion of many aspects of terrorism, ranging from terrorist ideology and terrorist organizations to counterterrorist measures.

Dunn, Jennifer L. 2002. *Courting Disaster: Intimate Stalking, Culture, and Criminal Justice.* New York: Aldine de Gruyter. Provides an intimate look at the nature of stalking through the victims' experiences.

Fox, James Alan, Jack Levin, and Kenna Quinet, 2005. *The Will to Kill: Making Sense of Senseless Murder.* Boston: Allyn and Bacon. Analyzes the nature of various forms of murder, including serial murder, school shootings, mass murder, and cult killings.

Holmes, Ronald M., and Stephen T. Holmes. 1998. *Serial Murder,* 2d ed. Thousand Oaks, Calif.: Sage Publications. Presents various types of serial killers, their behavioral patterns, and the motivations behind their killings.

Levin, Jack, and James Alan Fox. 2002. *Dead Lines: Essays in Murder and Mayhem.* Boston: Allyn and Bacon. A series of essays about homicide, school shootings, workplace violence, hate crimes, serial murder, the culture of killing, guns, official responses to murder, capital punishment, and crime victims.

Levin, Jack, and Gordana Rabrenovic. 2004. *Why We Hate.* Amherst, N.Y.: Prometheus Books. Discusses the various sources of hate crime and ways of combating it.

Mann, Coramae Richey. 1996. *When Women Kill.* Albany: State University of New York Press. An analysis of both qualitative and quantitative data on nearly 300 women arrested for homicide in six large U.S. cities.

Martinez, J. Michael, William D. Richardson, and D. Brandon Hornsby, eds. 2002. *The Leviathan's Choice: Capital Punishment in the Twentieth Century.* Lanham, Md.: Rowman & Littlefield. A collection of articles presenting various perspectives on the death penalty, including the philosophical, theological, social science, and legal perspectives.

Mullen, Paul E., Michele Pathe, and Rosemary Purcell. 2000. *Stalkers and Their Victims.* Cambridge, U.K.: Cambridge University Press. Discusses numerous aspects of stalking, from the epidemiology of stalking to various types of stalkers and stalking situations.

Reuter, Christoph. 2004. *My Life as a Weapon: A Modern History of Suicide Bombing.* Princeton, N.J.: Princeton University Press. An analysis of suicide bombings in different parts of the world.

Smith, M. Dwayne, and Margaret A. Zahn, eds. 1999. *Homicide: A Sourcebook of Social Research.* Thousand Oaks, Calif.: Sage Publications. A collection of detailed analyses of the theories, methodologies, substantive studies, and prevention of homicide.

Vanden Heuvel, Katrina. 2002. *A Just Response: The Nation on Terrorism, Democracy, and September 11, 2001.* New York: Thunder's Mouth Press/ Nation Books. A collection of essays on the meanings and implications of the September 11 terrorist attacks.

Weitz, Eric D. 2003. *A Century of Genocide: Utopias of Race and Nation.* Princeton, N.J.: Princeton University Press. Shows how the zealous attempt to create a homogeneous utopia led the leaders of nations as well as the masses of ordinary people to genocide.

CRITICAL THINKING QUESTIONS

1. Analyze the various forms of homicide discussed in this chapter. What are the similarities and differences among them?

2. Genocide is the most horrendous kind of killing. How can it be prevented?

CHAPTER

5 Rape and Child Molestation

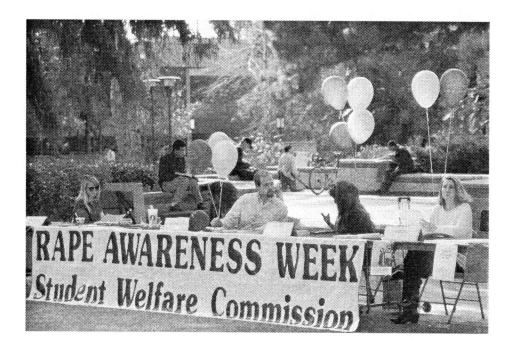

On one afternoon in Kosovo, Yugoslovia, Serbian paramilitary forces pulled 10 young Albanian women out of a refugee convoy of trucks, cars, and tractors that were fleeing the civil war between Albanians and Serbs. Then 10 Serbian soldiers raped the women in an open field about 30 feet from the road, which the victims' families could see with horror and helplessness while they themselves were held at gunpoint by other soldiers. An hour later the Serbians slashed the victims' pants around their thighs and put the women on a truck with their families. Crying, the women said, among other things, "Better dead than what they did to us" (Bumiller, 1999).

As in other wars in the past, sexual violence against women was relatively common in Kosovo. The problem is also prevalent in peacetime in other countries. According to a nationwide survey in the United States, 22 percent of women ages 18 to 90 reported having been sexually assaulted (Elliott et al., 2004). In other studies, rape victims were found to make up less than 22 percent of U.S. women. Still, the most conservative estimate has put the average woman's chance of being raped at "an appalling 1 in 10" (Russell and Bolen, 2000; Koss, 1995). Also significantly, the overwhelming majority of these women know their rapists.

In this chapter we will first explore the patterns of rape, seeking answers to such questions as: Who is likely to rape? How are rapes generally planned and executed? What is involved in different forms of rape? Why can't the victim be blamed for the rape? We will in turn examine the reactions of both victims and law enforcers to rapes, analyze the pervasive culture that encourages men to assault women sexually, discuss the major explanations for rape, and look at the issue about men being victims of rape. Finally we will analyze the problem of child molestation.

Patterns of Rape

Certain patterns can be detected in rape. Let us first see what kind of men are likely to rape and how they plan and carry out such a crime. Then we will take a close look at the nature of gang rape, acquaintance or date rape, and rape on the college campus along with the controversial issue of victim-precipitated rape.

Racial, Age, and Situational Factors

In his classic analysis of 646 rape cases from the Philadelphia police files for the years 1958 and 1960, sociologist Menachem Amir (1971) found that most of the rapists were poor. He also found that blacks were more likely than whites to be both rapists and victims. Amir further discovered that, contrary to the then widespread white fear of black men being more likely to rape white women than black, rape was mostly *intraracial*—black men raping black women and white men raping white women. In about 95 percent of the rapes in Philadelphia, both offenders and victims were of the same race; in only 3 percent were the rapists black and their victims white. In other words, rape was as intraracial as murder. The intraracial nature of rape can be attributed to at least two factors. One is the unusually severe legal penalty against blacks who raped white women. Another reason is racial segregation, which made black women more accessible than white women to those black men who are inclined to express their aggression in rape.

But today rape has become considerably less intraracial—or more interracial. Already by the early 1980s black-against-white rapes had soared to 19 percent (from 3 percent in the late 1950s and early 1960s) of all rapes committed by both blacks and whites (Wilbanks, 1985). This may have resulted from increased racial integration and hence more contact between potential offenders and victims of different races. But at least two other factors continue to operate in such rapes: (1) as members of an oppressed minority, some African-American men may want to "get even" at the white society by raping its women, and (2) the white-dominated society has enshrined the white female as the ideal of sexual attractiveness (LaFree, 1982). It should be pointed out, though, that most rapes still involve members of the same race.

Age is another factor in the relationship between rapists and their victims. Females from the age of 1 year all the way up to above the age of 80 are subject to rape. The age group most vulnerable to rape, however, is 16 to 20 years of age. In intraracial rapes, offenders are generally somewhat older than their victims. But in *inter*racial rapes, black offenders tend to be *younger* than their white victims. This does not mean that the black offenders prefer older white women. Instead, it is largely a matter of availability, because many of these black–white rape episodes involve the commission of burglary or robbery in addition to rape (Russell, 1984). While this may reflect black hostility toward white society, as suggested, it may also reflect the influence of a sexist society. Burglars and robbers usually feel that "if you rob a woman, you might as well rape her too—the rape is free" (Lear, 1972). Such criminals simply consider rape "an added bonus" to their property crime (Scully, 1990).

There is also a situational factor in rape. The number of rapes, especially gang rapes, tends to increase during the hot summer months. Most significant is the finding that most rapes occur on weekends (Michael and Zumpe, 1983). Does summer increase the heat of passion and hence the likelihood of rape? No, summer merely increases the social interaction between potential offender and victim that makes rape more likely to happen. Most rapes also involve drinking on the part of offenders, just like most homicides. The use of alcohol serves as an excuse for sexual aggression ("It wasn't my fault; I was drunk"). Because this excuse is to a significant degree socially acceptable, it helps reduce the inhibition against raping as it does against killing. But compared with murderers, rapists are generally less violent, less likely to have previous arrest records for aggravated assault. Since rapists are not as violent as murderers, most rapes do not happen as explosively or impulsively as murders do; they do not spring from a sudden, uncontrolled sexual desire. Instead, rapes are mostly planned.

Planning and Execution

Since most rapes involve acquaintances, friends, or lovers, the planning largely entails the offender using sweet talk, romantic moves, alcoholic beverages, or some other means to induce the woman to have sex, and then single-mindedly striving to achieve his aim without paying any attention to her wishes.

But rapists operate differently if they do not know the victim well or at all. In such cases, offenders tend to choose women who, they believe, are vulnerable to attack. Such targets are in a disadvantaged situation so that they cannot react appropriately or swiftly to the threat of rape. Examples include a mentally challenged girl, a sleeping female, an old woman, or a young woman under the influence of alcohol or drugs. Other women are also more vulnerable to rape if they appear passive or submissive, lacking in assertiveness or confidence. A woman is said to suggest submissiveness to a potential rapist if she "walks slowly and tentatively, stares at the ground and moves her arms and legs in short, jerky motions." Yet some rapists prefer the opposite type of women—those who appear too aggressive or domineering. As many convicted rapists in one study indicated, "they wanted to put a particular uppity woman in her place" (Bart and O'Brien, 1985). Apparently, women who project confidence without appearing too aggressive are less subject to rape.

If they cannot easily determine the vulnerability of a woman, rapists will likely work out a strategy to test her. They might first try to determine whether or not their selected target is a friendly and helpful person. A rapist might approach a woman on the street and ask her for a light or a street direction. If she provides it, he may proceed to ask her an intimate question, make some sexually suggestive remarks, put his arm around her, or touch her in a sexually provocative place to see how she reacts. If she reacts submissively or fearfully, he knows that she can be intimidated into submitting to his sexual demands. Another rapist might ask a woman to let him into her house to make an emergency phone call or for any other bogus reason. If the woman falls for such a ploy, the rapist may establish her as a prospective victim. An example follows:

> The rapist would walk into an apartment house and ring several doorbells asking for "Sally." When he found a woman who was helpful, attractive and presumably alone, he would explain how hot and tired he was and ask for a drink of water. Then he asked to use the bathroom so he could look around and make sure the victim was alone. Finally he would ask for a second drink of water and then approach the victim as she stood at the kitchen sink. With a knife at her throat and cut off from help, the victim usually capitulated. (Selkin, 1975)

After they have successfully identified a target for rape, the offenders initially do not resort to intimidation with such violent means as brandishing a weapon or administering a brutal beating. The majority of rapes involve only verbal coercion and nonphysical aggression, such as "Don't scream or I'll cut you to pieces," and "If you don't take your clothes off, I'll kill you!" Rapists ordinarily become more violent only when they are ready to carry out the crime. According to Pauline Bart and Patricia O'Brien (1985), the majority of the rapists in their study were rough—pushing, shoving, slapping, or choking their victims. Some rapists would not merely subject their victims to forced intercourse; they would also force them to submit to oral or anal sodomy and repeated vaginal assault. Sometimes rapists make jokes at their victims' expense. After he was through, one rapist proclaimed to his victim: "I'll marry you if you get pregnant" (Macdonald, 1995, 1971).

Gang Rape

Of all the rapes studied by Amir (1971), 43 percent were gang rapes. The most significant fact about these rapes is that the perpetrators are largely adolescents aged 10 to 19. Most of these young rapists come from lower-class families, and are members of street gangs. They find their victims in several ways. First, they may cruise an area looking for a female hitchhiker to pick up and drive the unsuspecting victim to a deserted area to rape her. Second, they may use a knife or gun to kidnap a woman from the street at night. Third, a member of the gang may make a date with a woman and then drive her, without her knowledge or consent, to a predetermined location where he and other members will rape her (Scully, 1990).

Occurring less frequently are gang rapes on college campuses, committed by middle- and upper-class youths. Gang rape takes place at various kinds of schools: large state universities, well-known liberal arts colleges, religious schools, and Ivy League institutions, where gang rape is often referred to as "running a train" on the victim. There is a pattern to the way campus gang rapes occur: At a party, the men encourage a woman to drink or take drugs and rape her when she gets drunk or high on drugs (Sanday, 1990).

Why do those lower-class adolescents and college men participate in gang rapes? Psychiatrists generally interpret gang rape as an expression of latent homosexuality, arguing that the fellow rapists have an unconscious wish to have sex with each other (Sanday, 1990). Such an interpretation, however, makes as much sense as the suggestion that several men who rob a store together unconsciously want to rob each other or that a bunch of guys who go hunting together have a latent wish to kill each other. It seems more convincing to theorize that participation in a gang rape fulfills a social need more than a sexual desire, particularly for young boys who feel peer pressure to prove that they are not "chicken" (Groth and Birnbaum, 1979).

Similarly, college men who share a close relationship may find it hard to resist the pressure to participate in a gang rape because they are afraid of having their masculinity questioned. Moreover, through their camaraderie, they can playfully urge each other to participate in a gang rape without seeing it as a serious crime. This may explain why fraternity brothers and college athletes on some campuses are more likely than other students to engage in gang rape (Schwartz and DeKeseredy, 1997; O'sullivan, 1991). In fact, the likelihood of committing gang rape is relatively great in other similarly cohesive or tightly knit groups. Examples are the Serbian soldiers gang-raping Muslim women in Bosnia in the early 1990s, Japanese soldiers gang-raping women in China and other Asian countries during World War II, and U.S. soldiers gang-raping women in Vietnam during the Vietnam War.

Acquaintance Rape

Compared with their counterparts in stranger rape, the offenders in acquaintance or date rape are more likely to use verbal or psychological coercion and less likely to resort to guns or knives. Verbal coercion may involve pressuring the victim by saying "C'mon, I know you really want it"; psychological coercion may involve making the victim feel inadequate as an object by ignoring her wishes when she says "Stop it!" Also, while stranger rapists typically premeditate the rape, acquaintance rapists tend more to premeditate only a sexual relation, which leads to rape when the victim refuses and the offender brushes her refusal aside, often assuming that she means yes when saying no (Jasper, 1992). Most victims of acquaintance rape see themselves as victims, but they are more likely than victims of stranger rape to blame the rape partly on themselves, such as for being careless or trusting the man too much (Bechhofer and Parrot, 1991). As one victim of acquaintance rape said,

> One summer while I was in college, I worked at a hamburger stand. There was a regular there. He seemed like a nice guy, and we'd gotten to know each other pretty well. He asked if I wanted to come over to his apartment that afternoon when I got off work and listen to a record he'd been telling me about. Once we were up there, he grabbed me, and when I pulled away, he turned up the music really loud and said I'd better not fight unless I wanted to lose some teeth. The music was blasting away—no one could have heard me if I yelled—and I knew he wasn't kidding, so I just let him do it. Afterward I told him what a jerk he was and tried to make him feel bad, but *I was the one who felt awful—how could I have been so stupid to let something like that happen, how could I have been so dumb?* (Mithers, 1980)

Acquaintance rape has always been a common offense. In the 1950s Clifford Kirkpatrick and Eugene Kanin (1957) asked a representative sample of 291 college women whether they had been sexually assaulted during the academic year. More than half (55.7%) replied that they had—at least once. Their experiences ranged from forced necking to forced petting to forced vaginal penetration. In the late 1970s, Kanin and Stanley Parcell (1981) did a follow-up study and found about the same result. In the mid-1980s *Ms.* magazine also found a similarly high incidence of sexual offense in its nationwide survey of more than 7,000 college students on 35 campuses: 52 percent of all the women surveyed had encountered some form of sexual assault. The *Ms.* survey further showed that 15 percent were actually raped—forced to have sexual intercourse. Similar studies in the 1990s can be expected to show about the same result. In short, of all college women, *more than half* are sexually assaulted in one way or another and about *15 percent* are forcibly raped by their dates (Jackson, 1996; Koss et al., 1987; Sweet, 1985).

Acquaintance rape is this common because it appears to be an extension of, rather than a departure from, the conventional pattern of male sexual behavior. In our culture, where men are expected to be aggressive rather than shy in dealing with women, young men can easily go too far and use too much force to execute a sexual conquest. Not surprisingly, as suggested by one study, the more sexually active they are, the more likely they are to commit date rape (Kanin, 1985). Moreover, most of the rapists and even many of their victims do not regard date rape as real rape. In the *Ms.* survey, about 8 percent of the college men admitted to committing the sexual offenses that can be legally defined as rapes or attempted rapes, but virtually none of these men identified themselves as rapists. In the same survey, of the women who had been raped, nearly 75 percent did not identify their experiences as rape. They simply found it hard to believe that someone they knew could have raped them (Koss, 1995; Jasper, 1992; Sweet, 1985; Shotland and Goodstein, 1983).

Campus Rape

As we have observed, rape is particularly prevalent on college campuses, with about 15 percent of college women having been sexually assaulted. But most of the campus rapists, and even the majority of their victims, do not see the offense as forcible rape. Why not? The reason, as has been suggested, lies in the culture of the larger society that defines aggressiveness with women—rather than gentleness—as a highly desirable quality for young men to have. Campus rape, in other words, represents an extension of this culturally idealized male behavior. Thus the more sexually active men, who can be said to have acquired the highly desirable masculine trait as proven by their great success with women, are more likely than other men to commit date rape (Mohler-Kuo et al., 2004; Gilbert, 1995; Koss, 1995; Kanin, 1985).

While the larger society exerts its cultural influence on the college campus, is there something unique about the campus itself that also encourages sexual aggression? The answer from researchers on campus rape is yes. In her analysis of small tribal societies Peggy Sanday (1981) found that many are "rape-free" and a few "rape-prone." Rape-free societies have a culture that discourages sexual aggression while rape-prone societies have a culture that encourages it. More recently, Sanday (1996b) observed that there are also rape-free campuses and rape-prone campuses. On a rape-free campus, sexual assault is treated as a serious offense punishable by expulsion, fraternities discourage heavy drinking, women are respected as friends rather than used as sex objects, and gays and lesbians are accepted in the same way as straights. But on a rape-prone campus, sexual assault is not seriously dealt with, heavy drinking is encouraged, taking advantage of an intoxicated woman is accepted, bragging about sexual conquests is prevalent, homophobia is rampant, and pornography is a popular guide to female sexuality. Thus we can expect a higher incidence of sexual offense on rape-prone campuses.

Other researchers have made similar observations about what causes the high incidence of campus rape. Patricia Martin and Robert Hummer (1995) conclude from their study of fraternities that such student groups contribute heavily to campus rape in a number of ways through their unique norms and practices. First, the brotherhood norm requires "sticking together," which discourages anyone's stopping rapes when they occur or reporting them to outsiders. This form of "participation" effectively condones and encourages sexual violence. Second, fraternity norms emphasize the value of maleness and masculinity over femaleness and femininity, causing members to devalue women by using them as mere sex objects, which can lead to rapes when women resist. Third, certain fraternity practices that often lead to coercive sex include excessive use of alcohol and pressure from fellow members to prove one's masculinity through sexual conquests. Studies on male athletes have also found them to be more rape-prone than other students. The athletes subscribe to the same norms and practices as the fraternity brothers (Adams-Curtis and Forbes, 2004; Benedict, 1998; Crosset et al., 1996).

The Myth of Victim Precipitation

In his classic study of the rapes in Philadelphia, Amir (1971) found that 19 percent were precipitated by the victims themselves. He refers to this kind of offense as "victim-precipitated rape," explaining that "the victim actually—or so it was interpreted by the offender—agreed to sexual relations but retracted before the actual act or did not resist strongly enough when the suggestion was made by the offender." A common victim behavior that Amir interprets as an invitation to sexual intercourse occurs when a woman agrees to have a drink or ride with a stranger. The implication here is that the victim is as much to blame as her offender. The following case has been given as an example of victim-precipitated rape:

> An 18-year-old girl was standing in the parking lot of a hamburger drive-in when some men in a car called to her to come over to the car. When she reached the car, she thought she recognized one of the men so she sat in the front seat and started talking to them. Suddenly the driver started the car and drove off. They explained that they were looking for a friend. As they were driving, one of the men asked, "Do you want to fuck?" She laughed and said no. After stopping briefly at another drive-in, the man sitting alongside her put a gun to her head and said, "Are you scared?" She replied, "I don't like having a gun to my head and I am scared shitless, but I don't feel like crying and begging you because I don't feel like hassling you. You won't get any enjoyment out of being sadistic to me." The man turned to the men in the back of the car and said, "Well, what about it, do you want to or not?" They agreed to go ahead and rape her. (Macdonald, 1971)

The concept of victim-precipitated rape reflects a *biased*, male-centered view rather than an accurate description of the crime, and it has drawn criticisms for being a sexist myth. In the example quoted above, the young woman can be said to have "asked for it" only from a biased or rationalizing perspective. As attorney Camille LeGrand (1973) says, "Hitchhiking and walking alone at night in a rough neighborhood may be considered behavior encouraging a sexual attack. This view of what a *man* can assume to be a sexual invitation is unreasonable, because when the female hitchhiker first sets out to get a ride, she normally is not expecting—or hoping for—a sexual encounter."

Sociologist Eugene Kanin (1984) also argues that the concept of victim precipitation, which has been applied to some homicides as discussed in the preceding chapter, is not applicable to rapes. But Kanin contends that some victims do "contribute" in some way to being raped, in the same way as a man contributes to the burglary of his house by failing to stop newspaper delivery while away on vacation. Thus Kanin suggests using the term *victim contribution* to describe those cases of rape in which the victims have willingly engaged in deep kissing or some other form of advanced intimacy prior to the occurrence of the assault.

There could also be problems, however, with the concept of victim contribution. Most important, it amounts to suggesting that virtually all dating women contribute to rape because they usually engage in uncoerced intimacy with their dates. We should note that rape victims only contribute to the *pre*rape intimacy, comparable to the way the man whose house is burglarized contributes to the burglary by failing to stop newspaper delivery while away on vacation. The rape victims cannot be said to contribute to the rape itself because they try to stop it at the moment of the crime, just as the burglary victim cannot be said to contribute to the burglary if he had come home and tried to stop it. In brief, a fundamental difference exists between prerape intimacy, which does not involve the use of force and hence is not a crime, and rape itself, which involves the use of force and therefore is a crime.

Many men, however, do not seem to recognize this difference between consensual prerape intimacy and forced sex. According to one study, 50 percent of the young men interviewed consider it "acceptable for a man to force a girl to have sexual intercourse when she initially consents but then changes her mind, or when she has sexually excited him" (Shotland and Goodstein, 1983). A more recent study found that 76 percent of high school male students regard forced sex as acceptable under similar circumstances (White and Humphrey, 1991). These young men, in effect, blame the victim. It reflects the popular myth that it is her fault if she is flirting, if she is attractively dressed, if she is in the man's perception "a tease," if she joins him for a drink, if she invites him to her apartment for coffee after having gone to a movie with him, or, sometimes, even if she only says "hello" to him at the office (Morris and Cubbins, 1992; Burt, 1991).

Consequences of Rape

Rape is in a way unique, different from murder, robbery, and most other crimes. While each of these other crimes is largely a finished act after it has occurred, rape is more likely to be a continuing process, in which the survivor keeps on suffering after the rape is over. Let us examine the survivor's experiences in the aftermath of the sexual assault.

The Rape Survivor's Response

The response to rape varies from one survivor to another. At one extreme are the survivors who show a lack of concern. One such survivor, when asked what happened between the two attacks of rape by her assailant, replied, "We went out for hamburgers." Some fall asleep after the rape; others are more upset over the theft of a purse, a ring, a cell phone, or similar property than over the rape; some survivors may voluntarily engage in sexual relations with their assailant when they meet him again after the rape; other survivors may later marry their rapists, whom they may or may not have met prior to the rape (Macdonald, 1995, 1971). At the opposite extreme are the survivors who are so traumatized that they sink into deep depression, attempt to commit suicide, or actually kill themselves. In between these two extremes are the great majority who initially experience shock, disbelief, anger, anxiety, or depression, but eventually pull themselves out of it.

This diversity of reactions to rape is apparently related to such factors as the degree of violence, the age of the survivor, her social class or cultural background, and prior sexual experience. If she has been violently raped, is relatively young, comes from a middle- or upper-class family, or has had no or little previous sexual experience, she is likely to suffer relatively severe consequences. Other factors also have a significant impact on how rape survivors feel. The trauma will be much greater, for example, if the survivor has experienced a major life change (divorce, separation, or unemployment) within a year prior to the rape (Ruch, Chandler, and Harter, 1980). Similarly, survivors of stranger rape are far more likely than survivors of acquaintance rape to have the most persistent depression, fear, and interpersonal problems because stranger rapes are generally more violent. But survivors of acquaintance rape suffer more from self-blame, primarily because society holds them responsible in some way. They also distrust men more and longer, because their earlier trust in men has been betrayed through rape (Gidycz and Koss, 1991; Katz, 1991; Mandoki and Burkhart, 1991).

Most rape survivors go through two phases of disorganization before they gradually and finally regain their ability to live normally. From the time immediately following the rape to a few days or weeks thereafter is the *acute phase* of disorganization. During this phase most survivors succumb to *extreme* fear, shock, humiliation, embarrassment, self-blame, or anxiety. After this initial, acute phase is over, survivors generally go through a *longer, lingering phase* of disorganization, which often lasts for a few months, but may persist for several years. In this phase survivors experience a variety of phobic reactions, including the fear of being alone and fear of sex. Understandably, survivors suffer from an increased risk of divorce, reduced income, and unemployment (Byrne et al., 1999; Burgess, 1995).

You may notice the nature of the survivors' feelings: Fear, depression, anxiety, and self-blame are inward-directed. Other possible feelings are outward-directed, such as anger, revenge, and the courage to have the rapist kept behind bars. While most rape survivors are gnawed by the passive, inward-directed feelings, a few others express the outward-directed feelings. One rape survivor with these feelings said, "I have fantasies about cutting off his dick and balls," and another said, "Never in my life had I felt such hate for another human being. I wish I had jammed my fingers into his eyes" (Madigan and Gamble, 1991). Interestingly, such active, angry survivors tend to feel better about themselves and swing back faster to their normal lives. As Pauline Bart and Patricia O'Brien (1984) have found, rape survivors who have resisted their attacker by screaming and kicking readjust more easily to life than passive survivors who have yielded to crying and pleading. Survivors of acquaintance rape can also recover faster if they learn to see the rape as totally their attacker's fault (Gidycz and Koss, 1991).

The Feeling of Being Raped Again

In the 1960s and 1970s both popular writers and social scientists published many horror stories about how police officers were grossly insensitive in dealing with rape survivors. For example, when a survivor gave a calm, rational account of the rape, she was asked, "What are you, some kind of sociologist?" If the woman was not physically attractive, her report of rape was dismissed as just another fantasy of a sex-starved woman. A middle-aged mother who reported having been raped might be asked by a young policeman: "Did he come?" (Geis and Geis, 1979).

When those blatant insults from the police were added to the physical and psychological injury from the rapist, survivors of sexual assault could not help feeling that they were being raped again. Although the "second rape" by the police described above is only psychological, the impact can be just as painful or traumatic as that of the first rape by the criminal (Madigan and Gamble, 1991). Today, police officers are generally much more polite and respectful, but many survivors continue to suffer the second rape because the police tend to make them feel responsible for the first rape by questioning their moral character. In many cases police officers ask a woman who comes to report being raped whether, for example, "she agreed to have drinks with the man, accepted or offered him a ride, or left with him after a party," whether she "has ever been arrested for soliciting or is a known prostitute," or whether she has resisted by squirming, struggling, and screaming even if the rape was carried out with a gun or knife (Madigan and Gamble, 1991). The presumption behind these questions is that the rape survivor might have "asked for it." The police in effect blame the victim rather than the criminal.

If the police find their "blame the victim" presumption proven wrong, they will proceed to file a complaint against the alleged rapist. In the court, however, the woman is likely to suffer another psychological rape. This is largely because defense attorneys focus on the victim's sexual history or reputation in order to discredit her. In effect, they put her on trial, accusing her of having "asked for it." Since the mid-1970s there have been some legal reforms. At least eight states have renamed rape "criminal sexual assault" or some other term designed to focus the law on what the alleged criminal rather than the victim did. Nearly all states have tried to make the rape survivor's day in court less horrendous by enacting "rape shield" laws, which ostensibly prohibit the admissibility of evidence regarding the victim's previous sexual experience. Nevertheless, defense lawyers can still get around the rape shield laws by subtly revealing the rape survivor's sexual history.

In one typical case, for example, the defense called the jury's attention to the fact that the rape survivor's address was the same as that of her boyfriend, whom she had known for just one week. This was obviously meant to suggest that she was sexually immoral. The tactic worked, as one juror later admitted, "We weren't supposed to judge her as to her past relations, but it came out that she was living with her boyfriend of one week. It was hard not to judge her" (LaFree, Reskin, and Visher, 1985). Many defense lawyers continue to use similar tactics to put the victim on trial. They will dig out testimony about the victim's drinking, drug use, extramarital sex, birth of an illegitimate child, prior acquaintance or sex between her and the alleged rapist, or some other aspect of her lifestyle that can be used to make jurors question her character and credibility (Sanday, 1996a; Vachss, 1994).

Many judges allow such evidence to be presented to the jury because they believe that without it the defendant cannot get a fair trial. This is what a judge did in 1993 at the trial of four young men in Glen Ridge, New Jersey, who were charged with raping a 17-year-old woman. The judge allowed in the evidence of the woman's past experiences of sexual promiscuity on the ground that the defendants could only get a fair trial if they were allowed to use the evidence. In presenting the evidence, the defense argued that the woman had willingly performed the sex acts with the young men (Lewin, 1993). Similarly, in 2004, the judge at the trial of basketball player Kobe Bryant let the defense present the evidence about the accuser's previous sexual activities with somebody else. The ensuing public scorn and ridicule forced her to withdraw from the trial.

The Culture of Rape

Obviously many societies openly condemn rape as a serious crime. Less obviously, however, those same societies have a hidden culture of rape—a culture that encourages men to sexually assault women. The rape culture does not affect all men in the same way; otherwise, all men would rape. Some men are more inclined than others to rape, though they all live under the influence of the same culture. Research has suggested that those who are immature, irresponsible, and lacking in social conscience are more influenced by the rape culture (Sapp et al., 1999; Rapaport and Burkhart, 1984). But what is the nature of this rape culture? We can see it through the prevailing attitudes toward women as well as through the popular concept of male and female sex roles.

Treating Women Like Men's Property

On the face of it the law against rape appears to protect the interests of the female. Actually it protects to a larger degree the interests of the male. This is because the female is treated like a piece of property that before marriage belongs to her father and after marriage belongs to her husband. If a man rapes an unmarried girl, he is, in effect, considered to be committing the crime of vandalism against her father. If a man rapes a married woman, he is considered to be committing the crime against her husband. Thus statutory rape laws "help preserve the 'market value' of virginal young women as potential brides, rather than [protect] the naive girls from sexual exploitation" (LeGrand, 1973). As for forcible rape laws, Susan Griffin (1971) explains:

> The laws against rape exist to protect rights of the male as possessor of the female body, and not the right of the female over her own body. Even . . . the laws themselves are clear: [In some states a man cannot be] accused of raping his wife. How can any man steal what already belongs to him? It is in the sense of rape as theft of another man's property that Kate Millett writes, "Traditionally rape has been viewed as an offense one male commits against another—a matter of abusing his woman." In raping another man's woman, a man may aggrandize his own manhood and concurrently reduce that of another man. Thus a man's honor is not subject directly to rape, but only indirectly, through "his" woman.

In marriage men traditionally feel entitled to use their wives as a sexual commodity in any way they want. As one senator opposed to making marital rape a crime said, "When you get married, you kind of expect you're going to get a little sex" (Blakely, 1983).

The absence of marital-rape laws in some states, and the rarity of husbands being imprisoned for raping their wives in all the other states, reflects the treatment of women as men's property. This component of the rape culture also comes across in other ways: For example, when a woman has been raped, it is often said that she has been "ravaged," "ravished," "despoiled," or "ruined." These words connote the idea that a raped woman is like a piece of property that has been damaged. Further, when a man's wife has been raped, he tends to feel as if she is less "lovable" than before—in about the same way as he would feel about a piece of damaged property. If he regarded her as a human being who has feelings rather than an object that does not have feelings, logically the husband should show her more love, affection, or understanding—particularly because, after being raped, she needs emotional support as a human being the most. Instead, her husband tends to show her less love than before, as if she had turned into a piece of damaged property with no feeling and very little value. This is why many men say something like "I can't see how I can face my wife again if she has been raped." It is not surprising that rape has the tendency to wreck or strain the victim's relationship with her husband, fiancé, or boyfriend. In fact, 75 to 85 percent of the marriages in which the wife has been raped end in divorce within two years following the sexual assault (Gordon and Riger, 1989).

Continuing to uncover these parallel assumptions, it is accepted that the more often an object has been used, the less valuable it is considered. Similarly, in a society where women are treated as sex objects, the more often a woman has engaged in sex with various men, the less valuable a property she is judged to be. A woman with very little value is referred to as a "cheap woman," "loose woman," "easy lay," "slut," or "whore." Thus, just as a man who steals or damages another's relatively worthless property can easily get away with it, so a man who ravages a relatively "cheap" woman—"common" property—can get away with it. This may be why it is difficult for a rapist to be convicted if his victim is known to have engaged in sexual relations with more than two men—and it is virtually impossible for the rapist to be convicted if his victim is a known prostitute. Also, since black or poor women are considered as less valuable sex objects than white or rich women, raping the former carries a lesser risk of conviction than raping the latter. Raping a woman who is simultaneously African-American, poor, and sexually experienced is especially unlikely to result in conviction. This is why, in a case involving the rape of a young, poor, black woman, a juror argued for acquittal by saying that "a girl her age from 'that kind of neighborhood' probably wasn't a virgin anyway" (LaFree, Reskin, and Visher, 1985). In fact, many convicted rapists themselves do not feel guilty for having raped known prostitutes, "loose" women, "promiscuous" women, or women with an "illegitimate" child. The rapists apparently see these women as cheap ("available") sexual commodities that men are entitled to use (Scully and Marolla, 1984).

Lastly, the widespread availability of pornography, especially the type that shows violence against women, reinforces the popular image of women as men's sex objects. By degrading women in this way, pornography increases men's callousness toward women. As several studies have shown, extended exposure to pornography tends to cause men to trivialize rape. After viewing pornography for some time, the men in these studies advocated less severe punishment for rapists and expressed less sympathy for the victims (Segal, 1993; Linz, Donnerstein, and Penrod, 1984; Zillman and Bryant, 1982). Pornography apparently encourages rape by producing sexual callousness toward women. This does not mean that pornography by itself causes rape, as it does not have the same impact on all men. But it does make certain men dangerous to women. As research has demonstrated, pornography tends to incite violent, angry men to rape (Gray, 1982).

Since women are culturally defined as men's property, men may find it difficult to respect women as human beings. It is through a lack of respect for women that men are encouraged to rape women, as rape expresses the very essence of this lack of respect for women. Not surprisingly, as sociologists Diana Scully and Joseph Marolla (1985) found in their interviews with 114 convicted rapists, "the overwhelming majority of these rapists indicated they never thought they would go to prison for what they did." These men regard women as sexual objects that they are entitled to use for pleasure, or as one young rapist confided to Scully, "Rape is a man's right. If a woman doesn't want to give it, the man should take it. Women have no right to say no. Women are made to have sex. It's all they are good for. Some women would rather take a beating, but they always give in; it's what they are for" (Scully and Marolla, 1985).

Using Women in Men's Masculinity Contests

In a society that places a high premium on competition, men are pressured to engage in what may be called a masculinity contest to prove their male prowess and to earn a macho reputation among peers (Fields, 1993). To come out a winner, a man has to make out with the largest number of women possible.

> And that means sex under whatever conditions the particular man can stand. Whether in a whorehouse or the backseat of a Toyota, the object is to score. However, your score counts more if you don't pay for it in cold hard cash. The most respected player in the game is the one who best outwits the most females by coaxing, lying, maneuvering; the one who, with the least actual cost to himself, gets the most females to give him the most sex. (Medea and Thompson, 1974)

This masculinity contest is comparable to such competitive sports as football, baseball, soccer, and tennis. In any one of these sports, the players need an object— say, a ball—to grab, hit, kick, or smash. Their goal is to score, and they couldn't care less whether they hurt the ball. Similarly, in the masculinity contest, the male participants need an object—namely, a woman—to play with. They don't care whether they may end up humiliating, degrading, hurting, or terrifying her as a human being. Their goal is to score, as was well illustrated in 1993 by the Spur Posse, a gang of high school boys in the Los Angeles suburb of Lakewood. Members of this group competed with one another to score points for sexual conquests, one point for each sexual encounter, whether the girl consented or not. In such a masculinity contest, men see the woman as merely an object, often referring to her as a "piece of meat," a "piece of ass," a "box," or a "whore." A victim of a gang rape reported that she was indeed treated that way; after they had finished with her, one of the rapists said, "Let's dump this one and find another piece of meat" (Medea and Thompson, 1974).

Such a dehumanizing attitude toward women can further be found in the language that men use to refer to sexual intercourse as if it were a manly game of violence and conquest. American soldiers in Vietnam used to speak of dragging women into the woods for a little "boom boom," as if the penis—the rape weapon—sounded like a gun. To "bang" a woman—to have sex with her—also has the violent sound of a gun. Words, such as *whacking off, screwing, fucking, scoring, shooting off, and knocking up,* also give off the tough sound of conquest (Blakely, 1983). This dehumanizing language and attitude toward women may encourage men to play the masculinity game. Whether they will actually do so depends on at least two things: (1) the social pressure to play the game and (2) learning some basic pointers for playing it.

The social pressure often comes from friends who ask something like "Did you score?" "Had any lately?" "Does she put out?" If you answer no, they may say, "What's the matter? You ain't got no balls?" Such social pressure tends to make men, especially teenage males, afraid of showing any sign of "femininity"—being soft, gentle, and considerate. It also tends to make them want to show off their "masculine" qualities—being aggressive, forceful, and violent. A likely consequence is that these men will engage in sexual violence, of one degree or another, against women at some point. As research has shown, the most important factor that distinguishes sexually aggressive males from others is the peer pressure, which comes from sexually aggressive friends (Alder, 1985).

As to the pointers for playing the masculinity game, they come with the masculine role that men have been taught to play. This role requires that the man take the active part in achieving the social and then the sexual relations with a woman. He should be as aggressive as possible to carry out his sexual conquest. He need not concern himself with how much force he is allowed to use. Our culture puts that burden on the woman, who is held responsible for determining the limit of the force he is allowed. But even when the woman bluntly tells him to stop or puts up a fight to ward off his sexual advances, he may still ignore her resistance (Sanday, 1996a; Fillion, 1991). Men often get this lesson in sexual conquest from the stereotype of the television or movie hero who forcefully, persistently embraces and kisses the heroine despite her strong resistance and is finally rewarded by her melting in his arms. In real life such sexual aggression may lead to forcible rape.

The Myth That Women Ask for It

There is a popular myth that women have a secret wish to be raped. As shown by various studies, most people believe that women have an unconscious rape wish. This myth is expressed in various ways and often: "She asked for it," "She actually wanted it," "She lied about it (or consented to sex but later decided to "cry rape")," and "She was not really hurt (or it was only a form of sex, though without her consent)" (Lonsway and Fitzgerald, 1994; Brinson, 1992). In essence, many people—particularly men—hold the victim responsible for the rape. They assume that the victim did something that provoked the man to rape her. That "something" involves being in the "wrong" place (going to a bar or walking alone at night), wearing the "wrong" clothes (short shorts, miniskirts, or some other sexy dress), or turning the man on (letting him kiss or pet her) (Vachss, 1994; Brinson, 1992).

These blame-the-victim rationalizations reflect society's sexist attempt to "put women in their place," denying them the freedom that men enjoy. The rationalizations also stem from the popular assumption that rape is only sexually motivated. This explains why men tend to blame physically unattractive women more than attractive ones for rape. They find it difficult to believe that a man would try very hard to have sex with an unattractive woman if she keeps on resisting. They assume that, since it is less easy for unattractive women to attract men, they would be more inclined to encourage rapes by flirting, dressing sexily, or in some other way presenting a sexually provocative appearance. In short, men tend to consider unattractive women more likely to fantasize about rape and ask for it when a rapist appears (Vachss, 1994; Deitz et al., 1984; Thornton and Ryckman, 1983).

The myth about women wanting to be raped is understandably popular with rapists, which may help explain why they committed the crime in the first place. According to various studies, most convicted rapists, even those serving long prison terms, deny their culpability. Stubbornly, they insist that their victims have encouraged and enjoyed the experience, or that their victims have seduced them, meant yes while saying no to the sexual assault, and eventually relaxed and enjoyed the rape (Vachss, 1994; Scully and Marolla, 1985; Selkin, 1975). The willing-victim myth also prevails in the courtroom. While a man charged with rape is presumed innocent until proven guilty, the rape victim is often presumed guilty until proven innocent of provoking the rape. In the past, defense lawyers often argued to the court how impossible it is to rape a woman if she resists with statements such as "You can't thread a moving needle" or "You can't put a pencil through a moving doughnut." Today, most defense lawyers have abandoned such crude tactics to suggest that the victim "has asked for it." But they manage to convey the same message by emphasizing that she has willingly danced with him at a bar, accepted his invitation to go to his apartment, or asked him to wear a condom before the intercourse. These less blatant tactics often result in the acquittal of the accused rapist because many jurors are influenced by the same popular myth (Vachss, 1994; LaFree, Reskin, and Visher, 1985).

Because of the willing-victim myth, when a woman declines a man's sexual invitation, he is likely to keep on pressuring her: "What's the matter, are you frigid?

Oh, come on, you know you really want to." If he eventually rapes her, he will assume that she has consented, even though she has strongly resisted all along (Sanday, 1996a; Vachss, 1994).

Socializing Girls to Be Victims

To make it easier for men to rape women, the rape culture teaches girls to play the stereotypically feminine role. In contrast to boys, who are taught to be "snips and snails and puppy dogs' tails," girls are taught to be "sugar and spice and everything nice." In other words, while boys learn to be tough and active, girls learn to be sweet and passive. Girls also learn from the movies and other mass media that women like macho men and expect such men to be rough with them. Slasher films and rock videos, in particular, teach young women to associate sex with violence. In learning all this as part of the feminine role, the girl acquires two tendencies that make her a potential victim of rape. One is to be "feminine"— passive, gentle, weak, childlike, and dependent on men. The other is to be submissive to aggressive or violent men.

To be feminine means that she is physically unaggressive and psychologically unprepared to defend herself in hand-to-hand combat. Thus, when she encounters her would-be rapist, especially one who is her acquaintance or date, she is unlikely to gouge his eyes, kick him in the groin or genitals, or otherwise blind, maim, or kill him. Being ladylike also involves being submissive to men. A "lady" does not shout, scream, scratch, hit, or otherwise make a scene when she is offended by a man. In public places such as buses, subways, elevators, and theaters, she is not supposed to react aggressively to sexual harassment. She is expected to find it too embarrassing to make a public scene in response to such "sex grabs" as the touching of her legs or behind by a molesting male (Weis and Borges, 1973). It is, therefore, not surprising that, as studies have suggested, traditionally passive or submissive women are the ideal victims for rapists. They are more likely than assertive women to be chosen as potential victims, and when they are approached by a potential rapist, they are also more likely to end up raped (Bart and O'Brien, 1985; Myers, Templer, and Brown, 1984).

Why Men Rape Women

Various researchers have tried to explain why some men are more likely than others to rape women or why some groups or societies have a higher incidence of forcible rape. Psychologists generally attribute rape to some psychological problem in the offender. Sociologists, on the other hand, see rapists as basically normal, psychologically no different from the average population. Various sociologists, however, explain rape differently: Some use a social-psychological theory to attribute rape to sexual permissiveness in society and others rely on a feminist theory to view rape as an expression of gender inequality. These three theories are positivist in nature, focusing on the causation of rape.

Global Perspective: Wartime Rape

Throughout history, when a conquering army destroyed or confiscated the conquered population's property, it also raped the women as if they were part of that property. During World War II, German soldiers raped massive numbers of Jewish and Russian women after occupying many villages and cities in Europe, and the Japanese army systematically raped women and girls as it invaded Korea, China, and various Southeast Asian countries. In 1971, when the Pakistani army marched into Bangladesh, soldiers were first shown pornographic movies and then let loose to rape at least 200,000 women. In 1992 Serbian soldiers in Bosnia raped thousands of Muslim women as part of an "ethnic cleansing" campaign. In 1994 the Hutus in Rwanda, who at that time dominated the country, raped immense numbers of minority Tutsi women. In 1999 when the Serbian forces took over Kosovo, they raped ethnic Albanian women. In 2004 pro-government Arab militias in Sudan used rape as a weapon of war to humiliate black African women in the region where rebels were fighting the government. All these rapes reflect the universally shared attitude that women are men's property, the same attitude in the U.S. culture that we have discussed.

Given that attitude it is not surprising that wartime rapes are especially dehumanizing and brutal. In Bosnia, for example, the victims were corralled like cattle in concentration camps where they were repeatedly raped, often in front of family members, neighbors, and other prisoners. The women were not only subjected to extreme humiliation; they were sexually tortured as well. As one victim says, "They would ask women if they had male relatives; I saw them ask this of one woman and they brought her 14-year-old son and forced him to rape her. If a man couldn't rape, he would use a bottle or a gun or he would urinate on me." Worse, many women were killed after being raped. Those who did survive became extremely traumatized from being raped by many men for many months. This is particularly true of traditional and conservative Muslim women who had never even been seen naked by their husbands.

After having been raped by foreign soldiers, women tend to be regarded as irreparably damaged property and therefore valueless. In some traditional countries, their husbands or other male relatives would throw them out of their homes as they would a piece of junk. Sometimes they would even kill the victims. In the minds of those men, though, their raped relatives have brought their family unbearable dishonor and shame.

Sources: Lacey, 2004; McGirk, 2002; Frederick, 2001; Barstow, 2000.

Psychological Theory: Sexual Inadequacy

Generally, psychologists, psychiatrists, and psychoanalysts agree that rapists suffer from some personality defects or emotional disturbance. "The majority of such offenders are not insane," write two psychologists, "nor are they simply healthy and aggressive young men 'sowing some wild oats.' The rapist is, in fact, a person who has serious psychological difficulties which handicap him in his relationships to other people and which he discharges, when he is under stress, through sexual [violence]" (Groth, 1983; Groth and Birnbaum, 1979). And a group of psychiatrists state, "It is true that classic neurotic symptoms are a rarity, but all types of character neuroses, character disorders, and more severe borderline and psychotic states are represented in rapists. It is equally clear that there are some specific characteristics present in rapists which differentiate them from other criminals and from other sexual offenders" (Cohen et al., 1971). One psychologist sums up all this by saying, "What's wrong with a sex offender is what's between his ears, not his legs" (Gelman et al., 1994).

Disagreement abounds over what the *specific* psychological problem is. The problem that has been theorized to reside in rapists ranges from feelings of sexual inadequacy to fear of homosexual tendency to sexual addiction (Herman, 1995; Goldner, 1972). According to a typical psychological theory, the rapist is a man who, as the result of his unpleasant childhood experiences, has developed such a personality defect that he cannot relate successfully to women—a defect called "sexual inadequacy." This inadequacy drives the rapist to indulge in fantasy and then act out this fantasy by raping a woman. Here is how a rapist describes his fantasy:

> I had a complete fantasy life that involved my being stronger than all men, irresistible to all women, a doer of great things. . . . I had fantasies about the woman I was raping, how she felt physically, where she had been in life, some resentment that she's done things in life without me. I had a longing to do things in general with people. Sometimes I'd verbalize these fantasies if the woman was quite submissive, otherwise I'd just take the trip within myself. (Selkin, 1975)

But psychological theories such as this can explain only a few cases of rape. True, there are some rapists who, because of their psychological problems, cannot relate to women well. However, they make up only a small minority of rapists. In prisons, for example, the majority of rapists appear quite normal, no different from other convicts who have committed robbery, theft, or some other nonsexual crime. In an experimental study in which the subjects were asked to chat with a woman for as long as they wanted, the convicted rapists were just as skilled and relaxed as the nonrapists (Scully, 1990; Alder, 1984).

The psychological theory of sexual inadequacy is even less applicable to the countless rapists, especially acquaintance rapists, outside of prisons. Far from sexually inadequate, most of these rapists are highly skillful in dealing with women. In fact, as indicated by Eugene Kanin's (1985) study, the date rapists in college are far more heterosexually successful than other male students—they have had more dates and more consensual sexual experiences (see also Rapaport and Posey, 1991).

Social Psychological Theory: Sexual Permissiveness

Sociologist Duncan Chappell and his colleagues (1971) ask why the rate of rape is higher in some societies than in others. The reason, they theorized, is that the society with a higher rape rate is, ironically, more sexually permissive—full of opportunities for men to have consensual nonmarital sex with women. Why would more men resort to force to get sex in a society where it is relatively easy to get sex without the use of force? The answer, according to the theorists, lies in the concept of relative frustration: When encountering the *same* experience of being rejected by a woman, the men in a sexually permissive society feel *more frustrated* than the men in a sexually restrictive society in which premarital and other nonmarital sex is prohibited. But why?

In a sexually restrictive society, a man is more able to take a woman's rejection in stride. This is because he can protect his ego by rationalizing that she has rejected him not because he is in some way undesirable but because the restrictive society prevents her from accepting his sexual invitation. He may take comfort from the fact that women are too sexually conservative, too afraid to engage in nonmarital sex, that their religion condemns such sex, or that laws against nonmarital sex are too stringent. In a sexually permissive society the rejected man cannot use this kind of rationalization. Instead, he is more likely to take the woman's rebuff personally, seeing that it is he himself who is responsible for his own failure to win the woman's favors. As a consequence, he is likely to feel hurt, thereby experiencing sexual frustration. This sexual frustration is said to drive many men in a permissive society such as the United States or Sweden to rape women (Geis and Geis, 1979; Chappell et al., 1971).

In short, the social atmosphere of sexual permissiveness produces a great number of rapes because it generates a great deal of relative frustration by causing men to take a woman's rejection personally. This theory may explain why modern societies such as the United States and Sweden have higher rates of rape today than a century ago or why modern societies have higher rates than traditional societies. It seems obvious that modern societies are more sexually permissive than traditional ones. Feminists, however, question the theory's assumption that rape is mostly sexually motivated. To feminists, rape is primarily motivated by the man's desire to dominate the woman because of gender inequality.

Feminist Theory: Gender Inequality

The social-psychological theory of sexual permissiveness seems to suggest that gender equality produces more rapes than does sexual inequality. This is because relative gender equality is more prevalent in the more sexually permissive societies such as Sweden and other industrialized Western societies than in the more sexually restrictive, traditional societies in the developing world. But feminist theorists blame rape on sexual inequality. To feminists, rape is primarily an expression of men's dominance over women, which in turn is a reflection of society's sexual inequality. Rape, then, serves to intimidate women, keeping them in their place to maintain sexual inequality (Edwards, 1993; Peterson, 1992; Schwendinger and Schwendinger, 1983; Brownmiller, 1975).

The evidence on rape as an expression of male dominance exists everywhere. All over the world, no matter which society we go to, we are bound to find that the overwhelming majority of rapes involve men raping women rather than women raping men. At the same time, men generally have greater physical, political, or economic power than women. We may therefore conclude that rape is largely an expression of male power over women. An abundance of more specific evidence also exists to support the feminist theory. In her study of tribal societies, for example, Peggy Sanday (1981) found that some of these societies are relatively free of rapes while others are full of rapes. She discovered that male dominance is a key feature of rape-prone societies, defined as societies in which rape is treated as a ceremonial expression of masculinity or where men are allowed to use rape to punish or threaten women. Other researchers have further found that the incidence of rape is high in colleges where masculinity and male dominance are highly valued (Schwartz and DeKeseredy, 1997; Martin and Hummer, 1995).

Nevertheless, the feminist theory of gender inequality has drawn fire for exaggerating the influence of male dominance on rape. As the major inspiration of the theory, Susan Brownmiller (1975) has often been faulted for arguing that "from prehistoric times to the present, I believe, rape has played a critical function. It is nothing more or less than a conscious process of intimidation by which *all men* keep *all women* in a state of fear." But critics have observed that not all men would use rape to intimidate all women, and that it is easy to think of numerous men who do not want to dominate women by raping them, especially if the women are their mothers and daughters. Through her forceful statement, however, Brownmiller probably means to say that rape is a primary expression—rather than the sole expression—of male dominance.

Males as Victims

According to popular belief, men are simply "too big," "too strong," or "too much in control" to be sexually assaulted. But men can and do become victims of rape in prison as well as outside the prison.

Inside the Prison

The experience of a man being raped by another in the prison is very common. It is much more prevalent than man-on-woman rape is outside the prison. About one in five inmates in U.S. prisons have been raped, compared with one in ten females in the larger society. Moreover, while the female rape victims typically get raped only once, the male victims are raped multiple times. Why so many more rapes in prison? The reasons include: (1) The general public has little or no sympathy for convicts. (2) The rapists go unpunished. (3) The "wolves" (rapists) are not segregated from the "punks" (the victims). And (4) rape is used as a prison-management tool to pacify violent inmates so that they will not turn against the staff (Lehrer, 2001; Cahill, 1985; Lockwood, 1985).

In an average state prison system, virtually every slightly built young man is approached for sex within one or two days after arrival. Many of these young men are repeatedly raped by gangs of inmates. Some of these victims commit suicide; others manage to escape gang rape by seeking protection from a more powerful inmate. However, they have to pay for that protection by serving as the protector's slaves, providing sexual services as well as keeping house for their "masters." Sometimes punks are forced into prostitution so that they can earn such goods as cigarettes for their keepers. Some new inmates are lured into a trap for forced sex. They are offered goodies such as cigarettes, drugs, or extra food stolen from the kitchen, and after a day or so the gift giver will demand sexual repayment. Sometimes the new inmate is lured into gambling, rolling up large debts, and then being told to "pay or fuck" (Lehrer, 2001; Knowles, 1999; Davis, 1982). This stratagem for forced sex is basically the same as that often used by male rapists on their prospective female victims in the larger society: offering a drink at a bar, a dose of sweet talk, an invitation into his apartment, and then forcibly demanding sex.

Male rapists and their male victims in prison are comparable to male rapists and their female victims in the larger society in several ways. The rapists within the prison, like the rapists without, are heterosexual. Moreover, the prison rapists are like the men who rape women outside the prison (and the male victims in prison are like the female victims outside) in that both types of rapists are generally older, heavier, taller, and more violent than their victims. However, compared with heterosexual rapes outside the prison, same-sex rapes in prison are much more likely to be interracial—blacks raping whites. Still, the two types of rape are similar in the sense that both involve members of the *dominant* group (the males outside the prison and the blacks inside) raping members of the *subordinate* group (the females outside and the whites inside).

Common sense may suggest that the rape in prison is intended to relieve one's sexual deprivation. But that is not the primary motive for prison rape. If an inmate simply wants to relieve his sexual deprivation, masturbation would be a much more convenient and normal method of relief than same-sex rape. Instead, the primary motive for same-sex rape is the need to subjugate and humiliate the victim, as evidenced by the fact that the prison rapists often use such language as "Fight or fuck," "We're going to take away your manhood," "You'll have to give up some face," and "We're gonna make a girl out of you." Of course, this does not mean that the rape serves *only* to express the need for dominance—if it did, the offenders should be content only to bully or beat up others. The rape, then, is also sexually motivated. But the drive for power appears to be a stronger motivation for the rape in prison (Lehrer, 2001; Knowles, 1999; Davis, 1982). The same is true of the majority of the men who rape other men in the larger society. As one such rapist says:

> I had the guy so frightened I could have made him do anything I wanted. I didn't have an erection. I wasn't interested in sex. I felt powerful, and hurting him excited me. Making him suck me was more to degrade him than for my physical satisfaction. (McMullen, 1990)

Outside the Prison

In the larger society, the risk of a man being raped by another man or by a woman is still far less than the risk of a woman being sexually assaulted by a man.

According to a national survey, only 3.8 percent of men have ever suffered sexual assault compared to 22 percent of women (Elliott et al., 2004). Surveys on U.S. campuses reveal considerably more male victims: 12 to 48 percent of male college students are forced or pressured to have sex, more commonly known as nonconsensual sex. But virtually all of these sexual coercions are not legally and popularly considered rapes because they involve women using verbal pressure such as pleading, demands, or blackmail rather than physical force. In the fewer cases where men rape men, however, most offenders do use physical force, with sodomy being the most common mode of assault (Gillespie, 1996; Struckman-Johnson, 1991). Male offenders are more likely than their female counterparts to use physical force, apparently because the men are generally stronger than the women. But another reason is that the men's victims are much more likely than the women's victims to be strangers, who tend to put up relatively strong resistance. On the other hand, female offenders are more likely to use verbal pressure because their victims are more likely to be their acquaintances.

Although male offenders are more likely than their female peers to be strangers to the victim, nearly half the male offenders know their victim as their peer, coworker, subordinate, or date. These acquaintance rapes include attacks by men meeting their victims at parties or bars, gang rapes in the Navy and other military settings, and seduction with pressure by trusted men, such as doctors, psychotherapists, priests, and teachers. Most victims are in their late teens or early twenties. More than half of the victims are heterosexual, so are more than half of the offenders. The rapist assaults his victim mostly with an intent to punish or dominate, rather than for sexual pleasure (Scarce, 1997; Struckman-Johnson, 1991).

Same-sex rape can be illustrated with a few actual cases of a man sexually assaulting a man: (1) A heterosexual man became intoxicated at an office party. He let his boss drive him home. He passed out in the car, but he soon woke up to find himself in the backseat, with his pants down, being anally entered by the boss. (2) A college male student, who was gay, met an older man at a bar. He went to the older man's apartment, where he was sodomized despite his protests. (3) Three Navy men overpowered, beat, and dragged a shipmate to a secluded area of the ship to rape him, but the victim escaped. Three weeks later the same attackers overpowered the victim and then two of the assailants held him down while the third raped him anally (Struckman-Johnson, 1991).

The male victim reacts in about the same way to same-sex rape as the female victim does to heterosexual rape. The reactions include shock, self-blame, shame, anger, and depression. These reactions are more distressing to men than women because men are expected to be strong, aggressive, and avoidant of sexual contact with other men. Given this male-role expectation, the male victim is also more likely to control his emotion by denying or minimizing the trauma of rape. Still, unlike the female victim, the male victim tends to feel a loss of masculinity. As one victim said, "Hell, I've got no manhood left. He's made me into a woman" (Elliott et al., 2004; Pelka, 1995; Struckman-Johnson, 1991).

Can Women Rape Men?

Women can rape men because rape, as feminists emphasize, is basically an expression of power. As we have seen, male prison rapists are more powerful than their male victims. Similarly, the rapists in the larger society are more powerful than their female victims. Since men are typically in a position of power in relation to women, rapes characteristically involve men as the aggressors and women as the victims. But men are not always in the power position; neither are women always vulnerable. Therefore, to the extent that a woman can overpower a man in a sexual encounter, she is able to rape him.

If it is sociologically possible for a woman to rape a man, is it physiologically possible? To the general public, the answer may appear to be "no," because it is assumed that men cannot perform sexually if frightened or anxious. But medical doctors have observed that "all anxieties are not the same. Neither are all men the same. Some men can and do have erections while they are anxious" (Sarrel and Masters, 1982; Sarrel and Sarrel, 1981). Further, even if some men cannot engage in sexual intercourse under stress or duress, they still are vulnerable to rape because they can be forced to perform oral sex or other sex acts that are meant to humiliate them but fulfill their attackers' need for asserting power and dominance.

Therefore, it should not be surprising that there are actual cases of women using physical force to rape men, but such rapes are *extremely rare*. Presumably, if there is a trend for women to become increasingly powerful, there may well be more women raping men. The cases that have occurred so far usually involve a single victim and two or more offenders—an apparent attempt on the part of the women to compensate for their traditional lack of power. As John Macdonald (1995) reports:

> A 37-year-old man was accosted late one evening by two women who forced him at gunpoint inside an abandoned building. They made him undress, tied his hands, manipulated him to erection and had intercourse with him a number of times. When he could no longer maintain an erection, they abused his genitals and rectum. When he fainted, they untied his hands and left him.

However, instead of using physical force as illustrated here, most female offenders resort to verbal persuasion and other nonviolent methods. Examples include an older woman seducing a teenage boy or younger man, a female babysitter sitting on a younger boy and forcing his penis into her vagina, and a female college student persistently "getting fresh" with her date until he gives in to intercourse (Struckman-Johnson, 1991). We may argue, though, that the use of verbal persuasion alone does not legally constitute rape if the victim is no longer under the age of consent.

The use of physical force is a different matter. It is rape and may traumatize the male victim as much as it does the female victim. He is likely to feel a loss of masculinity and consequently suffer such sexual dysfunction as impotence, premature ejaculation, or loss of sexual desire. But since most female offenders do not resort to physical force, most male victims are far from being traumatized.

Therefore, the most common effect is avoidance of aggressive women and pressured sex (Struckman-Johnson, 1991). As things stand now, even those male victims who are badly shaken by the more violent assault may not get much sympathy. "A former police officer in San Diego," report Philip Sarrel and Lorna Sarrel (1981), "told us that a few years ago a sailor came into his precinct house to report that he had been raped by a woman. The police in the station house thought he must be drunk, out of his mind, or simply weaving a good tale. They laughed him out the door."

Child Molestation

Child molestation can be considered a form of rape because the victims are too young and hence not legally capable of giving their consent.

Some Basic Facts

There are all kinds of studies giving vastly different estimates of how common child molestation is. It is impossible, therefore, to know with any certainty the true

Social Profile: Child Molesters

Compared with men who rape adult women, men who molest young girls have the following characteristics: (1) Molesters are much older; most are over 35 years of age, while most rapists are under 20. (2) Molesters are more likely than rapists to have been abused as children. (3) Molesters are more gentle and passive, while rapists are tougher and rougher. (4) Molesters are less likely to resort to physical force or vaginal penetration and more likely to restrict themselves to fondling the victim. (5) Molesters are much less capable than rapists of getting along with adult members of the opposite sex—less skilled, more nervous, and less assertive in interacting with women. (6) Most molesters commit the offense against the same child for a certain length of time, while rapists attack different victims. (7) Most molesters admit their guilt, while most rapists refuse to do so.

All this suggests that child molesters fail to meet the sexist cultural standard of "masculinity"—being dominant over women. This may explain why they are scorned and often raped by their tougher fellow inmates in prison. Their lack of masculinity may also explain why, unlike rapists who resort to rape to dominate women, child molesters feel inadequate with adult women but dominant over children. Moreover, while the culture of rape—which is related to the ideal of masculinity and male domination over females in society—encourages rapists to blame their victims, this same culture fails to have the same impact on molesters. This is why, unlike rapists, most molesters fully and frankly admit their guilt. Nonetheless, child molesters are at bottom similar to rapists: Both victimize a person who is less powerful than they are.

Sources: Bolen, 2001; Lanning, 1992; Groth and Birnbaum, 1979; McCaghy, 1968.

incidence of this sex offense. But we can have more confidence about the accuracy of these basic facts: (1) Girls are far more likely than boys to be molested. (2) The overwhelming majority of child molesters are men rather than women. (3) Molesters are more likely to be acquainted with, than to be strangers to, their victims. (4) The molester is usually unmarried; never or rarely dates; and lives alone or with his parents. (5) While only a few molesters have serious mental problems, most have a personality disorder characterized by "a relative lack of human attachments and social relations," as shown by their social incompetence or deficiency in social skills (Bolen, 2001; Macdonald, 1995; Lanning, 1992).

Another basic fact concerns the effects of child molestation on the victim. A review of 45 such studies has clearly demonstrated that molested children are more likely than other children to suffer from various problems. The problems include posttraumatic stress disorders (such as nightmares or nervousness), behavior problems (hyperactivity, immaturity, delinquency, or running away), sexualized behaviors (putting objects in vaginas or anuses, or excessive masturbation), and poor self-esteem (Bruni, 1997; Kendall-Tackett, Williams, and Finkelhor, 1993).

Molesting Boys

In the Social Profile box we discussed men who molest young girls. Men also molest young boys. There is some evidence that most of these molesters are not gay. Although they molest children of their own gender, they are usually married, have no sexual interest in other men, and do not identify themselves as gays. There are, of course, gay molesters, such as the pedophile priests that recently scandalized their church. But they are a minority. Whether gay or straight, however, the men who molest boys are not much different from those who victimize girls. They are by and large emotionally troubled. More specifically, they are lacking in human attachments, obsessed with their own fantasies, unable to feel empathy for others, and inclined to control and dominate less-powerful others. As for their victims, they are more likely than other boys to grow up to become child abusers themselves (Bolen, 2001; Finkelhor, 1984).

What about women who molest young boys? This type of molester is extremely rare. Perhaps due to their extreme rarity, they have not become a popular subject of scholarly investigation. It is also quite possible that, like the general public, researchers feel that if a woman molests a young boy she could hardly do any harm without a penis or, related to this attitude, that he should consider himself "lucky" (Mathis, 1972). In fact, this kind of sex can anger the boy so much that he may later as an adult take it out on other women by raping them. In an investigation of 83 rapists in a California prison, two researchers found that 59 percent of them had been molested as children by older women, as compared with another study of college students, only 3 percent of whom had been molested by older women (Petrovich and Templer, 1984).

There is, however, a gender difference in the way victims deal with the anger caused by their victimization. Men who have been molested as boys by older women or men are likely to *act out* their smoldering anger from the sexual traumas by becoming rapists or child molesters themselves. In contrast, women who have been molested as children appear more likely to *internalize* their anger by becoming victims of additional abuse, such as rape victims, wife-abuse victims, drug addicts, or prostitutes (Finkelhor, 1984; Russell, 1984). This gender difference can be attributed to traditional sex-role socialization, which encourages boys to be aggressive and girls to be passive.

The Scandal of Pedophile Priests

Early in 2002, the media started reporting that a few Roman Catholic priests in the United States were found to have sexually molested children in their care. This trickle of cases turned into a flood several months later, with child-molesting priests reported in virtually every region of the country. For many years the church hierarchy had protected the child molesters by silencing the victims and their parents while transferring the molesters to other posts—and new potential victims. In one case, for example, Boston's Cardinal Bernard Law allegedly moved the Rev. John Geoghan in 1984 from one parish to another even after he was told that Geoghan had molested children. Geoghan was finally sentenced to nine to ten years in prison in February 2002 for fondling a 10-year-old boy, but he had been accused of molesting more than 130 children over a period of thirty years (Cannon and Sheler, 2002).

As a result, many people now wrongly conclude that the majority of priests are child molesters. The fact is that only a few priests are. Probably only about 4 or 5 percent of Catholic priests are pedophiles, most being emotionally troubled, socially incompetent, or sexually immature. The great majority of priests are normal and mature. The general public also believes the myth that the celibate, sexless life imposed by the Catholic Church on its priests frustrates them so much as to drive them into perversion and molestation. If this were true, the majority of priests would have become child molesters. Instead, the majority, both straight and gay, keep their vows of celibacy and lead healthy and productive lives serving their church and community. What, then, could have caused the church to have child-molesting priests?

One reason, say some observers, is the absence of women and married men serving as priests. As has been observed, women rarely commit sexual abuse against children. It is also obvious that most women are more emotionally and sexually mature than the priests who molest children. So are most married men, when compared to child-molesting priests. Therefore, if numerous women and married men became priests, the scandal of child molestation might not have blown up in the church.

Another reason for the presence of deviant priests in the church, critics argue, is the declining number of priests and candidates for priesthood. The number of U.S. priests has dropped from 60,000 to 40,000 over the last four decades and an average of 1,200 priests have left the priesthood annually during the last three decades, mostly to marry (Berry, 2000). And because of the church's continuing refusal to ordain women and married men as well as its rejection of many increasingly popular American practices such as birth control, divorce, and remarriage, considerably fewer men are interested in joining the priesthood. Thus, the argument goes, the church hierarchy has become so desperate that it has lowered its recruitment standards. As a result, emotionally and sexually immature men who would later molest children were allowed into the priesthood.

And the third reason offered for the child-molestation scandal is the church leaders' failure to dismiss offending priests from their jobs. Such priests were often placed in new positions where they would have continued access to vulnerable children. The church leaders in effect aided and abetted child molestation. A major cause of such behavior is the culture of secrecy in which the church hierarchy operates. Specifically, church leaders are required to "keep in confidence anything that, if revealed, would cause a scandal or harm to the church" (McGeary, 2002). Church leaders were thus under pressure to refrain from firing a priest for child molestation; to do so, according to their calculation, would invite publicity for the scandalous act and thus hurt their church. In addition, there is the church's culture of forgiveness, which encourages protection of the offender as a sinner to be pardoned, rather than as a criminal to be turned over to the police.

Summary

1. What are the major patterns of rape? Blacks are more likely than whites to commit rape. Rapes are mostly intraracial, though interracial rapes are more common today than before. Females between ages 16 and 20 are most vulnerable to rape. Most rapists plan their assault rather than act it out impulsively. Gang rape involves mostly young men pressuring each other to prove their masculinity by raping the same woman. More common than stranger rape, acquaintance rape is an extension of men's socially accepted aggressive sexual behavior. Campus rape is relatively prevalent because of the influence of the rape-prone culture. The myth of victim precipitation in effect blames the rape survivor for having asked to be raped.

2. What consequences does rape have for its survivors? Most survivors are beset with anxiety and guilt. A few, but increasingly more, survivors feel outraged and revengeful, and they have also stimulated the growth of organizations for helping rape survivors and other women fight sexual attack. There have been legal reforms to treat rape survivors better, but they are still made to feel that they have "asked for it."

3. What is the culture of rape? It is made up of the prevailing male attitudes toward women as well as the traditional ideas of appropriate sex roles. In such a culture, women are treated as if they were men's property; women are used as objects to enable men to prove their masculinity; women are believed to have a secret desire to be raped; and girls are taught to play the feminine, submissive role. All these jointly encourage men to rape. **What does the global perspective reveal about wartime rape?** The army that invades a country tends to rape its women, treating them as if they are the conquered country's property.

4. Why do men rape women? Psychological theory attributes rape to a psychological problem, such as the offender's feelings of sexual inadequacy. Social psychological theory traces the source of rape to a sexually permissive culture that intensifies the male's feeling of rejection by women and thus increases his sexual frustration. Feminist theory explains that since rape serves to preserve male dominance in a sexually unequal society, men are likely to assault women.

5. What is the nature of same-sex rape in prison? In many respects, male-against-male rape in prison is comparable to male-against-female rape in the larger society. It is basically a phenomenon of a more powerful person raping a smaller, weaker person; it is an expression of dominance more than sexual desire. **How can men be raped in the larger society?** Men can be raped by other men as well as pressured by women to engage in nonconsensual sex. Male offenders are more likely to be strangers to their victims while female offenders tend to be acquaintances. More than half of the male victims are heterosexual, so are half of the offenders. **Can women rape men?** Yes. To the extent that some men are weak and submissive and some women are powerful and aggressive, women can rape men. But most

such rapes involve verbal pressure rather than physical force.

6. What are some of the common characteristics of child molestation? Most victims are likely to be girls; most child molesters are men; molesters are more likely to be acquainted with, not strangers to, their victims; and molesters tend to lack social skills. **What is the social profile of child molesters?** Compared to rapists of women, child molesters are older, more likely to have been abused themselves, more gentle and passive, less likely to resort to physical force, less skilled in interacting with women, more likely to victimize the same child repeatedly, and more likely to admit their guilt. **What could have caused the scandal of child molestation in the U.S. Catholic church?** Some suggested causes are: (1) the lack of women and married men as priests, (2) the declining numbers of priests and candidates for priesthood, which has lowered the recruitment standard and allowed child molesters to become priests, and (3) keeping rather than dismissing child-molesting priests.

FURTHER READING

Barstow, Anne Llewellyn (ed.). 2000. *War's Dirty Secret: Rape, Prostitution, and Other Crimes Against Women.* Cleveland, Ohio: Pilgrim Press. A collection of articles about how rape is used as a weapon of war.

Benedict, Jeffrey R. 1998. *Athletes and Acquaintance Rape.* Thousand Oaks, Calif.: Sage Publications. A detailed analysis of three court cases involving athletes charged with committing acquaintance rape, showing why such rape is relatively common in sports.

Bolen, Rebecca M. 2001. *Child Sexual Abuse: Its Scope and Our Failure.* New York: Kluwer Academic/Plenum Publishers. Discusses the history of child sexual abuse, the scope of the abuse, and professional responses to the problem.

Brownmiller, Susan. 1975. *Against Our Will: Men, Women, and Rape.* New York: Simon & Schuster. A hard-hitting classic on how men use rape to intimidate and keep women in their place.

Cahill, Ann J. 2001. *Rethinking Rape.* Ithaca, N.Y.: Cornell University Press. Analyzing the nature of rape from the feminist perspective.

Fairstein, Linda. 1993. *Sexual Violence: Our War Against Rape.* New York: William Morrow. An analysis of rape from the author's vantage point as chief of New York's Sex Crime Prosecution Unit for nearly 20 years.

Henry, Nicola, Tony Ward, and Matt Hirschberg. 2004. "A Multifactorial Model of Wartime Rape." *Aggression and Violent Behavior,* 9, 535–562. An analysis of how wartime rape has its roots in peacetime culture.

Jackson, Thomas L. (ed.). 1996. *Acquaintance Rape: Assessment, Treatment, and Prevention.* Sarasota, Fla.: Professional Resource Press. A collection of articles on various aspects of acquaintance rape, including its impact on victims, treatment of victims, and prevention of the sexual assault.

Madigan, Lee, and Nancy C. Gamble. 1991. *The Second Rape: Society's Continued Betrayal of the Victim.* New York: Lexington Books. A critical analysis of the various ways society makes the rape survivor's life worse.

Russell, Diana E. H., and Rebecca M. Bolen. 2000. *The Epidemic of Rape and Child Sexual Abuse in the United States.* Thousand Oaks, Calif.: Sage Publications. An evaluation of the prevalence of rape and child molestation that concludes that the problem is very widespread.

Sanday, Peggy Reeves. 1996. *A Woman Scorned: Acquaintance Rape on Trial.* New York: Doubleday. Illustrates how the U.S. culture and legal system help make victims of acquaintance rape responsible for their own victimization.

Scarce, Michael. 1997. *Male on Male Rape: The Hidden Toll of Stigma and Shame.* New York: Insight Books. The first-ever book-length analysis of male rape outside of prison settings.

Schwartz, Martin D., and Walter S. DeKeseredy. 1997. *Sexual Assault on the College Campus: The Role of Male Peer Support.* Thousand Oaks, Calif.: Sage Publications. Provides a critical review of various theories and studies on campus rape, and shows how male peer groups encourage college men to engage in sexual aggression.

Scully, Diana. 1990. *Understanding Sexual Violence: A Study of Convicted Rapists.* Boston: Unwin Hyman. An insightful analysis of how rapists see themselves and their crime.

CRITICAL THINKING QUESTIONS

1. The culture of rape is all around us. What can you do to resist it?

2. Can the Catholic church prevent more scandal about child molestation by its priests? If yes, why? If not, why not?

PART FOUR

Diverse Lifestyles

CHAPTER

9

Heterosexual Deviance

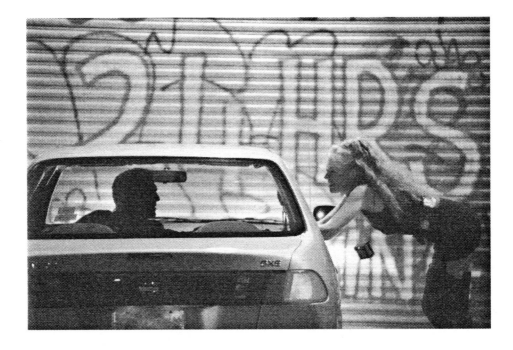

Jeanette Maier had worked for many years as a prostitute in New Orleans under various conditions. She had worked for pimps and sugar daddies as well as for strip joints and escort services. But somehow she still couldn't get rich. Then 10 years ago she heard about the Circuit, a vast nationwide network of over 100 brothels run by madams who make enormous sums of money swapping hookers with one another. Then, in her mid-thirties in 1996, Maier opened her own brothel and tried to join the Circuit. She called the madams in various cities and offered to send them her "girls" if they send theirs to her. Since then she's always had new faces in her bordello, which makes her fabulously rich. This is because the prostitutes who work for her through the Circuit fly around the country and stay at one place mostly for about a week only. The clients love the variety and will pay top dollar, sometimes spending thousands of bucks in one night. The women who temporarily work for Maier generally earn about $5,000 a week each and she as their madam gets half of those earnings (Campo-Flores, 2002).

This kind of prostitution, which involves women selling sex to men, is an example of heterosexual deviance. In this chapter, we will take a look at various aspects of prostitution. But first we will examine other forms of heterosexual deviance: teen sex, extramarital sex, pornography, sex deviance in cyberspace, phone sex, nude dancing, and sexual harassment.

Teen Sex

Most Americans today no longer consider premarital sex deviant as they did 20 or 30 years ago. More precisely, though, they find premarital sex acceptable for adults, but not for teenagers (Risman and Schwartz, 2002). It is okay for people aged 20 or older to engage in premarital sex, but it is still a no-no for those under age 20. Teenage sex, then, continues to be deviant in the eyes of U.S. society. The acceptability of premarital sex for adults apparently reflects the influence of the sexual revolution that has been going on since the 1960s. But why not for teenagers as well? Probably because teens are still *not* considered mature and responsible enough to have sex. Most adults seem to be afraid that if teens were allowed to have sex, they would end up having "illegitimate" babies (Goode, 2001). In fact, this seems to be a major reason for today's sex education programs that emphasize the importance of sexual abstinence.

Still, teenagers nowadays are much more likely than their peers of two or three decades ago to be sexually active. Teens now have sex younger, have more sexual partners, and are more likely to have "hookups" or one-night stands. Further teens are more likely to get an STD (sexually transmitted disease) such as herpes, gonorrhea, or HIV, and have the highest rate of premarital pregnancy in the industrial world. The sex education that urges teens to abstain from sex until marriage has worked in some ways, but with some unintended consequences. In some schools, for example, teens who have pledged abstinence tend to delay having sex for 18 months, but once they start having sex, they are less likely to use contraception. Also, partly because of the "just say no" emphasis in sex education, growing numbers of teens have been trying to maintain "technical virginity" by having oral sex, which they do not view as real sex, presumably because it cannot cause pregnancy (McGinn, 2004; Mulrine, 2002).

There is, however, a gender factor in teens having sex or abstaining from it. As shown by a study of youngsters aged 12 to 14, boys with high self-esteem are more likely to engage in sex, but girls with high self-esteem are more likely to abstain (Spencer et al., 2002). Apparently, the traditional double standard still holds sway over the teen world: Sexually active boys are looked up to as studs, while sexually active girls are looked down on as sluts. Girls are further caught in a double bind: If they continue to maintain their virginity, they risk being stigmatized as a tease. To get around both the "slut" and "tease" stigmas, many teenage girls become sexually active within a relationship—by having sex with their boyfriend or somebody they know well rather than a stranger or mere acquaintance (Dunn, 2004).

In the meantime two groups of adults continue to battle over what to do about teen sex. Conservative Christians want schools only to teach teenagers to abstain from sex, while liberals support a comprehensive sex-education program that teaches both abstinence and contraception. To the conservatives, the teaching of contraception contradicts the teaching of abstinence because the former will lead to sex. But to the liberals, teaching abstinence without contraception will leave teens defenseless against pregnancy and sexually transmitted diseases when they have sex, as some are bound to because the abstinence-only program cannot be expected to be 100 percent successful.

Thus, the nature of sex education varies from school to school. Among schools that teach sex education, about 51 percent discuss contraception but teach abstinence as the preferred option. Approximately 35 percent teach abstinence as the only option. The remaining 14 percent teach both options without emphasizing which is better. Research has shown the comprehensive program to be the most effective in reducing teen pregnancy and STDs (Irvine, 2002). But since 2002, a new sex education has emerged that may help boost the effectiveness of the abstinence-only program. It teaches only the health benefits of abstinence, totally ignoring the moral issues. Students are taught, for example, that the cervix of teenage girls is more vulnerable than that of adult women to certain STDs, particularly viral diseases such as HPV (human papillomavirus), so that a sexually active girl can still get the diseases even though her partner uses condoms (Parker-Pope, 2002).

Extramarital Sex

Extramarital sex, popularly known as adultery, infidelity, or an affair, is sex that a married person has with "the other" woman or man. An overwhelming majority of Americans frown on extramarital sex: Nearly 90 percent of men and 94 percent of women said in a national survey that they considered adultery "always wrong" or "almost always wrong." Not surprisingly, only a relatively small minority engage in extramarital sex: 25 percent of married men and 17 percent of married women reported having at least one affair. These data, however, can also be taken to suggest that adultery is very common because the ratios (25 and 17 percent) mean that at least 19 million American men and 12 million American women have committed adultery. "That's a helluva lot of people being unfaithful," said a sex researcher in Florida (Norman, 1998; Michael et al., 1994).

Seductive Myths

Although faithful to their spouses, most married Americans, especially men, wish at one time or another to have an extramarital affair. According to the classic Kinsey Report, over 70 percent of married men had such a wish in the late 1940s. While women tend to associate an affair with love more than sex, men are more likely to think of it as a sexual escapade (Glass and Wright, 1992). As a result, many men seem to believe in the myth that extramarital intercourse is far more exciting or satisfying than marital sex. But data show otherwise. Perhaps because extramarital copulation is mostly carried out in secrecy, and frequently charged with tension and guilt, the experience is far from gratifying. According to one study, two-thirds of married men rated their marital sex "very pleasurable," but fewer than half of the unfaithful husbands gave the same rating to their extramarital coitus. And 53 percent of married women regularly reached orgasm with their husbands, but only 39 percent of the straying wives did so in extramarital intercourse (Katchadourian, 1985).

Another myth about extramarital sex may be equally popular with both men and women: "People have affairs because they are oversexed." Research suggests, however, that those who engage in adultery are far from oversexed. They generally are much less sexually active—having a lot less sex—than monogamous couples (Adler, 1996; Pittman, 1993). If being oversexed is not the cause of infidelity, what is? The cause can be found in a set of social and cultural factors, as suggested by the fact that the incidence of extramarital sex varies from one group to another in the United States as well as from one culture to another in the world.

Cultural Variations

There are legitimate and illegitimate adulteries, and each appears in different forms in different cultures. First, consider the different forms of illegitimate adulteries. Among the Lozi of eastern Africa, adultery does not involve sexual intercourse. If a man walks with a married woman he is not related to, or if he gives her a beer, he has committed adultery. By contrast, in most other societies, illegitimate adulteries always involve copulation. To conservative Christians who interpret the Bible literally, even divorce and remarriage, which involves copulation, is condemned as adultery. As Jesus says in Mark 10:11, "Whoever divorces his wife and marries another commits adultery against her; and if she divorces her husband and marries another, she commits adultery." In various societies, however, women have historically been punished for adultery more harshly than men. In Muslim societies, for example, unfaithful wives could be stoned to death. Generally, because illegitimate adulteries are socially condemned, they do not occur frequently (Fisher, 1992; Lawson, 1988).

Legitimate adulteries, however, take place more often in societies where they are by definition socially approved. Among the Kofyar of Nigeria, a woman who is unhappy with her husband but does not want to divorce may, without seeking his consent, take an extra lover, who lives openly with her in her husband's house. A Kofyar man may do the same for the same reason. In many Italian towns on the Adriatic coast, virtually every married man has a lover whom he visits regularly. Most of these affairs are between men and women who are married to others. Sometimes younger male servants visit rich men's wives, while rich men occasionally copulate with their maids or cooks. But it is taboo for any married person to ever speak of his or her affair. This is because boasting, gossiping, or even whispering to others about one's dalliance can expose the extensive network of extramarital relationships, seriously threatening their highly cherished community cohesion and family life (Fisher, 1992). However, legitimate adulteries such as these do not exist in American society.

All this points to the significant influence of culture on extramarital sex. Whatever form of adultery a culture considers acceptable is likely to be prevalent. Research that focuses on U.S. society alone further suggests the influence of certain social factors on extramarital sex.

Social Factors

Under the influence of the same culture that basically discourages infidelity, some groups of Americans are nonetheless more likely than others to cheat on their spouses. As shown by various studies, extramarital sex is more common among those who have experienced premarital coitus than among those who have not; men are more likely than women to have an affair; the less religious generally have a higher incidence of extramarital sex than the more religious; and lower-income people are more likely than higher-income Americans to be unfaithful to their spouses (Duncombe et al., 2004; Janus and Janus, 1993).

Sociobiologists regard the gender difference in adultery as the most significant finding because it exists in virtually all societies. Sociobiologists trace it to humankind's long evolutionary past when men had to impregnate more women to produce more young so as to ensure the survival of their genes (Norman, 1998; Fisher, 1992). But the last thing that today's philandering men want is to produce babies. After all, most people, both male and female, now regard the primary purpose of sex as recreation rather than procreation. Far from scientific and valid, the evolutionary theory merely reflects the patriarchal belief that men should prove their masculinity by screwing around. It is this widely shared belief that causes men to philander more than women do. Most male philanderers also differ from their affair partners. The men tend to attach too little significance to the affair, being far from deeply in love with the women. But women tend to attach too much significance to the affair, believing that they no longer love their husband and that their affair partner is the true love of their life (Allan, 2004; Pittman, 1993).

Many affairs begin accidentally. The straying spouse may have drunk too much, got caught up in the moment, or just had a bad day. Here is how a typical accidental infidelity "just happens" to a 47-year-old college professor:

> I had my first affair with a young faculty member who was divorced. We had known each other for several years, and there was no great passion, but she was a woman and I a man. It was strange how it came about. We were both out of town at a professional conference. . . . The very first night, after some drinks, I found myself in bed with her. The sex was fine, but the guilt was awful. She kept telling me, "Grow up, we're both adults, and if we can give each other some pleasure, what's the sin in that?" It wasn't easy; I could see my poor sad-sack wife, and the dread of my kids ever finding out. The conference lasted a week but I carefully avoided my colleague for the rest of it. (Pittman, 1993)

Infidelity is likely to lead to divorce (Previti and Amato, 2004). But more often the betrayed wife or cuckolded husband strives to do whatever they can to save their marriage, although they initially feel deeply hurt and outraged. The marriage usually survives if the affair is stopped, brought into the open, and dealt with (Pittman, 1993).

Pornography

It is against the law to distribute what is called pornography—sexually explicit materials—in the media, but the law is not strictly enforced because the meaning of pornography is subject to different interpretations. A large majority of Americans are also opposed to the distribution as well as the consumption of pornography (Maguire and Pastore, 1996). Yet sexually explicit materials can be found everywhere, and most people, especially men, have used it. The recent film about *Hustler* magazine's founder, *The People vs. Larry Flynt,* raises the interminable controversy over whether the constitutional right to free speech allows even the most vulgar form of expression. Some would endlessly debate this kind of issue, but here we will focus more on what the producers and distributors of pornography sell and what effects the merchandise has on the consumers.

The Porn Industry

Pornography has become an enormous industry today. A major reason is that the demand for sexually explicit materials has soared over the last decade. The number of hard-core video rentals, for example, skyrocketed from only 75 million in 1985 to 665 million in 1996. Today, the United States has become by far the world's leading producer of hard-core videos, churning them out at the astonishing rate of about 150 new titles a week. Also widely consumed, though to a lesser extent than hard-core videos, are sex magazines, adult cable programming, peep shows, live sex acts, phone sex, and computer porn. The amount of money spent on all the adult materials ($10 billion in 2000) is much larger than Hollywood's domestic box office receipts or the entire revenue from rock and country music recordings. Strip clubs alone bring in more money than all the opera, ballet, and jazz and classical music performances combined (Egan, 2000; Schlosser, 1997).

The porn industry's fantastic growth has stemmed mostly from the invasion of pornographic videos into mainstream society. In the past, most people were too embarrassed to go to seedy movie theaters and adult bookstores, but today they can watch porn videos in the privacy of their homes. Not surprisingly, the number of those traditional suppliers of porn has declined. Now, not only mom-and-pop video stores but also cable-TV companies profit greatly from pornographic videos. Even large hotel chains such as Hyatt, Holiday Inn, and Marriott reportedly earn millions each year by making their guests feel at home with adult films to watch in their rooms (Ackman, 2004; Egan, 2000).

There is a wide spectrum of hard-core videos to meet every conceivable consumer demand: videos that feature gay, lesbian, straight, transsexual, interracial, or older couples; "cat fighting" videos that show naked women wrestling each other or joining forces to beat up a naked man; videos for sadomasochists, aficionados of bondage or spanking, or people fond of verbal abuse; and other kinds of videos too numerous to list. Other forms of pornography, particularly phone sex and computer porn, have also emerged on the scene, generating significant revenues for long-distance carriers such as AT&T (Egan, 2000; Schlosser, 1997).

The Effects of Pornography

Research has produced seemingly conflicting findings on the effects of pornography. Some studies seem to support the antiporn feminist and conservative view that pornography is harmful. Other studies appear to confirm the anticensorship, liberal view that pornography is harmless. Let us take a closer look at each of these two views and the studies supporting them.

Pornography as Harmful.   Some feminists support the idea that a woman has the legal right to free expression via pornography even though they may personally find the material distasteful. But many other feminists are opposed to pornography and want it banned because they believe that pornography is harmful to women.

To support this view, antiporn feminists usually point out many laboratory studies showing that exposure to violent pornography encourages male aggression against women (Linz and Malamuth, 1993; Donnerstein et al., 1987). In one experiment, for example, male subjects were divided into two groups: One watched a film depicting sexual violence against women; the other watched a nonviolent film. After seeing the movies, the subjects who had watched the violent film were more likely to adminster electrical shocks to women than were those who had watched the nonviolent film (Donnerstein et al., 1987). But we cannot generalize, as some feminists do, from the laboratory finding to what goes on in the larger society by insisting that violent pornography contributes significantly to the prevalence of antiwomen sexual aggression *in the society at large*. The reason is simply that, as research has indicated, *most* of the pornographic materials in the United States are not violent at all, and nonviolent pornography, which merely shows nudity and consensual sex, generally does not cause male aggression against women (Donnerstein et al., 1987).

Nevertheless, many feminists still assume that most pornography is violent—and that it leads to widespread violence against women in society. But many feminists also hold the convincing belief that pornography, if not violent, still degrades women by treating them as pieces of meat. Thus, cities such as Minneapolis, Indianapolis, and Los Angeles have considered or passed tougher laws to stop the spread of pornography, but they have been either defeated by lawmakers or overturned by courts on grounds that they violated the First Amendment guarantee of free speech. Some feminists have, however, argued that pornography should be prohibited because it violates the Fourteenth Amendment guarantee of equal protection of the law. Agreeing with this position, the Supreme Court of Canada has ruled that pornography does harm women by dehumanizing and degrading them. Ironically, though, the feminist fight for tougher antipornography laws receives considerable support from conservatives, who are opposed to the women's movement or gender equality (Wilkerson, 1993).

Aside from supporting the feminist view that pornography degrades women, conservatives believe that sexually explicit materials can destroy traditional family values and, thereby, the entire society. Often cited to support this belief is the research finding that long exposure to explicit depictions of common sex acts often leads men to seek portrayals of less common, more deviant practices, such as violent, sadomasochistic, or bestial sex. Such men are then more likely to engage in various deviant sexual activities, which they find exciting. At the same time, however, they become more likely to find conventional, monogamous, or marital sex boring. All this is considered to have "devastating consequences" for traditional monogamy, marriage, family, and society (Paul, 2004; Linz and Malamuth, 1993). There is, however, no clear-cut evidence that pornography wrecks many marriages, let alone threatens the survival of the society.

Pornography as Harmless.   Liberals may personally find pornography distasteful, but they are opposed to the censorship of sexually explicit material not only because it violates the freedom of expression but also because they view pornography as basically harmless.

To support their belief that pornography is harmless, liberals usually call on studies showing that, in the real world outside the laboratory, exposure to sexually explicit materials does not cause rape or other sex crimes. For example, the availability of pornography in the United States increased substantially between 1960 and 1969 but the incidence of rape did not go up as much during the same period. Similarly, the advent of the VCR has vastly increased the dissemination of hardcore videos, but the rate of rape has not increased to the same extent. U.S. cities with high circulation of sexually oriented magazines have basically the same rates of rape as cities with low circulation. In Denmark, in the late 1960s, after all legal prohibitions on the sale of pornography were removed, sex crimes did not rise but instead dropped sharply (Linz and Malamuth, 1993). To liberals, all these data strongly suggest that pornography is harmless.

It is more accurate to say, however, that *nonviolent* pornography is harmless because most of the sexually explicit material in the society at large is nonviolent. Considering everything that we have discussed, we may conclude that *nonviolent* pornography is harmless, as suggested by "real world" studies, but *violent* pornography is harmful, as shown by laboratory studies (Procida and Simon, 2003).

Sexual Deviance in Cyberspace

Since the early 1990s, the personal computer has become a common sight in homes. It is now widely used for seeking information and entertainment, e-mailing, shopping, and other activities and services. But it has also encouraged deviant sexual activities, especially in the forms of cybersex and cyberporn.

Cybersex

To experience cybersex, most people first find their partners by placing or answering personals on the Internet or by entering an online chat room. Then they exchange erotic e-mails, trade pornographic pictures of themselves, or engage in steamy conversations in the chat room, and in the process get sexually stimulated and, most often, masturbate. Some of these cybersex enthusiasts go offline to meet their partners in person. If the meeting is mutually satisfactory, they will have sex (Cooper, 2004; Wysocki, 1998; Lamb, 1998).

Most of the cybersex participants are white, male, and college-educated. Many, or about half, are married. Whether married or not, why do these people take part in cybersex? At least five reasons have emerged from an empirical study by sociologist Diane Wysocki (1998):

One reason is the need for *anonymity*. Unlike the real world in which sexual partners can see each other, the virtual, cybernetic world enables them to keep their true identities under wraps. They can thus take on whatever persona they want within the comfort of their home. If a man is shy and becomes tongue-tied when meeting partners face-to-face, online he can shed his shyness, feel bold, and turn chatty, projecting himself as the life of the party. Some women feel fat, old, and undesirable in person, but online they feel slim, young, wanted, and sexy—and this is the image they get across to the men on the other side of the electronic connection.

A second reason for participating in cybersex is the relative *ease and convenience* of finding sex partners. Trying to find a person with similar sexual attitudes and desires is difficult and time-consuming in the real world, where most of the people you meet do not share your interests. But it is much easier to find sex partners in the virtual world because it attracts only people with the same interests. This ease and convenience of finding a partner is especially important for people who are too busy to pursue friendships and sexual contacts on the face-to-face basis.

A third reason for engaging in cybersex is *sharing sexual fantasies.* Most people entertain sexual fantasies, such as engaging in sexual activities outdoors, having sex with more than one partner, or being a transvestite by wearing the clothing of the opposite sex. Since conventional society frowns on these fantasies, most people find them too embarrassing to share with others or even with their wives or husbands in the real world. But in the virtual world, where people with similar fantasies get together, the fantasies can be freely talked about and can even be turned easily into reality with willing partners.

A fourth reason for seeking online sex is the easy availability of partners as an *outlet for masturbation.* As a woman who is a regular participant in cybersex says, "I love it when the guy gets off . . . it starts with teasing and flirting . . . I usually rub my clit and we eventually get off. I most often am wearing a miniskirt or nude and it goes from there . . . usually the men are online for a hot chat and wanting to come" (Wysocki, 1998).

A fifth reason is the expectation that online sex can lead to *real sex* with a willing partner face-to-face. Most of the online partners find their sexual experience in the real world very satisfactory. But some find the experience disappointing because either one or both parties have lied online about their physical appearance. One man, for example, complains that some people he has met have not been completely honest: "[They] tell you how good of shape they're in . . . you know like 38-22-36 and 128 lbs . . . when you get there they are more like 180 or so . . . or they will tell you things like yes, I want to do this or that and when you meet it is different" (Wysocki, 1998).

Cyberporn

Cyberporn, or pornography in cyberspace, is not new. Soon after the Internet came on the technological scene, people started to trade dirty pictures on the Net. But amateur swapping has now given way to commercial ventures. By mid-1997, according to an online guide to cyberporn, there were already about 900 sex sites on the Web. Only one year later, this number had soared to somewhere between 20,000 and 30,000. These commercial sites vary in size from small outfits with just a few hundred paying members to major networks with thousands of subscribers. By 2001 the top five porn sites received nearly twice as many visitors as the top five news sites (Webb, 2001; Barnako, 1998; Weber, 1997).

Cyberporn has become big business, raking in some $700 million a year. Sex sites are comparable in popularity to sports or weather sites and have only slightly fewer visitors than business and travel sites. A onetime stripper's site brings in so much revenue that she has given up stripping for good. In her former profession, she made only $1,500 a month, but right after going on the Web, her monthly earnings jumped to somewhere between $10,000 and $15,000. A 23-year-old man formed a company called Internet Entertainment in 1997 and now makes $20 million annually by offering a wide range of online shows. One type, called "live video," features exotic nude dancers in full color on the computer screens of customers, who can chat on the phone with the gyrating performers. Customers can also click their way to different virtual rooms: In the "bedroom" the visitor can see a naked dancer rolling around on a giant mattress, and in the "health club" the performer works out on a step exerciser with no clothes on (Barnako, 1998; Weber, 1997).

Cyberporn has become so popular primarily because customers can view racy material in the privacy of their homes. They no longer have to sneak into a sleazy adult bookstore or the back room of a video shop. But the popularity of cyberporn has caused some parents to fear that children can easily look up pornographic material when going online. Curious about sex, youngsters may want to do so, and they can find the Web sites that provide what they are looking for. Theoretically, masses of youngsters will likely consume cyberporn, for several reasons: One, they can obtain the material in the privacy of their home, without having to walk into an adult bookstore or cinema. Two, they can download only the portions of the material that turn them on, rather than buy an entire magazine or video. And three, they can explore sex without risking public ridicule or communicable diseases (Elmer-Dewitt, 1995). But the reality is that the typical users of cyberporn are men over age 30, not teenagers (Webb, 2001).

Nevertheless, the U.S. Senate tried to pass a bill in 1995 prohibiting anyone from making "indecent" material available to children under 18. But the bill failed to become law, not only because many believed it violated the First Amendment guarantee of free speech but also because many feared it could transform the vast library of the Internet into a children's reading room where only subjects suitable for kids could be discussed (Elmer-Dewitt, 1995). However, the computer industry has come up with programs such as SurfWatch and Net Nanny that can block children's access to questionable material. In addition, most pornographic sites on the World Wide Web require an adult ID and a credit card (Onstad, 1996). Parents, too, can help solve the problem by raising their children to shun pornography.

There is, however, already a federal law that prohibits distributing obscene material across state lines. This law has been vigorously enforced against adults who sell or exchange child pornography via the Internet. For engaging in this kind of cyberporn, a growing number of people have been arrested in various states since 1995 (Nordland and Bartholet, 2001; Labaton, 1995).

Social Profile: Cyberporn Surfers

Contrary to popular belief, the typical regular consumers of cyberporn are not sex-crazed teenagers. They are, instead, older and married men. According to demographic data from the porn site Sex Tracker, two-thirds of the surfers are more than 30 years old and they are mostly married, white, and middle class. According to another study, 70 percent of the cyberporn traffic occurs during work hours, not at home after teens are let out of school. Teenagers are much less inclined to use cyberporn because it doesn't seem like a big deal to them; they have been growing up in an environment saturated with pornographic stimuli. But the same cyberporn may be more intriguing to older men because it is more striking than the porn they grew up with.

Research specifically on child porn in cyberspace has shown about the same demographics: Most users of child porn are white men in their thirties and forties. Their occupations, however, are highly diverse, ranging from the unemployed to taxi drivers to scientists and engineers. They can be considered pedophiles because of their attraction to young children and their discomfort with adult women. They often use child porn as masturbation aids. But they also like to trade their pornographic pictures with others in order to satisfy their "collector fetish," which is the same as normal people's desire to collect baseball cards, militaria, and Star Trek memorabilia. A broad spectrum of attitudes and opinions exists among child porn consumers. Some say that what they do is wrong, but others insist it is not. Some maintain that they are only interested in "innocent" fantasies, while others admit that they have molested young children.

Sources: Tuesday, 2002; Webb, 2001; Jenkins, 2001.

Phone Sex

In phone sex the operator, who is most likely a woman, essentially sells sexual fantasies to the caller, most likely a man. She is good at faking interest in the caller, talking about anything the caller wants, and playing along with whatever fantasies he has. The trick is to maximize profit by getting him to stay on the phone for as long as possible. If a caller says "I love you," the operator is likely to answer "I love you, too. Now what else do you want to do with me?" If the caller wants her to go down on him, she may pretend to do it by making the appropriate sound and saying the right things.

The operator is extremely unlikely to meet the caller for fear of getting beaten, raped, or even murdered. But she will do practically anything on the phone, regardless of what kind of man the caller is. As an operator says,

> There hasn't been a caller that I didn't really like. There have been callers that just basically ticked me off, but it's really not a like or dislike thing. I don't think of those callers as people that I like or dislike. It's just another John, you know? I mean, I'm a telephone whore, so this is just my trick. It's not that I like them or dislike them. (Flowers, 1998)

In other words, the operator has the typical business attitude toward her work. She needs the job primarily to make money, and she will sell her service to whoever the caller is.

There are five types of callers, says sociologist Amy Flowers, who spent four months working as an operator in a phone sex company while observing and interviewing 21 colleagues. Knowing what the five types are can help us understand the men's various reasons for engaging in this kind of sexual deviance.

First, *quick-sex callers,* the majority of customers, do not stay on the phone long enough to accumulate a hefty charge. They offer little or no conversation, usually asking the operator to perform a fast sex act. Second, *psychos* are violent and angry callers, who like to talk about beating or raping women. Third, *lonely, lovelorn callers* keep calling the same operator, proposing marriage, and making plans for the future with her, but refraining from discussion of sexual matters. Fourth, *sexually possessive callers* resemble the lovelorn for being infatuated with a particular operator, but they are jealous of her sexual involvement with other men and demand that she give sex only to him. And fifth, *likable callers* sound attractive, able to arouse the operator's personal or sexual interest. They are well spoken and educated with high-status professions as, for example, physicians, celebrities, and government officials. They often insist that they called the phone sex line "only out of curiosity" (Flowers, 1998).

Nude Dancing

Like phone sex, nude dancing enables the male customer to fulfill his fantasy of sexual intimacy with an attractive woman, except that only in nude dancing he can see the woman's partially clad or totally naked body. At topless bars and lingerie shows, the dancers are partly clothed but often do not wear panties so they can flash their customers. At nude clubs, however, the dancers remove all their clothing. Since they make most or all their money from tips, dancers do their best to please the customers. Not surprisingly, then, dancers pay only scant attention, if any, to the art and aesthetics of dancing, which they know is not the audience's interest. Instead, maximum effort is made to catch and hold the customers' attention on what they have come to the club to see. Thus, as customers seated near the edge of the stage are prepared with cash in hand to tip her, the dancer may move from one man to another exposing her vagina for his close-up view. She may later lie on her back, spread her legs, separate her labia, and repeatedly stroke her clitoris. If her vagina becomes profusely wet, she may snatch the baseball cap off the head of a client and wipe it between her legs and give it back to him (Schiff, 1999).

Most customers are working-class men. They are not only far from wealthy, they are also not good-looking, young, and assertive. In a patriarchal society where successful or wealthy older men often get trophy wives, it may be difficult or impossible for those working-class men to get a young and attractive woman to be romantically interested in them. In their everyday lives, such a woman might not even look at them or talk to them, let alone expose herself to them. But they can fantasize having such a woman treat them like a million bucks, and this fantasy is what the nude dancer seeks to fulfill (Schiff, 1999).

What about the dancer? What can she get out of this work? In 1999 she could expect to make $25,000 to $75,000 a year. This could be considered an excellent wage, given the fact that most nude dancers have only a high school education and few job skills. Unsurprisingly, money is by far the number one reason for becoming a nude dancer. Despite the high pay, though, nude dancing is still widely regarded as highly disreputable. But this does not seem to disturb most dancers, because they do not identify themselves with their stigmatized career. They identify themselves instead as wives, single mothers, or some other conventional role, and may not even tell family, friends, and others what they do. They feel that their dancing job does not reflect their true self, their true values and characteristics, who they really are. More positively, most dancers find their work empowering because it enables them to command so much attention and interest from an audience that it is willing to pay them handsomely (Wood, 2001; Schiff, 1999; Reid, Epstein, and Benson, 1995).

Sexual Harassment

Sexual harassment can be defined as an unwelcome act of a sexual nature. The U.S. Supreme Court has provided a more precise, legal definition: Sexual harassment is any sexual conduct that makes the workplace environment so hostile or abusive to the victims that they find it hard to perform their job.

The Supreme Court's definition came with its ruling on the suit that Teresa Harris filed against her former boss, Charles Hardy. In 1987 Harris quit her job in despair because she felt she had been sexually harassed by Hardy. According to

Harris, Hardy often asked her—and other female employees—to retrieve coins from the front pockets of his pants. He once asked Harris to go with him to a hotel room to negotiate her raise. And he routinely made such remarks to her as, "You're a woman; what do you know?" She spent six years trying to convince judges that she was sexually harassed in violation of federal law, but to no avail. The judges found Hardy's conduct not severe enough to "seriously affect her psychological well-being." But Harris persisted, and finally the Supreme Court ruled that sexual harassment does not have to inflict "severe psychological injury" on the victim. As the Court said, federal law "comes into play before the harassing conduct leads to a nervous breakdown" (Sachs, 1993). More recently, in 1998, the Supreme Court further broadened the definition of harassment: A female employee can sue her employer even if she gets a salary raise or promotion after resisting unwanted sexual advances from her supervisor (Lavelle, 1998).

Since the early 1990s, the number of harassment charges has increased substantially. To avoid being sued, many companies, as well as universities and colleges, have instituted antiharassment policies, guidelines, or educational programs, especially since 1998 when the Supreme Court ruled that companies can protect themselves against lawsuits only if they have a strong and effective program to prevent and discipline harassment (Lavelle, 1998). Even primary and high schools have started to prevent harassment after the Court ruled in 1999 that schools can be sued if they fail to stop a student from "severely" harassing another (Greenhouse, 1999).

The problem, however, is too prevalent to soon go away. According to various studies, about half of all working women have been sexually harassed at some point in their careers, and about 40 percent of college women have been harassed. Examples of harassment range from unwanted sexual remarks to actual rape. Also, among high school and junior high students, close to 70 percent of girls have been touched, groped, or pinched on school grounds. And as many as 1 in 10 students from kindergarten to twelfth grade may be subjected to some from of sexual harassment by teachers and other school employees (Gregory, 2004; Hendrie, 2004; Crouch, 2001; Reed, 2000).

Generally, sexual harassment reflects men's attempt to preserve their traditional dominance over women. Men are, therefore, more likely to harass a woman if they feel threatened by her "invasion" into their male-dominated world. This may explain why sexual harassment seems to occur most frequently in traditionally and heavily male-dominated occupations, such as the U.S. military. At bottom, however, sexual harassment is an expression of power, involving a more powerful person victimizing the less powerful, such as school employees taking advantage of their young charges. It is also possible for a female boss to sexually harass a male employee. But, given the predominance of men in positions of power, they are the offenders in most cases.

The World of Prostitution

Prostitution, the exchange of sex for money, is legal in many countries in Europe and elsewhere. By contrast, it is not legal in the United States, except in some counties of

Nevada. Nonetheless, prostitution has long been big business here. Every year billions of dollars are spent on the sexual favors of prostitutes, whose profit amounts to at least 10 times the annual budget of the U.S. Department of Justice. The number of prostitutes has been estimated to range from 84,000 to 336,000 (Potterat et al., 1990). But such estimates grossly underrepresent the real number of prostitutes because the figures are almost entirely derived from sex workers who are known to the police and fail to take into account those who are not. According to one survey that asked a nationwide sample of American women ages 18 to 64 whether they had ever had sex for money, nearly 6 percent said yes. This seemingly small percentage translates into a huge number—at least 4.2 million women (Janus and Janus, 1993). Although there are so many prostitutes, we know very little about them. Here we will take a look at various aspects of prostitution.

Myths about Prostitution

We often hear that prostitution is the oldest profession in the world. This is a myth, however, because priesthood is the oldest profession. We frequently encounter other myths about prostitutes such as those that follow.

First, it is often mentioned in both folklore and sometimes even in scientific literature that prostitutes typically are nymphomaniacs, having an insatiable desire for sexual intercourse with many men. This is male fantasy, not substantiated by facts. Before going into the sex business, most prostitutes did not have many more sex partners than other, average women. What is true is that prostitutes have started having sex at a younger age than other women (Perkins, 1991).

Second, some clinical psychologists assume just the opposite of the first myth: Prostitutes are sexually frigid. Actually, when they have sex with their husbands or boyfriends, prostitutes as a group are more responsive than other women—more able to achieve orgasm.

Third, there are two contradictory beliefs about how prostitutes treat their clients: On the one hand, they are believed to be nasty and hard-hearted—as evidenced by the popular saying "as cold as a whore's heart"—and on the other, they are romanticized as sweet and warmhearted—"a woman with a heart of gold." In reality, however, the average prostitute's attitude toward her clients is quite similar to that of anyone who provides services to a diverse clientele. Some clients she likes, a few others she dislikes, and toward most of them she simply feels neutral.

Fourth, according to popular belief, most prostitutes are drug addicts or have turned to prostitution to support their drug habits. It is true that the percentage of prostitutes who are drug addicts before or after entering the sex business is higher than the percentage of conventional women addicted to drugs. Young streetwalkers are particularly likely to be addicted to drugs, but the *majority* of prostitutes are not drug addicts (Perkins, 1991).

Fifth, it is widely believed that most prostitutes have been sexually abused as children. Indeed, as shown by many studies, most of the streetwalkers who start prostituting at a young age or prostitutes who have often been arrested by police or helped by social agencies have been victims of child abuse. But, unlike these prostitutes, most sex workers do not have a history of child abuse (Perkins, 1991).

Types of Prostitutes

There is a great variety of prostitutes. Some researchers have found as many as 18 different types (Benjamin and Masters, 1964). Most of these kinds are relatively rare, however, so we need to know only the more common types, namely, street-walkers, child and adolescent prostitutes, house prostitutes, and call girls. These sex workers are employed in a highly stratified occupation, so that they vary from one another in their status in prostitution, the price they charge, or the quality of their social and work life. The status, price, or life quality rises as one goes from street-walkers, who occupy the lowest status, to call girls, who have the highest status.

Streetwalkers.   In prostitution, soliciting customers on the street is probably the most ancient method. Generally, compared with most other types of prostitutes, streetwalkers are less educated, more likely to shoot drugs and get AIDS, and more often arrested by the police.

Streetwalkers normally use a standard method of soliciting. When a street-walker sees a potential customer strolling on a sidewalk, she is likely to smile at him. She may then say to him such things as: "Hi. How are you today?" or "Which direction are you heading?" If the man responds, she may ask, "Do you want company?" or "Want a date?" or "Wanna do something?" Then she tells him her price, although very often, the man himself takes the initiative and simply asks, "How much?" Once a deal is struck, she typically takes him to a hotel room.

Increasingly, streetwalkers solicit business from cruising motorists. For most of these transactions, the service is rendered in the car. Because many customers find their cars too cramped for intercourse, a large number of "car jobs" involve oral sex only. By contrast, virtually all the sexual services in hotel rooms involve vaginal intercourse. Wherever and however the sexual act is carried out, most streetwalkers, not being well paid, strive to minimize its duration. Thus, most of the sexual services in the room last 15 to 30 minutes, while most of the car jobs only 4 to 15 minutes (van Gelder and Kaplan, 1992; Freund et al., 1991). Many car customers may whine about the shortness of the service, but most streetwalkers consider their job finished when the customer ejaculates. And it does not take long for this to occur, as a streetwalker says, "The men who are driving around here are so excited and horny. When you touch that thing, well, it almost happens right away" (van Gelder and Kaplan, 1992). That's why, despite the complaint, most customers repeatedly return for the same kind of service.

Traditionally, streetwalkers tend to ply their trade in lower-class areas, where they can afford to solicit blatantly and openly, without much fear of getting arrested by the police. But in many suburban areas today streetwalkers are more careful to avoid arrest. This presents a problem, though. How can customers know the identity of a streetwalker if she camouflages it to avoid being too obtrusive to the general public? To solve this problem, streetwalkers resort to a unique strategy: alternating between actively soliciting when spotting a potential customer and discreetly blending into the street scene when seeing a police officer. Thus, most streetwalkers tend to stand near a bus or taxi stop, a public telephone booth, street corner, or hotel entrance. This enables a customer to distinguish a streetwalker from other pedestrians, and when she sees him approaching her she will know him to be a customer. At the same time, such public places enable a streetwalker to loiter like any other pedestrian when a police officer appears (Riccio, 1992).

The prospect of being arrested is not the only problem facing streetwalkers. More than other types of prostitutes, streetwalkers are often abused by customers, pimps, and even police. Customers frequently force them to engage in kinky sex, rape them, refuse to pay them, rob them, or beat them. Pimps regularly beat them, too. Policemen sometimes beat them or demand free sex. Serial killers often murder them one after another, while their families would not miss them and the police would not find them. Young streetwalkers, particularly those under age 16, are most likely to suffer these forms of victimization (Silbert and Pines, 1981). Older streetwalkers are more able to protect themselves. They know how to "manipulate anonymity" before soliciting, concealing their true identity while trying to determine which customers are trustworthy or dangerous (Merry, 1980).

Child and Adolescent Prostitutes.   Some prostitutes are only 8 to 12 years old. These child prostitutes are often called "baby pros." Most have been brought up in poor and chaotic families, where they are accustomed to seeing their mothers or older sisters engaged in sex with different men, in pornography, or in prostitution. Many have suffered physical or sexual abuse at the hands of their parents or other adults. Consequently, when first approached by a man with an offer to pay them for sex, they were "ready" to accept. Still too young, though, they continue to live with their parents and attend school, working as prostitutes only on a part-time basis.

Somewhat older than these children are adolescent prostitutes, aged 13 to 17. Most have also been brought up in disorganized families. They, too, have suffered physical or sexual abuse in childhood. But, unlike their younger counterparts, many adolescent prostitutes have run away from home and most have become heavy drug users. The need to support themselves, further intensified by the craving for drugs, is the most common motivation among the adolescents to sell sex for money (Weisberg, 1985). But often the pimp plays a significant role in their entry into prostitution. Alone in a large city, many young runaways from small towns or rural areas are fair game for pimps, who frequently look for new prey to entice or force into prostitution.

Adolescent prostitutes comprise only a small minority of prostitutes in the United States and other Western societies. The situation is different in poor countries, where far greater numbers of youngsters are forced or tricked into prostitution by pimps, parents, or poverty. In many poor villages in Thailand, many young girls are sold by penniless parents to brothel operators, are tricked into coming to big cities where they are forced to work in whorehouses, or are enticed to marry German tourists and then brought to Germany to serve as house prostitutes. In Nepal's poor Himalayan villages, some 7,000 adolescents are sold every year to the brothels in the Indian city of Bombay. In Brazil, about 25,000 girls from poor families have been forced into prostitution in remote Amazon mining camps. In Eastern Europe, many poor parents have forced their young daughters to sell sex, and those who work in brothels are often beaten to make them submit. As one official in a European aid group observes, "Many of the girls have broken teeth. They say they fell downstairs. But there are so many of them that either this business has the worst-maintained stairs in the world or these girls have been punched" (Perry and Sai, 2002; Kristof, 1996a; Hornblower, 1993).

Poverty is not the only driving force behind the prevalence of adolescent and child prostitution in those countries. A great demand for this kind of prostitution is another important factor. In recent years, the widespread belief among customers that very young sex partners are less likely to have AIDS has fueled a surging demand for youthful prostitution. In addition, many more tourists from rich, Western countries and Japan today flock to those poor countries for sex with children. These tourists know that they can exploit the children without any fear of being arrested for child abuse, as they would be in their home countries (Kristof, 1996a; Serrill, 1993; Simons, 1993).

House Prostitutes. A brothel is a place where prostitutes meet their customers and share their earnings with its operator. It has been variously referred to as a cathouse, whorehouse, parlor house, and bordello. Very often it is simply called a "joint" or "house." In the 1920s and 1930s many brothels existed in this country. Since 1945, most of them have been forced to shut down. Some houses today still operate openly in Nevada and clandestinely in other parts of the country.

In Nevada, where prostitution is legal, brothel prostitutes are fingerprinted and carry prostitute identification cards issued by the police or district attorneys. The women are generally required to have a weekly medical checkup. When a customer enters the house, the madam (proprietor) will direct a young woman to him. Before the sex act, most prostitutes in Nevada always make sure their clients wear condoms, though their counterparts in other states are less likely to do so (Hilts, 1987).

In many states where the brothel is covertly operated, the madam usually ensures that the potential client is not from the "pussy posse," which is what the vice squad is called in the sex industry. The madam will, of course, readily admit a regular customer. In cases in which she does not know him, she will first meet him at a nearby bar or send a cooperating cab driver to size him up. Only when convinced he is a genuine customer will the madam admit him into the brothel. Some prostitutes wait in the brothel, while others wait in their own apartments for phone calls from the madam, to whom she typically gives half her earnings. Since the clients often look for variety, the house prostitute usually does not work in a brothel for an extended period—the longest she will stay in one brothel is four or five years and the more enterprising ones will jet around the country to work in each city for only a few weeks. To minimize the risk of arrest, many houses simply operate as escort agencies (Campo-Flores, 2002; Potterat et al., 1990).

Most house prostitutes find that they have a distinct advantage over streetwalkers: Working in the house is safer and more secure. For lonely women, the brothel can offer opportunities for regular contact with other women, which may further blossom into friendship. Similar opportunities are rare for streetwalkers, because they have to work alone. But there are also disadvantages to working in a brothel. House prostitutes are not free to set their own working hours and must give half of their earnings to the house. These are restrictions that streetwalkers do not have. House prostitutes who work as escorts seem to have the best deal. Although they have to split the take 50/50 with the house, there are better opportunities for receiving a fat tip from a satisfied customer after a good night out. There is a downside to escort work, though, as one prostitute explains: "You are very vulnerable in the client's room and have no control over the situation, which can be pretty frightening if things get nasty . . . you could be dead" (Perkins, 1991).

Call Girls.   Occupying the highest status in the sex business, call girls have been referred to as "the aristocrats of prostitution" (Greenwald, 1970). As befitting this title, they usually charge from several hundred dollars for each sexual intercourse to, occasionally, even more. Every year they can earn as much as or more than a successful lawyer or doctor. They are generally better educated or more sophisticated than other types of prostitutes. They dress expensively, and they live in affluent neighborhoods. Call girls are acutely aware of their high status and will feel insulted if they are treated like an ordinary streetwalker or brothel prostitute. In fact, many call girls will not apply the term *prostitute* to themselves.

It is typical for a call girl to wait for customers to telephone her. Initially she gets a few clients through other call girls and advertisements. Later, and more important, her previously satisfied clients often recommend her to their friends, so she often receives calls from prospective customers who say, "I'm a friend of so-and-so; he gave me your number." Many call girls do not use personal telephones, though. They receive their calls from an answering service or machine, and this is the number they give to their clients.

Compared to lower-paid prostitutes, the call girl tends more to dress in good taste rather than poorly or garishly. She is skilled in making her commercial transaction appear noncommercial by, for example, acting like her clients' girlfriend in public. She may adhere to a professional code of ethics. For example, if a client is a prominent person, she would not even mention his name in her conversation with other call girls. She would not steal from her customers or let them overpay her when they are drunk and thus temptingly exploitable. She would do her best to satisfy her clients, even in cases where a client has difficulty getting an erection.

Most call girls claim that they fare much better than housewives and women with legitimate employment. They crow that they can afford to live in style because of the huge sums of money they are making. They also contend that they have found fulfillment of their desire for independence in their profession: "The difference between being a prostitute and being a wife is the security a wife's got. But it's also the difference in having a lot of men versus having just one. If you have a lot of men—like if you have 10 a day—then you're not dependent on any one of them. They can always be replaced . . . that's the thing I wanted—never to be dependent" (Rosenblum, 1975). While it is easy to accept their claim to the big buck and high living, it is harder to agree with their claim to independence. This is because call girls are heavily dependent on their customers for the high income they get, which requires taking orders from customers. Even in the case of a masochistic client, who likes to follow orders himself, the call girl still has to follow *his* order to give him orders (Rosenblum, 1975).

Social and Sexual Backgrounds

According to sociologist Roberta Perkins (1991), many studies give a distorted picture of prostitutes as child-abuse victims, heavy drug users, victims of low self-esteem, or as being socially immature, emotionally disturbed, or pitifully abnormal in some other way. These studies are biased, Perkins contends, because they have focused mostly on adolescent streetwalkers or prostitutes who have been arrested by police or helped by social agencies. Such prostitutes indeed have more problems in their lives than other sex workers. But they are a minority, representing only about 5 to 30 percent of all prostitutes, and they differ significantly from most other prostitutes (Perkins, 1991).

The prostitutes in Perkins' study, however, are a reasonably representative sample of the women in the sex business. Although these prostitutes are Australians, they are comparable to their counterparts in the United States and other Western societies. Perkins found that most prostitutes do not differ significantly from conventional women in their social and sexual backgrounds. For example:

■ They have the same desire as conventional women to be married and have a traditional family life. Among those who already have young children, there is a plan to quit turning tricks when the children are old enough to begin catching on to their mothers' stigmatized occupation. As one prostitute says, "My oldest son will be 13 this year, and I don't want to be at work much after that."

■ Prostitutes have about the same level of education as the general population of women. The percentages of prostitutes having been brought up in white-collar and blue-collar families are similar to those of conventional women.

■ Most prostitutes are not friendless, loveless, or particularly "promiscuous" in their private lives. Like most women, they live with their husbands, lovers, or children, or share apartments with friends. But since their occupation is highly stigmatized, they are significantly more likely than other women to be raped.

Reasons for Becoming Prostitutes

According to public opinion, the common reasons for entering prostitution are drug addiction, severe poverty, low self-esteem, and emotional problems. Most of these reasons have to do with personal, social-psychological deficiencies. Such problems have indeed driven most teenage streetwalkers into prostitution, but these young hustlers differ from the large majority of prostitutes. Thus, when prostitutes in a representative sample were asked why they become prostitutes, a different set of reasons emerged. The most common reasons are economic, such as wanting to make more money, being unemployed, supporting a family, or paying for an education, an overseas trip, a car, or some other specific thing. Money, then, is the most important reason for going into the sex business. This is no different from the reasons that most other people have for working in conventional businesses.

Those economic reasons, however, merely serve as a predisposing factor in entering prostitution. They are not enough for a woman to become a prostitute—she needs to know something about the business before entering it. Necessary knowledge usually comes from an acquaintance, as illustrated by the following accounts from two prostitutes (Perkins, 1991):

■ I needed some money because I was having legal hassles and my present job wasn't bringing in enough to pay for this. A girlfriend of mine had an escort agency, and this seemed the quickest way to get the amount of money I needed.

■ I met an old school friend, and we had lunch together. She told me she was a prostitute, and how much money she made. She asked me if I would [go out with] her one night. But the fellows kept asking for me, not her. So, I thought, I must be sitting on a gold mine. And that's how I started.

The Threat of AIDS from Customers

Although they are more likely than others to be infected with the AIDS virus, prostitutes in the United States and other Western countries do not have as high an incidence of AIDS virus infection as popularly believed. In a massive national survey of prostitutes in the early 1990s, the U.S. Centers for Disease Control found that the incidence of being diagnosed with the AIDS virus varied from zero percent among the house prostitutes in Nevada to 6.2 percent in San Francisco. The incidence was considerably higher, though, among prostitutes who used drugs intravenously. Fifty-seven percent of the drug-using prostitutes in New Jersey, for example, had the AIDS virus (Perkins, 1991). These prostitutes obviously contract the deadly virus from intravenous drug use, not from sex with customers. Most other prostitutes do not get the AIDS virus, not only because they do not use drugs but also because they often practice safe sex by having their customers wear condoms (Jackson et al., 1992; Modan et al., 1992).

The use of condoms is particularly critical to prostitutes because women are 10 times more likely to get the AIDS virus from men than men are to get it from women. But in many poor countries, where women are far more oppressed, most men refuse to wear condoms when having sex with prostitutes because of the belief that condoms diminish the pleasure. Consequently, the percentages of prostitutes infected with the AIDS virus are much higher in many poor countries than in the United States (Kristof, 1996a; Shenon, 1996). Here is a typical case of how those prostitutes get infected with the deadly virus:

When Pon and Tai were 15, a woman showed up one day in their village in Burma, just across the Thai border. She promised to take the two girls on a sightseeing tour of Bangkok. When they got there she dropped them off at a brothel. They were locked up, and their virginity was quickly sold for $40. Soon, they were forced to service four or five customers a day—up to a dozen on weekends—without payment. Fearful of AIDS, about which they learned from Thai television, they offered to buy clients condoms out of their meager tip money. Most men refused. Now both girls have tested HIV-positive . . . Pon, now 17, says, "The men knew about AIDS but didn't care. They certainly didn't care about us." (Moreau, 1992)

Recently, however, many prostitutes in the poor, developing countries of Asia, Africa, and Latin America have begun to insist that their customers wear condoms. If the men refuse, they are sent away. But in order to avoid rejecting customers who refuse to use a condom, an increasing number of prostitutes in these countries have begun to use the female condom, which is still rarely used in the United States and other Western countries (McNeil, 1999; Dugger, 1999).

The Subculture of Prostitution

Like any other profession, prostitutes hold certain beliefs about themselves and their work. One belief is that prostitutes are morally superior to conventional people. This is because prostitutes see themselves as honest and others as dishonest. To prostitutes, conventional women who marry so they can depend on their husbands for lifelong financial support—especially the young women who marry wealthy older men—are, in effect, prostitutes, except that they are not honest enough to regard themselves as such. Prostitutes also see their so-called respectable customers as hypocrites. As one prostitute says, "We come into continual contact with upright, respected citizens whose voices are loudly raised against us in public, and yet who visit us in private" (Hirschi, 1962). If most customers do not publicly condemn prostitutes, they in essence cheat on their wives by patronizing prostitutes. Many prostitutes, therefore, despise their customers, and try to exploit them by maximizing the fee and minimizing the service. Such an attitude and behavior is common among streetwalkers and other low-paid prostitutes who immerse themselves in the prostitution subculture by associating only with one another. Other prostitutes are less contemptuous and exploitative toward their customers. They include call girls and other higher-priced prostitutes who are less alienated from conventional society because their circle of friends includes straight people. These prostitutes are more likely to accept another, more positive aspect of the prostitution subculture to be true.

The more positive aspect of the subculture is the belief that prostitution is good for society because it performs many important services. One service is believed to involve preventing sex crimes; as one prostitute puts it, "I believe that there should be more prostitution houses and what have you, and then we wouldn't have so many of these perverted idiots, sex maniacs, all sorts of weird people running around." Another service is believed to involve contributing to marital success: "I could say that a prostitute has held more marriages together as part of her profession than any divorce counselor . . . the release of talking about an unhappy home situation may well have saved many a marriage, and possibly even lives, when nerves have been strained to a breaking point." Prostitutes liken themselves not only to marriage counselors but also to humanitarians, social workers, psychologists, or psychiatrists. One prostitute explains, "I don't regret doing it because I feel I help people. A lot of men that come over to see me don't come over for sex. They come over for companionship, someone to talk to. . . . They talk about sex. . . . A lot of them have problems" (Bryan, 1966; Hirschi, 1962).

This professional self-image has fueled civil rights movements among prostitutes in Western societies. In Great Britain, for example, prostitutes have long campaigned against the laws that prohibit public solicitation, as in streets, hotels, and bars, arguing that peaceful soliciting should be as lawful as peaceful picketing (*The Economist*, 1979). In the United States, prostitutes have formed unions in various cities with the aim of decriminalizing prostitution so that their working conditions can be improved and their sex work can be respected like any other legitimate profession. The most famous prostitutes' rights organization is COYOTE (Call Off Your Tired Ethics). It fights for full decriminalization and the elimination of all legal restrictions on prostitution. COYOTE argues that prostitutes have the right to sell sex because selling sex is no different from other kinds of work women do:

> A woman has the right to sell sexual services just as much as she has the right to sell her brains to a law firm where she works as a lawyer, or to sell her creative work to a museum when she works as an artist, or to sell her image to a photographer when she works as a model, or to sell her body when she works as a ballerina. (Jenness, 1990)

COYOTE asserts that arresting or jailing prostitutes violates their civil rights, and that their sex work should be respected and protected like other legitimate professions. However, most feminists have rejected COYOTE's crusade to turn prostitution into a legitimate, respectable profession, because they consider prostitution a form of sexual slavery—which they want prostitutes to get out of, not into. COYOTE has also failed to get support from most of the general public, legislators, and law enforcers (Weitzer, 1991).

Other Participants in Prostitution

Aside from prostitutes, three other kinds of people are involved in the so-called skin trade. They are the madam, the pimp, and the customer.

The Madam. The general public uses the term *madam* to refer to the owner or manager of a brothel; brothel owners themselves call one another "landlady." Most are former prostitutes with a great deal of experience "in the life" behind them. They run their establishments in about the same way as legitimate businesspeople run theirs, except that they must deal with problems arising from the illegal nature of their trade. There are three major forms of activities that the madam characteristically engages in. The first has to do with the employees, the second the customers, and the third the police.

The madam recruits her prostitutes largely through her current employees, but also from pimps and other madams. She trains the new employee to be clean, develop social skills, and observe such old customs of prostitution as asking for payment before giving the sexual service and refraining from getting emotionally involved or spending too much time with a customer. After the employees become professional, the madam supervises their work, keeps them happy, prevents quarrels and jealousy among them, and makes and enforces rules governing their behavior. The nature of her work is such that she usually functions as if she were the employees' mother. Some madams even insist that they are in effect running a charm school—where they teach social graces (*Time*, 1980).

The madam is responsible for finding customers. She keeps a "john book," which contains the customers' names and telephone numbers; she uses it when there is not much business in the house. Usually, customers call her. The madam's main concern is to make the client happy so that he will become a regular visitor. This means, among other things, that she has to find and hire new women constantly, because it is the variety of women that many customers look for in prostitution.

To avoid arrest, the madam must know how to deal with the police. She is usually skilled in recognizing a police officer disguised as a customer. As one madam says, albeit boastfully, "I could spot a copper a mile away—if I don't see him I can smell him" (Winick and Kinsie, 1971). Nonetheless, madams often have to work out some stable arrangements with the law officers. One arrangement involves bribing them. But more often the madam develops an understanding with the police that they will go through the motion of arresting her every now and then—thereby keeping up the appearance of performing their duty to appease the public's moral outrage against prostitution—while allowing her to continue her business. If all this cannot be done, a madam would ask her employees to wait for her calls at their own residences. Such a madam essentially runs a "call house"—euphemistically referred to in the sex business as "escort agency"—by maintaining a list of prostitutes on call. She simply sits by a telephone, gets calls from customers, and then sends prostitutes to customers, or sends customers to prostitutes, or arranges for both to meet in some other place.

The Pimp.   Many of the prostitutes who do not work for a madam work for a pimp. While the madam gets a large portion—usually about half—of her employees' earnings, the pimp typically gets all of them. Also, unlike the madam, who has to find customers for her prostitutes, the pimp generally just tells his prostitutes to go out in the street and hustle. He does not want to be bothered with the details of their working life. The pimp, then, is *not* what many dictionaries say he is— "a pander, a procurer, or a man who solicits customers for a prostitute in return for a share of the proceeds." Rather, he is simply a man who lives off the entire proceeds of one or more prostitutes. For this reason, most people in conventional society would consider him "the lowest of the low."

A pimp may have anywhere from one to twenty women, his "stable," but most pimps have only one or two women. Pimps and their stables live in a subculture that is in many ways the opposite of conventional culture. In the pimping subculture, men are extremely dominant, women are extremely submissive, and the ideal union is between a black man and several white women. Also, the men are obsessed with their own appearance, spending many hours a day on their hair, clothes, and jewelry in order to make themselves look beautiful. The women, who consider themselves "wives-in-law," are the real economic providers, working hard to support the household. Since the women routinely have sex with other men—their customers— paternity of their children often comes from outside the subcultural group. In this subculture, then, men are expected to demonstrate great style and creativity in the way they dress and groom themselves; women generally sleep during the day and work at night; money is worshiped as a god; conspicuous consumption is indulged in every day; and there is little concern for future security (Milner and Milner, 1972).

The pimp often resorts to violence to control his women. As a former prostitute says, "I saw a girl walk into a bar and hand the pimp a $100 bill. He took it and burned it in her face and turned around and knocked her down on the floor and kicked her and said, 'I told you, bitch, $200. I want $200, not $100.' Now she's gotta go out again and make not another hundred, but two hundred" (Millett, 1973). The pimp's violent method of controlling his women is apparently effective. According to one study, over 50 percent of the prostitutes who had been beaten by their pimps "accepted it as a way of life, felt they deserved it, or were flattered by it as a sign of caring" (Caplan, 1984; Silbert and Pines, 1981). According to another study, a pimp's women generally worship him as if he were a god. They invest in him all their hopes, dreams, and goals for the future. They wear his beatings proudly as symbols of his love. Everything that he does to them is considered right, proper, or admirable. When a prostitute was asked what her pimp did to deserve all her earnings, she replied, "He doesn't do *nothing*. But the way he does nothing is *beautiful*" (Sheehy, 1971). In short, as Kathleen Barry (1995) suggests, the prostitutes are so emotionally entangled with their pimp that they cannot see themselves being controlled by him.

The John.   In the argot of the sex trade, the prostitute's customer is called "john" or "trick." Research has shown that men who have slept with different women are more likely than monogamous men to become a john (Pitts et al., 2004; Michael et al., 1994). If sexually active men can get sex with conventional women for free, why would they want to buy sex from prostitutes? One reason, according to feminists, is that prostitution gives the customer the benefit of being a sexual master and the prostitute his sexual servant. As one prostitute says, "What they're buying, in a way, is power. You're supposed to please them. They can tell you what to do, and you're supposed to please them, follow their orders" (Overall, 1992). In this structure of power inequality between the sexes, the johns are, in effect, the prostitute's oppressors or victimizers.

Men also have other reasons for buying sex (Pitts et al., 2004; Winick and Kinsie, 1971; Benjamin and Masters, 1964). First is the desire to get quick, easy sex. Finding a willing woman for sex requires time, effort, or ability. There are men who do not have the time to find such a woman, particularly if they are too busy pursuing a career or if they are strangers in a city far away from their wives or girlfriends. There are also men who simply want to have sex—not conversation, not companionship, not cultivation of friendship or love. For these individuals, the ritual of dating—taking a woman to a restaurant, a movie, a bar, and possibly a bedroom—demands too much effort. They prefer a prostitute from whom they can effortlessly get what they want. There are yet other men who are too shy or are otherwise lacking the ability to attract and persuade a woman to go to bed with them. For such men, a prostitute can be easily gotten without risking rejection.

A second reason for going to a prostitute is the desire to get *untangled sex*. There are men who do not want to get seriously involved with women. They want to dodge emotional entanglements, obligations, or interpersonal conflict. More specifically, they want to avoid getting entangled with a woman in courtship or marriage; avoid being obligated to her if she becomes pregnant; or avoid the risk of breaking up a marriage—their own or the woman's if she is married. What these men want is impersonal, untangled sex, which can free them from the conventional strictures regarding the responsibility of sex. Sex of this kind is characteristically available from the prostitute. Here's how a john describes the straightforward, no-strings-attached sex: "I like the basic rawness of it . . . the basic honesty of it. There's a lot of honesty in that. You girl, me have sexual desire, you have the object of my sexual desire, me give you money, you give me what I want, no bullshit, no play, no games. . . . It's raw, honest, and it's good" (Holzman and Pines, 1982).

A third reason for patronizing prostitutes is the desire to get a *variety of sexual experiences.* There are men who want to have sex with a variety of women rather than with the same one only. Some men may want to engage in certain types of sex, such as oral sex, anal sex, or sadomasochistic sex, that turn off their wives or girlfriends. All these needs can be easily met with a visit to prostitutes.

The majority of the men who buy sex are *occasional johns,* while a few are *habitual* and *compulsive johns* (Greenwald, 1970). Occasional johns, who buy sex only occasionally, are psychologically normal. They are hardly different from most men who do not visit prostitutes (Pitts et al., 2004). But habitual and compulsive johns are less normal. Habitual johns want to get emotionally attached to one special prostitute. They are fond of asking the prostitute many questions, telling her about their lives, offering to help her in whatever way they can, or trying to make her enjoy having sex with them. Compulsive johns also seem a little abnormal: They cannot keep away from prostitutes. Generally, compulsive johns feel that sex is dirty and would not want to defile a "good" woman, so that they will copulate only with "bad" ones—namely, prostitutes. Some compulsive johns can be sexually potent only with prostitutes; they cannot have an erection with their wives or other conventional women.

Societal Reaction to Prostitution

In ancient civilizations, prostitution was not condemned as evil. It was even considered sacred by some religious sects, so that only priestesses had the privilege to practice it. Nowadays, it is regarded as an evil in virtually all societies; but in most societies, it is recognized as an evil that cannot be eradicated. Consequently, one of two situations usually prevails: (1) prostitution is legal but public solicitation for it is not, as is the case in many European and Asian countries (Davis, 1993), or (2) prostitution is illegal but the law is not strictly enforced, as is the case in the United States.

Before the turn of this century, prostitution was illegal but practiced openly in the United States, particularly in the Wild West, where prostitutes were as much a part of the new frontier as miners, cowboys, town preachers, and small merchants. In the early part of the twentieth century, various organizations, such as the YMCA and the American Purity Alliance, mounted an increasingly powerful campaign against prostitution. These vice crusaders eventually won; most brothels that had openly operated were closed down by the mid-1940s. Today, the few houses that continue to do business openly exist in several sparsely populated counties of Nevada, where prostitution is legal. In other parts of the country, where prostitution is not legal, the majority of prostitutes find their customers outside the house. The streetwalkers, who bear the brunt of law enforcement against prostitution, are periodically arrested. Soon after they pay a fine in court or are released from jail, however, they go right back to hustling on the street.

If prostitution is so tough to wipe out, why bother trying to enforce the antiprostitution laws? Conservatives have over the years developed the following rationales for the continued attempt at enforcement: (1) Prostitution often brings about mugging, robbery, or assault. (2) Prostitution provides a breeding ground for organized crime activities. (3) Prostitution helps spread the AIDS virus and other sexually transmitted diseases. (4) Prostitution often subjects innocent citizens to offensive public solicitation. (5) Prostitution is destructive to public morals, which enforcement of the laws helps to preserve (Bryant, 1977). Many feminists also condemn prostitution as degrading to women, robbing them of their dignity and worth as human beings. One feminist regards prostitution as "female sexual slavery" because she believes that most prostitutes, being controlled by pimps, cannot get out of it (Barry, 1995; Farley, 1994).

On the other hand, liberals have argued for the legalization of prostitution. They contend that most problems associated with prostitution stem largely from antiprostitution laws themselves. Treated as criminals, prostitutes are bound to operate secretly and stay as far away from the watchful eye of the law as possible. As a result, they and their customers are likely to commit crime against each other or transmit VD (venereal diseases) or AIDS to each other. If prostitution is legalized, liberals argue, those problems will disappear because specific statutes can be enacted to control prostitutes' activities. Prostitutes will be required to undergo regular medical checkups, be made to confine their business activities within a specified area, or be prohibited from soliciting on the street. Some liberals also argue that antiprostitution laws do not necessarily uphold national moral standards but instead encourage corruption among the police as well as moral hypocrisy and disrespect for the law among the general public. It is further argued that it costs too much to prosecute prostitutes and that precious law-enforcement efforts would be better employed against more serious crimes (*The Economist*, 2004; Quindlen, 1994).

The general public favors the conservative position over the liberal one. According to a survey, when Americans were asked whether they support or oppose the legalization of prostitution, 72 percent said "oppose" and only 23 percent said "support." Another survey also found significantly more people who want the current antiprostitution laws strictly enforced (Weitzer, 2000, 1991). However, no matter how strictly enforced the laws are, prostitution cannot be eradicated because of the substantial demand for it on the part of large numbers of ordinary men.

Global Perspective: Prostitution

Due to the poor economic condition after the collapse of the Soviet Union, many unemployed women in Russia and Eastern Europe have drifted into Western Europe and other prosperous countries to sell sex. In Germany, today, at least a quarter of the prostitutes originate from the former Communist world. In Israel, many newspaper ads offering "entertainment services" brag about "hot new Russians." In Japan, blond and blue-eyed Russian women have become the latest addition to fancy "hostess" bars. Even in deeply religious Saudi Arabia, many Russian women have arrived to work as prostitutes. Some of these women have chosen to enter the skin trade. But most have been forced into it after arriving in those foreign countries with phony promises of singing, dancing, modeling, or waitressing jobs—the promises having been given earlier by pimps or mafia-style criminals posing as businessmen in their home countries.

Many prostitutes in those prosperous countries have also come from Latin America. Most of these women also have been tricked and coerced into prostitution. They are offered legitimate-sounding jobs overseas, such as working in a night club. They are then given money for visas and airline tickets as well as cash to pass as tourists to immigration authorities. Once abroad, they are forced to work as prostitutes to pay a huge fee. Smuggling women this way has become attractive to organized criminals, who find it easier and cheaper than trafficking drugs and arms.

Many more poor women in Asia have also been lured into Western Europe, the United States, and Japan with promises of legitimate jobs only to be sold to brothels. Most of the Asian prostitutes, however, ply their trade in their home countries. Some of these women have come from poor villages to work in large cities and then are forced into prostitution. Others choose to sell their bodies. They all cater to not only local men but also hordes of Japanese and Western male tourists who come to the poor Asian countries primarily or solely for sex. In fact, prostitution has become a major component of those Asian countries' tourist industry, which represents a significant sector of their national economy.

One key factor behind the prevalence of prostitution in Asia is *abject poverty* in its rural areas. As Manju, a Nepalese prostitute in India, said, "Even if you work 24 hours a day in Nepal, you do not get enough to eat. One can endure anything except hunger. If I were a man, maybe I would have committed murder to fill my stomach. But as a woman, I became a prostitute." The rural poverty may have partly resulted from globalization. For example, large U.S. agribusinesses such as Dole and Del Monte have used up a massive expanse of farmland in the Philippines to plant pineapples and bananas for export, which drove many peasants out of their farms and caused widespread poverty. Another factor behind the prevalence of prostitution in Asia is *patriarchy*, the social and cultural system of men's domination over women. It forces poor women to sell their bodies as commodities while encouraging men to exploit them.

Sources: Wonders and Michalowski, 2004; Pratt, 2001; Pristina and Chisinau, 2001; Kuo, 2001; Hornblower, 1993.

Theories of Prostitution

There are at least three positivist theories about prostitution: functionalist, feminist, and social-psychological theories. Functionalist and feminist theories focus on prostitution, explaining why prostitution exists despite efforts to eradicate it. But social-psychological theory zeroes in on the individual prostitute, explaining why some women are more likely than others to become prostitutes.

Functionalist Theory

According to sociologist Kingsley Davis (1971), there are two reasons why prostitution exists. The first is the very system of *sexual morality* that ostensibly condemns prostitution but unintendedly or ironically causes prostitution to exist as a social institution. The moral system causes prostitution by creating advantages for it in at least two ways. First, the moral system divides sex into two types: Sex with one's spouse is part of a "meaningful" relationship and sex with a prostitute is "meaningless." This has the effect of encouraging men to go to a prostitute if they want to have "meaningless" sex. Second, by defining certain sex acts such as oral or anal sex as immoral and hence not to be indulged in with one's "moral" wife or girlfriend, the moral order encourages men to turn to "immoral" women—namely, prostitutes—for these sex acts. The moral system, in effect, creates a demand for prostitution.

Another reason for the existence of prostitution is also ironic: *prostitution's function of strengthening sexual morality.* More specifically, prostitution exists because it serves to strengthen sexual morality by "keeping the wives and daughters of the respectable citizenry pure" (Davis, 1971). In other words, the sex industry encourages men to go to prostitutes for premarital sex, extramarital sex, or other "immoral" sex so that they do not have to persuade or pressure "respectable" women to engage in the same "immoral" sex. By thus preserving the sexual morality of conventional women, who constitute nearly half of humankind, the level of a society's morality should be higher than if many women engage in the same sexual "immoralities" as prostitutes and men do.

In short, Davis's theory suggests that prostitution exists because the moral system paradoxically encourages it, and it in turn serves the important function of protecting "feminine virtue." This theory runs counter to the popular belief that "an evil such as prostitution cannot cause a good such as feminine virtue, or vice versa" (Davis, 1971).

There is some evidence to support the theory. In traditional Asian societies where prostitution is prevalent, "respectable" women are relatively unlikely to engage in "immoral" sex, while in modern Western societies where prostitution is less common, "respectable" women are more likely to get involved in "immoral" sex. Also, on many U.S. campuses, male students are more likely to think of having sex with college women than with prostitutes, so that they are more likely than their counterparts in Thailand to persuade or pressure college women to engage in premarital sex. There is, however, a basic problem with functionalist theory. It defines sexual morality and feminine virtue in sexist terms, implying that only women, particularly prostitutes, are immoral and virtueless when committing "meaningless" or "immoral" sex. That's why functionalist theory does *not* regard sexually "promiscuous" men, especially those who often patronize prostitutes, as a threat to the moral order.

Feminist Theory

To feminists, functionalist theory merely reflects a sexist society's view that "promiscuous" men are not a threat to the moral order, only "promiscuous" women such as prostitutes are. This explains why in a sexist society prostitutes are far more likely to be arrested than their male customers for committing the same sexual act. But why are "promiscuous" men not considered a threat to the moral order in the first place? Because the moral system reflects the larger patriarchal, gender-stratified system in which men dominate and exploit women.

According to feminist theory, the patriarchal system encourages prostitution by creating both demand and supply for it. On the demand side, boys are socialized under the influence of patriarchy to be dominant over girls, and when boys become adults, they are expected to desire sexual domination of women, which can be easily realized through sex with prostitutes. If a young man does not want to visit a prostitute, his peers will pressure him to do so, as we have observed in regard to college men in Thailand. On the supply side, girls are socialized to be submissive to boys and, later as adults, to men in work, play, or sex. At the same time, women are relegated to predominantly low-status employment, including prostitution. All this explains why prostitution is usually more prevalent in traditional societies marked by great gender inequality, when compared with more modern societies with less gender inequality.

While the patriarchal system with its gender inequality encourages prostitution, prostitution in turn reinforces patriarchy. Some feminists have observed that prostitution "serves to perpetuate women's social subordination" (Overall, 1992) or "perpetuates socially hegemonic belief which oppresses all women in many domains of their lives" (Miller, 1991). In other words, by selling their bodies as a commodity, prostitutes convey the message that women can be bought or used as an object. This directly reinforces the prevailing patriarchal "notion that all women are whores at heart; all women have a price" (Overall, 1992). Consequently, many men, for example, find this sexist joke funny: A man asks a woman, "Would you sleep with me for a million dollars?" The woman answers, "I guess I would." Then the man asks, "Would you sleep with me for five dollars?" The woman turns angry, saying, "What do you take me for?" But the man responds, "We've already established that; now we're just negotiating your price" (Overall, 1992). Learning from prostitutes that women can be bought like an object, as implied in this joke, many men will continue to support the patriarchal structure of gender inequality, which in turn encourages prostitution.

Social Psychological Theory

According to this theory, a combination of social and psychological factors causes some women to become prostitutes. These factors include the following:

- *Predisposing* factors—exemplified by such unpleasant experiences as struggling with parental "promiscuity," parental neglect, child abuse, or other traumatic events that cause psychological problems.

- *Attracting* factors—exemplified by the expectation based on popular belief that a woman can have an easy life or lots of money as a prostitute.

- *Precipitating* factors—exemplified by such social situations as being unemployed, meeting a prostitute friend, or being pressured by a pimp to sell sex (Brown, 1979; Benjamin and Masters, 1964).

Most psychologists and psychiatrists stress the predisposing factors as the key to entering prostitution. According to Harold Greenwald (1970), for example, prostitutes sell their sexual service because they have suffered parental neglect, rejection, or abuse in childhood and consequently have developed such abnormal symptoms as feelings of loneliness and unworthiness, lack of self-control, and inability to establish stable relations with others. This implies that a woman must be psychologically abnormal to become a prostitute.

From the sociological perspective, however, we need not assume that prostitutes are abnormal even if they have been abused by their parents. It seems largely a matter of emotional socialization that teaches the victim to be a normal prostitute, one who is able to detach herself emotionally from her johns. This is because parental abuse teaches the victim to detach herself emotionally from her parent and, by extension, anyone who treats her like an object in the same way as her parent does. With this emotional detachment, the victim may later find it easier to enter into prostitution, detaching herself emotionally from her customers, who in a way treat her as her abusive father has done, that is, as an object. In short, some women are more likely than others to become prostitutes not because they are abnormal, but because they are *normal* for being able to withhold affection from their customers in the same way as a normal child-abuse victim withholds affection from her parent. But this capacity for emotional detachment may only *predispose* a woman toward entering prostitution; it is not enough to cause her to sell sex. She is more likely to do so if the attracting and precipitating factors also appear in her experience, as has been suggested by the theory and some research (Perkins, 1991).

Summary

1. How does U.S. society view teenage sex? Most Americans consider teen sex unacceptable, apparently because of the presumption that teenagers are still not mature enough to handle sex responsibly. **Do teenagers conform to the society's expectation that they refrain from sex?** No. They are instead more sexually active than before. They also engage in oral sex more, which they do not see as real sex. But girls with high self-esteem are less likely to have sex, though boys with high self-esteem are more likely.

2. What are the myths about extramarital sex? One myth is that extramarital sex is more exciting or satisfying than marital sex. Another myth is that people have affairs because they are oversexed. **How does adultery vary from one culture to another?** Adultery is socially approved in some societies but not so in others. Legitimate adultery varies in form from one culture to another and so does illegitimate adultery. **Which groups of Americans are more likely than others to engage in extramarital sex?** The groups that are more likely to have an affair include men, the less religious, and lower-income persons.

3. How big is the pornography industry today? It has grown to be an enormous industry today, much more profitable than all the Hollywood movies distributed in the United States. **What are the effects of pornography?** Some argue that pornography is harmful, but others say it is harmless. Evidence suggests that while the erotic, nonviolent type of pornography is generally harmless, the violent type is harmful.

4. Why do some people engage in Internet sex? The reasons include being anonymous, the ease and convenience of finding sex partners online, being able to share sexual fantasies and turn them into realities, and seeking real sex with partners that one has met online. **What is cyberporn?** Cyberporn is sexually explicit material accessible via the Internet. It has become very popular today, and some parents fear that their children will be exposed to cyberporn. But there are ways to block children's access to it. **What is the social profile of cyberporn surfers?** Porn surfers are mostly over 30, married, white, and middle-class men. They tend to access cyberporn during work hours. Internet child porn consumers have about the same demographic backgrounds as porn surfers in general, but they are mostly pedophiles who like to use the porn for masturbation and collection.

5. Why do some men call the phone sex line? They want the phone sex operator to fulfill their sexual fantasies for one of five reasons: they are requesting quick sex, expressing anger, seeking love, demanding sex for oneself only, and being curious about the phone sex. **What is nude dancing all about?** In nude dancing the performer takes off all her clothes and shows customers her genitalia to encourage them to tip her generously. Most customers are working-class men who expect nude dancers to fulfill their sexual fantasies. The dancers make a relatively large amount of money and find their job disreputable but empowering.

6. **What is sexual harassment?** It is an unwelcome act of a sexual nature, but if it involves workers it means, according to the U.S. Supreme Court, any conduct that makes the workplace environment so hostile that the victim finds it harder to perform her job. **What causes sexual harassment?** An apparent cause is the threat posed by women to male dominance, which may explain why sexual harassment often occurs in traditionally and heavily male-dominated occupations.

7. **What are the popular myths about prostitutes?** The myths are that prostitutes are nymphomaniacs, that they are sexually frigid, that they are nasty and hard-hearted or sweet and warmhearted, that they are mostly drug addicts, and that they have been sexually abused as children. **Are all prostitutes largely the same?** No, there are many different types of prostitutes. They include—in ascending order of status, price, or life quality—streetwalkers, child and adolescent prostitutes, house prostitutes, and call girls.

8. **What kinds of backgrounds do prostitutes come from?** Most prostitutes have about the same social and sexual backgrounds as conventional women, desiring marriage and traditional family life, having the same level of education as other women, and being not particularly "promiscuous" in their private lives. **What have been their reasons for becoming prostitutes?** The most common reasons are economic, such as wanting to make more money, being unemployed, or supporting a family. **Are prostitutes very liable to get AIDS?** Yes, but prostitutes in Western countries are far less

likely than those in Third World countries to get the disease because condoms are often used. **What is the subculture of prostitution?** Prostitutes believe that they are morally superior to straights and that their so-called respectable customers are hypocrites. Prostitutes also regard their work as good for society because they compare it to the service rendered by a marriage counselor, social worker, or some other helping profession.

9. **Who are the prostitute's coparticipants in prostitution?** They include madams, pimps, and johns. The madam is a brothel owner or manager who employs prostitutes to serve her customers. The pimp is primarily the prostitute's nonworking lover or husband, who often uses violence to keep her under his thumb. The john visits prostitutes to enjoy being a sexual master or to seek quick and easy sex, untangled sex, and sexual variety. **How do conservatives and liberals want to deal with prostitution?** Conservatives want strong enforcement of antiprostitution laws, believing that prostitution causes many problems, such as crime and disease. Liberals want to legalize prostitution, arguing that legalized prostitution can be more effectively controlled and that the very problems currently associated with illegal prostitution will disappear.

10. **How does prostitution vary from one society to another?** Prostitution in Eastern Europe is more likely than in the West to have resulted from young women being tricked or forced into the skin trade. Asian and Latin American prostitutes are also more likely to have the same experience. In Asia, prostitution is a significant part of the tourist industry, and it thrives from abject poverty and patriarchy.

11. **How do various theories explain prostitution?** According to functionalist theory, prostitution exists because it is encouraged

by society's system of sexual morality and prostitution in turn serves the function of strengthening sexual morality. According to feminist theory, the patriarchal system encourages prostitution by creating demand and supply for it, and prostitution in turn reinforces the patriarchal structure of gender inequality. Social psychological theory offers three factors—predisposing, attracting, and precipitating factors—to explain why some women are more likely than others to become prostitutes.

FURTHER READING

Barry, Kathleen. 1995. *The Prostitution of Sexuality.* New York: New York University Press. An analysis of how prostitution represents the essence of sexual exploitation that serves to oppress womankind.

Bruckert, Chris. 2002. *Taking It Off, Putting It On: Women in the Strip Trade.* Toronto: Women's Press. A sociological analysis of nude dancing based on interviews with fifteen strippers, illustrating the feminist theory that emphasizes the agency, or power, rather than helplessness of women in this deviant career.

Christopher, F. Scott. 2001. *To Dance the Dance: A Symbolic Interactional Exploration of Premarital Sexuality.* Mahwah, N.J.: Lawrence Erlbaum Associates. Discusses the nature of premarital sex among various age groups.

Clift, Stephen, and Simon Carter (eds.). 2000. *Tourism and Sex: Culture, Commerce and Coercion.* London: Pinter. A collection of articles on various dimensions of sex tourism in different cities around the world.

Crouch, Margaret A. 2001. *Thinking about Sexual Harassment: A Guide for the Perplexed.* New York: Oxford University Press. A historical, theoretical, and empirical analysis of sexual harassment.

Davis, Nanette J. (ed.). 1993. *Prostitution: An International Handbook on Trends, Problems, and Policies.* Westport, Conn.: Greenwood. A collection of articles on the problems of prostitution in various countries, showing the importance of outlawing and abolishing the sex business.

Duncombe, Jean et al. (eds.). 2004. *The State of Affairs: Explorations in Infidelity and Commitment.* Mahwah, N.J.: Lawrence Erlbaum Associates. A collection of articles covering the interpersonal, social, and cultural aspects of marital infidelity from different perspectives.

Fisher, Helen E. 1992. *Anatomy of Love: The Natural History of Monogamy, Adultery, and Divorce.* New York: Norton. A sociobiological attempt to explain the universality of adultery, though providing data on cultural differences in form and frequency of adultery.

Flowers, Amy. 1998. *The Fantasy Factory: An Insider's View of the Phone Sex Industry.* Philadelphia: University of Pennsylvania Press. Using participant observation, the author studies the operation of a phone sex company and interviews its employees.

Gibson, Pamela Church, and Roma Gibson (eds.). 1993. *Dirty Looks: Women, Pornography, Power.* London: British Film Institute. A volume of articles that deal mostly with nonviolent, erotic pornography, showing the harmlessness of pornography and the harmfulness of censorship.

Gregory, Raymond F. 2004. *Unwelcome and Unlawful: Sexual Harassment in the American Workplace.* Ithaca, N.Y.: Cornell University Press. A thorough analysis of sexual harassment of women by men, harassment of men by women, and same-sex harassment.

Hicks, George. 1995. *The Comfort Women: Japan's Brutal Regime of Enforced Prostitution in the Second World War.* New York: Norton. A documentation of how the Japanese army forced massive numbers of young women in Korea, China, and other Asian countries to become sex slaves for Japanese soldiers.

Irvine, Janice M. 2002. *Talk about Sex: The Battles over Sex Education in the United States.* Berkeley: University of California Press. An analysis of the clash between professional sex education advocates and the politicized Christian conservatives.

Jenkins, Philip. 2001. *Beyond Tolerance: Child Pornography on the Internet.* New York: New York University Press. Discussing the nature of Internet child porn and society's reactions to it.

Jenness, Valerie. 1993. *Making It Work: The Prostitutes' Rights Movement in Perspective.* Hawthorne, N.Y.: Aldine de Gruyter. An analysis of how the prostitutes' rights movement attempts to have prostitution publicly recognized as freely chosen work so that it can be decriminalized.

Linz, Daniel, and Neil Malamuth. 1993. *Pornography.* Newbury Park, Calif.: Sage Publications. Presenting the conservative, liberal, and feminist views of pornography as well as the data employed to support them.

O'Donohue, William (ed.). 1997. *Sexual Harassment: Theory, Research, and Treatment.* Boston: Allyn and Bacon. A series of articles dealing with many different issues about sexual harassment, including the legal concepts, epidemiology, theories, effects, and prevention of such deviant behavior.

Procida, Richard, and Rita J. Simon. 2003. *Global Perspectives on Social Issues: Pornography.* Lanham, Md.: Lexington Books. Presents diverse societal reactions to pornography in North America, Australia, Western and Eastern Europe, Asia, and Africa.

Ryan, Chris, and C. Michael Hall. 2001. *Sex Tourism: Marginal People and Liminalities.* London: Routledge. Discusses the history of sex tourism, the interactions between sex workers and tourists, and the relationship between sexual slavery and sex tourism.

Sturdevant, Saundra Pollock, and Brenda Stoltzfus. 1992. *Let the Good Times Roll: Prostitution and the U.S. Military in Asia.* New York: The New Press. Analyzing the oppressive life and work of bar girls in the Philippines, South Korea, and Okinawa under the dehumanizing shadow of the U.S. military.

Weitzer, Ronald (ed.). 2000. *Sex for Sale: Prostitution, Pornography, and the Sex Industry.* New York: Routledge. A collection of articles on various aspects of the sex industry, from the perspectives of sex workers and their customers to prostitutes as victims and the social control of sex work.

CRITICAL THINKING QUESTIONS

1. Do you approve of teen sex? Do you find adults' objection to teen sex justifiable? Defend the position you take on this issue.

2. Are phone sex and nude dancing harmful to young people? If yes, how and why are they harmful? If not, how can they be beneficial and why?

CHAPTER

10 Gays and Other Victims of Stigma

Gary and Greg, a gay couple both in their thirties, are known to neighbors in a small, fairly conservative town in central Pennsylvania simply as "the guys." They call each other "honey" in the stores, and their straight friends call them "uncle" and "uncle." At their offices, their straight coworkers seem more familiar with gay issues than the gay couple themselves. As Gary says, "They realize we have the same worries they do. Now in tax season, they'll say, "That sucks, you can't put Greg on your return." All this friendliness shown by straights to Gary and Greg in a conservative town represents significant progress in U.S. attitudes toward gays. Now, for the first time in U.S. history, only a minority (46 percent) of Americans consider homosexuality a sin. But at the same time, a majority (57 percent) are still opposed to gay marriage, while more than 32 states have passed new laws banning same-sex marriages (Leland, 2000). In this new century, then, U.S. society still has a long way to go toward treating gays the same as straights.

The continuing rejection of gays suggests that homosexuality is still a *social stigma,* something a person has or does that others see as bad in some way. A stigma is practically the same as deviance, so that all the deviances discussed in this text can be considered stigmas. It is a stigma to be a prostitute, a mental patient, a suicide, a child abuser, a murderer, a rapist, and so on. Some of these stigmas are *justifiable.* Murderers, rapists, and other nasty criminals, for example, deserve to get what is coming to them. But most stigmas are *unjustifiable* because people such as gays and lesbians, suicides, mental patients, the obese, and the tattooed do not hurt others, and yet they are stigmatized—punished as victims of stigma. In this chapter we will focus on gays and lesbians as well as other victims of unjustifiable stigma, including bisexuals, transgenderists, people with physical disabilities, the obese, and the tattooed. By studying these people as victims of stigma, we may get a clearer understanding of how and why conventional society treats them as deviants and how they react.

Myths about Homosexuality

According to one popular myth, gay men are typically effeminate and lesbians masculine. Gays are believed to walk like women, talk like women, or look like women, and lesbians are believed to walk, talk, or look like men. In reality it is difficult to differentiate most gays and lesbians from straights. Most gays look and behave just like most heterosexual men, and most lesbians look and behave just like most heterosexual women (Marcus, 1993; Dunkle and Francis, 1990).

A second myth is that gay men like to molest or seduce young children. The fact is that the great majority of gay men have no more sexual interest in young boys than the great majority of straight men have in little girls. Actually, most child molesters are male *heterosexuals.* For one year, between 1991 and 1992, at the Children's Hospital in Denver, Colorado, there were 387 cases of suspected child molestation. Only one perpetrator was gay; all the rest were heterosexual men (Marcus, 1993).

A third myth is that gays and lesbians consistently play one specific role—either as an active or passive partner—in their sexual activities. The active partner is assumed to perform oral sex on the passive partner. The truth is that most gays and lesbians engage in a lot of alternation between those two roles. Same-sex couples are also popularly expected to behave like traditional couples, one mate playing the role of dominant husband, the other the submissive wife. Again the reality is quite different: Partners in a same-sex relationship often resemble best friends, who, being equal, "share and share alike" so that *both* may cook, make money, or disclose deep feelings (Peplau, 1981).

According to a fourth myth, same-sex orientation is a symptom of mental illness. Some gays and lesbians, particularly those who go to psychiatrists, are perhaps emotionally disturbed, but so are some straights, especially those who go to psychiatrists. Therefore, just as it is wrong to conclude that straights are mentally ill, it is wrong to conclude that lesbians and gays are. This is one reason why the American Psychiatric Association has, since 1973, removed "homosexuality" from its *Diagnostic and Statistical Manual* as a mental illness. There are still some psychiatrists, psychoanalysts, and psychologists, though, who continue to believe that same-sex orientation is a mental illness that can be cured (Socarides et al., 1997).

A fifth myth is that lesbians and gays cannot be expected to have a satisfactory sex life because it is abnormal or unnatural. Research, however, has shown no real difference between gays/lesbians and straights in their physical capacity to enjoy sex. The basic difference involves styles of making love. Same-sex couples tend to treat sex as play, spending much time on foreplay—focusing on kissing and caressing various parts of the body—before directing attention specifically to genitals for reaching orgasm. Heterosexual couples are more likely to treat sex as work, bent on a quick attainment of orgasm (Masters and Johnson, 1979).

According to a sixth myth, gays and lesbians are obsessed with sex, having sex all the time. In reality, gay men have about as much sex as their heterosexual peers—two or three times a week. As for lesbians, they seem less interested in sex when compared to heterosexual women: no more than once a week for lesbians but two or three times a week for married heterosexual women (Blumstein and Schwartz, 1990).

Finally, a seventh myth suggests that most people are either completely gay or completely straight. In reality, as biologist-turned-sexologist Alfred Kinsey (1948) wrote,

> [People] do not represent two discrete populations, heterosexual and homosexual. The world is not to be divided into sheep and goats. . . . It is a fundamental of taxonomy that nature rarely deals with discrete categories. Only the human mind invents categories and tries to force facts into separate pigeon holes. The living world is a continuum in each and every one of its aspects.

The difference between the sexes is mostly a matter of *kind:* People are either male or female. But the difference between sexual orientations is a matter of *degree:* Some people are more, or less, heterosexual (or homosexual) than others. Thus Kinsey assigned people varying positions on a scale from one extreme of being exclusively heterosexual to the other extreme of being exclusively homosexual (see Figure 10.1).

Gays and Lesbians

Exclusively homosexual men and women are called gays and lesbians. In this section we will discuss how many they are, what they are like, how they "come out" (reveal to others their sexual orientation), their lifestyles, and various theories about why some people become homosexuals.

FIGURE 10.1 The Kinsey Heterosexual-Homosexual Continuum

Source: Adapted from Alfred C. Kinsey, Wardell B. Pomeroy, and Clyde E. Martin, *Sexual Behavior in the Human Male,* Philadelphia: W. B. Saunders, 1948, p. 638. Reproduced by permission of the Kinsey Institute for Sex Research, Inc.

How Many Are There?

How many gays and lesbians are there in the United States? The answer depends first on the definition of what constitutes being a gay or lesbian. It appears from various studies that a lesbian or gay is a person with one or more of these characteristics: *same-sex feeling*—being attracted to a person of the same gender, (2) *same-sex behavior*—having sex with a same-gender person, and (3) *identifying oneself as gay or lesbian.*

Keeping in mind these different definitions of same-sex orientation, let us consider the following data from a study of a representative sample of the U.S. adult population (Laumann et al., 1994; Michael et al., 1994):

- Persons with same-sex feeling: 6 percent of men; 4 percent of women
- Persons who have ever engaged in same-sex behavior: 9 percent of men; 4 percent of women
- Persons with gay or lesbian self-identification: 2.8 percent of men; 1.4 percent of women

Most of these numbers fall significantly below the 10 percent that gay activists have long cited from Kinsey's classic studies as the proportion of gays and lesbians.

In the late 1940s and early 1950s, Kinsey found that 10 percent of the U.S. adults were "predominantly" or "more or less exclusively homosexual." However, he discovered that only 2.5 percent were "exclusively homosexual," which is quite similar to the proportion of today's Americans identifying themselves as gay or lesbian, even though the people in Kinsey's survey were a not representative sample of the U.S. adult population (Voeller, 1990; Kinsey et al., 1953, 1948). Nonetheless, the real number of gays and lesbians must be higher than 2.5 percent because the homophobia in our society discourages identifying oneself as "homosexual," particularly among young people with same-sex orientations.

What Are Gays Like?

Compared with male heterosexuals, gay men are more likely to be "promiscuous"—sexually active (Blumstein and Schwartz, 1990). Contrary to popular belief, though, the greater likelihood of promiscuity among gay men does not originate from gayness itself. It is in the main a product of *heterosexual* society, which socializes men to be more sexually active than women. Through its male-dominated culture, heterosexual society imposes a double standard of sexual behavior on men and women. If a woman is very sexually active, she is likely to be scorned as a "slut," but a man with the same experience is more likely to be praised as a "stud." Men, then, are encouraged to be more sexually active. Since they have been brought up in the same heterosexual culture as straight men, gay men equally have learned to be sexually active. Not surprisingly, just as heterosexual men are more sexually active than heterosexual women, gay men are more sexually active than lesbians. But why are *gay men* more sexually active than *heterosexual men*? Because the prospect of a heterosexual encounter involves only one person (a man) eager for casual sex—the other person (a woman) less interested—but the prospect of a same-sex encounter involves two persons (both men) equally eager for casual sex.

Casual sex was extremely common among gay men during the heyday of the sexual revolution in the 1960s and 1970s. Since the AIDS crisis struck the gay community in the early 1980s, however, there has been a drastic shift from casual sex to monogamy. Afraid to play sexual "Russian roulette" by putting their lives on the line, gay men have greatly reduced the number of partners they have sex with. The streets and parks that used to bustle with men "cruising" for sex partners are nearly deserted. In gay newspapers and magazines, classified advertisements placed by men seeking "sex only" have declined significantly, while ads looking for "relationships" have increased. Ads for models or escorts have also decreased substantially, and gay men are more likely to seek out other men for baseball, soccer, choral groups, and other social activities as alternatives to bars, heavy drugs, and sex. Walking on the street, they are less likely to eye each other as potential sex partners and more likely to greet each other by saying hello and smiling (Feldman, 1985; Morin et al., 1984).

Today, while gay men are still more likely than straight men to be sexually active, the majority of gay men are involved in a steady, long-term relationship.

In fact, most male couples are as satisfied with their relationships as most heterosexual couples are with theirs (Peplau and Cochran, 1990). Given the homophobic society's opposition to same-sex marriages, it seems remarkable for male couples to pull off the same level of love and happiness that heterosexual couples enjoy. What is the secret? Some researchers have analyzed gay couples' various personal and social characteristics, such as age, education, income, religion, ethnicity, or living arrangements. None of these was found to be associated with male couples' satisfaction. But researchers did find greater satisfaction among couples with one partner's income being about equal to another's. This finding is similar to the evidence from several other studies that male couples are happier when they perceive their relationships as egalitarian (Peplau and Cochran, 1990). In an egalitarian relationship, both partners make decisions together as equals, which is likely to occur if their incomes are roughly similar rather than widely different. In short, it is power equality that helps ensure "marital" happiness among male couples.

What Are Lesbians Like?

Brought up in the same heterosexual society, lesbians are in some ways *like other women*, which therefore makes them appear different from gay men. On the other hand, having the same sexual orientation, lesbians are in some ways just like gay men, which makes them *unlike other women*.

Like Other Women. Like straight women, lesbians have been socialized to be less interested in casual sex and more interested in relationship and love. Thus they rarely look for one-night stands in gay bars, let alone go "cruising" in streets or parks. Lesbians are far more interested in making friends in the context of social gatherings, parties, mutual friends, and school. The relationship grows slowly, through a long process of knowing the other person, becoming good friends, dating, and cultivating deep affection. Usually, only after a fairly stable, prolonged, and affectionate bond has formed does sexual involvement take place (Nichols, 1990).

Also, like heterosexual women, a majority of lesbians carry on a comfortable relationship with straights by passing as one of them. The posture of heterosexuality is easy for lesbians to put on, because they—like other women—have been socialized to play the conventional female role. Some lesbians may look like men because of their severely tailored clothes, short hair, and masculine mannerisms, but the vast majority look like other women. Being a part of the straight community's social and occupational scene, lesbians can slip into its sexual scene as well. Thus, more than a third of lesbians exhibit a "partial bisexual style" by having sex with men, and about two-thirds are attracted to men (Rust, 1995; Nichols, 1990).

Finally, many lesbians have the same desire as heterosexual women to be mothers. They may decide to adopt a child or to bear one through artificial insemination. If they are already mothers by an earlier heterosexual marriage, they

may fight for custody of their children. Stumbling blocks, however, are sometimes thrown in their way. In 1995, for example, the Virginia Supreme Court ruled
in favor of a lower court that took away a child from his mother after declar-
ing her "an unfit parent" simply because she is a lesbian. Nevertheless, today,
lesbians are just as likely to be mothers as heterosexual women (Kantrowitz, 1996;
Henry, 1993).

By sharing those characteristics with heterosexual women, lesbians appear
different from gay men: less interested in casual sex, more involved socially
and sexually with straights, and more interested in raising children—67 percent of
lesbians are mothers, while only 27 percent of gay men are fathers (LeVay and
Nonas, 1995).

Unlike Other Women.   Lesbians are more likely than heterosexual women to
reject the traditional female role. In a study of lesbians and a control group of heterosexual women, only one-third of the former said that they saw themselves as
"appropriately feminine" (passive, dependent, or nonassertive) while most of the
latter considered themselves "feminine" (Saghir and Robins, 1980).

While still teenagers, lesbians are far and away less likely than their straight
peers to know their sexual identity. While virtually all heterosexual youths know
they are heterosexual, most adolescent lesbians are not aware or certain of being
lesbian. They, therefore, tend to see their same-sex attraction in a nonsexual way,
as the following description by a lesbian of her adolescent experience suggests.

> We started out just being friends and then it became something special. She taught
> me a lot of things. I love music and she taught me how to listen to it and appreciate
> it. She liked things I liked, like walking. We read a lot together. We read the Bible,
> we read verses to each other. We shared things together. We caressed each other
> and kissed. *I think it was a need to have someone there. And I was there and she was there
> and we just held on to each other.* (Simon and Gagnon, 1974)

By being different from heterosexual women in these ways, lesbians appear
similar to gay men. Just as lesbians are more likely to reject the traditional female
role, gay men are more likely to reject the traditional masculine role—by being,
for example, both tough and gentle rather than tough only. And like lesbians,
gay men are less likely than heterosexuals during adolescence to be aware of their
sexual orientation. But since males generally have sex at a younger age than
females, gay men identify themselves as gay earlier than lesbians do, as we will
see in the next section.

Coming Out

In the argot of the gay community, becoming openly gay is called "coming out,"
because it involves people *publicly* identifying themselves as gays or lesbians. It is
difficult for most gays and lesbians to come out by revealing their sexual orientation

to parents, friends, or coworkers, because the latter may react with shock, rejection, or worse.

Before coming out, many young gays and lesbians do not even *privately* identify themselves as being gay, even though they feel attracted to a person of the same sex. Sociologist Richard Troiden (1979) presents a detailed analysis of how most of the gay men he studied came to acquire their gay identity. The identity acquisition involved going through four stages of experience.

In the first stage, *sensitization*, the gays felt that they were different from their peers. As one recalled, "I never felt as if I fit in. I don't know why for sure. I felt different. I thought it was because I was more sensitive." Another expressed a similar feeling: "I felt different due to my interest in school, ineptness at sports, and the like." Most gays had these feelings when their puberty began, that is, at about age 13. A few, though, knew they were gay when they were as young as 6 or 7, but such men tend to have been "sissy boys" who always identified with women (Bawer, 1993).

In the second stage, *dissociation*, the gays, about 17 years of age, began to feel that they might be gay but refused to define themselves as such. One described how he was in this stage: "Before I was publicly labeled a faggot, I realized that I wasn't very interested in women. I had had enough experiences with girls to realize that while I was aroused by them, I was also aroused by males and wanted to have sex with them. However, I thought this was something I'd outgrow in time, something that would straighten itself out as I matured." In this stage of dissociation, they might deny their own gayness by being hostile to gays, calling them "faggots."

In the third stage, *coming out*, the gays, roughly at age 19, regarded their sexual feelings as definitely gay, got involved in the gay subculture, and redefined gayness as a positive and viable lifestyle. While the very act of coming out is usually very painful, frightening, or overwhelming, the resulting experience is often highly positive. It has been described as "an incredible sense of relief and renewal . . . like being born. The burden had been lifted from my shoulders. For the first time I felt like I had a life" (Marcus, 1993).

In the final stage, *commitment*, the gays, now mature adults, are committed to gayness as a way of life. They insist that they are happy being gay, that they would not change even if given the opportunity, and that they cannot see any benefit in choosing heterosexuality. Such a positive feeling even prevails among those who have lost their jobs or have been rejected by their families and children (Marcus, 1993).

Even after gays and lesbians have publicly revealed their sexual orientation, the process of coming out never ends. "Coming out is not something you do just once and then forget about," observes gay writer Eric Marcus (1993). "For gay and lesbian people who choose to live out of the closet, coming out is something you may do almost every day. There are all kinds of chance encounters and conversations that force gay people to decide whether to answer honestly or not." Every time somebody at a party or some other place asks questions such as "Are you married?" openly gay men and women are forced to come out again by saying something like, "No, because I am gay." This is likely to occur to gays and lesbians all the time simply because the society in which they live is predominantly heterosexual—so that most people routinely assume others to be heterosexual like themselves, and ask questions based on that assumption. Thus, even though they have come out, openly gay men and lesbians continue to face the same challenges from heterosexual society as those who remain in the closet.

Gay and Lesbian Lifestyles

Due to their same-sex orientation, gay and lesbian life differs in some ways from straight life. But most gays and lesbians live a normal, happy life, as most straights do.

Family and Children.   Lesbians and gays encounter the same prejudice and discrimination as other minority groups. But there is a basic difference. In nearly all cases, the parents of African Americans are African American, the parents of Hispanics are Hispanic, or the parents of Jews are Jewish. In contrast, virtually all the parents of gays and lesbians are *heterosexual*. Unlike the other minorities, gays and lesbians cannot always count on their families for support in dealing with society's homophobia. In fact, practically all parents are upset when they find out their son or daughter is gay. Some react with tears but eventually manage to deal with it in a loving way; others react with anger, refusing to have anything to do with the gay child. Actually, these parents are not to blame for their negative reaction. Because of societal homophobia, parents with a gay child are typically afraid of what friends, neighbors, relatives, or even strangers will think if they find out. The parents are in effect victims of society's antigay culture. Therefore, ironically, while their gay child has come out of the closet, they themselves go into the closet, hiding from others the fact that their child is gay. All these problems are less common today, thanks largely to groups such as Parents and Friends of Lesbians and Gays (P-FLAG), which help parents accept their child's same-sex orientation without fear or embarrassment (Johnson and Piore, 2004; Marcus, 1993).

What if parents are gay? How do their heterosexual children react? In cases where children have been raised since birth or early childhood in a household with two gay parents, there is no real news for them to react to. The child has learned to accept the fact that they have two daddies or two mommies at home. As they grow older, particularly in adolescence, they may face teasing or even ridicule. But most studies show no psychological disadvantages for children raised by lesbians or gays. Such children do not differ from others in their social adjustment or in their identity as a boy or girl. Further, they are no more likely than other children to become gay (Kantrowitz, 1996; Marcus, 1993). Today, children of gay parents find it easy to live normal lives like everybody else. They have even formed their own networks such as COLAGE (Children of Lesbians and Gays Everywhere).

Dating and Marriage. It is easier for gays and lesbians to find a date in a relatively large city than in a small town simply because there are many more gays and lesbians in the city. The places where they hang out include bars, restaurants, clubs, and organizations that cater to lesbians and gays. But, like straights, gays and lesbians can also meet in any place imaginable, such as at work, at social events, at the grocery store, or at the mall. At such places, though, most people are straight rather than gay. It is usually quite a challenge for people with same-sex orientation to differentiate gays from straights, but occasionally they can spot each other by such clues as the style of clothing or haircut popular among gays and lesbians.

When having dates, lesbians and gays mostly do what straights do. They may go to a restaurant, a movie, or some other social place. They tend, though, to avoid holding their date's hand or some other intimate act in public unless they are in a predominantly gay neighborhood. Since they, like straights, have been socialized to the standard boy–girl roles, they may initially be uncertain as to who should, for example, make the first move in getting a date. But most gays and lesbians quickly learn to do what a specific situation calls for, rather than rigidly acting out the traditional gender roles. Thus, who asks for a date depends on who is more interested or bold, who pays for dinner depends on who asked for the date or who makes more money, and so on. When they fall in love, they will get married. But, since they cannot get a marriage license, same-sex couples do not have the same legal protections and financial benefits as heterosexual couples, such as the right to be on each other's insurance and pension plans or receive the Social Security survivor's benefits. In recent years, though, several cities such as San Francisco have granted unmarried couples, both gay and straight, a legal document called a "domestic partnership agreement," which can be used to gain family benefits from employers, insurance companies, health clubs, and other commercial establishments. But no states have legalized same-sex marriage (Cloud, 1998).

Politics, Education, and Religion. Because the Democratic Party has often espoused policies sympathetic to the sexual minority, gays and lesbians are most likely to be Democrats. Straights have about the same party affiliations. But gays and lesbians are much more politically active than straights: While straight Democrats are somewhat less likely than straight Republicans to vote, gay/lesbian Democrats are much more likely than gay/lesbian Republicans to vote (LeVay and Nonas, 1995). Apparently, homophobia makes the sexual minority more eager than the sexual majority to vote for gay-friendly candidates.

Lesbians and gays are generally better educated than straights. Some scholars attribute this to higher IQ among gays and lesbians. According to others, the stress of belonging to a stigmatized group drives many gay and lesbian teenagers into an "overachiever" mode (LeVay and Nonas, 1995). Perhaps, with few or no friends to socialize with because of antigay ostracism, lesbian and gay youngsters spend more time reading and studying than their straight peers do. Homophobia has also made the suicide rate among gay youth much higher than among straight youth. In response to this problem, some high schools in a few cities have set up counseling programs for gay and lesbian students, as well as programs designed to reduce the fear, prejudice, or hostility that straight students have toward gay people (Marcus, 1993).

Although many churches and synagogues condemn same-sex practices, gays and lesbians belong to various major faiths and denominations in about the same proportions as heterosexuals. Moreover, lesbians and gays are no more unreligious than straights (LeVay and Nonas, 1995). But gays and lesbians usually attend churches and synagogues that they know will welcome them. These gay and lesbian worshipers, along with their pastors and rabbis, believe that God loves them as much as anybody else. They do not regard their own sexuality as sinful in the same way that straights do not consider their own sexuality as sinful. An increasing number of pastors and other religious officials agree, to such an extent, that they are willing to perform same-sex marriage ceremonies (Niebuhr, 1998; Marcus, 1993).

Theories of Homosexuality

Scholars and researchers in various disciplines are mostly positivists trying to explain why some individuals become gays or lesbians. Their explanations may be classified into three major types: biological, psychoanalytic, and sociological theories.

Biological Theories.   Same-sex orientation has been linked to at least three kinds of biological factors: hormones, genes, and the brain.

According to the *hormone theory,* gay men have lower levels of male sex hormones than straight men, and lesbians have fewer female sex hormones than male sex hormones, while straight women have more female sex hormones. But most studies have found no hormonal difference between gays and straights (Burr, 1996; Porter, 1996).

According to the *genetic theory,* people are born, rather than bred to be, gay. Studies have suggested that the probability of two siblings becoming gay together is significantly higher among *identical* twins than among *fraternal* twins. This is taken to mean that same-sex orientation is largely determined by genes because identical twins are more genetically alike than fraternal twins. But the findings, critics point out, do not necessarily mean that same-sex orientation can be traced to genes. According to critics, social environment may contribute to the development of same-sex orientation because, when compared with fraternal twins, identical twins are more likely to elicit similar reactions from others. If parents react to an identical twin boy by treating him as if he were a girl, they will most likely treat his twin brother in the same way. Given similar experiences, identical twins are likely to develop similar behavior patterns, including same-sex orientation (Wickelgren, 1999; Alessio, 1996).

The *brain theory* comes from a study in which Simon LeVay (1996) examined brain tissues from deceased gay and straight men. The researcher found, among other things, a difference in the size of the hypothalamus, the cluster of neurons, or nervous tissues, in the brain's lower area, which controls sex drive and body temperature. The gays' hypothalamus was less than half the size of the straights'. Le Vay concluded that a relatively small brain could make a person gay. Critics of this theory argue that it could be the other way around, that is, that AIDS (which killed all the gay subjects that LeVay studied) or same-sex activities may change brain size, as suggested by the evidence that the brain's neural networks can change in response to certain experiences. In people who read braille after becoming blind, for example, the area of the brain controlling the reading finger usually grows larger (Ridley, 1996).

Psychiatric Theories. For many years, most psychiatrists regarded same-sex orientation as a form of mental disorder. But, in 1973, the American Psychiatric Association (APA) decided to define *homosexuality* as normal. Still, today the APA continues to find some, though not most, gays and lesbians to be suffering from what it calls *sexual orientation disturbance*. Most psychiatrists would help these troubled gays to accept their same-sex orientation and feel comfortable with themselves. But some psychiatrists would try to "cure" the "patients" of their same-sex orientation. Such psychiatrists continue to hold the belief that same-sex orientation is characterized by "hidden but incapacitating fears of the opposite sex" (Socarides et al., 1997; Berger, 1994).

This pathological fear is often attributed to an abnormal parent–son relationship. A young boy is said to become gay later in life if he has a domineering, overprotective, or seductive mother and a weak, detached, or hostile father. Alienated from his father, the boy will not look upon him as a model for learning the masculine role. Instead, being driven by his hostile father into the arms of his loving mother, the boy will cling excessively to her, identify himself with her, and fail to develop a strong masculine identity. As a consequence, the theory argues, the boy will likely grow up to become gay (Socarides et al., 1997; Herman and Duberman, 1995).

Many psychiatrists have found most of their gay patients to have had disturbed relationships with their parents, but these patients do not represent the majority of the gay population. Numerous studies on average, *non*patient gays have found them to be no different from heterosexuals in parent–child relationships (Ross and Arrindell, 1988).

Sociological Theories. A basic problem with biological theories is their assumption that same-sex orientation is universally the same. Were this true, we should expect different societies to have about the same incidence of gayness or lesbianism. The reality is that same-sex orientation varies greatly in form and frequency from one society to another.

Though relatively rare in many Western societies today, same-sex practices have been and are common in other societies, from ancient Greece and ancient Japan to the present-day Azande of Africa and various New Guinea societies. In some of these societies, male teenagers have sex regularly with older men as a normal way of growing up but later in their adulthood marry women and have children (Herdt, 1990). This suggests that society has much to do with the development of same-sex orientation. To most sociologists, then, same-sex orientation is just like heterosexuality, both developing from past social experiences. Only the specific nature of their social experiences differs.

While they do not believe that certain hormones, genes, or brain size causes same-sex orientation, many sociologists assume that gays and lesbians may be born with a biological *predisposition* that makes them more likely than other children to be attracted to members of the same sex. By itself, however, this biological predisposition does not automatically cause a person to become gay or lesbian. As suggested by societal variations in the incidence of same-sex orientation, society can check—or encourage—it through some social forces such as *socialization* and *social approval* (Dickermann, 1995; Bullough, 1993).

Socialization may involve children acquiring sexual orientation from physical contact with parents during the sensitive period between birth and age 3. As research has suggested, if a mother kisses, touches, or caresses her little girl much more than her little boy, as expected by the predominantly heterosexual society, then both the girl and the boy are likely to become heterosexual. If, contrary to the expectation of heterosexual society, the mother has much more physical contact with the boy than the girl, the boy will likely grow up to be gay and the girl, lesbian. Thus, parents can socialize, though often unintentionally, their children to feel like members of the opposite sex by treating them as such. Parents can also *intentionally* socialize children toward becoming gay or, for that matter, straight. But since their society condemns homosexuality and supports heterosexuality, parents are pressured to socialize their youngsters to become straight much more than gay, which explains why heterosexual adults far outnumber their homosexual counterparts (Fleishman, 1983).

In short, the origin of homosexuality is both biological and sociological. Growing up to become gay is like growing up to become left-handed. To grow up left-handed, one is usually first born with the *tendency* to be left-handed but, in order to become a lefty *as an adult*, the child must be socialized or allowed to use the left hand. Thus in societies such as the United States where left-handedness is socially approved there are relatively many left-handed adults. But left-handedness among adults is much less common in societies such as China where left-handedness is frowned on and left-handed children are taught or pressured to stop using their left hand. About the same social force can cause children born with the homosexual *tendency* to grow up gay—or straight.

The sociologists who basically agree with what has just been discussed are *positivists,* who regard same-sex orientation as real and, therefore, seek to explain how it has come about. Other sociologists may be *constructionists,* who are *not* interested in seeking the cause of same-sex orientation because they see the phenomenon not as real in and of itself but only as a social construct—society's definition of same-sex orientation as undesirable. To constructionists, then, how gays and lesbians live their lives depends on how society treats them, not on their sexual orientation. Constructionists are, therefore, mostly interested in studying societal responses to same-sex orientation, such as various expressions of homophobia, and how those responses affect the lives of gays and lesbians, as we discuss later in this chapter.

Same-Sex Practices among Straights and Bisexuals

As Kinsey suggested, many straights are not exclusively heterosexual, so it should not be surprising that some straights and all bisexuals do engage in same-sex activities. Although they may not see themselves as gays or lesbians, homophobes generally regard this kind of straight as "homosexual."

Trades

The straights whose sexual feelings and experiences are predominantly heterosexual and only incidentally gay are called trades. All trades are males. They are, or have been, married, and seek same-sex experiences mostly as a means of releasing tension. Were cheap brothels easily accessible to them, they would frequent them. They want other men to go down on them but refuse to reciprocate. They will not fellate other men because they consider themselves straight and have a masculine self-image. Defining themselves as straight and masculine, they tend to treat their partner's mouth as if it were a woman's vagina. Many trades find their male sex-objects in public parks and rest rooms. In his classic study of same-sex activities in public rest rooms, Laud Humphreys (1970) found that most trades come from lower classes, are Roman Catholics, and do not get enough sex with their wives.

Street Hustlers

This type of straight resembles the trade in having predominantly heterosexual feelings, but engages in a greater volume of same-sex activities. Like trades, all street hustlers are males. They are usually lower-class teenage boys who consider themselves heterosexual and masculine. But they frequently make money from letting adults perform oral sex on them, although, like the trade, they often refuse to reciprocate sexually. Many street hustlers have grown up in broken homes, could not get along with parents, or have run away from home. They are lonely and penniless at the time of their initial hustling experience. They generally do not take the initiative to start hustling; it is, instead, some older men who encourage them to do so. Here is how a young runaway, Eddie, got his first trick:

After arriving in the city by bus, Eddie was standing in the bus terminal, "getting my bearings," when the customer approached. . . . The man inquired, "Where are you staying?" "No place. Actually, I'm looking for my uncle." He suggested that they go to his place so they could look in the telephone book for the uncle's address. Shortly after they arrived at the customer's home, the man asked, "Have you ever had your dick sucked?" Eddie replied, "What? No!" He was shocked by the query, for "that was something I never heard of down in Selma, Alabama." The man said, "Well, how would you like to make $100?" Eddie accepted the offer. (Luckenbill, 1985)

Once youngsters such as Eddie are introduced into prostitution, they would search for customers by standing around particular streets, parks, bus stations, or bookstore entrances. Since they are basically heterosexual, they are likely to abandon homosexual prostitution when they reach adulthood. There are, of course, street hustlers who continue prostituting themselves by finding customers in the gay bars or through escort agencies, but they are likely to have seen themselves as gay in the first place (Luckenbill, 1986, 1985).

Situationals

Some straight men and women would engage in same-sex acts in situations in which the opportunity presents itself. These situational "gays" and "lesbians" can be found among prison inmates, priests, stripteasers, and others in one-sex situations (Blumenfeld and Raymond, 1993). They are predominantly heterosexual, see themselves as heterosexuals, and are able to abandon same-sex activities if circumstances permit. But they are compelled or tempted by their life in a unisexual institution to resort to sexual release with same-sex others. Among strippers, for example, the availability of opportunities for same-sex contacts is considered comparable to having a martini after a hard day's or night's work. As one stripper says, "I usually don't get kicks out of other women, not really, but there are times. Sometimes you come home and you are just too tired to work at it. Then it's nice to have a woman around. You can lay down on the floor, relax, watch TV, and let her do it" (McCaghy and Skipper, 1969).

However, opportunities for same-sex involvement are not only available in one-sex institutions. Straight women who find something lacking in their marriage may have a lesbian lover on the side, although they do not see themselves as lesbians. As one such a woman says, "I don't consider myself gay. I simply can't relate to that for me. I need a romantic involvement in my life and it happens to be with Victoria, but I was with a man before this. I love my husband in a way. I need the kind of anchoring or stability he gives me. . . . But I also have a romantic side" (Ponse, 1984). In fact, situational lesbianism has become an "in thing" at some colleges. It involves a straight female student experimenting sexually with a member of the same sex. Such students are known as "LUGs" (lesbians until graduation) or "four-year lesbians" because they give up their same-sex activities when leaving college. As a 25-year-old woman who has been a LUG at Wellesley College explains, "It was a real lesbian experience. It was a unique, phenomenal experience. Now it's not an issue anymore. I'm going to marry Richard" (Rimer, 1993).

Bisexuals

Bisexuals can be found among men as well as women. The bisexual is about equally straight and gay. Most bisexuals are married to members of the opposite sex, but also have sexual relations with others of the same sex. In some cases only one spouse, most likely the husband, is bisexual. In other cases both husband and wife are bisexual:

> Happily married for 10 years, Richard Sharrard, a dance instructor, and Tina Tessina, a psychotherapist and writer, blend in nicely enough with their neighbors in the middle-class community of Long Beach, California. But the couple's life-style is far from ordinary: Richard and Tina are openly and unapologetically bisexual. During their unusually flexible marriage, Richard has enjoyed liaisons with half a dozen men, while Tina has taken two female lovers. (Toufexis, 1992a)

According to popular belief, bisexuals are *basically straights* with a taste for exotic adventure or *essentially gay* and unwilling to acknowledge their true sexual orientation. However, most of these individuals do not see themselves as either straight in some ways or gay in other ways but as *totally unique persons with a third kind of sexual identity*. Thus they do not consider their bisexuality "a walk on the wild side" or "a run from reality" but a legitimate and healthy identity (Leland, 1995; Rust, 1995). As lovers, bisexuals appear to be more sensitive and empathic than others because their bisexual orientation enables them to see things from more than one perspective. Nonetheless, many bisexuals still cannot transcend the societal expectation that they are either basically straight or gay. Not surprisingly, they are racked by discomfort and conflict. As a bisexual explains, "Your feet are in both camps, but your heart is in neither. You have the opportunity to experience a kind of richness, but you constantly feel you have to make a choice" (Toufexis, 1992a).

This problem is likely to continue because bisexuals usually have sex with either straights or gays rather than with other bisexuals. The problem will diminish, though, if bisexuals develop their own bisexual community to the same extent as gays and lesbians have formed their own. Like the gay community, the bisexual community will be able to strengthen its members' unique sexual identity so that they can enjoy sex with one another without being torn with guilt and other psychological problems. The bisexual community will also bring social harmony to our multicultural society because bisexuals are uniquely qualified to mediate between the lesbian and gay community and the larger heterosexual society (LeVay and Nonas, 1995).

Homophobia

The word *homophobia* originally meant only the fear of same-sex orientation, but now it refers more broadly to antigay prejudice and discrimination. Homophobia is also called "heterosexism" for being comparable to racism and sexism. This is because the sexual minority often encounters prejudice and discrimination for their same-sex orientation in about the same way as racial minorities and women do for their skin color and gender.

The Homophobic View of Homosexuality

In the United States and other Western societies, the view of same-sex orientation as deviant can be traced to the Judeo-Christian scripture, where same-sex practices are strongly condemned:

> You shall not lie with a male as with a woman; it is an abomination. (Leviticus 18:22)
>   If a man lies with a male as with a woman, both of them have committed an abomination; they shall be put to death, their blood is upon them. (Leviticus 20:13)

It is from these biblical passages that many ultraconservative, fundamentalist Christians get their idea about same-sex orientation as an "abomination" that should be punished by death. But most homophobes today presumably would not go that far by interpreting the Bible so literally. If they do, they would have to condemn many heterosexuals to death for committing adultery, having sex with a menstruating woman, telling fortunes, or cursing one's parent. This is because in the same book of Leviticus, all these practices are also condemned as abominations punishable by death. Nonetheless, all homophobes still regard same-sex orientation as deviant in some way. Why? Usually, an act is considered deviant if it deviates from a *norm*. What, then, is the norm that most homophobes use to define same-sex orientation as deviant?

On the face of it, the norm may appear to be simply that sex should only involve persons of different genders. But the norm that is often used to condemn same-sex practices is more than simply gender-related, as can be discerned from standard arguments that oppose same-sex marriages. In 1996, for example, the Hawaiian legislators who opposed same-sex marriage argued that marriage is "intended for the *propagation* of the human race by man-woman units." And former Vice President Dan Quayle's speechwriter, Lisa Schiffren (1996), contends, "'Same-sex marriage' is inherently incompatible with our culture's understanding of the institution. Marriage is essentially a lifelong compact between a man and woman committed to sexual exclusivity and the *creation* and nurture of offspring." Even if Schiffren is persuaded that gay couples can have "lifelong sexual exclusivity" and "nurture" children just as heterosexual couples can, she still will consider same-sex marriage deviant, because such marriage *cannot create* offspring. It is, therefore, clear that procreation or reproduction is often used as the norm for defining same-sex marriage—and, by extension, same-sex orientation—as deviant.

The reproductive norm is a holdover from the past when the purpose of marital sex was widely believed to be procreation. Logically, according to this anachronistic norm, any sex engaged in without any intention of producing a baby is deviant. This means that the vast majority of married heterosexual couples today are deviant because they routinely engage in sex for *pleasure* or *love* alone rather than for procreation. Among the married heterosexuals who violate the reproductive norm are not only average couples but also infertile or childless couples, couples who marry past childbearing age, couples who use birth-control methods, and couples who engage in oral or other nonreproductive sex. If premarital sex, extramarital sex, or masturbation committed by countless other heterosexuals are also taken into account, it seems clear that all of the straights violate the reproductive norm as lesbians and gays do. Nevertheless, homophobic society illogically uses the same norm to define the sexual minority as deviant and the sexual majority (heterosexuals) as normal.

The Nature and Extent of Homophobia

Homophobia is both a negative *attitude* (hence prejudice) toward gays and lesbians and an unjust *action* (discrimination) against them. As an antigay attitude, homophobia is, therefore, covert and invisible. It may be in the form of an unfavorable *belief* about same-sex orientation—as, for example, abominable, evil, or unnatural. It may also be in the form of a negative *feeling* (such as fear, disgust, or hatred) toward lesbians and gays. Antigay discrimination, however, is overt and observable, in the form of an unfair action against the sexual minority (such as denying them jobs, calling them names, or assaulting them).

It is difficult to assess the extent of homophobia in U.S. society, but if homophobia involves condemning same-sex orientation as morally wrong, then nearly half of Americans may be considered homophobic. Asked in a national poll whether same-sex relationships between consenting adults are morally wrong, 46 percent indicated yes (Leland, 2000). Most Americans are, however, antigay in regard to other highly emotional issues. According to other surveys, 57 percent do not want the sexual-minority members to be legally married, and 56 percent do not want them to raise children. In the 2004 presidential election, the voters in 11 states overwhelmingly approved the constitutional amendment to ban same-sex marriages (Leland, 2000; Berke, 1998).

However, if homophobia involves denying the sexual minority the same civil rights enjoyed by the sexual majority, then most Americans do not appear to be homophobic: Over 83 percent say that gays and lesbians should have equal rights in job opportunities. And 50 to 58 percent also say that gays and lesbians should get health insurance, inheritance, and social security (Leland, 2000).

In short, U.S. society is deeply ambivalent about its sexual minority, torn between an uneasy feeling about their same-sex orientation and a democratic tolerance for them as citizens (Wolfe, 1998).

The Impact of Homophobia

Homophobia strongly affects virtually all aspects of gay and lesbian life. The problems that homophobia creates for its targets can be social or psychological in nature.

Social Problems. The social problems caused by antigay forces in the lives of gays and lesbians have recently become well known because they are often presented in the media. To cite just a few examples: Gays and lesbians cannot get legally married; same-sex couples are denied health insurance and other benefits enjoyed by heterosexual couples; and people with the same-sex orientation are often rejected by straight family members and friends, shunned or ostracized by fellow employees, discharged from the military for revealing their sexual orientation, and prohibited from discussing same-sex orientation with students in public schools. Indeed, there are countless other problems suffered by gays and lesbians as victims of antigay prejudice and discrimination (Blumenfeld, 1992). Due to the prevalence of homophobia, then, lesbians and gays have to struggle harder than straights to succeed and live a happy life in the same society.

Psychological Problems. Homosexuality does not cause mental health problems, just as heterosexuality does not. But the homophobic nature of society does make lesbians and gays more likely to develop some psychological problems, such as constant tension, self-hatred, and depression, which in turn lead to higher rates of suicide and alcohol and drug abuse among gays and lesbians than among straights. Running through these problems is the failure to achieve a harmonious integration of one's diverse identities (O'Hanlan, 1996; LeVay and Nonas, 1995).

Raised in a predominantly heterosexual and homophobic society, gays and lesbians, like straights, usually grow up identifying themselves as loving sons or daughters to their heterosexual parents, as fun-to-be-with persons to their heterosexual friends, and as productive or respected members to various heterosexual groups and organizations. But all these self-identities are based on conformity to the heterosexual way of life, and are, therefore, in conflict with their sexual self-identity as gays and lesbians. The conflict itself creates tension and restlessness. Some gays and lesbians try to resolve the conflict by assimilating into the straight world and outwardly carrying on like heterosexuals, but they tend to feel miserable for living a lie, for betraying their true self, or for deceiving their significant others. Other lesbians and gays try to resolve the identity conflict by leaving the straight world for the gay community, but many still feel the need to commute, physically or emotionally, between their new gay and old straight worlds (LeVay and Nonas, 1995). Thus the identity conflict that causes tension and other psychological problems is likely to remain as long as homophobia continues to hold sway in society. But through constant support from fellow gays and lesbians as well as from sympathetic straights, most members of the sexual minority manage to transcend those psychological problems and to live a relatively normal, happy life, like most heterosexuals do.

Social Profile: Homophobes

Not all straights are homophobic, but some are. The more homophobic have certain characteristics that distinguish them from straight people. They are generally:

- Less educated and less well-off
- More conservative—socially, politically, religiously, and sexually
- More negative toward racial and ethnic minorities
- More supportive of traditional gender roles, in which men are supposed to be aggressive and women gentle
- Men who see themselves as "masculine" and women who see themselves as "feminine"
- More likely to stereotype as "homosexual" a man whom they consider to be "feminine" in some way and a woman whom they consider to be "manly"
- Older, except in cases of extreme violence against gays, known as gay bashing or hate crime, which are more common among young men
- Less likely to know personally someone who is gay or lesbian
- More likely to be influenced by peers
- More likely to be men than women

Why are heterosexual men more homophobic than women? According to one explanation, straight men, accustomed to playing the stereotypically masculine role, do not want other men to look at them the way they themselves look at women. They are afraid of becoming what women in a sexist society often are: an object of unwanted sexual attention.

Sources: Wilkinson, 2004; Kite and Whitley, 1996; Blumenfeld and Raymond, 1993; Berrill, 1992.

AIDS, Gays, and Straights

When AIDS first broke out in the early 1980s, virtually all the victims were gay men. Today, notably, gay men are much less likely to get AIDS, thanks to dramatic increases in safer sex practices such as monogamy and condom use (Altman, 1999; Gagnon, Levine, and Nardi, 1997). The majority of *new* AIDS cases do not appear among gay men but among intravenous drug users, who often share contaminated needles when shooting drugs and consequently pass the AIDS virus on to one another. But, having been exposed to the virus longer, gay men still make up the largest proportion of AIDS patients today.

In the 1980s, the homophobic society blamed the emergence of AIDS on "promiscuity" among gay men. AIDS was then associated with the same-sex orientation itself, and the disease was called the "gay plague." Discrimination against gays visibly soared. Suspected of being infected with the AIDS virus simply because they were known as gays, gays were often denied insurance coverage, fired from their jobs, and evicted from their apartments. Those who were actually infected with the virus or ill with AIDS also received shabby treatment from society. Even the U.S. Justice Department said it was legal for employers to discriminate against

AIDS-infected employees if the discrimination was based on fear of contagion. Often, those who were ill with AIDS could not even see their gay lovers or have them attend their funerals because their families prohibited it. Physical attacks on gays also became more common.

Some well-known conservatives fanned the hostility toward gays further with inflammatory public statements. Patrick Buchanan, a conservative columnist, made the argument that AIDS is a fitting punishment for gays: "They have declared war upon Nature, and now Nature is exacting an awful retribution." Some conservatives even demanded that gays be incarcerated "until and unless they can be cleansed of their medical problems" (Bayer, 1985). Because they wanted to see gays punished with AIDS, many conservatives were opposed to any government attempt to develop a vaccine against the deadly disease. They declared that by showing compassion in developing the vaccine the government was in effect approving and supporting gayness as a normal, legitimate lifestyle (Marcus, 1993).

But today the general public has become less condemnatory toward gays and more sympathetic to those with AIDS. Most states have passed laws protecting AIDS victims against job dismissal and other discriminations. A number of factors have caused this turnaround in public sentiment: (1) A growing number of *heterosexuals,* including not only drug addicts but children and babies, have been afflicted with AIDS. (2) Many widely admired and loved celebrities, such as actor Rock Hudson and dancer Rudolf Nureyev, were brought to light as gay when they died of AIDS. (3) The media have often portrayed AIDS-infected gays and their gay companions and friends in a positive way, as courageous, compassionate, and hardworking people. (4) The AIDS crisis has galvanized thousands of otherwise apathetic gays and lesbians into joining the fight against the disease, thereby gaining respect from the general public—because the gays' anti-AIDS crusade also helped slow the spread of the disease among *heterosexuals* (LeVay and Nonas, 1995; Marcus, 1993).

Fighting Homophobia

For more than 50 years now gays and lesbians in the United States have been fighting for equal rights in a homophobic society. The gay rights movement began in the late 1940s with the discovery among many individual gays and lesbians that they were not alone. This "gay awakening" resulted in large part from the widely publicized Kinsey report that millions of men and women had engaged in same-sex activities. At first the gay and lesbian organizations focused on educating the public about same-sex orientation, counseling gays and lesbians in trouble, and providing them with recreational services.

Then, in June 1969, the police raided the Stonewall Inn, a gay bar in New York, simply for being gay. The patrons, who used to be cowed by such raids, reacted by throwing bottles and stones at the police. This violent reaction against police harassment soon led many young gays and lesbians to form militant organizations. They tried to confront the country with the fact that gays are an oppressed minority group, whose aspiration for respectability is no different from that of African Americans, Hispanics, women, migrant farm workers, and the like. They marched in great numbers, shouting such slogans as "Two-four-six-eight, gay is twice as good as straight!" "Three-five-seven-nine, Lesbians are mighty fine!" and "Gay Power!" They also resorted to dramatic confrontation tactics in dealing with antigay political figures. One such tactic was "zapping"—disrupting, for example, a Foran for Governor rally in Chicago in 1971 by marching, dancing, and chanting "Ho, ho, hey, hey, freaking fags are here to stay" as well as "Foran is a macho pig" (Humphreys, 1972). By the mid-1970s the militant fervor had cooled, and there was renewed concern with providing counseling and other social services to gays who needed them.

The cooling of the gay militancy apparently resulted from the many victories achieved by the gay power movement between the early and mid-1970s. A dozen states legalized consensual sex between same-sex adults. The school boards in some cities banned discrimination in the hiring of gay teachers, and a number of court decisions upheld the gay's right to teach. The Bank of America, IBM, NBC, AT&T, and other big corporations, as well as the Civil Service Commission, announced their willingness to hire gays and lesbians. The American Psychiatric Association stopped listing same-sex orientation as a psychiatric disorder. And more than 300 same-sex marriages were performed in a church in Los Angeles.

With the outbreak of AIDS in the early 1980s, the lesbian and gay rights movement began to shift into high gear again. At first, efforts were focused on fighting the disease. Gays and lesbians provided care for the sick and dying, presented AIDS education programs, lobbied for increased government funding for AIDS research, pressured medical researchers and drug companies to go all out searching for treatments and a cure, and fought discrimination against people with AIDS or HIV. Then, in the early 1990s, a few young people at the forefront of the AIDS battle began to reinvigorate the lesbian and gay rights movement with confrontational tactics. Giving themselves such militant names as "Queer Nation" and "Queer Action," they shouted their demands for equal rights in the streets, city halls, and suburban shopping malls. They staged gay-pride marches, with some appearing in drag, wearing nipple rings, kissing each other ostentatiously, or exhibiting some other anticonventional behavior. They even organized a massive march on Washington in 1993, shouting slogans like "We're here! We're queer! Get used to it!" (Marcus, 1992). But given today's conservative climate, those gay militants may have hurt rather than helped the cause of equal rights for gays. As gay writer Bruce Bawer (1993) explains, the confrontational and exhibitionist derring-dos in gay-pride marches helped "perpetuate the widespread view of homosexuals as freaks, outlaws, sex addicts, and sexual exhibitionists."

However, the majority of gay-rights activists are far from militant. Consider, for example, the Human Rights Campaign, the largest lesbian and gay organization. Its members are moderate, engaging in the same campaigning, fund-raising, and lobbying tactics as conventional interest groups. They also emphasize the importance of equal rights in the same way as other minority groups. They have, in a word, mainstreamed. Thus gays and lesbians have become an important, powerful political force. They can now count on an increasing number of leaders from both political parties to take their equal rights seriously. Many states and cities have passed laws to protect the sexual minority against discrimination. Massachusetts has become the first state to legalize same-sex marriages. But homophobia remains throughout the society, and antigay forces continue their efforts to oppose gay rights by arguing that gay-rights laws not only give the sexual minority special treatment but also encourage gay lifestyles and threaten traditional marriages (Rosenberg, 2004; Lacayo, 2004; Levay and Nonas, 1995). Actually, the sexual minority only wants the same rights as other Americans, not wanting to attempt the impossible task of turning straights into gays and destroying traditional marriages.

Global Perspective: Homophobia

As we have seen earlier, the homophobia in the United States makes life difficult for gays and lesbians. They have a hard time getting legally married, are often rejected or ostracized by straights, experience tension or depression, and suffer other social and psychological problems. In Japan, too, homosexuals are often denied, though quietly or politely, opportunities for jobs and loans for housing. But the problems created by homophobia are even more serious in less affluent societies. The International Gay and Lesbian Human Rights Commission has documented many cases of abuse committed by the governments in less developed countries against the sexual minority. The cases include gays or lesbians being beaten, raped, imprisoned, and institutionalized. One gay man in Romania, for example, reported that he and his partner were arrested after the police were told about their gay love. While in jail, other inmates raped him, and when he disclosed the rapes in court, the warden beat him.

In Russia, since the law against sodomy was abolished in 1993, personal ads in newspapers under sections labeled "Man to Man" have become as frank and easy to find as they are in New York City. But homophobia among the general public remains stronger in Russia than in the United States. According to a recent poll, 47 percent of the Russians said that gays should be executed or isolated, while only 29 percent said they ought to be left alone. Understandably, most Russian gays and lesbians are fearful of being beaten up by straights and of losing their jobs if they are discovered to be gay. As a result, Russian homosexuals are much more likely than their U.S. peers to stay in the closet.

In the African nation of Zimbabwe, the president has publicly announced that homosexuals have no legal rights, calling them "sodomists and perverts" and "worse than dogs and pigs." When 70 U.S. Congress members signed a letter of protest, the Zimbabwean president said, "Let the Americans keep their sodomy, bestiality—stupid and foolish ways." The Zimbabwean citizens are also intolerant of the sexual minority, especially lesbians. The family of a lesbian, for example, is reported to have "locked her up and had a man rape her so she would get pregnant. After she ran off and had an abortion, they caught her and did it again. Now she has the baby and is forced to live with the man." Similar atrocities are inflicted on homosexuals in other parts of Africa. In Egypt, for example, the police often entrap men through gay-related advertisements on the Internet. Once arrested, the gays tend to be beaten and tortured in jail, which sometimes results in deaths.

Sources: Allam, 2004; Hawkins, 2000; McNeil, 1998, 1995; Dunlap, 1995; Specter, 1995.

Other Victims of Social Stigma

Like gays and lesbians, many other groups are unjustly stigmatized—judged as undesirable and mistreated in some way. Here we turn our attention to some of those groups.

Transgenderists: Transsexuals, Intersexuals, and Transvestites

A new concept called *transgenderism* emerged in the 1990s to refer to those having the characteristics of both sexes. Most people, including straights, gays, lesbians, and bisexuals are either male or female, but transgenderists, also called transpeople, are both. Thus, transpeople include transsexuals, who belong to one sex but feel like members of the opposite sex; intersexuals (hermaphrodites), who are simultaneously male and female for being born with organs of both sexes; and transvestites (cross-dressers), who sporadically or permanently wear clothes associated with the opposite sex. They are all stigmatized, suffering as victims of social stigma.

There are many more male, or male-to-female, transsexuals than female transsexuals. The predominance of transsexuality among men has been attributed to women being the primary socializer of children in most families. If both a boy and a girl end up getting too attached to their mother and identifying themselves with her, only the boy is likely to become a transsexual because his mother is a member of the opposite sex. Both male and female transsexuals typically go through a "rite of passage," moving from one status to another. Male transsexuals first have partial and ambivalent feeling of being feminine, then gradually feel more and more certain about being women, and finally completely identify themselves as women. They may undergo hormone treatments or sex-change operations to become complete members of the desired opposite sex (Nanda, 2000).

Intersexuals are born having both male and female characteristics, but are forced to become either male or female. This is because pediatric surgeons routinely change their ambiguous sex to either male or female when they are still infants. Most operations involve changing the intersexual infants into girls instead of boys, primarily because of surgical convenience. As a surgeon said, "You can make a hole, but you can't build a pole" (Goode, 2001; Hendrix, 1993). However, transgenderism has emerged as a social movement that encourages the freedom to choose any form of gender identity beyond the conventional binary view that there are supposed to be only two, opposite sexes. As a result, the decision on sex-reassignment surgery is now more client-centered and less determined by the medical profession (Gorman and Cole, 2004; Nanda, 2000).

Transvestites are heterosexuals who cross-dress to obtain erotic gratification or satisfy an irresistible urge to look like a member of the opposite sex. Most are men. They are by definition distinguishable from individuals who cross-dress for show or fashion, such as men performing on stage as female impersonators or women projecting a masculine look wearing a pantsuit with a tie. Because transvestites are heterosexual, they are also distinguishable from drag queens and drag kings, who are gays and lesbians wearing clothing associated with the opposite sex. One final distinction is that gays and lesbians may flaunt their cross-dressing in public, while transvestites usually keep theirs private for fear of being ridiculed and harassed if they go public (Suthrell, 2004).

In fact, transvestites are not the only ones subject to verbal and physical harassment. So are other transgenderists, such as transsexuals and intersexuals, if the public knows they are different from the average men and women. That's why they often try to *pass* as "real" men and "real" women in order to conceal their true identity as transgenderists. Passing successfully, however, is no simple matter. Many transsexuals, for example, have to resort to electrolysis, hormone treatment, voice therapy, breast binding, mastectomy, and plastic surgery. Still, they suffer frequently from discrimination at the hand of "normal" people, even more than do gays and lesbians (Seligman, 2003; Namaste, 2000).

People with Physical Disabilities

Studies on the stigma of physical disabilities tend to distort reality by assuming that people with disabilities are *always* less desirable than "normal" people. This distortion seems to come from the influence of common sense that pervades the society. Thus, a common assumption is that compared to an average sighted person, an average blind person is less competent in walking from one place to another. But this is not necessarily true. It is true only because an unfair criterion is used, which allows the sighted to walk with their eyes open. But if we use the fairer criterion of who can best walk with eyes closed, then the blind person will definitely be more competent. That is often the essence of what stigma really is: not the disability itself but the judging of the disability by using criteria of competence that are *biased* in favor of so-called normal people.

The literature on disabilities also tends to give the impression that a person's disability is the *core* or even the *totality* of his or her self. This is unreal because the self of most people with disabilities consists of many different parts, such as being a son, daughter, parent, spouse, worker, rights activist, church member, or a quiet, kind, gentle, understanding, or wise person, and so on, many of which may be more important than being a disabled person. As a person with cerebral palsy says,

> My name is not cerebral palsy. There's a lot more to me than my disability and the problems surrounding it. That's what I call the disability trap. This country has a telethon mentality toward disability that thinks disabled people are not supposed to talk about anything but their disabilities. (Hebl and Kleck, 2000).

It is even more unreal to suggest that a disability can define the *totality* of a person's self as if he or she is already six feet under. Only dead people are totally disabled. In short, people with disabilities have many different roles to play so that they cannot be said to be mostly or totally defined by their disabilities.

Other reviewers of the literature on the stigma of disabilities have found similar, unsubstantiated assumptions (Link and Phelan, 2001; Fine and Asch, 1988):

- Disability resides solely in biology or the body.
- The disabled person's problems result from the disability-produced impairment.
- The disabled person is a victim of the disability.
- Disability is central to the disabled person's self-concept, self-definition, social comparisons, and reference groups.
- Having a disability is the same as needing help and social support.

These erroneous assumptions largely stem from the researcher's misleading definition of the stigma of disabilities, which focuses on the disability in the person rather than on the subjective, biased perception that normal people have of the disability. In reality, then, the stigma is not the disability in the disabled person; it is the perception held by normal people (Link and Phelan, 2001). Only in one sense can the stigma be a disability, but it is not located in the disabled person. It resides instead in the perception of normal people, and it often makes the disabled person's life more difficult. As a disabled person says, "My disability is how people respond to my disability" (Gill, 2001). This is comparable to what a victim of racism may say, "My problem is how racists respond to my skin color." So, to understand the stigma of disabilities, we should focus on stigma as a negative and often disabling perception in normal people and its impact on the disabled.

Certain characteristics of stigma can be found in normal people. First, stigma is *powerful*. As Bruce Link and Jo Phelan (2001) say, "it takes power to stigmatize." It is the powerful, namely the nondisabled majority, who are able to stigmatize the powerless, the disabled. The powerless may engage in reverse stigmatization by viewing the powerful as insensitive, stupid, or arrogant, but it does not mean much because it cannot significantly affect the powerful. But the powerful stigmatizers can greatly impact the lives of the disabled because they control educational institutions, employment, housing, health care, and other major life domains.

A second characteristic of stigma is the *stereotype* of disabled people as helpless, weak, and dependent, as shown by "Jerry's kids" on the annual Jerry Lewis telethons for muscular dystrophy. This is why many nondisabled people like to help wheelchair users without first asking the disabled if they need help. The stereotype of the disabled as helpless and dependent tends to make it difficult for the normal person to show disabled people respect rather than pity because the stereotype makes it impossible to know and appreciate the disabled's heroic effort to live with their disabilities and their admirable ability to achieve many things, such as finding increased meaning and value in life. The stereotype also tends to make even a compassionate normal person help the disabled in order to feel superior (Gill, 2001).

A third characteristic of stigma is whether normal people perceive a disability as *controllable or uncontrollable*. Normal people are likely to feel unsympathetic and hostile to the disabled person who has brought on his or her condition, such as contracting AIDS through sexual promiscuity and drug abuse. Apparently, normal people feel that these AIDS patients are responsible for their illness and deserve to be punished for it. More sympathy is given to those who become disabled beyond their control, such as those getting AIDS from blood transfusions (Hebl and Kleck, 2000).

A fourth characteristic of stigma is how normal people *express* it through their behaviors in the presence of a disabled person. They usually feel uncomfortable and distressed, which show up in forms of behavior that vary from one individual to another. These behaviors include fidgeting, staring, lack of eye contact, avoidance, physical distancing, expressions of sympathy, and acting as if the disability does not exist. They may also laugh at, joke about, or overcompensate their dislike with feigned hospitality toward the disabled. One behavior that the disabled find particularly disturbing is the tendency of the nondisabled to help them without being asked. The disabled often consider this helpful act an expression of pity and nervousness rather than genuine compassion and respect (Gill, 2001; Hebl and Kleck, 2000).

The stigma imputed to disabilities is bound to affect the lives of the disabled. Most people with disabilities have to struggle with employment discrimination, educational segregation, and environmental obstacles. They are also likely to have some difficulty being "welcomed as helpful neighbors, reliable friends, desired lovers, competent spouses and parents." Some disabled people become activists fighting discrimination in various spheres of social life, such as employment, public accommodation, and public services. Many other disabled people strive to get along with the nondisabled by helping them to feel good about interacting with the disabled. Thus, they may "use humor to put others at ease, tactfully ignore others' lack of tact, respond graciously to others' intrusive curiosity, and routinely sacrifice their interpersonal equality to accept unsolicited help from others who need to feel superior through helping" (Gill, 2001; Hebl and Kleck, 2000).

The Obese

Americans are getting fatter. About 31 percent of U.S. adults are now obese, twice the rate of 20 years ago. Many more Americans can be expected to join the ranks of the obese soon because a whopping 66 percent are already overweight. (According to the National Institutes of Health, "overweight" is 21 percent lighter than "obese.") The major culprit is overeating, especially of high-fat and high-sugar foods. Appetites have grown so big that businesses over the last two decades have greatly increased the amount of food served in restaurants and the quantity of potato chips, soft drinks, and other junk foods sold in grocery stores and from vending machines. Another reason for being overweight is the lack of physical exercise (Lemonick, 2004; Spake, 2002; Winslow and Landers, 2002).

Logically, because there are many more obese and overweight Americans, being heavy should become more acceptable or less stigmatized. But, ironically, the social stigma attached to fatness has increased, so that many more Americans, especially the women among them, feel unhappy about their figures. The reason is that over the last several decades the U.S. paragon of feminine beauty has gotten much thinner, with many fashion models now looking almost anorexic.

The stigma attached to heaviness, however, varies in strength from group to group. In the United States and other developed countries, obesity is more prevalent among the poor, but in poor countries the well-to-do are more likely to be fat. Thus, since the poor are generally less respectable than others, the stigma for being heavy is stronger in rich countries than in poor. But there is also a racial factor. Being heavy is more prominent among African Americans than whites, so that heavy is more acceptable and less likely to be stigmatized in the black community. Finally, the amount of stigmatization depends on what the general nonfat public thinks is the cause of fatness. If it thinks the cause is overeating and lack of exercise, which is taken to mean the person is self-indulgent and lazy, then the stigma for obesity is greater. If obesity is attributed to genetic inheritance, which is beyond the heavy person's control, then the stigma is less great. But due to the lack of data on this issue, we do not know for sure which public opinion predominates (Goode, 2004; Winslow and Landers, 2002).

The stigma of fatness has brought on three kinds of consequences. First, some female victims *internalize* the stigma, agreeing with the stigmatizing others that they are to blame for their obesity. Some of these women feel depressed and isolated while others turn to diet and exercise. Second, some heavy women *reject* the stigma, getting together to form a group expressing their pride in being heavy and to fight anti-fat discrimination. And third, the stigma for fatness has spawned a *huge industry* selling diet books, exercise programs and equipments, diet pills, liposuction, bariatric surgery, and mechanical devices for reducing weight without moving a muscle—some of which turn out to be downright fraudulent or incapable of achieving the hoped-for results (Goode, 2004; Falk, 2001).

The Tattooed

Tattoos have long been popular with drunken sailors, criminals, gangsters, prostitutes, and other disreputable people. They are used to express the identity of the wearers—who they are, what they believe in, or how they feel about the world (Vail, 2004). If you see a man sporting a tattoo on his arms that says "Kill the Pigs," you will know how he feels about the police—you can be sure he is not a worshiper of law and order (Vail, 2004; Dalrymple, 2002). Because tattoos have long been associated with disreputable characters, their wearers are usually stigmatized. But since the early 1990s, tattoos have been gaining popularity among college students, young professionals, and other middle-class, respectable people, including many women.

Why do people want to be tattooed? One reason is that they intend to seek freedom from the constraints of their relatively conservative middle-class lives by becoming a little deviant. And they see that they can experience this freedom by getting tattooed just like the drunken sailors and other deviants. For young people such as college students, for example, becoming tattooed means independence from parents and other authorities. Another reason for wanting to be tattooed is to be as "cool" as the people who sport nice-looking tattoos on TV and in other public places. There are an increasing number of individuals with tattoos in advertisements, professional athletes with tattoos, and even such famous U.S. icons as Barbie with tattoos (Irwin, 2001).

However attracted they are to the idea of getting tattooed, those people still would not hastily go out to get a tattoo because they have to contend with some aversions to deviancy. One major aversion stems from the fear of damaging relationships with parents, who usually disapprove of tattoos because they not only are associated with disreputable characters but also threaten both the family's social status and the tattoo wearer's future career. How, then, can this aversion be overcome to make tattooing possible? In other words, how can tattoos be de-stigmatized or legitimated so that the tattooed can maintain their middle-class status with all its advantages? This can be done in four ways, according to the findings of sociologist Katherine Irwin (2001), who interviewed 43 clients of a tattoo shop.

The first way involves *condemning the condemner* of tattoos. As one of Irwin's interviewees explains, "If someone wants to treat me differently because of the tattoo I would have on my ankle, that is a pretty shitty person. It would not be someone that I want to deal with anyway." This negative, antagonistic attitude toward the critic of tattoos may facilitate the decision to get a tattoo. But it may not be effective for achieving the desired goal of having one's status as a tattooed person accepted by others. The other strategies for attaining this goal are much more effective.

The second strategy involves *using conventional motivations* to justify the desire for tattoos. Such motivations exist in cases where people get a tattoo to commemorate special events in their lives, such as graduation from college, finishing final exams, getting married, or having a baby.

The third strategy involves *committing oneself to a conventional life*. This can be seen in people who prove that while getting tattooed they remain active in various conventional pursuits such as school, family, and careers. As a young man in Irwin's study says, "How could my dad really oppose? I'm everything he could want a kid to be. I'm a serious student. I get great grades. I am doing well in a career that I love and he loves. I'm married. Someday soon I will give him plenty of grandchildren. With all that, what difference is a tattoo going to make?"

And the fourth strategy involves *conforming to conventional aesthetics*. To achieve this, many middle-class tattooees avoid having the antisocial, violent, and other shocking, "in your face" images popular with bikers, skinheads, punk rockers, and other deviants emblazoned on their bodies. Instead, they go for small, discreet tattoos that show butterflies, flowers, and other images that would please rather than offend others.

With those strategies for de-stigmatizing tattoos, middle-class people have helped increase the acceptance and popularity of tattoos in conventional society. Ironically, though, while their initial desire to get tattooed was to seek *freedom* from conventional society, they have ended up using their tattoos to strengthen their *connection* to conventional society.

Summary

1. What are the popular myths about the sexual minority? One myth is that gay men are effeminate, while lesbians are manly. Other myths hold that gay men often molest young children, that gays and lesbians are restricted to either the active or passive role, are mentally ill, have an unsatisfactory sex life, and are obsessed with sex.

2. How many gays and lesbians are there in the United States? About 2.5 percent of U.S. adults see themselves as gay or lesbian. **What are some of the characteristics of gays and lesbians?** Gay men are more likely than straight men to be sexually active, but the majority of gay men are involved in long-term relationships characterized by power equality between partners. Lesbians resemble heterosexual women in having been socialized to desire long-term relationships, in having a comfortable relationship with straights, and in having the desire to be mothers. But compared with conventional women, lesbians are less likely to play the traditional female role and less aware of their same-sex orientation during adolescence.

3. What is "coming out"? It involves people revealing to others that they are gay or lesbian. **What does the process of coming out entail?** It entails going through four stages of experience: sensitization, dissociation, coming out, and commitment. **What are the other aspects of the gay and lesbian life like?** Despite the homophobia around them, lesbians and gays manage to live relatively normal, happy lives. They get along well with their straight parents and children. They date and get married like straights, except that their marriages are not legally recognized. They are mostly Democrats, better educated than straights, and belong to religious organizations as straights do.

4. What are the theories of homosexuality? According to biological theories, same-sex orientation can be traced to hormones, genes, and the brain. According to some psychiatrists, "homosexuality" is a form of mental illness that stems from strained parent-son relationships. Sociologists who hold the essentialist view of deviant behavior attribute the development of same-sex orientation to cross-gender socialization in childhood, but sociologists who embrace the constructionist view are more interested in studying homophobic reactions to gays and lesbians.

5. Do people who do not identify themselves as gay or lesbians engage in same-sex practices? Some do. They are called trades, street hustlers, situationals, and bisexuals.

6. How does homophobic society "deviantize" gays and lesbians? By using the anachronistic norm that people may only engage in reproductive sex. **What is homophobia and how widespread is it in the United States?** Homophobia is antigay prejudice and discrimination. The general public is deeply ambivalent about gays and lesbians. While it opposes their lifestyle, it nonetheless supports most equal rights for the sexual minority. **What is the impact of homophobia on the sexual minority?** Homophobia creates some social and psychological problems for gays and lesbians. **What is the social profile of homophobes?** They are distinguishable from others for being less educated, less well-off, more conservative, and more negative toward racial/ethnic minorities.

7. How has the AIDS crisis affected gays and lesbians? The sexual minority is more likely to practice safer sex now than before. When AIDS first emerged in the 1980s, however, homophobia grew more intense and gross insensitivity toward AIDS victims became common. However, today the general public has become more sympathetic due to factors such as the growing number of heterosexuals afflicted with AIDS and the effort of gays and lesbians to fight the disease for everybody.

8. What is the nature of the gay and lesbian rights movement? Most gay organizations were initially service-oriented, counseling gays in trouble or providing them with recreational activities. But in the late 1960s and early 1970s, they became militant, aiming to end antigay discriminations in all aspects of life. This brought some victories for the sexual minority, which cooled the militancy. Because the outbreak of the AIDS crisis led to greater homophobia in the 1980s, some gay activists have become militant again, but the majority have remained moderate, engaging in antihomophobic activities much like any conventional interest group.

9. What is the condition of homophobia in other countries? Homophobia is generally more serious in less affluent societies than in the United States. Gays and lesbians are known to have been beaten, raped, imprisoned, and institutionalized. In Russia nearly half of the population say that gays should be executed or isolated. In Zimbabwe and Egypt, gays tend to be beaten and tortured in jail.

10. Who are the transgenderists? Transgenderists have the characteristics of both genders rather than those of only one. Common examples are transsexuals, intersexuals, and transvestites. They usually pass as "normal" men or women to avoid harassment in conventional society. **What are disabled people like?** Contrary to what common sense suggests, they are not totally or mostly defined by their disabilities because they play many roles that have nothing to do with being disabled. **What is the stigma of disabilities like?** It has these characteristics: (1) It comes from powerful people; (2) it involves stereotyping the disabled as helpless; (3) it hurts the victim more if the latter's disability is controllable; and (4) it is expressed through "normal" people's behavior.

11. Why are more American women today stigmatized for being fat? Because food consumption has increased and the standard of feminine beauty has gotten thinner. **What consequences does the stigma of fatness bring?** Some of its victims accept the stigma, others reject it, and a huge industry has emerged to help the victims get slim. **How do middle-class people overcome the stigma of tattoos?** By condemning the condemner, using conventional motivations to justify the desire for tattoos, committing themselves to conventional life, and conforming to conventional aesthetics.

FURTHER READING

Albrecht, Gary L., Katherine D. Seelman, and Michael Bury (eds.). 2001. *Handbook of Disability Studies.* A collection of articles reviewing the literature on many aspects of disability, including the experiences of being disabled and the social factors behind disability.

Beemyn, Brett, and Mickey Eliason (eds.). 1996. *Queer Studies: A Lesbian, Gay, Bisexual, and Transgender Anthology.* A collection of articles on various dimensions of same-sex attractions and practices.

Blumenfeld, Warren J. (ed.). 1992. *Homophobia: How We All Pay the Price.* Boston: Beacon. A collection of articles on various aspects of homophobia, ranging from sources and manifestations of the problem to ways of breaking free from it.

Blumenfeld, Warren J., and Diane Raymond. 1993. *Looking at Gay and Lesbian Life.* Boston: Beacon. Discusses many different issues about homosexuality, including gay sex, causes of homosexuality, homophobia, the gay rights movement, and AIDS.

Byne, William, and Bruce Parsons. 1993. "Human sexual orientation: The biologic theories reappraised." *Archives of General Psychiatry, 50* (March), 228–239. An examination of various biological theories, which concludes that genes or hormones per se do not directly influence sexual orientation.

Falk, Gerhard. 2001. *Stigma: How We Treat Outsiders.* Amherst, N.Y.: Prometheus Books. A survey of various types of socially stigmatized groups, including the mentally ill, the obese, the mentally challenged, the homeless, and alcoholics.

Garber, Marjorie. 2000. *Bisexuality and the Eroticism of Everyday Life.* New York: Routledge. Analyzing various aspects of bisexuality, such as its culture, politics, and history, its normal sex, and its unique eroticisms.

Harris, Daniel. 1997. *The Rise and Fall of Gay Culture.* New York: Hyperion. A critical analysis of how the increasing assimilation of gays into mainstream society robs the gay culture of its distinctive sensibility and other values.

Heatherton, Todd F. et al. (eds.). 2000. *The Social Psychology of Stigma.* New York: Guilford Press. A collection of articles dealing with the development of stigma, its impact on the victims, and the interaction between the stigmatizers and their victims.

Katz, Jonathan Ned. 1995. *The Invention of HeteroSEXU- ALITY.* New York: Dutton Books. A social constructionist analysis of how the concept of heterosexuality—the basis for defining homosexuality as deviant in psychiatry and society in general—did not exist until about a century ago.

Kotula, Dean. 2002. *The Phallus Palace.* Los Angeles, Calif.: Alyson Publications. A full presentation of how it feels to be a female-to-male transsexual and how he is treated by others.

LeVay, Simon, and Elisabeth Nonas. 1995. *City of Friends: A Portrait of the Gay and Lesbian Community in America.* Cambridge, Mass.: The MIT Press. A highly informative guide into the community and lives of gay and lesbian Americans.

Marcus, Eric. 1992. *Making History: The Struggle for Gay and Lesbian Equal Rights.* New York: HarperCollins. An interesting and enlightening collection of autobiographical accounts of various stages of the gay rights movement.

Miller, Nancy B., and Catherine C. Sammons. 1999. *Everybody's Different: Understanding and Changing Our Reactions to Disabilities.* Baltimore, Md.: Paul Brookes Publishing. Close-up view of various kinds of disabilities.

Miller, Neil. 1992. *Out in the World: Gay and Lesbian Life from Buenos Aires to Bangkok.* New York: Random House. A close-up view of same-sex experiences in 12 countries, most quite different from the gay life in the United States.

Nanda, Serena. 2000. *Gender Diversity: Crosscultural Variations.* Prospect Heights, Ill.: Waveland Press. A wide-ranging examination of transgender practices throughout the world.

Seidman, Steven. 2002. *Beyond the Closet: The Transformation of Gay and Lesbian Life.* New York: Routledge. Shows how U.S. gays and lesbians have emerged from the closet to join mainstream society but more as tolerated minorities than equal citizens.

Suthrell, Charlotte. 2004. *Unzipping Gender: Sex, Cross-Dressing and Culture.* Oxford, U.K.: Berg. A cross-cultural study of transvestism, revealing the greater social acceptance of cross-dressing in India than in Britain.

Swain, John et al. (eds.). 2004. *Disabling Barriers— Enabling Environments,* 2nd ed. London: Sage Publications. A collection of articles presenting the social perspectives on disability, people's views of their own disability, the problems faced by the disabled, and the support offered to the disabled.

Vaid, Urvashi. 1995. *Virtual Equality: The Mainstreaming of Gay and Lesbian Liberation.* New York: Anchor Books. Shows how mainstreamed gays and lesbians are only virtually—but not really—equal to straights.

Warner, Michael. 1999. *The Trouble with Normal: Sex, Politics, and the Ethics of Queer Life.* New York: Free Press. A provocative analysis of conventional sex and marriage as well as gay life and politics.

CRITICAL THINKING QUESTIONS

1. If some heterosexual people engage in homosexual activities, what would you consider them to be? Straight or gay or what? Explain your answer.

2. Can the victims of stigma that we have discussed get rid of the stigma? If yes, how? If not, why not?

PART FIVE

Substance Use and Abuse

CHAPTER

11 Legal and Illegal Drug Use

A successful, extremely well-paid advertising executive, David, aged 25, smokes marijuana every day, usually at night, after work. "I use marijuana to relax," he explains, "to contemplate, and to enjoy myself. It makes me feel good, and I get a lot of insight from it. I'm more able to perceive who the other person is, and suspend all of life's petty 'games.' Anyway, I feel good when I'm stoned. That's why I do it. That's why I do it *regularly*. . . . It's fun. Food tastes better, sex is more expressive and enjoyable—yes, pot is an aphrodisiac, at least it is for me—I enjoy music more, I use my imagination more listening to music. . . . When someone asks me, why do I smoke dope, I answer, why not? There are no negatives, only positives. Really. Why not?" (Goode, 1999).

Is David a drug abuser? Objectively, he is not, because he does not use the drug to the extent of losing his job, his health, or his life. But the general public would consider him a drug abuser, simply because the drug in question, marijuana, is *illegal*. If David were regularly smoking cigarettes or drinking wine rather than using marijuana, he would *not* be considered a drug abuser, because tobacco and alcohol are *legal* drugs. The public also assumes that illegal drugs are always more dangerous than legal drugs, and that most users of illegal drugs are hopelessly hooked on the substances. Thus, in this chapter we will first discuss why this is not the case. We will then analyze the effects of various illegal drugs and the connection between such drugs, on the one hand, and AIDS and crime, on the other. We will also examine the extent of illegal drug use, the characteristics of the drug users, the process of becoming a drug user, theories of drug use, and the war on drugs. Finally, we will zero in on the use of OxyContin and tobacco as examples of legal drugs.

Drug Use in Perspective

Contrary to popular belief, *legal* drugs may in some ways be more dangerous than illegal ones. First, the use of such legal drugs as alcoholic beverages and tobacco cigarettes is considerably more prevalent than the use of such illegal drugs as marijuana, heroin, and cocaine. Some 18 million Americans are alcoholics and 55 million are regular smokers, compared with only 5.5 million users of illegal drugs. Other legal drugs, such as sedatives, tranquilizers, and stimulants, though less popular than alcohol and tobacco, are still more widely used than such illegal drugs as heroin and cocaine. Not surprisingly, the use of legal drugs, particularly alcohol and tobacco, causes far more death, sickness, violent crime, economic loss, and other social problems than the use of illegal drugs. For example, every year just two legal drugs—alcohol and tobacco—kill at least 60 times as many Americans as do all the illegal drugs combined (Falco, 1992).

Contrary to popular assumption, then, legal prohibition—or, more generally, societal disapproval—of a drug does not necessarily indicate how dangerous the drug really is. Instead, the disapproval reflects more the temper of the time and place. Opium is today an illegal drug and is widely condemned as a panopathogen (a cause of all ills), but in the last two centuries it was a legal drug and was popularly praised as a panacea (a cure for all ills). In contrast, cigarette smoking is legal in all countries today, but in the seventeenth century it was illegal in most countries and the smoker was harshly punished in some. The penalty for smoking, for example, included death in Turkey and China, removal of noses in Russia, and slitting of lips in Hindustan (Goode, 1999).

In assuming that illegal drugs are more dangerous than legal ones, the general public also believes that people who use illegal drugs typically become addicted, compulsive, or heavy users. But empirical evidence suggests that most people who use illicit drugs do so only experimentally, occasionally, or moderately, without sliding down the slippery slope to compulsive and uncontrollable use. This is because the majority of drug users have the ability to draw the line on what they do. Drugs by themselves do not have the power to pull users down the slippery slope. There are, of course, real horrors in drug use, but they befall only a few, not most, users (Goode, 1999).

Illegal Drugs: Their Effects and Users

Most drugs can be differentiated into three categories according to their effects on the user's central nervous system—the brain and spinal cord. One category includes *stimulants* ("uppers") such as cocaine, crack, caffeine, and nicotine. These drugs can stimulate the activity of the central nervous system, temporarily producing alertness and excitation as well as suppressing fatigue and sluggishness. Another category consists of *depressants* ("downers") such as heroin, PCP, morphine, and aspirin. In direct contrast to stimulants, depressants reduce the activity of the nervous system, so they can relax muscles, relieve anxiety, alleviate pain, create euphoria, or induce sleep. The third category comprises *hallucinogens* (psychedelics) such as LSD and MDMA ("ecstasy"). These drugs can disturb the nervous system, altering the user's perception of reality. Most illicit drugs belong in only one of these three categories of drugs, but marijuana does not. Marijuana is in a class by itself, because it can affect the user in the same way as each of the three types of drugs. Thus some experts have classified marijuana as a stimulant, others have categorized it as a depressant, and still others have regarded it as a hallucinogen.

No matter what kind of drug they are, they do not by themselves produce the effects mentioned above. Certain factors also influence the effects of drugs. One factor is the *dosage:* The higher the dosage or amount of a drug, the stronger its effect on the user. A second factor is the *purity* (or *potency*) of the drug: The more psychoactive substance (such as the chemical THC in marijuana) there is in the drug—or the more actual heroin or cocaine there is in a batch of heroin or cocaine—the easier it is to get "high." A third factor is *drug mixing:* Snorting cocaine while high on marijuana, or taking an injection of "speedball" (a combination of cocaine and heroin) has a synergistic or multiplier effect, which is many times more powerful than either of the two drugs taken separately. A fourth factor is the method of *administration:* Intravenous injection ("mainlining")—putting a drug directly into the bloodstream—produces a stronger effect than intramuscular injection ("skin popping"), which involves injecting the drug into the arm or leg muscles. Smoking cocaine in the form of crack also has a more powerful effect than snorting it. And a fifth factor is the degree of *habituation:* A drug has a greater effect on occasional users than chronic users (Goode, 1999). Keeping in mind these factors that influence drug effects, let us now take a closer look at the effects and users of today's three most-often-used illegal drugs and three newly popular ones.

Marijuana

Marijuana is the most widely used illegal drug in the United States. It is derived from the Indian hemp plant called *Cannabis sativa*. The top of the plant produces a sticky resin containing a psychoactive substance. A small portion of this psychoactive resin flows downward and coats the lower part of the plant. What is typically sold and bought as marijuana ("grass," "weed," "pot," or "dope") in the United States comes from the entire plant. But when only the top of the plant is harvested, the product is *hashish*, which is far more psychoactively potent than marijuana. Both marijuana and hashish can be eaten or drunk, but are more commonly smoked in the form of cigarettes ("joints" or "reefers"). The cannabis plant can grow all over the world, but the better grades come from the United States, Mexico, Jamaica, and Thailand.

When it was first used in ancient times, marijuana was considered a sacred and useful drug, as suggested by the following passages from ancient Indian literature:

> To the Hindu the hemp plant is holy. A guardian lives in bhang [marijuana]. . . . Bhang is the joy giver, the sky flier, the heavenly guide, the poor man's heaven, the soother of grief . . . No god or man is as good as the religious drinker of bhang. The students of the scriptures of Benares are given bhang before they sit to study. At holy places, yogis take deep draughts of bhang, that they may enter their thoughts on the Eternal. . . . By the help of bhang, ascetics pass days without food or drink. The supporting power of bhang has brought many a Hindu family safe through the miseries of famine. (quoted in Szasz, 1974a)

Yet there has been a great deal of opposition toward using marijuana in our society. This has distorted the judgment of both lay and scientific people about its effects. In the early 1950s, the former head of the Bureau of Narcotics expressed the popular view of the effects of marijuana this way: "In the earliest stages of intoxication the willpower is destroyed and inhibitions and restraints are released; moral barricades are broken down and often debauchery and sexuality result. Where mental instability is inherent, behavior is generally violent" (Anslinger and Thompkins, 1953). But later many researchers found that marijuana tends to inhibit rather than induce aggressive behavior. In an experimental study by two of these researchers, subjects who had taken relatively high doses of marijuana responded less aggressively to provocation than did those who had taken a lower dose (Myerscough and Taylor, 1985).

Today many people, particularly government scientists, argue that there are serious health hazards in smoking marijuana. Smokers can experience short-term effects such as memory loss, anxiety, and increased heart rate. Chronic smokers can eventually develop cancer, respiratory diseases, and heart problems. But critics point out that the majority of marijuana users do not suffer lasting harm while the drug's mild intoxicating effects are no more dangerous than those of alcohol and tobacco (Williams, 2003).

However, if smoked in large doses for an extended period, marijuana can be *physically* addictive. If marijuana use is discontinued, the user will suffer withdrawal symptoms such as mild nausea, restlessness, and loss of appetite, though not as serious as those caused by addiction to heroin and other hard drugs. Marijuana can also be *psychologically* addictive, but only mildly so, because it is not as immensely pleasurable as cocaine or heroin. If used to the point of intoxication, marijuana can create problems in the same way as alcoholic beverages. It can, for example, impair intellectual judgment, short-term memory, and human psychomotor function. It can thus hamper reading or studying. It can also undermine the performance of car drivers and airline pilots (Murray, 1986; Yesavage et al., 1985). But when used moderately, marijuana can create euphoria, heighten sensitivity, improve perception, and increase appetite (Falco, 1992). Marijuana can also be used for medical purposes, particularly for the benefit of the very ill. In the purified form under the trade name Marinol, or when smoked like a cigarette, marijuana has proven effective for controlling nausea and relieving pain in seriously ill patients with AIDS, cancer, and other diseases (Conant, 1997; Cowley, 1997; Doblin and Kleiman, 1993).

Many people believe that marijuana is a "gateway" to harder drugs. Indeed, considerable research has shown that almost all heroin and cocaine users started out with weed (Kandel and Jessor, 2002). But such a finding does not mean that marijuana use inevitably leads to hard drugs in the sense of marijuana itself being the cause of the drug escalation. The cause more likely lies in the marijuana user's involvement with friends who use hard drugs. In other words, pot smokers use heroin or cocaine largely because they have friends already using the hard drug (Goode, 1999).

Heroin

This drug, also called "P-dope" on the street, was first produced in 1898 from morphine, which was in turn first derived in 1803 from opium. Both morphine and heroin are analgesics (painkillers) and have been used as such. But heroin use is now a major source of our society's concern with the problem of drug abuse. Most of our heroin comes from opium poppies harvested in the Golden Triangle of Southeast Asia (Burma, Thailand, and Laos), the Golden Crescent of South Asia (Pakistan, Afghanistan, and Iran), Mexico, and Colombia.

Heroin can be smoked, sniffed through the nose, taken orally, or injected into the skin, a muscle, or a vein. Injection of the substance into a vein, or mainlining, produces the quickest and most intense high. Traditionally, mainlining has been by far the most common method of ingestion. But fear of AIDS and the greatly increased potency of today's heroin have made smoking or snorting increasingly popular. Taken in moderate doses, heroin not only can dull pain but also diminish anxiety and tension. Most important, heroin can induce euphoria—the feeling of a "flash," "rush," or intense orgasmlike sensation. Actually, heroin itself does not bring about the euphoric feeling; the user has to *learn* to achieve the sense of pleasure from heroin injection. The novice user typically encounters an unpleasant experience from the first shot. Yet the negative experience can easily be rationalized, thus opening the way for taking more heroin trips. Here's how a young woman described her first heroin experience with her boyfriend:

> The rush was so powerful that he almost fell down. He turned white and began to sweat profusely. . . . I, too, began to sweat and tremble. If anyone had seen . . . us walking out of the house, he would have called an ambulance, we could barely

walk. For some insane reason, we had decided to drive home immediately after shooting up . . . I had to keep pulling over to throw up on the side of the road . . . I was truly surprised that we both didn't die that very first night. I was more physically miserable than I had ever been before. The whole night was spent vomiting. The thing that surprises me is that we didn't forget about heroin right then and there. It was horrible! But we later decided that our dear friend had given us too much. So I decided to give it another chance. (Goode, 1999)

Once users try heroin several times, as this woman did, they feel an extreme pleasure from the drug experience. Many heroin users, both male and female, claim that the heroin rush is more satisfying than orgasm and the heroin high far more glorious and pleasurable than anything the nonuser could possibly experience. This, however, can easily lead to psychological dependence on the drug. Furthermore, heroin is physically addictive. If deprived of it for just one day, the addict may suffer withdrawal sickness. Those symptoms include profuse sweating, running nose, watering eyes, chills, cramps, nausea, and diarrhea (Chase, 1996a).

To relieve or avoid these withdrawal symptoms, the addict obviously has to keep on using heroin. This has led many researchers to believe that once people become addicted, they can no longer experience the pleasurable effects of preaddiction drug use—that addicts use heroin only for *avoiding* the withdrawal distress. As the influential drug researcher Alfred Lindesmith (1968) wrote, "The critical experience in the fixation process is not the positive euphoria produced by the drug but rather the relief of the pain that invariably appears when a physically dependent person stops using the drug." But William McAuliffe and Robert Gordon (1974) presented data to show that, contrary to Lindesmith's belief, addicts do continue to experience *euphoria* following each injection of heroin. McAuliffe and Gordon argued that if it were not for the promise of euphoria, addicts would not persistently take the trouble to steal and hustle to get money for the next fix, and that if they only wanted to avoid withdrawal distress, they would quickly seek help at some drug treatment center. But this is not the case.

Both interpretations may well miss the mark. They above all reflect the researchers' own perceptions of what the experience of the drug effect means to them rather than to the addicts, who were not asked how they themselves actually felt. According to an ethnographic study, which encouraged addicts to express their feelings, most heroin addicts seek *something between* withdrawal avoidance and euphoria—more than the desperate avoidance of withdrawal distress but less than the intense euphoria they initially experienced. What they seek is "a temporary calm and serenity, feelings of normalcy, relaxation, and capability to provide them with a respite from the bleak harshness of their lives. It is the pursuit of normalcy rather than of euphoria that propels these heroin users to continue to use the substance." The pursuit of normalcy, however, does not involve the frantic, pathetic search for relief from the pain of withdrawal symptoms. Instead, heroin addicts see themselves in control rather than as "down-and-out dope fiends." They have a sense of pride in being able to achieve normalcy in a society that has relegated them to a lowly status (Hanson et al., 1985).

Although heroin is addictive, most users do not become addicts. A major reason is that heroin users typically get less and less pleasure from the drug after their early experiences of euphoria. As a former user says, "Luckily, it was no longer feeling good enough to make it worth getting busted for. . . . Heroin had lost its immense power over me. It simply wasn't worth it. The magic ceased to happen long ago. There's only the memory. . . . Right now I'd rather go out for a good dinner than shoot a bag of heroin" (Goode, 1981). There is also no truth to the old saw that "once a junkie, always a junkie." One study shows that, among the returning Vietnam veterans in 1971 who had been addicted to heroin while overseas, over 90 percent were no longer addicted about eight months after their return home (Maddux and Desmond, 1980; Robins, 1973). Even if permanently addicted to heroin, people do not necessarily suffer severe damage to their health. The drug may be harmless when compared with other psychoactive drugs. Unlike cigarette smoking and alcohol drinking, prolonged use of heroin does not necessarily damage the organs, tissues, or cells of the human body. As long as heroin addicts do not neglect other aspects of their lives, they can remain as healthy as the nonuser. As Jerome Jaffe (1965), the physician who later served as President Nixon's adviser on drug problems, observed,

> The addict who is able to obtain an adequate supply of the drug through legitimate channels and has adequate funds, usually dresses properly, maintains his nutrition, and is able to discharge his social and occupational obligations with reasonable efficiency. He usually remains in good health, suffers little inconvenience, and is, in general, difficult to distinguish from other persons.

A good example is the physician addict. Although they use a much greater quantity of narcotics than "street junkies," physician addicts generally manage to maintain their health and practice their profession. They are only less efficient in their work when compared with their addiction-free colleagues (Coombs, 1997).

On the other hand, street junkies are far more likely to suffer the consequences of narcotics laws. Because of these laws, heroin's black market prices are usually so high that the addicts, who are mostly poor, have to spend a great deal of their time frantically searching for money to buy the next fix. The frantic search for money tends to involve the user in committing burglaries, shoplifting, gambling, prostitution, and other acquisitive crimes, which creates a great deal of stress and strain. By the time they get enough money to buy a packet of "junk," they are likely to be both physically drained and emotionally stressed out. In addition, there is no way for them to know how pure or potent the packet is—its heroin content may range from zero to 99 percent. If they are used to no more than 5 percent heroin and happen to buy a packet of 50 percent, they may die of an overdose (Smolowe, 1993).

Cocaine and Crack

Also known as "coke," "snow," and "toot," cocaine is derived from the leaves of coca plants. At least 90 percent of the coca plants in the world are grown on the mountains of Peru and Bolivia, whose governments sometimes treasure the crop as one of their major exports. The coca leaves, however, are processed into cocaine in Colombia, and from there the final product is smuggled into the United States (Wren, 1997).

Before it became illegal at the turn of this century, cocaine was commonly used as a local anesthetic, for offsetting fatigue and depression, and for curing morphine addiction and stomach disorder. It was even chosen as the official remedy of the Hay Fever Association. Sigmund Freud, the founder of psychoanalysis, not only prescribed cocaine for his patients to treat those ills, but also used the drug himself to stay alert and ward off melancholy. Cocaine was also a major ingredient in numerous patent medicines and in many soft drinks, such as Coca-Cola. In 1885, a well-known pharmaceutical company promoted cocaine as a wonder drug, claiming that it could "supply the place of food, make the coward brave, the silent eloquent, free the victims of alcohol and opium habit from their bondage, and, as an anesthetic, render the sufferer insensitive to pain." One of the best, most popular wines in the late nineteenth century, marketed under the name of Vin Mariani, contained some cocaine. It won endorsement from Pope Leo XIII, Pope Pius X, President McKinley, the kings of four countries (Spain, Greece, Norway, and Sweden), and many famous writers and artists. The French sculptor who designed the Statue of Liberty swore that if he had only drunk Vin Mariani earlier, he would have been able to build that lady hundreds of meters higher (Musto, 1986; Goode, 1981).

By the turn of the twentieth century, when laws were passed to make cocaine illegal, it had become widely used as a pleasure drug. At that time most of the users were the powerless, such as African Americans, lower-class whites, and criminals. But since the 1960s cocaine has become a symbol of wealth or status, mostly used by affluent whites. It is the most expensive drug, sometimes called "the champagne of drugs" or "caviar among drugs." Usually snorted, the drug is in the form of white powder—hence also called "powder cocaine." One can seek a greater high by resorting to "freebasing," which involves purifying the drug with ether and then smoking it. Since 1986, however, an increasing number of youths, especially those from poor and working-class families, have used crack cocaine—or simply, "crack." It is a less pure form of cocaine but can still produce an intense high because users typically smoke it rather than snort it. Crack is much cheaper than pure cocaine, which may explain its popular use among the poor and the young.

As a stimulant, cocaine increases the heartbeat and raises blood pressure and body temperature. A snort in each nostril can produce a euphoric lift that lasts for half an hour or so. The cocaine high may be described objectively as an intensely vivid, sensation-sharpening experience. In the view of users themselves, the drug (1) provides exhilaration—a sense of elation, well-being, or a voluptuous, joyous feeling; (2) enhances self-confidence, supplying a sense of mastery and competence in what the user does; and (3) increases energy and suppresses fatigue, enabling the user to continue physical and mental activity more intensely and longer—such as by working for two or three days and nights straight without any sleep. Some users claim that cocaine is an aphrodisiac, but most deny it. There is increasing evidence that sustained use of cocaine can cause sexual dysfunction and impotence (Goode, 1981).

Cocaine is physically addictive; it produces such withdrawal symptoms as exhaustion and stomach cramps after its use is discontinued. Cocaine is particularly noteworthy for being extremely psychologically addictive, due largely to the high quality of pleasure the user can derive from it. Coming down from a high usually causes such a deep gloom that the only remedy is more cocaine. Bigger doses follow, and soon the urge becomes a total obsession, with all its devastating consequences. As one cocaine user said, "I even hocked my wife's wedding ring. That's not me. Whoever said cocaine isn't addicting should be shot" (Rosenfeld, 1985). The powerful psychological addiction to cocaine has been demonstrated in laboratory experiments with animals. Once hooked on cocaine, rats and monkeys will prefer the drug to food, even though they have not eaten all day. They will keep on pressing the bar (which they have been trained to do) for a cocaine reward until they drop from exhaustion. Crack is even more addictive than plain cocaine. The rush comes and goes so much more quickly and intensely that the crack user can get hooked much faster. According to the National Institute on Drug Abuse, crack addiction develops after only six to ten weeks, while it takes three to four years for users to get hooked on regular cocaine. When snorted, the coke reaches the brain in about eight minutes to produce a much milder high than that from crack. But crack hits the brain within only seconds in an intensified, concentrated form (Lamar, 1986).

Most people who use cocaine find their experience positive. But the drug can also be extremely dangerous if taken in large doses or used frequently for an extended time. It can cause insomnia, impotence, extreme irritability, paranoia and other symptoms of psychosis, and the sensation of bugs crawling under the skin. A single overdose can also produce an effect like "lighting a fire in the brain," triggering severe headaches, nausea, and convulsions with the possibility of total respiratory and cardiovascular collapse. Crack puts its users even at higher risks. Since it swiftly and dramatically increases blood pressure and heart rate, crack can more easily lead to heart attacks and deaths. Most users of cocaine, however, do not experience these effects, primarily because they use cocaine moderately and infrequently.

Meth and Roofies

Meth (methamphetamine), an injectable stimulant known on the street as "speed," "crank," or "crystal," has, since 1995, risen dramatically in popularity among drug users throughout the western United States. The drug itself is not new. During the Second World War, soldiers on both sides used it to reduce fatigue and enhance performance. Hitler was widely believed to be a meth addict. Later, in the 1960s, President John Kennedy also used the drug, and soon it caught on among so-called speed freaks. But because it was extremely expensive as well as difficult to obtain, meth was never close to being as widely used as cocaine. Today, however, largely because Mexican drug traffickers have made meth easily available in the West, its use has increased sharply in that region, where meth has supplanted cocaine as the drug of choice. Meth has also spread to many rural areas in the Midwest, and is now making its way to the East. A growing number of users are white, 18- to 34-year-old working-class men and women, who like the fact that the high from meth lasts four or five times longer than that from cocaine. When used initially, meth is known to suppress appetite, create euphoria, boost self-confidence, and provide a burst of energy. But after users develop a tolerance for the drug, depression is likely to set in, followed by intense paranoia (Johnson, 2004; Kirn, 1998; Witkin, 1995).

Unlike meth, which is a stimulant, another recently popular drug is a depressant. In tablet form, the drug is known on the street as "roofies," "rope," "the forget pill," and "roach." It is related to the sedative Valium but is 10 times stronger. Roofies is actually Rohypnol, a prescription drug for severe insomnia. Rohypnol is sold over the counter in some 60 countries, and much of the drug used on the street in the United States is smuggled from Mexico and Colombia. The drug is particularly popular with teenagers in the South and Southwest, who like to combine the drug with alcohol for a quick high. This practice is apparently dangerous—it is what sent the grunge-rock star Kurt Cobain into a coma a month before he committed suicide. Like strong liquor, roofies make some users aggressive and fearless, but they often cause blackouts, with a total loss of memory. Consequently, some men use roofies to knock women out and then rape them, and it is from this use that the drug is also known as "the date-rape drug." The drug has also caused a great deal of concern about its potential for addiction and lethal overdosing (Cannon, 1999; Seligmann and King, 1996).

Ecstasy

The most recently popular illegal drug is Ecstasy, which chemists call MDMA (methylenedioxymethamphetamine). Since 1992, the number of people who use the drug for the first time has soared extraordinarily (see Figure 11.1). The drug is popular with high school and college students and relatively affluent young adults, who typically swallow the drug as a pill at a dance club or party. Ecstasy is a psychedelic, a mood-altering drug. Most of its users report that they feel happier, their mind gets clearer, and their memory improves. They also feel a stronger desire for human connection so that they become compassionate and forgiving toward others. They are thus more inclined to, for example, embrace people, which is why Ecstasy is nicknamed the "hug drug." In short, according to its users, the drug provides a new, better perspective on life. Here is how an Ecstasy user describes how the drug has changed his life:

> Since I've started rolling I'm healthier. I don't smoke, I don't drink, I exercise, I take vitamins. I've gotten interested in meditation. This whole scene for me has been the best thing personally. I've become a better human being. I've become much more calm, much more considerate. I don't freak out about stupid things anymore (Klam, 2001).

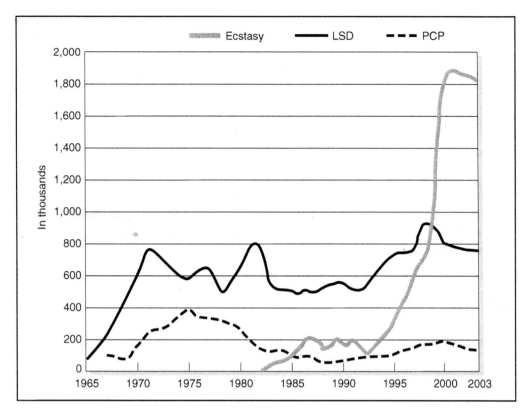

FIGURE 11.1   Annual Numbers of New Users of Hallucinogens

Source: National Household Survey on Drug Abuse (NHSDA), 2004.

But to the U.S. government and some scientists, the drug is dangerous. In 1985, when the law making Ecstasy illegal was passed, there were false rumors that the drug caused Parkinson's disease and that it could turn your spine into jelly or liquid. In recent years a series of studies have shown that rats and monkeys given large doses of Ecstasy suffered brain damage. As a result, some scientists conclude that even one dose of Ecstasy can damage your brain. Such a conclusion is unwarranted. High doses of Ecstasy like those given to the rats and monkeys are indeed dangerous, but so is swallowing a whole bottle of Tylenol, which can wreck your liver and cause you to die. But human users of Ecstasy typically take only a small dose of the drug.

Using Ecstasy does have at least two big problems. One is that the specific doses of Ecstasy may be impure, containing foreign substances that can kill. The other problem is that Ecstasy can cause a body to overheat. If people do not drink enough water to quench the enormous thirst, they may experience dehydration, organ failure, or brain damage. On the other hand, drinking too much water may cause death from thinned-out blood (Klam, 2001).

Social Dimensions of Drug Use

Drug use is not an individual behavior, engaged in simply by one person and affecting one person alone. It is social behavior, involving many drug users and affecting not only the drug user but also many other people—in fact, the entire society. Here we focus on four social dimensions of drug use: the extent of drug use in the United States, how U.S. society reacts to drug use, the impact of drug use on the spread of AIDS, and the influence of drug use on crime.

The Extent of Drug Use

The use of illegal drugs is quite common in the United States. About 12 percent of the U.S. population age 12 or older use illicit drugs every year, half of them at least once a month. Of various age groups, young adults (ages 18 to 25) have the highest rate of drug use and teenagers (ages 12 to 17) the second highest. The United States as a whole has the highest rate of drug use among the industrial countries of the world, and U.S. high school seniors also have the highest rate among their peers in the industrial world (NHSDA, 2001; Sallett, Goode, and Pooler, 1999; Currie, 1993).

All this, however, should not be blown out of proportion. It is true that the United States leads the industrial nations in drug use. It is not true that drug use is so pervasive that it invades every nook and cranny, enslaving all classes of Americans to the same extent. Most drug problems, especially the most serious ones, such as drug addiction, death from drug overdose, or drug-related homicide, are for the most part confined to the lower classes, particularly to socially and economically oppressed minorities. Drug use and overdose among the nonpoor, middle class, or affluent is generally far less common (Massing, 1998; Currie, 1993).

In fact, for Americans as a whole, the rate of drug use steadily declined from 1980 to 1992, and since 1992 the rate has remained about the same. But for teenagers, the rate has been rising, driven mostly by white youngsters smoking pot, so that today first-time users of marijuana outnumber users of any other drug (see Table 11.1). The sharpest increase in drug use has occurred among young teens, around age 13 (Sallett, Goode, and Pooler, 1999). Another noteworthy finding: African-American students in secondary school are now less likely than their white peers to use drugs because they are more likely to have observed at close hand how drugs wreck lives in black communities (Wren, 1996; Bogert, 1994).

Moral Panic: Societal Reaction to Drug Use

Because drug use is widely condemned as deviant and dangerous, society tends to respond with a moral panic regardless of what the facts about the problem are (Goode and Ben-Yehuda, 1994). Thus, the general public often seems to be seized with the terrible vision of huge masses of Americans shooting heroin, snorting cocaine, smoking pot, or using meth, roofies, or some other illicit drug. Even in the midst of a declining drug use in the 1980s, *Newsweek* (1986) declared:

TABLE 11.1   First-Time Users of Drugs in 2000

Drug	Number of People Using the Drug for the First Time
Marijuana	2.4 million
Ecstasy	1.9 million
Cocaine	0.9 million
Meth	0.3 million
Heroin	0.2 million

Source: National Household Survey on Drug Abuse, 2001.

An epidemic is abroad in America, as pervasive and as dangerous in its way as the plagues of medieval times. . . . It has taken lives, wrecked careers, broken homes, invaded schools, incited crimes, tainted businesses, toppled heroes, corrupted policemen and politicians, bled billions from the economy and in some measure infected every corner of our public and private lives.

In the year when the rate of drug use hit bottom, Mathea Falco (1992), former assistant secretary of state for international narcotics matters and drug-abuse adviser to Bill Clinton during the presidential campaign, also proclaimed:

The horrors of drug abuse have become depressingly familiar: crack-addicted mothers abandoning their babies; young children dealing drugs instead of going to school; innocent citizens killed in gang shoot-outs; and sports stars dying from overdoses. . . . Drug abuse is at the heart of what many people think has gone wrong with America. It appears as either the cause or the effect of a wide range of problems which seem out of control: urban blight, the destruction of families, the failure of schools, the loss of economic productivity.

Such displays of moral panic about drug use are difficult to justify. Of course, illegal drugs can be extremely dangerous—if used improperly, incessantly, or excessively. But the majority of users use drugs responsibly—experimentally, occasionally, or moderately. If this were not the case, the huge numbers of baby boomers who used drugs in the 1960s, including President Clinton, would today have become hopeless junkies and the whole nation would have gone to the dogs. Should we, then, shut our eyes to our society's drug problem? Absolutely not. But instead of succumbing to moral panic, the family, school, and media can be more effective by calmly doing such things as providing youngsters with valid rather than "scare" information about drugs or encouraging them to avoid drugs (as has been successfully done with smoking) or to use drugs responsibly to avoid harming themselves or others (as has been successfully done with drinking and driving).

Drugs and AIDS

Intravenous (IV) injection of an illegal drug can spread HIV, the virus that causes AIDS, from one user to another. Most drug users with AIDS are addicted to heroin, and they have caught the deadly disease from sharing needles with other addicts. The connection between drugs and AIDS is remarkably strong in the United States. IV drug users with AIDS make up less than 10 percent of all AIDS cases in Holland, Sweden, and Canada. By sharp contrast, this figure is over 30 percent in the United States. The proportion is considerably higher in some U.S. cities: 40 percent in New York City and 65 percent in Newark. In fact, the spread of the AIDS virus has virtually stopped among gays, but continues among IV drug users (CDC, 2003; Currie, 1993). Why?

A major factor behind the sharp drop in the new incidence of AIDS among gays is the practice of safe sex. But many IV drug users refuse to practice safe needle use, continuing to share needles and rejecting clean needles even if easily available (Decker and Rosenfeld, 1992; Sibthorpe et al., 1991). Why do they take the terrible risk of HIV infection? One reason is that they are drug addicts rather than occasional drug users. Their craving for drugs is so overwhelming that they must shoot up right away and cannot be bothered with taking precautions (Sibthorpe et al., 1991). Another reason is that the essence of the addict's lifestyle is risk taking: "Their habit alone is daily dalliance with mortality. Given a life filled with risks—overdoses, hepatitis, jail—the threat of dying from AIDS seems, to many, merely redundant" (Goode, 1999). A third reason has to do with the difference in social background between the gays who practice safe sex and the IV drug addicts who spurn safe needle use. Most of the gays are relatively well-off white men, but the majority of the addicts are poor African Americans and Hispanics. Deprived of the opportunities for material success in a society that discriminates against them, the addicts are compelled to seek social status through bravado and daring. This includes taking a dangerous drug, especially one that is widely known to be capable of killing the user. In other words, it is overwhelming poverty that makes life so bleak and empty that the risk-taking involved in unsafe drug use appears challenging and thrilling (Currie, 1993).

Drugs and Crime

Research in the United States and other countries has clearly shown a strong link between drug use and crime: People who use illegal drugs generally commit more crime than those who do not. It has been found that close to half of the crime suspects arrested in the United States had used illegal drugs in the prior three days while 55 percent of their counterparts in England had done the same. It is also a well-known fact that in the United States as drug use has declined since the 1980s so has the crime rate (Wren, 1999; Walchak, 1996). Does all this mean that drug use causes crime? The answer is yes, according to *drug enslavement theory*. The answer is no, according to *general deviance syndrome theory*.

According to drug enslavement theory, drug users are forced into a life of crime because they cannot afford to pay for their prohibitively expensive drug habits unless they rob or steal to get the money for their next fix. This may be true of "deficit users," who live in poverty, have inadequate education, lack job skills, face racial discrimination, and suffer other social disadvantages because they are relatively poor, uneducated, and economically unskilled. But the theory cannot be applied to "leisure users," who are well-off enough to find it unnecessary to commit crime for the purpose of raising funds for drug purchases (Harrison, 1992).

According to general deviance syndrome theory, the high correlation between drug use and crime does not mean that drug use causes crime because most drug users with a criminal record have committed crime *before* using drugs. Becoming a drug user and continuing to commit crime as a drug user are cut from the same cloth—that is, from a general tendency toward deviance. Those with a general deviance syndrome are likely to get involved not only in one form of deviant activities (such as crime) but also in other forms of deviance (such as drug use and drug-related criminality). This syndrome was found in about 77 percent of the drug users in a study conducted at a Denver drug abuse center, while the syndrome was absent in the remaining 23 percent—who committed offenses only after becoming drug users (Swan, 1993). It seems clear that drug use does not by itself cause crime for most users, but drug use does *intensify* criminal tendency or *increase* the frequency of criminal activity. This may explain the "astronomical" number of offenses committed by drug users.

Drugs and Socioeconomic Status

Socioeconomic status—measured in terms of education, occupation, and income—is significantly related to the type of illicit drug being used. People of higher status tend to use certain drugs, whereas people of lower status tend to use other drugs (Goode, 1999).

There is a strong connection between higher status and marijuana. The higher the status, the more likely the use of marijuana. The drug is particularly popular among college and high school students; marijuana is by far their number one drug of choice.

Heroin is far and away the most popular among lower-status people, particularly those who live in poor, inner-city neighborhoods. The affluent, including their children of high school or college age, typically stay away from heroin. This has long been so, and even in the 1960s, when massive numbers of college and high school students experimented with all kinds of drugs, heroin remained at the very bottom of their drug choice. But since the mid-1990s more affluent whites have turned on to heroin, primarily because the drug is now pure enough to snort or smoke, with no risk of getting AIDS from sharing contaminated needles (Wren, 1999; Leland, 1996).

Cocaine has long been associated with affluent people because of its high cost. Today, the drug is still more popular among the affluent than among the poor.

But since the drug is much less expensive today, less affluent people have increasingly used it. The cheapest form of cocaine, crack, is particularly popular with the poor. In fact, crack has been called "the poor person's drug."

As for meth and roofies, they seem to have a special allure among working-class and young people. As has been suggested, some working-class persons use meth to seek euphoria, an enhanced self-confidence, and a burst of energy, and some working-class women use the drug to lose weight because it can suppress appetite. Roofies are also popular with young people, particularly those who like to drink, because as a depressant the drug has the same effect as alcohol, except of course, that it is far more potent. It also seems popular with the working class. As for Ecstasy, it is often associated with high school and college students and young professionals.

While we have discussed users of different drugs separately, we should nonetheless note that the use of a particular drug does not necessarily mean that the individual uses or will continue to use only that drug. Most people who use drugs tend to use more than one type. In addition, under peer influence, they tend to graduate from using relatively soft drugs, such as cigarettes, liquor, or marijuana, to using "harder" drugs, such as heroin and cocaine. Still, most drug users favor a certain drug over others.

Becoming a Drug User

In their classic study of heroin use, Isidor Chein and his associates (1964) distinguished four stages in the process of becoming involved with the drug. These stages are *experimentation, occasional use* (once a week or less), *regular use* (once a day or more), and *futile efforts to break the habit.* Chein and his associates further note that a user may go through all these stages or may stop at any stage. One person may experiment but not repeat the experiment. Another may use heroin occasionally but never regularly. A third person may become a regular user but manage to break the habit. And a fourth person may go through all the stages to become hooked on heroin, despite strenuous efforts to kick the habit.

Among the users of various drugs, heroin users seem most likely to escalate into the last, fourth stage (addiction), while users of marijuana, cocaine, and other illicit drugs remain in the earlier stages (experimental, occasional, and regular use).

Heroin is most addictive not only because of its chemical properties but, perhaps more important, because the majority of its users are relatively poor and use the drug to cope with the stresses of their life problems, such as low-paying jobs, unemployment, and racism. Since the relief brought by the drug is transitory and the stresses always recur, extended use of heroin is likely to occur; and since the drug is extremely addictive, its users have the greatest chance of getting hooked. On the other hand, users of marijuana, cocaine, and other drugs may be less likely to get addicted to the drugs because, unlike heroin users, they are mostly young people who use drugs for about the same reason they go to the movies, to a party, or out on a date—that is, drugs are a part of their social lives or recreational activities. As a nationwide study of high school seniors found, the reasons most often cited by users of marijuana and cocaine are "to have a good time with friends," "to feel good or get high," and "to see what it's like." Very few of the students mentioned "to get away from my problems," "to deal with anger and frustration," or "to get through the day" (Johnston et al., 1986). Therefore, without the compulsion to use drugs for dealing with difficult, intractable problems, they are more likely to remain occasional users.

Whatever stage drug users may end up in, how do they get involved in drugs in the first place? They usually have been offered the drug by their friends in a simple, casual way. This can be illustrated by the following accounts of how two young men had their first experiences with heroin (Chein et al., 1964):

> It was raining, and I was tired. I was standing in a doorway when this friend of mine came by. He said, "Want a pick-up [injection]?" I said "Sure," so we popped [took a shot].

> I was at a party. Everybody was having a good time. I wanted to be one of the crowd. I thought, if it didn't hurt them it wouldn't hurt me. That started the ball rolling. They were sniffing it that time. Two or three pulled out a few caps [heroin capsules] and said, "Here, if you want to, try." I accepted. They weren't trying to addict me; they just gave it to me.

Contrary to popular belief, it is not the strange drug peddler, the "merchant of death," who pushes drugs on the innocent young. Instead, it is their friends who introduce them to drug use (Osgood et al., 1996).

Once having tried the drug, would-be users may go through a learning process—with explicit or implicit instruction from their drug-introducing friends. Howard Becker (1963) has identified three steps in the process of learning to become a marijuana user.

The first step is learning the *technique* to get high. Since beginners tend to smoke marijuana like an ordinary cigarette, they may fail to induce the desired drug effects. Thus they may watch their experienced friends smoke or they may receive direct coaching from them on the proper way of smoking grass, such as inhaling deeply and then holding the smoke in the lungs long enough for the bloodstream to absorb the psychoactive substance of marijuana.

Becker's second step is learning to *recognize* the drug effects. After learning the proper technique of smoking marijuana, new users may still not get high. So they have to learn from friends that having cold feet, rubbery legs, intense hunger, and unawareness of the passage of time are some of the signs of a marijuana high.

The third step is learning to *enjoy* the drug effects. While being high, novices may have such feelings as dizziness, thirst, and tingling of the scalp; they may misjudge time and distance or feel themselves to be simultaneously at two places; they may hear or otherwise sense things in strange ways. These feelings may be unpleasant or even frightening to beginning drug users. They must learn to redefine these sensations as pleasurable; otherwise they will not use the drug again. New marijuana users usually learn to enjoy these experiences because of the encouragement and reassurances of experienced friends. These friends may tell them such things as, "You sure are lucky; I'd give anything to get that high myself. I haven't been that high in years."

With the use of cocaine, heroin, or other illegal drugs, the beginner may also have to learn the first step—the technique of using the drug. But the second and third steps—learning to recognize and enjoy the drug effects—may not be necessary, because the effects are usually more clear-cut and predictable than the effects of marijuana. In virtually all cases of initial cocaine use, for example, the user feels its effect as extremely pleasurable. Hence, there is no need for users of cocaine and other drugs to learn to recognize and enjoy the drug effects.

Social Profile: Illegal Drug Users

Illegal drug users are generally distinguishable from nonusers for having certain social and social psychological characteristics. First, users are more likely to be male than female. This reflects the greater general tendency for men to engage in deviant activities. While men are only *slightly* more likely than women to use drugs at all, they are *considerably* more likely to use drugs regularly and *extremely* more likely to use drugs so heavily as to become addicts.

Second, drug users are relatively young. The age group with the highest rate of drug use is 18 to 25 years old. Within this group, more drug users are older teenagers (aged 18 or 19) than are young adults (aged 24 or 25). The higher rate of drug use among younger people can be attributed to freedom from parental control and, more important, freedom from adult responsibilities such as employment, marriage, and child rearing. Research has long established that the unemployed, unmarried, and childless are more likely than those with jobs, spouses, and children to use drugs.

Third, drug users learn to use drugs from parents and peers. Users usually have parents who use legal drugs such as tobacco cigarettes, alcoholic beverages, and prescription drugs for relieving tension and combating insomnia. From parents, then, drug users first learn to use legal drugs—before turning to illegal ones. When used for the first time, the drugs are usually given by friends. Unsurprisingly, drug users have at least a few friends who also use the same drugs. Whether they will continue to use the drugs for an extended period also depends significantly on their friends' drug use.

Fourth, drug users in high school, when compared with nonusing peers, are more likely to cut classes, skip whole days of school, drop out of school, avoid religious activities, and frequently go out in the evening for fun and recreation. In other words, young drug users are not as strongly tied to three major social institutions—the school, the church, and the home—as the nonusers.

Sources: Goode, 1999; Molotsky, 1999; Osgood et al., 1996.

What Causes Illegal Drug Use?

There are over 40 positivist theories about some aspect of drug use. Some of these theories are designed to explain why some individuals are more likely than others to use or abuse drugs. These explanatory theories can be divided into three major types: biological, psychological, and sociological. According to biological theories, the causes of drug addiction inhere in biological factors, such as an inborn high tolerance for drugs or a metabolic disorder that creates a craving for an illicit drug in about the same way that diabetes creates a craving for insulin. According to psychological theories, the causes of drug use are specific personality traits, such as low self-esteem or unconventionality. And according to sociological theories, drug use stems from social forces, such as the drug subculture or peer influence (Goode, 1999). The first type of theory is the least credible, because scientific research has largely failed to support it. Also, the so-called biological causes could well be the effects of drug abuse. There are ample data to support the other two types of theory, and here we will discuss three specific examples.

Economic Deprivation Theory

After reviewing various studies conducted on drug use since the early 1950s, Elliott Currie (1993) concludes that "the link between drug abuse and deprivation is one of the strongest in 40 years of careful research." More specifically, he writes:

> Forty years of accumulated research, then, confirms that endemic drug abuse is intimately related to conditions of mass social deprivation, economic marginality, and cultural and community breakdown—in Europe as in the United States, in the eighties and nineties as in the sixties, among poor whites and Hispanics as well as inner-city blacks.

Currie further explains *why* poor people turn to drugs in response to poverty-related social conditions. An important first reason is that drugs can fulfill the need for *status*. In the larger, conventional society, the poor are denied legitimate avenues of attaining esteem, a sense of respect, or even a sense of community. As a consequence, there has developed in the poor neighborhood a drug culture that serves as an alternative source of esteem and respect. As one researcher found, "being in the drug culture is just like being a movie star. So many people depend on you, want to stop you in the street. The police is always on you. . . . You are a very important person." A second reason is that drugs can help the user *cope* with the harsh, oppressive realities of poverty. As Currie writes, "Drugs become a way of getting away from daily problems, medicating emotional anguish, relieving stress, escaping pain." A third reason is that drugs can provide a sense of *structure* or *purpose* to shattered lives. In the absence of steady work or stable family life, the poor cannot find the sense of structure that the nonpoor have. As a substitute, drug use helps relieve monotony and purposelessness among the poor. A fourth, unavoidable reason is that the poor communities are *saturated* with illicit drugs.

Given the pervasiveness and easy availability of drugs along with the ubiquity of drug users, it is easy to drift passively into drug use without considering its consequences (Currie, 1993).

In short, grinding poverty can force people to use drugs as a way of meeting normal human needs that have been systematically thwarted by society. It is obvious that this kind of theory is useful for explaining drug use among the poor, but it is equally obvious that it cannot explain drug use among the affluent.

Cognitive Association Theory

While economic deprivation theory is intended to explain both drug use and abuse, cognitive association theory is designed to explain drug addiction alone. As Alfred Lindesmith (1968) explains,

> The power of the [drug] habit is derived basically from effects which follow when the drug is removed rather than from any positive effects which its presence in the body produces. Addiction occurs only when [drugs] are used to alleviate withdrawal distress, after this distress had been properly understood. . . . If the individual fails to conceive of his distress as withdrawal distress brought about by the absence of [the drugs], he does not become addicted, but, if he does, addiction is quickly and permanently established through further use of the drug.

Lindesmith has collected convincing data to support the theory. He found that, among patients who had been given morphine to kill their postsurgery pain, some later became addicted to the drug but others did not. The difference had to do with whether the patients *knew* that their nausea and other symptoms of withdrawal sickness were caused by their suddenly discontinuing the use of morphine. Those who did—in other words, "cognitively associated" the withdrawal distress with their prior use of morphine—ended up addicted to the drug because they demanded that they be given more morphine. By contrast, patients who experienced the same withdrawal sickness *without* knowing the cause of it did not become addicted. Why not? Because they were assured by their doctor that the discomfort was normal for a patient recovering from surgery and that it would eventually stop by itself. These patients then "toughed it out"—rather than demanding more morphine.

In sum, the cause of addiction is the drug user's *cognitive association* between withdrawal distress and prior drug use. To bolster the theory, Lindesmith further observes that the mentally ill, the mentally challenged, young children, and animals usually are immune to addiction because they cannot understand the meaning of withdrawal symptoms even if it is explained to them. The theory can also explain why people with average intelligence can easily get hooked on drugs once they experience withdrawal distress. However, a deeper reason for addiction, we may argue, is that most people in a modern, hedonistic society want to eliminate distress instantly rather than stoically endure it until it passes.

Social Psychological Theory

From various studies we can derive a number of sociological and psychological factors that lead people from virtually all walks of life into drug use.

Among the sociological factors, some exert their influence from the higher societal or cultural level, while others more directly affect individuals in their immediate milieu consisting of family, friends, schoolmates, neighbors, coworkers, and others they meet often.

A prime example of societal factors is the legal drug culture of our society. Such psychoactive drugs as alcoholic beverages, tobacco cigarettes, and various sedatives and tranquilizers are pushed on the general public either directly or indirectly. Each year, the alcohol and tobacco industries spend millions of dollars on advertising—coaxing and seducing people to use their drugs. The pharmaceutical industry sends its sales representatives into doctors' offices with free samples of legal uppers and downers, and these "reps" talk the physicians into pushing the drugs on their patients. On the other hand, the general public demands these drugs to help ease their physical aches and pains, their psychological stresses and strains, a sense of social incompetence and awkwardness, or existential emptiness and boredom. Given this drug culture, many people become accustomed to using legal drugs, which makes it easy to try illegal ones. This is why many people use illegal drugs only after they have drunk or smoked, and many teenagers use illicit drugs only after they have long seen their parents drink or smoke. If a youngster says, "My parents drink—why can't I smoke grass?" it is difficult for adults to talk down that argument.

The social factors that more immediately sway individuals toward drug use can be drawn from various deviance theories, such as social control, differential association, social learning, structured strain, deviant opportunity, and deviant subculture theories. Their significance has been demonstrated by current research. Since these general theories have been discussed in some detail in Chapters 2 and 3, we will mention here only the variables that have been found most useful for explaining drug use. They are (1) lack of attachment to conventional persons or institutions, such as parents, teachers, clergy, and employers, or family, school, religion, and work, (2) having friends who use drugs, (3) being a member of a drug-using subculture, and (4) easy access to drugs (Kaplan et al., 1986; Marcos, Bahr, and Johnson, 1986; Elliott et al., 1985).

As for the psychological reasons behind drug use, research has found the following factors significant: poor self-concept, low self-esteem, self-rejection; feelings of distress, powerlessness, or hopelessness; being unconventional or rebellious; receptivity to uncertainty, risk taking, or new experience; and expecting drugs to enhance status or mitigate life's problems (Kaplan et al., 1986; Jurich and Polson, 1984). Clinical evidence further suggests that people with a certain type of personal problem tend to prefer one particular drug after experimenting with various substances. They tend to use that preferred drug regularly because it helps relieve their specific problem. For example, those who are restless, aggressive, or given to violent eruptions tend to use heroin regularly because they find that it helps them "feel normal, calm, mellow, soothed, and relaxed." Those who often feel depressed, fatigued, bored, or shy are inclined to choose cocaine because they feel that it helps make them energetic, self-assured, and sociable (Khantzian, 1985).

The War on Drugs

The war on drugs consists of two basic strategies. One is *punitive:* using law enforcement to stop the supply of drugs and punish drug sellers and users. The other is *supportive:* using drug prevention (or education) and treatment to reduce the demand for drugs and help drug addicts. The U.S. government devotes most of its antidrug budget to law enforcement. One result is a sharp increase in the incarceration of drug offenders. Can this emphasis on law enforcement over drug prevention and treatment solve the drug problem? Let us first analyze the punitive strategy by looking at how it has been applied in the past and how it is applied today. Then we will see how reaction to the punitive strategy has sparked a debate over legalizing drugs. Finally, we will examine the application of the supportive strategy to solving drug problems.

Historical Pattern

Historically, the war on drugs has turned out to be a war on powerless groups, particularly minorities.

The first attempt to battle drug use appeared in the form of a city ordinance against opium dens in San Francisco in 1875. The custom of opium smoking had earlier been introduced to this country by Chinese coolies, unskilled laborers who were imported to work on railroad construction crews. At first, their opium dens were tolerated. But soon the Chinese labor pool was seen to present a threat to the white labor market because they were hired and worked long hours for low wages. The white laborers started a campaign against the Chinese and their opium dens. The campaign, effectively led by the president of the American Federation of Labor, conjured "a terrible picture of how the Chinese entice little white boys and girls into becoming 'opium fiends,' [who were] condemned to spend their days in the back of laundry rooms" (Hill, 1973).

Consequently, a number of cities followed San Francisco in passing ordinances against opium dens. The antiopium laws were, in practice, anti-Chinese laws, because they provided "a legal basis for unrestrained and arbitrary police raids and searches of Chinese premises" (Helmer, 1975). In 1909 Congress enacted a law prohibiting the importation of opium for smoking. Then, in 1914, Congress passed the Harrison Narcotic Act outlawing the sale or possession of opium and its derivatives. By this time a socially undesirable class, including prostitutes, thieves, and hoodlums, had been known to use the forbidden drugs and, therefore, became "dope fiends" in the wake of the new law. In contrast, opiate users of higher social status were largely unaffected by the law since they were able legally to obtain the drugs from their physicians—the Harrison Act did not prohibit opiate use for "legitimate medical purposes."

Around 1900, many state laws and municipal ordinances were also enacted against the use of another drug—cocaine. These anticocaine laws were, in reality, antiblack laws. In those days, cocaine was widely used by blacks, but whites fearfully believed that a cocaine high could spur blacks to violence against whites, stimulate sexual assaults by black men on white women, improve blacks' pistol marksmanship, make blacks invulnerable to bullets, give blacks superhuman strength, and make them cunning and efficient. The anticocaine laws, then, were useful for controlling blacks and keeping them in "their place."

In 1937 Congress passed the Marihuana Tax Act. This antimarijuana law was, in effect, an anti-Hispanic law. The Mexican migrant workers in the West and Southwest had been known to smoke marijuana, and Anglo Americans, holding a strong prejudice against them, had spread rumors that "weed" often led the Mexicans to commit murder, rape, and other horrible crimes. In 1936, for example, a Colorado newspaper editor wrote to the Bureau of Narcotics: "I wish I could show you what a small marijuana cigarette can do to one of our degenerate Spanish-speaking residents. That's why our problem is so great: the greatest percentage of our population is composed of Spanish-speaking persons, most of whom are low mentally, because of social and racial conditions" (Himmelstein, 1983; Musto, 1973).

In the 1950s the social problem of heroin use was blamed on the communists. They were believed to push heroin as part of their conspiracy against the United States. The Narcotic Drug Control Act, enacted in 1956, was indeed very tough on heroin peddlers: It provided the death penalty for the sale of heroin to a person under 18 by one over 18 (Szasz, 1974a).

In the 1960s horror stories about the effects of marijuana and other illicit drugs were widely publicized. One such story came in 1968 from Pennsylvania's governor, who subsequently became chairman of President Nixon's Marijuana and Drug Abuse Commission. The governor told the press that six college students stared at the sun while under the influence of LSD and were consequently blinded. Although the story was later exposed as a hoax, the general public had already erupted with fear about LSD and other illicit drugs. Then, many new federal and state laws were enacted to increase the severity of punishment for illicit drug use. All these harsh laws served to punish the youth who dared reject conventional values, scorn the establishment, and protest U.S. involvement in the Vietnam War.

Since the late 1960s, however, large numbers of conventional, middle-class whites have used drugs, particularly marijuana. Professional athletes, movie stars, rock stars, business executives, and other successful, respectable people have turned cocaine into a status drug. Drug use has stopped being associated exclusively with powerless minorities, anti-establishment youths, and social undesirables. Consequently, affluent, respectable drug users, instead of being treated like dangerous criminals, are today more likely to go free or receive light sentences. Nevertheless, racial minorities, particularly African Americans, continue to suffer the brunt of antidrug law enforcement.

Punitive Strategy: Law Enforcement

Compared with their affluent and white counterparts, the poor and minority drug users are more often arrested or imprisoned. African Americans, for example, constitute only 12 percent of the U.S. population, but they usually make up over 50 percent of all arrests for various drug offenses. The majority of people convicted of crack cocaine offenses in federal court are also African Americans, who receive much longer sentences than well-off white offenders convicted of selling powder cocaine. All this suggests how today's law enforcement against drugs continues the historical pattern of drug laws against minorities. Today's law enforcement does more than discriminate against African Americans and Hispanics; it worsens their drug problems by siphoning off government funds that could have been used for drug education and treatment programs. Thus, poor black and Hispanic communities continue to have the highest rates of drug addiction and other severe drug problems in U.S. society (Friedman, 1998).

Law enforcement is also aimed at poor foreign countries that produce most of the illicit drugs consumed in the United States. Our government has gone to great lengths in urging these countries to eradicate their narcotic plants. Millions of U.S. dollars have been offered in return for the destruction of the plants, and threats to cut off U.S. aid or oppose international lending have often been made to countries that fail to reduce drug production. Even U.S. soldiers and advisers have been dispatched to Latin American countries to destroy cocaine-producing plants and pursue drug lords. The U.S. Customs Service has also caught many people for trying to smuggle illicit drugs into the United States. In addition, the DEA (Federal Drug Enforcement Agency) and other law-enforcement agencies have often made headline news seizing tons of illicit drugs throughout the country.

Nevertheless, drugs are still easily available on the street, for the most part because as long as the demand for them is great, there are always some countries and many smugglers to supply them (Wren, 1996).

Debate over Legalizing Drugs

The apparent failure of the law-enforcement approach has led to calls for legalization of drugs. Advocates of legalization contend that, like Prohibition (of alcohol) in the 1920s, current drug laws do more harm than good. They are said to generate many crimes, including homicides. As Milton Friedman (1989) argues, "Addicts are driven to associate with criminals to get the drugs [and] become criminals themselves to finance the habit." The drug laws are also said to encourage official corruption because huge profits from drug sales enable the criminals to bribe police to "look the other way." By legalizing drugs, the proponents argue, the government can take away obscene profits from drug traffickers, end police corruption, and reduce crime drastically. Finally, legalizers believe that with legalization the huge amount of money currently spent on law enforcement can be used for drug treatment and education, which will dramatically reduce drug use and addiction (Friedman, 1998; Carter, 1989).

But most Americans oppose legalization. They fear that, if drugs are legalized, drug use and addiction will skyrocket (Walters, 2002). As William Bennett (1989), a former national drug policy director, says, "After the repeal of Prohibition, consumption of alcohol soared by 350%." A soaring rate of drug use and addiction, according to another opponent, will hurt the poor and minorities that already suffer the most even more (Rosenthal, 1995). Sociologist Elliott Currie (1993) also argues that legalization cannot solve the problem of widespread drug abuse and crime because the root cause of the problem is poverty, racism, or inequality. Thus, Currie proposes that the government eradicate the cause of the problem by providing employment to all, increasing the minimum wage, expanding the Job Corps, increasing health care for the poor, offering paid family leave, providing affordable housing, and reducing social inequality.

A third approach to controlling the drug problem has recently emerged. It involves striking a middle ground between all-out criminalization and outright legalization. To these "middle grounders," all-out criminalization can lead to great increases in such problems as crime and corruption, just as the legalization advocates have pointed out. But the middle grounders also argue that outright legalization can cause drug use and addiction to soar, just as the criminalization supporters have pointed out. The solution, then, is to reduce harm from these two different kinds of problems. It may involve, for example, legalizing the sale of a small amount of marijuana to adults while criminalizing the sale of marijuana to minors or the sale of hard drugs to anybody. This is already a reality in the Netherlands. Whether it will catch on in the United States is still hard to tell (Goode, 2004a).

Supportive Strategy: Prevention and Treatment

While the U.S. government pays more attention to the punitive strategy, the supportive strategy of preventing drug use via education and treatment for addicts and their drug addiction nonetheless exists. To prevent drug use, school programs, television commercials, and other educational efforts are focused on increasing public awareness of the harmfulness of drugs. Treatment involves hospitals, public-health agencies, and drug-treatment centers in programs for people with drug problems. Let's take a closer look at each of these two types of supportive strategy in the war on drugs.

Drug Prevention. The most popular program of drug prevention is the Project D.A.R.E. (Drug Abuse Resistance Education). Adopted by more than 60 percent of the U.S. school districts, DARE involves a police officer teaching a drug education class at a local school. The aim of the program is to prevent drug use by teaching students about the perils of drug use and then showing them how to develop social skills, raise self-esteem, resist peer pressure to use drugs, and seek drug-free alternatives, such as tutoring younger children or developing a hobby. According to its administrators and supporters, DARE has, since its establishment in 1982, proven successful in achieving its goal (DeJong, 1986). But researchers have found otherwise: DARE does not significantly prevent drug use, although it does enhance children's self-esteem, polish their social skills, and improve their attitudes toward police (Elliott, 1995).

Nonetheless, parents of most children who have participated in the DARE curriculum seem to agree with its administrators that the program works. They can see that their own children do not use drugs. But they do not realize that, as researchers have generally discovered, DARE works only for children who, like their own, are unlikely to use drugs in the first place. More precisely, then, DARE does prevent drug use by *reinforcing* the existing antidrug attitude that most children have learned from parents. The fact remains that DARE—and other similar programs—does not work for children who are already at risk of using drugs. Who are these children? They are children with the following experiences:

- Family history of alcoholism
- Family history of criminality
- Poor parental child-rearing practices, such as lax supervision and constant criticism
- Parental drug use or permissive attitudes toward drugs
- Early antisocial behavior in school, especially aggressiveness
- Alienation and low commitment to getting an education
- Academic failure in middle to late elementary school education
- Socializing with friends who take drugs (Levine, 1986)

Apparently, drug education alone cannot work for children with these problems unless the family, school, community, and the larger society also work together to deal with the impact of these problems on the children.

Drug Treatment. Three kinds of treatment exist for drug addicts. The first, *chemical treatment*, may include detoxification and maintenance therapy. *Detoxification* involves the use of a nonnarcotic chemical or a required rest to bring the patient into a drug-free state. Detoxification by itself cannot cure addiction because the craving for drugs remains, but it makes the patient more amenable to psychotherapy or other treatment programs designed to cure addiction. *Maintenance therapy* involves a treatment center giving the patient a drug that has almost the same chemical makeup as that of the illicit drug. The substitute drug, such as methadone for heroin addicts, is able to prevent withdrawal distress and can be used regularly as a safe alternative to the street drug or as a supplement to a treatment designed to cure addiction (Massing, 1998).

A second type of drug treatment is *psychological therapy,* including aversion therapy, personal therapy, and group therapy. *Aversion therapy* involves making patients associate their drug of choice with some unpleasant experience. Thus, if drug addicts undergo a program where they are administered an electric shock every time they use their drug of choice, they are likely to stop using the drug. *Personal therapy* involves a psychotherapist helping patients discover and then seek to eliminate the psychological causes of their drug abuse, such as low self-esteem or inability to form sound relationships with others. *Group therapy* involves a group of drug addicts discussing and sharing with each other their lives and personal experiences with drug abuse.

A third type of drug treatment is *therapeutic community*. This involves drug addicts living together like members of a family. Cut off from outside contacts, including family and friends, these addicts support each other, helping each other live a drug-free life. The better-known therapeutic communities are Synanon, Odyssey House, and Phoenix House, but they can even be found in many prisons (Early, 1996).

It is difficult, if not impossible, to determine which of these treatments works better than others because patients in different programs vary in such significant factors as age, ethnicity, employment status, length of drug use, and degree of addiction. Thus, for example, a program that treats with great success patients who are only mildly addicted to drugs *cannot* be said to be more successful than another program that treats with little success patients who are heavily addicted. But many studies suggest that any treatment method can work better if the patients are employed and can earn a good income, receive adequate support from others such as family and friends, or are free from a drug-abuse subculture (Abadinsky, 1993).

Abusing Prescription Drugs, Particularly OxyContin

Drugs prescribed by doctors for patients can be used either licitly or illicitly. The licit use of prescription drugs is meant to eliminate the patient's complaints, such as pain, stress, and fatigue. On the other hand, the illicit use of prescription drugs occurs when nonpatients get high. The misuse has skyrocketed over the last decade, with the abuse of painkillers rising much more sharply than the abuse of tranquilizers, stimulants, and sedatives (see Figure 11.2). Men and whites are more likely than women, blacks, and Hispanics to abuse prescription drugs. Also, people with some college education are more likely than those with less education to abuse these drugs. Apparently, then, the abuse of prescription drugs is mostly a middle-class problem (Kalb, 2001).

The skyrocketing abuse of painkillers, particularly OxyContin, seems to have gotten its fuel from the medical establishment and the pharmaceutical industry. For a long time before 1990, doctors usually paid little attention to their patients' complaints about pain. As the complaints grew increasingly urgent and prevalent, the doctors in the early 1990s began to be much more aggressive in treating the problem. This caused pharmaceutical companies to produce many different painkilling drugs in large quantities. Then, for the next 10 years, these companies launched aggressive marketing campaigns to sell their drugs. One common strategy involved buttering up doctors with free trips and paid speaking engagements. Thus, a pharmaceutical company would pay the transportation and hotel expenses for hundreds of doctors to attend weekend conferences at popular

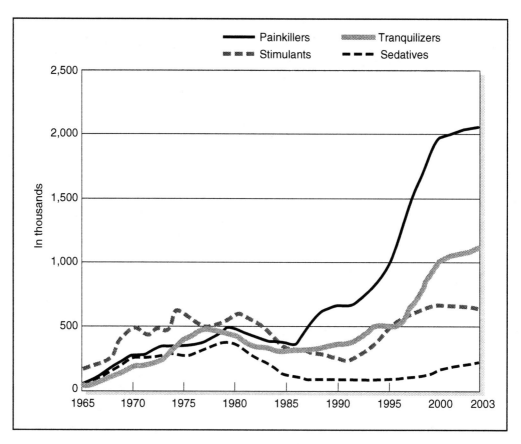

FIGURE 11.2   Soaring Numbers of New Illicit Users of Prescription Drugs

Source: National Household Survey on Drug Abuse (NHSDA), 2004.

resorts to discuss pain management. The company would also recruit and pay doctors to speak to other doctors at numerous "pain management" seminars all over the country. At those meetings doctors were encouraged to treat their patients with powerful painkillers, particularly OxyContin, the most abused prescription drug (Meier and Petersen, 2001).

Unfortunately, many doctors who were prodded to prescribe OxyContin and other painkillers did not have much experience dealing with such drugs. As a result, they often could not tell if a patient really needed a painkilling drug, and so prescribed it for many patients that lied to get the drug to abuse or sell to others. With pharmaceutical companies flooding the market with painkillers and other prescription drugs and with some doctors too quick to prescribe the drugs, the door to abusing the drugs swung wide open. Many abusers turn into "doctor shoppers," visiting different doctors to get more drugs. This is easy to do. As one abuser said, "I'd walk in and tell them I had a migraine; that's all I had to say." Some abusers obtain drugs by committing fraud, such as using bogus prescriptions or using a doctor's name to phone in prescriptions to pharmacies. Some abusers get drugs by using stolen prescription pads from doctors or breaking into pharmacies or the homes of patients with legitimate prescriptions. Some buy drugs from dealers or patients at prices above those charged by pharmacies. Since 2004, however, the U.S. Drug Enforcement Administration has intensified its regulation of OxyContin and other painkillers (Spencer, 2004; Kalb, 2001).

OxyContin is most popular with abusers of prescription drugs because it is by far the most powerful painkiller, most effective in eliminating severe pain. OxyContin also offers pain relief three times longer than other drugs because of its time-release feature. Licit, legitimate users get these benefits from the drug by swallowing it with water. But abusers can get an almost immediate and much more powerful rush by crushing the drug and snorting it. Understandably, it is relatively easy to become compulsive about taking the drug, to the point where it threatens the abuser's health or social and professional life (Adler, 2004; Kalb, 2001).

Smoking Cigarettes

As suggested before, compared with illegal drugs, legal drugs are far more prevalent and, over time, much more dangerous. The use of alcohol is the subject of the next chapter. Here we take a look at the smoking of tobacco cigarettes.

Since 1964, when the U.S. Surgeon General first announced the conclusion of a scientific study that smoking is causally related to lung cancer, there have been many reports about the serious health hazards of smoking. Consequently, laws have required warning labels for cigarettes, restriction of tobacco advertising and promotion, and smoke-free workplaces and public areas. In recent years the government has even forced the tobacco industry to pay more than $500 billion over 25 years ($20 billion annually) for health-care costs, an enormous sum in view of the fact that the tobacco business takes in around $30 billion a year. All these efforts have reduced smoking by about 40 percent over the last 40 years, and now the percentage of smokers in the United States is among the lowest in the world (Sullum, 1998; Pollack, 1997).

Still, too many Americans continue to smoke regularly, making up at least 25 percent of the U.S. population. Worse, since 1990, smoking among teenagers has gone up sharply. Now, for any given month, more than one-third of high school students smoke. Most of these young smokers are very likely to continue smoking in their adult lives, because research has shown that 75 percent of adult smokers started before age 18.

As teenagers, whites are much more likely than blacks to smoke. Among adults, however, African Americans are more likely to smoke. Of various racial or ethnic groups, Native Americans have the highest percentage of smokers and Asian Americans the lowest. These racial differences in smoking may have something to do with education. Generally, as many studies have shown, the prevalence of smoking is three times higher among people with less than 12 years of education compared to those with more than 16 years of education. Ethnic groups with less education are thus more likely than other groups to smoke. There is also a gender factor in smoking: Within most ethnic groups, there are many more male smokers than female smokers, the exception being that, among white teenagers, females are just as likely to smoke (McMurray, 2004; SAMHSA, 2002; AHA, 1998).

Given the terrible health hazards of smoking, why do smokers continue to smoke rather than quit? Are they irrational, or do they fail to appreciate the hazards of smoking? Many smokers have become addicted, so that they cannot quit. But others continue to smoke even if they could quit because to them the benefits of smoking outweigh the costs. The benefits include releasing tension, feeling relaxed, and enjoying quiet companionship or lively conversation. It is, however, more than these benefits that cause smokers to continue smoking. Smokers are simply much less risk averse than nonsmokers. Contrary to popular belief, most smokers are acutely aware of the hazards of smoking. In fact, they tend to greatly overrate the risks of smoking. In one study, for example, smokers placed the risk of lung cancer at 38 percent, while a more realistic risk is lower than 10 percent (Blizzard, 2004b; Viscusi, 1992).

Whatever benefits smokers claim to enjoy from tobacco use, nonsmokers can still assert their right to be protected from harmful secondhand smoke. But smokers can claim their right to risk their own health by smoking. Faced with this conflict between smokers and nonsmokers, the government has so far tried to bring about a smoke-free society but one in which only smoking in public places is prohibited, not smoking per se.

Global Perspective: Smoking

Since the 1960s smoking has become less and less prevalent in the United States, Western Europe, and other developed countries. By contrast, the prevalence of smoking has become increasingly higher in the developing countries of Africa, Asia, and Latin America as well as Eastern Europe. As a result, today, there are many more smokers in developing countries than in developed ones. A major reason for the rising prevalence of smoking in developing countries is the lack of laws that require warning smokers of the hazards of smoking, restrict tobacco advertising and promotion, and prohibit smoking at workplaces and public indoor areas. These are the kind of laws that have significantly reduced smoking in developed countries.

During the second half of the last century the prevalence of smoking was higher in developed than in developing countries. Thus the incidence of death from smoking between 1980 and 2000 was higher in developed countries, but it began to decline in the beginning of the current century. Due to the currently higher incidence of smoking in developing countries, smoking-related deaths are expected to become more prevalent in 30 years or so in those relatively poor countries.

In both developed and developing countries, men are more likely than women to smoke. But the ratio of male to female smokers is much greater in developing countries, a reflection of the greater gender inequality in the Third World. But the prevalence of female smokers in these countries has increased rapidly, largely a result of the tobacco industry's efforts to promote smoking among women. Tobacco companies, for example, often advertise their products with the seductive images of female smokers being modern, sophisticated, emancipated, full of vitality, slim, and sexy. The companies also promote female smoking with special brands of cigarettes for women, which are long, slim, lowtar, light-colored, or menthol.

All over the world, the overwhelming majority of smokers begin to light up before reaching adulthood. The most common factor in youthful smoking is peer pressure: Young people are likely to smoke if their friends smoke. Another factor is the popular view among youth of tobacco use as normal or "cool." Supporting these two factors are the tobacco industry's advertising and promotion, easy access to cigarettes, and relatively low prices.

Sources: Mackay and Eriksen, 2002; Peto and Lopez, 2001.

Summary

1. How can illegal drug use be put in proper perspective? We should recognize that illegal drugs are not as widely used and dangerous as some legal drugs. Societal reaction to drugs varies with time and place. Moreover, illegal drugs are for the most part used moderately rather than uncontrollably.

2. What are the effects of various illegal drugs? As a stimulant, marijuana can produce euphoria, heighten sensitivity, improve perception, and increase appetite. It has even proven beneficial to the very ill. But if used to the point of intoxication, marijuana can impair judgment and memory. It is also addictive, and its users are more likely than nonusers to use hard drugs as well. As a depressant, heroin can soothe pain, anxiety, and tension—as well as produce what the user considers to be euphoria. It is highly addictive. Heroin addicts do not necessarily have their health or careers ruined by the drug, but they may suffer both effects if they

are not socially privileged and financially successful. As a stimulant, cocaine sharpens the senses, provides exhilaration, enhances self-confidence, and boosts energy. It is also extremely addictive. Crack, the cheaper and smokable form of cocaine, is even more powerful and addictive. Meth and roofies are popular drugs, the former a stimulant and the latter a depressant. The latest popular drug is Ecstasy, which makes most of its users feel good and have a better perspective on life, despite government warnings that it is a dangerous drug.

3. What is the extent of drug use in the United States? The United States has the highest rate of drug use in the industrial world, but most of the drug problems are confined to the lower classes. Drug use in U.S. society steadily declined from 1980 until 1992, when it began to rise, largely fueled by young whites smoking pot. **How does U.S. society react to drug use by Americans?** It usually reacts with moral panic, imagining drug use as a much more serious problem than it is.

4. Why are intravenous drug users very likely to get AIDS? IV drug users are reluctant to take precautions by avoiding the sharing of needles. The reasons for such reluctance include an overwhelming need for immediate drug experience, the user's risk-taking lifestyle, and the bleakness and emptiness of life resulting from grinding poverty. **Does drug use cause crime?** The answer is yes according to drug enslavement theory, but no according to general deviance syndrome theory.

5. How is drug use related to socioeconomic status? Users of marijuana and powder cocaine are more likely to be relatively affluent, while users of heroin and crack cocaine are more likely to be poor. Users of meth and roofies seem largely working-class and young. Ecstasy users are mostly students and young professionals. **What is the social profile of illegal drug users?** Illegal drug users tend to be male and young, have drug-using parents and friends, and lack strong ties to social institutions.

6. How does a person become a drug user? There are four stages in the process of becoming an illegal drug user: experimentation, occasional use, regular use, and addiction. A user may go through all these stages until becoming an addict, or may stop at the first, second, or third stage. In Becker's classic study of pot smokers, the smoker characteristically learns three things in a sequential manner: how to get high on the drug, how to recognize the nature of the high, and how to enjoy the high.

7. What causes drug use and addiction? According to Currie's economic deprivation theory, severe poverty causes the victims to use drugs to fulfill their need for status, to cope with the oppressive realities of poverty,

and to gain a sense of purpose in their shattered lives with the easy availability of drugs in their community. Lindesmith's cognitive association theory says that we can become addicted to heroin if we associate our withdrawal distress with our previous use of the drug. Finally, according to social psychological theory, both sociological and psychological factors are involved in drug use—the former exemplified by the legal drug culture and lack of social control, and the latter by poor self-concept and low self-esteem.

8. What is the nature of the war on drugs? The war on drugs consists of two basic strategies. One is punitive, involving the use of law enforcement to stop the supply of drugs and punish drug sellers and users. The other strategy is supportive, involving the use of drug prevention or education to reduce the demand for drugs and the use of treatment to help drug addicts.

9. Why is OxyContin most popular with abusers of prescription drugs? When the drug is crushed and snorted, it can immediately deliver a powerful rush. But its popularity has created such a great demand that abusers commit fraud, burglary, and other crimes to get it. **What is the nature of smoking?** Although smoking can cause serious illnesses, at least 25 percent of Americans smoke regularly, primarily because they believe that the benefits of smoking outweigh the costs.

10. What is the situation of smoking in the world? In the second half of the last century, smoking was more prevalent in affluent countries than in poor countries. But today smoking is more common in poor countries due to the lack of laws that discourage tobacco use. In both affluent and poor countries, men are more likely than women to smoke and most smokers begin to light up at a young age.

FURTHER READING

Cherry, Andrew, Mary E. Dillon, and Douglas Rugh (eds.). 2002. *Substance Abuse: A Global View.* Westport, Conn.: Greenwood. A series of articles discussing the problem of drug abuse in 13 countries.

Coombs, Robert Holman. 1997. *Drug-Impaired Professionals.* Cambridge, Mass.: Harvard University Press. An interview-based analysis of the nature and causes of drug addiction among doctors, lawyers, and other professionals.

Currie, Elliott. 1993. *Reckoning: Drugs, the Cities, and the American Future.* New York: Hill and Wang. An analysis of the drug problems in largely poor minority neighborhoods of large cities across the United States.

Decker, Scott, and Richard Rosenfeld. 1992. "Intravenous drug use and the AIDS epidemic: Findings from a 20-city sample of arrestees." *Crime & Delinquency,* 36, 492–509. Shows how AIDS counseling alone—without drug treatment—largely fails to reduce high-risk drug use.

Early, Kevin E. (ed.). 1996. *Drug Treatment Behind Bars: Prison-Based Strategies for Change.* Westport, Conn.: Praeger. A collection of articles on the therapeutic communities in U.S. prisons.

Erickson, Patricia G., and Yuet W. Cheung. 1992. "Drug crime and legal control: Lessons from the Canadian experience." *Contemporary Drug Problems,* 19, 247–277. A study of past prohibitions on alcohol, heroin, cannabis, and cocaine in Canada, which shows the ineffectiveness of excessive reliance on the criminal law for curbing drug use.

Falco, Mathea. 1992. *The Making of a Drug-Free America: Programs That Work.* New York: Times Books. Showcasing effective programs on drug prevention, treatment, and law enforcement.

Gately, Iain. 2002. *Tobacco: The Story of How Tobacco Seduced the World.* New York: Grove. A readable and entertaining history of the weed, showing how it spread throughout the world and, in the process, influenced important global events such as the Atlantic slave trade, the American Revolution, and the opening of international trade.

Goldberg, Ted. 1999. *Demystifying Drugs: A Psychological Perspective.* New York: St. Martin's. Discusses how and why people use drugs as well as how the Swedish and Dutch societies deal with drug abuse.

Goode, Erich. 1999. *Drugs in American Society,* 5th ed. New York: McGraw-Hill. A comprehensive text on the subject, covering drug use in general, many specific drugs such as alcohol, marijuana, and cocaine, and theories of drug use.

Hanson, Bill, George Beschner, James M. Walters, and Elliott Bovelle (eds.). 1985. *Life with Heroin: Voices from the Inner City.* Lexington, Mass.: Lexington Books. A sensitive probe into the subjective world of poor African-American users of heroin.

Harrison, Lana D. 1992. "International perspectives on the interface of drug use and criminal behavior." *Contemporary Drug Problems,* 19, 181–201. A cross-national analysis of how the drugs–crime connection exists mostly among the lower classes but is weaker in countries with stronger welfare systems.

Harrison, Lana, and Joseph Gfroerer. 1992. "The intersection of drug use and criminal behavior: Results from the national household survey on drug abuse." *Crime & Delinquency,* 38, 422–443. Suggests a strong link between drugs and crime in the United States, although young age, poverty, and minority status are also strongly related to crime.

Kandel, Denise B. (ed.). 2002. *Stages and Pathways of Drug Involvement: Examining the Gateway Hypothesis.* Cambridge, UK: Cambridge University Press. An anthology of diverse articles presenting various theoretical and empirical analyses of the famous idea that the use of licit or less harmful drugs often leads to the use of harder or more dangerous drugs.

Massing, Michael. 1998. *The Fix.* New York: Simon & Schuster. An analysis of the U.S. drug problem with practical recommendations for treatment as opposed to law enforcement.

South, Nigel (ed.). 1999. *Drugs: Cultures, Controls and Everyday Life.* Thousand Oaks, Calif.: Sage Publications. A collection of articles dealing with the cultural influences on drug use and various societies' efforts to control it.

Sussman, Steve, and Susan L. Ames. 2001. *The Social Psychology of Drug Abuse.* Philadelphia: Open University Press. A review of studies focusing on social and psychological factors in drug abuse.

Venturelli, Peter J. 1994. *Drug Use in America: Social, Cultural, and Political Perspectives.* Boston: Jones and Bartlett. An anthology of articles on drug use among youth, women, and minorities as well as on drug prevention and decriminalization.

CRITICAL THINKING QUESTIONS

1. If in fighting the war on drugs you had to choose between law enforcement and prevention/treatment, which would you opt for? Why?

2. Some smokers believe that in a free country people should be allowed to smoke even though smoking can kill them. Should smoking be allowed as long as the smoke doesn't get into nonsmokers' lungs? Or should it be banned? Defend your position.

CHAPTER

12 Drinking and Alcoholism

On a typical American campus, serious weekend partying begins on Friday. Asked after midnight, "Why do you drink so much?" most students give a succinct answer. "Stress!" says a business major outside a bar. Watched by a bored bouncer, he staggers away. . . . "Stress," whispers a female student as she leans on a wall to avoid falling. Nearby are two bull-necked young men, one wearing a T-shirt with the slogan "Take Me Drunk, I'm Home" and the other's stating, "From Zero to Horny in 2.5 Beers." They lift up the disoriented and giggling young woman by the ankles over a beer keg. Hanging upside down, she seizes its plastic hose and begins to gulp. . . . "Outrageous, awesome, major stress," says a third student outside a club, helping her too-drunk-to-walk friend get into a car. The

317

friend, hair soaked with beer, promptly hangs out the window, hiccuping for a few seconds and then vomiting (Matthews, 1993).

Binge drinking, which is often defined by researchers as the consumption of five or more consecutive drinks for men and four or more for women, is relatively common on U.S. campuses. According to a national survey, about 44 percent of the students binge at least once within a two-week period (Wechsler et al., 2002). Stress is a contributing factor as most binge-drinking students believe, but other factors are also involved. In this chapter we will discuss those factors along with other facets of drinking and alcoholism.

The Extent of Drinking and Alcoholism

Despite the prevalence of binge drinking on the campuses, most Americans do not become alcoholics, who by definition have lost control over drinking and consequently have problems with health, work, or personal relationships. Only about 6 percent of U.S. adults are alcoholics. About 63 percent drink alcoholic beverages such as liquor, wine, or beer. These are moderate drinkers, among whom the men consume no more than two drinks a day and the women no more than one drink. And a large minority, 37 percent of the adult population, are teetotalers, who completely abstain from drinking (Blizzard, 2004a; SAMHSA, 2002). Globally, Americans also appear to be moderate drinkers, ranking neither among the heavy-drinking nations nor among the practically dry ones. This pattern of moderate drinking has become more popular since the early 1980s. Since that time, moreover, abstinence has increased and heavy drinking has declined, chiefly because of rising health consciousness and caution about the hazards of drinking and driving (Chase, 1996b).

Still, alcohol is far more widely used than all illegal drugs, and its abuse is the most widespread of all drug abuses. Alcoholism is also one of our nation's biggest health problems, surpassed only by heart disease and cancer, and drunk driving is the number one cause of death among young people (ages 16 to 24). The economic cost of alcohol problems is enormous, as much as $90 billion a year in reduced industrial production, illness, and traffic accidents (Rivara, 2004; Brake, 1994; Heien and Pittman, 1993).

Myths about Alcohol Abuse

Though prevalent and serious, alcohol problems do not seem to shock the general public. If we, as hosts or hostesses, continually invite our guests to have another drink, we are not considered dope pushers at all. Most important, the beer and liquor commercials vie with one another in pushing the drug on a massive audience. It is little wonder that only a small minority of Americans see alcohol use and abuse as a serious problem; most would rather consider the use of other drugs—marijuana, cocaine, and heroin—a serious problem. From this lack of public concern about drinking, there have emerged a number of misconceptions about alcohol and its abuse. Although some of the popular beliefs (e.g., "Drinking on an empty stomach can get you drunk fast") are indeed correct, many are false.

One commonly held notion is the myth that most alcoholics, who have long been disparaged as "skid-row bums," are homeless. The fact is that homeless alcoholics constitute only a very small minority—less than 5 percent—of the entire alcoholic population in the United States. The overwhelming majority of alcoholics are ordinary people who live with their families.

A second, widely believed idea is that mixing different kinds of alcoholic drinks can make a person drunk faster. Actually, it is not the mixture of different drinks, but the total amount of alcohol consumed and the length of time taken to consume it that determine the speed of intoxication.

A third belief held by many people is that drinking black coffee or dousing one's head with cold water can sober one up. In fact, there is no effective method for getting over intoxication other than waiting for the alcohol to leave the body—with the length of the waiting period depending on the percentage of alcohol in the bloodstream.

A fourth popular misconception is that drinking only beer is unlikely to make one an alcoholic. The truth is that beer drinkers are more likely to become alcoholics when compared with drinkers of gin, Scotch, or any other kind of alcoholic beverage. Perhaps because beer is less potent than the other drinks, people tend to drink it for hours on end, and extended, heavy drinking is very likely to lead to alcoholism.

According to a fifth—and seductive—myth, sex becomes more exciting after several drinks. However, since alcohol is a depressant rather than a stimulant of the central nervous system, a drinker may find it more difficult to perform sexually even if he or she feels less inhibited. As Shakespeare writes in *Macbeth*, drinking "provokes the desire, but it takes away the performance." A common problem with heavy drinking for men is loss of erections, particularly among the middle-aged. Also, a drunk man trying to arouse his partner sensitively is like a gorilla trying to play a violin (Hammond and Jorgensen, 1981).

What Alcohol Does to Its Users

Ever since Stone Age people became intoxicated from drinking the liquid oozing from fruit left too long in a warm place, alcohol has been bringing both joy and grief to humankind. Today, for example, most Americans who drink do get a great deal of enjoyment from it, but some end up getting misery from it by becoming alcoholics. Alcohol plays a significant role in holy ceremonies, making people feel religious, but it also has a hand in most cases of murder and aggravated assault. These conflicting effects of alcohol have spawned conflicting ideas in the folk wisdom about alcohol. For example, one Chinese proverb says that "Three glasses of wine can set everything right," yet another states that "Medicine may heal imaginary sickness but wine can never dispel real sorrow." In the Bible we are told that

"Wine maketh glad the heart of man," but we are also warned that "Wine is a mocker, strong drink is raging" (Fort, 1973). What exactly does alcohol do to or for its users? Let's take a closer look.

Mental and Physical Impact

Alcohol is a drug since it affects our mental and physical activity. Although it is not a stimulant, alcohol is popularly thought of as one. A stimulant increases the functional activity of the body and mind. But alcohol is a depressant; it belongs to the same class of drugs as anesthetics, sedatives, and narcotics. As a depressant, alcohol reduces our mental and bodily functioning.

> At the sensorimotor level . . . alcohol is an incompetence producer. Its effects on the drinker's equilibrium, for instance, may result in his stumbling, bumping into things, knocking them over, falling down. . . . In addition, things may be dropped or otherwise broken, judgments of time and distance may be thrown askew, tasks may be poorly executed. . . . What is more, we all know that when a person is drunk, these sorts of alcohol-produced failings are both unintentional and beyond the drinker's power to overcome by sheer volition. (MacAndrew and Edgerton, 1969)

Alcohol, then, greatly reduces the drinker's sensorimotor skill—that is, mental and physical functional activity. By itself, however, alcohol does not diminish the drinker's moral competence (Graham et al., 1979; MacAndrew and Edgerton, 1969). It does not, for example, cause people to insult their friends or to make an unwelcome pass at a member of the opposite sex. But the general public believes that alcohol produces moral failings. This popular belief, in the manner of a self-fulfilling prophecy, is so strong that many people in our society do indeed show moral failings after a few drinks. When sober again, they insist that alcohol has made them behave badly, thereby exculpating themselves, with the support of the general public.

Knowing that they will not be condemned for their immoral behavior while drunk, many men in our society often try to get themselves and their women friends drunk. But not all achieve their goal. Some are able to get drunk enough to feel uninhibited; others may get too sick or too drowsy to do or feel anything. This is because one group is more, or less, intoxicated than the other. What is it that determines the different degrees of intoxication? A number of factors:

1. A small-sized person may become intoxicated after drinking only one beer, but a large-sized person may stay sober after three or four. Because alcohol is diluted in the bloodstream, a 100-pound woman cannot tolerate as much liquor as a 200-pound man.

2. The higher the percentage of alcohol in a beverage, the quicker the intoxicating effect. Thus a 90-proof whiskey (containing 45 percent alcohol) is more powerful than a 6-proof beer (containing 3 percent alcohol). Obviously, the greater the amount of alcohol consumed, the more potent the intoxicating effect.

3. Alcohol is not digested as food; it goes through the walls of the stomach and small intestine and is absorbed directly into the bloodstream. So food in the stomach can retard absorption of alcohol and weaken its intoxicating impact; on the other hand, drinking on an empty stomach will result in quick absorption and quicker intoxication.

4. An individual with a higher level of tolerance for alcohol—through more frequent, heavier drinking—will become less intoxicated than one with lower tolerance if both consume the same amount of alcohol.

Health Effects

A small intake of alcohol can be socially, psychologically, and even physically beneficial. Studies have shown, for example, that occasional or moderate drinking helps rural whites alleviate the tension and pressure of their harsh lives. The aged residents of nursing homes who drink alcoholic beverages moderately also enjoy improved sleep, heightened morale, and general well-being. Moreover, moderate drinkers are generally healthier, live longer, or have lower death rates than abstainers. Moderate drinkers are also much less likely than teetotalers to suffer from heart disease (Burros, 1996). But the fact that a little bit is good does not mean that a lot would be better. The key, encouraging word here is *moderate*, which, as we have mentioned, means having two drinks a day for men and one drink a day for women. If men and women consume more, they are likely to harm their health in various ways.

The most common damage done to the body by immoderate, heavy drinking involves the liver. The constant intake of alcohol, coupled with malnutrition common among problem drinkers, can destroy liver cells and thereby cause fat to accumulate in the liver. The resulting scarred and fatty liver—a condition called *cirrhosis* of the liver—is a major cause of serious illness and premature death in heavy drinkers. Cirrhosis can also lead to sexual impotence. Although at least 60 percent of all cirrhotics who have stopped drinking recover from the disease within five years, their sexual impotence persists (Andreasen and Black, 2001).

Heavy drinking is also likely to cause heart disease and strokes. For one thing, heavy drinkers tend to have clogged blood vessels in the heart and thus suffer from *coronary heart attacks* more often than moderate drinkers. In addition, they are likely to suffer from *cardiomyopathy*, which involves the weakening of the heart muscle, or *hemorrhagic strokes*, which occur when a blood vessel in the brain leaks or ruptures (Mukamal and Rimm, 2001).

When combined with heavy smoking, heavy drinking further increases the risk of developing cancer of the mouth, throat, and other areas of the body that are frequently assaulted by alcohol. The causal impact of alcohol abuse on these cancers seems more indirect than direct: (1) Alcohol acts as an irritant to the tissues of mouth, throat, and other related organs, thereby making them more vulnerable to *carcinogens* (cancer-causing agents) that invade them. (2) Some alcoholic beverages carry their own carcinogens. (3) Poor diet in the heavy drinker facilitates the work of these carcinogens. And (4) the heavy use of alcohol enhances the cancer-causing impact of smoking (Bagnardi et al., 2001).

Finally, heavy use of alcohol can cause a whole array of other health problems, such as:

- Impaired memory and ability to learn

- Premature aging, with neuropsychological performance more characteristic of much older persons

- Fetal alcohol syndrome, characterized by damage to the fetus's central nervous system, small infant weight and size, and various birth defects (Stark, 1987; Miller, 1986).

Social Consequences

Moderate drinking can bring social benefits, such as sociability and hospitality or relaxation and recreation with others, but excessive use of alcohol helps bring about a number of negative social consequences. One is a relatively high rate of *automobile accidents*, the leading cause of death among young people in the United States. Over half of each year's automobile deaths and injuries can be traced to excessive drinking. As the National Institute on Alcohol Abuse and Alcoholism has found, "Most people killed in traffic accidents after drinking . . . have very high blood alcohol concentration, averaging twice the level of alcohol considered legally impairing" (NIAAA, 1983). A certain group of young people are especially likely to get involved in auto accidents and deaths. Compared with their peers, they are not just more likely to drink excessively but to use illicit drugs, violate various traffic laws, enjoy taking risks, and exhibit aggressiveness or hostility toward others (Donovan, 1993).

Another consequence is a high rate of *criminal offenses*. Offenses directly related to drinking include public drunkenness, driving while intoxicated, disorderly conduct, vagrancy, and violation of liquor laws. Such offenses result in so many arrests that they put a severe strain on the operation of the criminal justice system. Since 1970, many treatment programs for problem drinkers have helped reduce the number of arrests for alcohol-related offenses, but such offenses still constitute the largest arrest category today (U.S. Census Bureau, 2004). The majority (over 90 percent) of the crimes committed by students on college campuses are also alcohol-related. The perpetrators usually commit multiple crimes, including vandalism, fighting, theft, and alcohol violations. They are more likely than other students to have low grade-point averages, to be athletes, and to drink heavily (Engs and Hanson, 1994; Towson State, 1993).

Heavy drinking further plays a significant part, albeit indirectly, in the commission of more serious, violent crimes, such as homicide, aggravated assault, and forcible rape. As Figure 12.1 indicates, alcohol is implicated in 42 percent of all violent crimes in the United States. Those who commit these crimes seem to use alcohol as an excuse for expressing their aggression. Alcohol can thus become dynamite in the hands of an aggressive person. In one experimental study, subjects with a history of arguments and other aggressive acts were more likely to get involved in interpersonal aggression after they had done some heavy drinking (Boyatzis, 1975).

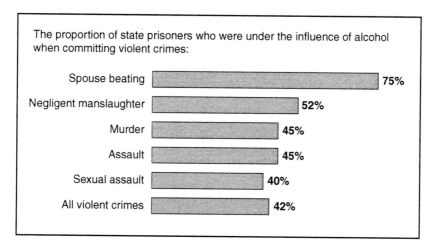

The proportion of state prisoners who were under the influence of alcohol when committing violent crimes:

Spouse beating	75%
Negligent manslaughter	52%
Murder	45%
Assault	45%
Sexual assault	40%
All violent crimes	42%

FIGURE 12.1   Alcohol and Violent Crimes

Source: U.S. Department of Justice, Bureau of Justice Statistics, 1999, 2004.

Social Factors in Drinking

Some Americans are more likely than others to use or abuse alcohol. The difference lies in a number of social factors, such as gender and age, racial and ethnic background, religious affiliation, socioeconomic status, and regional location.

Gender and Age

Drinking is a characteristically male activity. Compared with women, men are not only more likely to drink but also more likely to consume more when they drink and far more likely to get into trouble with drinking. It has been estimated that men are at least four times more likely than women to become alcoholic. But this gender difference has been narrowing over the years, as women have been achieving more equality in various aspects of life. According to many studies, over the last 30 years a significant increase in drinking as well as drinking problems has occurred among college women. The researchers attribute this finding to the women's greater career pressures, their stronger desire for achieving gender equality by behaving like "one of the boys," and declining social stigma about women getting drunk. Nevertheless, men still drink more and have more alcohol problems than women (Blizzard, 2004a; Rowe, 1995; Gross, 1993; Hanson and Engs, 1992).

One reason for the gender difference is that drinking and drunkenness are more socially acceptable for males than for females. Another reason is that, as a result of gender-role socialization men are more concerned with their masculinity, such as their need for dominance and emotional control, which is further reinforced by the peer pressure to "drink like a man" (Carey, 1993). Research has indeed shown a strong link between masculine concerns and alcohol use or abuse (Huselid and Cooper, 1992).

Apparently more concerned with their masculinity than older men, young men are more likely to drink and to do so heavily. But the age difference in alcohol consumption among women is not as great as that among men, because women are generally uninterested in being masculine. Younger women, though, are still significantly prone to drink more than older women. This suggests that the age factor can have its own, independent influence on drinking, without being affected by the gender factor (Blizzard, 2004a; Breslow and Smothers, 2004; Hanson, 1995).

Racial and Ethnic Background

Americans of different races and ethnicities tend to have different rates of alcohol use and abuse. Apparently, the culture of the countries from which their ancestors came continues to influence the drinking pattern of today's Americans.

African Americans.   Compared with whites as a broad group, African Americans are less likely to drink but significantly more likely to become alcoholics. Moreover, as they get older, African-American heavy drinkers are more likely than their white peers to continue drinking heavily (Nielsen, 1999). Thus, as a group, African Americans suffer from a higher rate of alcohol-related diseases, such as alcohol fatty liver, hepatitis, liver cirrhosis, and esophageal cancer (Herd, 1991). This is largely because African Americans have a much higher rate of *poverty*—and many studies have indeed indicated a strong link between poverty and drinking problems. The alcoholism among poor African Americans can be said to reflect a futile attempt to use alcohol "as a mechanism to escape the stresses of poverty, discrimination, and deprivation" (Neff and Husaini, 1985). Poor blacks, some research suggests, are more likely to abuse alcohol because poverty has caused them to have low self-esteem and little racial pride (Harper and Saifnoorian, 1991). By contrast, middle-and upper-class blacks have higher self-esteem and greater racial pride, which enables them to benefit from traditional Afrocentric values of kinship and spirituality that discourage alcohol abuse. Not surprisingly, many studies have found black college students to be much less likely to use and abuse alcohol than even their white peers, let alone poor blacks (Hanson, 1995; Herd, 1991).

Hispanic Americans.   Like African Americans, Hispanic Americans are also more likely than Anglos to drink heavily. This has long been attributed to the Hispanic value of machismo, which emphasizes the importance of masculinity in the form of male dominance, toughness, and honor. But, according to more recent research, machismo does *not* affect heavy drinking among Hispanics: Hispanics who drink heavily show no greater interest in machismo when compared with those who drink in moderation. Ironically, though, machismo affects heavy drinking among Anglos (Neff et al., 1991). Apparently, in Hispanic culture, men are not expected to prove their machismo through heavy drinking but rather through some other means, such as exhibiting physical courage or sexual prowess. The social expectation for men to prove their manhood through heavy drinking appears instead to be a part of the Anglo culture. A more credible explanation for the higher rate of drinking problems among Hispanics is their higher rate of poverty. Generally, more successful Hispanic groups, such as Cubans and Dominicans, are less likely than others, such as Puerto Ricans and Guatemalans, to abuse alcohol (Hanson, 1995).

Native Americans.   Compared with African and Hispanic Americans, Native Americans have more serious problems with alcohol. They suffer from higher rates of such problems as alcoholic cirrhosis, arrests for public drunkenness, and alcohol-related accidental deaths. These problems have been attributed to socio-cultural factors, particularly the fact that the life of Native Americans as a poor minority is filled with stress, while the traditional culture that provides them with a sense of pride and dignity has been diminished or destroyed through long years of colonization by Europeans and other immigrants (Schaefer, 1981). However, it is doubtful that the same alcohol problems plague all of the Native American tribes, who, after all, number over 300. While Native Americans as a group have more drinking problems than other Americans, some tribes do have few problems and others have many. Generally, tribes with "an individualistic hunting-gathering tradition" have a higher incidence of alcohol abuse than tribes with "an agricultural tradition stressing communal values and ceremonies" (Hanson, 1995).

Irish Americans.   Irish Americans have one of the highest rates of alcoholism in U.S. society. A major reason can be traced to the traditional Irish culture, which accepts heavy drinking as normal and treats the drunk as a lovable person:

> [In Ireland] drunkenness . . . is laughable, pleasurable, somewhat exciting, a punctuation of dull routine to be watched and applauded, and drunken men are handled with care and affection. The drunkard is handled with maternal affection, often referred to as "the poor boy," with a special connotation of sympathy, love, pity, and sorrow. If married, the drunkard is compassionately classed by his wife with "the min, God help us!" The man who is drunk is sometimes regarded with envy by the man who is sober (Bales, 1962).

Italian and Chinese Americans.   Americans of Italian or Chinese ancestry have one of the lowest rates of alcoholism, although they often drink. This is largely because Italian Americans usually drink with meals, do not encourage solitary drinking as a means of drowning sorrows, and have strong sanctions against drunkenness. Similarly, Chinese Americans drink a lot but are relatively free from alcoholism. Like the Italians, the Chinese usually drink with meals, particularly on such special occasions as family ceremonies (births, weddings, rites for the dead) and national and religious celebrations. The Chinese do not think of drunken behavior as funny or comical. They look at it with contempt because they believe that drunkenness can seriously disrupt interpersonal relationships and that only moderate, controlled drinking is a social lubricant (Hanson, 1995).

Religious Affiliation

American Jews start drinking at a very young age, but they have one of the lowest rates of alcohol problems. This has been the case for many years and is still true today. The reason has long been assumed to be the culture of Orthodox Judaism— more specifically, the fact that Jews use wine only for religious rituals and consider it sacrilegious to use the alcohol to get drunk. But sociologist Barry Glassner (1991) finds that Orthodox Judaism cannot fully explain the persistent low rate of drinking problems among Jews. Many Jews today are no longer very religious; instead, they are nominal, nonpracticing, or inactive Jews, who do not go to the synagogue or keep kosher. Instead, there are four factors that reinforce each other in protecting Jews against alcoholism.

One is the widespread belief among Jews that excessive drinking is a non-Jewish characteristic, while *moderate drinking* is a *Jewish trait.* Jews often use the Yiddish expression *shikker vie a goy* (drunk as a Gentile) and feel that it is not Jewish to get drunk. A second factor that protects Jews against alcoholism is the practice of *moderate drinking since childhood.* They have as children had many opportunities to learn to associate drinking with special positive events, such as religious services, weddings, or dinners. On such occasions, controlled drinking is expected, and excessive drinking is condemned. A third factor is the support for moderate drinking and disapproval of excessive drinking that Jews receive from *their peers.* This kind of peer support and pressure is effective in insulating Jews from alcohol abuse because most of their friends are Jewish. A fourth factor is the Jews' *conscious attempts to avoid excessive drinking* even under social pressures—from non-Jews—to do otherwise. If they are encouraged by non-Jews to drink more than they wish, Jews will often simply say no or will take a few sips rather than gulp down the whole drink (Glassner, 1991).

Conservative Protestants such as Pentecostals and Southern Baptists prohibit the use of alcohol by the faithful. Thus, they have the largest proportion of non-drinkers and the lowest proportion of heavy drinkers when compared with Catholics and liberal Protestants. But if they drink, conservative Protestants are more likely to end up being problem drinkers. One explanation is that conservative Protestants, having been brought up in a religion that preaches total abstinence from liquor, have not learned how to drink in moderation. Another explanation is that the drinking problem of conservative Protestants who drink is merely a part of their overall pattern of deviation from their religious training. Thus, whatever causes their larger pattern of deviance, such as broken homes or joblessness, also causes their alcohol abuse (Galen and Rogers, 2004; Orcutt, 1991).

Socioeconomic Status

Proportionately more people of the higher socioeconomic levels drink when compared with those of the lower levels. Yet there are more problem drinkers and alcoholics from the lower classes. There may be two explanations for this paradoxical finding. One is that drinkers of different classes use alcohol for different purposes. Drinkers of higher social classes seem more likely to use alcohol as a facilitator of social interaction, but lower-class drinkers tend more to drink as a way of trying to solve personal problems. This may explain why, when drinking, lower-class persons drink significantly more and faster than higher-class persons (Hunter, Hannon, and Marchi, 1982). It is apparent that a large consumption of alcohol can make the lower-class drinkers lose self-control, which in turn makes it harder to solve problems. They may in consequence keep drinking to attempt to achieve a goal that gets progressively harder to achieve the more they drink. Another explanation is that there may in fact be no real difference in alcoholism between the higher and lower classes. Lower-class people may only *appear* more prone to alcoholism because they are not as successful as the higher classes in hiding problem drinking.

The first explanation appears more convincing because the lower classes do have a greater number of distressful life experiences that are associated with drinking problems. Such experiences include family breakdown (marital violence, separation, or divorce) and job loss. Research has consistently found that people with these kinds of experiences suffer from higher rates of alcoholism than those without (Catalano et al., 1993).

Regional Location

Alcohol consumption is highest in the Northeast, lowest in the South, and intermediate in the Midwest and West (see Figure 12.2). The states that have higher rates of alcohol use are generally more urbanized, which suggests that cities and suburbs have proportionately more drinkers than rural areas and small towns. One explanation for the greater consumption of alcohol in more urbanized regions attributes it to the greater stresses and strains of their urban life. Another explanation is that regions with higher rates of alcohol use probably have more favorable attitudes toward alcohol, less legal restrictions, and weaker traditions of temperance or prohibition against alcohol.

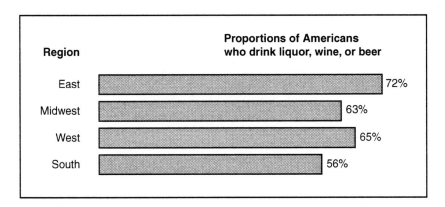

FIGURE 12.2   Prevalence of Drinking by Regions
Source: The Gallup Poll Tuesday Briefing, August 24, 2004.

While the South has the lowest level of alcohol consumption, it has the highest rate of drunkenness. In fact, compared with other regions, the South has higher rates of alcoholism and alcohol-related fights, accidents, and problems with work, the police, spouses, and friends (Hilton, 1991). In other words, Southerners are less likely than others to drink, but if they do drink, they are more likely to become problem drinkers. This apparent contradiction between less alcohol consumption and more problem drinking in the South should not be surprising. It is analogous to what we have observed in regard to the religiously conservative and the lower class, who are less likely than others to drink but, if drinking, are more likely to abuse alcohol. The reasons given earlier are (1) the failure to learn moderate drinking in the case of the religiously conservative and (2) the use of alcohol as a futile attempt to solve personal problems in the case of the lower class. What about the reason for the higher rate of drinking problems in the South? The reason is having a higher proportion of religiously conservative and lower-class people than other regions.

Global Perspective: Drinking

Throughout the world, liquor and beer have, over the last quarter century, become much more popular while wine has gotten less so. The consumption of alcoholic beverages as a whole, however, varies from one society to another. Generally, more affluent societies consume greater quantities of alcohol than do poorer societies. The prosperous Western European and North American societies, for example, consume more alcohol than the less economically developed countries in Southeast Asia and in the Middle East. Among prosperous countries, though, France, Germany, and Britain consume more alcohol than do the United States and Canada. Drinking even more than the Europeans are the Russians, who consume the most alcohol in the world.

The Russians have been beset with the habit of heavy drinking since they invented vodka, their favorite liquor, 500 years ago. The key reason is apparently the benefits the Russian drinker can obtain from vodka. As a Russian writer explains, "Vodka has provided access to a private life that is closed to the state, a place where it is possible to relax, to forget your troubles, to engage in sex with the illusion of free choice." Heavy drinking has gotten worse since the dissolution of the Soviet Union in the early 1990s, which has brought along severe social and economic problems. Unemployment or poverty has hit more people, the income of the employed has fallen, the prices of goods and services have gone up, and thieves and killers have proliferated. These problems in turn make social life less active. In the past, people often visited friends, patronized cafés and restaurants, went to the movies, attended sports events, or participated in some other social activities. But nowadays people tend to stay home and get drunk.

In Russia as well as in other countries where the prevalence of drinking is high, the gender difference in drinking is relatively small, with the percentage of male drinkers only slightly exceeding that of female drinkers. But in Islamic countries, which prohibit alcohol use, or in Southeast Asian countries, which are relatively traditional, drinking is almost entirely confined to men, so that drinking by women appears extremely rare.

As the traditional Asian countries become increasingly prosperous, their prevalence of drinking is expected to rise. India and China, the world's most populous countries, are already showing an increase in drinking. Another significant trend is the rising incidence of young people in Europe switching from light or moderate drinking with meals to heavy drinking without meals. This problem can be attributed to the alcohol industry's aggressive marketing to the European youth. After all, liquor and beer companies often promote youthful drinking by sponsoring fun events and putting their banners on Web pages. Young people are thus led to believe that alcohol use is indispensable to recreation, fun, and partying.

Source: Rehm et al., 2003; Erofeyev, 2002; Hagmann, 2001; Levin, Jones, and Braithwaite, 1998.

What Is Alcoholism?

There is no universally accepted definition of alcoholism. The most popular definition was offered by the World Health Organization in 1952: "Alcoholics are those excessive drinkers whose dependence upon alcohol has attained such a degree that it shows . . . an interference with their bodily and mental health, their interpersonal relations, and their smooth social and economic functioning" (Cahalan, 1970). This elaborate definition can be boiled down to a shorter sentence like the one offered more recently by psychiatrist Donald Goodwin (1991): "Alcoholism involves a compulsion to drink, causing damage to self and others." Thus alcoholics can be identified on the basis of certain problems that they have as a result of drinking. But those just given in the two definitions are too broad, not specific enough. In a 1991 report from the National Institute on Alcohol Abuse and Alcoholism (NIAAA), specific problems are presented in the form of 33 statements, of which 10 are presented here:

1. I have often taken a drink the first thing when I get up in the morning.
2. I deliberately tried to cut down or quit drinking but was unable to do so.
3. Once I started drinking it was difficult for me to stop before I became completely intoxicated.
4. I have had a quick drink when no one was looking.
5. I have skipped a number of regular meals while drinking.
6. I have awakened the next day not being able to remember some of the things I had done while drinking.
7. I have lost a job, or nearly lost one, because of my drinking.
8. My drinking contributed to getting hurt in an accident (in a car or elsewhere).
9. A physician suggested I cut down on drinking.
10. I have stayed away from work or gone to work late because of a hangover.

According to NIAAA, if a person says yes to at least one of those statements, that person may be identified as an alcoholic. But there is no certainty that a person having any one of these problems is necessarily an alcoholic. Consider the implication of statement 10. Many college students have occasionally stayed away from class because of a hangover from having drunk too much at a party the night before, but they are not necessarily alcoholics, because such experience has occurred only once or twice rather than repeatedly. It is safe to say, however, that the more of the listed problems people have, the more likely they are alcoholics. The problems can be classified into four types (Schuckit, 1984):

1. *Excessive drinking* over an extended period.
2. *Psychological addiction,* an irresistible craving for alcohol.
3. *Physical addiction,* experiencing physical discomfort when drinking stops.
4. *Alcohol-related problems,* such as divorce, car accident, or inability to work because of uncontrolled drinking.

Once a person is identified as an alcoholic, social scientists may still disagree on how to label the alcoholic's problem. Some label it *alcoholism* because they consider it a disease, but others call it *problem drinking* because they see it as a behavior. Still others simply regard alcoholism as chronic drinking, more serious than problem drinking. For our purposes, we use interchangeably various labels, including not only alcoholism and problem drinking but also abusive drinking, uncontrolled drinking, and alcohol abuse. But no matter what label we use, it is intended to mean having those four problems.

Becoming an Alcoholic

When people take a drink for the first time in their lives, they do not immediately, nor inevitably, become alcoholics (Hasin, Grant, and Endicott, 1990). They usually go through a sequence of events that may culminate in being totally dependent on alcohol. That sequence, according to E. M. Jellinek (1952) the influential pioneer in the study of alcoholism, consists of four stages.

Social Drinker

In the first, prealcoholic stage, prospective alcoholics *begin as social drinkers.* Through drinking, they discover their ability to experience some relief from tensions (Orcutt, 1993). But the more they drink, the less their tolerance for tensions; the less their tolerance for tensions, the more they want to drink to seek relief. This results in a vicious circle of more and more episodes of drunkenness and hangover. At the same time, the more individuals drink, the greater their tolerance for alcohol, so that they have to consume more and more alcohol to get drunk. These experiences increase the psychological and physiological impact of alcohol on the drinker. But people in this stage can still control their drinking so that they can continue to function normally in their occupational and social world.

Psychologically Addicted

In this second stage, social drinkers begin to show signs of abusing alcohol if they start to experience blackouts. A *blackout* is an attack of amnesia or memory loss, but it is quite different from passing out. When people drink beyond their alcohol-tolerance level, they may pass out on the spot, totally incapable of interacting with others. On the other hand, individuals experiencing blackouts may be the life of the party, or at least talk with others and move about freely; but the next day they cannot remember what they did.

By now they have become *psychologically addicted* to alcohol, having a strong craving for the drug. The craving is so great that they will drink a lot, drink alone, and drink in the morning. Such excessive drinking begins to hurt their relations with relatives, friends, and fellow workers, and they may feel guilty about drinking too much. Still, they feel they could not help having the strong attraction to alcohol. But they still can stop abusing alcohol if they are determined to do so.

Physically Addicted

In this third stage, the drinkers become *physically addicted* in the sense of having chills, shakes, and other withdrawal distresses when not drinking. By now they could not stop drinking even if they wanted to, because they have lost control over drinking. Therefore, once they start drinking, they tend to keep doing so until the supply is gone or they are too drunk to continue. Although they cannot control their drinking, they typically insist that they can stop if they really want to. To prove that they can, they will go on the wagon for a while or change their drinking patterns—switching types of liquor, trying different ways of mixing it, and altering speeds of consuming it.

But the more these drinkers think they can control their drinking—and the more they try to control it—the more they lose control. Consequently, they begin to invent excuses and rationalizations for drinking. They may, for example, blame their spouses or bosses for causing so much tension that they need to drink for relief. The drinking can break up their relations to bosses, friends, and family. This makes them become even more attached to liquor, and, as a result, they often skip meals in favor of liquor. They are nonetheless still capable of being gregarious and sociable (Morey, Skinner, and Blashfield, 1984).

Hitting Bottom

In this last stage, the alcoholic becomes isolated and withdrawn from others. They now *hit bottom* with total dependence on alcohol, exhibiting spectacular, bizarre behavior. A typical example is drinking and being intoxicated continuously for several days without doing anything else. They are haunted by the tremendous fear that alcohol may be taken away from them. They must have a drink just to be able to get up in the morning. They may be so far gone that to get liquor into their mouths becomes an almost impossible task to perform. But they usually work very hard at it—spending hours stumbling, crawling, vomiting, trembling, and failing to achieve the goal three or four times before finally succeeding in keeping a drink down. Since they rarely eat, they often suffer from malnutrition. They also suffer from delirium tremens, which can produce terrifying hallucinations—such as seeing millions of little flies chasing, suffocating, or eating them.

College Students and Alcohol

Since the late 1980s, many college students have hit the bottle with reckless abandon while an increasing number have abstained from alcohol. As we have suggested at the beginning of this chapter, those alcohol abusers are binge drinkers, men who gulp down five or more drinks in a row and women who put away four or more. What kind of students are these bingers? What has made them go on a binge in the first place?

Binge Drinking in College

Most college students (nearly 56 percent) drink in moderation or abstain from alcohol. In fact, more students today abstain than did in the early 1990s. But over the same period, the relatively high incidence of binge drinking has remained constant. Some 44.4 percent of students engaged in binge drinking in 2001; 44 percent did in 1993. Compared with moderate drinkers and abstainers, binge drinkers are more likely to run into trouble with the police, injure themselves or others, have academic and interpersonal problems, and ride in cars with drivers who are drunk or high. Binge drinkers also cause "secondhand effects" on others, with the latter having their study or sleep interrupted, being forced to take care of drunken students, and getting insulted or humiliated (Wechsler et al., 2002).

Binge drinking started to become a serious problem on many campuses in the late 1980s, about the same time the legal drinking age was raised to 21 throughout the country. Before the enactment of this drinking age law, drinking took place in the open, where it could be supervised by police, security guards, and even health-care workers. After the drinking age went up, drinking did not stop. It simply moved underground to homes, cars, and frat-house basements where, hidden from adults and authorities, it could get out of hand and lead to binge drinking.

More importantly, most students today have not learned and practiced moderate drinking as their peers did before students under 21 were legally denied access to liquor. When all students were allowed to drink, they learned to do so responsibly at college-sponsored events, where alcoholic beverages were served. They also learned to drink in moderation at the homes of professors who invited them to dinners and receptions. But this kind of drinking experience is no longer available to students. So, Jack Hitt (1999) was able to quip: "Why do college students drink so stupidly? Because drinking intelligently is against the law."

Since it is unlawful for most students to drink even moderately, over the last decade college administrators have tried to combat binge drinking with alcohol-free festivals and rock concerts, no-drinking dorms, abstinent fraternities, and the like. The emphasis is on abstinence. But binge drinking remains as prevalent as before (Wechsler et al., 2002).

At a few schools, though, significant headway has been made against binge drinking. In 1996 sociologist Wesley Perkins of Hobart and William Smith Colleges in New York discovered from a survey at his school that students *believed* their peers to be drinking five times a week while in *reality* they were drinking only twice a week. Students at other schools were also found to overestimate their peers' drinking. As a result, Perkins theorized that students would drink in accordance with the real drinking norm at their school if they know it. To test his theory, he used posters and newspaper ads to publicize the fact that most students drank only a little. Over the next two years, Perkins observed a significant drop in excessive drinking. When the same tactic was tried out at several other colleges, the reduction in heavy drinking was also significant (Kluger, 2001). These schools, however, are not a representative sample of U.S. universities and colleges.

Social Profile: College Binge Drinkers

College binge drinkers tend to have the following characteristics:

- Being male
- Being white
- Aged 18 to 23
- Traditional, full-time students, never married, and living independently of their parents
- Having parents with a college degree
- Engaging in risky behaviors, such as smoking pot or cigarettes
- Being involved in athletics
- Being fraternity members
- Having indulged in binge drinking as high school seniors

Unlike moderate drinkers, who drink to have fun, bingers drink to get drunk. At least four factors lie behind the binging. One is the stress from having to work hard for good grades. Another is the social pressure to get drunk so as to fit in and not be seen by others as uptight or antisocial. A third factor is the adoption of a party-centered lifestyle as an important part of college life. A fourth factor is the *belief* that binge drinking is the norm on the campus even if it is really not so.

Sources: Hoover, 2004; Mattern and Neighbors, 2004; Wechsler et al., 2002; Goldberg, 1998.

Women and Alcohol

Compared with men, women are generally more vulnerable to alcohol and less able to hold their liquor. Still, women are increasingly likely to drink and turn into alcoholics—as if they are trying to catch up with men. Here we will discuss why women are more likely to drink today and how women alcoholics differ from their male peers.

Why More Women Drink Today

Scientists have discovered in recent years that moderate drinking is good for health, especially the heart. Moderate drinkers have a better chance of avoiding heart disease and can expect to live longer than teetotalers. But for a woman moderate drinking also increases the risk of getting breast cancer, colon cancer, hip fracture, and infertility. In addition to this vulnerability to alcohol, women's bodies are less able than men's to tolerate drinking, for a number of reasons. First, women generally have smaller bodies and thus less blood volume to dilute alcohol. Second, women have more body fat and less body water, resulting in less alcohol dilution. And third, women have a smaller amount of the stomach enzyme that neutralizes and removes alcohol from the bloodstream. As a result of these differences, a woman drinking the same amount as a man will accumulate more alcohol in her bloodstream, which will affect her more powerfully (HWHW, 2000).

Despite those physiological disadvantages, more women drink today than ever before. Women generally still lag behind men in alcohol use, but this is no longer the case for female youth. In the latest national survey, published in 2002, among current drinkers 42 percent of females are aged 12 or older, compared with 55 percent of males. But for young people aged 12 to 17, females already have about the same rate of alcohol use as males—17.3 percent for females versus 17.2 percent for males (SAMHSA, 2002).

Why, then, do more women drink today? The main reason is apparently the increased power and freedom women enjoy, thanks to greater gender equality in U.S. society. Support for this observation is available from some historical and cross-cultural evidence. In colonial America, upper-class women, who by definition had a great deal of power in society, were free to drink in public. Nowadays, the rates of drinking among women are higher in Western societies, where there is a great deal of gender equality, than in non-Western societies, where there is less gender equality. In the United States, young women enjoy so much gender equality that they are considerably more likely to drink than older women and as likely in the 12 to 17 age group to drink as their male peers. Perhaps most significantly, at all-women colleges, bastions of feminism, the prevalence of binge drinking in the years 1993 to 2001 soared 125 percent (SAMHSA, 2002; Jersild, 2001). All this has prompted an older-generation feminist to say, "Going toe to toe with men is a feminist act [but] going drink for drink with them isn't" (Ehrenreich, 2002).

Nonetheless, the impact of increased gender equality on drinking among women seems irresistible. The many women now working full-time outside the home are more likely than stay-at-home moms to drink. Similarly, those women who have most benefited from greater gender equality, women who are white, business executives, unmarried, or young, are more likely than nonwhite, lower-paid, married, and older women to use alcohol. It is also noteworthy, as Devon Jersild (2002) observed, that "many girls and young women today associate drinking with independence, glamour, and the kind of power once reserved for men." As a college woman said, "To be able to drink like a guy is kind of a badge of honor. For me, it's a feminism thing" (Jersild, 2002).

Alcoholism among Women

Perhaps because they are generally expected not to drink as heavily as men, women tend not to be diagnosed as alcoholics, even when they are known to drink like fish. "I used to carry a big purse full of beer into my psychiatrist's office and drink right through the sessions," recalled a woman about her past alcoholism. "He never said a word to me about it. As I look back, I think I was probably challenging him to say something, to help me. But he never dealt with it." Unable or unwilling to see alcoholism as the source of their female patients' distraught states, doctors often diagnose the problem as merely "nerves," anxiety, depression, or some other emotional ailment and proceed to prescribe tranquilizers, antidepressants, and other psychoactive drugs, which they are far less likely to do for male patients. It is little wonder that women alcoholics are twice as likely as their male counterparts to be addicted to other drugs besides alcohol (Sandmeier, 1992).

The medical profession probably should not be faulted for their lack of knowledge about female alcoholics because most researchers in the field have long studied only male alcoholics, even though at least 25 percent of alcoholics are women. Consequently, doctors tend to rely on popular stereotypes of women alcoholics as loud and rude like male alcoholics or sexually promiscuous like prostitutes. But since most women alcoholics do not behave that way, it is hard for doctors to diagnose them with alcoholism (Jersild, 2001).

The few studies that have been done on women alcoholics show them to be different in some ways from their male peers. First, women are more likely to have a family history of alcoholism. Second, women are more likely to have experienced a stressful event, such as physical or sexual abuse, traumatic loss of loved ones, or loneliness, that precipitates alcoholic drinking. Third, women have their first drink and first intoxication at an older age. Fourth, women often drink abusively after their husbands or boyfriends have become heavy drinkers, but men rarely join their wives or girlfriends in becoming abusive drinkers. Fifth, women drink more at home, while men drink more in bars or other public places. And sixth, women have greater problems with both physical and social functioning, more bodily pain, and poorer physical and mental health (Jersild, 2001; H&MW, 2001).

What Causes Alcoholism?

Researchers from various academic disciplines have offered different positivist theories about the development of alcoholism. Medical scientists and psychiatrists believe that some people are genetically vulnerable to alcoholism. Psychologists attribute alcoholism to certain personality traits collectively called the alcoholic personality. And sociologists ascribe alcoholism to a unique set of environmental factors. Let's take a close look at each theory.

A Biological Predisposition

Some medical scientists have long assumed that alcoholism originates from various physical problems such as nutritional deficiencies, glandular disorders, and malfunctions of the central nervous system. Each of these physical factors is thought to cause a strong craving for alcohol, which then leads to alcoholism. But the medical scientists have been criticized for confusing effect with cause. The physical problems that the medical scientists assume are the causes of alcoholism may well be the effects of alcoholism. In other words, the prolonged, frequent, and heavy consumption of alcoholic beverages is very likely to damage the alcoholic's health, bringing on those physical problems.

Medical and psychiatric researchers have also argued that alcoholism is genetically determined. To support this argument, they point to studies showing, for example, that identical twins have higher concordance rates for alcoholism than fraternal twins. (That is, if an identical twin is alcoholic, the chances of the other identical twin becoming alcoholic are relatively high, but if a fraternal twin is alcoholic, the chances of the other fraternal twin becoming alcoholic are significantly lower.) Since identical twins are more genetically alike than fraternal twins, it is assumed that the cause of alcoholism is genetic.

In the early 1990s, some medical researchers purportedly discovered the so-called *A1 gene,* which is supposed to make people vulnerable to alcoholism. The A1 gene was found to deprive its carrier of the feeling of pleasure. Therefore, according to the researchers, people born with this defective gene are driven to constantly use alcohol—or some other drug—as a means of seeking the pleasure that genetically normal people can enjoy without excessive drinking. In analyzing the blood of 159 people, the researchers found the A1 gene in 50 percent of the alcoholics they studied, compared with only 21 percent of nonalcoholics (Noble et al., 1991; Parsian et al., 1991).

Another kind of evidence is also used to support the genetic theory of alcoholism. According to many studies, a majority (two-thirds to three-fourths) of Chinese and Japanese have a "flushing response" to alcohol. After they drink a small amount of alcohol (fewer than one or two beers), their faces and upper body parts will blush, to be accompanied by a sensation of warmth, nausea, and general discomfort. Because of this physiological reaction, apparently genetic in origin, many Asians cannot tolerate heavy drinking and, therefore, are unlikely to become alcoholics. By contrast, Caucasians, particularly white males, do not have this response. As a consequence, they are more able to literally hold their liquor—capable of guzzling a large quantity of alcohol without getting drunk. Given their greater tolerance for alcohol, they are more likely to become alcoholics (Nakawatase et al., 1993; Goodwin, 1991).

All this suggests that the biological factor may contribute to the development of alcoholism. But there is no direct evidence that the biological factor causes alcoholism. The biological factor can, at best, only serve as a predisposition to drink excessively, but whether people with that predisposition will actually become alcoholics depends on social and psychological factors (Bower, 1992).

The Alcoholic Personality

Many psychologists attribute alcoholism to one or more negative personality traits. These traits include being antisocial, rebellious, egocentric, gregarious, hyperactive, passive-dependent, depressed, anxious, and hostile. Alcoholics are also assumed to have weak ego, poor self-concept, low frustration tolerance, and neurotic guilt. Such personality deficits have supposedly been found in alcoholics (Donovan, 1986). There is no consensus among the personality researchers as to how many of those traits make up what they call the *alcoholic personality*. To some, only one trait—especially being *antisocial*—reflects the alcoholic personality; to others, many more constitute the alcoholic personality. Another problem with the personality theories is that the traits are often contradictory, such as being hyperactive versus depressed or being hostile versus gregarious. A third problem is that most of the personality researchers focus on adults who have become alcoholics rather than using the prospective, longitudinal method of examining children and then reexamining them when they become adults. As a result, the effects of alcoholism are often confused with the causes. There is evidence that chronic drinking causes rather than results from impulsivity, low self-esteem, anxiety, or depression (Vaillant, 1995; Vaillant and Milofsky, 1982).

Other psychologists consider the need for *dependency* to be the key factor in the development of alcoholism. According to William McCord and Joan McCord (1960), for example, the alcoholic's need for dependency stems largely from a stressful and erratic home environment where the mother often comforts the child with loving indulgence but also often terrifies the child with outright rejection. These conflicting childhood experiences are said to intensify the individual's need for love—the need for dependence on others. But this heightened need is not easy to satisfy, so that the individual becomes overwhelmed with *anxiety*, which in turn leads the person to use alcohol in order to get rid of the anxiety. But David McClelland and his colleagues (1972) contend that the need for *power*, rather than the need for dependency, is the driving force behind alcoholism. As McClelland says, "Societies and individuals with accentuated needs for personalized power are more likely to drink more heavily in order to get the feeling of strength they need so much more than others."

While McClelland regards the concern for power as the cause of alcoholism, the McCords do not necessarily disagree. This is because the McCords acknowledge the power desire as the other, *conscious* aspect of the same alcoholic personality that is characterized by the *unconscious* need for dependency. In these psychoanalytic terms, heavy drinking can be said to provide an appearance of toughness to make the alcoholic feel consciously like a powerful person, which in turn suppresses (i.e., keeps unconscious) the alcoholic's anxiety as a dependent person. In effect, heavy drinking simultaneously fulfills both the conscious need for power and the unconscious need for dependency. It is difficult, however, to demonstrate empirically the concept of the unconscious.

Social and Cultural Forces

In sociology there are two major explanations for alcoholism. One is a strictly sociological theory, useful for explaining why some *groups* have higher alcoholism rates than others. The other theory is social-psychological, explaining why some *individuals* become alcoholics but others do not.

Explaining Individual Differences. According to a classic social-psychological theory in sociology, the unique factor that turns individuals into alcoholics is the fit between vulnerable personality traits on the one hand, and certain drinking-group values and activities on the other (Trice, 1966). This fit will come about under the following four conditions:

1. People must have the qualifications to be a candidate for alcoholism, namely, the vulnerable personality features. These personality features are the same as some of those identified by psychologists as the traits of the alcoholic personality. As Harrison Trice (1966) says, "A potential alcoholic has intense dependency needs and sharp feelings of worthlessness, self-hate, and inadequacy, which produce an unusual need to be looked upon by others and by himself as a 'man.'" Such dependent individuals have deep anxiety about their own adequacy, which makes them highly susceptible to the influence of drinking groups.

2. Once they join drinking groups, they find that they fit right in. Members of drinking groups characteristically believe that drinking is a sign of masculine prowess. They are fond of encouraging a new member to "drink like a man," and praising him for being able to "hold his liquor." This is what the prospective male alcoholic badly needs because of his "unusual need to be looked upon by others and by himself as a 'man.'"

3. After drinking and enjoying his status as "a man" for some time, the individual finds it necessary to consume more and more liquor to prove his manhood. He reaches the point where he becomes an excessive drinker who has lost self-control. It is at this point that his drinking groups stop rewarding him for his alcohol consumption and start rejecting him as a loser. This is because the same social value that encourages a person to drink like a man also emphasizes the importance of self-control—presumably another aspect of the same masculine character.

4. After being ostracized by the drinking groups that initially encouraged the use of alcohol, the abusive, uncontrolled drinkers seek out more tolerant drinking companions, namely, other abusive, uncontrolled drinkers. In such company, the abusive drinkers encourage each other to drink more and more, until finally they are securely locked into alcoholism.

In short, psychologically vulnerable individuals and their drinking peers come together to generate a force that gradually causes the individuals to become alcoholics.

Explaining Group Differences. According to another classic sociological theory, three factors work together to create a high rate of alcoholism: (1) the production of acute inner tensions in people by their culture, (2) a culturally induced attitude toward drinking as a means of relieving those inner tensions, and (3) the failure of the culture to provide suitable substitute means for resolving the inner tensions (Bales, 1946).

To take the first factor, *culturally produced inner tensions* include feelings of anxiety, guilt, conflict, suppressed hostility, and sexual frustration. To show the way in which a culture can bring about these inner tensions in its members, Bales presented the case of Irish peasants, noted for their drunkenness during the past several centuries. Irish parents instilled fear, insecurity, and anxiety in their children by disciplining them with the threat of "boogey men," "spooks," and "fairies," and by smothering them with affection at one moment and beating them in a fit of anger at the next. The boys often had to stay on the farm, continuing to work for their father until he retired or died. "So long as they stayed on the farm," Bales observed, "they had to work for him as 'boys' and were treated as boys, even though they might be 45 or 50 years old." This created a huge reservoir of suppressed hostility against the father. Kept under the father's thumb as "boys," these physically mature men could neither marry nor dally in premarital sexual escapades. Such a situation generated powerful sexual tensions.

Acute inner tensions can become a powerful motivating force for compulsive drinking if *the culture has induced in people the attitude that liquor is excellent for relieving the tensions and many other problems,* the second factor. The Irish farmers are said to have such a culture. When going to fairs to buy or sell livestock, they treat each other with a few drinks in order to "soften the other guy up," so that they typically come home in a heavy state of intoxication. But their wives usually treat them with care and affection; their mothers lovingly call them "my poor boy"; and their friends, acquaintances, and others regard their intoxication with envy instead of pity. The Irish also consider alcohol an effective folk remedy for "keeping the cold out of the stomach," curing stomachache, combating insomnia, increasing the feeling of physical and sexual strength, and even getting rid of hangovers. With this attitude, the Irish find it natural to resort to drinking as a means of drowning their personal problems as well. The result is their relatively high rate of alcoholism.

In coping with a culturally induced stress, people will turn to alcohol if they *cannot find another method of resolving the stress,* the third factor. For Jews and Italians, eating seems to be the method of dealing with tension. Many Muslims are said to turn to hashish as well as strong tea and coffee. The Brahmins in India and the Japanese are believed to rely on opium. As a result of their having culturally approved alternatives to the use of alcohol for resolving tension, these groups have low rates of alcoholism. But the Irish, being without an alternative to drinking, have a higher rate of alcoholism.

Of the three types of theories, the sociological theories appear the most satisfactory. As psychologists McCord and McCord (1960) wrote, "Sociologists have produced impressive evidence demonstrating that rates of alcoholism are significantly related to the social factors." But we should not overgeneralize. People who are psychologically vulnerable and exposed by peers to heavy drinking do not necessarily become alcoholics, nor do the majority of the Irish indulge in excessive drinking. What the sociological theories suggest is that people with those social and cultural experiences are more likely than others to become alcoholics.

Controlling Alcohol Use and Abuse

Like illegal drug use, alcohol use or abuse has been subjected to various attempts to control it, but has proven to be a persistent aspect of American life.

Legal Measures

One way to control alcohol use involves the coercive power of the law. Let us see how this has been carried out in the past and present.

The Past.   In colonial days, the Puritans enjoyed drinking beer and rum in moderation. They condemned only excessive drinking. Then, in the early nineteenth century, there arose a crusade for total abstinence. This crusade, often called the Temperance movement, eventually culminated in the enactment of the Eighteenth Amendment (popularly known as "Prohibition") in 1919. During the next 14 years, drunkenness did not disappear from the face of America. On the contrary, Prohibition turned out to be such a disastrous failure that it was repealed by the Twenty-first Amendment in 1933 (Gusfield, 1991; Wilkinson, 1970).

In some ways similar to the efforts past and present at outlawing psychoactive drugs discussed in the preceding chapter, Prohibition originated chiefly from an attempt to control the powerless segments of society. In postcolonial America, the temperance movement first emerged as an attempt on the part of the aristocracy of wealth to control the new upsurge of democracy among the masses, who happened to engage in some drinking. Later the emergent, dominant middle classes (independent farmers, small-business owners, and self-employed professionals) used the temperance movement to stir up prejudice and discrimination against Irish and German immigrants, Catholics and Jews, and the urban lower classes. The middle classes felt that their puritanical values of hard work were threatened by the "ne'er-do-well, unambitious, and irreligious" immigrants and poor Americans who traditionally drank. But by the time Prohibition came into effect, a new, more powerful group (salaried professionals, white-collar workers, and managerial employees) had begun to emerge from within the middle class. Unlike the old middle class, who advocated total abstinence from drinking, the new one supported moderate use of alcohol, which contributed to the demise of Prohibition. Since then, moderate drinking, as opposed to total abstinence, has continued to be the norm of not just the middle class but of most Americans as well (Gusfield, 1991).

The Present.   In the 1990s the Clinton administration wanted to discourage alcohol abuse by imposing a "sin tax" on hard liquor, though not on beer or wine. The increased tax on liquor was designed to help pay some of the enormous, multibillion-dollar expenses for treating diseases caused by heavy drinking. This seemed to be a sensible measure against alcohol abuse, a far cry from the total prohibition of alcohol in the past. But the liquor lobby was so powerful that Clinton changed his mind. In fact, for the last four decades, the excise taxes on various alcoholic beverages have remained relatively low. This has contributed to the low price of alcohol, which has, along with aggressive marketing, encouraged widespread drinking, especially among teenagers (Serdula, 2004; Cohn and Hager, 1993).

However, a crusade against teenage drinking and drunk driving has been quite successful. Since 1982 many organizations such as MADD (Mothers Against Drunk Driving) and SADD (Students Against Drunk Driving) have effectively aroused public outrage at drunk driving for causing many traffic deaths. Their biggest achievement has come from lobbying the federal and state governments to raise the minimum drinking age to 21, and by the late 1980s virtually all the states had. As a result, the number of alcohol-related car crashes, along with teenage drinking per se, has declined significantly. There is a limit to what the drinking age law can accomplish, though. The law has helped create a phenomenon called *front-loading,* in which underage young people drink alcohol beverages in private before attending a social event where proof of legal age is required for drinking (Serdula, 2004; Gorman, 1994; Hughes and Dodder, 1992).

Therapeutic Approaches

While the law against drunk driving or underage drinking treats alcohol users and abusers as offenders, the therapeutic way of dealing with drinking problems is based on the assumption that abusive drinkers are patients who need help.

Detox and Treatment Centers.   In the early 1970s the popular belief in alcoholism as a disease led to the enactment of laws in over 20 states that treat alcohol abusers as patients rather than criminals. In those states today, violators of the public drunkenness law are no longer thrown into jail. They are instead taken to public detoxification centers for treatment and then, if necessary, sent to halfway houses or aftercare facilities where they are helped to stay "on the wagon." Unfortunately, many who have come out of detox centers or halfway houses will go back in again. In fact, research has shown that "detox doors revolve much faster than jail doors." The major reason is that many patients refuse to see themselves as alcoholics and to follow the center's rules for making a recovery (such as attending meetings or talking about drinking problems), two major conditions that have been proven essential for recovering from alcoholism (Rubington, 1991).

For other alcoholics, who do not violate the public drunkenness law, there are numerous community-based alcohol treatment centers throughout the country. These centers provide mostly outpatient services, offering hospitalization only as a last resort. Services primarily include psychological counseling and therapy because the centers are most often operated under the guidance of psychiatrists and psychologists. Much of the psychological treatment involves the use of aversion therapy or a combination of this with group therapy. Group therapy brings together a number of alcoholics (and, in many cases, their spouses and children) and tries to guide them back to sobriety through a series of sessions that include lectures, educational films, and discussions about drinking problems. Aversion therapy calls for the use of electric shock or nausea-inducing drugs designed to condition the alcoholic to feel sick at the very odor of liquor. Generally, this aversion therapy is effective only for a short time—the urge to drink returns within 6 to 12 months. The combination of this therapy with group treatment is more effective. However, most centers are underutilized, so that the enormity of alcohol abuse in the society as a whole remains largely untouched (Roman and Blum, 1991). A more popular—and effective—method does not involve any professional therapist, but simply alcoholics and ex-alcoholics themselves. It is the AA (Alcoholics Anonymous) method.

Alcoholics Anonymous.   Founded in 1935, AA is today the largest and most successful organization for helping alcoholics (Weisner et al., 1995). The only requirement for joining AA is the desire to stop drinking. Once having joined the organization, new members may choose another AA member as a sponsor. Sponsors are recovering alcoholics ready to come to a new member's aid whenever needed. The treatment involves attending a series of meetings where any number of alcoholics share their drinking histories. These meetings may be held in offices, schools, churches, lodges, or private homes, and they are open to alcoholics and nonalcoholics alike. At a typical meeting, a volunteer "leader" will begin by saying something like "Hello, I'm John, and I'm an alcoholic." He or she may then introduce some AA members who will discuss their experiences with alcohol as well as their recovery from the drinking problem. Afterward, others may follow suit, relating their own experiences. A crucial part of these sessions is that one admit to oneself and other AA members that one is an alcoholic and is powerless over alcohol.

This program is widely considered the most successful method ever devised for coping with alcoholism. Not surprisingly, it has spawned similar organizations such as Al-Anon (for spouses and other close relatives and friends of alcoholics) and Alateen (for alcoholics' teenage children). Their aim is to help members understand alcoholism and themselves, as well as learn how to live with and help their alcoholic relatives. AA meetings, along with recovery dorms, are also available to students in a growing number of colleges. Apparently, the effectiveness of the AA method is due in great measure to the *group support* provided to alcoholics by people who have deep, personal understanding of drinking problems. Group support is particularly important for alcoholics because they are typically "escape drinkers" (who drink alone in a futile attempt to solve personal problems) rather than social drinkers (who participate in drinking with other people for dietary, religious, or social reasons as the Italians, Jews, Chinese, or higher-status people characteristically do). Research has suggested that AA offers what those alcoholics have always sought before they started to drink heavily, namely, social acceptance, a more positive identity, and feelings of normalcy and confidence, the benefits of group support (Karlin-Resnick, 2004; Hurlburt, Gade, and Fuqua, 1984). AA can provide those benefits because it has effectively become its members' family. As a member said at an AA meeting,

> I lost everything. Family, home, wives, kids, job, everything. Even my parents turned against me. . . . I finally found you people. Now you're my family. Wherever I go, you're there. . . . You give me everything I ever wanted and ever looked for. I feel like I'm needed again. (Denzin, 1991)

Can Alcoholics Learn to Drink Moderately? AA assumes that alcoholism is an incurable disease. This is why AA often pronounces "once an alcoholic, always an alcoholic." Since they are not expected to fully recover, even members who have remained sober for years are always considered to be, and are called, recovering—*not* recovered—alcoholics. To continue staying sober, AA insists, recovering alcoholics must completely stay on the wagon. Even taking a small sip of wine, AA believes, will cause recovering alcoholics to relapse into uncontrolled drinking because they still have the disease. Therefore, to AA, alcoholics can never learn to drink moderately, and to talk about moderate drinking can only give alcoholics an excuse to keep on drinking.

But an increasing number of researchers argue that alcoholism is not a disease over which the problem drinker has no control. It is, instead, an unhealthy behavior pattern that can be changed by learning to engage in controlled, moderate drinking. According to moderation theorists, studies in the United States have shown that many alcoholics can learn to drink moderately without suffering a relapse, and studies in many European countries have also demonstrated the ability of alcoholics to learn to drink in moderation without relapsing into uncontrolled drinking (Rotgers, 1996; Sobell and Sobell, 1993). We should note, however, that most of these alcoholics may well be merely "problem drinkers" who have not developed a severe addiction to alcohol. But for "hard-core alcoholics," who have long been severely addicted to the drug, AA's insistence on abstinence may still be the safer way of dealing with the addiction (Rivera, 2000; Marriott, 1995).

Summary

1. **What is the extent of drinking and alcoholism in the United States?** Most Americans drink, but only moderately, while a large minority (one-third) abstain from drinking and a small minority (6 percent) suffer from alcoholism.

2. **What are some popular myths about alcohol use?** They are as follows: alcoholics are mostly homeless; mixing different kinds of drinks accelerates intoxication; drinking black coffee or pouring cold water on the head can get rid of drunkenness; drinking only beer cannot make one an alcoholic; and sex becomes more exciting after several drinks.

3. **What are the effects of alcohol?** Alcohol is a depressant drug, and as such, it reduces the drinker's mental and physical ability but not moral competence. How much the mental and physical ability declines depends on the level of intoxication—the percentage of alcohol in the bloodstream. The latter, in turn, depends on such factors as the body size and weight of the drinker, the type and amount of alcoholic beverages consumed, the quantity of food in the stomach, and the drinker's level of tolerance for alcohol. Taken in moderate amounts, alcohol can provide some health and social benefits. But heavy drinking is likely to damage the liver, bring about sexual impotence, and cause heart disease, strokes, cancer, and other health problems. Alcohol abuse further contributes to a number of social problems such as automobile injuries and deaths and criminal offenses.

4. **Who is more likely than others to use or abuse alcohol?** Those who are more likely to drink are whites, males, young adults, liberal Protestants and Catholics, higher-status persons, and residents of the Northeast and West. But those who are more likely to end up as alcoholics are lower-status persons, and African, Hispanic, Irish, and Native Americans.

5. **What is the global pattern of drinking?** Alcohol consumption is greater in affluent societies than in poor countries. Among people in affluent societies, Europeans drink more than North Americans, with Russians consuming the largest amount of alcohol. Young people in Europe are now more inclined to engage in heavy drinking than before. In these affluent countries women are only somewhat less likely than men to drink, but in Islamic and Southeast Asian countries it is extremely rare for women to consume alcohol.

6. **What is alcoholism?** It involves drinking excessively, being psychologically and physically addicted, and experiencing alcohol-related problems. **How does a person become an alcoholic?** The person first begins as a social drinker, then becomes psychologically and physically addicted, and finally hits bottom with total dependence on alcohol.

7. **What causes binge drinking in college?** The lack of opportunities to learn responsible, moderate drinking because of the drinking-age law. **Who's likely to go on a binge?** Binge drinkers are likely to be, among other things, white males, relatively young traditional full-time students, athletes and fraternity members, and engaged in risky activities. **What could explain the rise in drinking among women, especially female youths?** The increase in gender equality, which encourages women to drink like men. **How do women alcoholics differ from their male peers?** Women alcoholics are more likely to have a family history of alcoholism, experience stressful events, have

the first drink older, abuse alcohol to be like their spouse, drink at home, and suffer more physically, mentally, and socially.

8. What causes alcoholism? According to the biological theory, alcoholism is brought on by some problem inside the body such as a nutritional deficiency, a defective gene, or a lack of flushing response. Psychologists attribute alcoholism to the alcoholic personality, which includes being antisocial, the need for being dependent on others, and the need for power. According to one classic sociological theory, alcoholism develops from a social situation in which psychologically vulnerable individuals are pressured by drinking companions to drink heavily. According to another sociological theory, a culture causes alcoholism by producing acute inner tensions in people, encouraging people to view drinking as useful for relieving tensions, and failing to provide suitable substitutes for alcohol in reducing stress.

9. How has U.S. society tried to control alcohol abuse? By legal and therapeutic methods. The law prohibiting the sale of alcohol in the 1920s and early 1930s failed to eradicate drunkenness, and the prohibition reflected an attempt to control the powerless segments of society. The Clinton administration planned to discourage alcohol abuse but to no avail. Still, the crusade against teenage drinking and drunk driving since the early 1980s has produced positive results. Therapeutic approaches have also been used to control alcohol abuse. They include treating public drunkenness as a disease rather than a crime, providing treatment at community centers, and offering social support through groups organized by alcoholics themselves, of which the largest and most successful is Alcoholics Anonymous. AA insists that alcoholics must completely abstain from drinking, but a growing number of researchers find that alcoholics (more precisely, problem drinkers) can learn to drink in moderation.

FURTHER READING

Catalano, Ralph, et al. 1993. "Job loss and alcohol abuse: A test using data from the epidemiologic catchment area project." *Journal of Health and Social Behavior,* 34 (September), 215–225. Alcohol abuse is found to be more common among those who have been laid off than among those who have not.

Clark, Walter B, and Michael E. Hilton (eds.). 1991. *Alcohol: Drinking Practices and Problems.* Albany, N.Y.: State University of New York Press. A collection of articles presenting the results of several survey studies on alcohol use and abuse in the United States.

Denzin, Norman K. 1993. *The Alcoholic Society: Addiction and Recovery of the Self.* New Brunswick, N.J.: Transaction. Analyzing the various scholarly views on alcoholism and the experiences of drinking as well as recovering from alcoholism.

Edwards, Griffith. 2002. *Alcohol: The World's Favorite Drug.* New York: St. Martin's. A wide-ranging analysis of scientific facts about alcohol and its impact on people, illustrated with case studies.

Grant, Marcus, and Jorge Litvak (eds.). 1998. *Drinking Patterns and Their Consequences.* Washington, D.C.: Taylor & Francis. A collection of articles about social, cultural, and personal factors in drinking; policies and programs on alcohol use and abuse; and new approaches to controlling alcohol problems.

Heath, Dwight B. (ed.). 1995. *International Handbook on Alcohol and Culture.* Westport, Conn.: Greenwood. A collection of articles on the drinking norms and practices of 27 countries.

Jersild, Devon. 2001. *Happy Hours: Alcohol in a Woman's Life.* New York: HarperCollins. Presenting a mix of scientific data and personal stories about various aspects of drinking and alcoholism among women.

Martin, Jack K., Paul M. Roman, and Terry C. Blum. 1996. "Job stress, drinking networks, and social support at work: A comprehensive model of employees' problem drinking behaviors." *Sociological Quarterly, 37,* 579–599. A study of how stressful working conditions, drinking networks, and social support at work influence problem drinking among employees.

Orcutt, James D. 1993. "Happy hour and social lubrication: Evidence on mood-setting rituals of drinking time." *Journal of Drug Issues, 23,* 389–407. This study indicates a reduction in stress among college students when they engage in social drinking during weekday evenings.

Perkins, H. Wesley. 1992. "Gender patterns in consequences of collegiate alcohol abuse: A 10-year study of trends in an undergraduate population." *Journal of Studies on Alcohol, 53,* 458–462. The data show that college men continue to

have many more alcohol abuse and alcohol-related problems than college women.

Pittman, David J., and Helene Raskin White (eds.). 1991. *Society, Culture, and Drinking Patterns Reexamined.* New Brunswick, N.J.: Rutgers Center of Alcohol Studies. A large collection of articles presenting the social scientific views on various aspects of alcohol use and abuse.

Roman, Paul M. (ed.). 1991. *Alcohol: The Development of Sociological Perspectives on Use and Abuse.* New Brunswick, N.J.: Rutgers Center of Alcohol Studies. A set of essays on the contributions made by sociologists to the understanding of drinking and alcoholism.

Sayette, Michael A., et al. 1993. "Alcohol and aggression: A social information processing analysis." *Journal of Studies on Alcohol, 54,* 399–407. Alcohol use is found to be associated with aggressive responses to provocation.

CRITICAL THINKING QUESTIONS

1. Of the various social factors in drinking, which one would affect you the most and which one the least? Why?

2. How and why has the women's movement for gender equality unintendedly led many young women to the bottle?

PART SIX

Inequality in Deviance

CHAPTER
13 Privileged Deviance

As the boss of the worldwide conglomerate Tyco, Dennis Kozlowski made tons of money for his corporation and for himself. In one decade, he went on a frenzied shopping spree, spending more than $60 billion to buy 200 major corporations and hundreds of smaller ones. As a result, Tyco, once a relatively small industrial-parts manufacturer with $3 billion in yearly sales, turned into a global colossus that annually pulled in $36 billion, selling everything from diapers to fire alarms. For that feat, he rewarded himself with more than $300 million in total compensation in his last three years with the company. For himself he acquired, among other things, three Harley-Davidson motorcycles, a 130-foot sailing yacht, a private plane, and lavish homes in four states. Unfortunately, in the summer of 2002, he was first charged with failing to pay $1 million in sales tax on art purchases and then with stealing $600 million from Tyco (Eisenberg, 2002; Hill, 2002).

Kozlowski's alleged crimes may be called *privileged deviance,* highly profitable deviance that typically occurs among privileged people, the relatively rich and powerful. Privileged deviance can be divided into *white-collar deviance* and *governmental deviance.* In this chapter we will take a closer look at the sociological definition of white-collar deviance, the characteristics of corporate and occupational deviance (the subtypes of white-collar deviance), and the uniqueness and explanations of white-collar deviance. We will then analyze various facets of governmental deviance, including its causes.

What Is White-Collar Deviance?

When sociologist Edwin Sutherland first introduced the concept of white-collar crime in 1939, he defined it as an offense committed by "the upper, white- collar class, which is composed of respectable, or at least respected, business and professional men." Ten years later Sutherland (1949) tried to flesh out the concept:

> White-collar crime may be defined approximately as a crime committed by a person of respectability and high social status in the course of his occupation. Consequently, it excludes many crimes of the upper class, such as most of their cases of murder, adultery, and intoxication, since these are not customarily a part of their occupational procedures.

In this classic definition, two things characterize white-collar crime: (1) It is *occupationally* related, carried out during the course of the offender's occupation, and the occupation involved is *white-collar* as opposed to blue-collar. (2) The economic deviant is a relatively *respectable, high-status* person. By "high-status persons," Sutherland referred to people ranging from business managers and executives to "wage-earning class, which wears good clothes at work, such as clerks in stores" (Sutherland, 1956).

What distinguishes the commission of white-collar crime from the commission of blue-collar or street crime is more than the act itself. It also involves *how* the act is executed. Thus, white collars are more likely to commit an offense with skill, with sophistication, or, most important, with the resources of power, influence, or respectability for avoiding detection, prosecution, or conviction. If blue collars try to commit the same act, they usually do not—and, perhaps, cannot—do it in the same way as white collars. This is why blue collars are far more likely to be arrested, prosecuted, or convicted if they commit the same crimes as white collars (Shapiro, 1990).

While talking about high-status people engaging in economic deviance, Sutherland also had in mind *corporations* participating in similar deviant activities. The concept of corporate deviance was crucial for understanding the sociological nature of white-collar deviance in general. See how Sutherland used the examples of corporate deviance to show what he thought was the absurdity of explaining deviance in psychological terms:

> We have no reason to think that General Motors has an inferiority complex or that the Aluminum Company of America has a frustration-aggression complex or that U.S. Steel has an Oedipus complex, or that the Armour Company has a death wish or that the DuPonts desire to return to the womb. (Sutherland, 1956)

Therefore, for our purposes, white-collar deviance includes both occupational and corporate deviance. It may be noteworthy that we broaden the concept of white-collar *crime* by replacing it with "white-collar *deviance*." This is because what sociologists have traditionally called white-collar crime includes not just criminal offenses but civil and other noncriminal offenses. (A civil offense is legally not a crime because it involves violating a civil rather than a criminal law.) We use the term *white-collar deviance* to refer to both criminal and noncriminal forms of economic deviance carried out by high-status people as part of their occupation for personal gain (hence *occupational deviance*) or on behalf of their corporation (hence *corporate deviance*).

Corporate Deviance

Corporate deviance typically takes place in corporations, carried out by executives for their companies' benefits and their own. It can be divided into four major types: deviance against employees, deviance against customers, deviance against the government, and deviance against the environment.

Deviance against Employees

For many years corporations have been expected to ensure that their employees remain free from known hazards in the work environment. This expectation was finally turned into a law in 1970, and a federal agency, known as OSHA (Occupational Safety and Health Administration), was established to enforce the law. But many workers today are still exposed to various kinds of pollutants in the work environment, for example, coal dust, cotton dust, and radiation. Although these substances have been found to cause cancer, leukemia, and other serious illnesses, corporations tend to ignore or deny the problem rather than take corrective action, such as eliminating the exposures to make their plants safer (Frank, 1993).

Sociologists David Ermann and Richard Lundman (2002) have suggested three reasons for corporations' tendencies to be negligent about their employees' health and safety. The most obvious and important reason is corporate concern with *profit maximization*. Corporate executives are inclined to ignore health hazards in their plants because elimination of these hazards will eat into their companies' profits.

A second reason for the negligence about workers' safety is the nature of *corporate structure*. One of the major characteristics of corporations is that executives are rewarded for seeking short-term success only. Thus, in determining whether to ignore or eliminate health hazards, corporate executives tend to focus on how great a profit they will derive from a certain decision in a few months or years rather than in 10 or 20 years. It is no wonder that they usually decide against spending what appears, at the moment, to be a large amount of money to improve their employees' working conditions. They simply fail to consider the long-term consequences of such a decision, such as facing the high cost of numerous lawsuits filed against them by their many disabled employees. Another important characteristic of corporate structure is that it motivates executives to judge employees' worth impersonally, focusing only on their contribution to production. As a result, employees tend to be treated as if they were machines—and as machines, they are easily replaceable. If some workers become disabled or die, others can be found easily and quickly to take their place. Such a callous attitude toward employees can understandably lead corporate executives to disregard employee health and safety.

A third reason for corporate deviance against employees is *the government's reluctance to take action against offending corporations*. OSHA often avoids using threats or penalties to deter offenses; instead, negotiation and persuasion are routinely employed to obtain compliance. In cases where citations and fines are used as a last resort, the companies are allowed to have their penalties reduced if they correct their "deficiencies." In addition to this weak enforcement policy, the government has cut back on OSHA enforcement personnel. Moreover, many states prohibit injured employees from suing their employers unless they are able to prove that the injury was intentional. In other words, employers cannot be sued for negligence (Frank, 1993).

Deviance against Customers

There are many different forms of corporate deviance against customers. The most common ones involve dangerous foods, unsafe products, frauds, deceptive advertising, and antitrust violations.

Dangerous Foods. The food industry has been known to seek greater profits by selling adulterated or contaminated foods. Meat-packing companies often sell their products without being certain that the meat is safe for human consumption. That's why health experts advise consumers to make sure that their hamburgers are cooked fully. Still, in 1993, nearly 400 people were stricken with *E. coli*, a dangerous colon bacterium, after eating hamburgers at Jack in the Box restaurants. Four children later died from the bacterial infection. According to the U.S. Agriculture Department and state health officials, the bacteria could have been killed if Jack in the Box had cooked the hamburgers to a higher temperature (155 degrees instead of 140). But the problem originated in the slaughterhouse where the meat had been contaminated with feces (McDowell, 1996).

Foods can also be adulterated. Hormel Company, for example, has once taken stale meat returned by its retail-store customers and then "reconditioned," repackaged, and resold it for a higher profit to other stores—without the legally required reinspection by the U.S. Department of Agriculture officer in charge. As a researcher found, "Spareribs returned for sliminess, discoloration, and stickiness were rejuvenated through curing and smoking, renamed Windsor Loins, and sold in ghetto stores for more than fresh pork chops" (Wellford, 1972).

In fact, it is customary for the food industry to use all kinds of chemical additives in its products, many of which have been suspected by government scientists to cause cancer and other diseases. The apparent purpose is not only to keep the foods from spoiling, but to make them look fresh and appealing as well as to give them the right taste and aroma. Sodium nitrites and nitrates, for example, are added to keep meat products looking blood-red. However, the real purpose behind all this is the pursuit of the big buck. As one food marketer says, "The profit margin on food additives is fantastically good, much better than the profit margins on basic, traditional foods" (Simon, 2002).

Unsafe Products. The profit motive also underlies the manufacturing and selling of unsafe products by car, drug, tobacco, and other industries. Tobacco companies, for example, have long known that smoking causes cancer and is addictive, but they continue to make and sell cigarettes (Noah, 1997). Dealing in unsafe products also appears frequently in the pharmaceutical industry. Drug companies are often found committing such product-safety offenses as the sale of impure, overstrength, out-of-date, or nonsterile products. The far more serious offense of fraudulent safety-testing of drugs has also been uncovered many times. Experimental rats and monkeys that had developed terrible symptoms like tumors and blindness in drug trials were replaced by healthy animals. Dead animals were "resurrected" in lab reports—rats that had died from using a new drug reappeared later in the data as alive (Braithwaite, 1993). Falsification of clinical data such as these has set drug companies afoul of the law. In 1990, for example, Bolar's high-blood-pressure drug, generic Dyazide, was recalled because it was found defective and the company was fined $10 million for having forged documents in seeking FDA approval (Gorman, 1992). (The FDA is the federal government's Food and Drug Administration.)

More prevalent than presenting grossly phony data to the FDA is the profit-driven tendency to withhold data from the FDA about a drug's negative side effects. Consequently, many potentially dangerous drugs get FDA approval, and the consumers are, in effect, used as guinea pigs. After using the drugs at their own expense, sometimes for a lengthy period of time, consumers will know whether the medical products are dangerous. Of course, by the time they discover the danger, it is too late. They have already suffered and sometimes died. When this happens, the general public is bound to be greatly scandalized. One of the drug scandals of the 1990s involves Dow Corning's silicone-gel breast implants. In 1992 some customers complained that the implants leaked, ruptured, or caused autoimmune disorders. The FDA was forced to investigate, and found from the company's internal documents that the manufacturer of the breast implants knew about the problems way back in the mid-1970s (Pontell and Calavita, 1993).

Frauds. Fraudulent practices can be found in various industries such as banking, insurance, real estate, and securities. They are all extremely lucrative, largely made possible by inadequate government control. Let's take a closer look at the nature of bank and insurance frauds.

One of the greatest bank frauds in recent U.S. history involves a number of savings and loan (S&L or thrift) institutions in the 1980s, which cost taxpayers an astounding $1.4 trillion. In a span of only five years, from 1987 through 1992, a staggering 95,045 criminal charges were filed against S&L officials. The suspected frauds can be divided into three types: (1) illegal nonbanking activities—violating banking laws by engaging in unsafe practices, such as concentrating investment in one high-risk area, say, construction loans, without having conducted any marketability study; (2) collective embezzlement—using ownership of an S&L to steal depositors' money, which has prompted a California state official to say, "The best way to rob a bank is to own one"; and (3) covering up—falsifying records to make the institutions look normal or financially healthy. A major cause of all these frauds was the dismantling of "most of the regulatory infrastructure that had kept the thrift industry together for decades" (Pontell and Calavita, 1993; also see Truell and Gurwin, 1992).

Fraud is also a big problem in the insurance industry. Insolvencies among insurance companies are common, often the result of insiders' fraudulent activities. Government regulation is even more inadequate in the insurance industry. There are federal agencies policing banks, savings and loans, securities, and commodities, but there is none for the insurance industry. There are state agencies for regulating insurance, but they are mostly inefficient. They are typically underfunded and understaffed; New Mexico, for example, has only five staff regulators to monitor 1,600 insurance companies. The most common insurance frauds include phony assets and small-business scams. In the phony assets scheme, an insurance company lies about its assets to show that it has the sufficient amount required by law. In small-business scams, a firm administers an MEWA ("Multiple Employer Welfare Arrangement," whereby several small employers combine their money to insure health coverage for their workers) and simply steals the money until it cannot pay any claims (Headden and Witkin, 1993).

Deceptive Advertising. Closely similar to fraud is deceptive advertising. Most advertising is mere puffery, an exaggerated claim for a product. Examples follow (Simon, 2002):

> "Nestle makes the very best chocolate"
>
> "GM—always a step ahead"
>
> "Wheaties, Breakfast of Champions"
>
> "Every kid in America loves Jell-O brand gelatin"
>
> "Seagram's, America's Number One Gin"

Although these claims are false, they are legal. It is also legal to use misleading labels to make food products appear much healthier or less fattening than they actually are.

Pam and other cooking sprays, for example, can boast they are fat-free and calorie-free although they are made of 100% fat (Parker-Pope, 2003).

But another form of false advertising is illegal because it involves products with more serious consequences for the consumer, as the following case illustrates (Simon, 2002):

> The Federal Trade Commission ruled that Anacin had falsely advertised its product by claiming that it: (1) relieved nervousness, tension, stress, fatigue, and depression; (2) was stronger than aspirin; (3) brought relief within twenty-two seconds; (4) was highly recommended over aspirin by doctors; and (5) was more effective for relieving pain than any other analgesic available without prescription.

For such an illegal act, however, the company is not subject to punishment as a common criminal. The offender is merely required to sign a document stating an agreement to stop the illegal activity. Obviously, the intent of the law here is not to punish the offender, but to stop the illegal action and prevent further damage (Coleman, 1994).

Antitrust Violations. Antitrust laws prohibit companies from conspiring to reduce or eliminate competition. If there is little or no competition, prices will go up and consumers will have no choice but to pay them. To violate the antitrust laws, companies selling the same kind of products usually get together to fix prices that are abnormally high. Sometimes corporations prevent new competition from entering the market, as can be illustrated by the two largest credit-card companies, Visa and MasterCard, barring banks from issuing American Express and Discover cards (Frank and Wilke, 1997). Antitrust violations consequently can produce enormous profits. Although profit is an obvious prod to antitrust violations, at least three subtle forces may be at work also: (1) a history of cooperation among corporations; (2) an oligopolistic market, dominated by only a few companies, which makes co-operation easy; and (3) a lack of public awareness of antitrust violations (Ermann and Lundman, 2002).

These three elements of antitrust violations can be found in the baby-food industry. Virtually every U.S. family with an infant has bought baby formula, a commercial concoction of milk and vitamins. A few parents may complain about the high price of baby formula, but most do not know that the high price stems largely from antitrust violations. These violations involve three formula companies that, with a long-standing cozy relationship, have dominated the formula industry. Their antitrust violations started in 1980 when the largest of the three companies, Abbott Laboratories, conspired with the other two to prevent a new competitor, Nestle, from entering the formula market in the United States. More specifically, Abbott persuaded its two rivals to agree to a formula-industry code of business practice that prohibits, among other things, consumer advertising. This has hampered Nestle's ability to sell its formula because it relied heavily on advertising. Abbott and the other two giant companies did not have to advertise because they depended on hospitals and doctors to market their products. Since they have dominated the market, they have been able to keep the price of their formulas very high (Wilke, 2004; Jamieson, 1994; Burton, 1993b).

Deviance against the Government

Most corporate deviance against the government involves tax evasion. But tax evasion by corporations is not always illegal. Because of their pervasive and powerful political influence, large corporations can legally evade taxes through tax breaks provided by legislation and through tax loopholes made possible by the complexity of tax laws. This is why, according to a Congressional study, the top 148 corporations paid less than half of the official tax rate on profits and 10 percent of these corporations paid no taxes at all (Sloan, 1997; Coleman, 1994).

But taking advantage of the loopholes may go too far and become illegal. Consider, for example, the law that exempts from taxation the profit made by U.S. companies located abroad. To take advantage of this loophole, many giant American companies make themselves multinational corporations by setting up subsidiaries in foreign countries that have very low corporate tax rates and then making it appear that most of their profits are earned abroad. Suppose an item is produced in the United States at a cost of $100 and is sold to an Irish subsidiary for $100. Because there is no profit from this transaction, no U.S. tax is paid. But then the subsidiary resells the item for $200, earning a $100 profit. The company pays only a 4 percent tax ($4) in Ireland, thereby evading the 48 percent tax in the United States. With the Irish subsidiary, then, the American company evades a lot of taxes by making it appear that most of its profits come from the foreign subsidiary (Martz, 1991).

In committing deviance against the government, corporations do not evade payment of taxes alone. They also give huge sums of campaign donations to both political parties to influence legislation toward favoring their business interests (Sabato and Simpson, 1996; Hunt, 1995). Moreover, in today's global economy, giant U.S. corporations may even bribe foreign governments or engage in some other activities abroad that are forbidden by U.S. law. An example is Baxter International Inc., the world's largest hospital-supply company, which in 1993 pleaded guilty to a felony charge of violating the U.S. law that prohibits cooperating with the Arab boycott of Israel. Since 1985 Baxter had tried to enter the vast, lucrative market of the Arab world. Arab boycott authorities would not cooperate unless Baxter first ceased its business in Israel, which Baxter finally did (Burton, 1993a). Most of the illegal activities engaged in by U.S. companies involve giving bribes worth millions of dollars to foreign officials. Still, compared with their European and Asian counterparts, U.S. corporations are much less likely to use payoffs to do business abroad, an extremely common practice in the global economy (Milbank and Brauchli, 1995).

Deviance against the Environment

Most corporations in one way or another dump their wastes onto the land and into the air and water, primarily because they find it too costly to develop ecologically safer alternatives or antipollution devices. They are also unwilling to clean up the mess or to assume liability for the health of citizens affected by it, because to do so would cut into their profits. According to the U.S. Congress, corporations in the petrochemical, metals, electrical, and transportation industries are the more severe polluters of the environment (Barnett, 1993).

Environmental pollution affects practically all of us in some way. As Ralph Nader (1970) said, "The efflux from motor vehicles, plants, and incineration of sulfur oxides, hydrocarbons, carbon monoxide, oxides of nitrogen, particulates, and many more contaminants amounts to compulsory consumption of violence by most Americans. There is no full escape from such violent ingestions, for breathing is required." According to one EPA (Environmental Protection Agency) study, residents in poor or minority neighborhoods suffer significantly more than others. This is because landfills, garbage incinerators, toxic dump sites, and environmentally hazardous plants tend to be located near the homes of the poor and minorities (Suro, 1993).

The federal government has, since the early 1970s, tried to combat environmental pollution but with little success throughout the decade. Then, in 1980, Congress passed a law called the Comprehensive Environmental Response Compensation and Liability Act, popularly referred to as the Superfund program, intended to clean up some of the worst uncontrolled hazardous waste sites in the nation. In the early 1980s the Superfund program got off to a shaky start because the EPA was "soft" on environmental offenses. Many corporations that polluted the environment were left alone, and the few guilty ones were given every opportunity to negotiate cleanup settlements with the EPA. However, toward the late 1980s, the EPA aggressively began to enforce the Superfund law against guilty corporations. Today, these corporations are under a great deal of EPA pressure to pay for the cleanup. The industry and its insurance companies, though, have been advocating that all the cleanup costs be paid for through taxation. They argue that the general public should help pay for the cleanup because it has enjoyed many products of the industry, having in effect benefited from the production that created hazardous wastes (Barnett, 1993). Given today's widespread opposition to higher taxes, it is doubtful that the general public would like the idea of shelling out more money. Besides, many hold the corporations rather than themselves responsible for industrial waste.

Social Profile: Corporate Crooks

In 2002 many corporate executives were reported to have engaged in illegal business activities. The most notorious ones included:

- Kenneth Lay and his fellow executives at Enron, a huge energy trading company. They plunged Enron into bankruptcy—the biggest ever in U.S. history—by pocketing millions of dollars from defrauding investors, employees, and pensioners.
- The top executives of the accounting firm Arthur Andersen. They were widely reported to have cooked the books of their client Enron and then shredded the incriminating documents. The shredding caused some executives to be convicted of obstructing justice.

(continued)

Social Profile: Continued

- Scott Sullivan, chief financial officer at WorldCom, a global communications corporation, and his fellow executive Buford Yates. They were charged with masterminding a $7.2 billion securities fraud, which included pumping up the company's earnings to keep its stock price high. The charges carry as much as $2.25 million in fines and 65 years in prison.
- The founder of Adelphia, a cable television company, and his two sons. As the company's top executives, they were convicted of defrauding investors out of more than $250 million and giving themselves $2.3 billion in hidden loans from the company.
- The founder and chief executive of ImClone, a biopharmaceutical company. He was found guilty of securities fraud, obstruction of justice, and bank fraud. Domestic-style queen Martha Stewart was also convicted of obstructing the federal investigation into her insider trading of ImClone stocks.

Those corporate crooks, along with the CEOs (chief executive officers) of 23 companies under investigation for illegal accounting abuses, earned 70 percent more than the CEOs at 300 other large corporations. Specifically, the pay for the crooked CEOs averaged $62 million from 1999 to 2001, compared with $36 million for the CEOs at the other companies. As a whole, the shady CEOs at the 23 companies took home a total of $1.4 billion in those three years when the value of their companies plummeted by $530 billion and 162,000 of their employees lost their jobs. Apparently, excessive, sky-high compensation tends to encourage illegal business practices. It makes the executives feel that they, unlike their lowly and dispensable workers, are above the law.

But, more important, those corrupt executives were the product of the business deregulation that has run amok for more than two decades. Their criminal activities are, therefore, not much different from the legal business practices at many U.S. corporations liberated by the same deregulation. Consider, for example, the following legal practices: (1) moving the corporate headquarters, without people, to Bermuda and other such places to evade U.S. taxes, (2) overpaying executives and granting them huge stock options and interest-free loans even when they do their jobs poorly, causing their company to lose money, (3) increasing executive pay for cutting costs by firing masses of workers, which distracts attention from executive mismanagement, (4) stacking the board of directors with insiders and friends who will shower lavish compensation on executives and turn a blind eye to their wrongdoing, and (5) giving campaign contributions to candidates from *both* major parties to ensure government subsidies, tax breaks, and other favors.

Sources: Frank et al., 2004; Rawe, 2004; Lavelle and Prasso, 2002.

Occupational Deviance

Compared with the offenses committed by corporations, those perpetrated by individual white-collar employees for their own gain are usually less costly to the victims. But they still cost considerably more than the common crimes committed by the lower classes. There are many different forms of deviant activities in white-collar occupations, but we will analyze only the most common and costly ones.

Employee Theft

Theft by employees from the companies where they work is extremely common and costly. In the 1990s, it accounted for at least 2 percent of sales, costing an estimated $120 billion a year (Buss, 1993). Both businesses and consumers suffer. Because of employee theft, more than a thousand businesses go under every year, and the remaining, nonetheless successful businesses pass the cost of employee theft to consumers by raising prices. According to various expert estimates, about 30 percent of U.S. employees plan to steal from their employer, another 30 percent are basically good employees but may occasionally succumb to the temptation, and 40 percent are basically honest (Buss, 1993). Employee theft is probably the most pervasive and costly form of property deviance of any kind in the United States.

Most employee thieves are middle class. They are "predominantly solid, respectable citizens who pay taxes, root for major league stars, believe in the 'American way of life' and the virtues of hard work and honesty, and are quickly angered by the thought of welfare chiselers, street hoodlums, and the permissiveness and immorality, which they believe is upsetting an established social order" (Altheide et al., 1978). Why, then, do these straight arrows steal? Various researchers have provided at least four explanations (Hollinger and Clark, 1983; Altheide et al., 1978; Conklin, 1977):

1. Employee theft has much to do with *large and impersonal* corporations. Employees tend to feel little or no loyalty to such corporations, regarding them as abstract entities rather than real people. To the employee thief, stealing from a large and impersonal company is like stealing from nobody. The general public may feel the same way. As Jack Douglas and Frances Waksler (1982) say, "If someone steals your $20 calculator, you may well expect sympathy from others; if an employee of IBM steals one, people are less likely to say 'Poor IBM.'"

2. A society with a tradition of *union–management conflict,* such as the United States, tends to have a high incidence of employee theft, because workers feel exploited by and resentful toward the company. Employee theft is thus an expression of the workers' desire to get back at the company. That's why employee theft is more common in cases where workers feel underpaid or abused by their employers, or frustrated by lack of promotions or salary raises. Such workers regard their stealing not as real theft but as an informal compensation, which they feel they fully deserve (Greenberg, 1996).

3. Workers may steal if they *find their jobs too boring.* Stealing on the job, then, becomes interesting and challenging. One study of employee thieves in a midwestern clothing store found that those who stole for the satisfaction of getting away with it outnumbered those who stole for money alone or on impulse. When not stealing, employees unhappy with their jobs tend to engage in various counterproductive activities, such as doing sloppy work, coming to work late or leaving early, taking extra-long lunch hours or coffee breaks, using a sick leave without being sick, and drinking or using drugs on the job.

4. Employee thieves do not see themselves as criminals. This *noncriminal self-image* receives ample reinforcement from the popular stereotype of real criminals as those who commit street crime. Moreover, for fear of bad publicity, many companies are reluctant to have their crooked employees prosecuted. They merely fire the culprits, who later can get hired by other companies because their former employer does not want to publicize the theft. Some of the victimized firms play along with their thieving employees, pretending not to know what is going on. Since they pay the workers low wages, they expect them to supplement their meager income by taking home some merchandise.

Embezzlement

Embezzlement is a form of employee theft, but "embezzlement" is often used to refer to the stealing of money, while "employee theft" usually denotes stealing merchandise. Though less costly than employee theft, embezzlement in the 1990s cost $27.2 billion in one year, and commercial banks lost about five times as much money to embezzlers as they did to armed robbers (Thompson et al., 1992; Conklin, 1977).

Embezzlers range from relatively low-level employees to top executives. Many low-level employees who embezzle are middle-class bank tellers who occasionally steal several hundred dollars to solve some financial problems such as overdue bills or medical expenses. Top-level employees, of course, would make away with much more. In 1991, for example, Donald Houde, a trusted nine-year employee who was the systems director of Denver's Mile Hi Cablevision, was discovered to have embezzled $30,000 every month from the cable television company until he got caught. By then his loot had accumulated to nearly $2 million (Thompson et al., 1992).

Like Houde, most embezzlers are in management positions. Typically, they are white males in their thirties, well-paid, married with one or two children, and living in a respectable neighborhood. Embezzlers are basically hardworking, honest people; some are even pillars of their communities. Why do they steal? According to a classic explanation by sociologist Donald Cressey (1971), prospective embezzlers usually go through a social-psychological process that consists of three phases.

In the first phase, they encounter what they perceive to be an *unshareable* financial problem. They are too embarrassed to share this problem with their spouses, friends, or other people who are ordinarily available for help in financial matters. The reasons include being heavily in debt from gambling, or having a mistress, or simply feeling too much pride to ask others for help.

In the second phase, the individuals become aware of an *opportunity* for secretly solving the financial problem. The opportunity is typically embedded in the very position of trust that they hold by virtue of their respectable occupation.

And in the final, third phase, which is the most crucial, they *rationalize* away the criminal nature of embezzlement, defining the act as merely getting a temporary loan rather than as committing a theft. They expect to return the money later. As one embezzler put it, "I figured that if you could use something and help yourself and replace it and not hurt anybody, it was all right" (Coleman, 1994).

This rationalization clinches the decision to carry out the embezzlement. However, compared with those in higher positions in a company, people in lower positions are less likely to rationalize—they tend more to admit that their embezzlement is a crime (Benson, 1985; Zeits, 1981).

Financial Frauds

The most common form of financial frauds involves the failure to pay income taxes. Over half of all taxpayers have been found to evade taxes to some extent. Middle- and upper-income people, especially businesspeople and lawyers, are the most common culprits. Why is tax evasion so prevalent? A major reason is the complexity of income tax laws. There are numerous ambiguous legal definitions of what constitutes income, deductions, depreciation, exemptions, and credits. These items can, therefore, be computed and manipulated in different ways, with the result that people with the same income end up paying different amounts of taxes. In effect, how much people pay depends on how well they play the "tax game." Generally, because of being able to hire smart tax accountants or lawyers, higher-income persons can play the game better than others (Coleman, 1994). The richest ones can thus boast that they pay little or no taxes; as Leona Helmsley, one of the wealthiest real estate entrepreneurs in the United States, once said, "Only little people pay taxes."

Less common than tax evasion is violation of securities law. But since most violators are professional stockbrokers and stock traders, the cost per violation is much higher. A popular form of violation by stockbrokers is defrauding customers through sales of worthless securities. Suppose a male stockbroker personally owns a lot of stock in a company that is on the verge of bankruptcy. He gets his friends on Wall Street to put out phony news releases and market analyses that make the stock look like a sure winner. After providing this fraudulent information to his clients, the stockbroker sells them all his stock. The clients, of course, lose a bundle when the company goes under and the stock hits bottom. Increasingly more prevalent than this securities fraud are sweepstakes schemes, phony Internet stocks, and identity theft, such as using someone else's social security number or other personal data to get credit cards or loans (Eaton, 1999).

Another form of securities violation is insider trading. It involves an insider of a company, such as its owner or one of its executives, buying or selling its stock on confidential information not available to the general public, such as advance knowledge about a new product or unanticipated company profits or losses. Insiders can make a killing if they buy a lot of stock in their company before the public knows about the new product or unanticipated profit because the price of the stock will rise significantly after the release of the information. Such insider trading puts the general public at a distinct disadvantage, undermining the fair and honest operation of our securities markets (Szockyj, 1993).

Profitable Computer Crimes

There is a wide range of deviant acts that are considered computer crimes. They include electronic embezzlement, online financial theft, computer hacking, Internet vandalism, dissemination of computer viruses, electronic spying, phone phreaking, and Internet pornography (Carter and Bannister, 2002; Rosoff, Pontell, and Tillman, 2002). Some of these crimes do not involve financial gain, for example, online vandalism, which may involve defacing the Web pages of business corporations and government agencies. Another example is so-called ethical, "white hat" hacking, which entails breaking into computer systems in order to improve the machines of some security-conscious companies. Other computer crimes are highly profitable, typically committed by white-collar individuals in computer-related occupations. These are the crimes we will focus on here.

The most common forms of profitable computer crime are probably online theft and fraud. An example is identity theft, or more specifically, stealing credit card numbers, social security numbers, and other personal information, which can be used to buy anything online for free because the purchases are charged to the owners of those card numbers. This online theft, if compared with bank robbery, is obviously much more convenient to execute and extremely profitable if it is pulled off. Consider, for example, computer technician Carlos Salgado. In 1997 he managed to steal more than 100,000 credit card numbers by using a ready-made computer-intrusion program that he found on the Web to hack into several e-commerce databases on the Internet. Those cards had a combined credit line of more than one billion dollars. Unfortunately for Salgado, the FBI caught him, and after pleading guilty he was sentenced to two and a half years in prison. As for online fraud, it may involve, for example, perpetrating investment scams, offering bogus e-commerce opportunities, and rigging Internet auctions by using shills to drive up the bidding (Hansen, 2004).

Most people who commit online theft are the victimized companies' skilled employees, authorized computer users, and trusted insiders. This is because "the easiest way into a computer is usually the front door" (Carter and Bannister, 2002; Rosoff, Pontell, and Tillman, 2002). Online fraud, however, seems largely the work of white-collar workers committing the crime on the side. These computer crimes have soared for several reasons. One is the ubiquity of the computer and the Internet. Another is the rising education level of society because computer crime requires more, rather than less, education. A third reason is that law-enforcement officials do not have enough staff or expertise to catch and keep up with fast-growing numbers of online crooks (wingfield, 2004). A fourth reason is the relatively light punishment for computer crime even if it costs the victims a thousand times more than bank robbery. As we have seen above, the more-than-one-billion-dollar theft brought the convicted criminal only two and half years in prison. The light punishment not only may explain the enormous increase in computer crimes, but also reflects a key feature of white-collar offenses in general.

Deviance in the Professions

There are as many forms of professional deviance as there are professions. Here we focus on just three: medical misconduct, lawyerly lawlessness, and accounting abuse.

Medical Misconduct.   Many forms of criminal conduct take place in the medical profession. We will discuss just a few.

One is *fee splitting*, which involves a doctor receiving kickbacks from another for referring patients. The doctor who receives the kickbacks is usually a general practitioner referring his patients to a surgeon or specialist. Fee splitting not only hits the patients in their pocketbooks; it can also maim or kill them. The reason is that doctors who seek kickbacks typically send their patients to the surgeon who splits the largest fee rather than the surgeon who does the best surgery. Unfortunately, the surgeon who splits the largest fee tends to be the worst, most dangerous surgeon, who, because of incompetence, must offer maximum kickbacks to get business (Green, 1990).

A second form of medical misconduct is *unnecessary surgery*. In one study in which 1,356 patients recommended for surgery were examined, researchers at Cornell Medical School found that 25 percent of the operations were not needed. The figures were even higher for certain parts of the body: 50 percent of pacemaker implants, 36 percent of eye surgeries, 31 percent of gall-bladder removals, 29 percent of prostate surgeries, 43 percent of hemorrhoid operations, and 32 percent of knee surgeries (Green, 1990). The basic cause of these unnecessary operations is apparently the desire for maximum profits rather than honest misdiagnosis. As research has shown, surgeons who are highly paid by insurance companies on a fee-for-service basis perform considerably more operations than surgeons who are paid much less by HMOs (health maintenance organizations) on a flat salary (Coleman, 1994).

A third form of medical misconduct is *fraudulently claiming payment* for services. This usually involves billing insurance companies and the state and federal Medicaid and Medicare programs for services never rendered, double-billing them for services rendered, or billing them for expensive physician services when, in fact, the services have been performed by nurses or other nonphysicians. Such fraudulent practices seem particularly common among doctors who lack competency and success in their profession and work in poor neighborhoods (Coleman, 1994).

Lawyerly Lawlessness.   Legal lawlessness is widespread, marked mostly by the practice of overcharging clients. According to an auditor who works full-time investigating lawyers' bills, overcharging appears in about 90 percent of the cases he is hired to examine. In one survey, more than 60 percent of lawyers themselves said that they had personal knowledge of bill padding (Budiansky et al., 1995).

The opportunities for profiteering have much to do with the intangible nature of legal work. Unlike plumbers, who render a tangible, visible service by unclogging a stuffed drain or fixing a leaky faucet, lawyers often provide such intangible services as giving a few words of advice, making a telephone call, filling out and filing a form, writing a letter, preparing a document, talking to another attorney or a government agent, negotiating with somebody, or some other similar action that the client is rarely able to observe. Therefore, although any of these actions may take only a few minutes, an attorney can charge an hour's or even several hours' fee for them. It is difficult for the clients to dispute the high fee, because they cannot see what the lawyer does behind closed doors (Stevens, 1995; Green, 1990).

Even when the clients can see the lawyer in action, especially at court appearances, there are still ample opportunities for fraudulent charging of fees. For one thing, a lawyer can intentionally delay the resolution of a case so as to have more court appearances and charge the client accordingly. Lawyers are tempted to engage in this confidence game if the client is rich. But a confidence game can also be played on poor clients, though by the reverse of delay. This tactic involves shortening the duration of a case in order to maximize the number of clients and hence the profit the lawyer can have. The lawyer can pretend to work hard on the client's behalf while persuading the client to plead guilty so that the case can be brought to a quick conclusion (Coleman, 1994).

Regardless of how they inflate their hours of service, this tendency in lawyers has inspired jokes such as this one: "A lawyer appeared at the gates of heaven and began loudly protesting that he was only 42—much too young to die. 'That's funny,' St. Peter replied. 'According to the hours you've billed, we thought you were 93.'" (Budiansky et al., 1995).

Accounting Abuse. In preparing tax returns for companies and individuals, accountants may assist their clients in falsifying their income or deductions in order to pay less taxes. But this is not a profitable area for accounting abuses, because tax preparation provides only a small portion (no more than 23 percent in 1993) of the accounting profession's revenues. Most of the profession's $46 billion annual revenues comes from examining corporations' financial statements. Thus, most of the abuse involves fraud or negligence in the course of doing audits (Wells, 1993).

The job of auditing a corporation's books to make certain that their accounting is accurate is extremely important in ensuring the stability and health of the nation's economy. If a company is truly as well run as the accountant says it is, then the bank that lends it money and the public that invests in it by buying its stock and becoming its shareholders have a good chance of earning a profit later. But if the accountant says the company is financially sound and strong while, in fact, it is about to go bankrupt, as Enron was, the bank and investors will likely lose their money. But the bank itself can also collude with crooked companies in defrauding their shareholders and investors, with assistance from the lender's own accountants in covering up the seedy deals. In 1993, accountants faced more than 4,000 liability suits—double the total of seven years earlier—and as much as $15 billion in damages. Most of these suits charged the accountants with failure to uncover fraud (Wells, 1993).

The major cause of this accounting abuse is obviously the conflict of interest that is built into the accountant's position as an auditor paid by the company to audit itself. Accountants find it hard to resist the proverbial temptation of not biting the hand that feeds them. They may insist that they can be totally independent of the company so as to be able to examine its books objectively, but the fact

remains that they are financially dependent on that company. If they overzeal-
ously investigate the company, they will lose the job the next time around. In short,
the conflict of interest prevents accountants from doing what they are supposed to
do—detect fraud in the company they audit (Wells, 1993).

What Makes White-Collar Deviance Unique?

White-collar deviance is distinguishable from common crime in a number of ways.
The most distinctive aspect of white-collar deviance is the rational execution of the
offense to maximize profit, along with the use of power, influence, or respectability
to minimize detection. Equally distinctive but less obvious are: (1) the deviant's
respectable self-image, (2) the victim's unwitting cooperation, and (3) society's relative indifference toward the offense.

The Deviant's Respectable Self-Image

White-collar deviants typically see themselves as respectable individuals rather
than as common criminals. This self-image plays an important part in the perpe-
tration of various white-collar deviances.

White-collar deviants usually express their respectable self-image through
certain rationalizations. Corporate executives convicted of price fixing have been
found to argue that their unlawful price-fixing schemes are far from being criminal.
Instead, they view themselves as having really served a worthwhile purpose for the
nation's economy by "stabilizing prices," and they congratulate themselves for
having effectively helped their companies by "recovering costs." There is no such
thing as price fixing in their book. Embezzlers, as we have observed, tend to define
their stealing as only "borrowing," insisting that they will pay the money back
soon. Perpetrators of the more common employee theft feel that they actually do
not steal anything from their companies because the companies are believed to
make up the losses by using them as tax deductions and charging customers higher
prices. Tax offenders tend to see themselves as victims rather than offenders. They
would argue that they are just unlucky enough to get caught for doing something
that practically everyone else does. As a convicted tax offender said, "Everybody
cheats on their income tax, 95 percent of the people. Even if it's for $10 it's the same
principle. I didn't cheat. I just didn't know how to report it" (Benson, 1985).

What all these different types of white-collar offenders have in common is
their denial of criminal intent. They admit that they have committed the act that
landed them in prison, but regard their actions as mistakes only, not acts motivated by a guilty, criminal mind. In short, they find it hard to see themselves as real
criminals. As one businessman, who is in prison for price fixing, said about himself: "Having been in business for 33 years, you don't just automatically become a
criminal overnight" (Benson, 1985). Even Charles Keating, who was in prison for
conviction on numerous counts of bank fraud and racketeering in 1989, never
admitted guilt for his actions (Zagorin, 1997).

The Victim's Unwitting Cooperation

In contrast to such common crimes as murder, robbery, rape, and assault, white-collar deviance requires an unwitting cooperation from its victims. This cooperation is unwitting because it is based on the victim's carelessness or ignorance. In a home improvement scheme, for example, the victims do not bother to check the work history of the fraudulent company that solicits them, and they sign a contract without examining its contents for such matters as the true price and the credit terms. Some victims purchase goods through the mail without checking the reputation of the firm. Doctors may prescribe untested drugs after having relied on only the drug company's salespeople and advertising. Lest we blame the victims, we should realize the difficulty for them to know they are being victimized, even if they want to find out the true nature of their victimization. Grocery shoppers, for example, are hard put to detect such dangerous substances as residues of hormones, antibiotics, pesticides, and nitrites in the meat they buy.

Society's Relative Indifference

While ignorance or carelessness leads the victim to cooperate unknowingly with white-collar deviants, society's indifference to their offense is a blessing knowingly bestowed on them. Generally, little effort is made to catch white-collar deviants, and if, on rare occasions, they are caught, they seldom go to jail. Even if they are sent to prison, they are not likely to be placed in a harsh institution or to stay there for long.

Since the early 1980s, however, there have been some signs that our society has become more concerned about white-collar deviance. Many large corporations have been prosecuted for illegal activities. In 1985 a Chicago judge gave the most severe sentence ever (25 years) to three company executives for an employee's death resulting from their failure to correct unsafe plant conditions. The day after the sentencing, the *Detroit Free Press* asked its readers if murder is "too harsh a charge for negligent employers." An overwhelming 80 percent of those calling in said no (Cahan et al., 1985). Sociologists have also found that respondents in their studies rated white-collar offenses as serious as street crimes (Geis, 1984). More recently, in the early 2000s, most Americans wanted white-collar crooks harshly punished for committing frauds that cost thousands of workers their jobs and pension funds. And when Enron's chief financial officer, Andrew Fastow, was charged with multiple frauds, prosecutors said that he could face up to 140 years in prison (Glater, 2002).

Does all this mean that justice can now be expected to be *collar*-blind? Hardly. Most obviously, not a single white-collar offender has been sentenced to death, let alone actually executed, for causing the deaths of many workers or customers, although many lower-class criminals have been executed for killing just one person. Moreover, most white-collar criminals, especially the big-time ones that steal hundreds of millions, continue to be punished less severely than street criminals. From 1987 through 1992, federal agents charged a staggering 95,045 white-collar individuals and corporate executives with various bank and S&L frauds, but more than 75 percent of these charges were dropped from prosecution. The few that were convicted of bank fraud received an average of only 2.4 years in prison, compared with 7.8 years for traditional bank robbery (Pizzo and Muolo, 1993).

It is doubtful that the government can wage an all-out war on white-collar crime because many such criminals are just too powerful, influential, or respectable. After a jury convicted a wealthy businessman of defrauding an S&L out of $55 million, the judge reduced his sentence to only six months in a halfway house—not a real prison—and a mere $2 million in restitution, letting him keep the remaining $53 million profit from the crime (Pizzo and Muolo, 1993). Judges are typically lenient with white-collar offenders. One reason is that most white-collar offenders have never had serious run-ins with the law. Another reason is that it is difficult to prove criminal intent: The criminal intent in robbing a liquor store may be obvious but not so in committing a business fraud that has been approved by the company's lawyers and accountants. Besides, it is difficult for the jury to find the white-collar criminal guilty in the first place. As one prosecutor says, "Look, I can wave a pair of bloody underwear in front of a jury and have their undivided attention. But I can wave a $100 million phony loan statement in front of the same jury and just watch their eyes glaze over" (Pizzo and Muolo, 1993). Their eyes glaze over not only because they find the loan statement boring, but also because they find it too complicated to understand (Jenkins, 2004; Glater, 2002; Eichenwald, 2002).

Causes of White-Collar Deviance

From analyzing the literature on white-collar crime, we can find three basic reasons why corporate executives and other white-collar personnel are likely to engage in deviant activities. These three reasons have to do with being in a higher social position than others, as suggested by the power theory in Chapter 3.

Deviant Motivation: Fear of Loss and Greed for Gain

Some evidence suggests that fear and greed have much to do with deviant activities in the white-collar world. It is well-known to Wall Street observers that fear and greed are the two most powerful human emotions driving the stock market. The fear of loss causes investors to sell stocks, which brings down their prices. If the fear is great and widely shared, it will cause a market crash. On the other hand, the greed for gain causes investors to buy more stocks, which raises their prices. If the greed is great and widely shared, it will cause a market boom. All this means in economic terms that when the supply of a stock rises—as a result of many investors wanting to sell their shares of the stock—its price falls, and when the demand for a stock rises—as a result of many investors wanting to buy more shares of the stock—its price rises.

Just as fear and greed drive the stock market, these motives seem to propel white-collar deviance. The fear of loss, such as the fear of losing one's house from mortgage foreclosure or the fear of a company going bankrupt, has been found to be associated with white-collar deviance. The deviance is characteristically the type that produces a relatively low profit or high risk of arrest, such as bank embezzlement and credit fraud. This usually involves low-level white-collar workers and small, new, or unsuccessful companies (Wheeler, 1991; Weisburd et al., 1991). The greed for gain—in order to prove to oneself how successful one can be or to turn an already large and successful corporation into an empire—is also likely to cause white-collar deviance. But the deviance is characteristically one that produces huge profit, such as buying political influence with huge donations or violating an antitrust law. It usually involves big-time executives and large, well-established, successful corporations. The greed is a by-product of success. As one researcher on white-collar crime says, "Greed is distinguished as a want that can never be satisfied: Success is ever-receding; having more leads to wanting more again" (Braithwaite, 1992).

The greed is not a psychological abnormality, though. It derives from the culture of competition, which celebrates greed as the engine of capitalism that drives people to get rich (Simpson and Piquero, 2002). This cultural encouragement of greed came through loud and clear when Ivan Boesky, before he was prosecuted and convicted of insider trading in the 1980s, was the honored commencement speaker at the School of Business Administration of the University of California at Berkeley. He told the graduates: "Greed is all right. . . . I want you to know that. I think greed is healthy. You can be greedy and still feel good about yourself." The audience roared with appreciative laughter and applause (Martz, 1986). The business graduates could identify with Boesky probably because greed is basically the same as excessive, boundless ambition, a product of the U.S. culture of success, which greatly emphasizes the importance of achieving material success in our lives.

In short, the greater the fear of loss or the greed for gain, the stronger the motivation for engaging in white-collar deviance.

Deviant Opportunity: The Benefit of High Position and Power

By itself the deviant motivation in the form of fear or greed is not enough to compel a person or corporation to engage in economic deviance. The deviance is more likely to occur if opportunities exist for carrying it out. Generally, the higher the individual's position is in a company, the more likely the "deviantly" motivated individual is to carry out a profitable deviant act, basically because of easier access to the company's resources. Thus managers, officers, or owners can be expected to be more likely than lower-level personnel to steal from the company. Relatively high status and prestige in society also make it easier to defraud unsuspecting victims because status and prestige lend the appearance of legitimacy and trustworthiness and reduce the target's guard against being victimized (Weisburd et al., 1991). A combination of high position, status, and prestige can thus provide the greatest opportunity for deviant activities, which in turn is likely to turn a deviant motivation into a deviant action.

For the same reason, the more power corporations have, the more likely they are to commit corporate crime. There is evidence to support this statement. In one study, for example, large corporations constituted only 42 percent of all companies investigated, but accounted for 70 percent of all violations—compared with 20 percent for medium-sized companies and 10 percent for small firms (Clinard and Yeager, 1980).

Weak Social Control: Lax Law Enforcement

It is widely known that law enforcers do not exercise as much control over white-collar deviance as over street crime. As we have indicated, for example, the penalty for bank fraud committed by a bank's executive or owner averages only 2.4 years in prison, compared with 7.8 years for bank robbery perpetrated by a lower-income person. As a result, white-collar crime by the rich and powerful can be expected to be more prevalent than street crime by the poor and powerless. Sometimes the government even directly encourages the rich to engage in deviance with its deregulation policies, as we can see from the proliferation of banking frauds in the 1980s after the government deregulated the banking industry (Glasberg and Skidmore, 1998).

Some studies, however, claim to have found that the overwhelming majority of white-collar criminals are far from rich and powerful but instead are pitiful middle-class people such as the bank teller who, saddled with overdue bills, embezzles only a few hundred dollars (Weisburd et al., 1991). The sample of such studies is usually a biased one, representing mostly the losers among white-collar criminals, namely, those who are prosecuted or convicted for their crimes. But the plain fact is that most white-collar criminals, particularly those who are rich and powerful, are not caught, which is, in fact, a powerful testimony to the relative lack of law enforcement against them.

Law enforcers are not entirely to blame for the weaker control experienced by more powerful deviants. The huge power commanded by such deviants plays a role too. In the pharmaceutical industry, for example, the government's regulatory agencies may try to confiscate drugs that have not been properly tested. But powerful drug companies can use their considerable resources to stop the confiscation. They may bribe the regulatory agents or pay unethical medical researchers to produce fraudulent evidence that the drugs are safe. To ensure against prosecution for bribery, some pharmaceutical companies even have employees who are, as part of their job description, responsible for going to jail. If a head has to "go on the chopping block," it would be the heads of these employees (Braithwaite, 1993, 1992).

In brief, more powerful corporations and individuals are more likely than others to engage in deviant activities because of weaker social control.

Governmental Deviance

Most of us seem to be ambivalent about our government officials. On the one hand, we expect them to break the law every now and then and we may, when seeing one of them get caught, remark, "There goes another crook." Mark Twain expressed this popular sentiment well when he said way back in 1894: "It could probably be shown with facts and figures that there is no distinctly American criminal class except Congress." On the other hand, we respect and admire them for being our leaders, often so much so that we would scramble in a crowd to get their autographs or shake their hands with a sense of pride and honor. Given these conflicting feelings of revulsion and respect, we nonetheless try to be objective in analyzing governmental deviance. This type of deviance essentially involves the abuse of power by government officials or politicians running for elected office. Here we focus on three types of governmental deviance: political corruption, election improprieties, and official violence.

Political Corruption

Political corruption is usually associated with graft or bribery—the abuse of power for personal gain. It may take the form of an outright bribe, in which case the public official accepts the money offered by a briber who expects a favor in return. Outright bribery routinely takes place in poor countries because it has become a part of their culture (Omestad, 1997). Outright bribery is far less common in the United States. The types of political corruption that occur more often in this country include kickbacks, management of public funds for personal gain, and illegal use of mail privileges.

Receiving Kickbacks from Businesses.   The federal government spends an enormous sum of taxpayer money on goods and services supplied by various businesses. The officials in charge of purchasing these goods and services may find it hard to resist kickbacks from the companies they are dealing with. To receive kickbacks, though, the officials will allow businesses to send the government outrageous bills. Thus, repair contractors and suppliers have been known to bill the government for work that was never done and for materials that were never delivered. Officials in the U.S. Defense Department are also known to have paid hundreds of dollars for a hammer and hundreds more for a toilet seat.

Abusive Management of Public Funds.   The management of public funds is a potential source of political corruption. City or state treasurers can be tempted to misuse the millions of dollars for personal gain, especially because there are many subtle, unprosecutable ways to do it. In deciding which bank to deposit an enormous sum of public money into, government officials may base their decision on whether it will profit themselves financially and politically. Thus, they may choose a bank of which they are shareholders; or a bank that will give their family members or business associates loans at low interest rates; or a bank that has promised to contribute substantially to their political campaigns.

Abusing the Frank.   The most common form of official corruption is probably the abuse of the frank—the privilege of sending mail free of charge. Our Founding Fathers intended the frank to be for official use only, namely, for answering letters from constituents. However, members of Congress routinely abuse the frank for personal purposes by sending out campaign information to ensure re-election. They, in effect, turn the franking system into a "taxpayer-funded propaganda machine" (Sabato and Simpson, 1996). As a Congressman explained to his new press aide, "We are going to mail, mail, mail and then mail some more. You're going to mail until you run out of ideas. Then you're going to talk to the rest of the staff and mail until they run out of ideas. After that you're going to come to me and mail until *I* run out of ideas. And when that happens, we're going to staple my picture to pages of the goddamn Yellow Book and mail them out, too, and lemme tell you, you can't *ever* run out of them sons of bitches" (Jackley, 1992).

Election Improprieties

Our representative democracy requires that we, the masses, have the right to choose our leaders. This right, however, often has little meaning to those who want to be our leaders. Therefore, various devious means are often used to win elections.

Denial of Voting Right.   The masses of citizenry are encouraged to participate in the presidential election. But in reality it is the electoral college—consisting of political leaders, not the populace—that selects the president. This should largely be blamed on the writers of the Constitution rather than on current political leaders, but it is important to realize that the "voters" are in a way bypassed to let political leaders decide who should be president (Simon, 2002).

Political Dirty Tricks.   Dirty tricks are often employed to ensure victory in an election. They include spreading rumors about the opponent's strange character, kinky sex life, or association with drug kingpins; having individuals in the audience at the opponent's rally heckle or ask embarrassing questions; defacing the opponent's billboards; and stealing the opponent's campaign mail. A more sophisticated form of dirty trick is the "telephone sleaze" in which campaign workers call voters, say they are conducting a nonpartisan survey, then ask loaded questions such as, "Did you know Senator Jones wants to vote against the banning of child pornography?" (Sabato and Simpson, 1996).

Campaign Finance Abuses.   Candidates for elected office often solicit and receive huge campaign contributions from monied interests (large corporations and wealthy individuals) and the donors expect the politicians to return the favor if elected. Incumbent legislators running *unopposed* also receive large contributions from the rich with the same expectation. As a result, the rich can gain access to the White House and Congress that ordinary citizens cannot. All this, in effect, involves the buying and selling of political influence or access to elected officials. Recently, for example, prominent bankers who had contributed heavily to Clinton's reelection campaign were invited to the White House to discuss banking regulations with the President and the nation's senior banking regulator, while executives of the giant tobacco company Philip Morris, a huge contributor to the Republicans, were able to discuss their concerns with Republican Congressional leaders (van Natta and Fritsch, 1997; Wertheimer, 1996).

Official Violence

There is a long history of governmental violence against various groups of citizens in the United States. The government, for example, drove Native Americans out of their lands and killed many of them in the early period of U.S. history. Today, most official violence involves police brutality against citizens, especially African and Hispanic Americans in large cities. When complaints of police brutality are brought against some officers, they are often dismissed as being without merit. If some complaints are admitted as legitimate, they are blamed on "only a few bad apples" in the police department. But these bad apples are usually kept on the force to rot rather than thrown out. Consequently, in nearly every large city's police department, there's a small group of officers committing most of the police brutality. Some police forces have begun to use a civilian review board to prevent police brutality, but most refuse to subject themselves to outside control, believing that they can police themselves (Kappeler, Sluder, and Alpert, 1998; Gleick, 1995; Herbert, 1995).

As a democracy, however, the United States commits *democide* (the killing of people by their government) to a much smaller extent than many other nations. For the twentieth century, democratic states account for only about 1 percent of all government-sponsored murders throughout the world. The vast majority of such killings have been carried out by Communist and authoritarian governments. The most notorious have been the Soviet Union, China, and the Khmer Rouge, which liquidated about one-third of the Cambodian population. Moreover, the governments of poorer nations commit democide on a larger scale than do richer nations. Apparently, the authorities in poor countries view life as cheap. But as the economy of these nations improves, the incidence of democide tends to decline, because "even ruthless dictators need tax revenue, and you can't collect taxes from dead people" (Scully, 1997).

Global Perspective: Official Corruption

Official corruption is a common practice around the world. Generally, the poorer a country is, the more corrupt its public officials are. In fact, in most of the world's poor countries, corruption is so prevalent that it is considered normal. There, people have to grease the public official's palm to obtain or retain business, to secure government contracts, or to pay for public service that is supposed to be free such as enrolling children in public school. Corruption hurts the poor more than others, because they spend more on bribes as a share of their small income while their access to badly needed public services is curtailed.

Official corruption discourages foreign investment in the corrupt country, which helps to retard its economic growth. This is a major reason why it is extremely difficult for many developing countries to climb out of their poverty. But corruption has helped a few East Asian countries, such as South Korea, Taiwan, Thailand, and Japan, become prosperous. This is because in exchange for bribes and kickbacks from large business companies, government officials offer cheap loans, tax benefits, protection against foreign imports, and other subsidies and support. Unfortunately, though, many developing countries are too poor to have the same large businesses and resource-rich governments that those newly industrialized East Asian countries have.

Research in various countries has indicated at least three major causes of official corruption. One is poverty, as suggested by the fact that corruption is much more common in developing countries than in developed ones. This is because the governments in poor countries do not have enough tax revenues to pay their public officials adequately on a regular basis. A second cause of corruption is a large population, which makes surveillance on a massive number of public officials difficult. This may explain why the world's largest country, China, and the fourth largest country, Indonesia, are among the most corrupt on earth while the tiny city state of Singapore is one of the least corrupt. And a third cause of corruption is the lack of democracy. This may explain the higher frequency of corruption in authoritarian countries, which generally do not have what democracies have: the anti-corruption surveillance by citizen groups, the press, and reform-minded politicians.

Sources: Rock and Bonnett, 2004 Transparency International, 2004; Xin and Rudel, 2004.

Official Ways of Neutralizing Deviance

Government officials take great care to cover up their deviant acts. Even after such acts have been uncovered, the officials rarely admit their guilt. Instead, they automatically attempt to neutralize their deviance—to make it appear as if they had done nothing wrong. Such an attempt has been called "the ritual of wiggle." There are different ways for government officials to wiggle out of their deviant activities. Let's take a look at their most common techniques of neutralization (Lieberman, 1973).

Denying the Obvious

Public officials tend to deny that any wrongdoing has occurred, no matter how strong the suspicion or how clear the reality. The denial is as frequently and honestly repeated as possible. Even a popular president like Ronald Reagan found it hard to tell the truth. In late 1986, when the arms deal with Iran shocked the nation, he insisted that he did not know of the diversion of funds to the Nicaraguan rebels, although it was clear to many Americans that he did. In a nationwide poll, 47 percent of the respondents said that he was "lying" (the exact word used in the question) while only 37 percent said that he was telling the truth (Church, 1986). More recently, former President Clinton denied that there was anything wrong with him having coffees or lunches in the White House with his wealthy contributors. He said, for example, "I think it is an appropriate thing and can be a good thing for the President and for the Secretary of the Treasury to meet with a group of bankers and listen to them and listen to their concerns" (Mitchell, 1997).

Ignoring the Deviance

If an illegal act is a private one committed by individual officials, they ignore it by disconnecting their phones, going into hiding or on a trip away from the press, or simply saying "no comment." If the government is supposed to take action against its officials for some lawbreaking, it resorts to evasive responses by insisting that the facts do not conclusively and absolutely warrant governmental intervention. The government, for example, has failed to address itself adequately to the issue of the legality of the United States' involvement in the Vietnam War. Even if they have been found guilty, officials still tend to act as if their deviance is not really deviant. In 1997, for example, after House Speaker Newt Gingrich was reprimanded and fined $300,000 for years of unethical conduct, he dismissed his misdeeds as only comparable to jaywalking (Weisman, 1997).

Accusing the Accuser

In the case of private offenses, the individual official may threaten or actually file a libel suit against the journalist who publicized the offense. Although it is almost impossible to prove libel, the official hopes that the suit will divert public attention from the official's own wrongdoing. The government hopes for the same thing when it accuses its accuser. This is why the Nixon administration often attacked the news media for distorting facts when its illegal activities were publicized. Also, when CBS-TV News broadcast its critical documentary *The Selling of the Pentagon,* a House committee launched an investigation into CBS-TV News rather than into the Defense Department. In 1992, when Senator Brock Adams of Washington State was accused by a woman for sexually molesting her, he claimed she was mentally ill, though eight other women had independently alleged similar sexual harassment by him (Trost and Thomas, 1993).

Promising to Take Action

When high government officials are under intense pressure to do something about a certain incident, they will publicly promise to take action to deal with it. Yet, behind the scenes, the promised action is not seriously carried out. In the 1970s, when the Watergate scandal broke, the Attorney General promised to make the Justice Department's investigation of the scandal "the most extensive, thorough and comprehensive investigation since the assassination of President Kennedy." But it was only a promise; nothing came of it. In the 1980s, when confronted with the scandal of selling arms to Iran and diverting funds to the Nicaraguan rebels,

President Reagan kept repeating that he wanted all the facts to come out. Yet he did not try very hard to get the facts out. He did not even demand from his aides, who were the key figures in the scandal, an accounting of what they did (Church, 1986). More recently, President Clinton repeatedly announced his intent to help clean up the system that effectively encourages politicians to sell access or influence for large campaign contributions. But he continued to raise funds for his political party by soliciting huge donations from big corporations and wealthy individuals (Mitchell, 1997).

Justifying the Deviance

This method of neutralization is rationalization par excellence. Although they have implicitly admitted their wrongdoing with their promise to deal with it, the guilty officials rationalize that it was necessary for them to commit the deviant act. This should not be surprising, because it has the support of the popular belief that the end sometimes justifies the means. Thus, many officials justify unlawful wiretapping on the grounds that the danger of not using it against suspected criminals or terrorists is too great. In the early 1970s, President Nixon, the CIA, and the FBI even justified domestic surveillance of U.S. citizens as in the interest of national security. In the 1950s and 1960s, top U.S. military and intelligence officials insisted that it was necessary to use unsuspecting Americans as guinea pigs for mind-control experiments by sneaking powerful mind-altering drugs into their drinks because there had been reports of Soviet success at mind control (Budiansky et al., 1994). In 1997 President Clinton defended his solicitation of big political donations, saying, "I do not believe you will ever get the politics out of politics. And that's not bad" (Mitchell, 1997). In 2004 the Secretary of Defense effectively approved torturing prisoners when he declared that detainees—especially unlawful combatants—should not get all the rights and privileges accorded prisoners of war under the Geneva Convention (Barry et al., 2004).

Causes of Governmental Deviance

A review of various studies on governmental deviance suggests at least three important causes of the problem: the superabundance of ambiguous laws, governmental complexity, and power.

Superabundance of Ambiguous Laws

Government officials operate under a *superabundance of ambiguous laws*—lack of clearcut laws for controlling official action. This enormous collection of ambiguous laws has been described by a legal scholar "as a wall of lattice-work: the thin strips of wood represent all of our legal rules, but the pervasive holes are very prominent; indeed, but for the holes there would be no design at all" (Lieberman, 1973). The "holes" referred to in the quote are popularly known as *loopholes,* meaning the ambiguity of laws through which the intent of the laws can be evaded. Therefore, the superabundance of ambiguous laws inevitably creates a "discretionary wilderness" where government officials are relatively free to rely on their own judgment and self-interest to interpret the law. The kind of interpretation opens up a great deal of opportunity for officials to engage in deviant activities, whenever they so desire, with impunity.

In fact, as is well known among historians studying the U.S. presidency, many laws are purposely ambiguous, designed to give presidents a lot of room to do their job. "The Reagan Administration," for example, "has followed the lead of its predecessors in emphasizing semantic interpretations to exempt its actions from various laws. As the Truman Administration called the Korean war a 'police action' to circumvent the necessity for a declaration of war, so the Reagan Administration has said that its assistance to the Nicaraguan rebels was part of a strategy of 'interdicting' supply lines to El Salvador's communist insurgents rather than of undermining the Sandinista Government of Nicaragua" (Tolchin, 1986). Earlier, Presidents Lyndon Johnson and Richard Nixon had also skirted the law when they sent troops into combat in Vietnam without the benefit of a congressional declaration of war. More recently, President Bill Clinton went around the law to raise money for his re-election campaign. Once, for example, after President Clinton received word that a rich man wanted to donate $5 million to his campaign fund, he instructed his White House deputy chief of staff to handle the matter, although it is against the law for a government official to raise campaign funds (Isikoff, 1997).

Governmental Complexity and Power

Given the intricate, complex nature of the government as a huge organization, it is inevitable that its members cannot have complete information and responsibility regarding what and how they should do their jobs in the organization. Due to this lack of information and responsibility, then, officials tend to get involved in deviant activities (Ermann and Lundman, 2002).

This explanation, however, implies that officials are not to blame for committing deviance because, given the lack of information and responsibility, they do not knowingly or intentionally get involved in deviance. Thus, the concept of governmental complexity can best be used to explain *unintentional* deviance among government officials. As for their *intentional* deviance, which essentially involves an abuse of power, it may be better explained by the power theory that we have developed in Chapter 3 and applied to white-collar deviance earlier in this chapter. According to the power theory, there are three reasons why government officials tend to purposely abuse their power: stronger deviant motivation, greater deviant opportunity, and weaker social control. Due to their relatively high position in society, governmental officials tend to be too ambitious, thereby more likely to experience relative deprivation, which would motivate them to employ deviant means to achieve their high goals. They are further encouraged to abuse their power because they enjoy abundant opportunities for doing so and are not subject to stringent social control, thanks again to their lofty position in society.

Summary

1. What is white-collar deviance? Traditionally called white-collar crime, white-collar deviance includes both criminal and noncriminal forms of economic deviance carried out by relatively high-status people as part of an occupation for their personal gain (hence occupational deviance) or on behalf of their corporation (hence corporate deviance).

2. What is the nature of corporate deviance? It can be divided into four types on the basis of who or what their victims are. Deviance against employees involves a corporation ignoring its employees' health and safety; deviance against customers involves a corporation dealing in dangerous foods or unsafe products, engaging in commercial frauds or deceptive advertising, and violating antitrust laws; deviance against the government includes evading payment of taxes, using campaign donations to buy influence, and bribing foreign governments or committing other illegal acts abroad; and deviance against the environment involves polluting the environment.

3. What is the social profile of corporate crooks? They are top corporate executives charged with fraud and other illegal business activities. They are much more highly paid than their already highly paid noncriminal peers. Their sky-high pay may cause them to feel that they are above the law, but their illegal business practices are not much different from the legal practices that result from too much deregulation.

4. What is the nature of occupational deviance? Carried out for the employees' own gain rather than on behalf of their company, occupational deviance includes employee theft, embezzlement, tax and securities violations, and deviance in such professions as medicine, law, and accounting.

5. How does white-collar deviance differ from common, street crime? White-collar deviance is distinguishable for its rational execution of the offense as well as the offender's respectable self-image, the victim's unwitting cooperation, and society's relative indifference toward the offense.

6. What causes white-collar deviance? Generally, the causes of white-collar deviance are stronger deviant motivation, greater deviant opportunity, and weaker social control. The motivation involves the fear of loss and greed for gain. The opportunity inheres in a higher position in a company or in the more powerful corporation. And weaker control comes from less stringent law enforcement against white-collar deviance.

7. What is the nature of governmental deviance? Government deviance involves the abuse of power by government officials or candidates for elected office. Such deviance appears in different forms, including political corruption, election improprieties, and official violence. Political corruption includes receiving kickbacks from businesses, abusing the management of public funds, and abusing the frank. Election improprieties include denial of the right to really elect the president, playing dirty tricks on the election opponent, and the buying and selling of political influence that favors the rich over ordinary citizens. Official violence involves mostly police brutality against crime suspects and innocent citizens, especially African and Hispanic Americans.

8. What are the nature and causes of official corruption around the world? Corruption is a common practice all over the world but more prevalent in poor countries, where it is considered normal. Corruption hurts the poor citizens more than the rich and usually retards the nation's economic growth. Causes of corruption include poverty, large population, and the lack of democracy.

9. What would government officials do if their illegal activities were revealed to the public? They would try to neutralize their deviance. This neutralization takes the form of denying the obvious, ignoring the deviance, accusing the accuser, promising to take action, and justifying the deviance.

10. What causes governmental deviance? The causes of governmental deviance include the superabundance of ambiguous laws, governmental complexity, and power that creates deviant motivation, deviant opportunity, and weak control.

FURTHER READING

Coleman, James William. 1994. *The Criminal Elite: The Sociology of White Collar Crime*, 3d ed. New York: St. Martin's. A comprehensive review of the literature on white-collar crime, dealing with the types, characteristics, origins, and legal control of the crime.

Croall, Hazel. 2001. *Understanding White Collar Crime.* Philadelphia: Open University Press. A concise text on white-collar crime, covering the nature, regulation, and explanation of the subject.

Ermann, M. David, and Richard J. Lundman (eds.). 2002. *Corporate and Governmental Deviance*, 6th ed. New York: Oxford University Press. A collection of articles dealing with the characteristics of elite deviance, its impact on people, and societal reactions to it.

Friedrichs, David O. 1996. *Trusted Criminals: White Collar Crime in Contemporary Society.* Belmont, Calif.: Wadsworth. A comprehensive text covering various types and characteristics of white-collar deviance.

Furnell, Steven. 2002. *Cybercrime: Vandalizing the Information Society.* London: Addison-Wesley. Discussing the nature and impact of computer crime, especially hacking, on society as a whole.

Green, Gary S. 1990. *Occupational Crime.* Chicago: Nelson-Hall. Deals with various kinds of crime committed in the course of one's occupation, as well as the concept, measurements, explanations, and control of occupational crime.

Poveda, Tony G. 1994. *Rethinking White-Collar Crime.* Westport, Conn.: Praeger. An analysis of the theoretical issues about the definition, explanation, and social control of white-collar crime.

Rosoff, Stephen M., Henry N. Pontell, and Robert H. Tillman. 2002. *Profit Without Honor: White-Collar Crime and the Looting of America*, 2d ed. Upper Saddle River, N.J.: Prentice Hall. Describing in great detail the nature of various forms of white-collar crime, including consumer fraud, governmental abuse of power, medical crime, and computer crime.

Sabato, Larry J., and Glenn R. Simpson. 1996. *Dirty Little Secrets: The Persistence of Corruption in American Politics.* New York: Times Book. Discusses how corruption flourishes in the current political system that serves big-money interests more than the ordinary citizenry.

Schlegel, Kip, and David Weisburd (eds.). 1992. *White-Collar Crime Reconsidered.* Boston: Northeastern University Press. A collection of articles by various sociological researchers on the definitions, theories, victimization, and control of white-collar crime.

Simon, David R. 2002. *Elite Deviance*, 7th ed. Boston: Allyn and Bacon. A survey of various forms of elite deviance, including corporate deviance, international deviance, and political deviance.

Simon, David R., and Frank E. Hagan. 1999. *White Collar Deviance.* Boston: Allyn and Bacon. Presents various aspects of white-collar deviance.

Shichor, David, Larry Gaines, and Richard Ball (eds.). 2002. *Readings in White-Collar Crime.* Prospect Heights, Ill.: Waveland Press. An anthology of articles dealing with the sociological definition of the subject, various forms of white-collar crime, and the treatment of white-collar criminals by the criminal justice system.

Shover, Neal, and John Paul Wright (eds.). 2001. *Crimes of Privilege: Readings in White-Collar Crime*. New York: Oxford University Press. A collection of articles covering the costs, opportunities, decision-making processes, characteristics, and controlling of white-collar crime.

Sutherland, Edwin H. 1983. *White Collar Crime: The Uncut Version*. New Haven, Conn.: Yale University Press. A classic on white-collar crime, with introductory remarks by contemporary sociologists Gilbert Geis and Colin Goff.

Weisburd, David, Elin Waring, and Ellen F. Chayet. 2001. *White-Collar Crime and Criminal Careers*. New York: Cambridge University Press. An analysis of the criminal careers of white-collar offenders who repeatedly run afoul of the law.

Weisburd, David, Stanton Wheeler, Elin Waring, and Nancy Bode. 1991. *Crimes of the Middle Classes: White-Collar Offenders in the Federal Courts*. New Haven, Conn.: Yale University Press. An empirical study of middle-class white-collar offenders who get caught for their crimes.

CRITICAL THINKING QUESTIONS

1. Free enterprise, the heart of capitalism, enables business to operate for profit without interference by government and is often credited with the affluence we enjoy as a society. Is corporate deviance, then, a necessary evil of capitalism, a price we have to pay for the affluence? Or is it an insufferable problem that can be eliminated without destroying capitalism? Whatever your answer, provide an explanation.

2. When they are known to have committed a deviant act, why don't politicians and government officials readily confess it to the public? If they do confess, under what circumstances would the public forgive them and under what circumstances would the public not forgive them?

14 Underprivileged Deviance

As a young man, Mani Chulpayev came to New York from Russia with his family in 1989. He first worked with his father, who owned several food carts, selling pretzels and sausages. Then he quit because, he said, "I was driven by greed." He went into extortion rackets with several fellow Russian immigrants. They made as much as $500 a week shaking down owners of furniture stores, restaurants, bakeries, and travel agencies. Chulpayev used pistols, knives, and stun guns to enforce payments from the victims. He also pimped prostitutes, two or three at a time, importing them from Moscow on six-month contracts. His luck finally ran out in 1998 when he was arrested after a furniture store proprietor complained to the F.B.I. about extortion. At the time he was in Los Angeles delivering a prostitute to a group of Russian doctors (Berkeley, 2002).

As a participant in organized crime, Chulpayev can be said to engage in *underprivileged deviance,* deviance that typically occurs among underprivileged people, who come from relatively poor and powerless backgrounds. Underprivileged deviance is generally distinguishable from privileged deviance in being less profitable or, in the case of successful organized crime, more disreputable and more liable to be punished and punished severely. In this chapter we will discuss examples of underprivileged deviance, including not only organized crime but also robbery, auto theft and carjacking, burglary, and shoplifting.

Robbery

Robbery is simultaneously both a property and a violent crime. It is a property crime because it involves illegally taking the victim's property; it is a violent crime for the use of violence or threat of violence against the victim in its commission. We will first examine these two connected facets of robbery, and then look at the patterns of robbery, such as where or when robbery usually occurs, what robbers are like, and why they commit robbery.

Robbery as a Property Crime

As a property crime, robbery is a relatively rational, calculated act, and as such, it involves making rational decisions. The decision making consists of a sequence of three elements: (1) deciding to rob mostly for financial gain, (2) deciding what target to rob, and (3) deciding how to carry out the robbery (Conklin, 1972).

Deciding to Rob for Money. For most robbers the decision to rob is based on their desire for money. But psychiatrists tend to assume that armed robbers are basically abnormal, suffering from a sense of inadequacy and failure and, therefore, committing robbery with a firearm as a way of seeking self-adequacy and power. One armed robber is quoted as saying, "When I have a gun in my hands nothing can stop me. It makes me feel important and strong. With a revolver you're somebody" (Gabor et al., 1987). This may be true of some robbers, but *most* robbers are *primarily* interested in money, just like the notorious Willie Sutton. When asked why he robbed banks, Sutton replied, "Because that's where the money is." The pursuit of power in robbery, if it exists, is only a *secondary* motive (Haran and Martin, 1984).

Deciding Which Target to Rob. Once they have decided to rob, would-be robbers have to select a certain target. Target selection is generally based on two factors: (1) Robbers usually consider *lucrative* establishments—such as banks, grocery stores, and other places where large sums of cash are available—as potential targets. (2) They usually select from among these targets one with a *lower risk of arrest.* Thus, most robbers choose, for example, to hold up a branch bank in an outlying commercial area with few people that is close to a highway, rather than the main bank in the busy central business district.

Deciding How to Rob.   This last decision involves varying degrees of planning. At one extreme, some robbers, particularly professional ones who are after a big score, plan their crimes with great care and minute detail. At the other extreme, some robbers, especially amateur ones who suddenly feel the need for a small sum of cash, commit robbery on the spur of the moment, with hardly any planning. The majority of robberies are more carefully planned than not, as evidenced by the relatively low rate of arrest for such a crime—usually only about one out of four robberies ends in arrest (FBI, 2002).

Robbery as a Violent Crime

There are two facets to robbery as a violent crime: One involves actual violence, the other potential violence. Because they do not carry a weapon, *unarmed robbers* usually have to resort to *actual violence* to subdue the victim; hence the crime is also called *strong-arm robbery*. But *armed robbers* tend more to rely only on *potential violence*—the threat of force—made to appear real and frightening to the victim by the sight of a weapon.

Unarmed Robbery and Actual Violence.   Unarmed or strong-arm robberies are often viewed by the public as less dangerous than armed robberies. But, in reality, the opposite is true: Unarmed robberies are far more likely to result in injury to the victims. According to one study, 66 percent of unarmed-robbery victims, compared to only 17 percent of armed-robbery victims, were injured (Feeney and Weir, 1975). Of course, armed robberies are more likely to result in the victim's death. But the likelihood of fatality is extremely small: Victims die in fewer than one percent of all robberies carried out with a gun (Wright, Rossi, and Daly, 1983; Feeney and Weir, 1975).

Unarmed robberies are more dangerous because offenders believe that victims are more likely to resist when there is no weapon involved than when there is a weapon. As one unarmed robber says, "In strongarms, you have to put [the victim] out of commission for a few minutes. When you haven't got a gun or knife, he won't do anything. He'll tell you to go to hell or turn on you. So all you can do is knock him out" (Luckenbill, 1981).

Armed Robbery and Potential Violence.   As a threat of force, potential violence in armed robbery rarely turns into real violence because the use of a weapon, particularly a firearm, often ensures the successful execution of the crime. There are four ways in which a weapon can help robbers accomplish their goal efficiently (Conklin, 1972).

First, the weapon creates a *buffer zone* between offender and victim. Many robbers believe that the firearm is the most effective weapon because it frightens the victim the most. With the firearm holding the victim at a distance, the robber can cover a large area and can also control many victims at the same time. Second, the weapon *intimidates* the victim, making it unnecessary for the robber to resort to violence. If the show of a weapon fails to intimidate the victims enough to give up their money, the offender often tries to increase the level of intimidation by cocking the pistol or holding it to the victim's head. If this attempt also fails, the robber may be compelled to use the weapon for the third purpose—to *make good the threat*. A few robbers stab or shoot the victim, but most simply strike—without seriously hurting—the victim on the side of the head or in the stomach to show that they "mean business." If this still does not work and the victim resists strongly, most robbers would not hesitate to kill the victim (Wright and Decker, 1997). According to an analysis of over 815 robberies reported to Chicago police, only a few (7 percent) of the victims did resist actively and most of these victims were killed (Meer, 1985). Fourth, the weapon *ensures escape* after the completion of the crime, as robbers use the weapon to prevent the victims, witnesses, and even police officers from interfering with their escape.

Patterns of Robbery

Robbery is basically a *big-city* crime. The robbery rate in large cities is many times higher than in rural areas. Relatedly, the more urbanized a region, the higher its rate of robbery. This is because, unlike homicide, which typically occurs between acquaintances as offender and victim, robbery involves mostly strangers—and opportunities abound for encountering strangers in large cities. Thus, as the northeastern states are more urbanized than the southern states, so the northeastern states have a higher robbery rate (U.S. Census Bureau, 2004–2005).

Robbery occurs most frequently in the *cold winter* months, reaching its peak in volume during the holiday season in December, when stores are making more money and people are carrying more cash with them on the streets. There are additional reasons for the higher frequency of robbery in the winter than in other seasons. The cold weather keeps most people off the streets, thereby making it easier for robbers to victimize lonely individuals without having any discouraging witnesses around. The cold weather also makes it look natural for robbers to wear a heavy coat, which is ideal for hiding a shotgun or other weapon. The increase in hours of darkness in the winter further enhances the opportunity for robbing without getting caught. All these factors involve the opportunity for committing robbery. Other factors have to do with the increased motivation for committing the crime. One such factor is a higher rate of unemployment in the winter, which largely comes from the loss of seasonal jobs such as construction, tourism, and other outdoor work. Another motivational factor is the economic pressure from the rising cost of living in the winter, because there is greater need for money to be spent on such goods as clothing, shelter, and heating (Landau and Fridman, 1993).

Most robberies (about six out of ten) take place *outdoors*, on the streets and highways. Of those that occur indoors, the general public assumes that a significant number take place in banks. But *bank robbery is relatively rare*, accounting for only about 6 percent of indoor robberies (see Figure 14.1). Since the early 1990s, though,

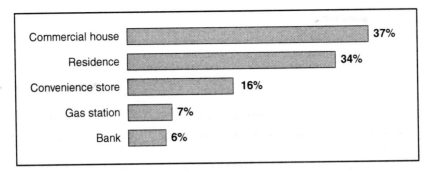

FIGURE 14.1 Locations of Indoor Robberies

Source: U.S. Census Bureau, *Statistical Abstract of the United States,* 2004–2005.

bank robbers have increased significantly. This is largely because it is much more convenient to rob banks today. Unlike the banks built in the past like fortresses, many banks today make themselves vulnerable to robbery by having potted plants, subdued lighting, long hours, and open teller stations in order to please customers. To avoid violence from angry robbers, bank tellers are instructed to quickly hand over the money without a fight, which makes it convenient even for a 12-year-old or an 80-year-old to rob the bank. The road system further makes it easy to pull off a robbery, since it takes less than a minute after the heist to zoom away on the freeway. This may explain why California, which has the nation's most extensive network of freeways, has more bank robberies than any other state (St. John, 2004; Hechinger, 2002; Johnston, 1997).

Most of the robberies today are *armed*. Over the years, armed robberies have increased faster than unarmed ones. Most of these robberies involve the use of firearms rather than knives and other cutting instruments, and are more likely to be committed by adults than youngsters. In contrast, unarmed robberies, which include purse snatching, mugging, and other violent confrontations, involve youngsters more often than adults. Compared with armed robberies, unarmed robberies also take place closer to the offender's home. This is largely due to the spontaneity and predominance of foot travel in unarmed robbery—as opposed to the planned nature of armed robbery and the common use of a vehicle in its commission (FBI, 2002; Capone and Nichols, 1976).

In contrast with violent crimes such as homicide and rape, which are predominantly intraracial in nature, robbery is more likely to be *interracial*—involving blacks robbing whites (Wilbanks, 1985). This is probably because robbery is more premeditated and impersonal than homicide and rape. "More premeditated" suggests that the robber, being more rational and calculative, would rather victimize people with more money than those with less, and "impersonal" implies that the robber would rather rob strangers than relatives, friends, or acquaintances. This victim profile—having more money and being strangers—is more likely to fit whites than blacks. Therefore, black offenders tend more to rob whites than other blacks.

Amateur and Professional Robbers

There are two kinds of robbers: amateurs and professionals. Compared with professionals, amateurs generally commit robbery for smaller sums of money with less planning and skill and higher risks of arrest. Adults are more likely than youngsters to be professionals, and youngsters tend more to be amateurs.

Amateur Robbers. Amateur robbers can further be divided into three types: (1) opportunist robbers, (2) addict robbers, and (3) alcoholic robbers (Haran and Martin, 1984; Conklin, 1972).

The majority of amateur robbers are *opportunist robbers*. Usually committing such forms of theft as larceny and shoplifting, opportunists infrequently rob. When they do rob, they tend to target individual persons rather than commercial establishments. Typical targets are older women with purses, drunks, cab drivers, and people who walk alone on dark or empty streets. The criteria for choosing such targets are the victim's easy accessibility and vulnerability rather than large sums of cash. Perhaps because such targets are easy to rob, opportunists rarely carry firearms and often have no weapon of any kind. Yet they are likely to form a gang, three or four young opportunists working together to overpower the victim in a strong-arm robbery. So the group itself operates as a weapon of sorts, comparable in threatening power to a knife.

Since the early 1980s, however, opportunist robbers have caused a surge in bank robberies, which are traditionally associated with professional robbers. This new breed of bank robber is mostly young and unsophisticated. There is little planning to their heists. Confederates are casually chosen and form loose groups thrown together "for the job." The robberies are so amateurishly conceived that the amount of loot is often the result of pure chance. The average take is about $3,000, but it does not seem much because it has to be split two, three, or four ways (Kaplan, 1991; Haran and Martin, 1984).

Addict robbers commit robbery to buy their next "fix." Like opportunists, addicts rarely go after lucrative targets and thus often commit robberies that yield small sums of money. But due to the high cost of their drug habit, the robbers desperately carry out more acts of property crime than the opportunist. Moreover, addicts are more reluctant to resort to physical force and thus more likely to use a firearm. Their robberies are often committed on the street against vulnerable targets for ready cash. Such targets often include drug dealers, who carry a lot of cash and as wanted criminals themselves can't call the police, and white folks, who are much less likely than blacks to offer resistance (Jacobs, 2000; Wright and Decker, 1997).

Among amateurs, *alcoholic robbers* are least likely to engage in robbery, and most likely to be caught when they rob. They usually do not plan their crime; neither do they try to make their crime easier by seeking a vulnerable victim. Instead, they often get involved in a situation that unexpectedly leads to a robbery. They may get into fistfights or drunkenly assault people, and then take away their victims' money as an afterthought. The random nature of the alcoholic's crime may be illustrated by one alcoholic who walked into a liquor store to buy a bottle of whiskey. After he had given the clerk the money to pay for it, the clerk asked whether he wanted anything else. At that instant, the alcoholic decided that he did, telling the clerk to hand over all the money in the register. Surprised and angered, the clerk refused. During the ensuing fight, the alcoholic managed to take some money and then fled.

Professional Robbers. Professionals carefully plan their robberies, execute them with one or more accomplices and with skill, and make away with large sums of money. There are two types of professional robbers, one more specialized in robbery than the other. The more specialized ones commit robbery almost exclusively; the less specialized, being also committed to other forms of crimes, commit robbery only occasionally but nonetheless with professional skill. The first type of professional robber was more common in the past, while the second type is more common today.

Professional robbers as a whole have a strong commitment to robbery as a way of earning a living, and seek a series of big scores to support an expensive, hedonistic lifestyle. After executing a robbery, professionals often leave the city for a few weeks, perhaps taking a trip to a resort area. Once there, they spend the money like millionaires, to satisfy luxurious whims and pleasures. When the supply of money is depleted, they will start developing specific plans for more robberies. At other times they just keep their eyes open, watching for possible scores. Since they are mostly interested in big scores, they will typically rob commercial establishments that contain large sums of money. Because these targets generally take greater precaution against theft than individuals do, professional robbers usually have developed considerably more skill and do more careful planning than amateur offenders, who usually rob individuals of smaller sums of money.

Professional robbers tend to see their crime as an honest enterprise. Unlike burglary and other thefts, which involve furtiveness or deception, robbery calls for an open, direct, face-to-face confrontation with the victim. It is this quality of candor that, in the eye of the professional robber, transforms the crime into an honest activity. Professional robbers even consider their crime more honest than the business activity of the companies they victimize. As one of them explains, "To me this is perfectly honest, because these companies are cheating people anyway. When you go and just take it from them, you are actually more honest than they are. Most of the time, anyway, they are insured and make more money from the caper than you do" (Irwin, 1970).

Causes of Robbery

Two positivist theories seem useful for explaining robbery. One focuses on the *motivation* to commit robbery and the other on the *opportunity* for committing robbery as the causes of the crime. According to the first theory, the motivation is socially created *relative deprivation*, the feeling of frustration from failing to realize a heightened expectation in the lower classes, and to the second theory, the opportunity is provided by the *economic abundance* in the larger society.

Relative Deprivation.   John Conklin (1972) has used the concept of relative deprivation to explain the surge in robbery rates in major U.S. cities during the 1960s. Conklin noticed that from 1960 to 1969 the social and economic condition of poor African Americans improved significantly as a result of the federal government's many antipoverty and civil rights programs. But at the same time the rates of robbery among poor African Americans also went up significantly. Conklin attributed this ironical increase in robbery rates to relative deprivation among the poor blacks: The absolute improvement in their life induced them to hold higher expectations of enjoying as many opportunities as whites, but when they failed to realize these expectations, they felt frustrated and, as a consequence, tended to commit robbery.

Economic Abundance.   Leroy Gould (1969) has used not only the concept of relative deprivation but also economic abundance to explain why the rate of property crime that had remained relatively low during the 1930–1943 period of economic scarcity rose sharply during the period of abundance from 1944–1965. As Gould says, "Increases in the amount of property would serve to increase the relative deprivation of those who were still not sharing in the ownership of the property, while at the same time *making it easier for these people to steal the property for their own use.*"

According to Gould, people with money problems feel particularly frustrated when they know that many others are doing very well because of the general affluence around them. At the same time, the society's economic abundance creates a lot of opportunities for committing robbery. Many banks, especially branch banks, are located close to highways and shopping centers—a convenience obviously designed for customers but tempting to robbers as well (Johnston, 1997; Duffala, 1976; Gould, 1969). The opportunities for robbery are also available in many other business establishments and private residences, where the robber can find a great deal of money, jewelry, and other precious objects. Since people have more money, they are also likely to carry more cash with them on the streets. In brief, economic abundance enhances what some sociologists have called "target suitability" for robbery (Cohen, Cantor, and Kluegel, 1981).

Auto Theft and Carjacking

Over the last 15 years or so various property crimes have declined significantly. But the decline in auto theft was much less when compared to robbery and burglary (see Table 14.1).

TABLE 14.1   Property Crimes, 1986–2002

| Crime | Rate per 100,000 population | | Change from 1986 to 2002 |
	1986	2002	
Auto theft	507.8	432.1	−15%
Robbery	225.1	145.9	−35%
Burglary	1,344.6	746.2	−45%

Source: U.S. Census Bureau, Statistical Abstract of the United States, 2004–2005.

Characteristics and Trends

Many people seem to associate auto theft with teenagers stealing a car for purposes of "joy riding"—driving the car for a while and then abandoning it. Indeed, joy riding was once quite common, especially in the 1960s and 1970s. But today most auto thieves steal cars in order to sell them for a quick and handsome profit. In fact, auto theft has become big business. Every year, about 1.2 million cars are stolen, costing at least $8 billion, which accounts for nearly half of all the property lost to crime (FBI, 2002).

The overwhelming majority of auto thefts do not involve any violence against the victim because the offender typically steals the car when the owner is not around. However, since 1990, there has been a trend toward the use of violence to force drivers to give up their cars. Cars have been hijacked at highway rest stops, gas stations, fast-food outlets, car washes, red lights, and shopping-mall parking lots. In a typical carjacking, a single robber puts a pistol to the head of a startled driver. Some carjackers would do a "bump and run" by staging a minor rear-end accident. When the unsuspecting motorist gets out to investigate the damage, one robber holds up the victim while the other drives off with the victim's car. A few of these carjackings are extremely violent, resulting in the victim being severely beaten or brutally killed (Hyatt, 1993; Witkin, 1992).

According to the U.S. Justice Department, every year in the 1990s there were about 49,000 attempted carjackings and in half of these cases the offender got away with the car. Most of the carjackers are African Americans, but so are most of their victims. The most vulnerable to carjacking are people who are most likely to become victims of violent crime in general. They include men more than women, blacks more than whites, Hispanics more than non-Hispanics, the divorced more than the married, and urban residents more than rural or suburban dwellers (Klaus, 1999).

Causes

The *motivation* for committing auto theft appears to be about the same as for other property crimes. Like other property criminals, car thieves have a strong motivation for monetary gain. Their criminal motivation derives largely from the poor, lower-class environment where they have suffered deprivation resulting from income inequality, racial discrimination, or society's failure to fulfill aspirations for decent jobs. But auto thieves are unique in being offered abundant *opportunities* for stealing cars (Rice and Smith, 2002).

First, *inadequate law-enforcement* makes it easy to steal cars without getting caught. Overwhelmed by violent crime, the police have too little time left for dealing with auto theft. Of the nation's 500,000 police officers, fewer than 3,000 (less than one percent) investigate auto theft. Moreover, prisons are so overcrowded with violent offenders that most car thieves do not serve any time—they are simply set free on probation. A second reason for auto theft is the *profitability* of stolen cars and car parts, the demand for which is relatively high. Some of this demand comes from foreign countries, to which some 200,000 "hot" cars are shipped a year, because a stolen American car can double or triple in value there. Auto-repair shops also like to buy the parts removed from stolen cars because the illegal items are sold cheaper and delivered faster than legal ones from the manufacturer. A third reason for auto theft is *insurance fraud*. To collect insurance money, a car owner can contract with a thief to steal the car, abandon the automobile on a city street for any thief to steal, or simply run the vehicle into a river (Christian, 1995; Witkin, 1992).

What about the upsurge in carjacking? The reason for this increase in carjacking is ironical: *the increased sophistication of the car's security devices*, such as the alarm systems, steering-wheel locks, and ignition-control systems. These antitheft devices are likely to encourage car thieves, particularly young amateurs, to hijack a car, because it is considerably easier to rob a motorist at gunpoint than to steal a car parked somewhere with its engine turned off (Bradsher, 1999; Witkin, 1992).

Burglary

Compared with other property crimes, burglary has declined the most (see Table 14.1). Nevertheless, burglars still steal more than $4 billion worth of property in a year, more than three times higher than the cost of auto thefts (Armes, 2004).

Modus Operandi

Burglars are characteristically rational and calculating in executing their crime. Thus, most burglaries are committed during the day when the homes are empty because the occupants are at work, at school, or out shopping. The most popular time for burglars to do their thing is between 9 and 11 A.M. and from 1 to 3 P.M. These are the hours when people are most likely to go out. Contrary to popular belief, burglaries are *not* crimes of the night, because breaking into a house at night may cause a confrontation with its occupants. There are exceptions, though. A few cat burglars may break into a home without waking up its occupants. This is especially easy to do in houses with loud window air conditioners. As a burglar says, "If you can't hear the air conditioner when you're asleep, you can't hear me when I break into your home." A few other burglars would work at night only if the family is away on vacation (Sussman, 1992; Cromwell, Olson, and Avary, 1991).

To ensure that the house they want to break into is empty, most burglars have a bag of tricks at their disposal. One common trick is to pass themselves off as a door-to-door salesperson. They knock on a door or ring a doorbell, ready to deliver a sales pitch. A similar stratagem is to knock on the door, ready to ask for a nonexistent person ("Is Mr. Smith home?") or directions to a nearby address. If nobody answers the door, they may quickly break into the house. But the more cautious burglars would leave a card in the door. If the card is still there the next day, it is a sure sign that the family is away. Another common trick is to get the prospective victim's name from the mailbox, look up the telephone number, and repeatedly make the call. If nobody answers, the house is assumed to be unoccupied (Cromwell, Olson, and Avary, 1991).

After making sure that nobody is in the house, most burglars still want to find out whether there is a burglar alarm. If there is, the burglars will go away. They will even pass over a house with a mere sign or window sticker that says the house is protected by an alarm system. They do not want to take chances with any-one who takes some precaution against burglary. As one burglar says, "Why take a chance? There's lots of places without alarms. Maybe they're bluffing, maybe they ain't." Dogs are another effective deterrent. Most burglars will stay away from a house if they know there is a dog in it. Even small dogs deter burglary, because, as one burglar explains, "Little dogs yap too much. The neighbors look to see what they are so excited about. I don't like little yapping dogs" (Cromwell, Olson, and Avary, 1991).

Causes of Burglary

Like other property crimes, burglary can be explained by deviant motivation and opportunity. But the specific nature of motivation and opportunity for burglary is not the same as that for other economic deviances.

In the case of burglaries, the primary motivation is the desire to obtain money to *meet expressive needs,* specifically the needs to maintain a "fast life," to party, and to use drugs and alcohol. Burglars have developed these needs from their street culture that emphasizes partying as the most important purpose of life (Wright and Decker, 1994).

The opportunity for committing burglary largely comes from the frequent *absence of capable guardians.* Capable guardians are people whose presence deters others from committing crime. Members of a family can become capable guardians against burglary simply by being present in their home. But there is no guardian-ship against burglary in many homes when husbands and wives go to work and children go to school. Moreover, the lack of community integration, as indicated by the absence of many neighbors watching each other's homes, reduces the neigh-bors' capability as antiburglary guardians (Lynch and Cantor, 1992).

Shoplifting

Shoplifting has become a scary word, conjuring up an image of thieves mingling with customers. Who wants to shop at a store known to be crawling with thieves? Understandably, store owners, to avoid frightening away customers, euphemistically refer to shoplifting as "shrinkage." Whatever it is called, shoplifting has become a serious problem in the United States. It costs U.S. shops about $13 billion a year. This is roughly equivalent to 2 percent of their total merchandise, compared with 1.5 percent for shops in Canada and less than 1 percent in Japan (Clarke, 2002; Adler, 2002; *The Economist,* 1991). Ultimately, however, it is the honest customers who are forced to pay for the cost of shoplifting because prices of goods are routinely raised to reduce the loss from shrinkage.

Social Profile: Shoplifters

Only a few shoplifters are *boosters,* professional criminals who shoplift for profit. Most shoplifters are *snitches,* amateurs who steal articles of small value for personal use.

Shoplifting is predominantly a juvenile offense. Individuals under age 21 are most likely to shoplift and, among these young people, those between ages 11 and 15 shoplift the most. This explains the increased incidence of shoplifting on nonschool days, afternoons and evenings, and late in the week, from Wednesday through Saturday. The youth of the common shoplifters further explains why the items most often stolen include beauty products, music CDs and movie videos, and apparel from athletic shoes to designer clothing.

The incidence of shoplifting is lowest for people above age 50. Still, older shoplifters are more often featured in newspaper and magazines than their numbers warrant, because they can offer heartrending stories like, "I'm tired of eating dog food, and I felt like eating a decent piece of meat." It is also extremely rare for movie stars and other celebrities to shoplift, but the few that are charged with the offense make headlines. They, unlike ordinary folks, are said to lack the intent to steal because they "unfortunately" suffer from kleptomania, a neurotic impulse to steal.

The general public seems to believe that shoplifting is mostly a female crime. Some criminologists have also assumed the same thing. But this assumption was based on old studies that dealt with *apprehended* shoplifters only. Apprehended shoplifters do not represent the population of shoplifters, most of whom are not caught by the police. In more recent studies, when random samples of ordinary people were asked whether they had shoplifted, men turned out to be more likely than women to commit the crime.

The lower class, the unemployed, the homeless, and drug addicts also have clearly higher rates of shoplifting. As for race, African Americans are more likely than whites to shoplift in cases where the items taken are relatively expensive, while whites are more inclined to take things of little value.

Sources: Adler, 2002; Clarke, 2002; Klemke, 1992.

Causes of Shoplifting

Like other property crimes, shoplifting can be explained by criminal motivation and opportunity. But a unique configuration of motivations and opportunities differentiates shoplifting from other crimes.

There are both economic and social psychological motivations for shoplifting. As for economic motivations, poverty is a factor, as suggested by the evidence that poor people are more likely than others to shoplift and that shoplifting becomes more common when unemployment is high. But severe economic hardship alone cannot explain most cases of shoplifting. In fact, many shoplifters are merely *frugal customers*, who can afford to buy the things they need, but are driven to steal by a desire to stretch their budget through bargain hunting, as encouraged by the consumption-driven society. Also, many young shoplifters commit the offense because they do not have the money to buy designer jeans, fancy shoes, and other fashionable items that enhance peer acceptance (Klemke, 1992).

Of the social psychological motivations for shoplifters, the most common is the *sense of thrill, excitement,* or *fun* that shoplifters expect to experience when committing the crime. Another important motivation is the *desire for social acceptance,* which makes youngsters, in particular, highly vulnerable to peer pressure. When asked why they shoplift, many would say "because my friends are doing it." A third motivation is a cluster of *rationalizations* that the shoplifter can use to justify the crime before committing it. Thus, many shoplifters deny responsibility (saying, for example, "My friends make me do it" or "I'm high or drunk"); deny injury to the victim ("It's only a cheap bottle of perfume" or "It's such a big store they won't miss it"); or argue that the victim deserves it ("It serves them right because they rip us off every time we buy something from them"). Armed with these rationalizations, shoplifters are able to decriminalize their offense, thereby continuing to see themselves as respectable, law-abiding citizens rather than as criminals (Klemke, 1992).

Those economic and social psychological motivations seem by themselves powerful enough to cause people to shoplift because the opportunities for shoplifting are so available to everybody. Anyone can, without any difficulty, walk into a store as a prospective shoplifter in the guise of a customer. And the risk of being apprehended for shoplifting is minimal, thanks to the laxness of law-enforcement against such offense. Even when a shoplifter is caught, most stores are reluctant to press charges for fear of publicity and possible liability over false arrest (Adler, 2002).

Organized Crime

The entertainment media, through vehicles like the movie *The Godfather,* first shown more than 30 years ago, often romanticizes mobsters as men of honor, courage, and toughness, but it also sensationalizes them as ruthless killers. Actually, the participants in organized crime, like the average Americans, try to achieve the American Dream, except by using more socially disreputable, deviant means. Let's take a closer look at organized crime.

Organizational Structure

There are many different organized crime groups in the United States, each consisting of members of the same race or ethnicity. The best known and most powerful is *the Mafia,* also called *la Cosa Nostra, the mob,* or *the syndicate.* Composed mostly of Italian Americans, the Mafia is a relatively loose, informal confederation of diverse groups of professional criminals operating independently in large cities around the country. Each group is known to law enforcers as a crime family identified by the name of its founder, such as Genovese, Gambino, or Bonanno. Each family consists of a *hierarchical structure* of positions, ranging from the highest to the lowest as follows: "don" or boss, underboss, lieutenants, counselor, and "soldiers" or button men (so-called because they do the bidding of the higher-ranking members when the latter "push the button"). The boss of each family directs the criminal activities of the members of his family.

Members are governed by *a code of conduct.* The most important rules in the code concern *loyalty* ("Be loyal to the family") and secrecy ("Don't squeal on fellow members"). If these rules are violated, the individual will be murdered. That's why the U.S. government has to spend an enormous sum of money on the witness-protection program, providing informers with new identities, houses in different locations, and new jobs.

Those two basic characteristics of organization—a well-defined hierarchy of positions and a code of conduct—also exist, with some variation, in many other ethnic crime groups, such as those dominated by African Americans, Hispanic Americans, and Asian Americans. But these ethnic gangs not only differ among themselves but also from the Italian-American Mafia in regard to the nature of their deviant activities.

Organized Crime Activities

The largest criminal organization is the 6,000-strong Herrera family founded by immigrants from Mexico, operating mostly in Southern California. They are notorious for smuggling heroin into the United States. Then there are some 200 Colombian crime families in Florida who engage in cocaine smuggling. Chinese, Vietnamese, Korean, and Japanese gangs have been found on the East and West Coasts, active in smuggling drugs and extorting money from businesses in their communities. Scores of other groups can be found in various cities: Israelis dominating insurance fraud in Los Angeles, Cubans running illegal gambling operations in Miami, Canadians engaging in gun-smuggling and money-laundering in Miami, Russians carrying out extortion and contract murders in New York, and so on (Kleinknecht, 1996; President's Commission, 1986). Despite their differences, all these groups have one thing in common: They specialize in one or two forms of economic deviance while confining their operation to a limited area, usually an ethnic community. In contrast, Italian-American crime groups operate *all over the country,* engaging in a *variety* of deviant activities, such as those disclosed below.

Selling Illegal Goods and Services.   The illegal goods and services sold by the Mafia include illicit gambling, loan sharking, and narcotics. *Illicit gambling* includes betting on horse races, lotteries, and sporting events. But it has become less profitable today because of the increasing legalization of lotteries and off-track betting. In the early 1990s illicit gambling brought in only about $2 billion a year, which was small potatoes in view of the Mafia's annual income of at least $60 billion (Angelo, 1992; President's Commission, 1986).

Far more profitable is *loan sharking,* the lending of money at exorbitantly high rates, typically more than 100 percent a year. In fact, when the economy is in a depression or recession, hordes of businesspeople and bill-payers are forced to borrow money from loan sharks at up to between 200 and 300 percent annual interest. Since customers can put up only their bodies as security for the loan (if they had valuable property, they would have gone to a legitimate loan company), it seems logical that the loan sharks may resort to violence or the threat of violence to ensure repayment. But the loan sharks hardly need to threaten violence, let alone actually use it, because they already have a bad *reputation* for being violent, which is enough to scare the borrowers (Block, 1991).

In the field of *illicit drugs,* the Italian-American Mafia operates for maximum profit at minimum risk of interference from law enforcers. They restrict their activities to importing and wholesale distribution, letting independent drug pushers take over the risky business of selling narcotics on the street. The narcotics trade is the most lucrative source of revenues for organized crime. Not surprisingly, the "new Mafias"—consisting of African Americans, Asians, or Hispanics—rely on drug trafficking as their *primary* source of income.

Engaging in Large-Scale Thefts and Racketeering.   The Mafia steals in a big way. Small-scale thefts such as holdups and burglaries are left to independent criminals. The mob turns to wholesale operations instead: They steal huge quantities of negotiable stocks and bonds as well as credit cards and airline tickets, whole carloads of merchandise (sometimes with the car itself) from docks, railway stations, and international airports, and millions of dollars' worth of automobiles, which they furnish with proper engine identification numbers and registration papers necessary for selling them. To sell these "hot" items, they have fences who work like big-time merchandising operators.

Another form of organized crime activity is known as racketeering. It may take the simple form of a "protection racket," which involves the extortion of money from legitimate businesspeople. They are given the proverbial offer they cannot refuse: The sale of the mob's "insurance policy" against such "accidents" as the burning of their stores and the breaking of their store windows or their heads—to be carried out by the mobsters if the businesspeople refuse to buy the "insurance." The more elaborate and more common form is *labor racketeering.* This involves the manipulation of workers' employers and unions. Racketeers may forcibly offer businesspeople a "sweetheart contract," whereby the employers pay them a fee for having their employees join the racketeers' nonexistent union; extort money from employers by threatening them with labor strife; or demand that the employing company put their relatives on the company's payroll.

Corrupting Public Officials.   To help ensure success in all the above patterns of activities, it may be necessary to corrupt the appropriate public officials. The mob usually targets three kinds of officials: law enforcers, politicians, and officials in licensing, supervisory, or regulatory agencies (Block, 1991). The manner of corruption is outright bribery or, in the case of politicians, contribution to a political campaign. The goal is to have their "political front person" pass laws favoring their interests and prevent the passage of laws damaging to their illegal activities, to have the police and other law enforcers ignore their criminal activities, or to get regulatory agencies to turn a blind eye to their illegal way of operating legitimate businesses—such as threatening competitors with violence.

Infiltrating Legitimate Businesses.   This activity is the most profitable and yet the safest for the mobsters to engage in. The types of businesses that they have infiltrated include Las Vegas casinos, nightclubs and restaurants, hotels and motels, trucking companies, wholesale food distributors, as well as the industries of banking and investment, insurance, real estate, electronics, health services, stock brokerage, and prepaid telephone cards. The Mafia's penetration into these legitimate businesses is so deep that many law-abiding citizens routinely deal with it. Even the FBI, always busy fighting organized crime, once unknowingly hired a mob's moving company (Raab, 1997; President's Commission, 1986). By acquiring any one of those legitimate businesses, the mobsters aim to achieve certain objectives: to gain respectability, to establish a legitimate source of income for paying taxes and thus avoid income tax prosecution, to invest "bad" money (from racketeering and other illegal activities) in a legitimate business for legitimate profit, and to use the legitimate business as a front for carrying out illegitimate schemes.

The most common objective of entering a legitimate business is the last one because it produces the most profit. An illegitimate scheme may involve insurance fraud: Taking over businesses and then hiring professional arsonists to burn buildings and their contents in order to then collect on the fire insurance. Increasingly, to avoid detection by law enforcers, the Mafia has resorted to the more sophisticated methods of fraud typically used by white-collar and corporate criminals like those we discussed in the preceding chapter.

Ethnicity and Organized Crime

The roots of organized crime reach deep into the American past. During the eighteenth century, there were pirates at many U.S. ports and rivers, as well as robbers, gamblers, and slave-snatchers operating mostly in the rural, frontier settings. The frontier lawlessness continued to reign throughout the nineteenth century. It spawned such legendary train- and bank-robbery gangs as the Reno brothers and the Jesse James gang.

Toward the end of the last century, many criminal gangs began to emerge in the cities. The major ones were Irish, Jewish, and Italian, but these three groups were not equally powerful at the same time. The Irish dominated the organized crime scene in the first two decades of this century, controlling large cities' political machinery and such industries as construction, trucking, public utilities, and the waterfront. Then, in the 1920s, the Jews took over the dominant position in organized crime, controlling gambling and labor racketeering. In the same decade Prohibition (the law against the manufacture and sale of liquor) began to prepare the Italians to succeed the Jews. By the end of Prohibition in the early 1930s, the Italians were firmly in control of organized crime. In fact, Italian dominance has continued to this day, largely because of Prohibition.

Prohibition ushered in a new era of organized crime. Before Prohibition, criminal groups were mostly local in the scope and extent of their activities, confined to single ethnic neighborhoods. During and after Prohibition, however, the Italian gangs went beyond the local setting to control criminal activities of more extensive territories—covering the entire country. Prohibition brought this about by making bootlegging a complex, large-scale operation. The illicit alcohol had to be manufactured, transported, and distributed to thousands of retail outlets across the country. Successful bootlegging required complex operations involving huge breweries and distillers, giant warehouses, fleets of tank cars and trucks, and protection from hijackers. It also required the bribery and cooperation of the Coast Guard, customs officials, politicians, and police. Since the liquor came from Europe or Canada, it further required international as well as interstate connections (Hills, 1980; Homer, 1974).

All this explains why the Mafia is the only crime group that exists in all the major U.S. cities today. But, since the early 1980s, the Mafia has lost some of its dominance over the underworld. The country's most celebrated Mafia boss in recent years, John Gotti, was finally convicted and sentenced to prison. Virtually all of the other Mafia bosses have also been put away. Every single one of the nation's 24 Mafia families has some members now doing time. The Mafia has also suffered severe internal problems. Threatened with long imprisonment unless they talk, many mafiosi are willing to violate the organization's sacred code of "omerta" (silence or secrecy) by testifying in court against fellow members. The Mafia membership is also shrinking because the crime families' children and grandchildren prefer to pursue conventional careers as lawyers, doctors, or businesspeople. Given all these problems plaguing the Mafia, criminal gangs of other ethnicities that have emerged over the last three decades are tempted to move in on the lucrative crime markets that the Italians have monopolized for the last 60 years (Corliss and Crittle, 2004; Griffin, 2003; Kleinknecht, 1996; Reuter, 1995).

But it will take some time for some of the new ethnic gangs to wrest the underworld leadership from the Italians. The history of ethnic succession in organized crime—the leadership first held by the Irish, then by the Jews, and finally by the Italians—suggests that an ethnic gang has to go through at least four stages before it can attain supremacy in the U.S. underworld. In the first stage, common street criminals get together to *form gangs in their own ethnic neighborhood* where they extort or otherwise victimize its residents. In the second stage, confined to the same area, different gangs are compelled to *compete with one another* in dominating the local crime scene. Frequent violent conflict occurs, including murders. In the third stage, the gangs *resolve their conflict* by forming a larger crime organization that allocates turfs to gangs and settles intergang disputes by peaceful means. The organization, stronger than each individual gang, is powerful enough to move its crime operations beyond the ethnic neighborhood and into the larger society. In the fourth stage, various ethnic crime organizations fight with one another, resulting in the emergence of *one ethnic organization as the victor,* which then dominates the underworld across the country. This is what the Italians have been doing since they became victorious over the Jews and Irish in the 1930s (O'Kane, 1992).

Today, African, Hispanic, Asian American, and other gangs are stuck in the second stage, as shown by the constant conflicts among ethnic gangs in their own ethnic neighborhoods. Most of the conflicts are drug-related, because the new ethnic gangs typically rely on drug trafficking as the primary source of their income. This is reminiscent of the 1930s when the Italians were also in the second stage, finding themselves locked in a liquor war comparable to the drug war of today. In fact, the new ethnic gangs seem to have taken over drug trafficking and other traditional street crime activities but only in their own ethnic communities, as the Italians did in the 1930s. But none of these new ethnic gangs—or the nonethnic motorcycle gangs—has managed to have the Mafia's success in developing a diversified portfolio that includes not just drug trafficking but many other crime activities throughout the country (Kleinknecht, 1996; Nordland, 1992). In short, the Mafia has been losing its power, but no other ethnic crime organization has emerged to replace it as the dominant force in organized crime.

The War on Organized Crime in the United States

In the 1980s the federal government began in earnest to crack down on organized crime. Special strike forces were set up in 26 cities to arrest and prosecute numerous mobsters and seize their assets. This was done by pulling together the resources of the Justice Department's lawyers; the FBI; the Drug Enforcement Administration; the Department of Labor; the Internal Revenue Service; the Customs and Postal Services; and the Bureau of Alcohol, Tobacco, and Firearms in order to ensure that the mobsters did not slip through the law-enforcement cracks. These federal agents also had the cooperation of local police, a far cry from the situation in the past when they distrusted each other and often collided in their organized-crime investigations. President Ronald Reagan also helped out by removing the limits on court-ordered wiretaps. With these electronic weapons, federal agents were able to listen in on countless conversations among mobsters in their cars, social clubs, and other places where they met. The federal agents were even successful in using the threat of heavy sentences to pressure many mafiosi to violate their crime family's centuries-old tradition of silence by testifying against their former partners. These turncoats were mostly the new generation, who found a long prison sentence too stiff a price to pay for family loyalty.

Because of the combination of all these factors, the war on organized crime showed impressive results. In only four years, from 1981 to 1985, 2,554 mafiosi were prosecuted and 809 convicted (Magnuson, 1986). The campaign against organized crime has been even more successful in the 1990s, as none of the nation's 24 Mafia families escaped successful prosecution (Nordland, 1992). By 2004 the bosses of four of New York's Mafia families have been convicted or imprisoned, with the last, fifth boss awaiting trial (Corliss and Crittle, 2004).

All this has undoubtedly dealt a serious blow to the Mafia. But it does not signal the death of organized crime. Those members of the crime families who have escaped the dragnet are now much more careful in concealing their activities and identities. They have begun to shift increasingly to more sophisticated, less detectable white-collar crimes (Raab, 1997, 1994). They have also stopped attracting public attention by shedding their former flamboyant lifestyles. It is doubtful that they would again behave like the mobster who turned himself into "a one-man parade" everywhere he went and impressed others by tipping a bartender $100 just for keeping the ice cubes cold (Pileggi, 1986).

Perhaps most important to the future, it seems impossible to stamp out organized crime because the two basic social causes of such deviance remain: (1) a strong demand for illicit drugs and other vices or a great opportunity for illicit gain in the white-collar and corporate world, and (2) a contingent of the ambitious poor or immigrants who cannot achieve the American Dream the conventional way.

Global Perspective: Organized Crime

A tour of the underworld in Italy, Japan, Hong Kong, and Russia reveals that organized crime in these countries resembles that in the United States in some ways but differs in other ways.

Like in the United States, organized crime is a crooked way for the ambitious poor youth to get rich. For example, recruits for the *Yakuza*, the crime family in Japan, are mostly lower-class youths who have been rejected by the business world. They include school dropouts, drug users, and members of motorcycle gangs. Before being initiated into the Yakuza, these social rejects must undergo an apprenticeship that usually lasts five years. They learn the values and customs of the syndicate, such as taking responsibility for one's failure by cutting off the little pinkie or, more important, being absolutely loyal to the boss, who is considered more important than one's wife and children, or life itself. At the end of the apprenticeship, the recruits join the Yakuza and earn four times as much as the average salaried person.

Organized crime is basically the same in most countries in that it is a hierarchical organization in which lower-level members are relatively obedient and loyal to their leaders. Members of the crime syndicate called Triad in Hong Kong, for example, have sworn absolute loyalty to the organization 36 times during the initiation ceremony so that they will always remember they have only two choices in their lives—loyalty to the Triad or death. Thus they are likely to become absolutely loyal, knowing that disloyalty is punishable by death. The exception is the organized crime in Russia. It is rife with distrust and betrayal, with members who are willing to sell out to the police to save their own skins.

The crime syndicate is unpredictable and volatile enough to project an image of *disorganized* rather than organized crime.

Organized crime in Russia is nonetheless more pervasive, influential, or powerful than in the United States. A large majority of commercial banks and private enterprises in Russia's major cities, for example, are forced to pay a tribute of 10 to 20 percent of their profit to organized crime. The reason is apparently economic: The capitalism in Russia is less mature than that in the United States so that organized crime in Russia is less controllable and more pervasive. Organized crime in Italy, Japan, and Hong Kong is also more pervasive than that in the United States, but the reason is mostly cultural: Organized crime in those foreign countries is more socially acceptable and integrated into the legitimate world of business and politics. In Italy, victims of robbery have a much greater chance of getting their possessions back if they seek help from the Mafia than if they go to the police. In Japan, the Yakuza is heavily involved not only in banking and other legitimate businesses but also in politics, as businesspeople and politicians actively seek out Yakuza as clients and providers of unique and essential services. In Hong Kong, the Triad has similarly penetrated into legitimate businesses.

Due to the underworld's deeper penetration into the conventional upperworld in those countries, it is extremely difficult, if not impossible, to get rid of organized crime. Given its limited influence in U.S. society, though, American authorities are more successful in keeping it under their thumb.

Sources: Thio, 2004; Friedman, 1999; Kaplan, 1998; Nicastro, 1992.

Summary

1. What are the characteristics of robbery? Robbery has the characteristics of both a property and a violent crime. As a property crime, robbery is a rational act, which involves making rational decisions about the execution of a robbery. As a violent crime, robbery is carried out with actual or potential violence against the victim; unarmed or strong-arm robbery involves actual violence, while armed robbery involves potential violence.

2. What are the patterns of robbery? Most robberies are committed in large cities, during the cold winter months, and most occur out-doors. While bank robbery is relatively rare, it has increased significantly. Most robberies are armed, and robberies are more interracial than such violent crimes as homicide and rape.

3. How do amateur robbers differ from professional robbers? The amateurs are generally younger, and tend to commit robbery for smaller sums of money with less planning and skill and a higher risk of arrest. In addition, professional robbers have a stronger commitment to robbery as a way of earning a living and see their crime as an honest enterprise. **What causes robbery?** According to sociological theories, the causes of robbery are relative deprivation in the lower classes and economic abundance in the larger society.

4. What are the characteristics of auto theft and carjacking? Most auto thieves steal cars for the purpose of selling them for a quick and handsome profit. While a great majority of auto thieves quietly steal cars left alone by their owners, a few thieves resort to violence by hijacking cars. **What causes auto theft and increase in carjacking?** The causes of auto theft include inadequate law enforcement against car theft, profitability of stolen cars and auto parts, and insurance fraud. The increased sophistication of the car's security devices is an additional factor behind the upsurge in carjacking.

5. How do burglars go about breaking and entering? They try to avoid confrontations with victims by breaking into empty houses, which explains why most burglaries occur during the day when people go out to work rather than during the night. **What causes burglary?** The causes include the offender's expressive needs for maintaining a fast life, partying, and using drugs and alcohol, and the deviant opportunity provided by the frequent absence of capable guardians against burglary.

6. What is the social profile of shoplifters? Shoplifters are mostly young people under age 21. They are more likely to be men and to be lower class, unemployed, homeless, or addicted to drugs. **What causes shoplifting?** Causes of shoplifting include economic motivations such as being poor and trying to be frugal and social psychological motivations such as the desires for thrill, social acceptance, and rationalizations.

7. What is the nature of organized crime as an organization? It has a well-defined hierarchy of positions and a code of conduct governing the behavior of members. **What crime activities do organized criminals participate in?** While most ethnic crime groups specialize in drug trafficking or only a few crimes, the Italian-American Mafia gets involved in many diverse deviances that include selling illegal goods and services, engaging in large-scale thefts and racketeering, corrupting public officials, and infiltrating legitimate businesses.

8. How is ethnicity associated with organized crime? Toward the end of the last century, the most powerful crime groups were Irish, Jewish, and Italian. Organized crime was first dominated by the Irish, then by the Jews, and finally, beginning in the 1930s, by the Italians. Prohibition—the period in which alcohol was made illegal—helped the Italians develop a nationwide dominance of organized crime, which continues to this day. Since the early 1980s, pressure from law enforcement has chipped away the Italian dominance, and other ethnic groups, particularly African, Hispanic, and Asian Americans, have emerged. But the Italian Mafia still retains its nationwide leadership in the underworld.

9. How has the U.S. government dealt with organized crime? Since the early 1980s, the federal government has consolidated its various law-enforcement efforts—with impressive results—toward putting organized crime out of business. Numerous mobsters, and their bosses, have been successfully prosecuted and put away. But the demise of organized crime is doubtful because the criminals tend to become more careful in concealing their activities and identities—and, perhaps most important, the basic social causes of organized crime continue to exist.

10. Is organized crime the same or different in various countries? It is basically the same in some ways, such as serving as a means for the ambitious poor to achieve success and operating as a hierarchical organization in which the rank and file swear their loyalty to their leaders. But organized crime is more pervasive and powerful in other countries than in the United States. Government attempts to crack down on organized crime are, therefore, less successful in other countries.

FURTHER READING

Albanese, Jay S., Dilip K. Das, and Arvind Verma (eds.). 2003. *Organized Crime: World Perspectives*. Upper Saddle River, N.J.: Prentice Hall. A collection of articles on the concept of organized crime, its nature and extent, and the methods of dealing with it in 20 different countries on all continents.

Block, Alan A. (ed.). 1991. *The Business of Crime: A Documentary Study of Organized Crime in the American Economy*. Boulder, Colo.: Westview. A collection of government reports on organized crime's infiltration and control of garment, air freight, waste disposal, and other industries.

Cromwell, Paul E., James N. Olson, and D'Aunn Wester Avary. 1991. *Breaking and Entering: An Ethnographic Analysis of Burglary*. Newbury Park, Calif.: Sage Publications. A thoroughgoing look into the world of burglary.

Handelman, Stephen. 1995. *Comrade Criminal: Russia's New Mafiya*. New Haven, Conn.: Yale University Press. Offers a guide to the frontierlike, ruthless, and chaotic world of organized crime in Russia.

Jacobs, Bruce A. 2000. *Robbing Drug Dealers: Violence beyond the Law*. New York: Aldine de Gruyter. An ethnographic analysis of what motivates robbers to stick up drug dealers and how they choose their targets, carry out the robbery, and deal with the retaliation from the victim.

Kenney, Dennis J., and James O. Finckenauer. 1995. *Organized Crime in America*. Belmont, Calif.: Wadsworth. A textbook on organized crime, covering its history, crime activities, and association with various groups of Americans, as well as the attempts to deal with organized crime.

Kleinknecht, William. 1996. *The New Ethnic Mobs: The Changing Face of Organized Crime in America*. New York: Free Press. A detailed presentation of organized crime among various ethnic minorities in the United States.

Klemke, Lloyd W. 1992. *The Sociology of Shoplifting: Boosters and Snitches Today*. Westport, Conn.: Praeger. A comprehensive theoretical and empirical analysis of various aspects of shoplifting.

O'Kane, James M. 1992. *The Crooked Ladder: Gangsters, Ethnicity, and the American Dream*. New Brunswick, N.J.: Transaction. An analysis of how a succession of ethnic minorities has been using organized crime to climb the ladder of success in the United States.

Rengert, George F., and John Wasilchick. 2000. *Suburban Burglary: A Tale of Two Suburbs*, 2d ed. Springfield, Ill.: Charles C Thomas. An empirical analysis of how burglars choose which communities and houses to break into.

Shover, Neal. 1996. *Great Pretenders: Pursuits and Careers of Persistent Thieves*. Boulder, Colo.: Westview. An ethnographic analysis of the experiences of criminals who persist in pursuing an unsuccessful career of committing robbery, burglary, and other property crimes.

Tunnell, Kenneth D. 1992. *Choosing Crime: The Criminal Calculus of Property Offenders*. Chicago: Nelson-Hall. An empirical study of robbers, burglars, auto thieves, and other property offenders with a focus on how they have come up with their motivation and decision to commit the crime.

Wright, Richard T., and Scott H. Decker. 1994. *Burglars on the Job: Streetlife and Residential Break-ins*. Boston: Northeastern University Press. A close-up analysis of how burglars do their crime and live their lives.

Wright, Richard T., and Scott H. Decker. 1997. *Armed Robbers in Action: Stickups and Street Culture*. Boston: Northeastern University Press. A detailed ethnographic analysis of how street robbers go about deciding to rob, choosing targets, and carrying out the offense.

CRITICAL THINKING QUESTIONS

1. Given what you have learned about robbery, how would you go about preventing robbery in your community?

2. Do you agree or disagree that it is impossible to get rid of organized crime? Why?

15

Serial Murder: Popular Myths and Empirical Realities

JAMES ALAN FOX AND JACK LEVIN

Since the early 1980s, Americans have become more aware of and concerned about a particularly dangerous class of murderers, known as serial killers. Characterized by the tendency to kill repeatedly (at least three or four victims) and often with increasing brutality, serial killers stalk their victims, one at a time, for weeks, months, or years, generally not stopping until they are caught.

The term *serial killer* was first used in the early 1980s (see Jenkins, 1994), although the phenomenon of repeat killing existed, of course, throughout recorded history. In the late 1800s, for example, Hermann Webster Mudgett (aka H. H. Holmes) murdered dozens of attractive young women in his Chicago "house of death," and the infamous Jack the Ripper stalked the streets of London, killing five prostitutes. Prior to the 1980s, repeat killers such as Mudgett and Jack the Ripper were generally described as mass murderers. The need for a special classification for repeat killers was later recognized because of the important differences between multiple murderers who kill simultaneously and those who kill serially (Levin & Fox, 1985). *Mass killers*—those who slaughter their victims in one event—tend to target people they know (e.g., family members or coworkers), often for the sake of revenge, using an efficient weapon of mass destruction (e.g., a high-powered firearm). As we shall describe below, serial murderers are different in all these respects, typically killing total strangers with their hands to achieve a sense of power and control over others.

A rising concern with serial killing has spawned a number of media presentations, resulting in the perpetrators of this type of murder becoming a regular staple of U.S. popular culture. A steady diet of television and movie productions could lead viewers to believe that serial killing is a common type of homicide. An increasing interest in serial homicide, however, has not been limited solely to the lay public. During the past two decades, the number, as well as the mix, of scholars devoting their attention to this crime has dramatically changed. Until the early 1980s, the literature exploring aspects of multiple homicide consisted almost exclusively of bizarre and atypical case studies contributed by forensic psychiatrists pertaining to their court-assigned clients. More recently, there has been a sig-

Author's Note: We contributed equally to this work; the order of authorship was determined alphabetically. We wish to acknowledge the able assistance of Stephanie Flagg.

Source: M. Dwayne Smith and Margaret A. Zahn (eds.), *Homicide: A Sourcebook of Social Research* (Thousand Oaks, CA: Sage, 1999), pp. 167–175. © 1999 by Sage Publications, Inc. Reprinted by permission of Sage Publications Inc.

nificant shift toward social scientists examining the cultural and social forces underlying the late 20th-century rise in serial murder as well as law enforcement operatives developing research-based investigative tools for tracking and apprehending serial offenders.

Author's Note: We contributed equally to this work; the order of authorship was determined alphabetically. We wish to acknowledge the able assistance of Stephanie Flagg.

Despite the shift in disciplinary focus, some basic assumptions of psychiatry appear to remain strong in the public mind. In particular, it is widely believed that the serial killer acts as a result of some individual pathology produced by traumatic childhood experiences. At the same time, a developing law enforcement perspective holds that the serial killer is a nomadic, sexual sadist who operates with a strict pattern to victim selection and crime scene behavior; this model has also contributed to myopic thinking in responding to serial murder. Unfortunately, these assumptions from both psychiatry and law enforcement may have retarded the development of new and more effective approaches to understanding this phenomenon. In an attempt to present a more balanced view, this chapter examines (serially, of course) several myths about serial killing/killers, some long-standing and others of recent origin, that have been embraced more on faith than on hard evidence.

Myth 1: There is an Epidemic of Serial Murder in the United States

Although interest in serial murder has unquestionably grown, the same may not necessarily be true for the incidence of this crime itself. Curiously enough, there may actually be more scholars studying serial murder than there are offenders committing it. Regrettably, it is virtually impossible to measure with any degree of precision the prevalence of serial murder today, or even less so to trace its long-term trends. One thing for certain, however, is that the problem is nowhere near epidemic proportions (Jenkins, 1994). . . .

The lack of any hard evidence concerning the prevalence of serial homicide has not prevented speculation within both academic and law enforcement fields. The "serial killer panic of 1983–85," as it has been described by Jenkins (1988), was fueled by some outrageous and unsupportable statistics promulgated by the U.S. Department of Justice to buttress its claim that the extent of serial murder was on the rise. Apparently, some government officials reasoned that because the number of unsolved homicides had surged from several hundred per year in the early 1960s to several thousand per year in the 1980s, the aggregate body count produced by serial killers could be as high as 5,000 annually (Fox & Levin, 1985). Unfortunately, this gross exaggeration was endorsed in some academic publications as well (see Egger, 1984; Holmes & DeBurger, 1988).

More sober thinking on the prevalence issue has occurred in recent years (Egger, 1990, 1998; Holmes & Holmes, 1998). Although still subject to the methodological limitations noted above in the identification of serial crimes, Hickey has attempted the most exhaustive measurement of the prevalence and trends in serial murder. In contrast to the Justice Department's estimate of thousands of victims annually, Hickey enumerated only 2,526 to 3,860 victims slain by 399 serial killers between 1800 and 1995. Moreover, between 1975 and 1995, the highest levels in the two centuries, Hickey identified only 153 perpetrators and as many as 1,400 victims, for an average annual tally of far less than 100 victims. Although Hickey's data collection strategy obviously ignored undetected cases, the extent of the problem is likely less than 1% of homicides in the country. Of course, that as much as 1% of the nation's murder problem can potentially be traced to but a few dozen individuals reminds us of the extreme deadliness of their predatory behavior.

Myth 2: Serial Killers are Unusual in Appearance and Lifestyle

As typically portrayed, television and cinematic versions of serial killers are either sinister-appearing creatures of the night or brilliant-but-evil master criminals. In reality, however, most tend to fit neither of these descriptions. Serial killers are generally White males in their late 20s or 30s who span a broad range of human qualities including appearance and intelligence.

Some serial killers are high school dropouts, and others might indeed be regarded as unappealing by conventional standards. At the same time, a few actually possess brilliance, charm, and attractiveness. Most serial killers, however, are fairly average, at least to the casual observer. In short, they are "extraordinarily ordinary"; ironically, part of the secret of their success is that they do not stand out in a crowd or attract negative attention to themselves. Instead, many of them look and act much like "the boy next door"; they hold full-time jobs, are married or involved in some other stable relationship, and are members of various local community groups. The one trait that tends to separate prolific serial killers from the norm is that they are exceptionally skillful in their presentation of self so that they appear beyond suspicion. This is part of the reason why they are so difficult to apprehend (Levin & Fox, 1985).

A related misconception is that serial killers, lacking stable employment or family responsibilities, are full-time predators who roam far and wide, often crossing state and regional boundaries in their quest for victims. Evidence to the contrary notwithstanding, serial killers have frequently been characterized as nomads whose compulsion to kill carries them hundreds of thousands of miles a year as they drift from state to state and region to region leaving scores of victims in their wake. This may be true of a few well-known and well-traveled individuals, but not for the vast majority of serial killers (Levin & Fox, 1985). According to Hickey (1997), only about a third of the serial killers in his database crossed state lines in their murder sprees. John Wayne Gacy, for example, killed all of his 33 young male victims at his Des Plaines, Illinois, home, conveniently burying most of them there as well. Gacy had a job, friends, and family but secretly killed on a part-time, opportunistic basis.

Myth 3: Serial Killers are all Insane

What makes serial killers so enigmatic—so irrational to many casual observers—is that they generally kill not for love, money, or revenge but for the fun of it. That is, they delight in the thrill, the sexual satisfaction, or the dominance that they achieve as they squeeze the last breath of life from their victims. At a purely superficial level, killing for the sake of pleasure seems nothing less than "crazy."

The basis for the serial killer's pursuit of pleasure is found in a strong tendency toward sexual sadism and an interest reflected in detailed fantasies of domination. Serial killers tie up their victims to watch them squirm and torture their victims to hear them scream. They rape, mutilate, sodomize, and degrade their victims to feel powerful, dominant, and superior.

Many individuals may have fantasies about torture and murder but are able to restrain themselves from ever translating their sadistic dreams into reality. Those who do not contain their urges to kill repeatedly for no apparent motive are assumed to suffer from some extreme form of mental illness. Indeed, some serial killers have clearly been driven by psychosis, such as Herbert Mullen of Santa Cruz, California, who killed 13 people during a 4-month period to avert an earthquake—at least that is what the voices commanded him to do (the voices also ordered him to burn his penis with a cigarette).

In either a legal or a medical sense, however, most serial killers are not insane or psychotic (see Levin & Fox, 1985; Leyton, 1986). They know right from wrong, know exactly what they are doing, and can control their desire to kill—but choose not to. They are more cruel than crazy. Their crimes may be sickening, but their minds are not necessarily sick. Most apparently do not suffer from hallucinations, a profound thought disorder, or major depression. Indeed, those assailants who are deeply confused or disoriented are generally not capable of the level of planning and organization necessary to conceal their identity from the authorities and, therefore, do not amass a large victim count.

Many serial killers seem instead to possess a personality disorder known as sociopathy (or antisocial personality). They lack a conscience, are remorseless, and care exclusively for their own needs and desires. Other people are regarded merely as tools to be manipulated for the purpose of maximizing their personal pleasure. Thus, if given to perverse sexual fantasy, sociopaths simply feel uninhibited by societal rules or by conscience from literally chasing their dreams in any way necessary for their fulfillment. . . .

Myth 4: All Serial Killers are Sociopaths

Although many serial killers tend to be sociopaths, totally lacking in concern for their victims, some actually do have a conscience but are able to neutralize or negate their feelings of remorse by rationalizing their behavior. They feel as though they are doing something good for society, or at least nothing that bad.

Milwaukee's cannibalistic killer, Jeffrey Dahmer, for example, actually viewed his crimes as a sign of love and affection. He told Tracy Edwards, a victim who managed to escape, that if he played his cards right, he too could give his heart to Jeff. Dahmer meant it quite literally, of course, but according to Edwards, he said it affectionately, not threateningly.

The powerful psychological process of *dehumanization* allows many serial killers to slaughter scores of innocent people by viewing them as worthless and therefore expendable. To the dehumanizer, prostitutes are seen as mere sex machines, gays are AIDS carriers, nursing home patients are vegetables, and homeless alcoholics are nothing more than human trash.

In a process related to this concept of dehumanization, many serial killers compartmentalize the world into two groups—those whom they care about versus everyone else. "Hillside Strangler" Kenneth Bianchi, for example, could be kind and loving to his wife and child as well as to his mother and friends yet be vicious and cruel to those he considered meaningless. He and his cousin started with prostitutes, but later, when they grew comfortable with killing, branched out to middle-class targets.

Myth 5: Serial Killers are Inspired by Pornography

Could Theodore Bundy have been right in his death row claim that pornography turned him into a vicious killer, or was he just making excuses to deflect blame? It should be no surprise that the vast majority of serial killers do have a keen interest in pornography, particularly sadistic magazines and films (Ressler, Burgess, & Douglas, 1988). Sadism is the source of their greatest pleasure, and so, of course, they experience it vicariously in their spare time, when not on the prowl themselves. That is, a preoccupation with pornography is a reflection, not the cause, of their own sexual desires. At most, pornography may reinforce sadistic impulses, but it cannot create them.

There is experimental evidence that frequent and prolonged exposure to violent pornography tends to desensitize "normal" men to the plight of victims of sexual abuse (Malamuth & Donnerstein, 1984). In the case of serial killers, however, it takes much more than pornography to create such an extreme and vicious personality.

Myth 6: Serial Killers are Products of Bad Childhoods

Whenever the case of an infamous serial killer is uncovered, journalists and behavioral scientists alike tend to search for clues in the killer's childhood that might explain the seemingly senseless or excessively brutal murders. Many writers have emphasized, for example, Theodore Bundy's concerns about being illegitimate, and biographers of Hillside Strangler Kenneth Bianchi capitalized on his having been adopted. . . .

It is true that the biographies of most serial killers reveal significant physical and psychological trauma at an early age. For example, based on in-depth interviews with 36 incarcerated murderers, Ressler et al. (1988) found evidence of psychological abuse (e.g., public humiliation) in 23 cases and physical trauma in 13 cases. Hickey (1997) reported that among a group of 62 male serial killers, 48% had been rejected as children by a parent or some other important person in their lives. Of course, these same types of experiences can be found in the biographies of many "normal" people as well. More specifically, although useful for characterizing the backgrounds of serial killers, the findings presented by Ressler et al. and Hickey lack a comparison group drawn from nonoffending populations for which the same operational definitions of trauma have been applied. Therefore, it is impossible to conclude that serial killers have suffered as children to any greater extent than others. . . .

Some neurologists and a growing number of psychiatrists suggest that serial killers have incurred serious injury to the limbic region of the brain resulting from severe or repeated head trauma, generally during childhood. As an example, psychiatrist Dorothy Lewis and neurologist Jonathan Pincus, along with other colleagues (1986), examined 15 murderers on Florida's death row and found that all showed signs of neurological irregularities. In addition, psychologist Joel Norris (1988) reported excessive spinal fluid found in the brain scan of serial killer Henry Lee Lucas. Norris argued that this abnormality reflected the possible damage caused by an earlier blow or a series of blows to Lucas's head.

It is critical that we place in some perspective the many case studies that have been used in an attempt to connect extreme violence to neurological impairment. Absent from the case study approach is any indication of the prevalence of individuals who did not act violently despite a history of trauma. Indeed, if head trauma were as strong a contributor to serial murder as some suggest, then we would have many times more of these killers than we actually do.

It is also important to recognize that neurological impairment must occur in combination with a host of environmental conditions to place an individual at risk for extreme acts of brutality. Dorothy Lewis cautions, "The neuropsychiatric problems alone don't make you violent. Probably the environmental factors in and of themselves don't make you a violent person. But when you put them together, you create a very dangerous character" ("Serial Killers," 1992). Similarly, Ressler asserts that no single childhood problem indicates future criminality: "There are a whole pot of conditions that have to be met" for violence to be predictable (quoted in Meddis, 1987, p. 3A). Head trauma and abuse, therefore, may be important risk factors, but they are neither necessary nor sufficient to make someone a serial killer. Rather, they are part of a long list of circumstances—including adoption, shyness, disfigurement, speech impediments, learning and physical disabilities, abandonment, death of a parent, academic and athletic inadequacies—that may make a child feel frustrated and rejected enough to predispose, but not predestine, him or her toward extreme violence.

Because so much emphasis has been placed on early childhood, developmental factors in making the transition into adulthood and middle age are often overlooked. Serial killers tend to be in their late 20s and 30s, if not older, when they first show outward signs of murderous behavior. If only early childhood and biological predisposition were involved, why do they not begin killing as adolescents or young adults? Many individuals suffer as children, but only some of them continue to experience profound disappointment and detachment regarding family, friends, and work. For example, Danny Rolling, who murdered several college students in Gainesville, Florida, may have had a childhood filled with frustration and abuse, but his eight-victim murder spree did not commence until he was 36 years old. After experiencing a painful divorce, he drifted from job to job, from state to state, from prison to prison, and finally from murder to murder (Fox & Levin, 1996).

Myth 7: Serial Killers can be Identified in Advance

Predicting dangerousness, particularly in an extreme form such as serial homicide, has been an elusive goal for those investigators who have attempted it. For example, Lewis, Lovely, Yeager, and Femina (1989) suggest that the interaction of neurological/psychiatric impairment and a history of abuse predicts violent crime, better even than previous violence itself. Unfortunately, this conclusion was based on retrospective "postdiction" with a sample of serious offenders, rather than a prospective attempt to predict violence within a general cross section.

It is often said that "hindsight is 20/20." This is especially true for serial murder. Following the apprehension of a serial killer, we often hear mixed reports that "he seemed like a nice guy, but there was something about him that wasn't quite right." Of course, there is often something about most people that may not seem "quite right." When such a person is exposed to be a serial murderer, however, we tend to focus on those warning signs in character and biography that were previously ignored. Even the stench emanating from Jeffrey Dahmer's apartment, which he had convincingly explained to the neighbors as the odor of spoiled meat from his broken freezer, was unexceptional until after the fact.

The methodological problems in predicting violence in advance are well known. For a category of violence as rare as serial murder, however, the low base rate and consequent false-positive dilemma are overwhelming. Simply put, there are thousands of White males in their late 20s or 30s who thirst for power, are sadistic, and lack strong internal controls; most emphatically, however, the vast majority of them will never kill anyone.

Myth 8: All Serial Killers are Sexual Sadists

Serial killers who rape, torture, sodomize, and mutilate their victims attract an inordinate amount of attention from the press, the public, and professionals as well. Although they may be the most fascinating type of serial killer, they are hardly the only type.

Expanding their analysis beyond the sexual sadist, Holmes and DeBurger (1988) were among the first to assemble a motivational typology of serial killing, classifying serial murderers into four broad categories: visionary (e.g., voices from God), mission-oriented (e.g., ridding the world of evil), hedonistic (e.g., killing for pleasure), and power/control-oriented (e.g., killing for dominance). Holmes and DeBurger further divided the hedonistic type into three subtypes: lust, thrill, and comfort (see also Holmes & Holmes, 1998). . . .

Modifying the Holmes-DeBurger framework, we suggest that serial murders can be reclassified into three categories, each with two subtypes:

1. Thrill
   a. Sexual sadism
   b. Dominance
2. Mission
   a. Reformist
   b. Visionary
3. Expedience
   a. Profit
   b. Protection

Most serial killings can be classified as thrill motivated, and the *sexual sadist* is the most common of all. In addition, a growing number of murders committed by hospital caretakers have been exposed in recent years; although not sexual in motivation, these acts of murder are perpetrated for the sake of *dominance* nevertheless.

A less common form of serial killing consists of mission-oriented killers who murder to further a cause. Through killing, the *reformist* attempts to rid the world of filth and evil, such as by killing prostitutes, gays, or homeless persons. Most self-proclaimed reformists are also motivated by thrill seeking but try to rationalize their murderous behavior. For example, Donald Harvey, who worked as an orderly in Cincinnati-area hospitals, confessed to killing 80 or more patients through the years. Although he was termed a mercy killer, Harvey actually enjoyed the dominance he achieved by playing God with the lives of other people.

In contrast to pseudoreformists, *visionary* killers, as rare as they may be, genuinely believe in their missions. They hear the voice of the devil or God instructing them to kill. Driven by these delusions, visionary killers tend to be psychotic, confused, and disorganized. Because their killings are impulsive and even frenzied, visionaries rarely remain on the street long enough to become prolific serial killers.

The final category of serial murder includes those who are motivated by the expedience of either profit or protection. The *profit-oriented* serial killer systematically murders as a critical element of the overall plan to dispose of victims to make money (e.g., Sacramento landlady Dorothea Puente murdered 9 elderly tenants to cash their social security checks). By contrast, the *protection-oriented* killer uses murder to cover up criminal activity (e.g., the Lewington brothers systematically robbed and murdered 10 people throughout Central Ohio).

Myth 9: Serial Killers Select Victims who Somehow Resemble Their Mothers

Shortly after the capture of Hillside Strangler Kenneth Bianchi, psychiatrists speculated that he tortured and murdered young women as an expression of hatred toward his mother, who had allegedly brutalized him as a youngster (Fox & Levin, 1994). Similarly, the execution of Theodore Bundy gave psychiatrists occasion to suggest that his victims served as surrogates for the real target he sought, his mother.

Although unresolved family conflicts may in some cases be a significant source of frustration, most serial killers have a more opportunistic or pragmatic basis for selecting their victims. Quite simply, they tend to prey on the most vulnerable targets—prostitutes, drug users, hitchhikers, and runaways, as well as older hospital patients (Levin & Fox, 1985). Part of the vulnerability concerns the ease with which these groups can be abducted or overtaken. Children and older persons are defenseless because of physical stature or disability; hitchhikers and prostitutes become vulnerable as soon as they enter the killer's vehicle; hospital patients are vulnerable in their total dependency on their caretakers.

Vulnerability is most acute in the case of prostitutes, which explains their relatively high rate of victimization by serial killers. A sexual sadist can cruise a red-light district, seeking out the woman who best fits his deadly sexual fantasies. When he finds her, she willingly complies with his wishes—until it is too late.

Another aspect of vulnerability is the ease with which the killers can avoid being detected following a murder. Serial killers of our time are often sly and crafty, fully realizing the ease with which they can prey on streetwalkers and escape detection, much less arrest. Because the disappearance of a prostitute is more likely to be considered by the police, at least initially, as a missing person rather than a victim of homicide, the search for the body can be delayed weeks or months. Also, potential witnesses to abductions in red-light districts tend to be unreliable sources of information or distrustful of the police.

Frail older persons, particularly those in hospitals and nursing homes, represent a class of victims that is at the mercy of a different type of serial killer, called "angels of death." Revelations by a Long Island nurse who poisoned his patients in a failed attempt to be a hero by resuscitating them and of two Grand Rapids nurses aides who murdered older patients to form a lovers' pact have horrified even the most jaded observers of crime.

Not only are persons who are old and infirm vulnerable to the misdeeds of their caretakers who may have a particularly warped sense of mercy, but hospital homicides are particularly difficult to detect and solve. Death among older patients is not uncommon, and suspicions are rarely aroused. Furthermore, should a curiously large volume of deaths occur within a short time on a particular nurse's shift, hospital administrators feel in a quandary. Not only are they reluctant to bring scandal and perhaps lawsuits to their own facility without sufficient proof, but most of the potentially incriminating evidence against a suspected employee is long buried with the victim.

Myth 10: Serial Killers Really Want to Get Caught

Despite the notion that serial killers are typically lacking in empathy and remorse, some observers insist that deeply repressed feelings of guilt may subconsciously motivate them to leave telltale clues for the police. Although this premise may be popular in media portrayals, most serial killers go to great lengths to avoid detection, such as carefully destroying crime scene evidence or disposing of their victims' bodies in hard-to-find dump sites.

There is an element of self-selection in defining serial killing. Only those offenders who have sufficient cunning and guile are able to avoid capture long enough to accumulate the number of victims necessary to be classified as serial killers. Most serial killers are careful, clever, and, to use the FBI's typology, organized. Of course, disorganized killers, because of their carelessness, tend to be caught quickly, often before they surpass the serial killer threshold of victim count.

Murders committed by a serial killer are typically difficult to solve because of lack of both motive and physical evidence. Unlike the usual homicide that involves an offender and a victim who know one another, serial murders are almost exclusively committed by strangers. Thus, the usual police strategy of identifying suspects by considering their possible motive, be it jealousy, revenge, or greed, is typically fruitless.

Another conventional approach to investigating homicides involves gathering forensic evidence—fibers, hairs, blood, and prints—from the scene of the crime. In the case of many serial murders, however, this can be rather difficult, if not impossible. The bodies of the victims are often found at desolate roadsides or in makeshift graves, exposed to rain, wind, and snow. Most of the potentially revealing crime scene evidence remains in the unknown killer's house or car.

Another part of the problem is that unlike those shown in the media, many serial killers do not leave unmistakable and unique "signatures" at their crime scenes. As a result, the police may not recognize multiple homicides as the work of the same perpetrator. Moreover, some serial killings, even if consistent in style, traverse jurisdictional boundaries. Thus, "linkage blindness" is a significant barrier to solving many cases of serial murder (Egger, 1984). . . .

From Myth to Reality

The study of serial homicide is in its infancy, less than two decades old. The pioneering scholars noted the pervasiveness and inaccuracy of longstanding psychiatric misconceptions regarding the state of mind of the serial killer. More recently, these unfounded images have been supplanted by newer myths, including those concerning the prevalence and apprehension of serial killers.

The mythology of serial killing has developed from a pervasive fascination with a crime about which so little is known. Most of the scholarly literature is based on conjecture, anecdote, and small samples, rather than rigorous and controlled research. The future credibility of this area of study will depend on the ability of criminologists to upgrade the standards of research on serial homicide. Only then will myths about serial murder give way to a reliable foundation of knowledge.

REFERENCES

Egger, S. A. (1984). A working definition of serial murder and the reduction of linkage blindness. *Journal of Police Science and Administration, 12*, 348–357.

Egger, S. A. (1990). *Serial murder: An elusive phenomenon*. Westport, CT: Praeger.

Egger, S. A. (1998). *The killers among us: An examination of serial murder and its investigation*. Upper Saddle River, NJ: Prentice Hall.

Fox, J. A., & Levin. J. (1985, December 1). Serial killers: How statistics mislead us. *Boston Herald*, p. 45.

Fox, J. A., & Levin, J. (1994). *Overkill. Mass murder and serial killing exposed*. New York: Plenum.

Fox, J. A., & Levin, J. (1996). *Killer on campus*. New York: Avon Books.

Hickey, E. W. (1997). *Serial murderers and their victims* (2nd ed.). Belmont, CA: Wadsworth.

Holmes, R. M., & DeBurger, J. (1988). *Serial murder*. Newbury Park, CA: Sage.

Holmes, R. M., & Holmes, S. T. (1998). *Serial murder* (2nd ed.). Thousand Oaks, CA: Sage.

Jenkins, P. (1988). Myth and murder. The serial killer panic of 1983–85. *Criminal Justice Research Bulletin* (No. 3). Huntsville, TX: Sam Houston State University.

Jenkins, P. (1994). *Using murder: The social construction of serial homicide*. New York: Walter de Gruyter.

Levin, J., & Fox, J. A. (1985). *Mass murder: America's growing menace*. New York: Plenum.

Lewis, D. O., Lovely, R., Yeager, C., & Femina, D. D. (1989). Toward a theory of the genesis of violence: A follow-up study of delinquents. *Journal of the American Academy of Child and Adolescent Psychiatry, 28*, 431–436.

Lewis, D. O., Pincus, J. H., Feldman, M., Jackson, L., & Bard, B. (1986). Psychiatric, neurological, and psychoeducational characteristics of 15 death row inmates in the United States. *American Journal of Psychiatry, 143*, 838–845.

Leyton, E. (1986). *Compulsive killers: The story of modern multiple murderers*. New York: New York University Press.

Malamuth, N. M., & Donnerstein, E. (1984). *Pornography and sexual aggression*. Orlando, FL: Academic Press.

Meddis, S. (1987, March 31). FBI: Possible to spot, help serial killers early. *USA Today*, p. 3A.

Norris, J. (1988). *Serial killers: The growing menace*. New York: Doubleday.

Ressler, R. K., Burgess, A. W., & Douglas, J. E. (1988). *Sexual homicide: Patterns and motives*. Lexington, MA: Lexington Books.

Serial killers. (1992, October 18). *NOVA*. Boston: WGBH-TV.

REVIEW QUESTIONS

1. Identify and discuss five myths about serial killers.

2. Distinguish between mass killers and serial killers.

3. What are the advantages of looking at serial killers sociologically, rather than psychologically or biologically?

What Triggers School Shootings?

MICHAEL S. KIMMEL AND MATTHEW MAHLER

Violence is one of the most urgent issues facing our nation's schools. All over the country, Americans are asking why some young people open fire, apparently randomly, killing or wounding other students and their teachers. Are these teenagers emotionally disturbed? Are they held in the thrall of media-generated violence—in video games, the Internet, rock or rap music? Are their parents to blame?

We begin our inquiry with an analysis of the extant commentary and literature on school violence. We argue that, unfortunately, there are significant lacunae in all of these accounts—the most significant of which is the fact that they all ignore the one factor that cuts across all cases of random school shootings—masculinity. Thus, we argue that any approach to understanding school shootings must take gender seriously—specifically the constellation of adolescent masculinity, homophobia, and violence. . . .

Missing the Mark

The concern over school shootings has prompted intense national debate, in recent years, over who or what is to blame. One need not look hard to find any number of "experts" who are willing to weigh in on the issue. Yet despite the legion of political and scientific commentaries on school shootings, these voices have all singularly and spectacularly missed the point. At the vanguard of the debates have been politicians. Some have argued that Goth music, Marilyn Manson, and violent video games are the causes of school shootings. Then-President Clinton argued that it might be the Internet; Newt Gingrich credited the 1960s; and Tom DeLay blamed daycare, the teaching of evolution, and "working mothers who take birth control pills." Political pundits and media commentators also have offered a host of possible explanations, of which one of the more popular answers has been violence in the media. "Parents don't realize that taking four year-olds to *True Lies*—a fun movie for adults but excessively violent—is poison

Source: Michael S. Kimmel and Matthew Mahler, "Adolescent Masculinity, Homophobia, and Violence," *American Behavioral Scientist*, vol. 46 (2003), pp. 1439–1458. © 2003 by Sage Publications, Inc. Reprinted by permission of Sage Publications, Inc.

to their brain," notes Michael Gurian. Alvin Poussaint, a psychiatrist at Harvard Medical School, wrote that

> in America, violence is considered fun to kids. They play video games where they chop people's heads off and blood gushes and it's fun, it's entertainment. It's like a game. And I think this is the psychology of these kids—this "Let's go out there and kill like on television."

And Sissela Bok (1999), in her erudite warning on violence, suggests that the Internet and violent video games, which "bring into homes depictions of graphic violence . . . never available to children and young people in the past," undermine kids' resilience and self-control.

For others, the staggering statistics linking youth violence and the availability of guns point to a possible cause. Firearms are the second leading cause of death to children between age 10 and 14 and the eighth leading cause of death to those age 1 to 4. In 1994, 80% of juvenile murderers used a firearm; in 1984, only 50% did. Barry Krisberg, president of the National Council on Crime and Delinquency, argues that both the media and guns are at fault. He says, "The violence in the media and the easy availability of guns are what is driving the slaughter of innocents." Or perhaps, if we are to believe National Rifle Association (NRA) president Charlton Heston, the problem is not that there are too many guns but that there are not enough guns. He argues that had there been armed guards in the schools, the shooting would have ended instantly. These accounts, however, that blame a media purportedly overly saturated by violence and a society infatuated with guns are undercut by two important facts, which are often conveniently forgotten amid the fracas. The first is that whereas the amount of violent media content has ostensibly been increasing, both youth violence, in general, and school violence, in particular, have actually been decreasing since 1980. And second, juvenile violence involving guns has been in decline since 1994 (largely as a result of the decline of the crack epidemic). As Michael Carneal, the boy who shot his classmates in Paducah, Kentucky, said, "I don't know why it happened, but I know it wasn't a movie" (Blank, 1998).

Finally, some have proposed psychological variables, including a history of childhood abuse, absent fathers, dominant mothers, violence in childhood, unstable family environment, or the mothers' fear of their children, as possible explanations. Although these explanations are all theoretically possible, empirically it appears as though none of them holds up. Almost all the shooters came from intact and relatively stable families, with no history of child abuse. If they had psychological problems at all, they were relatively minor. . . .

Most important for our argument is the fact that these studies have all missed gender. They use such broad terminology as "teen violence," "youth violence," "gang violence," "suburban violence," and "violence in the schools" as though girls are equal participants in this violence. Conspicuously absent is any mention of just who these youth or teens are who have committed the violence. They pay little or no attention to the obvious fact that *all the school shootings were committed by boys*—masculinity is the single greatest risk factor in school violence. . . .

But the analytic blindness of these studies runs deeper than gender. We can identify two different waves of school violence since 1980. In the first, from 1982 to 1991, the majority of all the school shootings were nonrandom (i.e., the victims were specifically targeted by the perpetrators). Most were in urban, inner-city schools and involved students of color. Virtually all involved handguns, all were sparked by disputes over girlfriends or drugs, and all were committed by boys.

These cases have not entirely disappeared, but they have declined dramatically. Since 1992, only 1 of the random school shootings occurred in inner-city schools (it was committed by a black student), whereas the remaining 22 have been committed by white students in suburban schools. Virtually all involved rifles, not handguns—a symbolic shift from urban to rural weaponry. However, once again, all shootings were committed by boys.

Who Shoots and Why?

Still, most students—white or non-white, male or female—are not violent, schools are predominantly safe, and school shootings are aberrations. As a public, we seem concerned with school shootings because its story is not "when children kill" but specifically when suburban white boys kill. To illustrate the distribution of shootings across the country, we have mapped all cases of random school shootings since 1982. There were five cases documented between 1982 and 1991; there have been 23 cases since 1992. School shootings do not occur uniformly or evenly in the United States, which makes one skeptical of uniform cultural explanations such as violent video games, musical tastes, Internet, television, and movies. School shootings are decidedly *not* a national trend. Of 28 school shootings between 1982 and 2001, all but 1 were in rural or suburban schools. All but 2 were committed by a white boy or boys. . . .

We undertook an analysis of secondary media reports on *random school shootings from 1982 to 2001.* Using the shooters' names as our search terms, we gathered articles from six major media sources—the three major weekly news magazines: *Time, Newsweek,* and *U.S. News and World Report* (in order from greatest circulation to least); and three major daily newspapers: *USA Today, The New York Times,* and the *Los Angeles Times.* In conducting our analysis, we found a striking pattern from the stories about the boys who committed the violence: Nearly all had stories of being constantly bullied, beat up, and, most significantly for this analysis, "gay-baited." Nearly all had stories of being mercilessly and constantly teased, picked on, and threatened. And most strikingly, it was *not* because they were gay (at least there is no evidence to suggest that any of them were gay) but because they were *different* from the other boys—shy, bookish, honor students, artistic, musical, theatrical, nonathletic, "geekish," or weird.

In a recent interview, the eminent gender theorist Eminem poignantly illustrated the role of "gay-baiting" in peer interactions. In his view, calling someone a "faggot" is not a slur on his sexuality but on his gender. He says,

> The lowest degrading thing that you can say to a man . . . is to call him a faggot and try to take away his manhood. . . . "Faggot" to me doesn't necessarily mean gay people. "Faggot" to me just means taking away your manhood.

In this rationalization, Eminem, perhaps unwittingly, speaks to the central connection between gender and sexuality and particularly to the association of gender nonconformity with homosexuality. Here, homophobia is far less about the irrational fears of gay people, or the fears that one might actually be gay or have gay tendencies, and more the fears that *heterosexuals* have that others might *(mis)perceive them as gay* (Kimmel, 1994). Research has indicated that homophobia is one of the organizing principles of heterosexual masculinity, a constitutive element in its construction. And as an organizing principle of masculinity, homophobia—the terror that others will see one as gay, as a failed man—underlies a significant amount of men's behavior, including their relationships with other men, women, and violence. One could say that homophobia is the hate that makes men straight.

There is much at stake for boys and, as a result, they engage in a variety of evasive strategies to make sure that no one gets the wrong idea about them (and their manhood). These range from the seemingly comic (although telling), such as two young boys occupying three movie seats by placing their coats on the seat between them, to the truly tragic, such as engaging in homophobic violence, bullying, menacing other boys, masochistic or sadistic games and rituals, excessive risk taking (drunk or aggressive driving), and even sexual predation and assault. The impact of homophobia is felt not only by gay and lesbian students but also by heterosexuals who are targeted by their peers for constant harassment, bullying, and gay-baiting. In many cases, gay-baiting is "misdirected" at heterosexual youth who may be somewhat gender nonconforming. This fact is clearly evidenced in many of the accounts we have gathered of the shootings.

For example, young Andy Williams, recently sentenced to 50 years to life in prison for shooting and killing two classmates in Santee, California, and wounding several others was described as "shy" and was "constantly picked on" by others in school. Like many of the others, bullies stole his clothes, his money, and his food, beat him up regularly, and locked him in his locker, among other daily taunts and humiliations. One boy's father baited him and called him a "queer" because he was overweight. . . .

In the videotape made the night before the shootings at Columbine High School, the site of the nation's most infamous school shooting, would-be killer Eric Harris says, "People constantly make fun of my face, my hair, my shirts." His fellow-killer Dylan Klebold adds, "I'm going to kill you all. You've been giving us shit for years." What Klebold said he had been receiving for years apparently included constant gay-baiting, being called "queer," "faggot," "homo," being pushed into lockers, grabbed in hallways, and mimicked and ridiculed with homophobic slurs. For some boys, high school is a constant homophobic gauntlet and they may respond by becoming withdrawn and sullen, using drugs or alcohol, becoming depressed or suicidal, or acting out in a blaze of overcompensating violent "glory."

The prevalence of this homophobic bullying, teasing, and violence is staggering. According to the Gay, Lesbian, Straight Education Network, 97% of students in public high school in Massachusetts reported regularly hearing homophobic remarks from their peers in 1993; 53% reported hearing anti-gay remarks by school staff (Bronski, 1999). The recent report *Hatred in the Hallways* paints a bleak picture of anti-gay harassment [and emphasizes how] gender performance—acting masculine—is perceived as a code for heterosexuality (Human Rights Watch, 2001). . . .

Let us be completely clear: Our hypotheses are decidedly *not* that gay and lesbian youth are more likely to open fire on their fellow students. In fact, from all available evidence, *none* of the school shooters was gay. But that is our organizing hypothesis: Homophobia—being constantly threatened and bullied *if you are gay* as well as the homophobic desire to make sure that others know that you are a "real man"—plays a pivotal role in these school shootings.

Why Boys and Not Girls?

Historically, no industrial society other than the United States has developed such a violent "boy culture," as historian E. Anthony Rotundo (1993) calls it in his book *American Manhood.* It is here where young boys, as late as the 1940s, actually carried a little chip of wood on their shoulders daring others to knock it off so that they might have a fight. It is astonishing to think that "carrying a chip on your shoulder" is literally true—a test of manhood for adolescent boys. And it is here in the United States where experts actually *prescribed* fighting for young boys' healthy masculine development. The celebrated psychologist G. Stanley Hall, who invented the term "adolescence," believed that a nonfighting boy was a "nonentity" and that it was "better even an occasional nose dented by a fist . . . than stagnation, general cynicism and censoriousness, bodily and psychic cowardice" (cited in Stearns, 1994). His disciple, J. Adams Puffer (1912), was even bold enough to suggest in his successful parental advice book *The Boy and His Gang* that it is not unreasonable for a boy to fight up to six times a week and maybe even more depending on the circumstances: $$$"There are times when every boy must defend his own rights if he is not to become a coward and lose the road to independence and true manhood (cited in Kimmel, 1996).

It is interesting to note that in a recently thwarted school shooting in New Bedford, Massachusetts, it was a young woman, Amylee Bowman, 17, who could not go through with the plot and decided to reveal the details to the authorities. Eric McKeehan, 17, one of the coconspirators, was described in media accounts as constantly angry, especially at being slighted by other students. The mother of a second boy accused in the plot said, "Eric has a temper. He says what's on his mind. He's been known to hit walls and lockers, but what teenage boy hasn't?" (Heslam & Richardson, 2001).

Indeed, what teenage boy hasn't? Eminem had that part right. Calling someone a "faggot" means questioning his manhood. And in this culture, when someone questions our manhood, we do not just get mad, we get even.

Why White Boys?

... All American men contend with a singular hegemonic vision of masculinity, a particular definition that is held up as the model against which we all measure ourselves. We thus come to know what it means to be a man in our culture by setting our definitions in opposition to a set of subordinated "others"—racial minorities, sexual minorities, and above all, women. As the sociologist Erving Goffman (1963) once wrote.

> In an important sense there is only one complete unblushing male in America: a young, married, white, heterosexual, father, of college education, fully employed, of good complexion, weight, and height, and a decent record in sports. . . . Any male who fails to qualify in any one of these ways is likely to view himself—during moments at least—as unworthy, incomplete, and inferior.

It is crucial to listen to those last few words. When we feel that we do not measure up we are likely to feel unworthy, incomplete, and inferior. It is here, from this place of unworthiness, incompleteness, and inferiority, that boys begin their efforts to prove themselves as men. And it is here where violence has its connections to masculinity. As James Gilligan (1966) says in his book *Violence*, violence has its origins in "the fear of shame and ridicule, and the overbearing need to prevent others from laughing at oneself by making them weep instead." Shame, inadequacy, vulnerability—all threaten the self; violence, meanwhile, is restorative, compensatory. . . .

Most important for our current discussion, though, is the fact that failure to see race while looking at gender will cause us to miss the real story. We know that African American boys face a multitude of challenges in schools—racial stereotypes, formal and informal tracking systems, low expectations, and underachievement. But the one thing they do not do is plan and execute random and arbitrary mass shootings. And this is particularly interesting because the classroom and academic achievement have [less attraction] for African American girls and African American boys. In their fascinating ethnographies of two inner-city public high schools, both Signithia Fordham (1996) and Ann Ferguson (2000) discuss these differences. When African American girls do well in school, their friends accuse them of "acting White." But when African American boys do well in school, their friends accuse them of "acting like girls." [Thus, simply by not doing well in school, the boys can easily feel masculine and no need to prove their manhood by committing school violence.]

Why These Particular Boys and Not Others who have had Similar Experiences?

Walk down any hallway in any middle school or high school in America and the single most common put-down that is heard is "That's so gay." It is deployed constantly, casually, unconsciously. Boys hear it if they try out for the school band or orchestra, if they are shy or small, physically weak and unathletic, if they are smart, wear glasses, or work hard in school. They hear it if they are seen to like girls too much or if they are too much "like" girls. They hear it if their body language, their clothing, or their musical preferences do not conform to the norms of their peers. And they hear it not as an assessment of their present or future sexual orientation but as a commentary on their masculinity.

But not all boys who are targeted like that open fire on their classmates and teachers. In fact, very few do. So how is it that some boys—many boys, in fact—resist? As Pedro Noguera (2001) writes in "The Trouble with Black Boys," "We know much less about resilience, perseverance, and the coping strategies employed by individuals whose lives are surrounded by hardships, than we do about those who succumb and become victims of their environment." What is the constellation of factors that facilitate resistance?

Perhaps there is what Robert Brooks, of Harvard Medical School, calls the "charismatic adult" who makes a substantial difference in the life of the child. Most often this is one or the other parent, but it can also be a teacher or some other influential figure in the life of the boy. Perhaps the boy develops an alternative substantive pole around which to organize competence. Gay-baiting suggests that he is a failure at the one thing he knows he wants to be and is expected to be—a man. If there is something else that he does well—a private passion, music, art—someplace where he feels valued—he can develop a pocket of resistance.

Similarly, the structures of his interactions also can make a decisive difference. A male friend, particularly one who is not also a target but one who seems to be successful at masculinity, can validate the boy's sense of himself as a man. But equally important may be the role of a female friend, a potential if not actual "girlfriend." Five of the school shooters had what they felt was serious girl trouble, especially rejection. Luke Woodham was crushed when his girlfriend broke up with him. "I didn't eat, I didn't sleep. It destroyed me," he testified at trial. She was apparently his primary target and was killed. Michael Carneal may have had a crush on one of his victims. Mitchell Johnson was upset that his girlfriend had broken up with him.

Although all the shooters have been boys, that does not mean that girls are inconsequential in boys' social worlds. It may be that the boys who are able to best resist the torments of incessant gay-baiting and bullying are those who have some girls among their friends, and perhaps even a girlfriend, that is, girls who can also validate their sense of masculinity (which other boys do as well) as well as their heterosexuality (which boys alone cannot do). If masculinity is largely a homosocial performance, then at least one male peer, who is himself successful, must approve of the performance. The successful demonstration of *heterosexual* masculinity requires not only the successful performance for other men but also some forms of "sexual" success with women.

These sorts of [social experiences—support from a charismatic adult, competence in something, and male or female friendship, or the lack of these]—will enable us to understand both what led some boys to commit these terrible acts and what enables other boys to develop the resources of resistance to daily homophobic bullying.

Conclusion

In a brilliant passage in *Asylums,* Erving Goffman (1961) touched on the interplay between repression and resistance:

> Without something to belong to, we have no stable self, and yet total commitment and attachment to any social unit implies a kind of selflessness. Our sense of being a person can come from being drawn into a wider social unit; our sense of selfhood can arise through the little ways in which we resist the pull. Our status is backed by the solid buildings of the world, while our sense of personal identity often resides in the cracks.

It is our task, as researchers concerned with gender and education, to understand how those social forces shape and mold young men's identities and to explore [their resources for] resistance, where they might carve out for themselves a masculinity that is authentic, solid, and confident.

REFERENCES

Blank, J. 1998, December. "The kid no one noticed." *U.S. News and World Report,* p. 27.

Bok, S. 1999. *Mayhem: Violence as Public Entertainment.* Cambridge, MA: Perseus. 16–8

Bronski, M. 1999, July. "Littleton, movies and gay kids." *Z Magazine.*

Ferguson, A. 2000. *Bad Boys: Public Schools in the Making of Black Masculinity.* Ann Arbor: University of Michigan Press.

Fordham, S. 1996. *Blacked Out: Dilemmas of Race, Identity, and Success at Capital High.* Chicago: University of Chicago Press.

Gilligan, J. 1996. *Violence.* New York: Vintage.

Goffman, E. 1961. *Asylums.* New York: Vintage.

Goffman, E. 1963. *Stigma: Notes on the Management of Spoiled Identity.* Englewood Cliffs, NJ: Prentice Hall.

Heslam, J., and F. Richardson. 2001, November 26. "Suspect labeled outcast, estranged from family." *Boston Herald,* p. 6.

Human Rights Watch. 2001. *Hatred in the Hallways: Violence and Discrimination against Lesbian, Gay, Bisexual, and Transgender Students in the U.S.* New York: Author.

Kimmel, M. 1994. "Masculinity as homophobia: Fear, shame and silence in the construction of gender identity." Pp. 119–141 in H. Brod and M. Kaufman (Eds.), *Theorizing Masculinities.* Newbury Park, CA: Sage.

Kimmel, M. 1996. *Manhood in America: A Cultural History.* New York: Free Press.

Noguera, P. 2001. "The trouble with black boys." *Harvard Journal of African American Public Policy,* 7 (Summer), 23–46.

Puffer, J. A. 1912. *The Boy and His Gang.* Boston: Houghton.

Rotundo, E. A. 1993. *American Manhood.* New York: Basic Books.

Stearns, P. 1994. *American Cool.* New York: New York University Press.

REVIEW QUESTIONS

1. Why do Kimmel and Mahler argue that terms such as "teen violence" are too broad?

2. What do most of the school shootings after 1992 have in common?

3. Do you agree with the premise of this article? Why or why not?

Unjustly Treating People with Disabilities

JEANIE AKAMANTI

If we are not disabled in one way or another now, we will be sooner or later. Disability in one form or another is inevitable for every one of us. We can get disabled from a car or motorcycle wreck, sporting injury, or being hurt on the job. If accidents such as these do not happen to us, we will with aging become disabled from, among other things, physical deterioration, mental decline, impaired mobility, or decreased vision. All such disabilities are partial, affecting a part rather than the entirety of our bodies. Even if, for some miraculous reason, we can escape from any of those partial disabilities, we still cannot get away from being totally disabled. That total disability will eventually come from death, the ultimate form of disability.

Given the inevitability and thus the normalcy of disability, people with disabilities are nonetheless treated as if they were abnormal. As a consequence, they suffer unjustly. They are, for example, three times more likely than other Americans to live in poverty and have lower household incomes (National Organization on Disability, 2000). When employed, they earn 57 percent less than people with no disabilities, and are paid less for the same work and the same position (Stoddard et al., 1998). Let us take a closer look at the specific ways people with disabilities are treated unjustly and the reasons for such treatment.

A Variety of Unjust Treatments

In situations where people without disabilities are shown respect, admiration, or solicitude, people with disabilities are usually shown just the opposite—disrespect, pity, the brush-off, or worse. Consider, for example, the experience of my friend Pam, who has muscular dystrophy. She cannot use her arms or legs, and has only limited use of one hand. She uses a power wheelchair and lets someone else prepare and cut up her food for her. Like any person with a disability, though, Pam is far from totally disabled. Contrary to popular belief, a person's disability does not represent the core or totality of that person's self (Thio, 2004). Not surprisingly,

Alex Thio and Thomas C. Calhoun (eds.), *Readings in Deviant Behavior*, Fourth Edition (Boston, MA: Allyn and Bacon, 2006), pp. 165–168. Copyright © 2006 Pearson Education, Inc. Reprinted by permission of Allyn and Bacon.

then, Pam is much more than being disabled from muscular dystrophy. She is also intelligent, articulate, and a computer whiz, and she makes beautiful pieces of art using her computer. Understandably, in the disability community, where people with disabilities are known as a whole person, there is nothing different or strange about Pam. But as soon as she goes out in the larger world, she is seen only as a disabled person and thus stigmatized as a deviant and treated accordingly.

Such treatment involves violating her very basic social right to go in the main entrance of a building along with everyone else. Once Pam went out for her birthday to a very expensive four-star restaurant. She had called in advance to inquire about access and was told there was an accessible entrance. Instead, she was confronted by twelve steep steps on her arrival, impossible to navigate in her 250-pound, solid frame, power wheelchair. There was no ramp to be seen. A friend went up and asked where the accessible entrance was. The maitre de indicated there was a "special" wheelchair entrance and directed her around the back. The special wheelchair entrance turned out to be the service entrance used to deliver the food and goods to the restaurant. Dressed in a black silk skirt and blouse, hair elegantly coiffed, and her ears sparkling with the new diamond earrings she had just received as a birthday present, Pam was ushered through the dark, smelly service entrance strewn with the dirt and debris of boxes of food being carried through—the so-called special wheelchair entrance. Further, she was separated from the rest of her party, who were asked to use the "normal" entrance.

Pam's experience reflects the absence or limitation of the rights of equality and inclusivity for people with disabilities. Like Pam, wheelchair users are singled out and treated differently by being sent to a special entrance. Most architectural structures, even new ones, are designed with a special wheelchair entrance for those with mobility impairments that is off to the side or even through a service entrance. Some buildings do not even have an accessible entrance. Contrary to popular belief and despite the passage of the Americans with Disabilities Act (ADA), private businesses are *not* required to provide access or accommodations. Businesses do not have to provide accessibility or accommodations if costs are considered unreasonable or pose an undue financial hardship (Johnson, 2003).

Moreover, the ADA does not require that entrances be made universally accessible. Universally accessible entrances can be used by anybody, those with or without disabilities. They include, though not limited to, those using assistive mobility devices such as a walker, scooter, or wheelchair. Most grocery stores are constructed this way—no steps, just smooth or level surfaces and automatic doors. Instead of a universal entrance, however, most new constructions offer a "special" entrance for persons with disabilities or mobility impairments. This reinforces the popular perception that people with disabilities are not normal and thus should be treated differently. In her book *Make Them Go Away*, Mary Johnson (2003) offers a compelling argument that the term *special* as applied to disability—as in "special" seating, "special" transportation, and "special" education—is simply a fancy word for segregation, discrimination, isolation, and exclusion. Even if the special entrance is not dank, dreary, and smelly like the one Pam had to use on her birthday, it still emphasizes that the user is different from and not as good or worthy as everyone else. "Special" as applied to disability, then, emphasizes that they are "not normal."

The lack of accessible entrances for people with disabilities, let alone universally accessible ones, is tantamount to violating the civil rights of people with disabilities. But most of the negative reactions to people with disabilities are not legally prohibited. Consider, for example, the experience of Jack, who has cerebral palsy. His motions are jerky and his speech can be difficult to understand because of slurring. He is also an honor roll student with a perfect grade point average, uses his computer to write and generate voice syntheses, and is witty and fun to be around. When he eats, an attendant cuts his food and puts it in his mouth. And Jack chews with his mouth open and drools when he eats. One night when having drinks and dinner with friends in a restaurant, the manager of the eating establishment came over and suggested that Jack's group would be more comfortable in the private back room. When Jack said they were fine, the manager went straight to the point. He said that some of the other guests had complained, saying Jack's appearance made them uncomfortable.

Generally, the more unusual the physical appearance of people with disabilities is, the more vulnerable they are to discrimination (Allesio, 2001). People like Jack are thus very likely to become targets of discrimination. But people with less visibly unusual disabilities than Jack's are more likely to be simply ignored and dismissed. Cahill and Eggleston (1995), for example, have showed that people who use wheelchairs in public are simply seen as "non-persons." Most people walk past them, while some talk about them as if they are absent, or glance at them without even looking at them, much less making eye contact or offering a casual greeting.

It is not just in everyday social interactions that people with disabilities are treated unjustly. Social policies control and regulate the social interaction and behavior of people with disabilities. These policies tend to create the façade that they are in place to help people with disabilities, but in reality they may limit where they can go, what they can do, and whether or not they can work. These policies sometimes even prohibit people with disabilities from getting married and bearing children. While claiming to be humanitarian and compassionate, these policies often engage in discrimination against people with disabilities.

When Pam was married, the government would only pay for twenty hours a week of personal and medical assistance for her. This was not enough to help her eat, dress, and have help getting to and from class and her part-time job. But because she was married, the policy set forth by the laws governing the Department of Rehabilitative Services demanded that her husband provide all the additional care she needed. This might seem reasonable until one notes that he was also working full time as well as taking care of all the household tasks such as shopping, cooking, cleaning, and laundry. There simply were not enough hours in the week for him to do everything, and he did not make enough to pay for all the care she needed. Pam's health was at risk because she did not have enough personal and medical assistance. When she was getting sick because she had not received enough personal assistance, the government agent suggested she get a divorce. After the divorce, the government gave her help with what she actually needed—eighty hours of care a week.

It is not just marriage that can create problems with the government policy. So can trying to work, as shown in Paul Longmore's (2003) book, *Why I Burned My Book*. Paul has post-polio syndrome. He is a quadriplegic and has only limited use of one hand. Sometimes he uses a ventilator to breathe. Paul also depends on government assistance to defray the estimated $40,000-a-year cost for personal assistance. Paul wrote a history book under the impression he could use the sale royalties to pay part, though not all, of these costs. Soon after it was published, he learned that if he made *any* money from the book he would lose the help he needed to pay for his personal and medical assistance. He could pay for some but not all the care he needed, leaving his health and life at risk. In protest, Paul publicly burned his book.

Because they are widely perceived as "not normal" and stigmatized as deviants, people with disabilities are likely to encounter prejudice and discrimination in the larger society. We have seen examples of these unjust treatments, but research is still needed to determine more precisely the prevalence or extent of each type of unjust treatment.

Why the Unjust Treatment?

There are two explanations for unjustly treating people with disabilities. One centers on the fear of becoming disabled. When people see or are around a person with disability, they are reminded that they could be in an accident or something could happen to render them disabled. Also, when seeing a very old person with some physical limitation or impairment, many people may fear that they too will likely suffer the same fate in old age. Whether disabled by accident or old age, people are afraid of and do not want to be reminded that they might become a person with a disability. By keeping the disabled hidden, out of sight, or in "special" isolated seating, people do not have to be reminded of their own vulnerability.

Another explanation for the unjust treatment of people with disabilities is that they are viewed as a threat to economic resources. More specifically, people with disabilities are regarded as *social junk,* who by definition cannot work or cost more for society to maintain than they contribute to society (Spitzer, 1975). People with disabilities are seen as economically wasteful because of their need for costly medical and personal care. Consequently, their lives, behaviors, and access to goods and services must be regulated and socially controlled through agencies such as Social Security and Public Aid. In order to control resources and save money, rules and policies are put into place to limit and regulate their social and economic participation. All this effectively means that rather than being regarded as individuals like everyone else, people with disabilities are seen as a deviant and expendable group and thus treated as objects and less than human.

Conclusion

These are just some of the examples of how people with disabilities are seen as deviants and discriminated against. They are denied basic civil and human rights such as the right to marry, eat in public, go through the front entrance, or have a job—namely the very same things that people without disabilities enjoy. Like everyone else, people with disabilities want to work and are able to work, and they also want to go to school, have families, and participate in social activities. But because they are stigmatized as deviants, they have to struggle with public policies and social practices that make life difficult for them.

REFERENCES

Allesio, John C. 2001. "Disabilities and Prejudice" in *Encyclopedia of Criminology and Deviant Behavior*, Vol. IV, edited by C. D. Bryant. Philadelphia: Brunner-Routledge.

Cahill, Spencer, and Robin Eggleston. 1995. "Reconsidering the Stigma of Physical Disability: Wheel-chair Use and Public Kindness." *The Sociological Quarterly* 36: 681–698.

Johnson, Mary. 2003. *Make Them Go Away. Clint Eastwood, Christopher Reeve and The Case Against Disability Rights*. Louisville, KY: Advocado Press.

Longmore, Paul K. 2003. *Why I Burned My Book and Other Essays on Disability*. Philadelphia: Temple University Press.

National Organization on Disability. 2000. "N.O.D./Harris Survey of Americans with Disabilities." Lou Harris and Associates, New York.

Spitzer, Steven. 1975. "Toward a Marxian Theory of Deviance." *Social Problems* 22: 638–651.

Stoddard, Susan et al. 1998. *Chartbook on Work and Disability in the United States*. United States Department of Education, National Institute on Disability and Rehabilitation Research, Washington, D.C.

Thio, Alex. 2004. *Deviant Behavior*, 7th ed. Boston: Allyn & Bacon.

REVIEW QUESTIONS

1. How do people with disabilities come to be labeled deviant?

2. Why does Mary Johnson argue that "special" equals segregation?

3. Do you agree with the author that people with disabilities in this society are seen as "social junk"?

Binge Drinking on College Campus

KEITH F. DURKIN, SCOTT E. WOLFE AND KARA LEWIS

Binge drinking, which involves the consumption of large quantities of alcohol in a single drinking episode, has been getting a lot of attention from the media, college administrators, healthcare professionals, and researchers in the behavioral sciences. Most researchers specifically define binge drinking as the consumption of at least five alcoholic drinks in a single sitting for men and four for women. A number of studies have revealed that this behavior is fairly common on college campuses, with a large minority (about 44 percent) of students having engaged in binge drinking during the previous two weeks (Wechsler et al., 1994; 2002b).

Consensus has been growing that binge drinking represents a very serious threat to the well-being of many of today's college students. Compared to other college students, binge drinkers have been found to be more likely to experience negative consequences as a result of their drinking. These include hangovers, blackouts, missing class, doing something they regret later, getting involved in physical fights and other arguments, and having trouble with the police. The tragic alcohol-related deaths of students at several colleges and universities further highlight the potentially fatal consequences of this activity.

Researchers have also found that binge drinkers can produce "secondhand effects" on non-drinking others by hurting them in some ways. These include verbally insulting or abusing the innocent victims, physically assaulting them, damaging the property around them, making unwelcome sexual advances on women, and disturbing others' sleep or studying (Wechsler et al., 2002a).

A number of recent studies have identified certain demographics associated with binge drinking on college campus. Men, for example, are much more likely than women to binge drink. White students are more likely than non-white students to drink excessively. And students who are athletes, fraternity brothers, or sorority sisters are more likely than other students to drink uncontrollably (Wechsler et al., 1994; 1995; NIAAA, 2002). But these demographics are merely correlates, not causes, of binge drinking. They cannot explain, for example, why men are more likely than women, or why some men are more likely than other men, to binge drink. It is thus important to know the causes of binge drinking.

Social Bond Theory

A promising source of such knowledge is Travis Hirschi's control theory of deviance, also known as social bond theory. This theory assumes that the motivation for deviant behavior is present in everyone but the motivation will lead to deviance only for some people—but not for others. The difference depends on the degree of bond between the individual and society. If the bond is weak, the individual will likely turn deviant, but if the bond is strong, the individual will likely not (Hirschi, 1969). This theory has been used to explain a wide variety of deviances including alcohol use, juvenile delinquency, marijuana use, and cheating on tests. The theory can also be used to explain binge drinking as a form of deviant behavior.

There are four elements of social bond. The first is *attachment* to others. This refers to the ties that an individual has to significant others such as family members, particularly parents, and friends. The second element of social bond is *commitment* to conformity, which refers to the willingness and determination to be a good student, a hardworking worker, or a religious person. The third element of social bond is *involvement* in conventional activities. This consists of spending long hours doing schoolwork, doing chores, working as a volunteer or for pay, and engaging in some other conventional activities. The fourth, final component of social bond is *belief* in morals, rules, and laws. This is the acceptance of a conventional value system, which can be expressed with respect for authority.

When applied to binge drinking, social bond theory effectively says that attachment to significant others, commitment to conformity, involvement in conventional activities, or belief in morality and other social values discourages people from drinking excessively, but the lack of any one of these four elements of social bond encourages them to have the drinking problem. The present study was designed to find out if this is indeed the case for binge drinking.

Methodology

Copies of a questionnaire called the First-Year College Student Lifestyle Inventory were administered to a sample of 361 freshmen at a private university in Ohio as part of their orientation activities during the beginning of the school year in September 2003. A similar questionnaire was given to mostly the same students toward the end of the school year in April 2004. However, thirty-six students of the original sample could not be contacted, largely because they had withdrawn from the university. On April 26, 2004, copies of the First-Year College Student Lifestyle Inventory were sent to the remaining 325 students. All students who responded by May 12 were eligible for a drawing to win one of five $50 Visa gift cards. On May 5, an additional copy of the questionnaire and cover letter were sent to all students who had not yet responded to the initial April 26 mailing. We received a total of 158 completed questionnaires in the second phase of data collection for a total response rate of 48.6 percent.

The dependent variable, binge drinking, was measured by asking male students to indicate how many times during the previous two weeks they had guzzled down five or more drinks in a row, and females how many times they had consumed four or more drinks successively. The questionnaire provided respondents with a definition of a drink as "a twelve-ounce beer or wine cooler, a shot of liquor, or a six- to eight-ounce glass of wine."

The questionnaire presented a variety of empirical indicators that reflect the various elements of social bond. The indicators of attachment to significant others, for example, were the statements that "I have a lot of respect for my parents," "My parents and I can talk about my future plans," and "I live with both of my parents." The indicators of the commitment to conformity included "Regular church attendance is important to me," "Prayer is an important part of my daily life," the number of times the subjects attended religious services, "I study hard in school," "Regular class attendance is important to me," and the student's grade point average. The indicators of the involvement in conventional activities were obtained from asking subjects how many hours a week they spent working, studying, and participating in extracurricular activities respectively. Finally, to get the indicators of the belief in morals and rules, the students were asked whether or not they agreed with statements such as "To get ahead you have to do some things which aren't right" and "It is okay to break the rules if you can get away with it." They were also asked if they respected the police, another indicator of the belief in social rules.

Results

At the beginning of the freshman year, 32 percent of the students engaged in binge drinking. These binge drinkers were indeed more likely than other students to have weaker social bond in terms of each of its four elements. But only in regard to commitment and belief was the difference between binge drinkers and nondrinkers large enough to be statistically significant. The other two elements, attachment and involvement, were not. Table 34.1 shows only the indicators of commitment and belief in which binge drinkers were significantly different from nondrinkers. First, those students who reported attending religious services less than once a month were more likely than other students to binge drink (38.1 percent vs. 24.6 percent). Second, those students with a high school GPA of B or lower were nearly two times more likely to binge drink than their peers with higher GPAs (50 percent vs. 28 percent). Third, students with a lower level of acceptance of conventional beliefs were more likely to binge drink than those with a higher level of moral beliefs (40.7 percent vs. 22.2 percent). Fourth, students with a low level of respect for authority were nearly twice as likely to become binge drinkers than students reporting a greater respect for authority (46.8 percent vs. 24.7 percent).

At the end of the freshman year, 36.1 percent percent of the students were binge drinkers, a slightly higher percentage than at the beginning of the school year. Binge drinkers differed somewhat from nondrinkers in regard to all the components of social bond, but the difference in most cases was not large enough to be

TABLE 34.1 Binge Drinking and Bond Indicators: Start of
Freshman Year

	Binge Drinker	
Social Bond Indicators	Yes (n = 113)	No (n = 245)
Commitment Component		
Church Attendance**		
More than once a month	24.6%	75.4%
Less than once a month	38.1%	61.9%
High School Grade Point Average**		
B+ or higher	28.0%	72.0%
B or lower	50.0%	50.0%
Belief Component		
Acceptance of Moral Beliefs**		
High	22.2%	77.8%
Low	40.7%	59.3%
Respect for Authority**		
High	24.7%	75.3%
Low	46.8%	53.2%

**Chi-square value statistically significant at p < .01

statistically significant. Only two indicators of commitment did significantly differentiate binge drinkers from non-drinkers, which are presented in Table 34.2. First, students who attended religious services less than once a month were almost twice as likely to binge drink than their peers who attended church more frequently (48.6 percent vs. 25.0 percent). Second, students with a low degree of religious commitment were more likely than other students to be binge drinkers (47.8 percent vs. 27.0 percent).

Discussion

As the results of the present study show, social bond theory receives mixed support as an explanation of binge drinking by college students. On the one hand, it appears that both the commitment and belief components of the social bond are negatively related to binge drinking. In other words, students who are committed to conformity (as shown by their religious practices and academic achievement) and hold beliefs that support morality and authority are less likely to binge drink than their peers. On the other hand, the attachment and involvement components of social bond appear much less useful in explaining binge drinking. As Leonard and Decker (1994) suggested, the elements of the social bond may work differently

TABLE 34.2   Binge Drinking and Bond Indicators: End of Freshman Year

Social Bond Indicators	Binge Drinker	
	Yes (n = 57)	No (n = 101)
Commitment Component		
Church Attendance**		
More than once a month	25.0%	75.0%
Less than once a month	48.6%	51.4%
Religious Commitment**		
High	27.0%	73.0%
Low	47.8%	52.2%

**Chi-square value statistically significant at p < .01

for various age groups. While commitment and belief may be important for college students, attachment to parents and involvement in conventional activities (which by definition are approved by authority figures) seem more powerful in preventing delinquency among juveniles.

REFERENCES

Hirschi, Travis. 1969. *Causes of Delinquency.* Berkeley: University of California Press.

Leonard, Kimberly K., and Scott H. Decker. 1994. "The Theory of Social Control: Does It Apply to The Very Young?" *Journal of Criminal Justice* 22: 89–105

NIAAA (National Institute on Alcohol Abuse and Alcoholism). 2002. *High-Risk Drinking in College: What We Know and What We Need to Learn.* Washington, D.C.: Author.

Wechsler, Henry, et al. 1994. "Health and Behavioral Consequences of Binge Drinking in College: A National Survey of Students at 140 Campuses." *Journal of the American Medical Association* 272: 1672–1677.

Wechsler, Henry, et al. 1995. "A Gender Specific Measure of Binge Drinking among College Students." *American Journal of Public Health* 85:92–985.

Wechsler, Henry, et al. 2002a. "Second Hand Effects of Student Alcohol Use Reported by Neighbors of Colleges: The Role of Alcohol Outlets." *Social Science and Medicine* 55:425–435.

Wechsler, Henry, et al. 2002b. "Trends in College Binge Drinking During a Period of Increased Prevention Efforts." *Journal of American College Health* 50: 203–217.

REVIEW QUESTIONS

1. What are the four elements of social bond theory?

2. Did the study in the article support social bond theory? Why or why not?

3. Do you believe that binge drinking "represents a very serious threat" to college students? Defend your answer.

46 Shoplifters: "The Devil Made Me Do It"

PAUL CROMWELL AND QUINT THURMAN

A 30-year-old male shoplifter: *"You know that cartoon where the guy has a little devil sitting on one shoulder and a little angel on the other? And one is telling him "Go ahead on, do it," and the angel is saying "No, don't do it." You know? . . . Sometimes when I'm thinking about boosting something, my angel don't show up."*

By blaming the devil for his shoplifting, the man is in effect saying that he is not responsible for his crime. He is, in other words, trying to neutralize, minimize, or expunge the guilt of committing the crime. Nearly five decades ago Gresham Sykes and David Matza (1957) introduced this idea of neutralization to explain juvenile delinquency. Their neutralization theory is an elaboration of Edwin Sutherland's proposition that individuals can learn to become criminal by developing, among other things, the "motives, drives, rationalizations, and attitudes favorable to violations of the law." Sykes and Matza theorized that if people can neutralize their guilt for their deviance with these rationalizations or justifications, such as blaming the devil rather than themselves for shoplifting, then they are likely to engage in deviant activities.

But since Sykes and Matza introduced this theory, there has developed a controversy over their contention that deviants must engage in neutralization *before* committing a deviant act. Some researchers have found that the neutralization usually occurs *after* the deviant act (Minor, 1981; Pogrebin, Poole, and Martinez, 1992). Unfortunately, our research here could not confirm or refute Sykes and Matza's theory that pre-deviance neutralizations cause deviant behavior. The reason is that the people we studied had already committed an offense so that if they engaged in neutralization they obviously did so after rather than before the

Source: Paul Cromwell and Quint Thurman, "'The Devil Made Me Do It': Use of Neutralizations by Shoplifters," *Deviant Behavior,* vol. 24 (2003), pp. 535–550. © 2001. Reproduced by permission of Taylor & Francis, Inc., www.taylorandfrancis.com.

offense was committed. But our research was able to find out if shoplifters tried to neutralize their offenses and how they went about doing it.

Sykes and Matza (1957) identified five techniques of neutralization commonly offered to justify deviant behavior. They are *denial of responsibility, denial of injury, denial of the victim, condemning the condemners,* and *appeal to higher loyalties.* Other, more recent researchers have identified five additional neutralization techniques. These include *defense of necessity, metaphor of the ledger, denial of the necessity of the law, the claim that everybody else is doing it,* and *the claim of entitlement* (Klockars, 1974; Minor, 1981; Coleman, 1994). Our research was intended to determine which of those techniques of neutralizations were popular with the adult shoplifters that we studied.

Methods

In 1997 and 1998 in Wichita, Kansas, we obtained access to a court-ordered diversion program for adult "first-offenders" charged with theft. Of these offenders, the majority were charged with misdemeanor shoplifting and required to attend an eight-hour therapeutic and education program as a condition for having their record expunged. A new group met each Saturday. The average group had 18 to 20 participants. The participants were encouraged by the program facilitator to discuss with the group the offense that brought them to the diversion program, why they did what they did, and how they felt about it. They were then engaged in a series of educational exercises and role playing activities. We participated in the sessions as observers, recording their stories and experiences and occasionally asking questions. The participants were told that we were researchers studying shoplifting. At the conclusion of each daily session, we approached attendees and asked them if we could interview them. We obtained interviews with 137 subjects from approximately 350 that we approached.

Out of the 137 subjects were 88 men and 49 women. As for their racial backgrounds, 78 were white, 42 African American, and 17 Hispanic. The average age of these people was 26. Although the diversion program was designed for first offenders, over one-half of the participants had been apprehended for shoplifting in the past. Subjects were promised anonymity and were administered a semistructured, open-ended questionnaire regarding their first shoplifting experiences, arrest or apprehension history, the role of co-offenders in the initial and subsequent shoplifting, reasons for shoplifting, emotional responses about the act and aftermath, attitude toward the victim, and their reasons and justifications for shoplifting. To test their commitment to conventional values, informants were specifically asked the question, "How do you feel about stealing from stores?" And, "Do you think that shoplifting is morally wrong?" Where appropriate, we probed and sought clarification and further information. Extensive field notes were kept and verbatim quotes were recorded whenever possible.

Findings

Nearly all of the subjects tried to neutralize their crime with some rationalization or justification. They presented a total of nine different neutralizations. Only five of the 137 informants failed to engage in neutralization. When asked how they felt about their illegal behavior, three of these subjects responded by admitting their guilt and expressing remorse, while the other two simply stated that they had nothing to say on that issue. As for the other majority of the subjects, many offered more than one neutralization for the same offense. One female respondent, for example, said, "*I don't know what comes over me. It's like, you know, is somebody else doing it, not me* [Denial of Responsibility]. *I'm really a good person. I wouldn't ever do something like that, stealing, you know, but I have to take things sometimes for my kids. They need stuff and I don't have any money to get it* [Defense of Necessity]." They frequently responded with a motivation (*I wanted the item and could not afford it*) followed by a neutralization (*Stores charge too much for stuff. They could sell things for half what they do and still make a profit. They're just too greedy*). Thus, in many cases, the motivation was linked to an excuse in such a way as to make the excuse a part of the motivation. The subjects were in effect explaining why they did the crime while justifying it at the same time. The following are examples of the nine neutralizations that our informants used when asked how they felt about their shoplifting.

Denial of Responsibility ("I Didn't Mean It")

Denial of responsibility frees the subjects from experiencing culpability for deviance by allowing them to perceive themselves as victims of their environment. They see themselves as being acted upon rather than acting. They thus attribute their deviant behavior to poor parenting, bad companions, some uncontrollable impulses within them, drug use, or drunkenness. Sykes and Matza (1957) describe the individual resorting to this neutralization as having a "billiard ball conception of himself in which he see himself as helplessly propelled into new situations."

> 26-year-old female: "*I admit that I lift. I do. But, you know, it's not really me—I mean, I don't believe in stealing. I'm a church-going person. It's just that sometimes something takes over me and I can't seem to not do it.*"
> 22-year-old female: "*I wasn't raised right. You know what I mean? Wasn't nobody to teach me right from wrong. I just ran with a bad group and my mamma didn't ever say nothin' about it. That's how I turned out this way—stealin' and stuff.*"
> 20-year-old male: "*If it wasn't for the bunch I ran with at school I never would have started taking things. We used to go the mall after school and everybody would have to steal something. If you didn't get anything, everybody called you names—chicken-shit and stuff like that.*"

Denial of Injury ("I didn't really hurt anybody")

Denial of injury allows the offenders to regard their behavior as having no harmful consequences to the victim. The victim such as a large store, insurance company, or wealthy person may be seen as easily able to afford the loss. Sometimes the crime is semantically recast, referred to in terms that make the offense trivial, such as when auto theft is called joyriding, or vandalism a prank.

> 19-year-old male: *"The stores are big. Make lotsa money. They don't even miss the little bit I get."*
>
> 28-year-old male: *"They write it off their taxes. Probably make a profit off it. So, nobody gets hurt. I get what I need and they come out O.K. too."*
>
> 20-year-old male: *"Them stores make billions. Did you ever hear of Sears going out of business from boosters?"*

Denial of the Victim ("They had it coming")

Denial of the victim facilitates deviance when it can be justified as retaliation upon a deserving victim. In the present study, informants frequently reported that the large stores from which they stole deserved to be victimized because they were believed to be charging high prices and making excessive profits at the expense of ordinary people.

> 48-year-old female: *"Stores deserve it. It don't matter if I boost $10,000 from one, they've made 10,000 times that much ripping off people. You could never steal enough to get even. . . . I don't really think I'm doing anything wrong. Just getting my share."*
>
> 29-year-old female: *"Dillons [food store chain] are totally bogus. A little plastic bag of groceries is $30, $25. Probably cost them $5. . . . Whatta they care about me? Why should I care about them? I take what I want. Don't feel guilty a bit. No sir. Not a bit."*
>
> 49-year-old female: *"I have a lot of anger about stores and the way they rip people off. Sometimes I think the consumer has to take things into their own hands."*

Condemning the Condemners ("The system is corrupt")

Condemning the condemners projects blame on law-makers and law-enforcers. It shifts the focus from the offender to those who disapprove of the criminal acts. This neutralization views the "system" as crooked and thus unable to justify making and enforcing rules it does not itself live by. Those who condemn the offender's behavior are viewed as hypocritical since many of them are believed to engage in deviant behavior themselves.

> 18-year-old male: *"I've heard of cops and lawyers and judges and all kind of rich dudes boosting. They no better than me. You know what I'm saying."*
>
> 35-year-old female: *"Big stores like J.C. Penney's—when they catch me with something—like two pairs of pants, they tell the police you had like 5 pairs of pants and 2 shirts or something like that. . . . What they do with the other 3 pairs of pants and shirts? Insurance company pays them off and they get richer—they's bigger crooks than me."*

> 22-year-old male: *"They thieves too. Just take it a different way. They may be smarter than me—use a computer or something like that—but they just as much a thief as me. Fuck 'em. Cops too. They all thieves. Least, I'm honest about it."*

Appeal to Higher Loyalties ("I didn't do it for myself")

Appeal to higher loyalties is called upon to legitimize a deviant act when the act is carried out to serve a nonselfish, noble purpose, such as meeting the demands of one's friends or taking care of the welfare of one's children.

> 17-year-old female: *"I never do it 'cept when I'm with my friends. Everybody be taking stuff and so I do too. You know—to be part of the group. Not to seem like I'm too good for 'em."*
>
> 28-year-old female: *"I like to get nice stuff for my kids, you know. I know it's not O.K., you know what I mean? But, I want my kids to dress nice and stuff."*

The Defense of Necessity ("I gotta do this")

The defense of necessity involves reducing guilt with the argument that the offender had no choice under the circumstances but to engage in a deviant act (Coleman, 1998). In the case of shoplifting, the defense of necessity is most often used when the offender considers the crime necessary to help the offender's family. The situation here may be similar to the appeal to higher loyalties except that it may also involve committing deviance for one's own needs such as when the person is suffering from hunger or starvation because of job loss. In other words, the appeal to higher loyalties calls for meeting only other-centered needs, but the defense of necessity encompasses either other-centered needs or self-centered needs or both.

> 32-year-old female: *"I had to take care of three children without help. I'd be willing to steal it to given them what they wanted."*
>
> 42-year-old male: *"I got laid off at Boeing last year and got behind on all my bills and couldn't get credit anywhere. My kids needed school clothes and money for supplies and stuff. We didn't have anything and I don't believe in going on welfare, you know. The first time I took some lunch meat at Dillons (grocery chain) so we'd have supper one night. After that I just started to take whatever we needed that day. I knew it was wrong, but I just didn't have any other choice. My family comes first."*

It's So Common ("Everybody does it")

Here the deviants try to neutralize their guilt feelings by reminding themselves that their deviant behavior is extremely common (Coleman, 1998). They apparently assume that if everybody does it and they themselves do not, they will feel like a sucker or a fool.

> 19-year-old female: *"Everybody I know do it. All my friends. My mother and her boyfriend are boosters and my sister is a big-time booster."*

17-year-old male: *"All my friends do it. When I'm with them it seems crazy not to take something too."*

35-year-old female: *"I bet you done did it too . . . when you was coming up. Like 12–13 years old. Everybody boosts."*

Justification by Comparison ("If I didn't do this, I'd be doing something worse")

We found this "new" neutralization only in our research, not in other sociologists' studies. This particular neutralization involves offenders justifying their actions by comparing their crimes to more serious offenses. With this neutralization, the offenders in effect argue that "I may be bad, but I could be worse."

40-year-old male: *"I gotta have $200 every day—day in and day out. I gotta boost a thousand, fifteen hundred dollars worth to get it. I just do what I gotta do. . . . Do I feel bad about what I do? Not really. If I wasn't boosting, I'd be robbing people and maybe somebody would get hurt or killed."*

37-year-old male: *Looka here. Shoplifting be a little thing. Not a crime really. I do it 'stead of robbing folks or breaking in they house. [Society] oughta be glad I boost, stead of them other things."*

19-year-old male: *"It's not thing. Not like its "jacking" people or something. Its just a little lifting."*

Postponement ("I'd think about it later")

Here is another neutralization we found in this research only. With this neutralization, the offenders refrain from thinking about the crime that they are going to commit or the crime that they have just committed. Instead, they say that they would deal with it later.

18-year-old male: *I just don't think about it. I mean, if you think about it, it seems wrong, but you can ignore that feeling sometimes. Put it aside and go on about what you gotta do.*

18-year-old male: *Dude, I just don't deal with those kinda things when I'm boosting. I might feel bad about it later, you know, but by then it's already over and I can't do anything about it then, you know?*

30-year-old female: *I worry about things like that later.*

Conclusion

We found widespread use of neutralizations among the shoplifters in our study. We even discovered two neutralizations that had not appeared in any other studies. These two rationalizations are Postponement and Justification by Comparison. But our research method could not resolve the complex issue of whether our informants neutralized *before* committing the crime. If our subjects did so, it could be used to support the conclusion that pre-crime neutralizations may cause criminal behavior. However, what we found was only the rationalizations our subjects offered *after* they had shoplifted. Neither have other researchers been able to find if pre-deviance neutralizations cause deviant behavior.

REFERENCES

Coleman, James W. 1998. *Criminal Elite: Understanding White Collar Crime.* New York: St. Martin's Press.

Klockars, Carl B. 1974. *The Professional Fence.* New York: Free Press.

Minor, William W. 1981. "Techniques of Neutralization: A Reconceptualization and Empirical Examination." *Journal of Research in Crime and Delinquency* (July) 295–318.

Pogrebin, M., E. Poole, and A. Martinez. 1992 "Accounts of Professional Misdeeds: The Sexual Exploitation of Clients by Psychotherapists." *Deviant Behavior* 13:229–252.

Sykes, Gresham M., and David Matza. 1957. "Techniques of Neutralization: A Theory of Delinquency." *American Sociological Review* 22(6):664–670.

REVIEW QUESTIONS

1. What are the five techniques of neutralization, according to Sykes and Matza?

2. What is "justification by comparison"?

3. Do you believe *postponement* can be used with other crimes? Support your answer.

REFERENCES

Abadinsky, Howard. 1993. Drug Abuse, 2d ed. Chicago: Nelson-Hall.

Ackman, Dan. 2004. "A star is porn." *Wall Street Journal*, August 27, p. W13.

Adams, Mike S. et al. 2003. "Labeling and delinquency." *Adolescence, 38*, 171–186.

Adams-Curtis, Leah E., and Gordon B. Forbes. 2004. "College women's experiences of sexual coercion: A review of cultural, perpetrator, victim, and situational variables." *Trauma, Violence, & Abuse, 5*, 91–122.

Adler, Jerry. 1996. "Adultery: A new furor over an old sin." *Newsweek*, September 30, 54–60.

Adler, Jerry. 2002. "The 'thrill' of theft." *Newsweek*, February 25, pp. 52–53.

Adler, Jerry. 2004. "In the grip of a deeper pain." *Newsweek*, October 20, pp. 48–49.

Agnew, Robert. 1992. "Foundation for a general strain theory of crime and delinquency." *Criminology, 30*, 47–87.

AHA (American Heart Association). 1998. "Tobacco smoke biostatistical fact sheet." http://www.amhrt.org.

Ahmadu, Fuambai. 2000. "Rites and wrongs: An insider/outsider reflects on power and excision." In Bettina Shell-Duncan and Ylva Hernlund (eds.), *Female "Circumcision" in Africa*. Boulder, Colo.: Lynne Rienner.

Akers, Ronald L. 1985. *Deviant Behavior: A Social Learning Approach*, 3d ed. Belmont, Calif.: Wadsworth.

Akers, Ronald L. and Gang Lee. 1999. "Age, social learning, and social bonding in adolescent substance use." *Deviant Behavior, 20*, 1–25.

Al-Arian, Laila. 2004. "Perceptions of U.S. in the Arab World." *Washington Report on Middle East Affairs*, September, pp. 69–70.

Albrect, Steven F. 2001. "Stalking, stalkers, and domestic violence: Relentless fear and obsessive intimacy." In Joseph A. Davis (ed.), *Stalking Crimes and Victim Protection*. Boca Raton, Fla.: CRC Press.

Alder, Christine. 1984. "The convicted rapist: A sexual or a violent offender?" *Criminal Justice and Behavior, 11*, 157–177.

Alder, Christine. 1985. "An exploration of self-reported sexually aggressive behavior." *Crime & Delinquency, 31*, 306–331.

Alessio, Vittoria. 1996. "Born to be gay?" *New Scientist, 151*, September 28, 32–35.

Allam, Abeer. 2004. "Egypt: Torture charged." *New York Times*, March 2, p. A6.

Allan, Graham. 2004. "Being unfaithful: His and her affairs." pp. 121–140 in Jean Duncombe et al., *The State of Affairs: Explorations in Infidelity and Commitment*. Mahwah, N.J.: Lawrence Erlbaum Associates.

Altheide, David L., et al. 1978. "The social meanings of employee theft." In John M. Johnson and Jack D. Douglas (eds.), *Crime at the Top*. Philadelphia: Lippincott.

Altman, Lawrence K. 1999. "New York study finds gay men using safer sex." *New York Times*, June 28, pp. A1, A17.

Alvarez, Alex. 2001. *Governments, Citizens, and Genocide*. Bloomington: Indiana University Press.

Amir, Menachem. 1971. *Patterns in Forcible Rape*. Chicago: University of Chicago Press.

Anderson, C. A. 1989. "Temperature and aggression: Ubiquitous effects of heat on occurrence of human violence." *Psychological Bulletin, 106*, 74–96.

Anderson, K. E., Hugh Lytton, and David M. Romney. 1986. "Mothers' interactions with normal and conduct-disordered boys: Who affects whom?" *Developmental Psychology, 22*, 604–609.

Andreasen, Nancy C., and Donald W. Black. 2001. *Introductory Textbook of Psychiatry*, 3d ed. Washington, D.C.: American Psychiatric Press.

Angelo, Bonnie. 1992. "Wanted: A new godfather." *Time*, April 13, p. 30.

Anslinger, Harry J., and W. S. Thompkins. 1953. *The Traffic in Narcotics*. New York: Funk and Wagnalls.

APA (American Psychiatric Association). 1994. *Diagnostic and Statistical Manual of Mental Disorders*, 4th ed. Washington, D.C.: APA.

Archer, Dane, and Rosemary Gartner. 1984. *Violence and Crime in Cross-National Perspective*. New Haven, Conn.: Yale University Press.

Armes, Audrie. 2004. "Keep your castle secure." *Family Safety & Health*, Fall, pp. 24–29.

Armstrong, Louise. 1993. *And They Call It Help: The Psychiatric Policing of America's Children*. Reading, Mass.: Addison-Wesley.

Arrigo, Bruce A., and Thomas J. Bernard. 1997. "Postmodern criminology in relation to radical and conflict criminology." *Critical Criminology, 8,* 39–60.

Athens, Lonnie. 1985. "Character contests and violent criminal conduct: A critique." *Sociological Quarterly, 26,* 419–431.

Avio, Kenneth L. 1979. "Capital punishment in Canada: A time-series analysis of the deterrence hypothesis." *Canadian Economic Review, 12,* 647–676.

Bachman, R., and Karl A. Pillemer. 1991. "Retirement: Does it affect marital conflict and violence?" *Journal of Elder Abuse and Neglect, 3,* 75–88.

Bagnardi, Vincenzo et al. 2001. "Alcohol consumption and the risk of cancer: A meta-analysis." *Alcohol Research & Health, 25,* 263–270.

Bailey, William C. 1984. "Poverty, inequality and city homicide rates: Some not so unexpected findings." *Criminology, 22,* 531–550.

Bailey, William C. 1998. "Deterrence, brutalization, and the death penalty: Another examination of Oklahoma's return to capital punishment." *Criminology, 36,* 711–733.

Baker, Jean A. 1998. "Are we missing the forest for the trees? Considering the social context of school violence." *Journal of School Psychology, 36,* 29–44.

Bales, Robert F. 1962. "Attitudes toward drinking in the Irish culture." In David J. Pittman and Charles R. Snyder (eds.), *Society, Culture, and Drinking Patterns.* New York: Wiley.

Bales, Robert Freed. 1946. "Cultural differences in rates of alcoholism." *Quarterly Journal of Studies on Alcohol, 6,* 480–499.

Balkan, Sheila, Ronald J. Berger, and Janet Schmidt. 1980. *Crime and Deviance in America: A Critical Approach.* Belmont, Calif.: Wadsworth.

Ball-Rokeach, Sandra J. 1973. "Values and violence: A test of the subculture of violence thesis." *American Sociological Review, 38,* 739–743.

Barnako, Frank. 1998. "Sex sites: $1 billion and growing fast." *CBS MarketWatch,* October 8.

Barnett, Harold C. 1993. "Crimes against the environment: Superfund enforcement at last." *The Annals of the American Academy of Political and Social Science, 525* (January), 119–133.

Barnett, Ola W., Cindy L. Miller-Perrin, and Robin D. Perrin. 2005. *Family Violence Across the Lifespan: An Introduction,* 2d ed. Thousand Oaks, Calif.: Sage Publications.

Baron, James N., and Peter C. Reiss. 1985. "Same time, next year: Aggregate analyses of the mass media and violent behavior." *American Sociological Review, 50,* 347–363.

Barry, John, et al. 2004. "Abu Ghraib and beyond." *Newsweek,* May 17, pp. 32–37.

Barry, Kathleen. 1995. *The Prostitution of Sexuality.* New York: New York University Press.

Barstow, Anne Llewellyn (ed.). 2000. *War's Dirty Secret.* Cleveland, Ohio: Pilgrim Press.

Barstow, Donald G. 2004. "Female genital mutilation." In Alex Thio and Thomas C. Calhoun (eds.), *Readings in Deviant Behavior,* 3d ed. Boston: Allyn and Bacon.

Bart, Pauline B., and Patricia H. O'Brien. 1984. "Stopping rape: Effective avoidance strategies." *Signs, 10,* 83–101.

Bart, Pauline B., and Patricia H. O'Brien. 1985. *Stopping Rape: Successful Survival Strategies.* New York: Pergamon.

Bawer, Bruce. 1993. *A Place at the Table: The Gay Individual in American Society.* New York: Poseidon Press.

Bayer, Ronald. 1985. "AIDS and the gay community: Between the specter and the promise of medicine." *Social Research, 52,* 588–589.

Beasley, James O. II. 2004. "Serial murder in America: Case studies of seven offenders." *Behavioral Sciences and the Law, 22,* 395–414.

Bechhofer, Laurie, and Andrea Parrot. 1991. "What is acquaintance rape?" In Andrea Parrot and Laurie Bechhofer (eds.), *Acquaintance Rape: The Hidden Crime.* New York: John Wiley & Sons.

Beck, Melinda. 1990. "Trading places." *Newsweek,* July 16, pp. 48–54.

Becker, Howard S. 1963. *Outsiders: Studies in the Sociology of Deviance.* New York: Free Press.

Becker, Howard S. 1974. "Labelling theory reconsidered." In Paul Rock and Mary McIntosh (eds.), *Deviance and Social Control.* London: Tavistock.

Beckerman, Nancy L. 1995. "Suicide in relation to AIDS." *Death Studies, 19,* 223–234.

Begley, Sharon. 1996. "Born happy?" *Newsweek,* October 14, pp. 78–80.

Begley, Sharon. 1999. "Why the young kill." *Newsweek,* May 3, pp. 32–35.

Begley, Sharon. 2004. "Alternative peer groups may offer way to deter some suicide bombers." *Wall Street Journal,* October 8, p. B1.

Belluck, Pam. 1998. "Black youths' rate of suicide rising sharply." *New York Times,* March 20, pp. A1, A18.

Benedict, Jeffrey R. 1998. *Athletes and Acquaintance Rape.* Thousand Oaks, Calif.: Sage Publications.

Benjamin, Harry, and R. E. L. Masters. 1964. *Prostitution and Morality.* New York: Julian.

Bennett, William J. 1989. "A response to Milton Friedman." *Wall Street Journal,* September 19, p. A32.

Benson, Michael L. 1985. "Denying the guilty mind: Accounting for involvement in white-collar crime." *Criminology, 23,* 585–607.

Berendzen, Richard, and Laura Palmer, 1993. *Come Here: A Man Overcomes the Tragic Aftermath of Childhood Sexual Abuse.* New York: Villard Books.

Bergen, Raquel Kennedy. 1996. *Wife Rape: Understanding the Response of Survivors and Service Providers.* Thousand Oaks, Calif.: Sage Publications.

Berger, Joseph. 1994. "The psychotherapeutic treatment of male homosexuality." *American Journal of Psychotherapy, 48,* 251–261.

Berger, Lawrence M. 2004. "Income, family structure, and child maltreatment risk." *Children and Youth Services Review, 26,* 725–748.

Berk, Richard A., and Phyllis J. Newton. 1985. "Does arrest really deter wife battery? An effort to replicate the findings of the Minneapolis spouse abuse experiment." *American Sociological Review, 50,* 253–262.

Berke, Richard L. 1998. "Chasing the polls on gay rights." *New York Times,* August 2, Section 4, p. 3.

Berkeley, Bill. 2002. "Code of betrayal, not silence, shines light on Russian mob." *New York Times,* August 19, pp. A1, A14.

Berrill, Kevin T. 1992. "Anti-gay violence and victimization in the United States: An overview." In Gregory M. Herek and Kevin T. Berrill (eds.), *Hate Crime.* Newbury Park, Calif.: Sage Publications.

Berry, Jason. 2000. *Lead Us Not Into Temptation.* Urbana, Ill.: University of Illinois Press.

Bettridge, Brenda J., and Olga Eizner Favreau. 1995. "Suicidal behavior among adolescent females: The cry for connection." In Silvia Sara Canetto and David Lester (eds.), *Women and Suicidal Behavior.* New York: Springer.

Blakely, Mary Kay. 1983. "The New Bedford gang rape." *Ms.,* July, p. 53.

Blank, Jonah, Jason Vest, and Suzie Parker. 1998. "The children of Jonesboro." *U.S. News & World Report,* April 6, pp. 16–22.

Blizzard, Rick. 2004a. "Americans and alcohol: Drink, drank, drunk?" *The Gallup Poll Tuesday Briefing.* August 24. www.gallup.com.

Blizzard, Rick. 2004b. "Smoking: Will education overpower addiction?" *The Gallup Poll Tuesday Brief.* August 31. www.gallup.com.

Block, Alan A. 1991. *The Business of Crime.* Boulder, Colo.: Westview.

Blumenfeld, Warren J. (ed.). 1992. *Homophobia: How We All Pay the Price.* Boston: Beacon.

Blumenfeld, Warren J., and Diane Raymond. 1993. *Looking at Gay and Lesbian Life.* Boston: Beacon.

Blumstein, Alfred. 1995. "Violence by young people: Why the deadly nexus?" *National Institute of Justice Journal,* August, pp. 2–9.

Blumstein, Philip, and Pepper Schwartz. 1990. "Intimate relationships and the creation of sexuality." In David P. McWhirter, et al. (eds.), *Homosexuality/Heterosexuality.* New York: Oxford University Press.

Bocij, Paul. 2004. *Cyberstalking: Harassment in the Internet Age and How to Protect Your Family.* Westport, Conn.: Praeger.

Boffey, Philip M. 1986. "Schizophrenia: Insights fail to halt rising toll." *New York Times,* March 16, p. 1.

Bogert, Carroll. 1994. "Good news on drugs from the inner city." *Newsweek,* February 14, pp. 28–29.

Bolen, Rebecca M. 2001. *Child Sexual Abuse: Its Scope and Our Failure.* New York: Kluwer Academic/ Plenum Publishers.

Bower, Bruce. 1992. "Alcoholism: Nurture may often outdo nature." *Science News, 141,* February 1, p. 69.

Bower, Bruce. 1994. "Mental disorders strike about half of U.S." *Science News,* January 22, p. 55.

Bowers, William J., and Glenn L. Pierce. 1980. "Deterrence or brutalization: What is the effect of execution?" *Crime and Delinquency, 26,* 453–484.

Boyatzis, Richard E. 1975. "The predisposition toward alcohol-related interpersonal aggression in men." *Journal of Studies on Alcohol, 36,* 1196–1207.

Bradsher, Keith. 1999. "For car thieves, a technological arms race." *New York Times,* March 28, Section 4, p. 3.

Braithwaite, John. 1989. *Crime, Shame and Reintegration.* New York: Cambridge University Press.

Braithwaite, John. 1992. "Poverty, power, and white-collar crime." In Kip Schlegel and David Weisburd (eds.), *White-Collar Crime Reconsidered.* Boston: Northeastern University Press.

Braithwaite, John. 1993. "Transnational regulation of the pharmaceutical industry." *The Annals of the American Academy of Political and Social Science, 525,* January, 13–14.

Braithwaite, John. 2000. "Shame and criminal justice." *Canadian Journal of Criminology,* July, 42, 281–299.

Brake, Mike. 1994. "Needed: A license to drink." *Newsweek,* March 14, p. 11.

Breault, K. D. 1986. "Suicide in America: A test of Durkheim's theory of religious and family integration, 1933–1980." *American Journal of Sociology, 92,* 628–656.

Breault, K. D. and Karen Barkey. 1982. "A comparative analysis of Durkheim's theory of egoistic suicide." *Sociological Quarterly, 24,* 321–331.

Breggin, Peter. 1997. *Empathy and the Creation of a Healing Presence.* New York: Springer.

Brener, N. et al. 2004. "Violence-related behaviors among high school students—United States, 1991–2003." *JAMA (Journal of American Medical Association), 292,* 1168–1169.

Breslow, Rosalind A., and Barbara Smothers. 2004. "Drinking patterns of older Americans: National health interview surveys, 1997–2001." *Journal of Studies on Alcohol, 65,* 232–240.

Brewer, John D. 2000. *Ethnography.* Buckingham, U.K.: Open University Press.

Brinson, Susan L. 1992. "The use and opposition of rape myths in prime-time television dramas." *Sex Roles, 27,* 359–375.

Brody, Jane E. 1997. "Quirks, oddities may be illnesses." *New York Times,* February 4, pp. B9, B11.

Brown, Judith K. 1992. "Introduction." In D. A. Counts, J. K. Brown, and J. C. Campbell (eds.), *Sanctions and Sanctuary: Cultural Perspectives on the Beating of Wives.* Boulder, Colo: Westview.

Brown, Marjorie E. 1979. "Teenage prostitution." *Adolescence, 14,* 665–680.

Browne, Angela. 1987. *Why Battered Women Kill.* New York: Free Press.

Brownmiller, Susan. 1975. *Against Our Will: Men, Women and Rape.* New York: Simon & Schuster.

Bruni, Frank. 1997. "In an age of consent, defining abuse by adults." *New York Times,* Section 4, p. 3.

Brush, Lisa D. 2003. "Effects of work on hitting and hurting." *Violence Against Women, 9,* 1213–1230.

Bryan, James H. 1966. "Occupational ideologies and individual attitudes of call girls." *Social Problems, 13,* 441–450.

Bryant, Marshall A. 1977. "Prostitution and the criminal justice system." *Journal of Police Science and Administration, 5,* 384.

Budiansky, Stephen, et al. 1995. "How lawyers abuse the law." *U.S. News & World Report,* January 30, pp. 50–56.

Bullough, Bonnie. 1993. "The causes of homosexuality: A scientific update." *Free Inquiry, 13* (Fall), 40–47.

Bumiller, Elisabeth. 1999. "Deny rape or be hated: Kosovo victims' choice." *New York Times,* June 22, pp. A1, A13.

Burgess, Ann Wolbert. 1995. "Rape trauma syndrome." In Patricia Searles and Ronald J. Berger (eds.), *Rape and Society.* Boulder, Colo.: Westview.

Burgess, Robert L., and Ronald L. Akers. 1966. "A differential association-reinforcement theory of criminal behavior." *Social Problems, 14,* 128–147.

Burr, Chandler. 1996. *A Separate Creation: The Search for the Biological Origins of Sexual Orientation.* New York: Hyperion.

Burros, Marian. 1996. "In an about-face, U.S. says alcohol has health benefits." *New York Times,* January 3, pp. A1, B6.

Burt, Martha R. 1991. "Rape myths and acquaintance rape." In Andrea Parrot and Laurie Bechhofer (eds.), *Acquaintance Rape.* New York: Wiley.

Burton, Thomas M. 1993a. "Caught in the act." *Wall Street Journal,* March 26, pp. A1, A5.

Burton, Thomas M. 1993b. "Spilled milk." *Wall Street Journal,* May 25, pp. A1, A6.

Burton, Velmer S. et al. 1998. "Gender, self-control, and crime." *Journal of Research in Crime and Delinquency 35,* 123–147.

Busch, Amy L., and Mindy S. Rosenberg. 2004. "Comparing women and men arrested for domestic violence: A preliminary report." *Journal of Family Violence, 19,* 49–57.

Buss, Dale. 1993. "Ways to curtail employee theft." *Nation's Business,* April, p. 36.

Butterfield, Fox. 1999. "Prisons brim with mentally ill, study finds." *New York Times,* July 12, p. A10.

Byrne, C. A., et al. 1999. "The socioeconomic impact of interpersonal violence on women." *Journal of Consulting and Clinical Psychology, 67;* 362–366.

Cahalan, Don. 1970. *Problem Drinkers.* San Francisco: Jossey-Bass.

Cahan, Vicky, et al. 1985. "A murder verdict jolts business." *Business Week,* July 1, p. 24.

Cahill, Tom. 1985. "Rape behind bars," *The Progressive,* November, p. 32.

Calhoun, Lawrence G., James W. Selby, and Michael E. Faulstich. 1980. "Reactions to the parents of the child suicide: A study of social impressions." *Journal of Consulting and Clinical Psychology, 48,* 535–536.

Campo-Flores, Arian. 2002. "A crackdown on call girls." *Newsweek,* September 2, p. 59.

Canetto, Silvia Sara, and David Lester (eds.). 1995. *Women and Suicidal Behavior.* New York: Springer.

Cannon, Angie. 1999. "Sex, drugs, and sudden death." *U.S. News & World Report,* May 24, p. 73.

Cannon, Angie, and Jeffrey L. Sheler. 2002. "Catholics in crisis." *U.S. News & World Report,* April 1, pp. 51–57.

Caplan, Gerald M. 1984. "The facts of life about teenage prostitution." *Crime & Delinquency, 30,* 69–74.

Capone, Donald L., and Woodrow W. Nichols, Jr. 1976. "Urban structure and criminal mobility." *American Behavioral Scientist, 20,* 199–213.

Carey, Kate B. 1993. "Situational determinants of heavy drinking among college students." *Journal of Counseling Psychology, 40,* 217–220.

Carlson, Margaret. 1995. "The sex-crime capital." *Time,* November 13, pp. 89–90.

Carrithers, David W. 1985. "The insanity defense and presidential peril." *Society, 22* (July/August), 22–27.

Carter, Bonnie Frank, and Allan Brooks. 1991. "Child and adolescent survivors of suicide." In Antoon A. Leenaars (ed.), *Life Span Perspectives of Suicide: Time-lines in the Suicide Process.* New York: Plenum.

Carter, David, and Andra J. Bannister. 2002. "Computer-related crime." In David Shichor, Larry Gaines, and Richard Ball (eds.), *Readings in White-Collar Crime.* Prospect Heights, Ill.: Waveland.

Carter, Hodding. 1989. "We're losing the drug war because prohibition never works." *Wall Street Journal,* July 13, p. A15.

Cashdan, Sheldon. 1972. *Abnormal Psychology.* Englewood Cliffs, N.J.: Prentice Hall.

Catalano, Ralph, et al. 1993. "Job loss and alcohol abuse: A test using data from the epidemiologic catchment area project." *Journal of Health and Social Behavior, 34,* 215–225.

Cazenave, N. A., and Murray A. Straus. 1990. "Race, class, network embeddedness, and family violence: A search for potent support systems." In M. A. Straus and R. J. Gelles (eds.), *Physical Violence in American Families.* New Brunswick, N.J.: Transaction.

CDC (Centers for Disease Control). 2003. "Drug-associated HIV transmission continues in the United States." www.cdc.gov/hiv/pubs/facts/idu.htm.

Chambliss, William J. 1969. *Crime and the Legal Process.* New York: McGraw-Hill.

Chambliss, William J., and Robert Seidman. 1971. *Law, Order, and Power.* Reading, Mass.: Addison-Wesley.

Chappell, Allison T. and Alex R. Piquero. 2004. "Applying social learning theory to police misconduct." *Deviant Behavior, 25,* 89–109.

Chappell, Duncan, Gilbert Geis, Stephen Schafer, and Larry Siegel, 1971. "Forcible rape: A comparative study of offenses known to the police in Boston and Los Angeles." In James M. Henslin (ed.), *Studies in the Sociology of Sex.* New York: Appleton-Century-Crofts.

Chase, Marilyn. 1996a. "Health journal." *Wall Street Journal,* August 26, p. B1.

Chase, Marilyn. 1996b. "Americans seem to drink a lot or hardly at all." *Wall Street Journal,* December 30, p. B1.

Chein, Isidor, Donald L. Gerard, Robert S. Lee, and Eva Rosenfeld. 1964. *The Road to H.* New York: Basic Books.

Cherry, Rona, and Laurence Cherry. 1973. "Depression: The common cold of mental ailments." *New York Times Magazine,* November 25, p. 38.

Chervyakov, Valerity V., et al. 2002. "The changing nature of murder in Russia." *Social Science and Medicine, 55,* 1713–1724.

Chesney-Lind, Meda. 1997. *The Female Offender: Girls, Women, and Crime.* Thousand Oaks, Calif.: Sage Publications.

Chiroro, Patrick et al. 2004. "Rape myth acceptance and rape proclivity: Expected dominance versus expected arousal as mediators in acquaintance-rape situations." *Journal of Interpersonal Violence, 19,* 427–442.

Christensen, Russ, and Peter W. Dowrick. 1983. "Myths of mid-winter depression." *Community Mental Health Journal, 19,* 177–186.

Christian, Nichole. 1995. "New generation of car thieves restructures the business." *Wall Street Journal,* July 19, p. B1.

Church, George J. 1986. "What he needs to know." *Time,* December 22, pp. 17–18.

Clarke, Ronald V. 2002. *Shoplifting.* Washington, D.C.: U.S. Department of Justice.

Clausen, John A., and Carol L. Huffine. 1975. "Sociocultural and social-psychological factors affecting social responses to mental disorder." *Journal of Health and Social Behavior, 16,* 405–420.

Clifton, A. Kay, and Dorothy E. Lee. 1995. "Gender socialization and women's suicidal behaviors." In Silvia Sara Canetto and David Lester (eds.), *Women and Suicidal Behavior.* New York: Springer.

Clinard, Marshall B., and Peter C. Yeager. 1980. *Corporate Crime.* New York: Free Press.

Cloud, John. 1998. "For better or worse." *Time,* October 26, pp. 43–44.

Cloud, John. 2001. "A license to kill?" *Time,* April 23, p. 66.

Cloward, Richard, and Lloyd E. Ohlin. 1960. *Delinquency and Opportunity: A Theory of Juvenile Gangs.* New York: Free Press.

Cochrane, Raymond. 1983. *The Social Creation of Mental Illness.* London: Longman.

Cohen, Albert K. 1955. *Delinquent Boys: The Culture of the Gang.* New York: Free Press.

Cohen, Lawrence E., David Cantor, and James R. Kluegel. 1981. "Robbery victimization in the

U.S.: An analysis of a nonrandom event." *Social Science Quarterly, 62,* 645–657.

Cohen, Murray, Ralph Garofalo, Richard Boucher, and Theoharis Seghorn. 1971. "The psychology of rapists." *Seminar in Psychiatry, 3,* 310.

Cohn, Bob, and Mary Hager. 1993. "The power of sin." *Newsweek,* October 4, p. 51.

Coleman, James William. 1994. *The Criminal Elite: The Sociology of White Collar Crime,* 3d ed. New York: St. Martin's.

Collier, Theresa J. 1993. "The stigma of mental illness." *Newsweek,* April 26, p. 16.

Colvin, Mark, and John Pauly. 1983. "A critique of criminology: Toward an integrated structural-Marxist theory of delinquency production." *American Journal of Sociology, 89,* 513–551.

Conant, Marcus. 1997. "This is smart medicine." *Newsweek,* February 3, p. 26.

Conklin, John E. 1972. *Robbery and the Criminal Justice System.* Philadelphia: Lippincott.

Conklin, John E. 1977. *"Illegal but Not Criminal": Business Crime in America.* Englewood Cliffs, N.J.: Prentice Hall.

Contexts. 2004. "From the polls: Assisted suicide." Summer, p. 58.

Cook, Philip J., and Mark H. Moore. 1999. "Guns, gun control, and homicide: A review of research and public policy." In M. Dwayne Smith and Margaret A. Zahn (eds.), *Homicide: A Sourcebook of Social Research.* Thousand Oaks, Calif.: Sage Publications.

Cookson, Peter W., Jr., and Caroline Hodges Persell. 1985. *Preparing for Power: America's Elite Boarding Schools.* New York: Basic Books.

Coombs, Robert Holman. 1997. *Drug-Impaired Professionals.* Cambridge, Mass.: Harvard University Press.

Cooper, Al. 2004. "Online sexual activity in the New Millennium." *Contemporary Sexuality,* March, pp. 1–8.

Corliss, Richard, and Simon Crittle. 2004. "The last don." *Time* March 29, pp. 44–52.

Corzine, Jay, Lin Huff-Dorzine, and Hugh P. Whitt. 1999. "Cultural and subcultural theories of homicide." In M. Dwayne Smith and Margaret A. Zahn (eds.), *Homicide: A Sourcebook of Social Research.* Thousand Oaks, Calif.: Sage Publications.

Cottle, Thomas J. 2004. "A teen suicide in the family." In Alex Thio and Thomas C. Calhoun (eds.), *Readings in Deviant Behavior,* 3d ed. Boston: Allyn and Bacon.

Cowley, Geoffrey. 1997. "Can marijuana be medicine?" *Newsweek,* February 3, pp. 22–27.

Coyne, James C., and Geraldine Downey. 1991. "Social factors and psychopathology: Stress, social support, and coping processes." *Annual Review of Psychology, 42,* 401–425.

Cressey, Donald R. 1971. *Other People's Money: A Study in the Social Psychology of Embezzlement.* Belmont, Calif.: Wadsworth.

Cromwell, Paul F., James N. Olson, and D'Aunn Wester Avary. 1991. *Breaking and Entering: An Ethnographic Analysis of Burglary.* Newbury Park, Calif.: Sage Publications.

Crossen, Cynthia. 1996. "Losing it." *Wall Street Journal,* December 3, pp. A1, A10:

Crosset, Todd W., J. Ptacek, M. A. Mcdonald, and J. R. Benedict. 1996. "Male student-athletes and violence against women: A survey of campus judicial affairs offices." *Violence Against Women, 2,* 163–179.

Cross-National Collaborative Group. 1992. "The changing rate of major depression: Cross-national comparisons." *JAMA (Journal of American Medical Association), 268,* 3098–3105.

Crouch, Margaret A. 2001. *Thinking about Sexual Harassment.* New York: Oxford University Press.

Currie, Elliott. 1993. *Reckoning: Drugs, the Cities, and the American Future.* New York: Hill and Wang.

Cuvelier, Monique. 2002. "Victim, not villain." *Psychology Today,* May/June, p. 23.

Dalrymple, Theodore. 2002. "Marks of shame." *National Review,* March 11, pp. 28–30.

Danigelis, Nick, and Whitney Pope. 1979. "Durkheim's theory of suicide as applied to the family: An empirical test." *Social Forces, 57,* 1081–1106.

Davies, Scott, and Julian Tanner. 2003. "The long arm of the law: Effects of labeling on employment." *Sociological Quarterly, 44,* 385–404.

Davis, Alan J. 1982. "Sexual assaults in the Philadelphia prison system and sheriff's vans." In Anthony M. Scacco, Jr. (ed.), *Male Rape.* New York: AMS Press.

Davis, Bernard D. 1990. "Right to die: Living wills are inadequate." *Wall Street Journal,* July 31, p. A12.

Davis, Kingsley. 1971. "Sexual behavior." In Robert Merton and Robert Nisbet (eds.), *Contemporary Social Problems,* 3d ed. New York: Harcourt Brace Jovanovich.

Davis, Nanette J. (ed.). 1993. *Prostitution: An International Handbook on Trends, Problems, and Policies.* Westport, Conn.: Greenwood.

Davis, Nanette J., and Clarice Stasz. 1990. *Social Control: The Production of Deviance in the Modern State.* New York: McGraw-Hill.

Davison, Gerald C., and John M. Neale. 1996. *Abnormal Psychology*, 6th ed. New York: Wiley.

Decker, Scott, and Richard Rosenfeld. 1992. "Intravenous drug use and the AIDS epidemic: Findings from a 20-city sample of arrestees." *Crime & Delinquency, 38*, 492–509.

Deitz, Sheila R., et al. 1984. "Attributions of responsibility for rape: The influence of observer empathy, victim resistance, and victim attractiveness." *Sex Roles, 10*, 261–280.

DeJong, William. 1986. "Project DARE: Teaching kids to say no to drugs and alcohol." *NIJ Reports*, no. 196, pp. 2–5.

DeKeseredy, Walter S., and Martin D. Schwartz. 1996. *Contemporary Criminology*. Belmont, Calif.: Wadsworth.

Demyttenaere, K., et al. 2004. "Prevalence of mental disorders in Europe: Results from the European Study of the Epidemiology of Mental Disorders project." *Acta Psychiatrica Scandinavica, 109*, 21–27.

Denham, Susanne A., Susan M. Renwick, and Robert W. Holt. 1991. "Working and playing together: Prediction of preschool social-emotional competence from mother-child interaction." *Child Development, 62*, 242–249.

Denzin, Norman K. 1991. "The AA group." In David J. Pittman and Helene Raskin White (eds.), *Society, Culture, and Drinking Patterns Reexamined*. New Brunswick, N.J.: Rutgers Center of Alcohol Studies.

Derfner, Larry. 2002. "After a suicide bomb." *U.S. News & World Report*, August 19, pp. 24–26.

Dickermann, Mildred. 1995. "Wilson's panchreston: The inclusive fitness hypothesis of sociobiology re-examined." *Journal of Homosexuality, 28*, 147–183.

Dickey, Christopher. 2002. "Inside suicide, inc." *Newsweek*, April 15, pp. 26–32.

Diller, Lawrence H. 1998. *Running on Ritalin*. New York: Bantam Books.

Dobash, Russell P., R. Emerson Dobash, Margo Wilson, and Martin Daly. 1992. "The myth of sexual symmetry in marital violence." *Social Problems, 39*, 71–91.

Doblin, Rich, and Mark A. R. Kleiman. 1993. "Marijuana as medicine." *Wall Street Journal*, February 19, p. A13.

Dobrzynski, Judith H. 1996. "For more and more job seekers, an aging parent is a big factor." *New York Times*, January 1, pp. 1, 24.

Dodge, David L. 1985. "The over-negativized conceptualization of deviance: A programmatic exploration." *Deviant Behavior, 6*, 17–37.

Dohrenwend, Bruce P. 1975. "Sociocultural and social-psychological factors in the genesis of mental disorders." *Journal of Health and Social Behavior, 16*, 365–392.

Dohrenwend, Bruce P., and Barbara Snell Dohrenwend. 1974. "Psychiatric disorders in urban settings." In S. Arietti and G. Caplan (eds.), *American Handbook of Psychiatry*. New York: Basic Books.

Dohrenwend, Bruce P., and Barbara Snell Dohrenwend. 1976. "Sex differences and psychiatric disorders." *American Journal of Sociology, 81*, 1447–1454.

Donnerstein, Edward, et al. 1987. *The Question of Pornography: Research Findings and Policy Implications*. New York: Free Press.

Donovan, James M. 1986. "An etiologic model of alcoholism." *American Journal of Psychiatry, 143*, 5–6.

Donovan, John E., 1993. "Young adult drinking-driving: Behavioral and psychosocial correlates." *Journal of Studies on Alcohol, 54*, 600–613.

Douglas, Jack D. 1967. *The Social Meanings of Suicide*. Princeton, N.J.: Princeton University Press.

Douglas, Jack D., and Frances C. Waksler. 1982. *The Sociology of Deviance*. Boston: Little, Brown.

Dubin, Louis I., and Bessie Bunzel. 1933. *To Be or Not To Be*. New York: Harrison Smith and Robert Haas.

Duffala, Dennis C. 1976. "Convenience stores, armed robbery, and physical environmental features." *American Behavioral Scientist, 20*, 227–246.

Duffy, Brian, and Angie Cannon. 2002. "The end of the road." *U.S. News & World Report*, November 4, pp. 19–30.

Dugger, Celia W. 1999. "Calcutta's prostitutes preach about condoms." *New York Times*, January 4, pp. A1, A8.

Duncombe, Jean et al. (eds.). 2004. *The State of Affairs: Explorations in Infidelity and Commitment*. Mahwah, N.J.: Lawrence Erlbaum Associates.

Dunkle, John H., and Patricia L. Francis. 1990. "The role of facial masculinity/femininity in the attribution of homosexuality." *Sex Roles, 23*, 157–167.

Dunlap, David W. 1995. "Two steps forward for homosexuals." *New York Times*, October 18, p. A12.

Dunn, Jennifer. 2004. "'Everyone knows who the sluts are': How young women get around the stigma." In Alex Thio and Thomas C. Calhoun (eds.), *Readings in Deviant Behavior*, 3d ed. Boston: Allyn and Bacon.

Durkheim, Émile. 1897/1966. *Suicide*. New York: Free Press.

Dutton, Donald G. 1986. "Wife assaulters' explanations for assault: The neutralization of selfpunishment." *Canadian Journal of Behavioral Sciences, 18,* 381–390.

Dutton, Donald G. 1994. "Patriarchy and wife assault: An ecological fallacy." *Violence and Victims, 9,* 167–182.

Early, Kevin E. 1992. *Religion and Suicide in the African-American Community.* Westport, Conn.: Greenwood.

Early, Kevin E. 1996. *Drug Treatment Behind Bars: Prison-Based Strategies for Change.* Westport, Conn.: Praeger.

Early, Kevin E., and Ronald L. Akers. 1995. "'It's a white thing': An exploration of beliefs about suicide in the African-American community." In Alex Thio and Thomas Calhoun (eds.), *Readings in Deviant Behavior.* New York: Harper-Collins.

Eaton, Leslie. 1999. "Assault with a fiscal weapon." *New York Times,* May 25, pp. C1, C25.

The Economist. 1979. "Sexual therapists." December 2, p. 26.

The Economist. 1991. "Shoplifting in America." January 19, p. 65.

The Economist, 2004. "It's their business." Vol. 372, September 4, p. 12.

Edmundson, Mark. 1999. "Save Sigmund Freud." *New York Times Magazine,* July 13, pp. 34–35.

Edwards, Hodee. 1993. "Rape defines sex." *Off Our Backs, 23* (August), 16–17.

Egan, Timothy. 2000. "Technology sent Wall Street into market for pornography." *New York Times,* October 23, pp. A1, A20.

Ehrenreich, Barbara. 2002. "Libation as liberation." *Time,* April 1, p. 62.

Ehrlich, Isaac. 1975. "The deterrent effect of capital punishment: A question of life and death." *American Economic Review, 65,* 397–417.

Eichenwald, Kurt. 2002. "White-collar defense stance: The criminal-less crime." *New York Times,* March 3, Section 4, p. 3.

Eigen, Joel Peter. 1981. "Punishing youth homicide offenders in Philadelphia," *Journal of Criminal Law and Criminology, 72,* 1075.

Einstadter, Werner, and Stuart Henry. 1995. *Criminological Theory: An Analysis of Its Underlying Assumptions.* Fort Worth, Texas: Harcourt Brace.

Eisenberg, Daniel. 2002. "Dennis the menace." *Time,* June 17, pp. 46–49.

Elliott, Diana M. et al. 2004. "Adult sexual assault: Prevalence, symptomatology, and sex differences in the general population." *Journal of Traumatic Stress, 17,* 203–211.

Elliott, Jeff. 1995. "Drug prevention placebo." *Reason, 26* (March), 14–21.

Elliott, Robert E., et al. 1985. *Explaining Delinquency and Drug Use.* Beverly Hills, Calif.: Sage Publications.

Elmer-Dewitt, Philip. 1995. "On a screen near you: Cyberporn." *Time,* July 3, pp. 38–45.

Empfield, Maureen, and Nicholas Bakalar. 2001. *Understanding Teenage Depression.* New York: Henry Holt.

Engs, Ruth C., and David J. Hanson. 1994. "Boozing and brawling on campus: A national study of violent problems associated with drinking over the past decade." *Journal of Criminal Justice, 22,* 171–180.

Erikson, Kai T. 1962. "Notes on the sociology of deviance." *Social Problems, 9,* 307–314.

Erlanger, Howard S. 1974. "The empirical status of the subculture of violence thesis." *Social Problems, 22,* 280–292.

Ermann, M. David, and Richard J. Lundman (eds.). 2002. *Corporate and Governmental Deviance: Problems of Organizational Behavior in Contemporary Society,* 6th ed. New York: Oxford University Press.

Erofeyev, Victor. 2002. "The Russian god." *New Yorker,* December 16, pp. 56–63.

Essex, Marilyn et al. 1981. "On Weinstein's 'Patient attitudes toward mental hospitalization: A review of quantitative research.'" *Journal of Health and Social Behavior, 21,* 393–396.

Falco, Mathea. 1992. *The Making of a Drug-Free America: Programs That Work.* New York: Times Books.

Falk, Gerhard. 2001. *Stigma: How We Treat Outsiders.* Amherst, N.Y.: Prometheus Books.

Farberow, Norman L. 1991. "Adult survivors after suicide: Research problems and needs." In Antoon A. Leenaars (ed.), *Life Span Perspectives of Suicide: Time-lines in the Suicide Process.* New York: Plenum.

Farley, Melissa. 1994. "Prostitution: The oldest use and abuse of women." *Off Our Backs, 24,* 14–15.

Farrington, David P. 1977. "The effects of public labelling." *British Journal of Criminology, 17,* 112–125.

FBI (Federal Bureau of Investigation). 2002. *Uniform Crime Reports.* Washington, D.C.: Government Printing Office.

FBI. 2004. *Uniform Crime Reports.* Washington, D.C.: Government Printing Office.

Feeney, Floyd, and Adrianne Weir. 1975. "The prevention and control of robbery." *Criminology, 13,* 104.

Feldman, Douglas A. 1985. "AIDS and social change." *Human Organization, 44,* 343–348.

Felson, Richard B., and Henry J. Steadman. 1983. "Situational factors in disputes leading to criminal violence." *Criminology, 21,* 39–74.

Ferrell, Jeff, and Mark S. Hamm (eds.). 1998. *Ethnography at the Edge: Crime, Deviance, and Field Research.* Boston: Northeastern University Press.

Fields, Suzanne. 1993. "Rape as sport: The culture is at the root." *Insight on the News, 9* (May 3), 19–20.

Fillion, Kate. 1991. "Rape on campus." *Chatelaine, 64* (August), 33–35.

Fine, M., and A. Asch. 1988. "Disability beyond stigma: Social interaction, discrimination, and activism." *Journal of Social Issues, 44,* 3–22.

Finkelhor, David. 1984. *Child Sexual Abuse: New Theory and Research.* New York: Free Press.

Finkelhor, David, et al. 1989. "Sexual abuse and its relationship to later sexual satisfaction, marital status, religion, and attitudes." *Journal of Interpersonal Violence, 4,* 379–399.

Firth, Raymond. 1961. "Suicide and risk-taking in Tikopia society." *Psychiatry, 24,* 4.

Fisher, Helen E. 1992. *Anatomy of Love: The Natural History of Monogamy, Adultery, and Divorce.* New York: Norton.

Fishman, Scott M., and David V. Sheehan. 1985. "Anxiety and panic: Their cause and treatment." *Psychology Today,* April, p. 26.

Fleishman, Ellen Gerschitz. 1983. "Sex-role acquisition, parental behavior, and sexual orientation: Some tentative hypotheses." *Sex Roles, 9,* 1051–1059.

Flowers, Amy. 1998. *The Fantasy Factory: An Insider's View of the Phone Sex Industry.* Philadelphia: University of Pennsylvania Press.

Foderaro, Lisa W. 1995. "Mentally ill gaining new rights, with the ill as their own lobby." *New York Times,* October 14, pp. 1, 8.

Folse, Kimberly A., and Dennis L. Peck. 1995. "A phenomenological analysis of suicide." In Alex Thio and Thomas Calhoun (eds.), *Readings in Deviant Behavior.* New York: HarperCollins.

Fort, Joel. 1973. *Alcohol: Our Biggest Drug Problem.* New York: McGraw-Hill.

Fox, James Alan. 1996. "Trends in juvenile offending." *National Institute of Justice Journal,* August, pp. 15–23.

Fox, James Alan, Jack Levin and Kenna Quinet. 2005. *The Will to Kill.* Boston: Allyn and Bacon.

Frank, Nancy. 1993. "Maiming and killing: Occupational health crimes." *The Annals of the American Academy of Political and Social Science, 525,* 107–118.

Frank, Robert, et al. 2004. "Scandal scorecard." *Wall Street Journal,* October 3, pp. B1, B4.

Frank, Stephen E., and John R. Wilke. 1997. "Visa, MasterCard may face antitrust suit." *Wall Street Journal,* February 7, p. A3.

Frederick, Sharon. 2001. *Rape: Weapon of Terror.* River Edge, N.J.: Global Publishing.

Fredriksen, K. I. 1989. "Adult protective services: A caseload analysis." *Journal of Interpersonal Violence, 4,* 245–250.

Freund, Matthew, et al. 1991. "Sexual behavior of clients with street prostitutes in Camden, N.J." *Journal of Sex Research, 28,* 579–591.

Friedman, Milton. 1989. "An open letter to Bill Bennett." *Wall Street Journal,* September 7, p. A18.

Friedman, Milton. 1998. "There's no justice in the war on drugs." *New York Times,* January 11, p. 19.

Friedman, Robert I. 1999. "White collar and dangerous." *New York Times,* August 27, p. A25.

Furr, Susan R. 2001. "Suicide and depression among college students: A decade later." *Professional Psychology: Research and Practice, 32,* 97–100.

Gabor, Thomas, et al. 1987. *Armed Robbery: Cops, Robbers, and Victims.* Springfield, Ill.: Charles C. Thomas.

Gagnon, John H., Martin Levine, and Peter Nardi (eds.). 1997. *Encounters with AIDS: The Impact of the HIV/AIDS Epidemic and the Gay and Lesbian Communities.* Chicago: University of Chicago Press.

Galea, S., et al. 2002. "Psychological sequelae of the September 11 terrorist attacks in New York City." *New England Journal of Medicine, 346,* 982–987.

Galen, Luke W., and William M. Rogers. 2004. "Religiosity, Alcohol expectancies, drinking motives and their interaction in the prediction of drinking among college students." *Journal of Studies on Alcohol, 65,* 469–476.

Gallagher, Bernard. 2002. *The Sociology of Mental Illness,* 4th ed. Upper Saddle River, N.J.: Prentice Hall.

Gamper, Catharine M. 2004. "Perceived social competence and rape myth endorsement." *Deviant Behavior, 25,* 133–150.

Gamwell, Lynn, and Nancy Tomes. 1995. *Madness in America: Cultural and Medical Perceptions of Mental Illness before 1914.* Ithaca, N.Y.: Cornell University Press.

Garfinkel, Harold. 1967. *Studies in Ethnomethodology.* Englewood Cliffs, N.J.: Prentice Hall.

Garland, David. 1993. *Punishment and Modern Society: A Study in Social Theory.* Chicago: University of Chicago Press.

Gauthier, DeAnn K., and William B. Bankston. 2004. "'Who kills whom' revisited: A sociological study of variation in the sex ratio of spouse killings." *Homicide Studies, 8,* 96–122.

Geis, Gilbert. 1984. "White-collar and corporate crime." In Robert F. Meier (ed.), *Major Forms of Crime*. Beverly Hills, Calif.: Sage Publications.

Geis, Gilbert, and Robley Geis. 1979. "Rape in Stockholm: Is permissiveness relevant?" *Criminology*, 17, 315.

Gelles, Richard J. 1985. "Family violence." *Annual Review of Sociology*, 11, 347–367.

Gelles, Richard J. 1995. *Contemporary Families: A Sociological View*. Thousand Oaks, Calif.: Sage Publications.

Gelles, Richard J. 1998. "Family violence." In Michael Tonry (ed.), *The Handbook of Crime and Punishment*. New York: Oxford University Press.

Gelles, Richard J., and Murray A. Straus. 1987. "The cost of family violence." *Public Health Reports*, 102, 638–641.

Gelles, Richard J., and Murray Straus. 1988. *Family Violence*. Beverly Hills, Calif.: Sage Publications.

Gelman, David, et al. 1994. "The rapist: An overview." In Karin L. Swisher , Carol Wekesser, and William Barbour (eds.), *Violence Against Women*. San Diego, Calif.: Greenhaven.

George, Robert, Fred Wulczyn, and David Funshel. 1994. "A foster care research agenda for the 90s." *Child Welfare*, 73, 525–549.

Gianelli, Diane M. 1999. "Oregon suicide report contains some surprises." *American Medical News*, 42, March 8, pp. 9, 11.

Gibbs, Nancy. 1993a. "R for Death." *Time*, May 31, p. 37.

Gibbs, Nancy. 1993b. "'Til death do us part." *Time*, January 18, p. 41.

Gibbs, Nancy. 1995. "Love and let die." In Robert Emmet Long (ed.), *Suicide*. New York: Wilson.

Gidycz, Christine A., and Mary P. Koss. 1991. "The effects of acquaintance rape on the female victim." In Andrea Parrot and Laurie Bechhofer (eds.), *Acquaintance Rape*. New York: Wiley.

Gilbert, Neil. 1995. "Realities and mythologies of rape." In Alex Thio and Thomas C. Calhoun (eds.), *Readings in Deviant Behavior*. New York: HarperCollins.

Gilgoff, Dan, and Jay Tolson. 2003. "Losing friends?" *U.S. News & World Report*, March 17, p. 40.

Gill, Carol J. 2001. "Divided understanding: The social experience of disability." In Gary L. Albrecht et al. (eds.), *Handbook of Disability Studies*. Thousand Oaks, Calif.: Sage Publications.

Gillespie, Michael, Valerie Hearn, and Robert A. Silverman. 1998. "Suicide following homicide in Canada." *Homicide Studies*, 2, 46–63.

Gillespie, Terry. 1996. "Rape crisis centers and 'male rape': a face of the backlash." In Marianne Hester et al. (eds.), *Women, Violence and Male Power*. Philadelphia: Open University Press.

Girard, Chris. 1993. "Age, gender, and suicide: A cross-national analysis." *American Sociological Review*, 58, 553–574.

Glasberg, D. S., and D. Skidmore. 1998. "The dialectics of white-collar crime: The anatomy of the savings and loan crisis and the case of Silverado Banking, Savings and Loan Association." *American Journal of Economics and Sociology*, 57, 423–449.

Glaser, Daniel. 1956. "Criminality theories and behavioral images." *American Journal of Sociology*, 61, 433–444.

Glass, Shirley P., and Thomas L. Wright. 1992. "Justifications for extramarital relationships: The association between attitudes, behaviors, and gender." *Journal of Sex Research*, 29, 361–387.

Glassner, Barry. 1991. "Jewish sobriety." In David J. Pittman and Helene Raskin White (eds.), *Society, Culture, and Drinking Patterns Reexamined*. New Brunswick, N.J.: Rutgers Center of Alcohol Studies.

Glater, Jonathan D. 2002. "Mad as hell: Hard time for white-collar crime." *New York Times*, July 28, Section 4, p. 5.

Gleick, Elizabeth. 1995. "The crooked blue line." *Time*, September 11, pp. 39–42.

Gleick, Elizabeth. 1996. "Putting the jail in jailbait." *Time*, January 29, pp. 33–34.

Goetting, Ann. 1989. "Patterns of marital homicide: A comparison of husbands and wives." *Journal of Comparative Family Studies*, 22, 341–354.

Goetting, Ann. 1995. *Homicide in Families and Other Social Populations*. New York: Springer.

Goffman, Erving. 1961. *Asylums*. Garden City, N.Y.: Anchor.

Gold, Martin. 1958. "Suicide, homicide, and the socialization of aggression." *American Journal of Sociology*, 43, 651–661.

Goldberg, Carey. 1998. "Little drop in college binge drinking." *New York Times*, September 11, p. A12.

Goldner, Norman S. 1972. "Rape as a heinous but understudied offense." *Journal of Criminal Law, Criminology and Police Science*, 63, 402–407.

Goldsmith, S. K., et al. 2002. *Reducing Suicide: A National Imperative*. Washington, D.C.: National Academies Press.

Goleman, Daniel. 1986. "Aid in day-to-day life seen as hope for schizophrenics." *New York Times*, March 19, pp. 1, 12.

Goleman, Daniel. 1992. "A rising cost of modernity: Depression." *New York Times*, December 8, p. B6.

Goode, Erica. 2002. "Antidepressants lift clouds, but lose 'miracle drug' label." *New York Times,* June 30, pp. 1, 18.

Goode, Erich. 1981. "Drugs and crime." In Abraham S. Blumberg (ed.), *Current Perspective on Criminal Behavior.* New York: Knopf.

Goode, Erich. 1991. "Positive deviance: A viable concept?" *Deviant Behavior, 12,* 289–309.

Goode, Erich. 1999. *Drugs in American Society.* 5th ed. New York: McGraw-Hill.

Goode, Erich. 2001. *Deviant Behavior,* 6th ed. Upper Saddle River, N.J.: Prentice Hall.

Goode, Erich. 2004a. "Legalize it? A bulletin from the war on drugs." *Contexts,* Summer, pp. 19–25.

Goode, Erich. 2004b. "The stigma of obesity." In Alex Thio and Thomas C. Calhoun (eds.), *Readings in Deviant Behavior,* 3d ed. Boston: Allyn and Bacon.

Goode, Erich, and Nachman Ben-Yehuda. 1994. *Moral Panics: The Social Construction of Deviance.* London: Blackwell.

Goodwin, Donald W. 1991. "The etiology of alcoholism." In David J. Pittman and Helene Raskin White (eds.), *Society, Culture, and Drinking Patterns Reexamined.* New Brunswick, N.J.: Rutgers Center of Alcohol Studies.

Gordon, Margaret T., and Stephanie Riger. 1989. *The Female Fear.* New York: Free Press.

Gorman, Christine. 1992. "Can drug firms be trusted?" *Time,* February 10, p. 43.

Gorman, Christine, and Wendy Cole. 2004. "Between the sexes." *Time,* March 1, pp. 54–56.

Gosselin, Denise Kindschi. 2000. *Heavy Hands: An Introduction to the Crimes of Domestic Violence.* Upper Saddle River, N.J.: Prentice Hall.

Gottesman, Irving I. 1995. "Genetic factors contribute to schizophrenia." In David Bender and Bruno Leone (eds.), *Mental Illness: Opposing Viewpoints.* San Diego, Calif.: Greenhaven.

Gottfredson, Michael R., and Travis Hirschi. 1990. *A General Theory of Crime.* Newbury Park, Calif.: Sage Publications.

Gould, Leroy C. 1969. "The changing structure of property crime in an affluent society." *Social Forces, 48,* 51.

Gove, Walter R. 1970. "Societal reaction as an explanation of mental illness: An evaluation." *American Sociological Review, 35,* 882.

Gove, Walter R. 1982. "Labeling theory's explanation of mental illness: An update of recent evidence." *Deviant Behavior, 3,* 307–327.

Gove, Walter R. 1984. "Gender differences in mental and physical illness: The effects of fixed roles and nurturant roles." *Social Science and Medicine, 19,* 77–84.

Gove, Walter R., and Michael Hughes. 1980. "Reexamining the ecological fallacy: A study in which aggregate data are critical in investigating the pathological effects of living alone." *Social Forces, 58,* 1157–1177.

Graham, Kathryn, William Turnbull, and Linda LaRocque. 1979. "Effects of alcohol on moral judgment." *Journal of Abnormal Psychology, 88,* 442–445.

Gray, Susan H. 1982. "Exposure to pornography and aggression toward women: The case of the angry male." *Social Problems, 29,* 387–398.

Green, Edward, and Russell P. Wakefield. 1979. "Patterns of middle and upper class homicide." *Journal of Criminal Law and Criminology, 70,* 172–181.

Green, Gary S. 1990. *Occupational Crime.* Chicago: Nelson-Hall.

Greenberg, David F. (ed.). 1981. *Crime and Capitalism: Readings in Marxist Criminology.* Palo Alto, Calif.: Mayfield.

Greenberg, Michael, and Dona Schneider. 1994. "Violence in American cities: Young black males is the answer, but what was the question?" *Social Science and Medicine, 39,* 179–187.

Greenberg, Scott. 1996. "Why do workers bite the hands that feed them? Employee theft as a social exchange process." *Research in Organizational Behavior, 18,* 111–156.

Greenhouse, Linda. 1999. "Sex harassment in class is ruled schools' liability." *New York Times,* May 15, pp. A1, A24.

Greenwald, Harold. 1970. *The Elegant Prostitute.* New York: Walker.

Greer, Frank I., and Rhona Strasberg Weinstein. 1979. "Suicide prevention outreach: Callers and noncallers compared." *Psychological Reports, 44,* 387–393.

Gregory, Raymond F. 2004. *Unwelcome and Unlawful: Sexual Harassment in the American Workplace.* Ithaca, N.Y.: Cornell University Press.

Griffin, Sean Patrick. 2003. "'Emerging' organized crime hypotheses in criminology textbooks: The case of African-American organized crime." *Journal of Criminal Justice Education, 14,* 287–300.

Griffin, Susan. 1971. "Rape: The all-American crime." *Ramparts,* September, pp. 4–5.

Gross, William C. 1993. "Gender and age differences in college students' alcohol consumption." *Psychological Reports, 72,* 211–216.

Grossman, Dave. 1995. *On Killing: The Psychological Cost of Learning to Kill in War and Society.* Boston: Little, Brown.

Groth, A. Nicholas. 1983. "Rape: Behavioral aspects." In S. H. Kadish (ed.), *Encyclopedia of Crime and Justice.* New York: Free Press.

Groth, A. Nicholas, and H. Jean Birnbaum. 1979. *Men Who Rape.* New York: Plenum.

Gruenbaum, Ellen. 2001. *The Female Circumcision Controversy: An Anthropological Perspective.* Philadelphia: University of Pennsylvania Press.

Gunnell, David, Helen Wehner, and Stephen Frankel. 1999. "Sex differences in suicide trends in England and Wales." *Lancet, 353,* 556–557.

Gusfield, Joseph R. 1991. "Status conflicts and the changing ideologies of the American temperance movement." In David J. Pittman and Charles R. Snyder (eds.), *Society, Culture, and Drinking Patterns.* New York: Wiley.

H&MW (Health & Medicine Week). 2001. "Study finds women at greater risk of harm by alcoholism." *H&MW,* April 2, pp. 13–14.

Hagmann, Michael. 2001. "Alcohol takes its toll on Europe's youth." *Bulletin of the World Health Organization, 79,* 380.

Hammond, D. Corydon, and Gary Q. Jorgensen. 1981. "Alcohol and sex: A volatile cocktail." *USA Today: The Magazine of the American Scene,* July, pp. 44–46.

Handel, Warren. 1982. *Ethnomethodology: How People Make Sense.* Englewood Cliffs, N.J.: Prentice Hall.

Hansen, Brian. 2004. "The proliferation of cyber-crimes." In Alex Thio and Thomas C. Calhoun (eds.), *Readings in Deviant Behavior,* 3d ed. Boston: Allyn and Bacon.

Hanson, Bill, et al. 1985. *Life with Heroin: Voices from the Inner City.* Lexington, Mass.: Health.

Hanson, David J. 1995. "The United States of America." In Dwight B. Heath (ed.), *International Handbook on Alcohol and Culture.* Westport, Conn.: Greenwood.

Hanson, David J., and Ruth C. Engs. 1992. "College students' drinking problems: A national study, 1982–1991." *Psychological Reports, 71,* 39–42.

Haran, James F., and John M. Martin. 1984. "The armed urban bank robber: A profile." *Federal Probation, 48* (December), 51.

Harman, Lesley, D. 1985. "Acceptable deviance as social control: The case of fashion and slang." *Deviant Behavior, 6,* 1–15.

Harper, Frederick D., and Elaheh Saifnoorian. 1991. "Drinking patterns among black Americans." In David J. Pittman and Helene Raskin White (eds.), *Society, Culture, and Drinking Patterns Reexamined.* New Brunswick, N.J.: Rutgers Center of Alcohol Studies.

Harries, Keith D. 1990. *Serious Violence: Patterns of Homicide and Assault in America.* Springfield, Ill.: Charles C. Thomas.

Harris Interactive. 2004. *Therapy in America 2004.* http://cms.psychologytoday.com/pto/topline_report_042904.pdf

Harrison, Lana D. 1992. "The drug-crime nexus in the USA." *Contemporary Drug Problems, 19,* 257–258.

Harry, Joseph. 1983. "Parasuicide, gender, and gender deviance." *Journal of Health and Social Behavior, 24,* 350–361.

Harry, Joseph, and Mary C. Sengstock. 1978. "Attribution, goals, and deviance." *American Sociological Review, 43,* 278–280.

Hasin, Deborah S., Bridget Grant, and Jean Endicott. 1990. "The natural history of alcohol abuse: Implications for definitions of alcohol use disorders." *American Journal of Psychiatry, 147,* 1537–1541.

Hawkins, Joseph R. 2000. "Japan's journey into homophobia." *Gay & Lesbian Review Worldwide, 7* (Winter), pp. 36–38.

Hayes, Lindsay M. 1995. *Prison Suicide: An Overview and Guide to Prevention.* Washington, D.C.: U.S. Department of Justice.

Headden, Susan, and Gordon Witkin. 1993. "Preying on the helpless." *U.S. News & World Report,* May 24, pp. 48–52.

Hebl, Michelle R., and Robert E. Kleck. 2000. "The social consequences of physical disability." In Todd F. Heatherton et al. (eds.), *The Social Psychology of Stigma.* New York: Guilford Press.

Hechinger, John. 2002. "Easy money." *Wall Street Journal,* October 8, pp. A1. A18.

Heckert, Alex, and Druann Maria Heckert. 2004. "A new typology of deviance: Integrating normative and reactivist definitions of deviance." *Deviant Behavior, 23,* 449–479.

Heckert, D. Alex, and Edward W. Gondolf. 2000. "The effect of perceptions of sanctions on batterer program outcomes." *Journal of Research in Crime and Delinquency, 37,* 369–346.

Heidensohn, Frances. 1995. *Women and Crime,* 2d ed. New York: New York University Press.

Heidensohn, Frances. 2002. "15. Gender and crime." pp. 491–530 in Mike Maguire and Rodney Morgan (eds.), *Oxford Handbook of Criminology,* New York: Oxford University Press.

Heien, Dale M., and David J. Pittman. 1993. "The external costs of alcohol abuse." *Journal of Studies on Alcohol, 54,* 302–307.

Helmer, John. 1975. *Drugs and Minority Oppression.* New York: Seabury.

Hendin, Herbert. 1979. "A saner policy on suicide." *Psychology Today,* May, p. 115.

Hendin, Herbert. 1995. *Suicide in America.* New York: Norton.

Hendin, Herbert. 1997. *Seduced by Death: Doctors, Patients, and the Dutch Cure.* New York: Norton.

Hendrie, Caroline. 2004. "Report examining sexual misconduct taps some nerves." *Education Week,* July 14, pp. 1–2.

Hendrix, Melissa. 1993. "Is it a boy or a girl?" *Johns Hopkins Magazine,* November, pp. 10–16.

Henry, Andrew, and James Short. 1954. *Suicide and Homicide.* New York: Free Press.

Henry, William A. III. 1993. "Gay parents: Under fire and on the rise." *Time,* September 20, pp. 68–71.

Henslin, James M. 1970. "Guilt and guilt neutralization: Response and adjustment to suicide." In Jack D. Douglas (ed.), *Deviance and Respectability.* New York: Basic Books.

Hepburn, John R. 1977. "Social control and the legal order: Legitimated repression in a capitalist state." *Contemporary Crises, 1,* 84.

Herbert, Bob. 1995. "Killer cops." *New York Times,* September 15, p. A15.

Herd, Denise. 1991. "Drinking patterns in the black population." In Walter B. Clark and Michael E. Hilton (eds.), *Alcohol in America.* Albany, N.Y.: State University of New York Press.

Herdt, Gilbert. 1990. "Developmental discontinuities and sexual orientation across cultures." In David P. McWhirter et al., *Homosexuality/Heterosexuality.* New York: Oxford University Press.

Herman, Ellen, and Martin B. Duberman. 1995. *Psychiatry, Psychology, and Homosexuality.* New York: Chelsea House.

Herman, Judith Lewis. 1995. "Considering sex offenders: A model of addiction." In Patricia Searles and Ronald J. Berger (eds.), *Rape and Society.* Boulder, Colo.: Westview.

Hess, John H., and Herbert E. Thomas. 1963. "Incompetency to stand trial: Procedures, results, and problems." *American Journal of Psychiatry, 119,* 713–720.

Hill, Andrew. 2002. "Ex-Tyco chairman free on $10m bail." *FT.com,* September 27.

Hill, Herbert. 1973. "Anti-oriental agitation and the rise of working-class racism." *Society, 10,* January/February, p. 52.

Hills, Stuart L. 1980. *Demystifying Social Deviance.* New York: McGraw-Hill.

Hilton, Michael E. 1991. "Regional diversity in U.S. drinking practices." In Walter B. Clark and Michael E. Hilton (eds.), *Alcohol in America: Drinking Practices and Problems.* Albany, N.Y.: State University of New York Press.

Hilts, Philip J. 1987. "AIDS infection found in 11% of U.S. prostitutes." *Washington Post,* March 27, pp. A1, A10.

Himmelstein, Jerome L. 1983. *The Strange Career of Marijuana: Politics and Ideology of Drug Control in America.* Westport, Conn.: Greenwood.

Hinrichsen, Gregory A., Nancy A. Hernandez, and Simcha Pollack. 1992. "Difficulties and rewards in family care of depressed older adults." *Gerontologist, 32,* 486–492.

Hirschi, Travis. 1962. "The professional prostitute." *Berkeley Journal of Sociology, 7,* 44–45.

Hirschi, Travis. 1969. *Causes of Delinquency.* Berkeley and Los Angeles: University of California Press, 1969.

Hirschi, Travis. 1973. "Procedural rules and the study of deviant behavior." *Social Problems, 21,* 166–171.

Hirschi, Travis, and Michael R. Gottfredson (eds.). 1994. *The Generality of Deviance.* New Brunswick, N.J.: Transaction.

Hirschi, Travis, and Michael Gottfredson. 2000. "In defense of self-control." *Theoretical Criminology, 4,* 55–69.

Hitt, Jack. 1999. "The battle of the binge." *New York Times Magazine,* October 24, pp. 31–32.

Hochstetler, Andy, Heith Copes, and Matt DeLisi. 2002. "Differential association in group and solo offending." *Journal of Criminal Justice, 30,* 559–566.

Hochstetler, Andy. 2004. "Interactional dynamics in robbery." pp. 303–307 in Alex Thio and Thomas C. Calhoun (eds.), *Readings in Deviant Behavior,* 3d ed. Boston: Allyn and Bacon.

Hollinger, Richard C., and John P. Clark. 1983. *Theft by Employees.* Lexington, Mass.: Lexington Books.

Holmes, Ronald M., and Stephen T. Holmes. 1992. "Understanding mass murder: A starting point." *Federal Probation, 56,* 53–61.

Holzman, Harold R., and Sharon Pines. 1982. "Buying sex: The phenomenology of being a john." *Deviant Behavior, 4,* 105.

Homer, Frederic D. 1974. *Guns and Garlic: Myths and Realities of Organized Crime.* West Lafayette, Ind.: Purdue University Press.

Hoover, Eric. 2004. "Studies find 'social norms' strategy reduces drinking at colleges." *Chronicle of Higher Education,* August 13, p. A32.

Hornblower, Margot. 1993. "The skin trade." *Time,* June 21, p. 45.

Horwitz, Allan V., Susan C. Reinhard, and Sandra Howell-White. 1996. "Caregiving as reciprocal exchange in families with seriously mentally ill members." *Journal of Health and Social Behavior, 37,* 149–162.

Hosenball, Mark. 2002. "Islamic cyberterror." *Newsweek*, May 20, p. 10.

Hughes, Stella P., and Richard A. Dodder. 1992. "Changing the legal minimum drinking age: Results of a longitudinal study." *Journal of Studies on Alcohol, 53*, 568–575.

Humphreys, Laud. 1970. "Tearoom trade: Impersonal sex in public places." *Transaction, 7*, 17–18.

Humphreys, Laud. 1972. *Out of the Closets*. Englewood Cliffs, N.J.: Prentice Hall.

Hunt, Albert R. 1995. "The best Congress money can buy." *Wall Street Journal*, September 7, p. A15.

Hunter, Patricia A., Roseann Hannon, and David Marchi. 1982. "Alcohol consumption in natural settings as a function of sex, age, and income level." *Journal of Studies on Alcohol, 43*, 387–392.

Hurlburt, Graham, Eldon Gade, and Dale Fuqua. 1984. "Personality differences between Alcoholics Anonymous members and nonmembers." *Journal of Studies on Alcohol, 45*, 170–171.

Huselid, Rebecca Farmer, and M. Lynne Cooper. 1992. "Gender roles as mediators of sex differences in adolescent alcohol use and abuse." *Journal of Health and Social Behavior, 33*, 348–362.

HWHW (Harvard Women's Health Watch). 2000. "Women and moderate drinking: Health in the balance." *HWHW*, November, pp. 2–3.

Hyatt, Ralph. 1993. "Carjacking: A sign of the times." *USA Today: The Magazine of the American Scene, 22*, September, pp. 40–41.

Ibrahim, Farah A. 1995. "Suicidal behavior in Asian-American women." In Silvia Sara Canetto and David Lester (eds.), *Women and Suicidal Behavior*. New York: Springer.

Irvine, Janice M. 2002. *Talk about Sex: The Battles over Sex Education in the United States*. Berkeley: University of California Press.

Irwin, Katherine. 2001. "Legitimating the first tattoo: Moral passage through informal interaction." *Symbolic Interaction, 24*, 49–73.

Irwin, John. 1970. *The Felon*. Englewood Cliffs, N.J.: Prentice Hall.

Isikoff, Michael. 1995. "Crack, coke and race." *Newsweek*, November 6, p. 77.

Isikoff, Michael. 1997. "The White House shell game." *Newsweek*, February 10, pp. 34–35.

Itzin, Catherine (ed.). 1993. *Pornography: Women, Violence, and Civil Liberties: A Radical View*. New York: Oxford University Press.

Jackley, John L. 1992. *Hill Rat: Blowing the Lid Off Congress*. Washington, D.C.: Regnery Gateway.

Jackson, James O. 1996. "The lost children." *Time*, March 25, pp. 44–45.

Jackson, Lois, et al. 1992. "Varied potential risks of HIV infection among prostitutes." *Social Science and Medicine, 35*, 281–286.

Jacobs, Bruce A. 2000. *Robbing Drug Dealers: Violence Beyond the Law*. New York: Aldine de Gruyter.

Jacobs, Jerry. 1967. "A phenomenological study of suicide notes." *Social Problems, 15*, 60–72.

Jaffe, Jerome H. 1965. "Drug addiction and drug abuse." In Louis S. Goodman and Alfred Gilman (eds.), *The Pharmacological Basis of Therapeutics*. New York: Macmillan.

Jamieson, Katherine M. 1994. *The Organization of Corporate Crime: Dynamics of Antitrust Violation*. Thousand Oaks, Calif.: Sage Publications.

Janus, Samuel S., and Cynthia L. Janus. 1993. *The Janus Report on Sexual Behavior*. New York: Wiley.

Jasper, Jann. 1992. "Rape: Are you at risk?" *New Woman, 22*, 80–86.

Jehl, Douglas, and David Rohde. 2004. "Captured Queda figure led way to information behind warning." *New York Times*, August 2, p. A1.

Jellinek, E. M. 1952. "Phases of alcohol addiction." *Quarterly Journal of Studies on Alcohol, 13*, 673–684.

Jenkins, Holman W. Jr. 2004. "Is corporate fraud too hard for juries?" *Wall Street Journal*, April 14, p. A15.

Jenkins, Philip. 2001. *Beyond Tolerance: Child Pornography on the Internet*. New York: New York University Press.

Jenness, Valerie. 1990. "From sex as sin to sex as work: COYOTE and the reorganization of prostitution as a social problem." *Social Problems, 37*, 403–420.

Jersild, Devon. 2001. *Happy Hours: Alcohol in a Woman's Life*. New York: HarperCollins.

Jersild, Devon. 2002. "Alcohol in the vulnerable lives of college women." *Chronicle of Higher Education*, May 31, pp. B19–11.

Johnson, Charles Felzen. 2004. "Child sexual abuse." *Lancet, 364*, 462–470.

Johnson, Dirk, and Adam Piore. 2004. "At home in two worlds." *Newsweek*, October 18, pp. 52–54.

Johnson, Dirk. 2004. "Policing a rural plague." *Newsweek*, March 8, p. 41.

Johnston, David. 1997. "The mystery of the violent bank jobs." *New York Times*, March 30, p. E4.

Johnston, Lloyd D., et al. 1986. *Drug Use Among American High School Students, College Students, and Other Young Adults*. Rockville, Md.: National Institute on Drug Abuse.

Jones, Peter, et al. 1993. "Premorbid social underachievement in schizophrenia: Results from the Camberwell Collaborative Psychosis Study." *British Journal of Psychiatry, 162*, 65–71.

Jurich, Anthony P., and Cheryl J. Polson. 1984. "Reasons for drug use: Comparison of drug users and abusers." *Psychological Reports, 55,* 371–378.

Kahan, Dan M. 1997. "It's a shame we have none." *Wall Street Journal,* January 15, p. A14.

Kalb, Claudia. 2001. "Playing with painkillers." *Newsweek,* April 9, pp. 45–48.

Kandel, Denise B., Richard Jessor. 2002. "The gateway hypothesis revisited." pp. 365–372 in Denise B. Kandel (ed.), *Stages and Pathways of Drug Involvement.* Cambridge, UK: Cambridge University Press.

Kanin, Eugene J. 1984. "Date rape: Unofficial criminals and victims." *Victimology: An International Journal, 9,* 95–108.

Kanin, Eugene J. 1985. "Date rapists: Differential sexual socialization and relative deprivation." *Archives of Sexual Behavior, 14,* 219–231.

Kanin, Eugene J., and Stanley R. Parcell. 1981. "Sexual aggression: A second look at the offended female." In Lee H. Bowker (ed.), *Women and Crime in America.* New York: Macmillan.

Kantor, Glenda, and Murray A. Straus. 1990. "The 'drunken bum' theory of wife beating." In M. A. Straus and R. J. Gelles (eds.), *Physical Violence in American Families.* New Brunswick, N.J.: Transaction.

Kantrowitz, Barbara. 1996. "Gay families come out." *Newsweek,* November 4, pp. 50–57.

Kaplan, David A. 1991. "The bank robbery boom." *Newsweek,* December 9, p. 63.

Kaplan, David E. 1998. "Yakuza Inc." *U.S. News & World Report,* April 13, pp. 40–47.

Kaplan, David E. 2003. "Playing offense." *U.S. News & World Report,* June 2, pp. 18–29.

Kaplan, David E., and Kevin Whitelaw. 2004. "Terror's new soldiers." *U.S. News & World Report,* November 1, pp. 34–35.

Kaplan, Howard B. 1972. *The Sociology of Mental Illness.* New Haven, Conn.: College and University Press.

Kaplan, Howard B., et al. 1986. "Escalation of marijuana use: Application of a general theory of deviant behavior." *Journal of Health and Social Behavior, 27,* 44–61.

Kappeler, Victor E., Mark Blumberg, and Gary W. Potter. 1993. *The Mythology of Crime and Criminal Justice.* Prospect Heights, Ill.: Waveland.

Kappeler, Victor E., Richard D. Sluder, and Geoffrey P. Alpert. 1998. *Forces of Deviance: Understanding the Dark Side of Policing,* 2d ed. Prospect Heights, Ill.: Waveland.

Karlin-Resnick, Joshua. 2004. "Helping students stay clean and sober." *Chronicle of Higher Education,* August 31, pp. A31–A33.

Kart, Gary S. 1990. *The Realities of Aging,* 3d ed. Boston: Allyn and Bacon.

Katchadourian, Herant. 1985. *Fundamentals of Human Sexuality,* 4th ed. New York: Holt, Rinehart and Winston.

Katz, Bonnie L. 1991. "The psychological impact of stranger versus nonstranger rape on victims' recovery." In Andrea Parrot and Laurie Bechhofer (eds.), *Acquaintance Rape.* New York: Wiley.

Katz, Jack. 1988. *Seductions of Crime: Moral and Sensual Attractions in Doing Evil.* New York: Basic Books.

Kaufman, Joan, and Edward Zigler. 1987. "Do abused children become abusive parents?" *American Journal of Orthopsychiatry, 57,* 186–192.

Kaufman, Joan, and Edward Zigler. 1993. "The intergenerational transmission of abuse is overstated." In Richard J. Gelles and Donileen R. Loseke (eds.), *Current Controversies on Family Violence.* Newbury Park, Calif.: Sage Publications.

Kaysen, Susanna. 1993. *Girl, Interrupted.* New York: Turtle Bay Books/Random House.

Kelley, Jack. 2001. "Wired for death." *USA Today,* June 26, p.12.

Kemp, Alan. 1998. *Abuse in the Family: An Introduction.* Pacific Grove, Calif.: Brooks/Cole.

Kempf, Kimberly L. 1993. "The empirical status of Hirschi's control theory." In Freda Adler and William S. Laufer (eds.), *New Directions in Criminological Theory.* New Brunswick, N.J.: Transaction.

Kendall-Tackett, Kathleen A., Linda Meyer Williams, and David Finkelhor. 1993. "Impact of sexual abuse on children: A review and synthesis of recent empirical studies." *Psychological Bulletin, 113,* 164–180.

Kendler, Kenneth S. 1983. "Overview: A current perspective on twin studies of schizophrenia." *American Journal of Psychiatry, 140,* 1413–1425.

Kessler, Ronald C., and Harold W. Neighbors. 1986. "A new perspective on the relationships among race, social class, and psychological distress." *Journal of Health and Social Behavior, 27,* 107–115.

Kessler, Ronald C., et al. 2004. "Prevalence, severity, and unmet need for treatment of mental disorders in the World Health Organization world mental health surveys." *JAMA (Journal of the American Medical Association),* 2581–2590.

Kessler, Ronald C., and James A. McRae, Jr. 1983. "Trends in the relationship between sex and attempted suicide." *Journal of Health and Social Behavior, 24*, 98–110.

Kessler, Ronald C., et al. 1985. "Social factors in psychopathology: Stress, social support, and coping processes." *Annual Review of Psychology, 36*, 560–561.

Kessler, Ronald, et al. 1994. "Lifetime and 12-month prevalence of DSM-III-psychiatric disorders in the United States." *Archives of General Psychiatry, 51*, 8–19.

Kety, Seymour S. 1974. "From rationalization to reason." *American Journal of Psychiatry, 131*, 957–963.

Khantzian, Edward J. 1985. "The self-medication hypothesis of addictive disorders: Focus on heroin and cocaine dependence." *American Journal of Psychiatry, 142*, 1259–1264.

King, David R. 1978. "The brutalization effect: Execution publicity and the incidence of homicide in South Carolina." *Social Forces, 57*, 683–687.

Kinsey, Alfred C., et al. 1948. *Sexual Behavior in the Human Male*. Philadelphia: Saunders.

Kinsey, Alfred C., et al. 1953. *Sexual Behavior in the Human Female*. Philadelphia: Saunders.

Kinzer, Stephen. 2001. "Why they don't know us." *New York Times*, November 11, pp. 4–5.

Kirkpatrick, Clifford, and Eugene Kanin. 1957. "Male sex aggression on a university campus." *American Sociological Review, 22*, 52–58.

Kirn, Walter. 1998. "Crank." *Time*, June 22, pp. 26–32.

Kite, Mary E., and Bernard E. Whitley, Jr. 1996. "Sex differences in attitudes toward homosexual persons, behaviors, and civil rights: A meta-analysis." *Personality and Social Psychology Bulletin, 22*, 336–353.

Kitsuse, John I. 1962. "Societal reaction to deviant behavior: Problems of theory and method." *Social Problems, 9*, 247–256.

Klam, Matthew. 2001. "Experiencing Ecstasy." *New York Times Magazine*, January 21, pp. 38–43, 64–79.

Klaus, Patsy. 1999. "Carjackings in the United States, 1992-96." *Bureau of Justice Statistics Special Report*, March, U.S. Department of Justice.

Kleck, Gary, and M. Hogan. 1999. "National case-control study of homicide offending and gun ownership." *Social Problems, 46*, 275–293.

Kleinfield, N.R., and Kit R. Roane. 1999. "Subway killing puts harsh light on the suspect's mental torment." *New York Times*, January 11, pp. A1, A18.

Kleinknecht, William. 1996. *The New Ethnic Mobs: The Changing Face of Organized Crime in America*. New York: Free Press.

Klemke, Lloyd W. 1992. *The Sociology of Shoplifting: Boosters and Snitches Today*. Westport, Conn.: Praeger.

Klinger, David A. 2001. "Suicidal intent in victim-precipitated homicide." *Homicide Studies, 5*, 206–226.

Kluger, Jeffrey. 2001. "How to manage teen drinking (the smart way)." *Time*, June 18, pp. 42–44.

Kluger, Jeffrey. 2003. "Medicating young minds." *Time*, November 3, pp. 48–57.

Knowles, Gordon James. 1999. "Male prison rape: A search for causation and prevention." *Howard Journal of Criminal Justice, 38*, 267–282.

Kolata, Gina. 1992. "The burdens of being overweight: Mistreatment and misconceptions." *New York Times*, November 22, pp. 1, 18.

Kolb, Lawrence C., and H. Keith H. Brodie. 1982. *Modern Clinical Psychiatry*, 10th ed. Philadelphia: Saunders.

Kotula, Dean. 2002. *The Phallus Palace*. Los Angeles: Alyson Publications.

Kopelowicz, Alex, and T. George Bidder. 1992. "Outcome of schizophrenia." *American Journal of Psychiatry, 149*, 426.

Koss, Mary P. 1995. "Hidden rape: Sexual aggression and victimization in a national sample of students in higher education." In Patricia Searles and Ronald J. Berger (eds.), *Rape and Society*. Boulder, Colo: Westview.

Koss, Mary P., et al. 1987. "The scope of rape: Incidence and prevalence of sexual aggression and victimization in a national sample of higher education students." *Journal of Consulting and Clinical Psychology, 55*, 162–170.

Kristof, Nicholas D. 1996a. "Asian childhoods sacrificed to prosperity's lust." *Time*, April 14, pp. 1, 6.

Kristof, Nicholas D. 1996b. "Guns: one nation bars, the other requires." *New York Times*, March 10, p. E3.

Krueger, Alan, and Jitka Maleckova. 2002. "Does poverty cause terrorism?" *New Republic*, June 24, pp. 27–33.

Krummel, Sabine. 2001. "The elderly are vulnerable to abuse." In J. D. Lloyd, *Family Violence*. San Diego, Calif.: Greenhaven.

Kuo, Michelle. 2000. "Asia's dirty secret." *Harvard International Review, 22* (summer), 42–45.

Kuo, Wen H. 1984. "Prevalence of depression among Asian-Americans." *Journal of Nervous and Mental Disease, 172*, 449–457.

Kuo, Wen H., and Yung-Mei Tsai. 1986. "Social networking, hardiness and immigrant's mental health." *Journal of Health and Social Behavior, 27*, 133–149.

Kurst-Swanger, Karel, and Jacqueline L. Petcosky. 2003. *Violence in the Home: Multidisciplinary Perspectives.* New York: Oxford University Press.

Kushner, Howard I. 1985. "Women and suicide in historical perspective." *Signs, 10,* 543.

Kushner, Howard I. 1995. "Women and suicidal behavior: Epidemiology, gender and lethality in historical perspective." In Silvia Sara Canetto and David Lester (eds.), *Women and Suicidal Behavior.* New York: Springer.

Kutchins, Herb, and Stuart A. Kirk. 1997. *Making Us Crazy.* New York: Free Press.

Labaton, Stephen. 1995. "As pornography arrests grow, so do plans for computer stings." *New York Times,* September 16, pp. 1, 8.

Labovitz, Sanford. 1968. "Variation in suicide rates." In Jack P. Gibbs (ed.), *Suicide.* New York: Harper & Row.

Lacayo, Richard. 2004. "For better or for worse?" *Time,* March 8, pp. 26–33.

Lacey, Marc. 2004. "Amnesty says Sudan militias use rape as weapon." *New York Times,* July 19, p. 9.

LaFree, Gary D. 1982. "Male power and female victimization." *American Journal of Sociology, 88,* 312–313.

LaFree, Gary D., Barbara F. Reskin, and Christy A. Visher. 1985. "Jurors' responses to victims' behavior and legal issues in sexual assault trials." *Social Problems, 32,* 389–406.

LaFree, Gary. 1999. "Homicide: Cross-national perspectives," 115–139 in M. Dwayne Smith and Margaret A. Zahn (eds.), *Studying and Preventing Homicide.* Thousand Oaks, Calif.: Sage Publications.

Laing, R. D. 1965. *The Divided Self.* Baltimore, Md.: Penguin Books.

Laing, R. D. 1967. *The Politics of Experience.* New York: Ballantine.

Laing, R. D. 1985. *Wisdom, Madness and Folly.* New York: McGraw-Hill.

Lamar, Jacob V. 1986. "Crack," *Time,* June 2, p. 17.

Lamb, Michael. 1998. "Cybersex: Research notes on the characteristics of the visitors to online chat rooms." *Deviant Behavior, 19,* 121–135.

Landau, Simha F., and Daniel Fridman. 1993. "The seasonality of violent crime: The case of robbery and homicide in Israel." *Journal of Research in Crime and Delinquency, 30,* 163–191.

Lanning, Kenneth V. 1992. *Child Molesters: A Behavioral Analysis.* Arlington, Va.: National Center for Missing and Exploited Children.

Laubscher, Leswin R. 2003. "Suicide in a South African town: A cultural psychological investigation." *South African Journal of Psychology, 33,* 133–143.

Lauderdale, Pat, Jerry Parker, Phil Smith-Cunnien, and James Inverarity. 1984. "External threat and the definition of deviance." *Journal of Personality and Social Psychology, 46,* 1058–1068.

Laumann, Edward O., et al. 1994. *The Social Organization of Sexuality: Sexual Practices in the United States.* Chicago: University of Chicago Press.

Lavelle, Louis, and Sheridan Prasso. 2002. "The fat wages of scandal." *Business Week,* September 9, p. 8.

Lavelle, Marianne. 1998. "The new rules of sexual harassment." *U.S. News & World Report,* July 6, pp. 30–31.

LaViolette, Allyce D., and Ola W. Barnett. 2000. *It Could Happen to Anyone: Why Battered Women Stay,* 2nd ed. Thousand Oaks, Calif.: Sage Publications.

Lawson, Andrea, and Gregory Fouts. 2004. "Mental illness in Disney animated films." *Canadian Journal of Psychiatry, 49,* 310–314.

Lawson, Annette. 1988. *Adultery: An Analysis of Love and Betrayal.* New York: Basic Books.

Leaning, Jennifer. 2004. "Diagnosing genocide—The case of Darfur." *New England Journal of Medicine, 351,* 735–738.

Lear, Martha Weinman. 1972. "Q. If you rape a woman and steal her TV, what can they get you for in New York? A. Stealing her TV." *New York Times Magazine,* January 30, pp. 62–63.

Lecomte, D., and P. Fornes. 1998. "Homicide followed by suicide: Paris and its suburbs, 1991-1996." *Journal of Forensic Sciences, 43,* 760–764.

LeGrand, Camille E. 1973. "Rape and rape laws: Sexism in society and law." *California Law Review, 61,* 929–930.

Lehrer, Eli. 2001. "Hell behind bars." *National Review,* February 5, pp. 24–25.

Leland, John. 1995. "Bisexuality." *Newsweek,* July 17, pp. 44–50.

Leland, John. 2000. "Shades of gay." *Newsweek,* March 20, pp. 46–49.

Lemelson, Robert. 2001. "Strange maladies." *Psychology Today,* December, pp. 60–64.

Lemert, Edwin M. 1951. *Social Pathology.* New York: McGraw-Hill.

Lemonick, Michael D. 2004. "How we grew so big." *Time,* June 7, pp. 66–74.

Leonard, Eileen B. 1982. *Women, Crime, and Society: A Critique of Criminology Theory.* New York: Longman.

Lester, David. 1985. "Accidental deaths as disguised suicides." *Psychological Reports, 56,* 626.

Lester, David. 1988. "Toward a theory of parasuicide." *Corrective and Social Psychiatry, 34,* 24–26.

Lester, David. 1990. "Suicide, homicide and the quality of life in various countries." *Acta Psychiatrica Scandinavica, 81,* 332–334.

Lester, David. 1991. "Childlessness, suicide and homicide." *Psychological Reports, 69,* 990.

Lester, David. 2000. *Why People Kill Themselves.* 4th ed. Springfield, Ill.: Charles C Thomas.

Lester, David, and Bruce L. Danto. 1993. *Suicide Behind Bars: Prediction and Prevention.* Philadelphia: Charles Press.

LeVay, Simon. 1996. *Queer Science: The Use and Abuse of Research into Homosexuality.* Cambridge, Mass.: MIT Press.

LeVay, Simon, and Elisabeth Nonas. 1995. *City of Friends: A Portrait of the Gay and Lesbian Community in America.* Cambridge, Mass.: MIT Press.

Levin, B. M., Anthony Jones, and Kim Braithwaite. 1998. "Principal factors of the spread of alcoholism in society in a time of social changes." *Russian Social Science Review, 39* (November/December), 38–50.

Levin, Jack, and James Alan Fox. 1985. *Mass Murder: America's Growing Menace.* New York: Plenum.

Levine, Art. 1986. "Drug education gets an F." *U.S. News & World Report,* October 13, pp. 63–64.

Levinson, David. 1988. "Family violence in a cross-cultural perspective." In V. B. Van Hasselt et al. (eds.), *Handbook of Family Violence.* New York: Plenum.

Lewis, Mindy. 2003. "Those who hold the keys are listening." *Newsweek,* October 6, p. 24.

Lewin, Tamar. 1993. "Rape and the accuser: A debate still rages on citing sexual past." *New York Times,* February 12, p. B12.

Lewin, Tamar. 1995. "Parents poll finds child abuse to be more common." *New York Times,* December 7, p. A17.

Lewis, Helen Block. 1985. "Depression vs. paranoia: Why are there sex differences in mental illness?" *Journal of Personality, 53,* 150–178.

Liddick, Don. 2004. "Political deviance: Two case studies." pp. 280–283 in Alex Thio and Thomas C. Calhoun (eds.), *Readings in Deviant Behavior,* 3d ed. Boston: Allyn and Bacon.

Lieberman, Jethro K. 1973. *How the Government Breaks the Law.* Baltimore, Md.: Penguin.

Liebling, Alison. 1992. *Suicides in Prison.* London: Routledge.

Lindesmith, Alfred R. 1968. *Addiction and Opiates.* Chicago: Aldine.

Link, Bruce G., Bruce P. Dohrenwend, and Andrew E. Skodol. 1986. "Socio-economic status and schizophrenia: Noisome occupational characteristics as a risk factor." *American Sociological Review, 51,* 242–258.

Link, Bruce G., Mary Clare Lennon, and Bruce P. Dohrenwend. 1993. "Socioeconomic status and depression: The role of occupations involving direction, control, and planning." *American Journal of Sociology, 98,* 1351–1387.

Link, Bruce G., Jerrold Mirotznik, and Francis T. Cullen. 1991. "The effectiveness of stigma coping orientations: Can negative consequences of mental illness labeling be avoided?" *Journal of Health and Social Behavior, 32,* 302–320.

Link, Bruce G., and Jo C. Phelan. 1999. "Public conceptions of mental illness: Labels, cause, dangerousness, and social distance." *American Journal of Public Health, 89,* 1328–1333.

Linz, Daniel, and Neil Malamuth. 1993. *Pornography.* Newbury Park, Calif.: Sage Publications.

Linz, Daniel, Edward Donnerstein, and Steven Penrod. 1984. "The effects of multiple exposures to filmed violence against women." *Journal of Communication, 34,* 130–147.

Liptak, Adam. 2002. "Judge blocks U.S. bid to ban suicide law." *New York Times,* April 18, p. A16.

Littlejohn, Christopher. 2004. "Rediscovering the 'social' in the biopsychosocial perspective." *Mental Health Practice, 8,* 14–17.

Lockwood, Daniel. 1985. "Issues in prison sexual violence." In Michael Braswell et al., *Prison Violence in America.* Cincinnati, Ohio: Anderson.

Lonsway, Kimberly A., and Louise F. Fitzgerald. 1994. "Rape myths are attitudes and generally false beliefs about rape." *Psychology of Women Quarterly, 18,* 133–164.

Luckenbill, David F. 1981. "Generating compliance: The case of robbery." *Urban Life, 10,* 25–46.

Luckenbill, David F. 1985. "Entering male prostitution." *Urban Life, 14,* 131–153.

Luckenbill, David F. 1986. "Deviant career mobility: The case of male prostitutes." *Social Problems, 33,* 283–296.

Lyman, Stanford M. 1995. "Without morals or mores: Deviance in postmodern social theory." *International Journal of Politics, Culture and Society, 9,* 197–235.

Lynch, James P., and David Cantor. 1992. "Ecological and behavioral influences on property victimization at home: Implications for opportunity theory." *Journal of Research in Crime and Delinquency, 29,* 335–362.

MacAndrew, Craig, and Robert B. Edgerton. 1969. *Drunken Comportment.* London: Nelson.

Macdonald, John M. 1971. *Rape.* Springfield, Ill.: Charles C Thomas.

Macdonald, John M. 1995. *Rape: Controversial Issues.* Springfield, Ill.: Charles C Thomas.

MacFarguhar, Neil. 2001. "Bin Laden and his followers adhere to an austere, stringent form of Islam." *New York Times,* October 7, p. B7.

Mackay, Judith, and Michael Eriksen. 2002. *The Tobacco Atlas.* Geneva, Switzerland: World Health Organization.

Maddux, J. F., and D. P. Desmond. 1980. "New light on the maturing out hypothesis in opioid dependence." *Bulletin on Narcotics, 32,* 15–25.

Madge, Nicola, and John G. Harvey. 1999. "Suicide among the young—The size of the problem." *Journal of Adolescence, 22,* 145–155.

Madigan, Lee, and Nancy C. Gamble. 1991. *The Second Rape: Society's Continued Betrayal of the Victim.* New York: Lexington Books.

Magnuson, Ed. 1986. "Headhunters," *Time,* December 1, p. 32.

Maguire, Kathleen, and Ann L. Pastore (eds.). 1996. *Sourcebook of Criminal Justice Statistics—1995.* Washington, D.C.: Government Printing Office.

Mancoske, Ronald J., et al. 1995. "Suicide risk among people living with AIDS." *Social Work, 40,* 783–787.

Mandoki, Catalina A., and Barry R. Burkhart. 1991. "Women as victims: Antecedents and consequences of acquaintance rape." In Andrea Parrot and Laurie Bechhofer (eds.), *Acquaintance Rape.* New York: Wiley.

Mann, Coramae Richey. 1996. *When Women Kill.* Albany, N.Y.: State University of New York Press.

Mao, Tse-tung. 1967. *Selected Works of Mao Tse-tung,* Vol. 1. Peking: Foreign Languages Press.

Marcos, Anastasios C., Stephen J. Bahr, and Richard E. Johnson. 1986. "Test of a bonding/association theory of adolescent drug use." *Social Forces, 65,* 135–169.

Marcus, Eric. 1992. *Making History: The Struggle for Gay and Lesbian Equal Rights.* New York: HarperCollins.

Marcus, Eric. 1993. *Is It a Choice?* San Francisco: HarperSanFrancisco.

Margolin, Leslie. 1992. "Deviance on record: Techniques for labeling child abusers in official documents." *Social Problems, 39,* 58–70.

Marks, Alan. 1980. "Socioeconomic status and suicide in the state of Washington: 1950–1971." *Psychological Reports, 46,* 924–926.

Marriott, Michel. 1995. "Half steps vs. 12 steps." *Newsweek,* March 27, p. 62.

Martin, Patricia Yancey, and Robert A. Hummer. 1995. "Fraternities and rape on campus." In Alex Thio and Thomas C. Calhoun (eds.), *Readings in Deviant Behavior.* New York: HarperCollins.

Martin, Patti. 2001. *Teenage Blues Might Be More.* Asbury Park, N.J.: Asbury Park Press.

Martin, William T. 1984. "Religiosity and United States suicide rates, 1972–1978." *Journal of Clinical Psychology, 40,* 1166–1169.

Martz, Larry. 1986. "True greed." *Newsweek,* December 1, p. 48.

Martz, Larry. 1991. "The corporate shell game." *Newsweek,* April 15, pp. 48–49.

Marx, Gary T. 1981. "Ironies of social control: Authorities as contributors to deviance through escalation, nonenforcement, and covert facilitation." *Social Problems, 28,* 221–246.

Maso, Ilja. 2001. "Phenomenology and ethnography." In Paul Atkinson et al. (eds.), *Handbook of Ethnography.* London: Sage Publications.

Massing, Michael. 1998. *The Fix.* New York: Simon & Schuster.

Masters, William H., and Virginia E. Johnson. 1979. *Homosexuality in Perspective.* Boston: Little, Brown.

Mathis, James L. 1972. *Clear Thinking About Sexual Deviations.* Chicago: Nelson-Hall.

Mattern, Jody L., and Clayton Neighbors. 2004. "Social norms campaigns: Examining the relationship between change in perceived norms and changes in drinking levels." *Journal of Studies on Alcohol, 65,* 489–494.

Matthews, Anne. 1993. "The campus crime wave." *New York Times Magazine,* March 7, p. 41.

Matthews, Dawn D. (ed.). 2004. *Domestic Violence Sourcebook,* 2d ed. Detroit: Omnigraphics, Inc.

Mauro, Robert. 1996. "Suicide—not the answer." *Accent on Living, 41* (Winter), 68–69.

May, William F. 1991. "The molested." *Hastings Center Report, 21,* 9–17.

Mazzetti, Mark. 2004. "Rethinking the next wars." *U.S. News & World Report,* January 5, p. 70.

McAuliffe, William E., and Robert A. Gordon. 1974. "A test of Lindesmith's theory of addiction: The frequency of euphoria among long-term addicts." *American Journal of Sociology, 79,* 795–840.

McCaghy, Charles H. 1968. "Drinking and deviance disavowal: The case of child molesters." *Social Problems, 16,* 43–49.

McCaghy, Charles H., and James K. Skipper, Jr. 1969. "Lesbian behavior as an adaptation to the occupation of stripping." *Social Problems, 17,* 262–270.

McClelland, David C., et al. 1972. *The Drinking Man.* New York: Free Press.

McCord, William, and Joan McCord. 1960. *Origins of Alcoholism.* Stanford, Calif.: Stanford University Press.

McDowell, Bill. 1996. "Jack in the Box battles back with some help from a clown." *Advertising Age, 67,* November 25, p. 11.

McGeary, Johanna. 2002. "Can the church be saved?" *Time*, April 1, pp. 29–39.

McGinn, Daniel, and Ron Depasquale. 2004. "Taking depression on." *Newsweek*, August 23, pp. 59–60.

McGinn, Daniel. 2004. "Mating behavior 101." *Newsweek*, October 4, pp. 44–45.

McGirk, Tim. 2002. "Lifting the veil on sex slavery." *Time*, February 18, p. 8.

McIntosh, John L. 1991. "Epidemiology of suicide in the United States." In Antoon A. Leenaars (ed.), *Life Span Perspectives of Suicide: Time-lines in the Suicide Process*. New York: Plenum.

McKegney, F. Patrick, and Mary Alice O'Dowd. 1992. "Suicidality and HIV status." *American Journal of Psychiatry, 149,* 396–398.

McLanahan, Sara S., and Jennifer L. Glass. 1985. "A note on the trend in sex differences in psychological distress." *Journal of Health and Social Behavior, 26,* 328–336.

McMullen, Richie J. 1990. *Male Rape: Breaking the Silence on the Last Taboo.* London: GMP Publishers.

McMurray, Coleen. 2004. "Number of teen smokers holding steady." *The Gallup Poll Tuesday Briefing.* www.gallup.com.

McNeil, Donald G. 1998. "Mugabe attacks, and gay Zimbabweans fight back." *New York Times,* July 14, p. A4.

McNeil, Donald G., Jr. 1995. "For gay Zimbabweans, a difficult political climate." *New York Times,* September 10, p. 3.

McNeil, Donald G., Jr. 1999. "Condoms for women gain approval among Africans." *New York Times,* July 24, pp. A1, A6.

Medea, Andra, and Kathleen Thompson. 1974. *Against Rape.* New York: Farrar, Straus and Giroux.

Meer, Jeff. 1985. "Living through robbery." *Psychology Today,* May, p. 20.

Meier, Barry, and Melody Petersen. 2001. "Sales of painkiller grew rapidly, but success brought a high cost." *New York Times,* March 5, pp. A1, A15.

Meier, Robert F., Steven R. Burkett, and Carol A. Hickman. 1984. "Sanctions, peers, and deviance: Preliminary models of a social control process." *The Sociological Quarterly, 25,* 67–82.

Meiselman, Karin C. 1990. *Resolving the Trauma of Incest: Reintegration Therapy with Survivors.* San Francisco: Jossey-Bass.

Meloy, J. Reid et al. 2004. "A comparative analysis of North American adolescent and adult mass murderers." *Behavioral Sciences and the Law, 22,* 291–309.

Meloy, J. Reid, and Alan R. Felthous. 2004. "Introduction to this issue: Serial and mass homicide." *Behavioral Sciences and the Law, 22,* 289–290.

Menard, Scott. 1995. "A developmental test of Mertonian anomie theory." *Journal of Research in Crime and Delinquency, 31,* 136–174.

Merry, Engle. 1980. "Manipulating: Streetwalkers' strategies for safety in the city." *Ethnos, 45,* 157–175.

Merton, Robert K. 1938. "Social structure and anomie." *American Sociological Review, 3,* 672–682.

Merton, Robert K. 1957. *Social Theory and Social Structure,* rev. ed. New York: Free Press.

Messerschmidt, James W. 1986. *Capitalism, Patriarchy, and Crime: Toward a Socialist Feminist Criminology.* Totowa, N.J.: Rowman & Littlefield.

Messner, Steven F. 1982. "Poverty, inequality, and the urban homicide rate." *Criminology, 20,* 102–114.

Messner, Steven F. 1983. "Regional and racial effects on the urban homicide rate: The subculture of violence revisited." *American Journal of Sociology, 88,* 997–1007.

Messner, Steven F., and Reid M. Golden. 1992. "Racial inequality and racially disaggregated homicide rates: An assessment of alternative theoretical explanations." *Criminology, 30,* 421–445.

Messner, Steven F., and Richard Rosenfeld. 2001. *Crime and the American Dream,* 3d ed. Belmont, Calif.: Wadsworth.

Messner, Steven F., and Kenneth Tardiff. 1985. "The social ecology of urban homicide: An application of the routine activities' approach." *Criminology, 23,* 241–267.

Michael, Richard P., and Doris Zumpe. 1983. "Sexual violence in the United States and the role of season." *American Journal of Psychiatry, 140,* 883–886.

Michael, Robert T., et al. 1994. *Sex in America: A Definitive Survey.* Boston: Little, Brown.

Milbank, Dana, and Marcus W. Brauchli. 1995. "Greasing wheels." *Wall Street Journal,* September 29, pp. A1, A14.

Miller, Howard L., et al. 1984. "An analysis of the effects of suicide prevention facilities on suicide rates in the United States." *American Journal of Public Health, 74,* 340–343.

Miller, JoAnn L. 1991. "Prostitution in contemporary American society." In Elizabeth Grauerholz and Mary A. Koralewski (eds.), *Sexual Coercion.* Lexington, Mass.: Lexington Books.

Miller, Laurence. 1986. "Pickled brains age faster." *Psychology Today,* January, p. 16.

Miller, M., and D. Hemenway. 1999. "The relationship between firearms and suicide: A review of the literature." *Aggression and Violent Behavior*, 4, 59–75.

Millett, Kate. 1973. *The Prostitution Papers.* New York: Avon.

Mills, Linda G. 2003. *Insult to Injury: Rethinking Our Response to Intimate Abuse.* Princeton, N.J.: Princeton University Press.

Milner, Christina, and Richard Milner. 1972. *Black Players.* Boston: Little, Brown.

Mishara, Eric. 1983. "R. D. Laing's new home." *Omni*, August, p. 35.

Mitchell, Alison. 1997. "President regrets top U.S. regulator met with bankers." *New York Times*, January 29, pp. A1, A12.

Mitchell, Roger E., and Rudolf H. Moos. 1984. "Deficiencies in social support among depressed patients: Antecedents or consequences of stress?" *Journal of Health and Social Behavior, 25*, 438–452.

Mithers, Carol Lynn. 1980. "Date rape: When 'nice guys' won't take NO for an answer." *Mademoiselle*, November 8, pp. 210–211.

Mixson, Paula M. 1995. "An adult protective services perspective." *Journal of Elder Abuse and Neglect, 7*, no. 2–3, 69–87.

Modan, Baruch, et al. 1992. "Prevalence of HIV antibodies in transsexual and female prostitutes." *American Journal of Public Health, 82*, 590–591.

Moen, Phyllis, Julie Robison, and Donna Dempster-McClain. 1995. "Caregiving and women's well-being: A life course approach." *Journal of Health and Social Behavior, 36*, 259–273.

Moffatt, Gregory K. 2000. *Blind-Sided: Homicide Where It Is Least Expected.* Westport, Conn.: Praeger.

Mohler-Kuo, Meichun et al. 2004. "Correlates of rape while intoxicated in a national sample of college women." *Journal of Studies on Alcohol, 65*, 37–45.

Molotsky, Irvin. 1999. "Study links teen-age substance abuse and paternal ties." *New York Times*, August 31, p. A14.

Monahan, John. 1992. "Mental disorder and violent behavior." *American Psychologist*, April, pp. 511–521.

Monroe, Scott M., and Katholiki Hadjiyannakis. 2002. "The social environment and depression: Focusing on severe life stress." In Ian Gotlib and Constance Hammen (eds.), *Handbook of Depression.* New York: Guilford Press.

Moreau, Ron. 1992. "Sex and death in Thailand." *Newsweek*, July 20, p. 50.

Morey, Leslie C., Harvey A. Skinner, and Roger K. Blashfield. 1984. "A typology of alcohol abusers: Correlates and implications." *Journal of Abnormal Psychology, 93*, 408–417.

Morin, Stephen F., et al. 1984. "The psychological impact of AIDS on gay men." *American Psychologist, 39*, 1288–1293.

Morris, Allison. 1987. *Women, Crime, and Criminal Justice.* New York: Basil Blackwell.

Morris, Jeanette, and Lisa A. Cubbins. 1992. "Dating, drinking, and rape." *Psychology of Women, 16*, 179–191.

Morris, Monica B. 1977. *An Excursion into Creative Sociology.* New York: Columbia University Press.

Mukamal, Kenneth J., and Eric B. Rimm. 2001. "Alcohol's effects on the risk for coronary heart disease." *Alcohol Research & Health, 25*, 255–262.

Mullen, Paul E., et al. 2000. *Stalkers and Their Victims.* Cambridge, U.K.: Cambridge University Press.

Mulrine, Anna. 2001. "Where do hopes go?" *U.S. News & World Report*, May 7, pp. 41–44.

Mulrine, Anna. 2002. "Risky business." *U.S. News & World Report*, May 27, pp. 42–49.

Mulvihill, Donald J., and Melvin M. Tumin with Lynn A. Curtis. 1969. *Crimes of Violence*, Vol. 11. Washington, D.C.: Government Printing Office.

Murray, John B. 1986. "Marijuana's effects on human cognitive functions, psychomotor functions, and personality." *Journal of General Psychology, 113*, 25–40.

Musto, David F. 1973. *The American Disease: Origins of Narcotic Control.* New Haven, Conn.: Yale University Press.

Musto, David F. 1986. "Lessons of the first cocaine epidemic." *Wall Street Journal*, June 11, p. 30.

Myers, Mary Beth, Donald Templer, and Ric Brown. 1984. "Coping ability of women who become victims of rape." *Journal of Consulting and Clinical Psychology, 52*, 73–78.

Myerscough, Rodney, and Stuart Taylor. 1985. "The effects of marijuana on human physical aggression." *Journal of Personality and Social Psychology, 49*, 1541–1546.

Nader, Ralph. 1970. "Foreword" to John C. Esposito, *Vanishing Air.* New York: Grossman, p. viii.

Nakawatase, Tomoko V., et al. 1993. "The association between fast-flushing response and alcohol use among Japanese Americans." *Journal of Studies on Alcohol, 54*, 48–53.

Namaste, Viviane K. 2000. *Invisible Lives: The Erasure of Transsexual and Transgendered People.* Chicago: University of Chicago Press.

Nanda, Serena. 2000. *Gender Diversity: Crosscultural Variations.* Prospect Heights, Ill.: Waveland.

Nathan, Debbie. 1995. "Justice in Wenatchee." *New York Times*, December 19, p. A19.

Neff, James Alan, and Baqar A. Husaini. 1985. "Stress-buffer properties of alcohol consumption: The role of urbanicity and religious identification." *Journal of Health and Social Behavior, 26*, 207–222.

Neff, James Alan, et al. 1991. "Machismo, self-esteem, education and high maximum drinking among Anglo, black and Mexican-American male drinkers." *Journal of Studies on Alcohol, 52*, 458–463.

Nelson, Roxanne. 2004. "Oregon court upholds assisted-suicide law." *The Lancet, 363*, 1877.

Nettler, Gwynn. 1974. "On telling who's crazy." *American Sociological Review, 39*, 893–894.

NewsRx.com. 2004. "Asian suicide rate higher in women." April 22.

Newsweek. 1986. "Editorial: The plague among us," June 16, p. 15.

Newton, Michael. 2004. *The Encyclopedia of High-Tech Crime and Crime-Fighting.* New York: Facts on File.

NHSDA (National Household Survey on Drug Abuse). 2001. *National Survey on Drug Abuse.* Washington, D.C.: Government Printing Office.

NIAAA (National Institute on Alcohol Abuse and Alcoholism). 1983. *Alcohol and Health.* Rockville, Md.: NIAAA.

Nicastro, Franco. 1992. "All is quiet in Corleone." *World Press Review,* December, p. 13.

Nichols, Margaret. 1990. "Lesbian relationships: Implications for the study of sexuality and gender." In David P. McWhirter, et al. (eds.), *Homosexuality/Heterosexuality.* New York: Oxford University Press.

Niebuhr, Gustav. 1998. "Laws aside, some in clergy quietly bless gay 'marriage'." *New York Times,* April 17, pp. A1, A20.

Nielsen, Amie L. 1999. "Testing Sampson and Laub's life course theory: age, race/ethnicity, and drunkenness." *Deviant Behavior, 20*, 129–151.

Noah, Timothy. 1997. "OK, OK, cigarettes do kill." *U.S. News & World Report,* March 31, pp. 29–30.

Noble, Ernest P., et al. 1991. "Allelic association of the D_2 dopamine receptor gene with receptor-binding characteristics in alcoholism." *Archives of General Psychiatry, 48*, 648–654.

Nordland, Rod. 1992. "The 'Velcro Don': Wiseguys finish last." *Newsweek,* April 13, p. 35.

Nordland, Rod, and Jeffrey Bartholet. 2001. "The web's dark secret." *Newsweek,* March 19, pp. 44–51.

Norman, Michael. 1998. "Getting serious about adultery." *New York Times,* July 4, pp. A13, A15.

Norris, Frank H. et al. 2002. "The epidemiology of sex differences in PTSD across developmental, societal, and research contexts." In Rachel Kimerling, Paige Ouimette, and Jessica Wolfe (eds.), *Gender and PTSD.* New York: Guilford.

Norris, Joel. 1989. *Serial Killers.* New York: Anchor Books.

O'Boyle, Michael, and Elisif A. A. Brandon. 1998. "Suicide attempts, substance abuse, and personality." *Journal of Substance Abuse Treatment, 15*, 353–356.

O'Hanlan, Katherine A. 1996. "Homophobia is a health hazard." *USA Today: The Magazine of the American Scene, 125*, November, pp. 26–29.

O'Kane, James M. 1992. *The Crooked Ladder: Gangsters, Ethnicity, and the American Dream.* New Brunswick, N.J.: Transaction.

Omestad, Thomas. 1997. "Bye-bye to bribes." *U.S. News & World Report,* December 22, pp. 39–44.

Onstad, Katrina. 1996. "The cyberporn flap: An update." *Canadian Business, 69*, Fall, p. 58.

Orcutt, James D. 1991. "Beyond the 'exotic and the pathologic': Alcohol problems, norm qualities, and sociological theories of deviance." In Paul M. Roman (ed.), *Alcohol: The Development of Sociological Perspectives on Use and Abuse.* New Brunswick, N.J.: Rutgers Center of Alcohol Studies.

Orcutt, James D. 1993. "Happy hour and social lubrication: Evidence on mood-setting rituals of drinking time." *Journal of Drug Issues, 23*, 389–407.

Osborne, Lawrence. 2001. "Regional disturbances." *New York Times Magazine,* May 6, pp. 100–102.

Osgood, D. Wayne, et al. 1996. "Routine activities and individual deviant behavior." *American Sociological Review, 61*, 635–655.

O'Sullivan, Chris S. 1991. "Acquaintance gang rape on campus." In Andrea Parrot and Laurie Bechhofer (eds.), *Acquaintance Rape.* New York: Wiley.

Overall, Christine. 1992. "What's wrong with prostitution? Evaluating sex work." *Signs, 17*, 705–724.

Parker, Robert Nash. 1989. "Poverty, subculture of violence, and type of homicide." *Social Forces, 67*, 983–1007.

Parker, Robert Nash, with Linda-Anne Rebhun. 1995. *Alcohol and Homicide: A Deadly Combination of Two American Traditions.* Albany, N.Y.: State University of New York Press.

Parker-Pope, Tara. 2002. "A new reason for teens to avoid sex: It could be harmful to their health." *Wall Street Journal,* August 27, p. D1.

Parker-Pope, Tara. 2003. "A 'fat-free' product that's 100% fat: How food labels legally mislead." *Wall Street Journal,* July 15, p. D1.

Parnaby, Patrick F., and Vincent F. Sacco. 2004. "Fame and strain: The contributions of Mertonian deviance theory to an understanding of the relationship between celebrity and deviant behavior." *Deviant Behavior, 25,* 1–26.

Parsian, Abbas, et al. 1991. "Alcoholism and alleles of the human D2 dopamine receptor locus: Studies of association and linkage." *Archives of General Psychiatry, 48,* 655–663.

Passas, Nikos, and Robert Agnew (eds.). 1997. *The Future of Anomie Theory.* Boston: Northeastern University Press.

Paul, Pamela. 2004. "The porn factor." *Time,* January 19, pp. 99–100.

Paveza, Gregory J., et al. 1992. "Severe family violence and Alzheimer's disease: Prevalence and risk factors." *Gerontologist, 32,* 493–497.

Pearson, Veronica, and Meng Liu. 2002. "Ling's death: An ethnography of a Chinese woman's suicide." *Suicide and Life-Threatening Behavior, 32,* 347–358.

Peck, Dennis L. 1984. "Lethality of method of suicide among a youthful sample of committers: An examination of the intent hypothesis." *Psychological Reports, 55,* 861–862.

Peck, Dennis L. 1985–1986. "Completed suicides: Correlates of choice of method." *Omega, 16,* 309–323.

Peck, M., and A. Schrut. 1971. "Suicidal behavior among college students." *HSMHA Health Report, 86,* 149–156.

Pelka, Fred. 1995. "Raped: A male survivor breaks his silence." In Patricia Searles and Ronald J. Berger (eds.), *Rape and Society.* Boulder, Colo.: Westview.

Pennebaker, James W., and Robin C. O'Heeron. 1984. "Confiding in others and illness rates among spouses of suicide and accidental-death victims." *Journal of Abnormal Psychology, 93,* 473–476.

Peplau, Letitia Anne. 1981. "What homosexuals want." *Psychology Today,* March, pp. 28–38.

Peplau, Letitia Anne, and Susan D. Cochran. 1990. "A relationship perspective on homosexuality." In David P. McWhirter et al. (eds.), *Homosexuality/Heterosexuality.* New York: Oxford University Press.

Perkins, Roberta. 1991. *Working Girls: Prostitutes, Their Life and Social Control.* Canberra: Australian Institute of Criminology.

Perry, Alex, and Mae Sai. 2002. "How I bought two slaves, to free them." *Time,* March 11, p. 7.

Pescosolido, Bernice A., and Robert Mendelsohn. 1986. "Social causation or social construction of suicide? An investigation into the social organization of official rates." *American Sociological Review, 51,* 80–101.

Peterson, Elicka S. 1999. "Murder as self-help: Women and intimate partner homicide." *Homicide Studies, 3,* 30–46.

Peterson, Ruth D. 1992. "Rape and dimensions of gender socioeconomic inequality in U.S. metropolitan areas." *Journal of Research in Crime & Delinquency, 29,* 162–177.

Peterson, Virginia. 2000. *Child Abuse: Fear in the Home.* Wylie, Tex,: Gale Group.

Peto, Richard, and Alan D. Lopez. 2001. "Future worldwide health effects of current smoking patterns." pp. 154 in C. Everett Koop, Clarence E. Pearson, and M. Roy Schwartz (eds.), *Critical Issues in Global Health.* San Francisco: Jossey-Bass.

Petrovich, Michael, and Donald I. Templer. 1984. "Heterosexual molestation of children who later became rapists." *Psychological Records, 54,* 810.

Phillips, David P. 1979. "Suicide, motor vehicle fatalities, and the mass media: Evidence toward a theory of suggestion." *American Journal of Sociology, 84,* 1150–1174.

Phillips, David P. 1980a. "Airplane accidents, murder, and the mass media: Towards a theory of imitation and suggestion." *Social Forces, 58,* 1001–1024.

Phillips, David P. 1980b. "The deterrent effect of capital punishment: New evidence on an old controversy." *American Journal of Sociology, 86,* 139–148.

Phillips, David P. 1981. "The complementary virtues of qualitative and quantitative research: Reply to Altheide." *Social Forces, 60,* 597–599.

Phillips, David P. 1983. "The impact of mass media violence on U.S. homicides." *American Sociological Review, 48,* 560–568.

Phillips, David P. 1993. "Adequacy of official suicide statistics for scientific research." *Suicide & Life-Threatening Behavior, 23,* 307–319.

Phillips, David P., and Kenneth A. Bollen. 1985. "Same time, last year: Selective data dredging for negative findings." *American Sociological Review, 50,* 364–371.

Pileggi, Nicholas. 1986. *Wiseguy: Life in a Mafia Family.* New York: Simon & Schuster.

Pillemer, Karl A., and David Finkelhor. 1988. "The prevalence of elder abuse: A random sample survey." *The Gerontologist, 28,* 51–57.

Pittman, Frank III. 1993. "Beyond betrayal: Life after infidelity." *Psychology Today,* May/June, p. 36.

Pitts, Marian K. et al. 2004. "Who pays for sex and why?" *Archives of Sexual Behavior, 33,* 353–358.

Pizzo, Stephen P., and Paul Muolo. 1993. "Take the money and run." *New York Times Magazine,* May 9, p. 26.

Platt, Steven. 1984. "Unemployment and suicidal behavior." *Social Science and Medicine, 19,* 93–115.

Pollack, Andrew. 1997. "Overseas, smoking is one of life's small pleasures." *New York Times,* August 17, p. E5.

Ponse, Barbara. 1984. "The problematic meanings of 'lesbian.'" In Jack D. Douglas (ed.), *The Sociology of Deviance.* Boston: Allyn and Bacon.

Pontell, Henry N., and Kitty Calavita. 1993. "White-collar crime in the savings and loan scandal." *The Annals of the American Academy of Political and Social Science, 525* (January), 31–45.

Porter, Roy. 1996. "Born that way?" *New York Times Book Review,* August 11, p. 8.

Potterat, John J., et al. 1990. "Estimating the prevalence and career longevity of prostitute women." *Journal of Sex Research, 27,* 233–243.

Pratt, Timothy. 2001. "Sex slavery packet: A growing concern in Latin America." *Christian Science Monitor,* January 11, p. 7.

Pratt, Travis C. and Francis T. Cullen. 2000. "The empirical status of Gottfredson and Hirschi's general theory of crime: A meta-analysis." *Criminology 38,* 931–964.

President's Commission on Organized Crime. 1986. *The Impact: Organized Crime Today.* Washington, D.C.: Government Printing Office.

Previti, Denise, and Paul R. Amato. 2004. "Is infidelity a cause or a consequence of poor marital quality?" *Journal of Social and Personal Relationships, 21,* 217–230.

Pridemore, William Alex. 2002. "Using newly available homicide data to debunk two myths about violence in an international context." *Homicide Studies, 5,* 267–275.

Pridemore, William Alex, and Andrew L. Spivak. 2003. "Patterns of suicide mortality in Russia." *Suicide and Life-Threatening Behavior, 33,* 132–150.

Pristina, Andrew Purvis, and Jan Stojaspal Chisinau. 2001. "Human slavery." *Time Europe,* February 19, pp. 18–21.

Pritchard, C., and D. S. Baldwin. 2002. "Elderly suicide rates in Asian and English-speaking countries." *Acta Psychiatrica Scandinavica, 105,* 271–275.

Procida, Richard, and Rita J. Simon. 2003. *Global Perspectives on Social Issues: Pornography.* Lanham, Md.: Lexington.

Psychology Today. 1976. "Wrist-cutting—a road to life, not death." April, p. 20.

Quindlen, Anna. 1994. "Sex for sale." *New York Times,* November 26, p. 15.

Quinney, Richard. 1974. *Critique of Legal Order: Crime Control in Capitalist Society.* Boston: Little, Brown.

Quinney, Richard. 1975. *Criminology.* Boston: Little, Brown.

Raab, Selwyn. 1994. "Mob tightens secretive style in retreat from prosecutors." *New York Times,* May 29, pp. 1, 13.

Raab, Selwyn. 1997. "Officials say mob is shifting crimes to new industries." *New York Times,* February 10, pp. A1, A10.

Rapaport, Karen R., and C. Dale Posey. 1991. "Sexually coercive college males." In Andrea Parrot and Laurie Bechhofer (eds.), *Acquaintance Rape.* New York: Wiley.

Rapaport, Karen, and Barry R. Burkhart. 1984. "Personality and attitudinal characteristics of sexually coercive college males." *Journal of Abnormal Psychology, 93,* 216–221.

Ratey, John J., and Catherine Johnson. 1997. *Shadow Syndromes.* New York: Pantheon Books.

Rawe, Julie. 2004. "The case against Ken Lay." *Time,* July 19, pp. 62–63.

Reed, Susan E. 2000. "New economy, same harassment problems." *New York Times,* August 12, Section 3, pp. 1, 11.

Rees, Matt. 2002. "Where to now?" *Time,* August 19, pp. 28–31.

Rehm, Jurgen, et al. 2003. "The global distribution of average volume of alcohol consumption and patterns of drinking." *European Addiction Research, 9,* 147–156.

Reid, Scott A., Jonathan Epstein, and D. E. Benson. 1995. "Does exotic dancing pay well but cost dearly?" In Alex Thio and Thomas C. Calhoun (eds.), *Readings in Deviant Behavior.* New York: HarperCollins.

Rein, Mei Ling. 2001. *Child Abuse: Betraying a Trust.* Detroit, Mich.: Gale Group.

Reuter, Peter. 1995. "The decline of the American Mafia." *Public Interest,* Summer, 89–99.

Riccio, R. 1992. "Street crime strategies: The changing schemata of streetwalkers." *Environment and Behavior, 24,* 555–570.

Rice, Kennon J., and William R. Smith. 2002. "Socioecological models of automotive theft: Integrating routine activity and social disorganization approaches." *Journal of Research in Crime and Delinquency, 39,* 304–336.

Richards, Bill. 1992. "Burden of proof." *Wall Street Journal,* December 8, pp. A1, A8.

Rickgarn, Ralph L. V. 1994. *Perspectives on College Student Suicide.* Amityville, N.Y.: Baywood.

Ridley, Mark. 1996. "The gay brain." *Natural History, 105* (August), 10–11.

Rimer, Sara. 1993. "Campus lesbians step into unfamiliar light." *New York Times*, June 5, p. 6.

Ripley, Amanda. 2002. "Why suicide bombing . . . is now all the rage." *Time*, April 15, pp. 32–39.

Risman, Barbara, and Pepper Schwartz. 2002. "After the sexual revolution: Gender politics in teen dating." *Contexts*. Spring, pp. 16–24.

Rivara, Frederick, et al. 2004. "Mortality attributable to harmful drinking in the United States, 2000." *Journal of Studies on Alcohol, 65*, 530–536.

Rivera, Elaine. 2000. "License to drink." *Time*, July 31, p. 47.

Robins, Lee N. 1973. *The Vietnam Drug User Returns*. Washington, D.C.: Government Printing Office.

Robins, Lee N., et al. 1984. "Lifetime prevalence of specific psychiatric disorders in three sites." *Archives of General Psychiatry, 41*, 949–958.

Rock, Michael T., and Heidi Bonnett. 2004. "The comparative politics of corruption: Accounting for the East Asian paradox in empirical studies of corruption, growth and investment." *World Development, 32*, 999–1017.

Rodgers, Bryan, and Susan L. Mann. 1993. "Rethinking the analysis of intergenerational social mobility: A comment on John W. Fox's 'Social class, mental illness, and social mobility.'" *Journal of Health and Social Behavior, 34*, 165–172.

Roman, Paul M., and Terry C. Blum. 1991. "The medicalized conception of alcohol-related problems: Some social sources and some social consequences of murkiness and confusion." In David J. Pittman and Helene Raskin White (eds.), *Society, Culture, and Drinking Patterns Reexamined*. New Brunswick, N.J.: Rutgers Center of Alcohol Studies.

Rose, Harold M., and Paula D. McClain. 1990. *Race, Place, and Risk: Black Homicide in Urban America*. Albany, N.Y.: State University of New York Press.

Rosenau, Pauline. 1992. *Postmodernism and the Social Sciences*. Princeton, N.J.: Princeton University Press.

Rosenberg, Debra. 2004. "The *Will & Grace* effect." *Newsweek*, May 24, pp.38–39.

Rosenblum, Karen E. 1975. "Female deviance and the female sex role: A preliminary investigation." *British Journal of Sociology, 26*, 169–185.

Rosenfeld, Barry. 2004. *Assisted Suicide and the Right to Die*. Washington, D.C.: American Psychological Association.

Rosenfeld, Sam A. 1985. "The lady is addictive." *Psychology Today*, January, p. 20.

Rosenhan, D. L. 1973. "On being sane in insane places." *Science*, January 19, p. 256.

Rosenthal, A. M. 1995. "The cruelest hoax." *New York Times*, January 3, p. A11.

Rosenthal, Elisabeth. 1999. "Suicide gains ground on women in rural China." *New York Times*, January 24, pp. 1, 8.

Rosoff, Stephen M., Henry N. Pontell, and Robert H. Tillman. 2002. *Profit without Honor: White-Collar Crime and the Looting of America*. Upper Saddle River, N.J.: Prentice Hall.

Rosoff, Stephen M. et al. 2002. *Profit Without Honor: White-Collar Crime and the Looting of America*, 2d ed. Upper Saddle River, N.J.: Prentice Hall.

Ross, Michael W., and Willem A. Arrindell. 1988. "Perceived parental rearing patterns of homosexual and heterosexual men." *Journal of Sex Research, 24*, 275–281.

Rotgers, Frederick, et al. 1996. *Treating Substance Abuse: Theory and Practice*. New York: Guilford.

Roubach, Michael. 2004. "Meaning, phenomenology, and being." *Inquiry, 47*, 189–199.

Rowe, Paul M. 1995. "Alcoholism in USA." *Lancet, 345*, April 1, 860.

Rubington, Earl. 1991. "The chronic drunkenness offender: Before and after decriminalization." In David J. Pittman and Helene Raskin White, (eds.), *Society, Culture, and Drinking Patterns Reexamined*. New Brunswick, N.J.: Rutgers Center of Alcohol Studies.

Ruch, Libby O., Susan Meyers Chandler, and Richard A. Harter. 1980. "Life change and rape impact." *Journal of Health and Social Behavior, 21*, 248–260.

Ruiz, Dorothy S. 1982. "Epidemiology of schizophrenia: Some diagnostic and sociocultural considerations." *Phylon, 43*, 315–326.

Russell, Diana E. H. 1984. *Sexual Exploitation*. Beverly Hills, Calif.: Sage Publications.

Russell, Diana E. H. 1990. *Rape in Marriage*. Bloomington Ind.: Indiana University Press.

Russell, Diana E. H., and Rebecca M. Bolen. 2000. *The Epidemic of Rape and Child Sexual Abuse in the United States*. Thousand Oaks, Calif.: Sage Publications.

Rust, Paula C. 1995. *Bisexuality and the Challenge to Lesbian Politics: Sex, Loyalty, and Revolution*. New York: New York University Press.

Sabato, Larry J., and Glenn R. Simpson. 1996. *Dirty Little Secrets*. New York: Times Books.

Sachs, Andrea. 1993. "9-Zip! I love it!" *Time*, November 22, pp. 44–45.

Saghir, Marcel T., and Eli Robins. 1980. "Clinical aspects of female homosexuality." In Judd Marmor (ed.), *Homosexual Behavior: A Modern Reappraisal*. New York: Basic Books.

Sallett, Alphonse, Erich Goode, and William Pooler. 1999. "The death of a paradigm? The onset and dynamics of an adolescent drug epidemic, 1991–1998." Unpublished paper.

SAMHSA (Substance Abuse and Mental Health Services Administration). 2002. *Annual Household Survey*. www.hhs.gov/news.

Sanday, Peggy Reeves. 1981. "The socio-cultural context of rape: A cross-cultural study." *Journal of Social Issues, 37,* 5–27.

Sanday, Peggy Reeves. 1990. *Fraternity Gang Rape: Sex, Brotherhood, and Privilege on Campus.* New York: New York University Press.

Sanday, Peggy Reeves. 1996a. *A Woman Scorned: Acquaintance Rape on Trial.* New York: Doubleday.

Sanday, Peggy Reeves. 1996b. "Rape-prone versus rape-free campus cultures." *Violence Against Women, 2,* 191–208.

Sandmaier, Marian. 1992. *The Invisible Alcoholics: Women and Alcohol,* 2d ed. Bradenton, Fla.: Blue Ridge Summit.

Santtila, Pekkam, et al. 2001. "The structure of crime-scene actions in Finnish homicides." *Homicide Studies, 5,* 363–387.

Sapp, M., et al. 1999. "Attitudes toward rape among African American male and female college students." *Journal of Counseling and Development, 77,* 204–208.

Sarrel, Philip M., and William H. Masters. 1982. "Sexual molestation of men by women." *Archives of Sexual Behavior, 11,* 117–131.

Sarrel, Philip, and Lorna Sarrel. 1981. "Can a man be raped by a woman?" *Redbook,* May, p. 94.

Satel, Sally. 1996. "The madness of deinstitutionalization." *Wall Street Journal,* February 20, p. A22.

Scarce, Michael. 1997. *Male on Male Rape: The Hidden Toll of Stigma and Shame.* New York: Insight books.

Schaefer, James M. 1981. "Firewater myths revisited: Review of findings and some new directions." *Journal of Studies on Alcohol,* Supplement No. 9 (January), 108–109.

Scheff, Thomas J. 1964. "Social condition for rationality: How urban and rural courts deal with the mentally ill." *American Behavioral Scientist, 7,* 21–27.

Scheff, Thomas J. 1966. *Being Mentally Ill.* Chicago: Aldine.

Scheff, Thomas J. 1974. "The labeling theory of mental illness." *American Sociological Review, 39,* 448–449.

Schiff, Frederick. 1999. "Nude dancing: Scenes of sexual celebration in a contested culture." *Journal of American Culture,* Winter, pp. 9–16.

Schiffren, Lisa. 1996. "Gay marriage, an oxymoron." *New York Times,* March 23, p. 37.

Schlenger, William, et al. 2002. "Psychological reactions to terrorist attacks: Findings from the National Study of Americans' Reactions to September 11." *JAMA, 288,* 581–588.

Schlosser, Eric. 1997. "The business of pornography." *U.S. News & World Report,* February 10, pp. 42–50.

Schmitt, Richard B. 1996. "Defenses down." *Wall Street Journal,* February 29, pp. A1, A6.

Schuckit, Marc A. 1984. "Overview: Epidemiology of alcoholism." In Marc A. Schuckit (ed.), *Alcohol Patterns and Problems.* New Brunswick, N.J.: Rutgers University Press.

Schur, Edwin M. 1984. *Labeling Women Deviant.* New York: Random House.

Schuster, Mark, et al. 2001. "National survey of stress reactions after the September 11, 2001 terrorist attacks." *New England Journal of Medicine, 345,* 1507–1512.

Schutz, Alfred. 1962. *Collected Papers I: The Problem of Social Reality.* Ed. Maurice Natanson. The Hague: Martinus Nijhoff.

Schwartz, Martin D. 1987. "Gender and injury in spousal assault." *Sociological Focus, 20,* 61–75.

Schwartz, Martin D., and Walter S. DeKeseredy. 1997. *Sexual Assault on the College Campus: The Role of Male Peer Support.* Thousand Oaks, Calif.: Sage Publications.

Schwartz, Sharon. 1991. "Women and depression: A Durkheimian perspective." *Social Science and Medicine, 32,* 127.

Schwendinger, Julia R., and Herman Schwendinger. 1983. *Rape and Inequality.* Beverly Hills, Calif.: Sage Publications.

Scull, Andrew. 1988. "Deviance and social control." In Neil J. Smelser (ed.), *Handbook of Sociology.* Newbury Park, Calif.: Sage Publications.

Scully, Diana. 1990. *Understanding Sexual Violence: A Study of Convicted Rapists.* Boston: Unwin Hyman.

Scully, Diana, and Joseph Marolla. 1984. "Convicted rapists' vocabulary of motive: Excuses and justifications." *Social Problems, 31,* 530–544.

Scully, Diana, and Joseph Marolla. 1985. "Riding the bull at Gilley's: Convicted rapists describe the rewards of rape." *Social Problems, 32,* 251–263.

Scully, Gerald W. 1997. *Murder by the state.* Paper published by the National Center for Policy Analysis at the University of Texas, Dallas.

Segal, Lynne. 1993. "Does pornography cause violence?: The search for evidence." In Pamela Church Gibson and Roma Gibson (eds.), *Dirty Looks: Women, Pornography, Power.* London: BFI Publishing.

Seidman, Steven. 2002. *Beyond the Closet: The Transformation of Gay and Lesbian Life*. New York: Routledge.

Seligman, Dan. 2003. "Transsexuals and the law." *Forbes*, October 13, pp.68–69.

Seligmann, Jean, and Patricia King. 1996. "'Roofies': The date-rape drug." *Newsweek*, February 26, p. 54.

Selkin, James. 1975. "Rape." *Psychology Today*, January, p. 74.

Sellin, Thorsten. 1938. *Culture Conflict and Crime*. New York: Social Science Research Council.

Serdula, Mary et al. 2004. "Trends in alcohol use and binge drinking, 1985–1999: Results of a multistate survey." *American Journal of Preventive Medicine, 26*, 294–98.

Serrill, Michael S. 1993. "Defiling the children." *Time*, June 21, pp. 53–55.

Shapiro, Joseph P. 1996. "The elderly's vulnerability to abuse is exaggerated." In A. E. Sadler (ed.), *Family Violence*. San Diego, Calif.: Greenhaven.

Shapiro, Susan P. 1990. "Collaring the crime, not the criminal: Reconsidering the concept of white-collar crime." *American Sociological Review, 55*, 346–365.

Sharpe, Anita. 1997. "Psyched up." *Wall Street Journal*, January 24, pp. A1, A11.

Sheehy, Gail. 1971. *Hustling*. New York: Delacorte.

Shellenbarger, Sue. 2001. "A colleague's suicide has a lasting impact on fellow employees." *Wall Street Journal*, June 13, p. B1.

Shenon, Philip. 1996. "AIDS epidemic, late to arrive, now explodes in populous Asia." *New York Times*, January 21, pp. 1, 8.

Shihadeh, Edward S., and James Flynn. 1996. "Segregation and crime: The effect of black social isolation on the rates of black urban violence." *Social Forces, 74*, 1325–1352.

Shneidman, Edwin S. 1975. "Classification of suicidal phenomena." In Simon Dinitz, Russell R. Dynes, and Alfred C. Clarke (eds.), *Deviance*. New York: Oxford University Press.

Short, James F. Jr. 1960. "Differential association as a hypothesis: problems of empirical testing." *Social Problems, 8*, 14–25.

Shotland, R. Lance, and Lynne Goodstein. 1983. "Just because she doesn't want to doesn't mean it's rape: An experimentally based causal model of the perception of rape in a dating situation." *Social Psychology Quarterly, 46*, 220–232.

Shrout, Patrick E., et al. 1992. "Mental health status among Puerto Ricans, Mexican Americans, and Non-Hispanic whites." *American Journal of Community Psychology, 20*, 729–749.

Sibthorpe, Beverly, et al. 1991. "Needle use and sexual practices: Differences in perception of personal risk of HIV among intravenous drug users." *Journal of Drug Issues, 21*, 699–712.

Siegal, Lewis J., and Jacob H. Friedman. 1955. "The threat of suicide." *Diseases of the Nervous System, 16*, 45.

Silbert, Mimi H., and Ayala M. Pines. 1981. "Occupational hazards of street prostitutes." *Criminal Justice and Behavior, 8*, 397–398.

Simmons, J. L. 1965. "Public stereotypes of deviants." *Social Problems, 13*, 223–224.

Simon, David R. 2002. *Elite Deviance*, 7th ed. Boston: Allyn and Bacon.

Simon, William, and John H. Gagnon. 1974. "The lesbians: A preliminary overview." In Gagnon and Simon (eds.), *Sexual Deviance*. New York: Harper & Row.

Simons, Marlise. 1993. "The sex market: Scourge on the world's children." *New York Times*, April 9, p. A3.

Simpson, Sally S., and Nicole Leeper Piquero. 2002. "Low self-control, organizational theory, and corporate crime." *Law & Society Review, 36*, 509–548.

Skrapec, Candice A. 2001. "Phenomenology and serial murder: Asking different questions." *Homicide Studies, 5*, 46–63.

Sky and Telescope. 1985. "The moon and murder." Vol. 70, p. 28.

Sloan, Allan. 1997. "A sexy new loophole." *Newsweek*, February 3, pp. 37–38.

Smith, Michael D. 1990. "Patriarchal ideology and wife beating: A test of a feminist hypothesis." *Violence and Victims, 5*, 257–273.

Smith, Wesley J. 1993. "The whispers of strangers." *Newsweek*, June 28, p. 8.

Smolowe, Jill. 1993. "Choose your poison." *Time*, July 26, p. 57.

Smyth, Angela, and Chris Thompson. 1990. *SAD: Seasonal Affective Disorder*. New York: Unwin.

Sobell, Mark B., and Linda C. Sobell. 1993. *Problem Drinkers: Guided Self-Change Treatment*. New York: Guilford.

Socall, Daniel W., and Thomas Holtgraves. 1992. "Attitudes toward the mentally ill." *The Sociological Quarterly, 33*, 435–445.

Socarides, Charles, et al. 1997. "Don't forsake homosexuals who want help." *Wall Street Journal*, January 9, p. A10.

Sontag, Deborah. 2002. "Who was responsible for Elizabeth Shin?" *New York Times Magazine*, April 28, pp. 57–61, 94, 139.

Spake, Amanda. 2002. "A fat nation." *U.S. News & World Report*, August 19, pp. 40–47.

Specter, Michael. 1995. "Gay Russians are 'free' now but still stay in fearful closet." *New York Times,* July 8, pp. 1, 4.

Spencer, Jane. 2004. "Crackdown on drugs hits chronic-pain patients." *Wall Street Journal,* March 16, pp. D1, D10.

Spencer, Jennifer, et al. 2002. "Self-esteem as a predictor of initiation of coitus in early adolescents." *Pediatrics, 109,* 581–584.

St. John, Warren. 2004. "Today's bank robber might look like a neighbor." *New York Times,* July 3, pp. A1, A16.

Stack, Steven. 1979. "Durkheim's theory of fatalistic suicide: A cross-national approach." *Journal of Social Psychology, 107,* 161–168.

Stack, Steven. 1982. "Suicide: A decade review of the sociological literature." *Deviant Behavior, 4,* 49–51.

Stack, Steven. 1983. "The effect of religious commitment on suicide: A cross-national analysis." *Journal of Health and Social Behavior, 24,* 362–374.

Stack, Steven. 1986. "A leveling off in young suicide." *Wall Street Journal,* May 28, p. 30.

Stack, Steven. 1987. "Celebrities and suicide: A taxonomy and analysis, 1948–1983." *American Sociological Review, 52,* 401–412.

Stack, Steven. 1991. "Social correlates of suicide by age: Media impacts." In Antoon A. Leenaars (ed.), *Life Span Perspectives of Suicide: Time-lines in the Suicide Process.* New York: Plenum.

Stack, Steven, and Jim Gundlach. 1992. "The effect of country music on suicide." *Social Forces, 71,* 211–218.

Stark, Elizabeth. 1987. "Forgotten victims: Children of alcoholics." *Psychology Today,* January, pp. 58–62.

Steffensmeier, Darrell. 1996. "Gender and crime: Toward a gendered theory of female offending." *Annual Review of Sociology, 22,* 459–487.

Steffensmeier, Renee Hoffman. 1984. "Suicide and the contemporary woman: Are male and female suicide rates converging?" *Sex Roles, 10,* 613–631.

Steinberg, Jacques. 1999. "The coming crime wave is washed up." *New York Times,* January 3, Section 4, p. 4.

Stephens, Joyce. 1995. "The pseudocidal female: A cautionary tale." In Silvia Sara Canetto and David Lester (eds.), *Women and Suicidal Behavior.* New York: Springer.

Stevens, Amy. 1995. "Ten ways (some) lawyers (sometimes) fudge bills." *Wall Street Journal,* January 13, pp. B1, B10.

Stolberg, Sheryl Gay. 1999. "Science looks at Littleton, and shrugs." *New York Times,* May 9, pp. 1, 4.

Straus, Murray A. 1991. "Discipline and deviance: Physical punishment of children and violence and other crime in adulthood." *Social Problems, 38,* 133–154.

Straus, Murray A., Richard J. Gelles, and Suzanne K. Steinmetz. 1980. *Behind Closed Doors.* Garden City, N.Y.: Anchor Books.

Struckman-Johnson, Cindy. 1991. "Male Victims of Acquaintance Rape." In Andrea Parrot and Laurie Bechhofer (eds.), *Acquaintance Rape.* New York: Wiley.

Stylianou, Stelios. 2002. "The relationship between elements and manifestations of low self-control in a general theory of crime: Two comments and a test." *Deviant Behavior, 23,* 531–557.

Suitor, Jill J., Karl Pillemer, and Murray A. Straus. 1990. "Marital violence in a life course perspective." In Murray A. Straus and Richard J. Gelles (eds.), *Physical Violence in American Families: Risk Factors and Adaptations to Violence in 8,145 Families.* New Brunswick, N.J.: Transaction.

Sullum, Jacob. 1998. *For Your Own Good: The Anti-Smoking Crusade and the Tyranny of Public Health.* New York: Free Press.

Suro, Roberto. 1993. "Pollution-weary minorities try civil rights tack." *New York Times,* January 11, pp. A1, A12.

Sussman, Vic. 1992. "To stop a thief." *U.S. News & World Report,* March 30, pp. 55–58.

Sutherland, Edwin H. 1939. *Principles of Criminology,* 3d ed. Philadelphia: Lippincott.

Sutherland, Edwin H. 1949. *White-Collar Crime.* New York: Holt, Rinehart and Winston.

Sutherland, Edwin H. 1956. "Crimes of corporations." In Albert K. Cohen, Alfred Lindesmith, and Karl Schuessler (eds.), *The Sutherland Papers.* Bloomington, Ind.: Indiana University Press.

Sutherland, Edwin H., and Donald R. Cressey. 1978. *Criminology,* 10th ed. Philadelphia: Lippincott.

Suthrell, Charlotte. 2004. *Unzipping Gender: Sex, Cross-Dressing and Culture.* Oxford, U.K.: Berg.

Swan, Neil. 1993. "Researcher's problem, which comes first: Drug abuse or antisocial behavior?" *NIDA (National Institute on Drug Abuse) Notes, 8* (May/June), 6–7.

Sweet, Ellen. 1985. "Date rape: The story of an epidemic and those who deny it." *Ms.,* October, p. 58.

Szasz, Thomas. 1974a. *Ceremonial Chemistry.* Garden City, N.Y.: Anchor.

Szasz, Thomas. 1974b. *The Myth of Mental Illness,* rev. ed. New York: Harper & Row.

Szasz, Thomas. 1994. "Mental illness is still a myth." *Society,* May/June, pp. 34–39.

Szockyj, Elizabeth. 1993. "Insider trading: The SEC meets Carl Karcher." *The Annals of the American Academy of Political and Social Science, 525* (January), 46–58.

Tannenbaum, Frank. 1938. *Crime and the Community.* New York: Columbia University Press.

Taylor, Steven J. 2004. "'You're not a retard, you're just wise.'" In Alex Thio and Thomas C. Calhoun (eds.), *Readings in Deviant Behavior,* 3d ed. Boston: Allyn and Bacon.

Thio, Alex. 1973. "Class bias in the sociology of deviance." *The American Sociologist, 8,* 1–12.

Thio, Alex. 2004. *Deviant Behavior,* 7th ed. Boston: Allyn and Bacon.

Thomas, Evan. 2002. "Descent into evil." *Newsweek,* November 4, pp. 21–38.

Thompson, Terri, et al. 1992. "Crime and the bottom line." *U.S. News & World Report,* April 13, p. 57.

Thornton, Bill, and Richard M. Ryckman. 1983. "The influence of a rape victim's physical attractiveness on observers' attributions of responsibility." *Human Relations, 36,* 549–562.

Time. 1980. "Deadwood's defunct houses." July 28, p. 77.

Tittle, Charles R. 1995. *Control Balance: Toward a General Theory of Deviance.* Boulder, Colo.: Westview.

Tolchin, Martin. 1986. "On breaking, or bending, or ignoring the law." *New York Times,* November 28, p. 12.

Torrey, E. Fuller. 1974. *The Death of Psychiatry.* Radnor, Pa.: Chilton.

Torrey, E. Fuller. 1997. *Out of the Shadows: Confronting America's Mental Illness Crisis.* New York: Wiley.

Totman, Jane. 1978. *The Murderers: A Psychosocial Study of Criminal Homicide.* San Francisco: R and E Research Associates.

Toubia, Nahid, and Susan Izett. 1998. *Female Genital Mutilation.* Geneva: World Health Organization.

Toufexis, Anastasia. 1992a. "Bisexuality: What is it?" *Time,* August 17, p. 49.

Toufexis, Anastasia. 1992b. "Do mad acts a madman make?" *Time,* February 3, p. 17.

Toufexis, Anastasia. 2002. "A psychiatrist's-eye view of murder and insanity." *New York Times,* April 23, p. D5.

Towson State. 1993. "A study on campus crime by Towson State University's Center for the Study and Prevention of Campus Violence," reported in *New York Times Magazine,* March 7, p. 40.

Trad, Paul V. 1991. "The ultimate stigma of mental illness." *American Journal of Psychotherapy, 45,* 463–466.

Transparency International. 2004. *Global Corruption Report 2004.* London: Pluto Press.

Trice, Harrison M. 1966. *Alcoholism in America.* New York: McGraw-Hill.

Troiden, Richard R. 1979. "Becoming homosexual: A model of gay identity acquisition." *Psychiatry, 42,* 362–373.

Trost, Cathy, and Paulette Thomas. 1993. "Sexual politics." *Wall Street Journal,* March 10, p. A6.

Truell, Peter, and Larry Gurwin. 1992. *False Profits: The Inside Story of BCCI, the World's Most Corrupt Financial Empire.* Boston: Houghton Mifflin.

Tuesday, Vince. 2002. "The naked truth about porn surfers." *Computerworld,* June 24, p. 40.

U.S. Census Bureau. 2004–2005. *Statistical Abstract of the United States.* Washington, D.C.: Government Printing Office.

U.S. Congress, Office of Technology Assessment. 1990. *Indian Adolescent Mental Health* (OTA-H-446). Washington, D.C.: Government Printing Office.

Unnithan, N. Prabha, Lin Huff-Corzine, Jay Corzine, and Hugh P. Whitt. 1994. *The Currents of Lethal Violence: An Integrated Model of Suicide and Homicide.* Albany: N.Y.: State University of New York Press.

Vachss, Alice S. 1994. *Sex Crimes: Ten Years on the Front Lines Prosecuting Rapists and Confronting Their Collaborators.* New York: Holt.

Vail, D. Angus. 2004. "Tattoos are like potato chips. . . You can't have just one." In Alex Thio and Thomas C. Calhoun (eds.), *Readings in Deviant Behavior,* 3d ed. Boston: Allyn and Bacon.

Vaillant, George E. 1995. *The Natural History of Alcoholism Revisited.* Cambridge, Mass.: Harvard University Press.

Vaillant, George E., and Eva S. Milofsky. 1982. "The etiology of alcoholism: A prospective viewpoint." *American Psychologist, 37,* 494–503.

Valentino, Benjamin A. 2004. *Final Solutions: Mass Killing and Genocide in the 20th Century.* Ithaca, N.Y.: Cornell University Press.

van Gelder, Paul J., and Charles D. Kaplan. 1992. "The finishing moment: Temporal and spatial features of sexual interactions between streetwalkers and car clients." *Human Organization, 51,* 253–263.

van Natta, Don Jr., and Jane Fritsch. 1997. "$250,000 buys donors' best access to Congress." *New York Times,* January 27, A1, A10.

van Poppel, Frans, and Lincoln H. Day. 1996. "A test of Durkheim's theory of suicide—Without committing the 'ecological fallacy'." *American Sociological Review, 61,* 500–507.

Vaughan, Diane. 1983. *Controlling Unlawful Organizational Behavior: Social Structure and Corporate Misconduct.* Chicago: University of Chicago Press.

Victor, Jeffrey S. 2004. "Sluts and wiggers: A study of the effects of derogatory labeling." *Deviant Behavior, 25,* 67–84.

Viscusi, W. Kip. 1992. *Smoking: Making the Risky Decision.* New York: Oxford University Press.

Voeller, Bruce. 1990. "Some uses and abuses of the Kinsey scale." In David P. McWhirter, Stephanie A. Sanders, and June Machover Reinisch (eds.), *Homosexuality/Heterosexuality.* New York: Oxford University Press.

Walchak, David G. 1996. "Drugs and violent crime." *Police Chief, 63,* March, p. 6.

Walker, Lenore F. 1990. *Terrifying Love: Why Battered Women Kill and How Society Responds.* New York: Harper Perennial.

Wallace, Harvey. 1996. *Family Violence: Legal, Medical, and Social Perspectives.* Boston, Mass.: Allyn and Bacon.

Waller, Willard. 1936. "Social problems and the mores." *American Sociological Review, 1,* 922–933.

Walters, John P. 2002. "Don't legalize drugs." *Wall Street Journal,* July 19, p. A10.

Wartik, Nancy. 1995. "Jerry's choice: Why are our children killing themselves?" In Robert Emmet Long (ed.), *Suicide.* New York: Wilson.

Wasserman, Ira. 1984. "Imitation and suicide: A reexamination of the Werther effect." *American Sociological Review, 49,* 427–436.

Webb, Gary. 2001. "Sex and the internet." *Yahoo! Internet Life, 7,* 88–98.

Weber, Thomas E. 1997. "The X files." *Wall Street Journal,* May 20, pp. A1, A8.

Wechsler, Henry, et al. 2002. "Trends in college binge drinking during a period of increased prevention efforts." *Journal of American College Health, 50,* 203–217.

Weicker, Lowell P., Jr. 1985. "Dangerous routine." *Psychology Today,* November, pp. 60–62.

Weinstein, Raymond M. 1981. "Mental patients' attitudes toward hospital staff." *Archives of General Psychiatry, 38,* 487.

Weinstein, Raymond M. 1983. "Labeling theory and the attitudes of mental patients: A review." *Journal of Health and Social Behavior, 24,* 70–84.

Weis, Kurt, and Sandra S. Borges. 1973. "Victimology and rape: The case of the legitimate victim." *Issues in Criminology, 8,* 81–85.

Weisberg, Kelly. 1985. *Children of the Night: A Study of Adolescent Prostitution.* Lexington: Lexington Books.

Weisburd, David, et al. 1991. *Crimes in the Middle Classes.* New Haven: Yale University Press.

Weisheit, Ralph. 1992. "Patterns of female crime." In Robert G. Culbertson and Ralph Weisheit

(eds.), *Order Under Law.* Prospect Heights, Ill.: Waveland.

Weisman, Steven R. 1997. "Spin nation." *New York Times,* January 26, p. 12.

Weisner, Constance, et al. 1995. "Trends in the treatment of alcohol problems in the U.S. general population, 1979 through 1990." *American Journal of Public Health, 85,* 55–60.

Weitz, Eric D. 2003. *A Century of Genocide: Utopias of Race and Nation.* Princeton, N.J.: Princeton University Press.

Weitzer, Ronald. 1991. "Prostitutes' rights in the United States: The failure of a movement." *Sociological Quarterly, 32,* 23–41.

Weitzer, Ronald. 2000. "Deficiencies in the sociology of sex work." *Sociology of Crime, Law and Deviance, 2,* 259–279.

Wellford, Harrison. 1972. *Sowing the Wind: A Report from Ralph Nader's Center for Study of Responsive Law on Food Safety and the Chemical Harvest.* New York: Grossman.

Wells, Joseph T. 1993. "Accountancy and white-collar crime." *The Annals of the American Academy of Political and Social Science, 525* (January), 86–87.

Wertheimer, Fred. 1996. "Stop soft money now." *New York Times Magazine,* December 22, pp. 38–39.

Wheeler, Stanton. 1991. "The problem of white-collar crime motivation." In Kip Schlegel and David Weisburd (eds.), *White-Collar Crime Reconsidered.* Boston: Northeastern University Press.

White, Jacquelyn W., and John A. Humphrey. 1991. "Young people's attitudes toward acquaintance rape." In Andrea Parrot and Laurie Bechhofer (eds.), *Acquaintance Rape.* New York: Wiley.

Wickelgren, Ingrid. 1999. "Discovery of 'gay gene' questioned." *Science,* April 23, p. 571.

Widom, Cathy Spatz. 1989. "The intergenerational transmission of violence." In Neil Alan Weiner and Marvin E. Wolfgang (eds.), *Pathways to Criminal Violence.* Newbury Park, Calif.: Sage Publications.

Wilbanks, William. 1984. *Murder in Miami: An Analysis of Homicide Patterns and Trends in Dade County (Miami) Florida, 1917–1983.* Lanham, Md.: University Press of America.

Wilbanks, William. 1985. "Is violent crime intraracial?" *Crime & Delinquency, 31,* 117–128.

Wilentz, Amy. 1985. "When brother kills brother." *Time,* September 16, p. 33.

Wilke, John R. 2004. "Price-fixing investigations sweep chemical industry." *Wall Street Journal,* June 22, pp. A1, A6.

Wilkerson, Isabel. 1993. "Foes of pornography and bigotry join forces." *New York Times,* March 12, p. A12.

Wilkins, James. 1967. "Suicidal Behavior." *American Sociological Review, 32,* 286–287.

Wilkinson, Kenneth P. 1984. "A research note on homicide and rurality." *Social Forces, 63,* 445–452.

Wilkinson, Rupert. 1970. *The Prevention of Drinking Problems.* New York: Oxford University Press.

Wilkinson, Wayne W. 2004. "Religiosity, authoritarianism, and homophobia: A multidimensional approach." *The International Journal for the Psychology of Religion. 14,* 55–67.

Will, George F. 2001. "Now, weapons of mass disruption?" *Newsweek,* October 29, p. 76.

Williams, Kirk R. 1984. "Economic source of homicide: Reestimating the effects of poverty and inequality." *American Sociological Review, 49,* 283–289.

Williams, Kirk R., and Susan Drake. 1980. "Social structure, crime and criminalization: An empirical examination of the conflict perspective." *The Sociological Quarterly, 21,* 563–575.

Williams, Mary E. 2003. *Marijuana.* San Diego, Calif.: Greenhaven Press.

Wilson, Margo I., and Martin Daly. 1992. "Who kills whom in spouse killings? On the exceptional sex ratio of spousal homicides in the United States." *Criminology, 30,* 189–215.

Wilson, Mitchell. 1993. "DSM-III and the transformation of American psychiatry: A history." *American Journal of Psychiatry, 150,* 399–410.

Winerip, Michael. 1999. "Bedlam on the streets." *New York Times Magazine,* May 23, pp. 42–49, 56, 65, 68–70.

Winerip, Michael. 2002. "The never-promised rose garden and the snake pit." *New York Times,* May 5, Section 4, p. 3.

Wingfield, Nick. 2004. "Problem for cops on eBay beat: Crooks keep getting smarter." *Wall Street Journal,* August 3, pp. A1, A8.

Winick, Charles, and Paul M. Kinsie. 1971. *The Lively Commerce.* Chicago: Quadrangle.

Winslow, Ron, and Peter Landers. 2002. "Obesity: A world-wide woe." *Wall Street Journal,* July 1, pp. B1, B4.

Witkin, Gordon. 1992. "Willing to kill for a car." *U.S. News & World Report,* September 21, pp. 40–43.

Witkin, Gordon. 1995. "A new drug gallops through the West." *U.S. News & World Report,* November 13, pp. 50–51.

Wittig, Monique. 1990. "The straight mind." In Russell Ferguson et al. (eds.), *Out There: Marginalization and Contemporary Culture.* Cambridge, Mass.: MIT Press.

Wolfe, Alan. 1998. "The homosexual exception." *New York Times Magazine,* February 8, pp. 46-47.

Wolfgang, Marvin E. 1958. *Patterns in Criminal Homicide.* Philadelphia: University of Pennsylvania Press, 1958.

Wolfgang, Marvin E. 1967. "A sociological analysis of criminal homicide." In Marvin E. Wolfgang (ed.), *Studies in Homicide.* New York: Harper & Row.

Wolfgang, Marvin E., and Franco Ferracuti. 1967. *The Subculture of Violence: Towards an Integrated Theory in Criminology.* London: Tavistock.

Wolpert, Lewis. 2000. *Malignant Sadness: The Anatomy of Depression.* New York: Free Press.

Wonders, Nancy A., and Raymond Michalowski. 2004. "The globalization of sex tourism." In Alex Thio and Thomas C. Calhoun (eds.), *Readings in Deviant Behavior,* 3d ed. Boston: Allyn and Bacon.

Wood, Elizabeth Anne. 2001. "Strip club dancers: Working in the fantasy factory." In Alex Thio and Thomas C. Calhoun (eds.), *Readings in Deviant Behavior,* 2d ed. Boston: Allyn and Bacon.

Wren, Christopher S. 1996. "Adolescent drug use rose in latest survey from 1995." *New York Times,* December 20, p. A8.

Wren, Christopher S. 1997. "Keeping cocaine resilient: Low cost and high profit." *New York Times,* March 4, pp. A1, A10.

Wren, Christopher S. 1999. "Study compares U.S. and English drug crimes." *New York Times,* May 14, p. A10.

Wright, Bradley R. E. et al. 2004. "Does the perceived risk of punishment deter criminally prone individuals? Rational choice, self-control, and crime." *Journal of Research in Crime and Delinquency, 41,* 180–213.

Wright, James D. 1995. "Ten essential observations on guns in America." *Society,* March/April, pp. 62–68.

Wright, James D., Joseph F. Sheley, and M. Dwayne Smith. 1992. "Kids, guns, and killing fields." *Society,* November/December, pp. 84–89.

Wright, James D., Peter H. Rossi, and Kathleen Daly. 1983. *Under the Gun: Weapons, Crime, and Violence in America.* New York: Aldine.

Wright, Richard T., and Scott H. Decker. 1994. *Burglars on the Job: Streetlife and Residential Break-ins.* Boston: Northeastern University Press.

Wright, Richard T., and Scott H. Decker. 1997. *Armed Robbers in Action: Stickups and Street Culture.* Boston: Northeastern University Press.

Wysocki, Diane Kholos. 1998. "Let your fingers do the talking: Sex on an adult chat-line." *Sexualities,* Vol. 1, pp. 425–452.

Xin, Xiaohui, and Thomas K. Rudel. 2004. "The context for political corruption: A cross-national analysis." *Social Science Quarterly, 85,* 294–309.

Yamamoto, J., et al. 1983. "Symptom checklist of normal subjects from Asian-Pacific islander population." *Pacific/Asian American Mental Health Research Center Research Review, 2,* 6–8.

Yardley, Jim. 2000. "Unmarried and living together till the sheriff do us part." *New York Times,* March 25, p. A7.

Yen, Hope. 2005. "High court to review assisted suicide law." *Yahoo! News,* February 22, http://story.news.yahoo.com.

Yesavage, Jerome A., et al. 1985. "Carry-over effects of marijuana intoxication on aircraft pilot performance: A preliminary report." *American Journal of Psychiatry, 142,* 1325–1329.

Yonkers, Kimberly A., and George Gurguis. 1995. "Gender differences in the prevalence and expression of anxiety disorders." In Mary V. Seeman (ed.), *Gender and Psychopathology.* Washington, D.C.: American Psychiatric Press.

Young, T. J. 1991. "Suicide and homicide among Native Americans: Anomie or social learning?" *Psychological Reports, 68,* 1137–1138.

Zagorin, Adam. 1997. "Charlie's an angel?" *Time,* February 3, pp. 36–38.

Zakaria, Fareed. 2001. "Why do they hate us?" *Newsweek,* October 15, pp. 22–40.

Zeisel, Hans. 1982. "A comment on 'The deterrent effect of capital punishment' by Phillips." *American Journal of Sociology, 88,* 167–169.

Zeits, Dorothy. 1981. *Women Who Embezzle or Defraud.* New York: Praeger.

Zillmann, Dolf, and Jennings Bryant. 1982. "Pornography, sexual callousness, and the trivialization of rape." *Journal of Communication, 32,* 10–21.

Zimmerman, Jacqueline Noll. 2003. *People Like Ourselves: Portrayals of Mental Illness in the Movies.* Lanham, Md.: The Scarecrow Press.

Zorza, Joan, and Laurie Woods. 1994. *Mandatory Arrest: Problems and Possibilities.* New York: National Center for Women and Family Law.

NAME INDEX

SUBJECT INDEX

A1 gene, 336
AA (Alcoholics Anonymous), 342–343
Absolutism, positivist perspective and, 5–6
Abstinence, 214, 215
Abstract meanings, 42
Abuse of the frank, 370–371
Accidental death, 42
Accounting abuse, 364–365
Accusing the accuser, 374
Acquaintance rape, 94–95
Acquired immunodeficiency syndrome. *See* AIDS
Acrophobia, 180
Addict robbers, 385
Addiction
  to alcohol. *See also* Alcoholism
    physical, 331
    psychological, 331
  cocaine, 298–299
  heroin, 298
  marijuana, 298–299
  prostitution and, 227
Administration, drug, 285
Adolescents
  alcoholism and, 318
  homicides committed by, 63
  lesbian, 254
  mental illness and, 185–186
  prostitutes, 229–230
  suicide and, 158–159
Adultery, 215–218
  illegitimate, 216
  legitimate, 216–217
Advertising, deceptive, 354–355
African Americans
  alcohol drinking and, 324
  drug use and, 305, 306
  gangs, 397
  as hate killing victims, 76–77
  women, raping of, 102

Age
  alcohol drinking and, 324
  of family abusers, 134
  mental illness and, 185–186
  rape and, 92
  suicide rates and, 154–156, 158–159
Aggravated assault, 60
Agoraphobia, 180
AIDS (acquired immuno-deficiency syndrome)
  gays and, 267–268
  heterosexuals and, 268
  illegal drug use and, 296
  prostitution and, 233–234
  responsibility for, 273–274
  suicide rates and, 160–161
Akers, Ronald, 27–28
al Qaeda, 78–79, 81
Alcohol drinking, 317–343
  college students and, 332–333
  consequences, social, 322–323
  controlling, 340–343
  effects of, 319–322
    on health, 321–322
    mental impact of, 320–321
    physical impact of, 320–321
  excessive. *See* Alcoholism
  extent of, 318
  family violence and, 122
  global perspective on, 328–329
  moderate
    alcoholics and, 343
    health effects of, 321
  myths about, 318–319
  physical addiction to, 331
  prohibition of. *See* Prohibition of alcohol
  psychological addiction to, 331
  regional locations and, 327–328
  religion and, 326
  social drinkers, 330

  social factors in, 323–329
  socioeconomic status and, 326–327
  women and, 334–335
Alcoholic personality, 337–338
Alcoholic robbers, 385–386
Alcoholics Anonymous (AA), 342–343
Alcoholism, 317–343
  among women, 335
  causes of, 336–340
  controlling, 340–343
  definition of, 329–330
  extent of, 318
  myths about, 318–319
  stages of developing, 330–332
  treatment approaches, 341–343
Altruistic suicide, 167, 168
American Dream, 25, . 33
Ancient Greece, mental illness and, 190–191
Anger, from child molestation, 115–116
Anomic suicide, 167
Anomie, 19, 20
Anomie-strain theory, 19–26, 33
  development of, 19
  differential illegitimate opportunity, 23–24
  evaluation of, 25–26
  goal-means gap, 19–22
  recent developments, 24–25
  status frustration and, 22–23
Anticocaine laws, 305
Antideviant ideas, 26
Antisocial personality, alcoholism and, 337
Antitrust violations, 355–356
Anxiety reaction, 180
Arguments, murder from, 68–69
Asian Americans, gangs, 397
Assault, 60
Association, with deviant individuals, 26–27

481